"[Anna Freud] comes alive wonderfully in Elisabeth Young-Bruehl's splendid pages...."

—Robert Coles, *Boston Globe*

"The authorized biography of Anna Freud, the world-famous child analyst, based on her intimate papers, is a scrupulously written documentary of immense value to readers who have wondered about the relation between Anna and the famous founding father of psychoanalysis, Sigmund Freud. Elisabeth Young-Bruehl's book is also a fascinating record of psychoanalytical politics in the years following Freud's death."

—Leon Edel

"A remarkable portrait of an intelligent, intensely private, enigmatic woman who was one of the great pioneers of child analysis...."

—Mary Mackey, *San Francisco Chronicle*

"Elisabeth Young-Bruehl's biography of Anna Freud is unusually successful and unusually fascinating.... [Young-Bruehl] is distinguished by painstaking attention to reliability; by sensitivity and good judgment ... and by a clear, sinewy prose...."

—Anne Chapman, *Cleveland Plain Dealer*

"We encounter the interior life of Anna Freud with a fullness and a level of intimacy rarely achieved in biography.... There is throughout a sensitivity of touch, a care in execution, and abiding sympathy...."

—Elizabeth Coleman, *Newsday*

"Both Young-Bruehl and Anna Freud have used this difficult life to illuminate some of human nature's hidden recesses and to illustrate something Lou Andreas-Salome once said to Anna: "It does not matter what fate one has if one only really lives it.""

—Jean Strouse, *Vogue*

ANNA FREUD

A BIOGRAPHY BY
ELISABETH YOUNG-BRUEHL

Second Edition

Yale University Press
New Haven and London

FOR M. T. BEECHER

Side by side with the exigencies of
life, love is the great educator.

Sigmund Freud
(*SE*, XIV, 312)

CONTENTS

ACKNOWLEDGMENTS
AND NOTES ON SOURCES

Lottie Newman, Anna Freud's editor and literary executor, invited me to undertake this biography, offering access to Anna Freud's papers and permission to quote them. She also gave me astute editorial and historical readings of my manuscript at various stages of its evolution, but she imposed no requirements as the authorizer. My gratitude for her confidence and her help is enormous, and it extends as well to Richard Newman, also a reader and supporter.

When I read through Anna Freud's literary estate, it was with Lottie Newman in New Haven; it is now in the Sigmund Freud Archives at the Library of Congress, where it will be reorganized according to the Library's principles. I have annotated my quotations from these papers by document title or by addresser/addressee/date for letters. Hopefully this will allow any future researchers to identify accurately the papers cited. Smaller numbers of my sources are located at the Freud Museum in London and at the Sigmund Freud House in Vienna; in my annotations I have indicated these locations where appropriate. To the capable and cooperative staffs of all three archives, my thanks. All translations from German papers are my own, but I am indebted for transcriptions, checking, and some rough drafting to my friend Charlotte Sempel Klenbort, to Hilda Damiata, Brigitte Molnar, John Gasiewski, and Corinne Arnold.

The literature on Freud, his family, and the history of psychoanalysis is vast, in many languages. It is also troubled by the fact that the Sigmund Freud Archives has until recently been inaccessible to scholars. The Archives' policy fostered the historical and biographical speculation that has been growing in the field since Freud's death and that became typical of it in the 1970s. There are many completely irreconcilable versions of Freud, layers of suppositions, rumors, and sheer inventions about his family, and very few serious histories of psychoanalysis—none of child analysis. Finding the preexisting context for my work to be so full of difficulties on the one hand, and so mapless on the other, I adopted several rules. I have offered here as much primary documentation as possible for each factual or interpretive statement that I make about Anna Freud's life—and where there are holes in the documentation, I say so; I have not used any statements in existing biographies of Freud or Anna Freud for which no primary documentation was cited; statements in published sources that were based upon uncited interview material have been disregarded; statements made to me in interviews have not been used unless corroborated by at least one other interviewee. Published memoirs and reminiscences have been very valuable to this biography; but some, like the recent account of the Freud family's life constructed from interviews with their housekeeper, I consider unreliable in almost every way and I have not used them.

The unpublished correspondences referred to most frequently in this biography are the following:

1. Sigmund Freud's correspondences with Jones and Ferenczi, both of which being prepared for publication (now in Sigmund Freud Archives) and Eitingon (transcript in Freud Museum, London). Citations from the Eitingon Letters are by permission of Sigmund Freud Copyrights, Wivenhoe, England

2. Sigmund Freud/Anna Freud, both sides, but neither complete, between 1908 and 1935

3. Lou Andreas-Salomé/Anna Freud, Anna Freud's side only, nearly complete, between 1921 and 1937 (both sides are being prepared for eventual publication)

4. Max Eitingon/Anna Freud, Anna Freud's side (Eitingon's seems not to have survived), between 1920 and 1942

5. Eva Rosenfeld/Anna Freud, Anna Freud's side (Rosenfeld's has not survived), nearly complete, between 1925 and 1932 (kindly lent to me by Victor Ross and Peter Heller, who is preparing the letters for publication)

6. Dorothy Burlingham/Anna Freud, Dorothy Burlingham's side only (Anna Freud's has not survived), between 1939 and 1940

7. August Aichhorn/Anna Freud, both sides nearly complete, a

few letters between 1924 and 1926 (Freud House, Vienna) and most between 1945 and 1948

8. Ernest Jones/Anna Freud, both sides, nearly complete, between 1927 and 1957 (all the prewar letters and some of the postwar ones are in the Institute of Psychoanalysis, London; the remainder of the postwar ones are with the Anna Freud estate, Sigmund Freud Archives)

9. Ernst Kris/Anna Freud, both sides nearly complete, between 1944 and 1957

10. Hans Lampl/Anna Freud, Lampl's side only (Anna Freud's is in Jeanne Lampl-de Groot's estate), nearly complete, between 1946 and 1958

11. Ralph Greenson/Anna Freud, both sides, nearly complete, between 1949 and 1979 (partly in Anna Freud's estate, partly with Hildi Greenson, Los Angeles)

I interviewed friends and colleagues of Anna Freud's in America and Europe. Most of her contemporaries have died, so the few survivors were particularly important sources: Anny Rosenberg Katan (Cleveland); Jeanne Lampl-de Groot (Amsterdam; d. 1987); Margarethe Rie Nunberg (New York; d. 1986); Josefine Stross (London); Anna Maenchen (Berkeley); and, a little younger, Hildi Greenson (Los Angeles). Anna Kris Wolff and Anton Kris talked with me about their parents, Marianne and Ernst Kris, and supplied helpful letters.

In the next generations of analysts, I interviewed only those who seemed to me, from my reading of Anna Freud's papers, to be particularly knowledgeable about her. I am grateful to her colleagues at the Anna Freud Center (formerly the Hampstead Clinic) for their hospitality and their helpfulness: Hansi Kennedy, Clifford Yorke, and George Moran, the administration; Gertrud Dann, Sophie Dann, and Ilse Hellman, colleagues since the Hampstead War Nursery; Joseph Sandler, Anne-Marie Sandler, and Doris Wills, early Hampstead graduates; Pauline Cohen, Barbara Grant, and Elizabeth Model, longtime staff members; Gina Bon, Anna Freud's secretary; Masud Khan. Manna Friedmann, the Hampstead nursery-school teacher, who helped care for Anna Freud in her last years, kept a journal (referred to in my notes as "Manna Friedmann's journal") that was invaluable for reconstructing Anna Freud's childhood as well as her last years. I am deeply grateful for access to this journal and for Manna Friedmann's trust.

In America, I concentrated my interviewing attention on Anna Freud's associates at the Yale Child Study Center and Yale University, particularly Alice Colonna, Albert Solnit, Joseph and Sonja Goldstein, and Jay Katz. Informally, at the Gardiner Seminar in Psychiatry and the Humanities, I gathered anecdotes and information from Samuel and Lucille Ritvo, Theodore and Ruth Lidz, and Peter Gay. My thanks to Hans Loewald for his helpfulness.

Katrina Burlingham Valenstein generously answered my questions about her mother, Dorothy Burlingham. But I decided not to carry my story into the generations of Anna Freud's nieces and nephews and their children or of Dorothy Burlingham's grandchildren, so I did not interview them.

I interviewed a number of Anna Freud's analysands (other than training analysands), whose names I will not mention here or in my notes—though I wish to thank them. In general, I have made it a policy not to quote letters to or from analysands or to discuss case material reflected in other letters (with one exception, in Chapter 10, where I did not think a breach of confidentiality was involved).

The John Simon Guggenheim Memorial Foundation of New York generously funded my work for the 1985–86 academic year. Wesleyan University granted me leave from my teaching responsibilities for that year and the next, and supplied me with a grant for travel to Vienna in 1987. The staff at Olin Library, Wesleyan, supplied gracious research support, and I have my meticulous copy editor, Pat Miller, to thank for her excellent collaboration.

My work on this biography is indebted to my friends Paul Schwaber and Rosemary Balsam, both analysts, who read it chapter by chapter; to my editor at Summit Books, Ileene Smith, who has been a superb reader and consultant; and to the dear friends who provide me with such good company in Chester—especially the one to whom I gratefully dedicate this biography of Anna Freud.

January 1988
Chester, Connecticut

PREFACE TO THE SECOND EDITION

This biography of Anna Freud was first published in 1988, four years after her death at the age of eighty-seven. Because it was the first biography of her (and remains the only one) to draw upon both the documents that constituted her literary estate and an extensive oral and interview history, *Anna Freud: A Biography* set the framework for understanding her and her achievements as a psychoanalyst. Although her literary estate has since received additions, several published correspondences not completely available to me have been published, biographical speculations about Freud have continued to appear, and quite a collection of articles, chapters of books, and books about Anna Freud has accumulated, I think it is accurate to say that in the past twenty years nothing has appeared that requires substantial factual amendment or interpretive emendment to the life story told here. So I have not altered the text for this 2008 twentieth-anniversary second edition from Yale University Press, where the original volume's fine editor, Ileene Smith, has overseen its publication again.

But much has changed around this biography during the past two decades, in psychoanalysis and in the wider world. I also think it is accurate to say that the Anna Freud who appears in these pages was largely obscured in much of the world for approximately the decade of the 1990s by an American-centered cultural episode known as the Freud Wars, which, though ended, still reverberate. But now, a decade into the twenty-first century, her work is once again, but in a different way, of great interest to child psychoanalysts and everyone concerned with child development. In this preface, I want to tour briefly for new readers these two periods of Anna Freud's new world.

When I was writing *Anna Freud* in the mid-1980s, the history of Freudian psychoanalysis existed almost entirely in biographies, and almost all of the biographies were of Freud himself. The second-generation Freudians, including Anna Freud, were hardly known outside of the profession, and only a few of their works—chiefly Jacques Lacan, Melanie Klein, and D. W. Winnicott—were taught in university programs that presented psychoanalysis. The situation is entirely different now, as there are biographies—at least one—of each of the major second-generation Freudians, and several histories (national or regional, not yet international) of psychoanalysis itself. In particular, the contribution of women to psychoanalysis has been studied and appreciated, and Anna Freud, along with other women analysts, is now featured on the many women's history Web sites that have emerged in the past two decades. Cultural historians concentrating on the social trauma that the Jewish psychoanalytic diaspora shared with the larger European diaspora have also explored Anna Freud's life, like those of her émigré contemporaries, in a number of works.

But in the mid-1980s, forty years after Freud's death, psychoanalysis still meant Freud. Psychoanalysis as a profession was practically without a written history or any historiographical reflection on why there was so little history. The standard biography was still Ernest Jones's monumental three-volume *The Life and Work of Sigmund Freud*, completed in the year of Freud's centenary, 1956, the first biography to be written with access to the huge trove of papers and correspondences that would later be closed away in the Sigmund Freud Archives, where their secret existence tantalized other biographers. Jones's work had, however, begun to be questioned in a complex revisionist literature, which started appearing in the 1960s and was then woven into the major Freud biography of the late 1980s, Peter Gay's *Freud: A Life for Our Times*, which appeared in the same year as this biography of Anna Freud. In the revisionist literature, Freud was properly criticized for his views of women, and the psychoanalytic movement was taken to task for its social conservativeness, which was quite at odds with its prewar progressiveness (when, for example, there were free psychoanalytic clinics for working-class Berliners and many analysts were socialists).

By the late 1980s, the heroic and virtuous Freud, depicted by Jones as a genius who had triumphed over his own neuroses using his own method, was widely—and rightly—understood as an idealization, an idealization that pushed other analysts, like the Hungarian Sandor Ferenczi, to the margins of the movement. But at the moment of correction, Freud was also besieged by the advance troops of a fault-finding campaign that eventually produced the full-scale culture clash popularly known as the Freud Wars. Although there were revisionists in the late 1980s (myself included) who simply wanted a less idealized, more complex Freud and a less prejudiced psychoanalysis, the anti-Freud warriors wanted to disprove psychoanalysis and implicate it as a socially pernicious pseudoscience by debunking its founder, argumentum ad hominem. Anna Freud had lived long enough to witness the beginnings of the assault upon her father's character and reputation, and by the time *Anna Freud: A Biography* was published, the assault was so advanced that she was being interpreted for general audiences as a rigid conservator of a harmful psychoanalysis. Despite my effort in the biography to show her innovativeness and originality, and despite the continued influence of her London clinic, her reputation fell under the shadow of the shadow Freud.

The story of the Freud Wars of the 1990s is too complex and many-faceted for brief summary, especially because it was also part of an even more complex, wider war of ideas—or, more accurately, of ideologies—aimed at debunking the major nineteenth-century scientific heirs of the Enlightenment. Many scientific questions became ideological questions to an extent that was novel because of the intellectual and technological sophistication of the ideologues, who were researchers and marketers, not totalitarians or residents of lunatic fringes, as had been the case with so many prewar anti-Enlightenment campaigns. Darwin's theory of evolution was attacked by theocrats who were expert propagandists for "intelligent design." Marx's theory, which, like most social scientific theories (and certainly like most theories of the dismal science of economics), was more speculative than the theory of evolution, was attacked by a new generation of anticommunists when that great mausoleum of Marxian thought, the Soviet Union, disappeared. "The end of history" was announced by triumphalist "neoliberal" ideologues. And Freudian psychoanalysis, which is both a theory and a treatment method, rich in variants and developments institutionalized as schools of thought and training programs, was reduced to a caricature of Freud himself and then dissected. Despite an enormous literature in books and journals that revised and extended his work, Freud was equated with psychoanalysis and his person was attacked with the purpose of showing that his ideas about the power of the unconscious in all of life were wrong and deleterious. As noted, there was little in the way of history of psychoanalysis to expose the caricature.

At the time, there was a widespread trend in American and European universities, loosely called postmodernism, which questioned all master

narratives or attempts to order huge ranges and historical sweeps of phenom-
ena into patterns stemming from first principles. Master narratives were said to
be instruments of power (as they certainly could be, given a will to use them
thus); and sometimes postmodernists argued that science generally, or even
theory generally, is just something constructed and manipulated by Western-
ers, patriarchs, powerful elites (as it certainly can be). But it was not from the
antitheoretical postmodernists, who were usually academics speaking to very
limited audiences in arcane languages, that the ideological critiques of
Charles Darwin, Karl Marx, and Freud came. People with broadly appealing
alternative theories—counternarratives—offered them.

The counternarrative to Freudian psychoanalysis was about Freud; it
was a Bad Freud Story (not matched by any similar story about Darwin or
Marx as persons) that exposed how he had suppressed true visions of reality
with his theory of unconscious motivation. The Bad Freud Story served
many groups, not just religious fundamentalists or ideologues of *rationally*
self-interested imperialistic democracy. Fundamentalists used bits of it to
suggest that modern science had corrupted modern people and threatened
the family (and particularly the family's control over women and children),
and democratic rugged individualists used other bits to argue that the psychoanalytic notion of the unconscious denies free will and rationality. But
the Bad Freud Story did not have a clear plot, and it did not appear at once.
Rather, it accumulated, growing up around the general charge against
Freud that he was an authoritarian who defended psychoanalysis with his
secret committee, exorcised dissidents, and censored dissident truths. (The
schism-filled history of psychoanalysis became more like the history of a religious cult or a Stalinist "cult of personality" as it was told and retold.) As the
psychoanalytic high priest or tribal chieftain, Freud permitted himself all
kinds of meddling in the lives of his colleagues and his patients, as well as all
kinds of exploitative prerogatives in his family (including an often-alleged
love affair with his wife's sister, and including his analysis of his daughter,
Anna, which had been presented unsensationalistically in this biography).
The story of Freud the physician doing harm was told so often that it underwent that slow transformation from unfounded gossipy allegation through
rumor to "fact" that is characteristic—we now know—of what is called
"celebrity culture," that is, culture where the features and foibles of the famous receive more attention than any idea and where ideas themselves,
both suspected and envied as implements of power, resemble public relations images. In the 1990s, Anna Freud, too, acquired an image—a popular
branding—as the aloof, cold, defensive administrator of her father's reputation and the keeper of the keys to his archive with all the damning secrets it
was imagined to contain.

For any historian old enough—like me—to have experienced earlier clashes between psychoanalysis and its critics, the Freud Wars of the late 1980s and 1990s had an obviously new and different tone and meaning. When feminist critics in the 1960s—following the pioneering postwar work of Simone de Beauvoir—raised their criticisms of Freud's views on female psychology, Freud himself was often charged with sexism or even misogyny. But he was also understood to be a Victorian patriarch, a person of his period, and the charges were usually tempered with statements about how important for women Freud's acknowledgment of their emotional lives and their sexuality had been, and how open Freud and his followers had been to the participation of women in psychoanalytic work and institutions. The feminist demand for revisions in psychoanalytic theory of female psychology met up with, and was inspired by, critical thinking within psychoanalysis itself, and not just by female psychoanalysts like Karen Horney or Clara Thompson. Freud's views on male psychology, in turn, became central to the feminist critique of sexism, as they are to this day. Slowly, the most Victorian and patriarchy-serving Freudian tenets lost their hold on psychoanalysis, as they lost at least some of their hold on the cultures in which psychoanalysts worked. (The problem that remained in psychoanalytic institutions, as it remained in the surrounding cultures, was not theoretical; it was sexual boundary violations.)

The same storyline unfolded over the bias in psychoanalysis against homosexuality, a prejudice that critics recognized as stronger among Freud's followers—particularly his American medical ones, but also the British ones (including Anna Freud and some Anna Freudians) and the Latin American ones—than it was in Freud himself, who had assumed that each and every human being makes a same-sex object choice unconsciously. In the 1990s, when psychoanalytic associations began to offer conference panels on homophobia rather than the conference panels on homosexuality as a pathology, which had been their fare earlier, the work of critique and reform could be seen in its success (even though redoubts of homophobic theorizing remained and remain to this day). Even the biographical question of whether Anna Freud was a sexually active homosexual or, as I concluded in this biography, an ascetic in a monogamous partnership with Dorothy Burlingham, can, perhaps, be considered today without the prejudices that surrounded it in the 1980s; perhaps it can even be seen as both unanswerable (since neither woman answered it) and as only a strand in the great weave of their remarkable love and work. The rise of religious fundamentalism around the world has had a terribly regressive effect on both the liberation of women and the liberation of sexual minorities, but it is now possible for psychoanalysis to weigh in against these regressions rather than participating in them and to be appreciative rather than judgmental of diversity in its own ranks.

But the Freud Wars were a different matter, reflecting, as I noted, a different moment in the wider world after the Cold War. Freud's character—even Freud's unconscious—had to be assassinated for psychoanalysis to be toppled. The most popularly successful and catalyzing ad hominem critic in the late 1980s was Jeffrey Masson, an academician trained as a psychoanalyst in Toronto, who makes an appearance in the last chapter of this biography, where he is portrayed spending time as a guest in Anna Freud's house (now the Freud Museum) researching his edition of Freud's correspondence in the 1890s with Wilhelm Fliess. Masson also gathered material for a book called *The Assault on Truth*, which was published in 1984, when Anna Freud was no longer alive to protest it. But not long afterward Masson began to self-destruct his own case by publishing a memoir, *Final Analysis* (1990), in which he hyperbolically portrays himself as a passionate truth-teller about Freud and the terrible corruption of the psychoanalytic movement, the roots of which could be traced to Freud's fundamental dishonesty, chronicled in the Fliess correspondence. After he had offered readers of his memoir's "Anna Freud and I" chapter some tidbits of gossip from the Freuds' octogenarian housekeeper ("she was cheap . . ."), Masson both belittled Anna Freud's lifetime of achievement and mocked her loyalty to her father.

The founding lie that Masson claimed to have exposed was, as the subtitle of *The Assault on Truth* put it, Freud's *Suppression of the Seduction Theory*. This theory, which had claimed childhood seduction as the ultimate cause of both hysterical and obsessional neurosis, was a theory about which Freud had been quite proud because it fulfilled the two criteria he had then for a psychoanalytic truth: reduction of a complex phenomenon to seduction as a single cause, and cure when the theory was applied to a case, which meant when the theory was explained to the patient. Freud had argued for this seduction theory in his early work on hysteria but then came to doubt it for clinical reasons—it did not, applied, or explained, cure his patients. Masson might have noted and questioned the two scientific criteria, which Freud himself later found inadequate and worked hard to abandon. But instead, single-mindedly bent on his ad hominem mission, Masson asserted that Freud *suppressed* (not abandoned) the seduction theory because he was concerned that espousing it, and thus exposing the high incidence of child sexual abuse in the city's middle class, from which Freud's adult patients came, would have meant ostracism from the Vienna psychiatric community and the destruction of his practice. Instead of continuing to claim that his female hysterical patients had been seduced as children or adolescents by their fathers or other men in their families, Freud had turned to the idea that girls often, out of unconscious desire for the father, which he began to call "the Oedipal complex," fantasized scenes of seduction. Masson asserted that this cowardly retreat into the domain of fantasy meant that Freud, and also most later Freudians, no longer believed what their female patients told them. With their belittling disbelief, they became just like the nineteenth-century psychiatrists Freud had once criticized for their obtuseness about female sexual desire. Courageous truth-telling had to wait one hundred years for Jeffrey Masson himself, who, for his honesty, paid the price of ostracism by the cold, father-worshipping Anna Freud, by the Board of the Sigmund Freud Archives, and by the entire Freudian psychoanalytic establishment.

Final Analysis is certainly a book of its personality-dissecting period, which had been so presciently analyzed by the critic Christopher Lasch in his *The Culture of Narcissism* (1979). But Masson's was a Bad Freud Story with a twist: to make his ad hominem case against Freud, Masson analyzed *himself* using Freud's science. He made an ad hominem case about himself by presenting his own Oedipus complex, which centered on his search for a good, genius father or a guru who would not use or betray women as Masson's own charming father had by having many mistresses (and telling his son that being a seducer is "in our blood," a kind of curse). But every man whom Masson had cast in the good father role proved to be a great narcissist who did abuse women, either in fact or, like Freud, by not listening to them and belittling them with theory. By offering this analysis, and admitting his loneliness and sadness at being a disappointed son who felt he had to protect women (including from himself as a seducer), Masson felt he could claim that his story had not influenced him as he made his case against Freud. He was only responding to what Freud really did—dishonestly blame the female victims of seduction for harm they had suffered. In my judgment, what Masson actually produced was a remarkably vivid example of the psychoanalytic rule of thumb that when people blame others in a scathing or polemical spirit, they reveal what they know themselves to be or to be capable of being. They are "projecting," and projecting the story of the hurts they have sustained and the lineaments of their own Oedipus complexes (the power of which had struck Freud so forcefully that he abandoned the theory that seduction is the sole cause of hysterical and obsessional neurosis).

Because he thought of himself as motivated not by unconscious fantasy but by his conscious, *rational* desire to tell the truth—about himself, as about Freud—Masson had no idea how he mistook Freud's struggle over the seduction theory for a betrayal of women. Only specialist readers, familiar with Freud's writings, would have known that Masson was a selective citer of Freud or that Masson simply did not believe what Freud said in the quotations he did offer. By omitting from consideration statements that clearly indicated that Freud had never denied or purposefully understated the existence of child sexual abuse, Masson made half a shocking case, but he was unable to make the other half by showing that Freud had ever recommended that therapists not believe their patients. In fact, the one technical recommendation that Freud did make was that therapists not suggest to their patients that the patients had been abused—this is the mistake he said (in his 1925 "Autobiographical Study") that he had made when he was applying the seduction theory. Generally, as Freud began to understand more about transference in the analytic situation, he moved away from didactically applying his theories to his patients. He understood that an analyst has to wait for the truth to come forward, out from under layers of repressed memories and fantasies. Telling patients what theory says their experience must have been, as he had done when he told the hysterical patient called Dora that she must really have loved the suitor whose advances she had said were unwelcome, drives patients away.

What Freud did claim was that a psychoanalyst would not be able to understand the effect of child sexual abuse *or any other early experience* without understanding the patient's Oedipal fantasies (and the patient's sexual constitution, he usually added). His specific claim was that not all patients who talk about being abused have been abused or have been abused in the way they say they have, because layers of fantasy shape their stories. (Only in the 1930s—as he noted in an essay called "Female Sexuality," for a specific example—did he begin to explore how actual seduction by the mother might be covered over by a fantasy of seduction by the father.) Freud argued (against his earlier position) that hysteria—like the other neuroses—should not be understood as having a *sole* cause. Neuroses are, rather, complexly determined ("over-determined" was his term). In fact, Freud's effort to free himself from his "find the sole cause" and "apply the theory" ways of thinking and treating was so multifaceted that many of his followers settled for something much more simple and self-flatteringly authoritative—disbelieving their patients. Some even asserted this as a technical rule (as Masson correctly reported). Freud's younger colleague Sandor Ferenczi and the members of his Budapest School, however, went in the opposite direction and argued that one should listen to patients on the assumption that there is always trauma *of some sort* as well as fantasy in what they say. They vastly enlarged the definition of trauma (and looked at pre-Oedipal trauma as well); they explored in great detail the effects of trauma. The Hungarians were more in the spirit of Freud; the analysts who disbelieved their patients had about as much relation to the mature Freud as the Social Darwinists who declared which races were not fit to survive had to Darwin.

As he developed psychoanalysis, Freud himself was not always clear or consistent on this crucial topic of how experiences in the external world are related to instinctual desire and fantasy, and he had to make major changes—for example, in his understanding of transference and his theory of anxiety—in order to compass the new complexities he discovered after his abandonment of the sole cause seduction theory and the crude original technique of applying theory to a case. But, by the late 1920s, when it came to declaring which of three sources of anxiety felt by the ego is the most fundamental, Freud surveyed all three—objective anxiety coming from situations of danger in the external world, neurotic anxiety coming from the instinctual drives, and moral anxiety coming from the superego—and said unequivocally (sounding like Ferenczi): "frightening instinctual situations can in the last resort be traced back to external situations of danger" (*New Introductory Lectures*, 1933, p. 117). Anna Freud elaborated the same point about the primacy of the external world and its traumas in her *The Ego and the Mechanisms of Defense* (1936), and she maintained this claim throughout her career, arguing for it against Melanie Klein, who emphasized the primacy of the frightening instinctual drives (particularly aggression). But for Masson and those who believed Masson's assault on Freud, once the "lie" about child sexual abuse had been told, there was no appreciation of external dangers and traumas in psychoanalysis, no truth at all in psychoanalysis.

For most of the 1990s the assault upon Freud's character, and upon psychoanalysis that was thought to be rooted in his character flaws, was conventional wisdom outside of the profession (and, not infrequently, within it). Pained psychoanalytic defenders came forth to fight with Masson's argumentum ad hominem—the argument he made about Freud, not the one he made in exposing himself, which seemed to go unappreciated—but the Bad Freud Story Masson had catalyzed proved compelling. And over the course of the decade the idea that Freud had been a dishonest thinker was used to support anti-Freudiansm on the second major front of the Freud Wars. This was a front that had no celebrity catalyst like Masson, although an American literary critic named Fredrick Crews led an influential charge into the pages of the *New York Review of Books* and then published a book called *The Memory Wars*. (Crews's memoir about why he had to reject what he had once loved had a title comparable to *Final Analysis*; it was, graphically, *Out of My System*, a book that described his propensity for total commitments followed by "enlightened" expulsions of what he had once loved.)

The memory wars began as the prevalence of child abuse became more obvious—or more undeniable—because social policies were instituted in the United States and Europe to make reporting of suspected abuse mandatory and to support legal prosecution of abusers. Adults claiming to have been sexually abused began to make their claims in court: they said that they had repressed memories of their childhood abuse and recovered those memories later, often in therapy. But as a wave of court cases made headlines, critics like Crews emerged who questioned whether there can be such a thing as a "recovered memory," which meant, ultimately, that the critics questioned Freud's notion that there is an unconscious into which memories are repressed. Ironically, on this memory wars front of the Freud Wars, the Bad Freud Story was that Freud was the originator of a therapeutic technique that involved suggesting to patients that they had been abused and then had repressed memory of that abuse. General readers would, of course, be appalled that Freudian-derived therapy could produce such a result; and general readers did not have the help that finally appeared in the best book for seriously weighing the questions involved, which was produced in 1997 at the Anna Freud Centre in London under the title *Recovered Memories of Abuse: True or False?*

So the generally believed Bad Freud, in other words, ended up being the one that Masson had wished for: a Freud who never abandoned the seduction theory but used it to help his patients, believing their stories of abuse and affirming them. In the memory wars, Freud of the seduction theory period stood as an example to generations of unethical and dishonest therapists who fostered—maybe even invented—the false accusations of abuse their clients took into court. This time Bad Freud did not blame the victim, he blamed the abuser—falsely.

Although they both fault Freud for dishonesty and reject his notion of the unconscious, the two Bad Freud Stories are, obviously, incompatible, but it seems to me that the same cultural situation stood behind the widespread acceptance of one or the other or even both of them among general readers and cultural commentators. That situation was that the general public was, as I just noted, finally becoming aware of how common child maltreatment is—not just sexual abuse, but abuse in many forms—and, rightly horrified, needed some explanation for why it had taken so long for child maltreatment to be recognized for the huge phenomenon and problem that it is. There had been a word for maltreatment of women as a group since the mid-1960s when "sexism" was coined, and that word, that concept, had helped people (and various scientific disciplines) think about why women are maltreated. But there was no similar word for the prejudice or bias against children that is structured into many families and into most societies; and there still is no such word, no "childism," to help us see that when a child is harmed children *as a group* are being unvalued, not thought worthy of protection and good care. It has been simpler and easier to say either that maltreated children have not been believed (by Freud) or that some child abuse is a fabrication of (Freudian) therapy than to consider why people abuse children (and have since long before any child or adult survivor might have been allowed to speak of it). Further, it has been simpler and easier for psychoanalysts themselves—starting with Freud—to focus on the question of how children (or adult survivors) tell the truth or fantasize or mingle truth and fantasy than to develop insights into pedophilia and incest, child pornography and child sex trafficking, child slavery and labor and soldiering, child battering, neglect, infanticide, and all the kinds of traumatic inadequacies of parenting and schooling and communal practices that make life miserable for so many children—in some times and places, for the majority of children.

Awareness about the pervasiveness of child maltreatment had developed since the early 1960s, when a psychoanalytically trained American researcher, Henry Kempe—student of Sandor Ferenczi's student Rene Spitz—had described "the battered child syndrome." It had grown after Kempe wrote about "Another Hidden Pediatric Problem: Child Sexual Abuse" in 1978 and helped move Congress to legislate both the mandatory reporting of suspected child abuse and neglect and the founding of the National Center for the Study of Child Abuse and Neglect, which Kempe directed and which became a model for European centers. But Kempe, who did so much to protect and treat children, was aware that study of maltreaters lagged behind study of victims. His original book of essays, *The Battered Child Syndrome* (1968), had reported only one in-depth study (by a psychoanalytic team) of child abusers, and this contained the difficult-to-hear news that the majority of child abusers (like the majority of abusers of women) are not, by psychiatric criteria, mentally ill and that the vast majority of maltreatment is interfamilial, not perpetrated by strangers. Abusing children, like abusing women, is often culturally sanctioned and is tied to the idea that all children are the property of their families.

While the phenomenon of child abuse and neglect was finally becoming widely discussed and to some extent addressed, another realization about the lives of children made its way from scientific research teams, including psychoanalytic ones, into the public consciousness and policy. Research from many natural and social scientific fields confirmed what child analysts had been arguing since the days of Anna Freud's Hampstead War Nursery: the first years of a child's life are absolutely critical for all later bodily and mental development, including (neuroscience research showed) brain development. If a child is maltreated in this crucial period, only the most intense work of repair (or extraordinary resilience) can restore the child to normal development. Freudian insights about the importance of childhood experience were refined by child development specialists of many varieties and directed right at the first three years (the period known as pre-Oedipal). The general public became more able to accept and understand the significance of good parenting, of secure, loving childhood attachments, and of basic good provisioning, as well as the significance of preventing child maltreatment in order to prevent a lifetime of pain and suffering. (In the United States, this general acceptance and understanding made possible policy initiatives like the Head Start program and other similar efforts, overriding the resistance of groups who felt that the government should not intervene in the lives of preschool children or interfere with parental child-property rights.) There was even, by the beginning of the twenty-first century, the beginnings of a broad effort to see maltreatment of children as a social problem comparable to the problem of sexism. The United Nations had helped spur this realization with its Convention on the Rights of the Child, which succeeded the Convention on the Rights of Women. Children, like adults, have rights; they are not the property of their parents or other adults.

As general awareness of "zero to three" and of the rights of children grew, the clamor of the Freud Wars died down and the real *casus belli* became clear: this really had been a battle about who to hold responsible for child abuse. The need to blame Freud diminished as the need to understand the sources of the problem of child abuse and neglect grew. Among psychoanalysts, who had felt beleaguered during the Freud Wars and had taken to fighting among themselves, as so commonly happens when a group feels that it has been misunderstood and stereotyped, a great desire arose to overcome the intellectual disorder and conflict among schools of theory and technique that had grown ever more intense and confusing during the 1990s. Eventually, in my estimation, the effects and aftereffects of the Freud Wars began to be salutary for the profession. In the domain of female psychology and then in the domain of homosexuality, psychoanalysis had been substantially reformed, but further reform in Freud's theory and technique had been needed: more attention to all the kinds of obstacles that family and social-cultural milieus present to healthy development had been needed, and more responsive—more "relational" (a word that became a manifesto)—ways of listening to patients had been needed. In institutional psychoanalysis, reform had also been needed, for many of the training institutions had grown hierarchical, arrogant, internally contentious, and unconnected to other scientific disciplines—including the ones where child maltreatment and child maltreaters were being studied with greater urgency. The Freud Wars, as unilluminating in themselves as any other kind of war, concealed a challenge to which psychoanalysts either had to rise or watch their science and their profession sink.

In the past decade, as the Freud Wars have passed, Anna Freud's reputation, which was so overshadowed in the United States and in Europe by the attack on her father and by the confusion it caused, has recovered. But that does not mean that the hopes she had for psychoanalysis have been—even now—fulfilled.

Anna Freud had argued all her working life (as I report in this biography) that the vitality of psychoanalysis—its continued healthy growth and development—depended upon adult analysts recognizing and incorporating into their work what child analysts were discovering, particularly about what family and social-cultural conditions are necessary for normal, healthy development. And she had argued that child analysis needed to be respected institutionally, not treated as a subspecialty with no rights in psychoanalytic training programs and societies—like a neglected child in the psychoanalytic family. Her father had acknowledged her work and the work of all the child analysts by declaring in 1925, "The future of analysis belongs to child analysis." But this message had never really been heard during her lifetime by the majority of adult analysts, despite the attention they gave to the controversy between Anna Freud and Melanie Klein over how child analysis should be conducted. A child analyst could not, in Anna Freud's lifetime, be accepted into the International Psychoanalytical Association without having done adult training as well—and that situation persists to this day.

During the 1980s and 1990s, however, most adult analysts finally acknowledged that the English pediatrician-psychoanalyst D. W. Winnicott had pointed the way to a middle ground on which the Anna Freud–Melanie Klein controversy could be resolved. Winnicott emerged as the most important contributor to analysis focused on not just the child but the mother- (or primary caretaker) child duo in the first years of life. As the 1990s unfolded, his work was the major psychoanalytic spur to the multidisciplinary concern with early childhood and early childhood relationships, as it was the spur to psychoanalytic concern with the therapeutic relationship as an interaction, an interplay, not an application of theory. But Winnicott was not as theoretically sophisticated a writer on these topics as was Hans Loewald in the United States, and he also was not a developmental thinker; his insights did not open into a full developmental framework for all of childhood and adolescence. For that broad framework, the seminal contributor remained Anna Freud, the great developmentalist. And that claim became widely accepted in the 1990s among child analysts and those who paid attention to child analysis. As Winnicott's influence grew, Anna Freud's grew with it and enhanced it—even though many Winnicottian analysts felt that she was a conservative in terms of technique and that she had been slow to assimilate the challenges posed by theorists who emphasized developmental gender differences and object preference differences and race, class, and cultural differences.

The most important strand in Anna Freud's postwar work—her focus on the problems she named "developmental disorders" (rather than the classically defined infantile neuroses) and her careful elaboration of the multitude of developmental lines that every child must travel on the way to healthy maturity—is now known to every child analyst, as it was to Winnicott himself, who always praised her developmental thinking and her attention to children's environments. (I have included as an appendix to this edition of her biography an article that presents Anna Freud's work with Dorothy Burlingham on mother-infant observation, work that was well known to Winnicott and all who developed this psychoanalytic concern with children's environments.) But many adult analysts, and certainly the general public, remained unaware that it was she who had really redefined therapy as developmental help and repair, as a way of giving children (and adults) who had failed to develop along one line or another, or many, a chance and an assist to get back on track.

Her legacy is most lively in child study centers around the world, and especially in her own Hampstead Clinic, now the Anna Freud Centre. But it has been modernized. Little of the Freudian language of instinctual drives remains, although respect for the unconscious and its power is everywhere, in combination with the Winnicottian attention to mother-child relations and with much attention to attachment theory, which originated with John Bowlby. (This is an approach focused on the various ways in which infants and children are attached to their primary caretakers and on how the various types of attachment—secure, insecure, ambivalent, disorganized—can play out as repetitively in later life as do unconscious pre-Oedipal and Oedipal fantasies.) The current directors of the Anna Freud Centre, Peter Fonagy, Mary Target, and Linda Mayes (also on staff at the Yale Child Study Center, where Anna Freud had such a fruitful affiliation late in her life, when she coauthored *In the Best Interests of the Child*), have developed their own version of attachment theory and used it to continue the Anna Freud tradition of linking psychoanalysis with other fields and with areas where it ought to have influence: family law, pediatrics, education, social work.

The new directors have also linked the Anna Freud Centre with University College London, where they teach in a graduate degree program in neuroscience and psychoanalysis. This partnership brings together the Anna Freudian emphasis on development with the revolution now in course within the field of neuroscience, where the human brain has come to be understood as a continually developing organism. Especially in the past twenty years, the idea that the brain is a machine with fixed parts fulfilling fixed functions has yielded to the knowledge (gained with use of new imaging techniques) that it is a vast, plastic, generative, and regenerative neuronal network, an ecosystem. The child's brain, like the child as a whole, must travel developmental lines, growing in complexity and creativity, and if it does not, in a critical period, achieve the kinds of neuronal connectivity that it needs, the brain will—as the child does—suffer developmental disorders. As the commitment to integrate the findings of neuroscience into psychoanalysis grows at the Anna Freud Centre (and more generally), her concepts of developmental lines, developmental disorders, and developmental help will have greater and wider influence.

Currently, there are also initiatives at the Anna Freud Centre to try to fulfill at last Anna Freud's old dream of having child analytic training be a fully acknowledged route to membership in the International Psychoanalytic Association, on a par with adult analysis. If this goal can be accomplished, the child analytic training program at the center, which had to be discontinued for financial reasons, may be ready for revival. Fundraising for renovations at the center have been more successful in recent years, and the center will soon have its own neuroscience laboratory and research program as well. If it can be revived, child training at the Anna Freud Centre will be even more multidisciplinary than it was in Anna Freud's lifetime.

In sum, the main reason, I think, that Anna Freud's legacy has been revitalized in recent years is that the emphasis on *development* at the core of Anna Freud's work was just what was needed in terms of theory and innovative technique in the period when the whole conceptualization of early childhood shifted. Her Hampstead War Nursery had been like an ideal residential Head Start program: a Head Start program in which children were not only helped to be ready for school and the world outside their families but in which the developmental obstacles that kept them from being ready were assessed and addressed. Among people involved with early childhood, the programs being innovated at the Anna Freud Centre—programs that took off from her work and adapted it for the new era—are also serving as models. For example, there is now a Mother-Infant Program at the Anna Freud Centre, in which mothers having trouble caring for and understanding their newborns can come and be helped by therapists specifically trained to pay attention to the developing mother-child relationship. They treat "the relationship as the patient." In the videos made of such treatments, a viewer can see relationships that are inhibited or impulsive, lacking emotional connection and mutual understanding, come to healthy life as the new mothers learn about themselves and become able to imagine their babies' needs; to interpret what their babies are "saying" with their body language, facial expressions, and wordless talk; and to be self-reflective and baby-reflective. As I watched one of these videos, I found myself imagining the joy it would have given Anna Freud to see, in microscopic detail with the help of the new technology, how therapists working in her tradition are discovering how complex and sensitive are the minds of those just starting out on the developmental roads for which she had made the pioneering maps.

Elisabeth Young-Bruehl
New York City and Toronto, March 2008

PREFACE TO THE
FIRST EDITION

ANNA FREUD, the youngest of Sigmund and Martha Freud's six children, was born in Vienna in 1895, the year to which her father attributed his discovery of the meaning of dreams, the key to his creation—psychoanalysis. To Anna Freud's reckoning, she and psychoanalysis were twins who started out competing for their father's attention.

By the time Anna Freud was thirty and a practicing psychoanalyst as well as a lecturer at the Vienna Psychoanalytic Institute on her specialty, child analysis, she and her twin were no longer rivals. They were merged. In 1936, for his eightieth birthday, she gave her father a book she had written, *The Ego and the Mechanisms of Defense*, which marked a reconfiguration of their lives: she was then the inheritor of her twin, the mother of psychoanalysis; the one to whom primary responsibility for its spirit, its future, was passed. Sigmund Freud, old, weak, faced with the imminent occupation of his homeland by the Nazis, the prospect of exile, called his daughter "Anna Antigone."

The Freud family escaped from Vienna to London in 1938, and Freud died the next year. Anna Freud, in partnership with her friend Dorothy Burlingham, an American, directed a war nursery and then a psychoanalytic training program and a clinic for children, the most renowned institution for child psychoanalysis in the world. During her forty-four years in London, she worked ceaselessly *für die Sache*, as her father had put it, "for the cause," marking her progress with volume after volume of seminal lectures and papers, *The Writings of Anna Freud*.

WHEN she died, in her eighty-sixth year, Anna Freud left behind two literary estates: her father's, which she and her brother Ernst had carefully protected and managed, and her own. She had arranged for both estates to be deposited in the Sigmund Freud Archives at the Library of Congress, Washington, D.C. Her home, 20 Maresfield Gardens, became a museum, a complement to the Freud House that she had helped to establish earlier at Berggasse 19 in Vienna, her birthplace.

Anna Freud's own literary estate resembled an archaeological site, keyed precisely to the day-by-day, year-by-year living of her life. She filed away every piece of paper that came to her at 20 Maresfield Gardens from the end of the Second World War to 1982, and she kept carbon copies of every typewritten communication that left the house. Her filing system was alphabetical by the names of her correspondents. At the end of each year, all the papers for the year were punched with two holes in their left margins and tied up with string into six-inch-thick booklike parcels. Each of the parcels was then labeled with its year and A–E, F–H, I–L, M–R, or S–Z. There were exactly five parcels for each year. The system never varied.

Underneath—chronologically—this precise, professional estate was another layer. Anna Freud took with her from Vienna to London a few of her youthful correspondences—chiefly fifteen years of letters from her older friend Lou Andreas-Salomé—and she later received from other correspondents letters she had written and they had saved. Unlike the postwar correspondences, these are highly personal, unprotected, without her later militant concern for privacy. The early letters reveal the openhearted, childlike mode that her intimates loved her for. In the decades when she had a public persona and international renown, this earlier Anna Freud remained, but far from the public realm—with Dorothy Burlingham, in their vacation houses, in her fantasy life.

The postwar typewritten correspondences are with friends, neighbors, colleagues, psychoanalytic societies, journals and institutions, admirers and fans. Parents wrote to Anna Freud asking for consultations; Viennese émigrés asked for references as they tried to establish themselves after the war; childless couples sought help with adoptions; aspiring psychoanalysts arranged training; autograph collectors sent pleas; magazines, children's homes, nurses' associations, clinics, universities, and political organizations wanted lectures, visits, advice, signatures, contact with the daughter of the Master. From old Viennese psychoanalytic friends, writing in German, came news, photographs of children and grandchildren, reports on clinical problems and writings. Younger analysts wrote asking for help with their projects, information about the history of psychoanalysis. Institutions of all sorts wanted to bestow honorary degrees, dedications, memberships, lectureships, plaques.

Anna Freud was as unable to leave a letter unanswered as she was to leave one unfiled. Only in her later years did she refuse importuning autograph seekers or decide against answering the clearly insane. To the kinds of letters most busy illustrious people would disregard, she responded gently and respectfully: "I am sorry that I have to disappoint you, but none of the courses in psychotherapy that I know of can be combined with Spiritual Healing." Her literary estate is dotted with little monuments to the psychopathology of everyday life and she—in an almost clinical s█████ █████ed each one.

In all of Anna Freud's postwar typewritten letters, there are only a few passages that could be described as intimate, confessional, autobiographical, or memoiristic. When she wished to write personally, in the unguarded mode of her prewar letters, she wrote by hand, away from her workplace, away from secretaries and dictation. Of her handwritten letters, she kept no copies; these were to be in the charge of her friends, for them in the immediate sense and left to their discretion in the longer term.

But the typewritten postwar letters, while not personal, are of course revelatory, in their details and in general. She appears in them as a woman of extraordinary energy, orderliness, productivity, clarity of mind, and altruism. But her desire to be in control is also everywhere apparent, though it is nowhere tyrannical: she was an enlightened despot, warmly sponsoring her subjects' wishes and asking of them that they be loyal in turn not to her personally but to psychoanalysis—as she understood it and represented it. Her expectations were often exhausting to her correspondents, except for those who were unconflicted in their identification with her and "the cause."

Anna Freud gave intense, focused attention to whatever was at hand. A friend once asked her which she thought was the most important of her projects and she replied without hesitation: "Whatever I am doing at the moment." She gave the same calm, restrained, self-aware, and discreet agility of mind to each task and every person, striving always for the appropriate course of action or response. Her letters to children show her in her alertness most clearly. She sent them double-spaced, capital-lettered messages designed not just for their reading levels but also for both the surfaces and the depths of their feelings. One of Dorothy Burlingham's grandchildren, who was due for minor surgery, got a chatty letter about a horse he knew, Smokey, and how Smokey went to the blacksmith whenever his feet grew too large for his shoes: "AND THAT HAPPENS TO PEOPLE SOMETIMES, TOO," she noted.

In Anna Freud's letters, there is no aspiration to understanding or influence beyond psychoanalysis. She was exclusively dedicated to her cause and single-minded in her efforts to live and work psychoanalytically. When she was eighty-five, a depressed young man sent her a lament about the chaotic state of the world, and she sent him a succinct statement of her credo: "I agree with you wholeheartedly that things are not as we would like them to be. However, my feeling is that there is only one way to deal with it, namely to try and be all right oneself, and to create around one at least a small circle where matters are arranged as one wants them to be."

In this biography of Anna Freud, I have tried to tell how Sigmund and Martha Freud's youngest child, jealous of psychoanalysis, became not only her father's successor and, in her own right, her generation's most scientifically exact and wide-ranging theoretical and clinical contributor, but also a woman whose life was, through and through, psychoanalytic. The eight volumes of *The Writings of Anna Freud* and the literary estate in its pre- and postwar layers were my materials. But I have also made this "life and work" with the work, psychoanalysis, as my method.

Sigmund Freud and his early followers initiated psychoanalytic biography writing, and advanced on the basis of their efforts two general characterizations about great intellectual creativity. Creative people were typically, they argued, virtuosos of daydreaming in their youths. Second, in their maturities, they do not tend to be extreme or pure types in psychosexual or emotional terms; they have in them nearly equal mixtures of femininity and masculinity, and of passivity and activity. Anna Freud does not challenge these generalizations. In her youth she was such a daydreamer that even her father was startled by the elaborateness of her creations. She also balanced in herself to quite remarkable effect a maternal, child-loving femininity and an adventurous, feisty masculinity—both enacted in quite conventional ways.

But Anna Freud's creativity, while it illustrates these accepted psychoanalytic generalizations, also suggests other, further possibilities. During her personal psychoanalysis and afterward, in an ongoing, lifelong self-analysis, Anna Freud reflected on herself and on how she came to love and to work as she did. In pieces, and without the intention—or the disguise—of an autobiographer, she wrote the psychoanalytic story of her creative development, and left it, fragmentary, unassembled, in her published papers and unpublished correspondences. For this story, it is my privilege to be the courier.

PART ONE

VIENNA

1

ANNERL

THE YOUNG NEUROLOGIST Sigmund Freud and his wife, Martha, started their family when they were living in the Suehnhaus, an apartment building raised by the emperor Franz Josef as a memorial on the site of the Ringtheater, which had burned to the ground in 1881. Rents from the "House of Atonement" were given to the needy families of the fire's nearly six hundred victims. In 1887, Mathilde Freud, the first baby born in the apartment house, received a present from the emperor.[1]

Otherwise, the Freuds were without public recognition and often quite worried about how to earn the rent they contributed to the emperor's philanthropy. Sigmund Freud had been received coolly in Viennese medical circles as he reported on his exciting and—he was convinced—important work with the pioneering neurologist Jean Martin Charcot at his Salpêtrière Clinic in Paris and with Hippolyte Bernheim, who headed the Nancy School and was famous for developing hypnotic techniques. Freud's first independent theoretical contribution, on male hysteria, was greeted with a similar lack of interest. Although he continued to lecture in his position as *Privatdozent* at Vienna University, his hopes for being hailed as an innovator were thwarted. Without publishing his results, Freud lectured about his comparative studies of hysterical and organic paralyses. But he concentrated his attention on his rounds three times a week among the infant patients at the Kassowitz Institute, his translations of books by Charcot and Bernheim, and his private neurological practice. In December 1887 he began to treat his patients with hypnotic suggestion.

Mathilde was an only child until 1889, when Jean Martin—named after Charcot—was born. A year and a half later, Oliver appeared, and the Freuds moved to more spacious quarters in the Berggasse, a noisy business street near the university's medical faculty. In addition to his family, their cook, and various nursemaids, Freud was financially responsible for his parents and his four unmarried sisters. The summer vacations that he so relished—and that the Viennese heat dictated—were taken modestly and near the city. After 1890, Freud traveled when he could to meet his Berlin friend the physician Wilhelm Fliess for "congresses" on their mutual scientific interests. Even though Freud remained friendly with his Viennese colleague and collaborator Josef Breuer, Fliess was the friend to whom he confided developments in his research into the etiology of hysteria and his experiments with a new technique, "the cathartic method," which was more lastingly therapeutic than hypnotic suggestion.

Ernst Freud was born in 1892, and a little sister, Sophie, in 1893, a financially constricted year that made the total of five children seem quite sufficient, particularly as they, like most Viennese children, were often ill with the many contagious diseases the city's stagnant air fostered, and their mother needed extra help. Then the family's situation, always unpredictable, improved in 1894 and the summer holiday that year included both a month in Reichenau, in the Semmering mountains, and a fortnight's stay with all the children on the Adriatic. But 1894 was not a calm year for Freud himself.

IN the year and a half before Anna Freud's birth in December 1895, her father struggled with diverse symptoms of what his last physician, Max Schur, diagnosed retrospectively as "paroxysmal tachycardia, with anginal pain and signs of left ventricular failure" resulting in "an organic myocardial lesion, most likely a coronary thrombosis in a small artery, or perhaps a postinfectious myocarditis, with temporarily increased nicotine sensitivity."[2] With this full display of medical regalia, Schur tried to resolve much after the fact a question for which Freud himself never had an answer. He could not determine whether he suffered from a chronic myocarditis, as his Viennese colleague Josef Breuer thought, or a nicotine toxicity or hypersensitivity, as his correspondence friend in Berlin, Wilhelm Fliess, thought. So Freud, at the age of thirty-eight, felt a dreadful uncertainty about whether he was a man awaiting death by heart attack or a hypochondriac.

Throughout 1894, Freud made efforts to give up his beloved cigars, and to keep working without them. Depressions came frequently and as he told Fliess "the libido has long since been subdued."[3] With "the hen" and "her five little chicks" off in Reichenau, Freud, waiting for his own departure from Vienna, contemplated what his death would mean: "Among the gloomy thoughts of the past few months there is one that is in second place, right after wife and children—namely, that I shall not be able to prove the sexual thesis any more. After all, one does not want to die either immediately or completely."[4]

Freud kept writing, when he could, on the cases that he and Breuer published the next year as *Studies on Hysteria*—the first major statement about "the sexual thesis," the sexual etiology of hysteria. By the end of the summer, after the Adriatic sojourn, his discomfort and his anxieties had abated. Martha Freud was not informed about the cardiac symptoms, because Freud did not want either to burden her with the possibility of his early death or to overstate a problem that might, with nicotine abstinence, disappear. As Josef Breuer became less and less Freud's confidant during the period when they brought *Studies on Hysteria* to its final form, which was much closer to Freud's views than to Breuer's, Wilhelm Fliess provided both essential support and the more hopeful diagnosis. In "that difficult time when I was forced to believe that I was very close to the end of my life," Freud reminded his friend, "it was your confidence that kept me going."[5]

Despite the subdued condition of Freud's libido, Martha Freud became pregnant for the sixth time in February of 1895, probably just before Fliess came to Vienna to perform nasal surgery on one of

Freud's patients, Emma Eckstein. The operation had horrifying consequences during the weeks when the Freuds learned that their family was unexpectedly going to grow by one more child. Emma Eckstein's condition mysteriously deteriorated after Fliess had performed the surgery and departed for Berlin. A specialist named Rosanes was called in to examine her, and he discovered that Fliess had left a strip of gauze in her nasal cavity. Taken by surprise, Rosanes decided to remove the strip immediately. Emma Eckstein had a severe hemorrhage and went into shock, but Rosanes was able to save her. Freud, who was present at this scene, had to leave and restore himself with a cognac. For weeks, Emma Eckstein was in danger from repeated hemorrhages and further surgical interventions were necessary.[6]

Throughout the spring and summer of 1895, Freud's letters to Fliess were filled with ambivalence. He had begun to distrust Fliess— or begun to acknowledge his distrust—but he also continued to feel intensely his need for Fliess's support and encouragement. On the same February trip to Vienna that had been so fateful for Emma Eckstein, Fliess had treated a sinus infection of Freud's with cocaine (and perhaps cauterization) and elaborated as he did so on his theory that Freud's cardiac symptoms also had nasal connections. Fliess's concern was then turned on himself in late March, when he underwent a series of nasal surgical procedures designed to cure headaches and sinus problems. Freud became quite skeptical about these operations, and he refused to go to Berlin for any further ministrations from Fliess for his own cardiac symptoms. An Easter holiday consisting of a long round-trip train ride and one precious day on the Adriatic was Freud's choice of cure.

While Freud was working on his writings and trying to put the Emma episode behind him, Fliess was elaborating a theory of organic periodicity that included speculations on female fertility during the menarche. Freud responded carefully in his letters to this theory and also let Fliess know that Martha was pregnant. Fliess soon informed Freud that his own wife was expecting their first child. The two discussed names for their children, and Freud was prepared, despite his ambivalence, to name a male child Wilhelm.[7]

Or, it might be argued, because of his ambivalence. The child Sigmund and Martha awaited was their sixth in eight years; and the youngest three had been born at intervals of only a little more than a year in 1891, 1892, and 1893. In the year of Sophie's birth, Mathilde, who was then six, had nearly died of diphtheria—a terrifying episode for her parents. In 1894, laced into his reports of his own difficulties, Freud made it clear to Fliess that Martha Freud was worn out and in need of more rest and recreation than she was getting. Neither their physical nor their mental energies—not to mention their finances— were entirely equal to the prospect of another child. Anna Freud herself maintained in her adulthood that if any acceptable, safe means of contraception had been available to her parents she would not have been born—an idea that it is unlikely she arrived at only by reading the many laments in Freud's published works about civilized society's need for contraception.[8]

During the spring, Freud—with the help of renewed smoking— worked on his *Studies on Hysteria* and a paper on anxiety neurosis. By the summer, he had made an enormous breakthrough in his work and in what he called his "self-analysis." But his progress on a technique for interpreting his dreams was not ready for public view, as he told Fliess in a curious metaphor: "saying anything now would be like sending a six-month-old embryo of a girl to a ball."[9] According to this image, Freud was gestating at a pace about two months ahead of his wife, and it seems that his project was not of the sex to be named Wilhelm.

A dream that Freud had just before his wife's thirty-fourth birthday, which appeared later in *The Interpretation of Dreams* under the title "Irma's injection," reflected at a remove the tumultuous medical events of the early spring and quite directly presented Martha Freud's pregnancy. Both of the dream referents were disguised in Freud's report—or rather twice disguised: once by the dream itself and once by Freud's presentation in his book. "Of each dream," Freud later told his colleague Carl Jung, "I explain only as much as is needed to bring out a specific point."[10]

As he interpreted "Irma's injection," Freud stressed one hidden wish that he saw ramifying through the dream's "plot." This was his wish to be exonerated for any lack of medical conscientiousness. He placed—or "displaced"—blame for Irma's condition on other doctors, though not on the figure of Fliess, who comes forth to aid Freud's search for exculpation. The theme of professional responsibility is intricately drawn out of the dream, but the female characters who came to Freud's mind as he "free-associated" to the central character, Irma, are left relatively uninterpreted except in relation to this theme. The wish that these female figures represented was not for public report, as Freud later told his friend Karl Abraham: "Sexual megalomania is hidden behind it, the three women, Mathilde, Sophie and Anna, are my daughters' three godmothers, and I have them all! There would be one simple therapy for widowhood, of course. All sorts of intimate things, naturally."[11] Freud did not—naturally—want his dream ideas about how to cure young widows suffering from enforced sexual abstinence to be presented to an uncomprehending public. Just as unacceptable would have been an analysis of why, as Freud said, "I was not treating either Irma or my wife very kindly in this dream."[12] They were both making complications, Irma by being a temptation and Martha Freud by being pregnant—a condition for which Freud may well have reproached himself. Irma was what Freud called a "condensation," a figure composed of other figures: she may well have had an element of the troubling Emma Eckstein in her, but she was mainly Anna Hammerschlag Lichtheim, a young widow Freud was then treating, who was related to Sophie Schwab, Sophie Freud's godmother, and friends with Mathilde Breuer, Mathilde Freud's godmother. In December 1895, Anna Hammerschlag Lichtheim became the godmother of Anna Freud.

The last months of Martha Freud's pregnancy, after the family's return to Vienna from the summer holiday, were difficult. Freud wrote to Fliess on September 31: " 'Wilhelm' or 'Anna' is behaving very badly and should see the light in November." And then on November 8: "Martha is already suffering pretty badly. I wish it were over." The child arrived a little behind schedule, but without difficulty. After two months, Freud could report: "Little Anna is flourishing; Martha took a long time to recover." Martha Freud could not or did not wish to nurse her new daughter, and no wet nurse was hired (as was the common practice and the Freuds' practice for at least one other of their children, Martin). By her fifth day, Anna Freud was, her father reported to Fliess, guzzling Gartner's whole milk, a baby formula.[13]

Fortunately, Freud's practice took a turn for the better soon after Anna's birth, and he was eager to interpret her presence as a good omen for the family. "We like to think that the baby has brought a doubling of my practice."[14] Even though the practice took a downturn the next spring, it rose again through the second half of the little daughter's first year. The family was secure enough to vacation in the summer of 1896 at Aussee, in Styria, and Freud was able to fulfill his dream of a month in Italy—Bologna, Venice, Ravenna, Florence—with his younger brother, Alexander. Martha Freud, also in need of a holiday, went off on her own for the first time since her wedding in 1886. She spent two weeks with her mother in Hamburg and then traveled home through Berlin where she stayed with the Fliess family and met the child who did get the name Wilhelm, Robert Wilhelm Fliess—a young man who, like the child who got the name Anna, grew up to be a psychoanalyst.

Soon after Martha Freud's stay at her mother's, when Anna Freud was just a year old, Martha's younger sister Minna Bernays came to join the Freud household. During the preceding ten years, Minna had been living either with her mother or in various private homes where she had worked as a lady's companion or governess. This decade was in stark contrast to her years as the fiancée of Ignaz Schoenberg, a Sanskrit scholar and a close friend of Sigmund Freud's; but Schoenberg had died of pulmonary tuberculosis, and Minna seems never again to have fallen in love.

Anna Freud's mother and her Tante Minna were quite unalike in temperament, though each reflected in her own way the Orthodox Jewish and rigorous North German mores with which they had grown up. Freud had remarked in the days when he was courting Martha and his friend Schoenberg was courting Minna that the quartet was made up of two types: the good ones, Martha and Schoenberg, and the wild, passionate ones, himself and Minna. He noted to his future wife: "That is why we get on better in a criss-cross arrangement; why two similar people like Minna and myself don't suit each other specially; why the two good-natured ones don't attract each other." His preference was for "someone delicate whom I could take care of."[15]

Minna was also quite a contrast to Martha in the quasi-maternal role she assumed after joining the Freud family. She was large, stately, impressively sure of herself, energetic, and given to expressing her opinions just as vigorously as their mother did. Martha was smaller, quieter, more retiring, sharp-witted but very seldom sharp-tongued. The sisters moved in different, if overlapping, spheres. Martha held sway over all matters domestic; she made sure that the household ran with completely non-Viennese efficiency and punctuality; that the meals were on the table exactly on schedule; that the servants were content as well as competent; that Freud's professional guests and their personal friends were graciously and warmly received. Minna was freer to participate in conversations with Freud's colleagues, and to leave the family to travel. She sometimes went with Freud on his journeys to Austrian spas or to Italy, and she was the first household member to act informally as Freud's personal secretary—a role later filled in turn by each of his three daughters.

Minna was also more interested than her sister in Sigmund Freud's psychoanalytic theories. Martha was quite able to cede to others, Minna included, the role of intellectual companion. She did this with remarkable tact later when Freud turned so intensely for support and intellectual exchange to his friend Wilhelm Fliess, a man whose position in the ranks of the good and good-natured ones, the Martha types, Freud extolled in an 1893 letter to Minna.[16] Frau Ida Fliess, by contrast, was jealous and played a role in subverting the friendship.

Martha's deference was not at all a matter of lack of intellectual confidence or ability; she chose to stay outside of the work sphere, to promote it by leaving Freud free to attract others to himself and his science, and to protect her love for her husband by letting others love the one dimension of him she found foreign—psychoanalysis. As Anna Freud remarked many years later: "So far as psychoanalysis was concerned, my mother never cooperated. . . . My mother believed in my father, not in psychoanalysis."[17]

From his study of Freud's and Martha Bernays's premarital correspondence, Freud's biographer Ernest Jones arrived at an opinion about the Bernays sisters that he did not express in his biography. Jones felt that Martha Bernays, despite her obvious strength of character, was unable to assert herself against her mother—a woman whom Anna Freud remembered, when she and Jones were corresponding about the biography, as despotic. Minna, on the other hand, though as much or more devoted to her mother than Martha was, could be quite unsparing with her criticisms. This difference between the sisters in relation to their mother was important to Freud, who had used it adroitly.

The occasion of Freud's maneuver was a quarrel that Jones decided to pass over for the sake of avoiding pain to Anna Freud's cousins: "the reasons for [the quarrel] cannot be given here."[18] Martha and Minna Bernays's brother, Eli, who was responsible for supporting the Bernays women as Freud was for supporting his sisters and parents, incurred Freud's wrath on a number of occasions before and after a peaceful interlude in 1883 during which he married Freud's oldest sister, Anna. Freud had furiously held Eli responsible for Frau Bernays's decision to remove herself and her two daughters from Vienna during their engagements. It was Freud's theory that Eli wanted his widowed mother, with whom he was locked in a struggle for the title of head of the household, sidelined in Hamburg. Freud accepted the relocation of his fiancée to Hamburg, but he drew the line when Eli, who had been entrusted with part of Martha's small dowry from an aunt, would not return the money and thus held up Freud's hopes for bringing his long engagement finally to an end. Three months before the marriage date in 1886, when Eli had evaded Martha's pleas for the money, Freud was ready to issue an ultimatum: Martha was to condemn her brother in no uncertain terms or they could not go ahead with their marriage. She refused. Freud then importuned Eli himself and avoided a rupture with his fiancée by getting the money, which had not been embezzled, as Freud thought, but simply tangled into Eli's complicated financial speculations. Peace was negotiated without the family rift that Martha had deemed intolerable.

She did not disagree with Freud's disapproval of Eli on moral grounds: Eli's financial troubles were compounded by his infidelity to Freud's sister and a number of illegitimate children to whom he gave money. But her family loyalty proved stronger than her moral outrage—and also stronger than Freud's desire to sweep his rival for family power out of the path of his marriage plans. Although he gave way to Martha's view, Freud did, however, as Jones noted, try to mitigate his bride's subordination to the real head of the Bernays household, the mother who ultimately commanded the loyalty. "Your father," Jones wrote to Anna Freud, "must have detested the old lady and he did a clever bit of weaning by bringing out a shift onto

Minna." Her younger sister became for Martha not so much a mother substitute as an ally for detaching herself from her mother's house and law—her personal law and her Orthodox Judaism. With Minna as his own ally, Freud also did not have to stand alone in his criticism of Frau Bernays or in his later efforts to raise his own children nonreligiously. Minna was the demilitarized zone. And Eli, fortunately, emigrated to America in 1892, from whence his children, the "American cousins," were always received graciously when they visited the Freuds and Tante Minna.

On the other side of the extended family, Martha and Minna stood together in a careful arrangement that both included and excluded Sigmund Freud's mother, Amalie. The older Frau Freud was widowed a year after Anna Freud's birth, not long after Minna came to Vienna, and Freud then made a habit of calling on her every Sunday morning. He visited there with the four sisters who remained with her, particularly the one he appreciated most, Dolfi (Adolphine), the youngest, who had nursed their father through his final illness. It was not uncommon in the Viennese middle class for the youngest girl in a large family to forgo marriage, staying on with the parents— as Anna Freud later did—and becoming the link between the parents and the other children's spouses. On Sunday evenings, Amalie, always escorted by Dolfi and often accompanied by the other daughters, dined with the Freuds. With Minna in the house, Martha was not—as it were—a single daughter-in-law; they could deal in tandem with the energetic, demanding, doting, and rather childish mother of Sigmund Freud.

MARTHA Freud and Minna Bernays—"the two mothers," as Freud called them—joined forces in ruling the household sphere.[19] But neither of them took full responsibility for the youngest child's needs. The woman who was what the psychoanalyst Anna Freud called the "primary caretaker," or the "psychological mother," was Josefine Cihlarz, a Catholic nursemaid, or *Kinderfrau*, hired when Anna Freud was born. Josefine also had responsibilities for the other younger children, Ernst and Sophie, but a governess took charge of the older ones, Mathilde, Martin, and Oliver.

Josefine cared for the little children at home, and for all on their daily walks in the public parks around the Ringstrasse. "I can still recall clearly our little procession," Martin Freud later wrote in his memoirs, "the baby lying in the pram [pushed by Josefine] and the taller children walking at its side, sometimes with their hands on its rails." Usually these promenades were peaceful, Martin recalled, but not during the demonstrations against Franz Josef's government that took place near the university or the parliament buildings. "On one of these . . . occasions our little detachment, commanded by Josefine, found itself between the rioters and [the Imperial] dragoons. It narrowly escaped being trampled down, perambulator and all, under the hooves of the cavalry. The incident was, of course, highly alarming."[20]

Josefine seems to have had a number of opportunities to be the dearly beloved rescuer. The one that fixed itself in Anna Freud's memory was not of the military sort that appealed to Martin. While the Freud household was asleep one night, the gas supply to the apartment immediately below them leaked and an explosion rocked the building. As the watchmaker who lived in the apartment scrambled to safety through a back window, Sigmund Freud rushed into the room where his boys slept to ask—Martin recalled—"Are the monkeys all right?" The nursemaid, Josefine, went immediately to grab Anna from her crib and only then came to check on the older children. No damage was done in the Freuds' apartment, and the only consequence for their living arrangements was the happy one— for them—that the watchmaker decided to give up his apartment. Sigmund Freud was able to rent its three rooms for an office, thus relieving the overcrowding in the "monkey" quarters.[21]

The consequence for Anna Freud was just as pleasant. Her brothers put to Josefine the question: "If there were a fire, who would you save first?" And she answered, unhesitatingly, "Anna." This story was passed along to Anna Freud when she was old enough to understand it, and it constituted proof of what she felt: that she was Josefine's favorite, Josefine's—in effect—only child.

When she was a toddler, Anna Freud offered a proof in deed of this special bond. On one of their expeditions to the Ringstrasse parks, she was playing near a bench on which Martha Freud sat watching over her children. Josefine disappeared from Anna's view for a moment, and Anna, in a panic, went racing off to look for her— even though her mother was nearby. The child got lost, and was found only after an anxious search through the park by everyone in the Freud contingent. Many years later, Anna Freud used this story to indicate that it was Josefine's attention that made her feel secure. She could also have said the same thing differently: that her behavior was a comment on how she felt about her mother. When she was grown up and a child analyst, Anna Freud put this emphasis at the center of a beautiful essay entitled "On Losing and Being Lost":

It is only when parental feelings are ineffective or too ambivalent, or when aggression is more effective than their love, or when the mother's emotions are temporarily engaged elsewhere. that children not only feel lost but, in fact, get lost. This usually happens under conditions that make rationalization easy, but which, on the other hand, are much too common to explain the specific event, such as crowds, a full department store, etc. It is interesting that children usually do not blame themselves for getting lost. An example of this was a little boy, lost in a store, who, after being reunited with his mother, accused her tearfully. "You losted me!" (not "I lost you!").[22]

In all of her memories of Josefine, Anna Freud stressed her *Kinderfrau*'s warm, sympathetic nature. She had an ability to empathize with children and animals that Anna Freud, who was passionate about animals, relayed with an anecdote. A neighbor's dog, unhappy on his leash in the garden behind the Berggasse apartment building, howled with such force and persistence that all the adult nerves in the Freud household were frayed—all but Josefine's. The *Kinderfrau*'s simple comment was—in saucy Viennese: "Dafür ist er ja ein Hund" ("He can't help it, he's a dog").

The stories about Josefine that Martin Freud set in his memoirs are, by contrast, focused on her rather severe judgments.[23] During another tumultuous day at the park, the Freud children "saw uniformed police, as always in pairs, leading between them somewhat disheveled students. Josefine ordered us not to look, giving it as her firm opinion that anybody arrested by the police must be a wicked criminal at whom a really good child should not look." Martha Freud, then, contradicted Josefine to explain that "a man arrested in political strife could very well be a brave man and, possibly, a noble character." In retrospect, Martin found this opinion of his mother's surprising, for she "could hardly have been more conservative or more law-abiding"; so he attributed her opinion to "her deep love of my father who, at heart, had always been a rebel against convention." About Josefine's attitude he offered not a comment but another story: "Josefine never failed to explain as we passed [the Mensa Academica, a canteen near the university buildings] that only very poor people, people destitute and without decent pride, would eat in such a place."

Martin's romantic memories show that the Josefine he knew and the Josefine Anna Freud knew were as different as their ages and their needs for her. But what all the Freud children appreciated about Josefine was her dedication to them. The boys, who loved to tease, tried her patience but realized that her notions about what was good for them would prevail. During a period most boys go through, rebellion against taking baths, one of them cited to Josefine the example of the Eskimos, who, he insisted in a scholarly tone, went for months without bathing and were none the worse for it. Taking these Eskimos not for a people living halfway around the world but for some disreputable Viennese, she reduced her young charges to laughter— and obedience: "Was gehen mich anderen Leut'kinder an?" ("What's it to me what other people's kids do?").

Josefine stayed with the Freud family until Anna Freud completed her first year of school. Then she left, married, and had a family of her own. For Anna Freud, she remained "meine alte Kinderfrau, meine alteste Beziehung und die allerwirklichste aus meiner Kinderzeit" ("my old nursemaid, the oldest relation and the most genuine of my childhood").[24] So the twenty-nine-year-old Anna Freud wrote to a friend after she had, the day before, attended Josefine's funeral in Vienna.

A s THE YOUNGEST CHILD, and the one the Freuds had clearly decided was to be their last, "Annerl"—as Anna Freud was called—was raised under somewhat altered household circumstances. The method of contraception that her parents resorted to was abstinence; and this modus vivendi coincided—probably not without a causal connection—with Freud's period of preparation for his most ambitious and preoccupying piece of writing, the enormous *Die Traumdeutung* (*The Interpretation of Dreams*). Freud's "self-analysis" was very agitating to him in 1896, particularly after the death of his father, Jakob, in the fall. The dream book was in Freud's mind in May 1897, and he drafted most of it during 1898 (up to the summer vacation); he then left it aside and finished it in the summer of 1899.[25] Freud was always careful to give his children as much of his attention as his practice, his lecturing, his correspondence, and his writing permitted, but the proportions did vary: more for the children in the summer, more for the work during the professional year, more for the writings in the intensely productive periods. Anna Freud was an infant and a toddler in a period of which her father later said: "Insight such as this falls to one's lot but once in a lifetime."[26]

The family's vacation schedule also altered. Not only did Martha Freud take her first vacation away from the family in Anna Freud's tenth month, but Sigmund and Martha Freud began, when Anna was one and a half, to take short vacations together at the end of the summers. In both 1897 and 1898, they made September excursions to northern Italy—though the later trip was not a joy to Frau Freud, who had to abandon their itinerary in Merano for recuperation from a stomach complaint. In 1900, when Anna Freud was four and a half, they went again to northern Italy. These journeys (interestingly enough, unmentioned in Martin's memoir, which is a veritable Book of Vacations) meant that the children either stayed on at the summer lodgings or returned to Vienna with Tante Minna, the governess, and Josefine.

The summer holidays when "Papa"—as the Freud children called their father—could be with them were richly remembered by all. When she was in her mid-twenties, Anna Freud reminisced about their mushroom-picking expeditions to her friend and confidante Lou Andreas-Salomé, who committed the description to her journal:

> Listening to Anna talk about her father . . . When they went collecting mushrooms he always told them to go into the wood quietly and he still does this; there must be no chattering and they must roll up the bags they have brought under their arms, so that the mushrooms shall not notice; when their father found one he would cover it quickly with his hat, as though it were a butterfly. The little children—and now his grandchildren—used

to believe what he said, while the bigger ones smiled at his credulity. . . . The children were paid in pennies for the mushrooms they had found, while the best mushroom of all (it was always Ernst who found it) got a florin. It was the quality and not the quantity of the mushrooms that mattered.[27]

These were the happy memories of later childhood, when Anna Freud had begun to get over the condition that made her early years miserable: "the experience of being left out by the big ones, of being only a bore to them, and of feeling bored and left alone."[28] As an older woman she told a friend:

There are two such occasions left in my memory which serve as a cover for all others. In the first, I was 4 or 5 years old and all the other five children had been invited to a circus by a visiting uncle; I had to stay at home because of a cold. . . . I felt very miserable and I have kept an attraction to circuses ever since. The second happened several years later on a summer holiday when the "others" all went off in a boat and left me at home, either because the boat was too full or I was "too little." This time I did not complain and my father, who was watching the scene, praised me and comforted me. That made me so happy that nothing else mattered.

In his memoir, Martin noted the kind of experience for which these two episodes may have served as a cover. During the three years that the family vacationed in Aussee—the first three years of Anna Freud's life:

. . . we were still very young children, the eldest being eleven and the youngest only three [in 1898]; but hardly a day passed without father taking us out for walks in the forest. My mother's organizing genius was not apparent [on the walks], but I think she had ruled that no child could join the expeditions with father until he was house-trained, or perhaps, one should say, forest-trained. Since it was felt that the presence of a governess or nursemaid on these delightful walks with father would add unwelcome constraint, the need for attention to this detail becomes obvious; my mother would never expect father to act as a nursemaid. As it happened his expeditionary force could never boast more than five explorers of tender age.[29]

The message of this discreetly oblique passage is that Anna Freud, not quite three years old, was neither house- nor forest-trained and had to endure being the only one of the troops to miss the mushroom picking. Toilet training, as the child analyst Anna Freud noted, was carried out in turn-of-the-century families like hers quite strictly and on a firm schedule—a schedule not adjusted to the particular needs of particular children. "One can say," she noted, "that the whole second year of life proceeds under the impact of these frequently very energetic efforts on the part of the adults to inculcate cleanliness."[30] In somewhat more technical psychoanalytic prose, she described the consequences for children like herself:

All too frequently, environmental pressure toward toilet training and condemnation of aggressions set in while the anal-sadistic phase is still at its peak. The infant may concur or identify with both these attitudes, which puts an end to any possible enjoyment of dirty matter or of the urge to attack and hurt people who are at the same time his most important love objects. The child's efforts to come to terms with the offending part within himself then lead to the precocious employment of defenses such as repression, reaction formation, and turning aggression against the self. Following this, there appear such manifestations as disgust with dirty hands, excessive tendencies toward orderliness, and repetitive behavior.[31]

Toilet training was the domain of womenfolk—not something, as Martin indicated, that Sigmund Freud would have been involved with. If Anna Freud battled over it and suffered the punishment of not being allowed on walks in the woods, the battle was with her mother figures. Martha Freud had a reputation among her children for her domineering attitudes toward how their bodily needs and drives should be approached. The boys loved to tell the story of her reaction to a suggestion from the governess that a doctor should be called to see a feverish Freud child. She snapped: "Wie kann ich den Doktor rufen, ich weiss selber noch nicht was dem Kind fehlt?" ("How can I telephone the doctor, I don't yet know myself what is the matter with the child?"). Anna Freud, who was not often able to find the humor in her mother's firmness, said simply: "My mother observed no rules, she made her own rules."[32]

Anna Freud's father, spared any responsibility for the day-to-day health discussions or for the toilet training, seems to have had a rather relaxed attitude toward "the urge to attack and hurt people" that is so typical of two- and three-year-olds. When Anna Freud was just two, he told Wilhelm Fliess by letter: "Recently Anna complained that Mathilde had eaten all the apples and demanded that [Mathilde's] belly be slit open (as happened to the wolf in the fairy tale of the little goat). She is turning into a charming child."[33]

Anna Freud fought on well past the second year, the year she had declared as the typical battle year of that era of child rearing, and the character result by the end of her childhood was an adventurous, fearless girl who was also very prim and orderly, even if not quite as meticulous as Oliver, who won the family prize in this domain. The adventurous side of her personality came to the fore with Martin and Ernst, and she seems to have associated it with the big boys' prerogatives. But she also associated it with her father's adventurousness. When Freud went to Athens in 1904 with his younger brother, Alexander, she—then aged eight—had missed him terribly. She told her father's biographer Ernest Jones in 1954: "I remember that he sent me a picture postcard from Athens which I still see most vividly although to my regret I cannot find it now. It showed a little girl in a bathing suit pushing a toy sailboat in blue waters and he had written underneath "Möcht'auch nach Athens!" ("Wish also for Athens!"), an allusion to my very many wishes at that time. At the time this meant to me, curiously enough, a sort of promise that he would take me there."[34]

When she was ten, Martin enjoyed taking her swimming, carrying "my small sister Anna on my back," in the south Tyrolean Lake Molveno. Later in that summer, he and Ernst took her out in a small sailboat on Lake Garda.

Quite cocksure in our seamanship, one day we invited our little sister Anna to join us, possibly to impress her with our efficiency as sailors. She came trustfully and, I may say, she recalls the incident better than I do. The south wind had freshened and a sea was rising, but this meant nothing to sailors like Ernst and me, not until we found our little ship becoming quite disobedient and doing what she liked. . . . My sister Anna recalls that her brothers asked her to lie flat in the bottom of the boat, evidently, I suppose, to save her head from being struck by the boom which was flying from side to side. . . . She recalls that she accepted the command gladly since she was enjoying the adventure tremendously and was not a bit afraid.

The family's one nonsailor and nonswimmer, Martha Freud, observing this adventure about to become a disaster, courageously commandeered a boat for hire at the dock and set out to rescue her children in their pitching, sloshing craft. Neither of the Freud parents was given to making an uproar over such incidents, and there were no recriminations.[35]

But Annerl's place was much more commonly the one that Martin presented in his description of the family's carriage trip between Lavarone and Lake Garda that summer. Two carriages were needed to transport the Freuds and their holiday baggage the twenty-five miles. In the rear carriage, Anna sat lodged between her parents, with Mathilde, who had been seriously ill the year before, quietly opposite. In the front carriage were the three boys and Sophie, adventurously alone with the Italian driver.

When she was not on larks with the boys, Anna Freud was a model good girl. She was, for example, as fastidious in her dress as any of the proper adults around her, and she did not like to be disheveled or unstarched. During their south Tyrolean vacation, one of her playmates, Anny Rosenberg, the seven-year-old daughter of one of Freud's pediatrician friends, who was also renowned in her family for not being a good girl, induced the ten-year-old Anna Freud to play near a creek. A large stone that Anny was using to build a dam slipped from her hands and hit the water. Anna Freud's pinafore and stockings were drenched. In tears, she ran home to change, ignoring Anny Rosenberg's challenge: "You could just let it dry!"

Sigmund Freud was, of course, skeptical about how accidental this accident had been: "Sometimes we contribute a little," he told Anny, and then impressed her by issuing no reprimands and making a joke of his daughter's distress. Even Anna Freud found the episode funny years later, when Anny Rosenberg, then a young physician seeking psychoanalytic training, challenged her again, this time by asking her childhood friend to be her analyst. Anna Freud was uncertain about whether she should consent, but Anny got her way by suggesting, "You aren't going to let a little splash stand in the way, are you?"

THE six Freud children developed in contrast to one another, as is common in large families, like Sigmund Freud's own, which was a family of seven, not including a boy who died in infancy or two much older stepbrothers. The six Freud children were divided into two groups of three. Martin's description reflected the family accounting system: "The three elder children, Mathilde, myself and Oliver, were born in the Suehnhaus; the three younger, Ernst, Sophie and Anna, were born in the flat at Berggasse 19, where the family lived for forty-seven years, from 1891 to 1938."[36] The older children had grown up with a shared nursemaid, and a shared governess during their early years of schooling.

But the age groupings did not dictate the play groupings. Martin and Ernst became playmates, sailing, ice-skating, and hiking partners, while Oliver went his own way, which was not the way of physical activity but of solitary intellectual projects. He enjoyed mathematics and drawing—eventually, mechanical engineering. Oliver was, from an early age, a precisionist, critical of Martin's cavalier attitude toward spelling, intolerant of any road signs or maps not perfectly executed. He was an excellent scholar, always at the top of his form. The young Oliver Freud's fascination with (in his father's words) "making plans of the mountains here [on vacation] just as he does with the underground lines and tramways in Vienna" was a source of amusement in the family.[37] Later, when he showed the excessive cleanliness, ritualistic orderliness, and indecisiveness symptomatic of an obsessional neurosis, the amusement all turned to worry—until Oliver was successfully treated by one of his father's younger colleagues.

When she was a child, Anna Freud received Martin's big-brotherly care. He taught her to swim and took her for hikes. But later she favored Ernst, the most stable and charming of the boys, and called him "my closest brother."[38] Oliver remained an enigma to her, although she appreciated his expertise. One of her playmates once asked her if she knew how to use the telephone; "No," she replied, "about such things we go to ask Oliver."

In Martin's memoir, Sophie is mentioned only in his opening

catalog of the siblings. His fond feeling is most obvious when he writes of Mathilde, his protective older sister, who several times rescued him from humiliations and threats to his "honor"—about which he cared a great deal. Anna Freud shared this perspective: she adored the protective, sensible Mathilde but mixed her strong love for Sophie with jealousy. Mathilde and Sophie, on the other hand, were united in their passion for handicrafts of all sorts, particularly knitting, and for smart clothes and the understated elegance their mother cultivated. Mathilde later ran a boutique specializing in handmade, handwoven clothes.

Sophie was her mother's favorite, and as a child she was very reluctant to share her mother's attentions. Anna Freud told a friend: "When my siblings and I had measles (long ago), my sister Sophie [age 7–8] was very ill, high fever and delirious. In the delirium she was heard to say over and over: 'I want my mummy, no not your mummy, I want my mummy.' "[39] She and Martha Freud often traveled together, and they spent stints of two weeks to two months together at Karlsbad in the years 1910 and 1911, when Sophie was ill and needed to "take the waters" at the spa.

Among the boys, Frau Freud favored Oliver, who was a beautiful child, dark-haired and dark-eyed ("Italian," remarked Martin with a little jealousy). He and Sophie were the most lovely of the children, and the most tractable. Freud also appreciated Oliver's intellect, and told his friend and fellow analyst Max Eitingon that before Oliver's obsessional symptoms had appeared, the boy had been "my pride and my secret hope."[40] As their children grew up, Frau Freud joined her husband in appreciating Ernst, the one who always found the best mushrooms, whom they called their "lucky child."[41] Ernst became quite independent: he told people who asked him why he became an architect that the profession was not one his father or any other member of the family knew anything about. Ernst did not, like Martin and Oliver, go through classical Gymnasium preparation; he went to a technical school and on to architectural study in Munich before he started to practice in Berlin.

Martin had a difficult relationship with his mother. Freud's analysis of it shows how little the bitter episode of Eli Bernays's interference in the Freuds' wedding plans had receded from Freud's memory: "He is not his mother's favorite son," Freud told his

Swiss analytic colleague Carl Jung, "on the contrary, she treats him almost unjustly, compensating at his expense for her overindulgence towards her brother, whom he resembles a good deal, whereas, strangely enough, I compensate in my treatment of him for my unfriendliness towards the same person (now in New York)."[42]

Freud adored for their girlish charms both Sophie and Mathilde, who Anna declared was his favorite while she was denying the persistent idea that Sophie was.[43] Mathilde was always held in the family as the standard of reasonableness and good nature. Her virtues would, her father reassured her in a letter that tells as much about him as about her, win her a trustworthy husband: "The more intelligent young men are sure to know what to look for in a wife—gentleness, cheerfulness, and the talent to make their life easier and more beautiful."[44] Freud did not feel that he had to reassure Sophie about her attractiveness. As a three-year-old at the 1896 wedding of Freud's sister Rosa to Heinrich Graf, Sophie was precious: "The loveliest part of the wedding, by the way, was our Sopherl—with curled hair and a wreath of forget-me-nots on her head."[45]

What he adored his little Annerl for was not her femininity, but something rather different: he called it *Unartigkeit*, naughtiness. In 1899, when she was three, he found her "cheeky," once even "beatified by naughtiness." Freud obviously enjoyed telling Fliess about his daughter's saucy, adventurous side: "Recently I was told that little Anna said on Tante Minna's birthday: 'On birthdays I am usually rather good.' "[46] He indulged his littlest at the midday meal when he entered the family quarters from his office and greeted her "by making a funny sound, something between a growl and a grunt."[47] This naughty side of Anna Freud was later covered over with goodness, but it never disappeared—especially because her father loved it.

Mathilde, who was a lively, intelligent student and a great reader, went through a period of hero-worshiping regard for the ancient Greeks, and then the Vikings, which delighted her father. But Anna was the one who made up stories, lived in stories, and had a peculiar insightfulness about the antiquities her father loved: "Little Anna [not yet three years old] has not inappropriately described a small Roman statuette I bought in Innsbruck as 'an old child.' "[48] Although she was known to Sigmund Freud's small circle of followers as the little girl in *The Interpretation of Dreams* who dreamed up a whole menu of goodies the night after she had been denied food because of a stomach ache, in her family Anna Freud was known more for her abilities as a daydreamer and a teller, later a writer, of elaborate tales with dozens of heroic characters.

Martin was the one, on the other hand, who had literary aspirations as a child. He wanted to be a poet and signed his letters "Dichter M.F." until his adolescence and lack of success put an end to what Freud called "his attacks of poetitis."[49] Martin wrapped himself in fantasies of being praised and elevated that were not unlike those his littlest sister created. His memoir reflects a "family romance" in which the emperor Franz Josef and the Imperial officers figure as the loved ones of a "stout royalist" and admirer of military uniforms and male athletic prowess; all criticism of his father is suppressed as Freud is raised into the domain of these "ego ideals." "To have a genius for a father is not a common experience," Martin noted laconically. "The son of a genius remains the son of a genius, and his chances of winning human approval of anything he may do hardly exist if he attempts to make any claim to a fame detached from that of his father."[50] Martin struggled continually with this feeling and the attachment to his father that it rested upon, but his more immediate difficulties came from the fact that he was, as Anna Freud noted, "the one to whom all the accidents happened"—including a skiing accident resulting in a broken thigh.[51] That his genius father understood such accidents as having very complex motives for avoiding other kinds of trials was probably not easy for Martin: "He had told me nothing about this projected skiing trip," Freud noted in his February 17, 1911, letter to Jung. "I knew that a few days before he had been in a fight in the barracks yard and was expecting to be called before a court of honor. As for the erotic or heterosexual motives, I heard of them only later . . ."[52]

The vocation for which Mathilde and Sophie were raised was marriage. Mathilde was a gracious teenager, spirited and surrounded by beaux. In 1909, she married a Viennese businessman, Robert Hollitscher, who was considerably older. But Mathilde, who had suffered through a number of serious childhood illnesses, including the nearly fatal diphtheria of 1893, was thwarted from motherhood by a dreadful episode. In 1905, when she was eighteen, she was operated on for appendicitis. The surgeon, Rosanes, the same man who had operated on Emma Eckstein back in 1895, who was an ear, nose, and throat specialist, wanted to try out a new method for ligature of blood vessels. But only a few hours after the operation, the blood vessels opened and Mathilde almost died of the internal bleeding and then the reopening of her wound. For days she lay in a sanatorium with a high fever—her family did not know whether she would live. The fever did break, and she eventually regained her health, but she had to undergo a number of smaller operations to remove cysts resulting from the first surgery. The only happy consequence of one of these operations was that she met Robert Hollitscher at the Merano pensione where she was sent to recuperate. But even after her marriage Mathilde was still in treatment, and she was never able to conceive.[53]

For Anna Freud, Sophie was the most difficult sibling, the focus of her jealousy—and Sophie awarded this honor to her little sister too. The *Kinderfrau*, Josefine, taught Anna Freud to knit so that she could participate in the family knitting circle, which included all the females in the house. The circle was headed up by Tante Minna, the most spectacular producer, who had taught both Mathilde and Sophie. But Anna Freud felt that her own work was worth little praise, particularly in comparison to Sophie's. And Sophie flatly declared that Anna was not good at knitting—a remark that her little sister remembered for the rest of her life. Still, Anna persisted in knitting to such an extent that her parents had to ask her—without success—to spend less time at it. "When I was a little girl and had a new [knitting] project, I had to start it at once," Anna Freud told a friend later in her life. "I have not lost that enthusiasm. My mother tried to moderate this habit, but she was not successful, I am still the same."[54]

Freud also tried to moderate what he called her "passionate excesses," but his entreaties resulted only in a conversion: she took up weaving. His efforts to understand her then brought him to one of his wilder anthropological speculations: that weaving is the one technique historically attributable to female ingenuity, and that it has served the unconscious motive for women of producing a cover for their "genital deficiency."[55]

Sophie's beauty was also hard for Anna Freud to bear. She felt herself to be lacking the slim waist and trim ankles that her sister had, and as she grew into her adolescence she favored the long-skirted traditional country dress, the dirndl, that disguised her waist and covered her thick ankles. She also developed a slightly hunched forward posture—one that hours of sitting over knitting aggravated—of the sort adolescents use for hiding. The two youngest Freuds developed their version of a common sisterly division of territories: "beauty" and "brains." Thus they lived up to their names and to the characters of the females in Freud's "Irma's injection" dream. Sophie was named after Sophie Schwab, an attractive niece of Professor Hammerschlag, Freud's revered instructor in Scripture and Hebrew. This Sophie was married to Josef Paneth, a doctor who had befriended Freud when they were colleagues at the Institute of Physiology, and the Paneths had raised a family. Anna had been named after Anna Hammerschlag Lichtheim, the same Professor Hammerschlag's very intelligent but quite plain daughter, who had been widowed after only a year of marriage. She was a schoolteacher as well as a patient of Freud's.[56]

Anna Freud even objected to her name because she thought it was common and plain, while "Sophie" was lovely and sophisticated. Her father tried to console her by pointing out that "Anna" was a palindrome, reading the same left to right as right to left.[57] But it was the child in him and not his child who enjoyed this kind of orthographic game.

Sophie was to Anna what Oliver was to Martin in their childhoods—a pretty competitor. "Oliver always inspired admiration from strangers we met, when his brothers could hardly attract a glance," Martin recalled. Martha Freud had been rather blunt with her oldest boy: she told him that "the fairy godmother who gives beauty to babies was not present at my birth; she had been replaced by another fairy who gave me a beautiful imagination."[58] While he cultivated this second-best gift, Martin drew attention to himself with exploits and adventures and was known as something of a mischief-maker, a card. Sigmund Freud remarked in a letter to Fliess about his two-and-a-half-year-old daughter: "Annerl is turning into a charming child; she is of the same type as Martin, physically and mentally."[59] (This remark did not appear in the first edition of the Fliess letters, which Anna Freud helped to prepare; it cannot have pleased her.) Like her name, this assessment too had a degree of self-fulfilling prophecy about it: for Anna Freud felt herself to have been passed over by the first fairy godmother and admired for her imaginativeness— initially for her saucy sayings, and later for her literary sensibility.

Aɴɴᴀ Fʀᴇᴜᴅ started school when she was almost six, in 1901. To get to her first private elementary school, she had to walk with Josefine, but a second school, where she went from 1903 to 1905, was in Grünentorgasse, only two blocks away, and she could go alone. During these years, the Freuds were living in much more reliable financial circumstances, in part due to the fact that Freud had finally, in 1902, been made a professor at the university, a position that meant much more prestige, which, in turn, meant more patients.

Most of the Freud children's schoolmates also came from professional families, but only the Jewish ones were ever their friends. Many of Anna Freud's peers were doctors' daughters, and she shared with them Sunday-afternoon parties at the home of Dr. Kassowitz, where they played with the children their fathers treated at the Kassowitz Institute. She associated with non-Jewish girls at school, but she was never invited to their homes. One time she brought home for a visit Hertha von Arnim-Eperjesy, a school friend who was both Gentile and aristocratic, but, as Anna Freud noted in a reflection on the social barriers separating Jews and non-Jews in Vienna before the First World War: "I was never invited back to her house, as I remember well."[60]

Anna Freud's school years were of the sort described in her favorite volume of poetry, Rainer Maria Rilke's *Das Buch der Bilder*.

> *Da rinnt der Schule lange Angst und Zeit*
> *mit Warten hin, mit lauter dumpfen Dingen.*
> *O Einsamkeit, o schweres Zeitverbringen* . . .

> *The school's stream of hours and anxiety*
> *winds on with waiting and dull things.*
> *O loneliness, o heavy marking of time* . . .[61]

She was often bored, and she turned into such a complainer that her family resorted to bribery. As she said to a friend late in her life, when her reputation for stoicism and fortitude was firmly set: "Can you imagine that I was a whiney child? I was promised a present if I did not whine for a whole day."[62] Elsa Reiss, who was principal of Anna's elementary school and renowned for her lively teaching, was engaged as a private tutor while Anna Freud prepared to enroll in the Salka Goldman Cottage Lyceum, a secondary school for girls between the ages of ten and sixteen. But this plan, though it provided a supplement to the boring schooling, also aggravated the younger Freud sisters' rivalry, for Sophie was included in the tutoring arrangement. Anna chafed at the slow pace of the lessons Fräulein Reiss designed for them both, and Sophie resented yielding to her sister any share of the tutor's attention.[63]

Anna Freud's attitude toward school was not exceptional in the family. All the children enjoyed their summer vacations too much to be eager for September. They had the chance to run wilder, to spend more time with their father, and to be out of the apartment that Anna Freud once described as "eleven rooms and one bathroom," a rather congested arrangement for nine family members and their help, which probably contributed to the high incidence of intestinal complaints in the family (including a duodenal ulcer for young Ernst). Anna Freud once noted in jest to a friend that it would have been very expensive for her to have developed any vanity—another bathroom would have been required.[64]

Martin, the family clown, was the main actor in an anecdote that captured the shared summer feeling. While the six children were returning to Vienna by train with the womenfolk, the boys began to devour all the provisions packed for the trip. Martha Freud delivered a lecture of the sort that bourgeois mothers of all nationalities use on such occasions: "Think of the miner's children who go without food for weeks at a time." To which Martin replied: "Sie sind auch nicht erholt zurueck-gekommen" ("They, however, are not coming home refreshed").[65]

All the children did well enough in school—and Oliver and Anna did quite well—but five of them, all but Mathilde, were hampered by their lisping. Anna Freud told Ernest Jones about this problem as she was responding to a remark of his about how Sigmund

Freud had lisped as a child—something she did not know. "Our lisping was quite atrocious so that all our teachers complained and said something had to be done about it, since otherwise we were quite clever children. But it spoilt every school performance for us."[66] A speech therapist was hired (interestingly enough, Martin later married a speech therapist) and the Freud lisping stopped. All that remained of it for public consideration was Sigmund Freud's clinical postulate: stammering and lisping are displacements upwards of conflicts over excremental functions.

Many of the teaching methods, which stressed learning by rote, were valuable to Anna Freud only as examples for her later work of how not to treat children. The Hebrew lessons she and her Jewish classmates took at the Reform synagogue on Saturday mornings were especially annoying. "We were taught the Hebrew letters on one side of the page, the German text on the other. Knowing the letters of the alphabet enabled us to 'read' the Hebrew text. But we were not taught the meaning of the words, and knowledge of the letters disappeared, of course, very quickly after the school years were over. . . . Neither I nor any of my classmates were able to read and translate even a simple Hebrew sentence."[67]

In Anna Freud's later work, investigations of children's school phobias and anxieties are prominent, and she had a good deal of personal experience to bring to her interest. In her own psychoanalysis, what she called "die alte Sommerabneigung gegen die Schule" ("the old summer aversion against school"[68]) was an important theme, as was the fact that she, dedicated to being on the holiday German speakers call *Sommerfrische* (summer restoration), nonetheless decided to become a schoolteacher and subject herself to the September ritual beyond the call of necessity. Before her analysis resolved the contradiction for her (and she left teaching), school remained the place where she tried hardest to be what her parents and her teachers wanted her to be. As she noted later to a schoolmate: "About me as a schoolgirl, people only wished that I would be more 'diligent,' and that is most certainly what I did become!"[69]

Anna Freud remembered writing and reading as the great antidotes to her boredom and restlessness in school. She became as intense a writer and reader as she was a knitter and weaver. Writing implements had an allure for her not unlike that exerted by knitting needles: "Pencils and pens in any form are favorites of mine, a predilection which I have brought along from early childhood. Nothing ever fascinated me as much as the shops where they were on display."[70]

Her memory for what she had read was remarkable, and her later psychoanalytic writings are full of references to children's books and the importance they have for children. These remarks have a quite autobiographical ring to them; but, at the least, they reflect a vivid memory of what reading was like, of the experience of reading. She encouraged her child analytic colleagues and students of later years to produce a brilliant—and little known—literature on children's books.[71]

From an early age, Anna Freud liked only stories that excluded the fantastic, the totally unreal. She preferred adventuring in the American wild West with the German yarn spinner Karl May or in India with Rudyard Kipling.

> At an age before independent reading, when children are read to or told stories my interest was restricted to those that "might be true." This did not mean that they had to be true stories in the ordinary sense of the word, but they were supposed not to contain elements which precluded their happening in reality. As soon as animals began to talk, or fairies and witches or ghosts to appear—in short, in the face of any unrealistic or supernatural element—my attention flagged and disappeared.[72]

Her tendency toward what she called "a realistic outlook" was of a piece with her daily desire, which was not for escape into unreality, but for being as grown-up as her siblings, being accepted and appreciated in her real family.

Among the poems and ballads known to German-speaking schoolchildren, Anna Freud tended to enjoy and memorize ones dealing with heroes and deeds of valor. Schiller's "Die Burgschaft" was one of her favorites, as was Heine's "Grenadiere" (which Robert Schumann set to music). The Heine poem was a source of great debate between Anna Freud and her closest school friend, a girl named Gertrud Baderle (later Hollstein). With Trude Baderle, Anna Freud considered the fate of two French grenadiers, captured in Russia during Napoleon's campaign, who tramped back through Germany only to find that "My Emperor, my Emperor is taken!" The soldiers dedicated themselves to awaiting the emperor's return: "What matters wife? What matters child? / With far greater cares I'm shaken," one of the stalwart soldiers announces in a line Anna Freud particularly liked. The last stanza rings out:

> *The Emperor will come and columns will wave,*
> *The swords will be flashing and rending,*
> *And I will rise full-armed from the grave,*
> *My Emperor, my Emperor defending!*

Trude Baderle was not inclined to idealize and identify with a self-sacrificing grenadier, dedicated in life and in death to his emperor, but Anna Freud was. And when—late in her life—she told another friend about her youthful emperor-faith, she seemed still amazed that anyone could have been a doubter. "As a child I thought why was everyone so surprised when he came? Of course, he had to come!"[73]

Much of Anna Freud's external inspiration for study seems to have come not from her teachers but from the visitors to her household and its Emperor. She was eager to emulate her father's extraordinary gifts as a linguist. English and French were available at school, and after the exciting visits made to her father by Ernest Jones, a Welshman, and Abraham Brill, an American, in 1908, she was determined to be able to speak English fluently. On the family's visits to the Dolomites and during a stay she made on her own in 1912 in Merano, she learned enough Italian to read newspapers and simple novels and to discover that she could not read Dante, even though her brother-in-law, Robert Hollitscher, made her a present of a beautiful edition of the *Commedia*, which she enjoyed for the illustrations. The other language of which she had a good knowledge was the one common among the analysts of her generational circle, who were passionate gardeners, even before they emigrated to England: botanical Latin. But of the rest of Latin and the whole of Greek, she was ignorant, as she did not have a Gymnasium education; and this lack made her, in later years, very self-conscious as a writer. In part because she was quite incapable of a style dense in classical and literary allusions, she cultivated—and raised to an art—a style of remarkable simplicity.

Despite her precocity, Anna Freud was not prepared for a Gymnasium education. She, like her sisters, went to the Lyceum, or high school, directed by Dr. Salka Goldman, where she took a basic curriculum: religious instruction, German composition, French, English, geography and history, arithmetic and geometry, science and penmanship. On her last two year-end reports, for 1910–11 and 1911–12, she received the very impressive *sehr gut* in every subject.[74] Nonetheless, in the matter of educating their daughters, the Freuds were more conservative than most of their friends.

Freud played a card game called tarok every Saturday evening with two of his pediatrician friends from the Kassowitz Institute, Oscar Rie and Ludwig Rosenberg—the two consultants who appear as Otto and Leopold in the dream called "Irma's injection"—and he discussed with them the progress of their daughters, who were Anna Freud's friends. Margarethe Rie went to a Gymnasium and her younger sister, Marianne, to a Lyceum, but when Marianne decided she wanted to be a doctor, she was privately tutored to catch up to the Gymnasium curriculum. Margarethe went on to become an actress—which was not a typical career for a Jewish professional's daughter. Frau Rie was a socially more independent woman than Martha Freud: she was an accomplished painter, though she never allowed herself the professionalism that she encouraged in her daughters. The Rosenbergs also had two daughters. The youngest—the rock thrower Anny Rosenberg—went to a Gymnasium and on to medical school. Sigmund Freud, who had little to say in praise of medical education, did not encourage any of his children toward it. But he was very sympathetic to women as practitioners of psychoanalysis, and he encouraged his friends' daughters into the field—as he encouraged his own, when she declared psychoanalysis as her direction.

Freud also gave Anna Freud her first introduction to psychoanalysis as a science when she was about fourteen. She remembered vividly an after-dinner walk with him in about 1909: as they passed by the beautiful homes near Vienna's Prater, he imparted a mysterious lesson. "You see those houses with their lovely facades? Things are not necessarily so lovely behind the facades. And so it is with human beings too."

The lessons were rather more technical at the Wednesday-evening meetings of the Vienna Psychoanalytic Society, where Anna Freud was allowed to sit on a little library ladder in the corner and listen to her father and his colleagues discussing one another's presentations. She was fascinated and wanted very much to go with her father to America to hear him deliver the lectures that were the triumph of his early years, when colleagues were few and his achievements still were regarded as a scandal. He had been issued an invitation by Dr. Stanley Hall, president of Clark University in Massachusetts, to give a brief introductory course in psychoanalytic theory and practice and to receive, in connection with the university's twentieth anniversary celebration, an honorary degree. Freud's colleagues Carl Jung, Sandor Ferenczi, Ernest Jones, and Abraham Brill were also invited. Anna Freud begged to go with her father, Jung, and Ferenczi on the transatlantic trip but was refused, and her disappointment was intense. She was, once again, too young.

Many years later, Anna Freud was in correspondence with a woman of exactly her own age who had met her father and his friends on that very trip. A relative of the American psychoneurologist James Putnam, she was charged with conducting the European visitors around Putnam's retreat, Sugar Maple Camp, in the Adirondacks, where they went after the Clark lectures. In the woods, the fourteen-year-old guide and her troops came across a dead porcupine. Freud was astonished, as he had made a joke in Vienna about the most efficient way to prevent anxiety in the face of an important task—to invent another task and focus attention on it. The secondary task he had concocted was to catch sight of a wild porcupine. Even his joking wishes came true on this trip, and the phrase "to find one's porcupine" became a talisman among his close colleagues. "I was very sorry at the time not to be taken along," Anna Freud told her correspondent. "You have no idea how often he told us about the walks through the woods and especially about the porcupine. He was most attracted to the porcupine, evidently, for he brought a metal one back to stand on his desk, and I still have it."[75] Having her father safely home from his adventure, with regret only for an intestinal complaint that he attributed to the frantic pace of American life and its unfamiliar cuisine, was consolation to Anna Freud for being left behind. But the real consolation came on the

occasion of Clark University's sixtieth anniversary celebration, in
1950, when Anna Freud herself was invited to lecture and to receive
an honorary degree—her first university degree of any sort.

*

THE YEAR before Freud's trip to America, in March 1908, Anna
Freud lost several weeks of school to an appendectomy. Her surgery,
unlike Mathilde's three years earlier, went without difficulty and her
recuperation was smooth. "Anna's operation went superbly," Freud
wrote to Mathilde, "and she endured it charmingly. Schnitzler is
certainly a real artist, but the operation can be done by anyone, and
[yours] was really not Rosanes's fault. Misfortunes happen now and
again, to one surgeon or another, and I wouldn't dare to say that
such a misfortune would never befall Schnitzler or Gerstner. And
what can one do but behave with dignity if one has been an innocent victim."[76] Mathilde had to live with what happened to her—
whether she did so in the manner her father recommended or not—
and Anna was fortunate. But Anna was also furious—for another
reason.

When the hospitalization and surgery were ordered, Martha
Freud, who received the news, did not tell her daughter about the
surgery. The twelve-year-old Anna went to the hospital under false
instructions, and was taken by surprise. "All I knew was that I was
going in for an examination." Whatever Sigmund Freud's role in
this deception was, Anna blamed it—when she later told the story—
squarely on her mother. The Freuds' tactic may have been influenced by their anxiety over Mathilde's experience, but Anna Freud
felt that it repeated a prerogative her mother had assumed throughout her school years. Martha Freud would conceal from Anna the
school test schedule, which was sent to parents, on the theory that
Anna would worry less if she did not know when the tests were up-
coming.

The episode of anger at her mother of course passed, and the
next summer Anna Freud traveled companionably with her mother
and wrote to her every day when they were parted. But she also

became insistent about how much she wanted to travel with her father—not just to America, but in the summer holidays. When Ernst and Oliver got to spend time during the summer of 1910, in Holland, with their father all to themselves, Anna was full of envy. The best she could do to be near him was to borrow a copy of his book called *Delusions and Dreams in Jensen's Gradiva* from his colleague Ludwig Jekels, whose sanatorium she was visiting with Tante Minna and Sophie.[77]

Freud wrote letters designed to restore the family to harmony while they were traveling to and fro. About the ongoing tension between Anna and Martha Freud's favorite, Sophie, which was apparently part of the reason why the family separated that summer, he sugested to Anna: "You should be generous with your sister, otherwise you two will end up like two of your aunts, who could never get along as children and as punishment could never part— for love and hate are not very different."[78]

Anna Freud took to signing her letters to Papa with hugs and kisses as well as passionate entreaties for letters—although the Freud family was not a hugging and kissing family. In the summer of 1911, she told her father—in the midst of her usual plea for letters—that she very much missed having him around to call her "*Schwarzer Teufel*" ("Black Devil"), the nickname in which he summarized her naughtiness.[79] Her longing for her father became increasingly dramatic and solicitous. She wrote from Klobenstein, in the Dolomites, where she, Sophie, Oliver, Martha, and Tante Minna were waiting for Freud's arrival from Vienna: "I look forward with great joy to your arrival, and I will take you to all the places where it is beautiful, for I know my way around a little by now. I think you will have more leisure to write here than in Karlsbad, for the train goes only once every hour and there are no carriages or automobiles [for visitors]."[80]

In the summers after her appendectomy, Anna Freud regained some of the weight she had lost and improved her posture, which had become more hunched. She then finished up her Matura diploma, the final degree at her Lyceum, in the early summer of 1912. But that fine accomplishment brought to the fore Anna Freud's unanswered question: "What am I going to be when I grow up?" And the question came just as her family got ready for a major reorganization: Sophie announced that she intended to marry a young man

from her mother's hometown, Max Halberstadt, a Hamburg pho-
tographer.

Anna was to have been sent off at the end of the summer vacation in the Dolomites for an eight-month tour of Sicily and Italy in
the company of Tante Minna. She was to enjoy the southern cli-
mate for the sake of her health, take time off to contemplate her
future, and make a miniature of a *grande tour* for the broadening of
her horizons. But Tante Minna was needed in Vienna, to run the
Berggasse household while Martha went to Hamburg to help the
engaged couple set up an apartment there.[81] So, instead of an Italian
tour, Anna Freud got an Italian vacation at the pensione in Merano
were Mathilde had recuperated under the care of Marie Rischavy,
Robert Hollitscher's widowed sister. Both Martha Freud and Tante
Minna were caught up in the exciting wedding preparations; Papa
wrote the letters from home.

Anna Freud wrote almost every day, and reported eagerly to
her father each time she put on half a kilogram of weight or spent
a day without backaches. She could not complain about the "spoiling" hospitality, but she did complain that her father did not write
often enough to "the one who is soon to be your only daughter."[82]
She nervously wondered whether she would ever be able to "stand
in for three" daughters, and she could not be reassured often enough
that he missed her.[83]

Freud informed Anna that she was to stay on in Merano through
the winter and not return to Vienna for Sophie's January wedding.
"The ceremony can be performed quite well without you, for that
matter also without guests, parties, etc., which you don't care for
anyhow. Your plans for school can easily wait till you have learned
to take your duties less seriously. They won't run away from you.
It can only do you good to be a little happy-go-lucky and enjoy
having such lovely sun in the middle of winter." This news delivered
and rationalized, Freud concluded: "So now, if you are reassured
that your stay in Merano won't be interrupted in the immediate
future, I can tell you that we all enjoy your letters very much but
that we also won't be worried if you feel too lazy to write every day.
The time of toil and trouble will come for you too, but you are
still quite young."[84]

To console her for her exile, which she did not find as pleasant as Freud hoped, she was given a new writing table and carpet for her room at home and a great springtime event to look forward to. After five months in Merano, her father came on his Easter vacation and took her for a brief tour of Verona, Venice—for four days— and Trieste. They returned to Vienna after a wonderful trip, and Anna Freud had become her father's new traveling companion— exactly what she had wanted since the American trip in 1909. The consolation was deep, but so was the bitterness Anna Freud felt at being left out of the wedding events. Some forty years after she first got marooned in Merano and then left out of the rite of passage Sophie made, Anna Freud wrote to a young woman of her acquaintance, an émigré to England, whose sister was getting married. "Thank you very much for your nice letter with the exciting news of [your sister's] marriage in Israel. This must be wonderful for her, but I can also imagine that it must be a difficult experience for you. I have had two older sisters myself and remember well what an upsetting experience it was when they married, especially the second one who married while I was absent from home so that I missed the whole ceremony."[85]

Freud suspected from his daughter's references to Sophie's wedding that her upset was not simple. He wrote her a calming letter that suggested she might be jealous of Max Halberstadt for his ability to win so quickly Sophie's love, from which Anna had always felt excluded.[86] In psychoanalytic terms, what he implied was that the wedding brought forth from her the "negative Oedipal" feelings a girl may have as she experiences a brother-in-law or father as a rival for a sister's or a mother's love. Freud's suggestion met with incredulity. On January 7, 1913, a week before the wedding, his daughter replied with a letter that shows the state of her self-understanding at the beginning of her eighteenth year.

DEAR PAPA,
I got your letter today and wanted to write you anyway, to thank you for your last letter, which made me very happy. I am now quite well again, and I hope that whatever I had will not recur—I wondered a great deal what it was, for I am not really sick. It irrupts in me, somehow, and then I am very tired and must worry about all kinds of things, which at other times are just a matter of course: about my being here, and that I do

nothing all day long when I am not sick, and similar things. I am no longer embroidering Sophie's tablecloth, and it is unpleasant when I think about that, for I would like to have finished it. Naturally, I think rather often about Sophie's wedding, but I am indifferent about Max, because he is a complete stranger to me; I don't really like him, but I am certainly not jealous of him. It is not really nice to say it, but I am glad that Sophie is getting married, because the unending quarrel between us was horrible for me. It was no matter for her, because she did not care for me, but I liked her very much and I always admired her a bit. I cannot, however, understand why she is marrying Max, for she hardly knows him. But I cannot think that his presence in Vienna and all that has any connection [as Freud had suggested] with how I feel and I truly do not know why I am sometimes quite well and sometimes not, and I would like very much to know, so that I can do something to help myself. I would like very much to be reasonable like Mathilde, and I don't know why with me everything takes so long. I am really very well, I like it here, and when I come back to Vienna I can start again all the things I like to do. But if I have a stupid day, everything looks wrong to me; for instance, today I cannot understand how it can sometimes be so stupid. I do not want to have it again, for I want to be a reasonable person or at least to become one, but I can't always help myself alone. When I had something like that in Vienna, I always talked with Trude [Baderle] about it and then everything was all right.

Please understand that I would not have written all this to you, because I do not want to worry you, if you had not written as you did. Now I am well and you will see that I will return to Vienna all strong and healthy, because [if] I want it absolutely then it does happen. I weighed myself today and I had gained another half a kilo, and I purposefully went for a long walk, which did not tire me as before. The weather and the sun are more and more beautiful and warm, and I look forward to the time when everything starts blooming—which won't be long here. Walks are much more beautiful here than in Vienna and you would have liked everything very much had you come here, which would have been so lovely. I send you many, many greetings and a kiss and could you please write to me soon again, for I will become more reasonable if you will help me.

YOUR ANNA

P.S. I could not write more to you, because I don't know more myself, but I certainly do not keep any secrets from you.

In the surviving correspondence between Anna Freud and her father, there is no direct reply to this confession. But after the wedding, Freud did send a general statement about what he and his wife hoped the time in Merano would help bring about in their youngest daughter—normal femininity.

You will have understood from the books you have read that you were so overzealous, restless and unsatisfied because you have run away like a child from many things of which a grown-up girl would not be afraid. We will notice a change when you no longer withdraw from the pleasures of your age but gladly enjoy what other girls enjoy. One hardly has energy for serious interests if one is too zealous, too sensitive, and remains removed from one's own life and nature; then one finds oneself troubled in the very things one wishes to take up.[87]

The "it" to which Anna Freud referred repeatedly in her letter is mysterious: something that was not a physical illness kept irrupting in her and making her feel exhausted and "stupid." Unlike Mathilde, who had recovered so reasonably from her appendectomy and its sequelae, Anna Freud—she seems to imply—had physically recovered five years earlier but had somehow become nonetheless unreasonable or what was then called "psychasthenic" (intellectually or cognitively slowed down for emotional reasons). A mild eating disturbance of the kind Freud associated with hysteria and its "conversion symptoms" is suggested, but there is no further contemporary information about either anorexia or the affliction called "it." In later years, however, Anna Freud would describe herself as "stupid" ("dumm") and exhausted when she was controlling a tendency to masturbate by daydreaming and constructing elaborate, involved "nice stories" with many characters and intricate plots.

An article called "Beating Fantasies and Daydreams" that Anna Freud wrote ten years after her stay in Merano discusses quite autobiographically a patient who made up such "nice stories."[88] This patient's storytelling dated from her eighth to tenth years, which for Anna Freud herself would have been 1903–1905, the years when she was preparing to enter her Lyceum. The patient's stories became more involved during her fourteenth or fifteenth year—1909 or 1910 in Anna Freud's life, a year or two after her appendectomy. (No mention is made in the patient's case of an operation or significant illness.) Both masturbation and intense daydreaming that substitutes for masturbatory pleasure are, of course, quite normal in childhood, but as one enters one's eighteenth year they are not—to use Anna Freud's rather self-chastising, moralistic word—"reasonable."

Sigmund Freud's understanding of masturbation conflicts and fantasies is recorded in the minutes of nine discussions held in the Vienna Psychoanalytic Society just before the Freuds decided that Anna should make an Italian tour.[89] The minutes indicate that during the period of Anna Freud's adolescent turmoil Freud had modified his earlier views: he had learned that masturbation takes different forms at different developmental stages, and he had questioned the "progressive" view of his colleague Stekel, who claimed that masturbation has entirely psychical causes and no injurious consequences. Of particular concern, Freud thought, are the injurious connections that can develop between masturbation and fantasies, particularly in hysteria, where "conversion symptoms" or psychosomatic illnesses are indications of sexual conflict, as in Freud's patient Dora. He concluded in the 1912 discussions that "we have not been able to pay as much attention to female as to male masturbation [in which] a special emphasis lies on the modifications in it that arise in relation to the subject's age." What he could say from his clinical experience with hysterics was that he thought "clitoridal sexuality," "a piece of masculine sexuality" in females, must be repressed in puberty for mature, vaginal female sexuality to emerge. Not until 1919, when Anna Freud was in analysis with him, did Freud extend his exploration of the connections between masturbation and fantasies beyond the hysteric's conversion symptoms and "so-called hypnoid states—absences during daydreams" and on toward the much more complex phenomenon to which it seems his daughter had given the simple title "it."

THE shift in the family configuration that Sophie's engagement and marriage represented was great. Anna was the only girl left at home. Martin lived at Berggasse 19 after his army service in 1910, but he spent his days at the university, studying first business and then law—

until the First World War required his army service for nearly five years. Ernst and Oliver studied in Munich and Berlin and came home only for holidays. The summers were no longer whole-family affairs; the older children and the two sons-in-law came and went, visiting rather than staying with the permanent foursome: Professor, Frau Professor, Tante Minna, and Anna.

Freud had felt the shift coming for years. In July 1909, just before he went to America, he wrote to Jung: "Little by little the young people are becoming independent and all of a sudden I have become the old man."⁹⁰ But he felt it acutely in the spring of 1912, when he realized that Sophie and Max Halberstadt would soon announce their engagement, despite the brevity of their acquaintance and the extremely small size of Max Halberstadt's income. Freud marked his feelings by starting an essay called "The Theme of the Three Caskets." The Freuds then spent the first part of their vacation at Karlsbad and the latter part near the Lago di Caldonazzo in northern Italy. A plan that Freud had made to visit his half brother in England was canceled when Mathilde was once again ill and Freud had to rush to Vienna to attend her. This emergency came after a series of anxieties: over an illness Freud's seventy-six-year-old mother suffered through in the spring; over the nearly fatal illness of Freud's colleague Ludwig Binswanger, whom he visited in June 1912;⁹¹ and over the morphine addiction of a new patient, Ernest Jones's mistress Loe Kann, a woman on whom Freud said he would have been pleased, were she not his patient, to expend his fantasies.

Freud recovered some of his good spirits by traveling to Rome at the end of the summer of 1912, but his moods were erratic. He found Sophie's wedding trying, and Sandor Ferenczi had to suggest to him that he not take the loss of his lovely daughter so much to heart, even to a heart so accustomed to self-analysis and aware of what Ferenczi called his "Sophie-Complex."⁹² The summer that followed, he told Ferenczi, "everything and everyone were too much for me."⁹³ In addition to the complicated family and practice affairs, two of his collaborators, the Viennese Stekel and the young Swiss Jung, had troubled him with their—to his mind—divergences from the true path of psychoanalytic research, so that he felt his hard-won, small confraternity to be endangered at the same time that his children were leaving home. The "subjective condition" for the

"Three Caskets" essay, Freud told Ferenczi, was the fact that, with
both his older girls married, "my closest companion will be my little
daughter."[94] But this subjective condition had as its near neighbor
the loss of his dissident "sons" and even his feeling that they were—
like the sons in his major work of 1912, *Totem and Taboo*—waiting
for or desiring his death.

Freud's essay traces the theme of "a man's choice between three
women" through Shakespeare's plays *The Merchant of Venice* and
King Lear, the myths and fairy tales of Cinderella, Psyche (in Apu-
leius's *The Golden Ass*), Paris's choice of Aphrodite, the Greek
Horae (goddesses of the seasons) and Moerae (Fates). (To this collection Freud might have added the dream "Irma's injection," with
its three female objects of his "sexual megalomania.") The essay ends
with a long reflection on how the third woman in the primeval myth
underlying these stories, who is always the youngest, pale and silent,
represents Death. "Eternal wisdom, clothed in the primeval myth,
bids the old man [Lear] renounce love, choose death, and make
friends with the necessity of dying."[95] The peroration of the essay
focuses on the "three inevitable relations that a man has with a
woman—the woman who bears him, the woman who is his mate,
and the woman who destroys him." But it is in vain, the final sentence reads, "that an old man yearns for the love of woman as he
had it first from his mother; the third of the Fates alone, the silent
Goddess of Death, will take him into her arms."

When Freud wrote his "Three Caskets" he was fifty-six years
old. He felt, then, that the foundational theories of psychoanalysis
had been securely set in preliminary formulations—particularly in
The Interpretation of Dreams and the *Three Essays on The Theory
of Sexuality*. Much of his effort was focused on the future of the psychoanalytic movement and the problem of succession. Somewhat flip-
pantly, he told Ferenczi to do a good job analyzing Ernest Jones,
their energetic young Welsh colleague, for they would need him:
"Put some stuffing in the clown, so we can make him a king . . .
our dear Swiss have become quite *meschugge*.[96] Help was needed
because Carl Jung, the heir apparent, the Gentile Freud imagined
playing Joshua to his Moses in the great drama of psychoanalysis,
was busy denying the heart of the science, the sexual etiology of the
neuroses.

In the fatiguing summer of 1912, and throughout the next year, into the summer of 1913, when he was quite visibly depressed—so that Anna Freud later remembered this summer as the only one in which she had known her father to be depressed[97]—Freud was a Lear. He was a man who felt himself caught in a "tragedy of ingratitude" from the recalcitrant psychoanalytic heir Jung and through the perfectly natural (and not for that any the less irrationally injurious) departure of the older daughters into marriages. "But the doomed man," as Freud wrote of Lear, "is not willing to renounce the love of women; he insists on hearing how much he is loved." In his youth, Freud had called his fiancée, Martha Bernays, "my Marty-Cordelia," and he had agreed with Josef Breuer, who also called his wife Cordelia, that a Cordelia type is "incapable of displaying affection to others, even including her own father."[98] Cordelia-like love continued to be for Freud, as his essay makes quite clear, deeply alluring.

With his remarkable self-honesty, Freud seems to have been trying to guard himself against asking too much of his youngest daughter—who loved her father as deeply and exclusively as any Cordelia. The Christmas of 1913 was the first with only one left of the six children who use to assemble around six little Christmas trees to receive their presents: "The house will be very still, three lonely ladies," Freud told Ferenczi, repeating his theme of the year in another key, with Martha, Tante Minna, and Anna in the familiar three roles.[99]

Freud knew that he wanted to keep his youngest at home: "We are no longer a family, only three old people," he told his colleague Karl Abraham early in 1914. "Even my little daughter wants to go to England by herself this year."[100] But Freud also tried to hear Anna as she spoke the anxiety of a youngest child suddenly finding herself at center stage, an only child of sorts. Her anxiety about being "wrecked by success," as Freud titled those who cannot bear fulfillment of their not very acceptable wishes, came to him by letter. "My little daughter," he told his friend Lou Andreas-Salomé, ". . . who is staying with her eighty-year-old grandmother in Ischl, has written to us in concern: 'How am I to make do for six children all by myself next year?' "[101] The little daughter was then eighteen.

2

IN TIMES OF WAR
AND DEATH

In June 1914, Anna Freud took the examination that allowed her to start an elementary-school teaching apprenticeship the next fall. It is unlikely that she already viewed the teaching as a preparation for future psychoanalytic work. But it is clear that her father had become interested in the possibilities of psychoanalytic work with children through the child cases colleagues like Carl Jung, Lou Andreas-Salomé, and Sandor Ferenczi had undertaken, and through the practice of Hermine von Hug-Hellmuth. Hug-Hellmuth was a teacher and an associate of the Vienna Society, whose first publication on "play therapy" came out in 1913. Freud viewed pedagogical applications of psychoanalysis as an important new departure, and he recommended Hug-Hellmuth's work to Sophie, whose first son, Ernst, was born in 1914.[1]

Anna Freud must have known of these developments, which all had a common source in Freud's case study of a five-year-old boy with a phobia, the 1909 "Little Hans" case. She had also given herself a short course in Freudian psychoanalysis while she was in Merano, where she celebrated her seventeenth birthday early in the winter of 1912–13: "I have read some of your books," she told her father, "but you should not be horrified by that, for I am already grown up and so it is no surprise that I am interested."[2] Teacher training did not then include instruction in child or developmental psychology that would have furthered Anna Freud's own effort to learn, but the Vienna Ministry of Education and the school administrators were not as hostile to psychoanalysis as the city's medical and psychiatric circles were.

Before she took her teacher's examination in June, Anna Freud suffered through a long bout of whooping cough and this made it impossible for her to accompany her father, as they had planned, on an Easter vacation trip to Italy. But a new equanimity and calm after her storm of 1912–13 were apparent in Anna Freud's response. When she realized that she would not be well in time, she suggested to her father that he take someone else in her place—and he called upon Sandor Ferenczi. She also made secure her plan to reward herself after her examination with a trip to England, where she planned to visit the Freud relatives in Manchester and to tour the southeast coast. Her Uncle Emmanuel had sent her instructions about how to reach Manchester and advice that his step brother, Sigmund, would have appreciated: "Now do just as your uncle tells you to!"

Escorted by Anna Hammerschlag Lichtheim, the family friend whose namesake she was, Anna Freud set out in the middle of July, less than a month after the Austrian crown heirs had been assassinated at Sarajevo. The Freuds evidently shared with the European heads of state the hope that war could be avoided. But only five days after Anna Freud's departure, Serbia was presented with an ultimatum by Austria-Hungary, and soon after, mobilizations began across the Continent. Martin Freud joined the Austrian Army as a gunner; Ernst, too, went off to the trenches; and Oliver, after he finished his examinations in engineering, joined the Army's corps of engineers.

The abbreviated tour of southeastern England that Anna Freud made was chaperoned by Loe Kann, Freud's former patient, a vivacious, willful, and quite wealthy Dutchwoman whose wedding to Herbert (called "Davy") Jones, an American, had taken place in Budapest that June, with Freud in attendance. Anna Freud had become friendly with Loe Kann during Loe's analysis with Freud in 1912, a period during which Loe was trying to decide whether to

end her troubled love affair with another Mr. Jones—Ernest Jones.
Loe Kann and Ernest Jones had gone to England together on a trial
basis, but she returned to Vienna in the fall of 1913 to renew her
analysis. Freud then felt that he had begun to make good progress
in unraveling her neurosis—and dealing with her addiction to morphine—but the result was her decision to marry "Jones the Second,"
as Ernest Jones called his rival. Jones the First, in the meanwhile,
went to Budapest for a few weeks of analysis with Sandor Ferenczi,
who found him to be a much more interesting and reliable man
than he had expected. After their marriage, Loe and Davy Jones
moved to England, where Ernest Jones was busy organizing the
London Psychoanalytic Society and living with a woman named
Lina, who had been Loe Kann's maid and companion and who had
first become Ernest Jones's mistress in 1912.[3]

Into this tangled web of relationships sailed the eighteen-year-
old Anna Freud. Ernest Jones, a short, sleek, terrierlike man, thirty-
five years old and still a bachelor despite his seven-year relationship
with Loe, met her boat from France with a bouquet of flowers. In a
little memoir she wrote about Ernest Jones in 1979, twenty-one years
after his death, Anna Freud gave a very refined version of the events
that followed.

Naturally I was flattered and impressed, though not without a
lurking suspicion that his interest was directed more to my father
than to myself, a circumstance to which I had become used.
However that may have been, he certainly did not show any lack
of attention. He put himself out considerably to fetch me from
the places where I stayed and to show me the beauties of England which he loved. There was a never forgotten trip in a boat
going up the river Thames. There was a book, *The Highways
and Byways of Sussex*, which remained in my possession for
many years. He also took every opportunity to correct my English.[4]

Jones also took the opportunity her visit offered to try to court
Anna Freud—with no success whatsoever. Nor did his attentions en-
dear him to Sigmund Freud, who was as suspicious of Jones's motives as he was worried by his daughter's unresolved, though muted,
symptoms. Warned by Loe Kann Jones, Freud sent a letter to Jones

suggesting that the courtship was inappropriate because Anna was too young and not yet interested in men, and a letter to his daughter full of parental prerogatives. "I know from the most reliable sources [i.e., Loe] that Doctor Jones has serious intentions of wooing you. It is the first time in your young life, and I have no thought of granting you the freedom of choice your two sisters enjoyed. For it has so happened that you have lived more intimately with us than they, and I would like to believe that you would find it more difficult to make such a decision for life without our—in this case my—consent." Having made his position quite clear, Freud than retreated a little: "Our wish is that you should not marry or become engaged while you are so young and inexperienced, before you have seen, learned and lived more and gotten to know more about people. The regret I would feel having you so far away from me [i.e., in England] I suppress—it would not make the other considerations easy to weigh."[5] Behind his paternal—indeed, paternalistic—words there is clearly a fear that Anna, so given to mysterious psychosomatic complaints and still so tied to him, would become, if too abruptly courted, a candidate for hysteria.

Freud suggested to his daughter that Ernest Jones, despite his many virtues, would not make a suitable husband. Jones was too old for her and he was, Freud argued, in need of an independent woman with more experience, not a refined young one. To his friend Sandor Ferenczi, Freud was openly annoyed. He noted that he had taken the occasion "to make clear to Anna immediately my relation to the business, because I don't want to mix up in it further, and I also don't want to lose the dear child to an obvious act of revenge—one opposing any rationality that speaks against it. And I do think that Loe will keep watch like a dragon."[6] As it became clear to him that Anna was not interested in Dr. Jones and that Dr. Jones was being nothing but pleasant and helpful, Freud slowly calmed down: "I will not do anything to interfere with their meetings. My little one will have to learn how to assert herself, but she will be adroit enough to avoid any kind of proposal [from Jones], which could only lead to disappointments. She herself is completely sure."[7]

When Ernest Jones, in his later capacity as Freud's biographer, read Freud's speculations about his desire to wreak revenge on Freud for Loe Kann's decision in favor of Jones the Second, he was also annoyed. He defended himself to Anna Freud almost thirty-nine years after the fact: "He seems to have forgotten the existence of the sexual instinct, for I had found you (and still do) most attractive. It is true I wanted to replace Loe, but I felt no resentment against her for her departure, it was a relief from a burden. In any case, I have always loved you, and in quite an honest fashion."[8] This declaration was signed "Yours always, Ernest" in a bold hand, many times larger than Jones's usual constricted script. Anna Freud ignored the topic and kept, in her next letter, right to the business of her father's biography.

In the biography, Jones, for whatever his own reasons might have been, said nothing at all about how Sigmund Freud's sexual instinct had played into the story. The Ferenczi correspondence of 1912 and 1913 has a number of little testimonies to the fact that Freud, who had thought of himself as a man too old and preoccupied for sexual interests, had found in Loe Kann "a jewel," "highly intelligent, deeply neurotic," someone who aroused his feeling "with full symptoms" and made him work at keeping his psychoanalytic neutrality.[9] Anna Freud might have been amused to learn this, for her own feelings were tied to Loe Kann Jones just as excitingly. "Today I wrote to Frau Jones in London," she told her father after she arrived in Southampton, "for I learned that she is already there. I dream very often of her, last night, too. I also heard that she had a bad [Channel] crossing and that she is not very well, I am very sorry about that, for you know that I am extraordinarily fond of her."[10] Throughout the next four years, while communications with England were nearly impossible, Anna Freud dreamed of Loe Kann Jones and imagined their reunion in peacetime. Loe was the first of a number of attractive, childless older women by whom Anna Freud was adopted and who shared generously with her their worldly wisdom and sophistication.

On the other hand, toward her erstwhile suitor Ernest Jones, Anna Freud displayed unfailing cordiality mingled with distrust and resentment that he never—despite his protests to the contrary—took her or her work seriously but treated her merely as an access to her father. Being an intermediary was a circumstance to which she had become accustomed, she said, but it was not one that she ever took for granted. After her trip to England, she was out of contact with

Ernest Jones until he wrote in January 1917. Then she sent in return not a letter but a postscript to one of her father's letters. The occasion was a recent birthday greeting that had made its way to Vienna by wartime courier: "Dear Dr. Jones! I must now send thanks for three birthday letters from you; and I see from this fact how much time has passed since my trip." After this double-edged opening, she offered a pointed account of her work.

> When you receive the *Zeitschrift* issues, perhaps you will find it interesting to note that last year I translated your essay against Janet, as well as Putnam's article. I also attended all of Papa's lectures, about which you wrote in your last letter.—Would you also give Frau Loe many warm geetings from me? Papa and I wrote to her at New Year's, but I wonder whether she received the letter. I would so very much like to hear from her. I remain with best wishes, your Anna Freud.[11]

Thus she made it quite clear, without a direct word, that the person in England to whom she had already written, the person from whom she really wanted to hear, was Loe Kann Jones.

It was also the Jones the Second couple who managed, very cleverly, Anna Freud's return to Austria from her English trip. She was visiting in a girls' boarding school, St. Leonards's, on the southeast coast of England, in the company of her cousin Rosi Winternitz, when Austria officially became England's enemy. Her communications with her family then had to go through the analyst van Emden and Jacobus Kann, Loe's brother, in Holland, while the Joneses arranged for her to join the party of the departing Austrian ambassador. This plan necessitated visits to the police for travel permits and visas. Sigmund Freud was pleased to hear from Davy Jones that "your daughter is frightfully brave, if you would see her you would be extremely proud of her behavior."[12] And Anna Freud was pleased to find that the English officials treated her politely and even, to her amazement, displayed none of the anti-Semitism she was accustomed to at home. She remembered vividly even as an old woman how thrilling she had found it to join a group of English soldiers at their mess in Southamptom. With the Austrian ambassador and his entourage, she sailed for Gibralter, then to Malta, and finally to Genoa, where she was able to get a train to Vienna.

This adventure was like something out of the pages of Anna Freud's favorite English author, Rudyard Kipling, whose "Service Songs"—"Take up the White Man's burden—Send forth the best ye breed—"—her father had sent her for a summer-vacation present in 1911.[13] Her reflection on the voyage home was not, however, Kiplingesque; she wrote a prose piece called "On the Ship" that was intended to contrast the peace at sea—"peace, which is here still the unchallenged ruler . . ."—with the war starting up on the land. She evokes "a deep blue, barely moving ocean, a hazy blue sky, and a small white ship, cautiously seeking its course," the setting for a group of passengers. "Behind them lies the island they have just left full of belligerent mood and unconfirmed, wild rumors, behind them lie days of tension, excitement and strain; ahead lies their own land, of which they have heard nothing for weeks, the unnerving uncertainty about the fate of their families, and the war with all its horrors and atrocities."[14]

THE FREUDS were in Vienna when their daughter returned, as their plans for August and September, like those of citizens on both sides of the European war, had been scrapped. Initially, Sigmund Freud was in a patriotic excitement over the war. He wrote glowing letters about the Austrian Army, in which Martin and Ernst were serving, and enjoyed a September visit with Sophie and Max in Hamburg, where he could feel connected to the German war effort. Throughout the fall and into 1915, he spoke eagerly about the coming victory of the Central Powers—though the date for that projected victory kept receding. But Freud's exhilarated mood did not survive the newspaper reports of hideous carnage on every battlefront, his worry over his sons, and his increasing isolation in Vienna. Only a few patients, mostly Hungarians, came for psychoanalysis; and Freud's colleagues and correspondents went into military service— Ferenczi and Eitingon in Hungary, Abraham in Germany—so that letters were few and visits almost impossible. To Jones Freud wrote warily: "What Jung and Adler have left of the movement is being ruined by the strife of nations. Our Association can as little be kept together as anything else that calls itself International."[15] As the strife of nations went on and on, it became, as Freud wrote in an essay called "Thoughts for the Times on War and Death," "more bloody and more destructive than any war of other days, because of the enormously increased perfection of weapons of attack and defense. . . . It tramples in blind fury on all that comes in its way."[16]

The psychoanalytic movement did certainly lose most of its international forums and exchanges during the war years, but Freud himself, on the other hand, rallied and began to use his solitude and his free hours for writing. He wrote a long case history of the patient known as "The Wolfman," and then he embarked upon a series of essays that he thought of entitling, as a group, *Introduction to Metapsychology* or *A General Review of the Transference Neuroses*. In an astonishing burst of productivity, he wrote twelve essays for this series between March and August 1915—and this was in addition to four other papers that were written or polished for publication in 1915. Even though only five of the twelve metapsychology papers were ever published, it is hardly an exaggeration to say that in the first years of the war Freud single-handedly kept the scientific momentum of the international psychoanalytic movement strong.

It almost seems as though the fervor Freud could no longer direct toward the war after he began to see the war for what it was— a prolonged, brutal horror—went instead into his work, into saving his work from the war. And he could, at the same time, give to his lifework, which he sometimes called his child—even his *Sorgenkind*, his problem child—the solicitous fatherly attention he could not give to his children. Not to his boys, whose postings he could only infer from the newspapers when they were unable to send cards or letters; and not to Sophie, whose husband, too, was called up while she remained in Hamburg; and not to Mathilde, who was close by in Vienna but often preoccupied with her husband's family and the difficulties of keeping their silk importing business going in wartime.

Anna Freud's eager beginning as an apprentice teacher was a great joy to her father—especially in contrast to the anxiety he felt about his other children and to the anxiety he had felt earlier about Anna's health. Anna is "industrious and delightful," he told Ferenczi in November 1914.[17] And by April 1915, Freud was even jokingly wishing she would not complete her course, so that she would not leave home: "Anna studies hard for the exam that means a regular teacher's post, but hopefully her lack of a singing voice [for the music segment of the exam] will hold her back." The littlest daughter had risen, finally, to the position in her father's esteem that had been the great wish of her childhood: "She is developing into a charmer, by the way, more delightful than any other of the children."[18]

Freud was quite frank, particularly in his letters to Ferenczi, about how hard it was for him to be losing his children and enduring what he called "das Los des Alters" ("the lot of old age"), being lonely and in need of signs of youthfulness and vigor.[19] How important his youngest daughter had become to him in the bleak times of the war is apparent in a letter he wrote in September 1915 after Anna and one of her sisters had departed from Konigsee, leaving their parents and Tante Minna to keep themselves company: "Today both daughters set out for Salzburg on their way home, and I noted with surprise, judging from the sinking of my mood, how thoroughly satiated my libido is by them. The little one is also an extraordinarily dear and interesting creature. Now I have left only my two old ones."[20]

After she had successfully passed the teacher's examination hurdle, with help from a singing tutor—Hedwig Hitschmann, the wife of one of Freud's analyst colleagues, who was a singer with the Vienna opera—Anna Freud wanted to participate in her father's effort to keep the psychoanalytic journals going. So she started in the summer of 1915 to translate into German one of the articles she mentioned to Jones, a piece by the American James Putnam, who had himself taken an interest in pedagogical applications of psychoanalysis and translated into English Hug-Hellmuth's work on "play therapy." When they were in separate locations during the vacation, Anna Freud wrote to her father asking for clarifications of psychoanalytic terms. "Transference," Freud replied to one query, "is a technical term referring to the patient's transference of his latent tender or hostile feelings to the doctor."[21] But even more important, they began to correspond about Anna Freud's dreams. She reported her dreams, and her father—when he thought it appropriate—replied with a suggestion or an interpretation. That the translating projects and the dream-interpretation exchanges fulfilled the same wish for closeness seems obvious in a brief report from July 1915: Anna told her father that she had dreamed of a meeting with him and James Putnam (whom she had never, in waking life, met) to discuss a problem of translation.[22]

It is not clear from Anna Freud's correspondence with her father whether she realized—or trusted—that his pride and affection for her were as his letters to Ferenczi show them to be. Only a year had passed since she set out to England in a state of doubt that her father had felt needed assuaging. He was not completely successful: "What you wrote about the esteem in the family would be very nice," she replied, "but I can't entirely believe that it is true. I don't believe, for instance, that it will make a great deal of difference at home when I am not there any longer. I think only I would feel the difference."[23] But she did feel confident enough to confide her dreams in her father—and to receive his interpretations.

MOST of the surviving father-daughter correspondence in the war period comes from the summer vacation months. In both 1915 and 1916, Anna Freud spent a month at her grandmother's in Ischl while her parents and Tante Minna were visiting the spas at Gastein or Karlsbad. Her translating activities and her dream life were surrounded by Freud aunts and female cousins. Freud's two widowed sisters, Rosa Graf, whose husband had died in 1908, and Pauline Winternitz, widowed in 1900, were in Ischl with their daughters, Caecilie Graf (called Mausi), four years younger than Anna, and Rose Beatrice Winternitz (called Rosi), a year younger than Anna.

The three cousins were expected to be friends, and they did spend a good deal of time together, but their relations were never easy. Anna Freud found Rosi unhappy and still suffering from a schizophrenic episode she had been through in 1913. Mausi, who looked upon Anna with—so Anna thought—"pitying contempt," was much more actively annoying.[24] The most that Anna would concede about Mausi in the summer of 1915 was that she "was not as bad as I thought."[25] When her father seized upon this little opportunity to try negotiating a rapport, Anna Freud snapped: "You should not believe that, because I got along with Mausi, I have changed my opinion, about which we have already talked. About her I am right."[26]

Within the cousin group, Anna Freud was the acknowledged leader when they went adventuring, but she did not get the position without a bit of teasing about the "good girl" caution and conservativeness that were always coupled with her verve. More than thirty years after their first summer together, Rosi Winternitz reminisced in a letter to Anna Freud.

> You told me that your father had said to you before you came to us, "This will be either the beginning or the end of the friendship between you two." In my memory, two excursions during that summer are clearest. On one, we walked to Lake Wolfgang and camped on the left shore, near the forest. We had a camp stove and prepared our meals. . . . I got angry at you because you always wanted to walk only on flat paths, instead of in the mountains. The other excursion was to Hallstadt. We took a boat and rowed from the landing across Gosaumuhle to Hallstadt. A thunderstorm approached, and we were very frightened that we might not reach the shore. We rowed with all our strength, though, and made it.

The widowed mothers made such a fuss over the rowing episode that Anna Freud, who was not accustomed to reproaches, wrote home and asked to leave. Her request was granted, and she joined the Rie family on their holiday until the aunts calmed down.

When they were not on excursions, the cousins went to the spa gardens in Ischl to wander and to visit the fruit stands. "Your Papa supplied us with money for those trips, and you were the chief administrator and treasurer," Rosi reminded Anna Freud. The troops wanted to have some pears, but their leader refused to spend all their funds and instead told them that the green pears brought to her mind a story. Rosi related it:

> Karl, the heir to the throne, had quarreled with his adviser and wanted to prove that he did not need him. So Karl went to St. Stephen's Church, was shown around, and then climbed the church tower. As he was leaving, he found that he had no money, and he could not leave the church until his identity was determined—the adviser had to be called in to get him off the hook, so miserably did his bid for independence turn out. The adviser said, "You see, Your Highness, you are green." And with

that you gave us the explanation for why you did not want to buy the pears—like them we would be green. Already back then you were the cleverest and most careful of the three of us.[27]

In her fantasy life and in her dreams, Anna Freud often identified with male story characters—as she did with the adviser in her joke—or took a male role. This tendency later became one of the most important focuses of her analysis. But she was, at the same time, very self-conscious about not being feminine or femininely attractive enough. For example, in the summer of 1916, she reported sadly to her father that she had left her hiking shoes by the doorway "and they are so big that when the Hausfrau saw them she said that a man must own them."[28] She was no less uninhibited in telling him that "the other day I also dreamed that I had to defend a milk farm belonging to us. But [my] sword was broken so that as I pulled it out [of its sheath] I was ashamed in front of the enemy."[29] This is the kind of scene that the psychoanalyst Anna Freud would later discuss as typical of "beating fantasies." A weak young man is dominated or symbolically castrated or beaten and the scene of humiliation is associated with pleasure in masturbation; the "beating fantasy" is a disguised, masochistically organized way of enjoying the exclusive love of a dominator (the father). Instead of saying "father loves only me," the fantasy says the more acceptable (or less incestuous) "father defeats or beats only me."

After she woke up from her dream of defending the farm, she told her father, "it was like 'you didn't lie in bed with your hands at the seam of your nightgown, as the rules require.' " The voice of her conscience—or, as her father would later term it, her superego, her internalization of parental voices—reminded her that the pleasure of masturbation toward which her dream was directed was forbidden. In this letter, it is not clear whether the command to keep her hands at her sides was a parental command or Anna Freud's technique for obeying a more general antimasturbation order; but what is clear is that she expected her father to know precisely what she meant.

Even the dreams in which Anna Freud cast herself in a classic turn-of-the-century "family romance" had a twist of forbidden excitement to them: "I dreamed that you were a king and I was a princess. Someone wanted to separate us by political intrigues. It was not at all nice and quite thrilling."[30] Freud did not interpret this dream. But he did make an effort when she had a dream of the sort he had labeled "Typical Dreams" in *The Interpretation of Dreams*. His response to an "examination dream" in which she was terrified of failing a school test had as its result that she stopped having examination dreams. But she jokingly reassured him that she was not left in dreamless peace: "As I never lack material, I now dream every night about Frau Jones [Loe Kann Jones] and last night that I became blind. It was absolutely terrible, but I have dreamed it often."[31]

THERE is no direct evidence from correspondence of how Anna Freud's complex inner life translated into her nearly six years of work as a teaching apprentice and then a certified teacher. From the Volksschule administrators' point of view, she was a delight. Dr. Salka Goldman, her superior at the Cottage Lyceum, praised her apprentice performance with third, fourth, and fifth graders during the 1915–16 and 1916–17 school years and her first venture as *Klassenlehrerin* (head teacher) for the second grade during 1917–18. She showed, Dr. Goldman wrote, "great zeal" for all her responsibilities, but she was particularly appreciated for her "conscientious preparations" and for her "gift for teaching" (*Lehrbegabung*). Her preparatory years were such a success that the Cottage Lyceum administration invited Anna Freud to stay on with a regular four-year contract starting in the fall of 1918. Dr. Goldman also hired Anna Freud on a part-time basis as her secretary and assistant, providing her with excellent preparation for the many later administrative positions she held.[32]

From the viewpoint of her little students, Anna Freud was an oasis of warmth and enthusiasm in the midst of their dreary, difficult wartime lives. At the age of nineteen, in 1915, she was less formidable to her charges than the predominantly older regular teachers; and at five feet three, she was not formidable in size either. She seemed so much like a schoolgirl that many of her children remembered her as wearing a blue school uniform when she wore—albeit uniformly— her favorite dark-blue skirt and coat. In retrospective testimonies, her former students remark again and again on the excellent discipline in Anna Freud's classrooms and on her remarkable attentiveness. "I remember," one of her boys wrote forty years after his time as her pupil, "that you were wearing a blue uniform and were entering many notes into a little book and I always wondered whether it was pertaining to child observation."[33] "She had only to look at us firmly and seriously to keep us in order," another recalled.[34] And Anna Freud herself was fond of telling how the discipline filtered down through the ranks: a visitor came to the class one day and began to nibble at his lunch before the appointed lunchtime—until the little boy next to him leaned over and said in a grown-up voice, "We don't eat during lessons in this class!"[35]

Like most children who start school under wartime rationing, Anna Freud's pupils played out all of the usual childhood fantasies in the medium of food. Instead of exaggerating her father's size or wealth or power, one little girl announced with complete conviction: "Der Vater will alleweil jeden Sonntag Fleisch essen" ("My father, he always eats meat every Sunday").[36] Many years later, a former pupil introduced himself from the American city to which he had emigrated before the Second World War: "I was a little insignificant boy who had a lot of earaches, and you even expressed yourself very sympathetically about it on some occasions." His most powerful memory was of Christmas 1917, a time of terrible food shortages in Vienna. It was the custom for the children to bring a small gift for their teacher, and to put it under the Christmas tree. "Unfortunately, my parents did not give me any gift to give to the teacher, and I found it most embarrassing." So he decided to offer up a cube of marmalade wrapped in paper that had been given to him for his morning snack. When the other children were at recess, he slipped this marmalade cube under the tree for Fräulein Freud. "I was in love with my teacher," he confessed, "and this was before the name of Freud meant anything to me."[37]

The cold wartime winters with little fuel for heating at home or at school were hard on everyone's health and nerves. Sigmund Freud once cranked out a piece of popular writing for a Hungarian journal in exchange for a sack of potatoes—much more useful during the winter shortages than currency—and this work became known as "the potato dish" ("Kartoffelschmarren").[38] A legend also grew up among the Freuds about the day that Martha, Tante Minna, and

Anna spent going through a bag of peas that Ernst had brought home on one of his military leaves: they opened each and every pea to remove the worms feasting within, and then cooked up the whole wormless remainder.[39] Everyone devoted a great deal of energy to securing food (and cigars for Freud) from Loe Kann's brother in Holland, the Freud relatives in England, and the colleagues in Hungary. Anna Freud took tutorial students after school hours for extra cash or food, and contributed to the household her salary, 2,000 kronen a year—as her father reported to Ferenczi proudly and with his usual exactitude about money.[40]

But there were limits to the concessions the Freud family was willing to make to the wartime conditions. The common practice in Vienna was for a family—or two—to spend evenings crowded into one room, with one stove going. But in the Freud household the living room was left to Martha and Tante Minna and the housekeeper, Fammi. Both Anna Freud and her father retired to their cold rooms to work, she on her class preparations and translations, he on his important summary volume called *Introductory Lectures on Psychoanalysis*. With his usual wry humor, Freud praised his daughter as the winter of 1917–18 approached for being "mit Feuereifer bei der Arbeit" ("at her work with fiery zeal").[41] But the combination of hunger, cold, and long hours of work left Anna Freud with an infection that was later diagnosed as tuberculosis. She shared this illness with huge numbers of Viennese and a good portion of the Austrian Army, including her brother Ernst, who did a stint in a sanatorium for his cure after the war. For mild cases, fresh air and good nutrition worked wonders—but in Vienna neither fresh air nor adequate food was to be had.

The first appearance of Anna Freud's infection occurred in January 1917. She was forced to take a three-week leave from school with influenza and a heavy cough. Because Freud could not find a place for her in the sanatoria in Breitenstein or the Semmering, she was sent to the suburb known as Sulz, in the Vienna Forest (Wienerwald), to recuperate. The episode passed, but in June she was down again with a serious ear infection, and from then on—for nearly five years—she had to be careful. Her uncertain health was one reason why she gave up schoolteaching after the war, in 1920. "After she gives up school on account of her health," Freud noted to Max Eitingon at that time, "Anna should remain free to move, and if possible she should spend parts of the winter in the south."[42]

Sandor Ferenczi provided a warm and sunny retreat for the Freuds in the summers of 1917 and 1918 by putting them in touch with Hungarian friends and relatives who had summer homes in Csorbató. "The Hungarians are uncouth and noisy," Freud reported, "but obliging and hospitable and friendship and loyalty are taking the form of generosity, with the result that we are able to wallow in a superfluity of bread, butter, sausages, eggs, and cigars, rather like the chief of a primitive tribe."[43]

In 1917, Anna went ahead of her parents, who visited first at the spa in Gastein. She spent lovely days with Ferenczi's mother and sister, eating well and (she wrote to her parents) riding horseback in dirndl and black stockings—for lack of a proper habit. Ferenczi's sister put her in touch with several of the local schoolteachers, and Anna Freud arranged to bring her Cottage Lyceum class to visit a Hungarian school the following summer. Also instrumental in these arrangements were Ferenczi's friends Lajos and Katá Levy. Dr. Levy, an analysand of Ferenczi's, was the director of the famous Jewish Hospital in Budapest, and his wife, Katá, was a social worker and the sister of Anton von Freund, a wealthy businessman. Von Freund's wife had been analyzed by Ferenczi, and he himself sought an analysis with Freud—one that became intensely charged when von Freund found out that he had a lethal abdominal cancer. The von Freunds were happy to have Anna Freud act as a kind of informal resident tutor for their little daughter, Vera, and Anna Freud was happy to take Katá Levy as her own quasi-maternal companion in lieu of Loe Kann Jones.

Anna Freud went with her father by boat to Hungary in the summer of 1918, and then they parted company. He went to Lomnicz, where Martha joined him after a visit with Sophie, and Anna went to the school near Budapest. She worked there as a teacher for several weeks, and then received her Viennese students for their visit. This was an experiment in what Anna Freud later called—using the American John Dewey's term—"project teaching." The students took Hungary as their "project," and they were to find out, by being there, by looking and listening, everything they could about Hungary; then when they returned to Vienna they were to continue their research in the library.

Anna Freud's personal project in Hungary was more specific. She had arranged to rejoin her parents, and meet up with her brother Ernst, in Budapest that September, just before she returned to Vienna to her regular teaching position. The others were to attend the first International Psychoanalytic Congress since before the outbreak of the war. She could stay only long enough to meet the psychoanalysts who would one day, she hoped, be her colleagues as well as her father's, for she had arranged to begin an analysis with her father when he returned to Vienna on the first of October. Freud had argued strongly for years that a personal analysis should be required of every psychoanalytic practitioner, and his Viennese colleague Hermann Nunberg brought a proposal to that effect before the Budapest meeting. The proposal was defeated, particularly because of opposition from two younger Viennese, Otto Rank and Victor Tausk, and was not successfully reintroduced until 1926. But in the Freud household, for Anna Freud, the proposal was in effect long before its acceptance. Her plan was to continue teaching during the analysis so that she could turn toward an analytic practice or toward psychoanalytically informed pedagogy; determining the right path would be part of the analytic work.

At the Congress, Sigmund Freud breached a tradition: rather than speaking extemporaneously, from notes carried in his head, he read his lecture. This was behavior he had always considered impolite and described as equivalent to offering a man a ride in a carriage and then attaching a rope to pull him along behind. The family members later protested. But Freud was making a very demanding, anxiety-inducing appearance: his first statement before colleagues—rather than the noninitiates who came to his wartime Vienna lectures—after four disunifying, draining years. He had to pull his troops together, and set them on a new path—one they would have to take without the aid of the Swiss who had departed with Carl Jung in 1913.

The first part of Freud's address, called "Lines of Advance in Psychoanalytic Therapy," carefully surveyed current questions about psychoanalytic technique and the necessity for finding ways to deal with patients' reluctances to recover. But the address ended with a stirring vision of psychoanalytic physicians working in institutes and clinics, extending the reach of the therapy beyond the confines of the upper classes and into "the wider social strata."[44] Freud hoped for the time when "the conscience of society will awake and remind it that the poor man should have just as much right to assistance for his mind as he now has to the life-saving help offered by surgery; and that the neuroses threaten public health no less than tuberculosis, and can be left as little as the latter to the impotent care of individual members of the community."

Many analysts took up the challenge of Freud's technical survey and developed therapies for psychotics (not just neurotics), for victims of physical traumas (like the "war neurotics" who were the main topic of the Budapest Congress), and sufferers from extreme forms of phobia. Among the new techniques was "child analysis," analytic therapy specifically designed for children and adolescents—a possibility Freud did not note in his survey. Many analysts also took Freud's advice and extended psychoanalysis through clinics and institutes into "the wider social strata." But the analyst for whom Freud's social vision became a credo most deeply and most lastingly was his daughter.

ALTHOUGH SHE had written poetry in school and as an exercise during her teacher training, Anna Freud had never written poetry from inner necessity before her psychoanalysis. But in October 1918, during the first month of her analysis, she began writing that poetry of the need to write poetry, which is as timeless as adolescence but which is also "modernist" and known for its debt to psychoanalysis.[45] Anna Freud wrote a poem called "Dichter" ("Poet," not poetess) in which she told her discovery in a stanza:

> Only when my mind was churned more deeply,
> When I was struggling with wild, dark forces,
> Did I, alone in my need, feel with fear
> That each poet sings but his own sorrow.

She could remember or read others' verses, she said, but they would not tell her story. Her illustrative metaphor came from the Old Testament, which she had been studying the previous spring for her final examination in religion. She wanted to call to her own heart, as King Saul had once called to David:

> *I would like to play the harp myself,*
> *To try the power of my own verse,*
> *Snatch up my soul from its despair,*
> *Do what cannot be done by others' words.*
>
> *My song should conquer night and pain,*
> *Reaching in triumph the realm of joy.*
> *In my own service, I would sing my soul—*
> *David would I be, and King Saul as well.*

Anna Freud's tendency to identify with male characters and to imagine younger men and older men—like the young Karl and his adviser—achieving harmony is present in this poem, but the characters are internalized. She is both, David and Saul, heart and soul. Such a declaration of self-sufficiency may also have been part of the transference relation to her father-analyst: that is, the common initial analysand's feeling: I will do it myself, you are there but you are not the (Jewish) king in my kingdom.

In the analysis and in the dreams she had that October, Anna Freud confirmed the possibility she had sensed before the Budapest Congress, that she could be released from her indecisiveness about what she wanted to be when she grew up. She also—more importantly—felt that she could be freed from her fearful inexperience for loving: "Love might now softly touch your heart." This was the final line of an eight-stanza poem called "Dreams" in which Anna Freud related a dream image of herself wandering "with bare feet / All the walks, tracks, gardens, streets" in a condition that she called "only one will"—not of divided will. The fifth and sixth stanzas contain the crucial self-portrait:

> *And so I am thinking: in your life*
> *You would have found several loves,*
> *Only clear sight was not given you,*
> *Your heart stood open to other thoughts.*

> *Tighter than the shoes upon your feet,*
> *Fears, obsessions, obstinance gripped*
> *Your mind; affectless, repulsed by things,*
> *You turned your longing in on yourself.*

She wanted to recover her barefoot, unconstrained childhood self, and to rid herself of what she called in semipsychoanalytic terms *Angst, Zwang, und Trotz.* (*Angst* is the general psychoanalysis term for anxiety, as in *Kastrationsangst;* the compound for obsessional neurosis is *Zwangsneurose; Trotz* is the word Freud often used for obstinacy, which, with *Sparsamkeit* and *Ordentlichkeit*, parsimony and orderliness, he considered an ingredient of "the anal erotic character.")

But, while she was imagining her future freedom, Anna Freud was also profoundly disturbed to discover that an interpretation of the world and of herself which she had built up was nothing but "a nice story," featuring a nice little person, which was untrue to the realities of life or character. The nice story served to repress a not-nice fantasy. (The mechanism of that kind of repression was the main subject of a paper her father started writing in December 1918, called " 'A Child Is Being Beaten.' ") In a long blank-verse lament entitled "Irrtum" ("Mistake"), Anna Freud made an effort to withdraw from the repression-story habits of a decade, and to let the dark, unpleasant fantasy material come through. This is the poem in full:

> *Once it seemed to me that I could play Fate,*
> *Could a Creator be. In the image of the world*
> *Where we are living, I would be busily*
> *Building a little world, for myself,*
> *Made with my own power, a miniature.*
>
> *So I studied for some years. Gestures*
> *I eagerly imprinted on my memory:*
> *I saw the hands in their revealing games,*
> *Saw the light that fell on excited faces,*
> *And lips, too, saw forming careless words.*
> *Greedily I drank life in until,*
> *Full of phantasms, life overflowed me.*
> *So many words of love I had noted,*
> *Gentle speaking, fears of doing harm,*
> *And people who, understanding, seek others.*

And what a sad bungler's work I made,
Which of the true world showed only half—
The lights only, not the shadows.
Fate's own work I misunderstood:
With blind, heavy hand it commands, kills,
Just like a man who pokes an anthill
With a cane, spreading destruction,
Unable to feel the tiny creatures' pain.
Where did I put hurt, rage, anger?
Fear of sudden death, of loneliness?
Where the ending, or the luck, that we,
in our need, steal from Fate like thieves?
I forgot pity, which as cold fear before
Our misfortunes, claws at our hearts.
For so long I have diluted my strength
With goodness, happiness, kind words,
For so long I have kept my eyes shut.
Only tonight have I grasped my mistake.
Instead of truly imitating the world,
I made an image of my own self;
Because I formed people out of me,
I refused anxiously to harm them,
lest I unknowingly my own flesh
cut, and lest I criminally
blood of my own blood spilt.

I am like a mother, who her own child
weakens with too much love; but not like Fate,
which I, powerless, had dared to impersonate.

It is interesting to note that the only female role in which Anna Freud imagined herself was that of mother.[46] This is the only one of her poems in which she is a mother, however, and as a mother she errs in just the direction she felt her own mother never went with her—"too much love."

"Mistake" was written in October, but its theme lingered, and on December 3, to mark her twenty-third birthday, Anna Freud wrote "Misstrauen" ("Mistrust"). This poem is addressed to an unnamed "you," who shares her own bent: "You want to find only the open form of things / You will not imagine hostile nature." She asks this "you" to consider:

> *And you really believe, because in bright*
> *Daylight my appearance has become familiar,*
> *That you can talk about how I think!*
> *Perhaps in the night I am a murderer?*
> *As we walk fearfully in dark places,*
> *Guided by only the touch of our hands,*
> *So we seem to stand blindly in life,*
> *Circled by doubts of foreignness in things.*

It is not clear who this "you" is—perhaps only a part of herself—but the "you" of another poem from that December is named. Anna Freud wrote the poem, called "Zuspruch" ("Encouragement"), for Heinz Rudolf Halberstadt, the baby born to her sister Sophie on December 8, 1918. To this child, Anna Freud imparted the lessons she had learned for herself: those about choosing a path in life; and those about acknowledging life's shadows as well as its light, the not-nice stories as well as the nice ones. Like a mother determined *not* to weaken her child with too much love, too much direction, too much protection, she gives the kind of bracing advice she was giving herself. The poem is in five stanzas, rhymed like a nursery song in the German original, and simpler, less self-consciously poetic in style than her other efforts.

> *Yes, by strange hands, and unasked*
> *You will be set down in strange rooms,*
> *Where you can turn your steps forward,*
> *Backward, any way, and as you like.*
>
> *Don't be foolish and ask the path*
> *When you see others going aimlessly.*
> *Try yourself! All those standers-by—*
> *Not one can tell you what is right.*
>
> *And you should find things your way,*
> *Testing them with your own hands.*
> *What's on the surface, what you see,*
> *Gives false notice of realities.*
>
> *Maybe you will have to wander*
> *Many paths, in the cold and dark.*
> *But who promised you that only*
> *For joy were you brought to this earth?*

Don't look too much—I counsel you—
At how your wishes get fulfilled.
And if some longing goes unmet, don't
Be astonished. We call that Life.

ANNA Freud had put fall 1918 dates on nine poems in the packet that she carefully saved and later took with her to England. There are also many undated poems in her collection, and some of these may also be records of the first several months of her analysis as well. But among the dated poems, the next is one from March 1919; then come several from the summer of 1919. That summer Anna Freud spent mostly with the Oscar Rie family, and in the company of the oldest Rie daughter, Margarethe (or Margretl), and Frau Melanie Rie, a lovely woman, who that summer joined Loe Kann Jones and Katá Levy in Anna Freud's collection of beautiful and good maternal older friends. The two young women had wonderful times together, hiking and sailing on the Konigsee as they had when they were children. They also talked about their analytic experiences: "I told her that I was in analysis with you," Anne Freud wrote to her father, "because she often talks about her therapy, and I did not think it was fair that I knew about her and she not about me."[47]

In the relaxing summertime, such a relief after the hard winter in Vienna—as hard materially as any during the war—Anna Freud imagined how lovely it would be to buy a little country house and retire to a life of making cheese and butter and working in the fields—with a little translating for the *Zeitschrift* to bring in money. Similarly, in a poem called "Sunday," she reflected on how waiting for Monday destroys the peacefulness of the day of rest. But she recognized her wish for Sunday and her country-idyll fantasy as echoes of her "old summer aversion against school," although she enjoyed it anyway, particularly as her night dreams were then so devoid of idyllic scenes, so violent and perplexing.

On the fifth of August she wrote to her father:

My different personalities leave me in peace now. But I dream every night very clearly and strangely. For example, yesterday: "I murdered somebody, or something like that. As punishment, I was put into a large room where there were many people, who could do with me what they pleased. The people wanted to tear me to bits and throw me out the window. I was frightened, but not terribly much. There was also an old gentleman among them, who all of the sudden took something down off the wall and gave half of it to me so that I might defend myself, driving the people back. Then I was guarded by two soldiers pointing rifles toward me. And then came the strangest thing: one soldier suddenly told me the true cause of Napoleon's death. He was guarded in this room, just as I was. He stood as I did by the open window and wanted to climb out it in order to go to the toilet. The soldiers thought he was attempting escape and shot him. One of them warned me that they would do the same to me." I think I would have a lot of associations to that! It seems that now mostly dire things happen in my dreams—killing, shooting or dying.[48]

The masculine cast of characters and the violence in her dreams, although they cannot be interpreted in any detail without the associations she did not write down, do seem to presage further dissolution for the nice stories she told herself about life and her own character. Such a development is indicated by her next wave of literary production. In December 1919, at about the time of her twenty-fourth birthday, Anna Freud began to work on short prose pieces that seem to be part of a novel or novella. She constructed a scene, largely through dialogue, in which a lover (male) returns to an unnamed place for an attempt at reconciliation with his estranged beloved (gender unspecified). He is rejected. The beloved says that "everything I had to tell you—and it was much—I spoke in the long days and evenings, after you had left." There is nothing more to say. In another scene, one partner in a married couple beseeches the other, who is ill and perhaps dying, for closeness, for permission to give comfort. The scene is in three parts, and from one to the next the estrangement between the partners grows, until, at the end, the beseeching one feels reproached, rejected. "You loved me with all my faults and rigidities for so long, only to push me from you today! Have you no longer any strength, so that you must tally up all my failings?"

In these prose pieces, something unspecified blocks the possibility of reconciliation, kindness, and harmony. In terms of Anna Freud's inner life, what this seems to have meant is that the nice stories she was accustomed to tell herself failed to keep from her consciousness fantasies that lay behind them—fantasies full of violence. There is no date on a long, free-form poem called "Nacht" ("Night"), but it too presents a rupture in which a story that Anna Freud had created as an adolescent is summoned up for comfort. This was a story involving a medieval character called Egon, a suffering young hero, and the emperor who holds Egon's fate in his hands. Like the earlier poem called "Mistake," this one begins with a moment of revelation:

> A fever is in me and drives me away. My mind
> Has been kept so tightly shut for years.
> But today a door stood open and out stumbled
> So wildly that which was long repressed.
> I have long known that many people already
> Have taken flight from their own egos—
> Out over land and sea, around the world—
> And yet in every inner fiber they have found
> That ego comes crawling along after them.
> So loathsomely familiar, so never new.
> For one hour, one day, I do so wish
> To be rid of my self, no longer to know
> My own face, my own poor hand,
> Just once not to feel my thoughts.
> That man, that drayman, would I be,
> His shoulder rubbed sore from the strap;
> That porter, his neck bent, burdened;
> Someone other, who has no need to cover up—
> As I have been doing for so very long,
> With satisfactions cleverly calculated,
> Yet so stingy, so pitiful, that the dog
> Sunning himself in the corner there
> Would never look up from his bone for them.

She then imagines herself "like the boy in the poor song" who is humiliated by being unable to close a door that has been opened. It would be better to walk out into the night and find "the sin which lures me" than to lie in bed, wanting to scream, afraid of breaking into pieces. This tumultuous stanza ends with an address to another unnamed "you," who is, perhaps, the one who forbade the "sin" (which is all but called masturbation) and who is, as the analyst, opening the door that has been closed on the subject of this sin.

> *Why are you happy, when I toss in my bed,*
> *When I stretch my arms wide but let them*
> *Fall empty on my body. Close the door!*

The image system of the poem shifts after this appeal, and Anna Freud portrays her "poor ego" ("Mein armes Ich") as a bird that sat for many years quietly in its cage and then flew out to wing its way wildly around her bedroom. She appeals to the bird to return and offers a bribe:

> *Just fly inside! And I will tell you*
> *Two stories on every day—the very*
> *Nicest that I know. If you are hungry*
> *And my stories do not satiate you,*
> *You can still have your own free will,*
> *No matter how bad it be!*

She finally coaxes the bird into the cage: "I will tell you a story right away / Listen: 'Egon said . . .'—Put your head under your wing!" When the story is offered, the cage door can be closed on this unruly ego and she can sleep for the night.

In this poem, Anna Freud gave up the tremendous struggle against what her father called "the return of the repressed" fantasy by resorting to a nice story, which controls the sinfulness. In the entire collection there is, in fact, no poem in which the nice stories are renounced successfully. Rather, the stories themselves changed form. The sorrows and disappointments that the nice stories had kept out of view were admitted into stories with no happily-ever-afters in them.

An undated poem shows how the motifs of Anna Freud's favorite medieval Egon story were transformed as her analysis progressed. A young hero meets two figures at a forest crossroads. One is Love, the other Glory. Love offered a rose, and Glory a sword for bringing death upon enemies. Before the hero can make up his mind, Love places the rose "in the golden hair of another." The hero then takes the sword from Glory and goes off with it—but not in a triumphant frame of mind:

Wearily I took the sword in my hand,
And unwillingly I went off to battle.
Soon the sword's sharp edge turned
My happiness into bitter sorrow . . .

As an old man the unhappy soldier sheathes his sword for good:

For all the glory my sword has won,
The old and the young do envy me,
But my heart still hungers after Love,
Which in the forest there I sacrificed.

This is not a story about being unable to wield a sword, or envying those (males) who have phallic swords to wield. The poem finds the glory of sword-wielding unsatisfactory, loveless. The hero is like Cyrano de Bergerac in the play by Edmond Rostand, which Anna Freud read for the first time during her analysis and immediately adored: Cyrano goes off to war without speaking his love for Roxane, and love passes him by—until it is too late. There is no redemption in Anna Freud's poem. But also no illusion.

For much of the summer of 1920, Anna Freud was in Gmain, again with the Rie family, relaxing and translating an English-language book by the Dutch psychologist Varendonck on daydreaming. Although the vacation was overshadowed somewhat when Oscar Rie became seriously ill and had to endure a slow, painful recuperation, it was nonetheless restful. In good health and happy, Anna Freud finished the summer in Berlin: "Everyone here says in a surprised manner," she wrote to Margarethe, "that I have grown . . . they are so stupid and do not notice that I am standing up straighter!"[49] Her letters were active, chatty, and gay: "Otherwise, I am not surprised— once again—by anything, by finding myself on a train, on a track leading everywhere, conversing with Papa, just letting things go well, while attempting to read a new, very difficult paper by him, telling myself stories in the meantime, and surprised only that all of you are not here."[50]

The summer joyousness was all the more welcome since the preceding six months had been so dreadful. December 1919 had been a happy month for the family. Martin, who had been captured in Italy and left stranded at the end of the war—largely incommunicado—in a military hospital, returned to Vienna and announced soon afterward that he would marry. Ernst and Oliver were at home for the December wedding, so that all the children were present except Sophie. But the time was otherwise a great strain. Martha Freud had had a case of pneumonia the preceding spring that lingered on in the form of fatigue and coughing, even after a two-month stay in a Salzburg sanatorium. Freud was worried by his wife's condition and also about his ability to provide for both her care and treatments for her sister Minna's persistent pleurisy. His income hardly kept stride with the wild inflation. Even the beginning of a flow of English and American training cases did not keep him from engaging an English tutor in case emigration to England proved the only way to escape financial catastrophe. For his publishing ventures, Freud was relying on the generosity of Anton von Freund, but currency export restrictions kept most of that generosity in Hungarian banks, useless to psychoanalysis. And then, at the beginning of January, von Freund, who was in Vienna trying through analytic work to stem his despair over the progress of his cancer, took a final turn for the worse. In less than three weeks, he was dead. Freud, who had spent many hours at the bedside of his friend and patient, was distraught.

Then the whole family took a terrible blow: an influenza epidemic that swept through Germany in the frigid third week of January caught Sophie Halberstadt. After only four days, before any of the family could reach Hamburg on the strike-ridden railroads, she died. Because of the rail strikes, only Ernst and Oliver could attend the funeral. They traveled from Berlin with Max Eitingon, who had taken von Freund's place on Freud's Committee of colleagues, and who, from 1920 on, was the helpful Berlin uncle for the five surviving Freud children and for the young widower, Max Halberstadt. In Vienna, Freud mourned in stunned, stoic reserve. Martha Freud, who had loved Sophie so dearly and spent—more than anyone else in the family—so much energy on helping the Halberstadts keep a happy family life during the war, was devastated: "My wife is quite overwhelmed," Freud wrote to Ferenczi. And of his youngest daughter he reported, simply, "Anna sicht schlect aus" ("Anna looks bad").[51]

Like her father, Anna Freud tried to overcome with work her grief at the loss of the sister she had so adored and so envied. Her health was still poor; even though the tuberculosis infection had re-

ceded, she had backaches and recurrent coughs. But when the school
year ended, she resigned her post and took on more translating work
for the psychoanalytic journals. Her resolve eventually to practice
psychoanalysis strengthened and Freud recognized her dedication by
giving her, in May, one of the gold-and-intaglio rings that the members of his Committee wore as signs of their allegiance. With the
loss of Sophie, Freud and his youngest daughter grew even closer in
their professional partnership.

Freud's hope that his movement would survive the death of its
chief patron, von Freund, was given a great buttressing by the opening in February 1920 of the Berlin Policlinic, an outpatient clinic
financed by Max Eitingon and housed in a building renovated by the
young architect Ernst Freud. Heartened, Freud finished a book called
Beyond the Pleasure Principle, which he had started in the spring of
1919, and gave an abstract of it to the Vienna Society on June 16,
1920; then he turned his attention to another long manuscript, *Group
Psychology and the Analysis of the Ego*, during the summer. In August, Anna Freud took the second manuscript to Eitingon and Karl
Abraham in Berlin—and apparently read it on the train herself. She
went to Berlin before traveling with her father to the Psychoanalytic Congress in Holland, where she hoped to have a long-awaited
reunion with Loe Kann Jones. In the course of her journey she also
stopped in Hamburg for one of her frequent visits to the Halberstadt household. Her nonprofessional work of mourning was centered
on Ernst and Heinz (called Heinerle), Sophie's boys, aged six and
thirteen months when their mother died.

Max Halberstadt's sister-in-law, who had lost her husband in the
war, helped Max with his children, as did a housemaid. Anna Freud
came whenever one of these women had to be away from the house—
as was the case for six weeks in the spring of 1922. Sharing the household management with Max's sister-in-law, Anna Freud felt identified
with her own mother, who had shared the Berggasse household
with Tante Minna. The sister-in-law was, Anna Freud said, "a good
Minna."⁵² In the summers after 1920, Max usually brought one or
both of the boys to the Freuds for part of their holidays, and Anna
Freud cared for them by herself. Max was remote and depressed after
his wife's death, and he took little pleasure in the Freud family—
or in much else. Mathilde and her husband, Robert Hollitscher, be-

came very attached to the little boy, Heinerle, and wanted to adopt him. Anna Freud, sensing that Ernst was the more troubled of the boys and the one who endeared himself less to the family, took a special interest in him—though he was so hurt and bewildered by the loss of his mother that he found it hard to reciprocate. Anna Freud was enormously patient with him, but once or twice she despaired: "for the first time in my life I am glad that I do not have any children, for if he were my child and behaved like he does, I could hardly bear it."[53]

Anna Freud had the idea in 1921 that she might informally adopt Ernst Halberstadt and bring him to live in the Berggasse apartment. She and her father discussed the possibility by letter and decided against it, because life with grandparents and great-aunt did not seem to offer the energetic flexibility a complicated boy of seven needed and specifically because Freud felt that his wife would find Ernstl too much. Martha Freud was not well in the years after her pneumonia and Sophie's death; she tired easily and was not restored by summer stays in the spas. Having guests was a difficult undertaking for her; she clung to fixed routines, and adapted not at all easily.[54]

AFTER Sophie's death, Anna Freud continued to work sporadically on prose pieces, and she eventually began to shape a novel called *Heinrich Mühsam* (Henry Laborious) out of them. Despite the tension in their friendship, she read pieces of the work to her cousin Mausi Graf when they met in the summers at their grandmother's in Ischl. Mausi seems to have understood Anna Freud's male-character stories to some extent, though Anna Freud did not entirely trust her reactions: "Even toward Mausi, my public, I was always careful."[55] But Anna Freud did say that she felt Mausi became like a sister, especially in the summers after Sophie's death. To her old quest for a perfect mother, Anna Freud added a quest for a living sister.

In 1920 and 1921, Anna Freud also experimented with little two- or three-sentence prose reflections. Obliquely, the loss of her real sister sounds in several of these pieces.

Lumberjacks are walking through the forest with axes and saws. And every time they have selected a victim, the crowns of the

trees rustle. They realize more clearly than ever before how
wonderful it is to stand erect when the one next to them
trembles and falls. (August 25, 1921)

Once again the woodcutter has done his job. Bare tree trunks
sway on heavy wagons down to the village, and withered
branches, pieces of bark, are piled up in neat heaps along the
path. But we are aware only of the empty space in the forest,
which only yesterday was filled with trees. (August 27, 1921)

Anna Freud's anxiety in imagining Sophie cut down was connected
to her own growing hope for herself as a person who would be able
to stand erect, enjoy a full life of love and happiness. She both identified with her sister's fate and rejected it. After she visited Alix
Strachey (a patient of Freud's and the wife of his English translator,
James Strachey) who was ill in Vienna, Anna Freud recorded the
mixture of her feelings precisely: "Her illness affected me intimately, despite the rather loose personal tie; half because she seemed
like myself lying there and still desiring to live for an interminable
time (as I find more and more that life is better than I thought it
would be) and the other—probably greater—half in remembering
my sister."[56]

   The prose pieces from these years are also permeated with questions about time, about the passage of time and the meaning of
past, present, future. These questions seem to come from deep
down in the analytic work—for which Anna Freud found an anal or
intestinal metaphor of considerable graphicness.

We are moles, who painstakingly make our tunnels through the
innards of time. With the gravedigger's tools our hands have
become, we reach into the firm walls of the years, to break
them slowly into pieces, clod by clod. We live trapped, between
the churned-up and examined past and a future that waits for
our work. As we crawl gropingly through a dark piece of the
present, our eyes are blinded to the brightness of the timeless
world above. (July 19, 1920)

She expressed continually a sense of being caught between the struggles of the present and an unknown future—the life and the love
that were only hopes.

We are imprisoned in the realm of life, like a sailor on his tiny boat, on an infinite ocean. Around us is the boundless expanse, which lures us on. But we have nothing except a pair of oars, impotent as the wings of a mosquito, and our aching hands. (August 15, 1920)

Just like a boy who tries to catch the fish in the brook with his hands, I stand on the shore of time, which flows by me; the hours run through my hands without leaving anything alive in them. But I don't stop scooping up time, as I lean over its stream. And in the glistening play of drops that the waves splash on my face, I forget about the booty I set out to bring home. (October, 1920)

In the 1918 poem called "Dreams," while she was wishing for a return of her barefooted childhood unconstraint, Anna Freud had noted that she might have found several loves had she not been distracted by "other thoughts" and turned in on herself. During her analysis, those loves did not get any more found than they had been before; but Anna Freud did find male friends who became very important to her and to her work.

In the course of her teaching apprenticeship, and then during the analysis, which went on until the spring of 1922, Anna Freud had a few brief flirtations. Her American cousin Edward Bernays, her senior by four years, traveled to Europe in the summer of 1920. She met him in Salzburg, where he was visiting their Uncle Alexander, and they went walking in the countryside together. But she kept her distance.

The only serious suitor was Hans Lampl, a schoolmate of Martin's, a Viennese, and from an impoverished family. Lampl, who was six years older than Anna Freud, had become friendly with all the Freud children, and had gone to parties with the Freud partygoers—Martin, Ernst, and Sophie. He also occasionally took Anna Freud to a party, even though she was definitely not—as a young woman or ever after—in favor of parties. Her social memories tended to be more connected to her father than to her escorts. She recalled one New Year's Eve, for example, when she and Lampl had stopped by her father's study on their way to a masquerade ball. Freud had interrupted his writing long enough to give them a coin—a krone—and then turned right back to see the New Year in alone at his desk.[57]

Lampl attended the University of Vienna's medical school and graduated in 1912. He then worked for eight years in a research group headed by Dr. Karl Landsteiner, who published on blood groups. Lampl was focused upon serology and two other fields, bacteriology and pathological anatomy, until 1920, when he decided to study psychoanalysis. His interest in psychoanalysis was older, however, and came from his friendship with the Freuds. Lampl had been attending Freud's lectures at the University of Vienna since 1912, when he reported on them by letter to Anna Freud, who was then in her exile in Merano. They attended together the 1916 lectures that were eventually published as the *Introductory Lectures on Psychoanalysis*.

Sigmund Freud was always friendly toward Hans Lampl. He discreetly supplied him with money so that he could go on school trips and skiing expeditions with Martin, and he made him gifts. Lampl kept for decades an expensive dressing gown given to him by Freud. But Freud was not interested in having Lampl as a son-in-law when the courtship became more serious. At the 1920 Hague Congress, which father, daughter, and suitor all attended, Lampl felt that he was the third—and shortest—side of a triangle. Thirty-six years after the event, he remembered: "There was a situation in Schwewenigen at the Hague Congress in which your father walked home alone and both of us continued on with Eitingon, singing "Carmen" as we went. It certainly did not disturb me that your father went on alone while I was with you!"[58]

It is not clear why Freud deemed Lampl unsuitable, but it is clear that father and daughter agreed in the conclusion. In the summer of 1921, she wrote to her father: "I am often together with Lampl in a friendly relationship, but I also have daily opportunities to confirm our judgment of him from last year and to rejoice that we judged correctly."[59] Lampl seems to have then involved himself with Anna Freud's cousin Mausi Graf, for Anna Freud reported to her father in November of 1920 that she had seen another cousin, Martha, the youngest of Marie Freud's three daughters, with her journalist fiancé Jakob Seidmann, in the company of Mausi Graf and Lampl. Martha, who called herself Tom and dressed as a man, seemed happy with her Jakob, but Mausi was not, Anna Freud felt, happy with "her Lampl."[60] Neither of the young women had, however, happy lives. Tom Seidmann, a talented illustrator of children's books, but always a complicated, restless woman, eventually committed suicide in 1930—a year after Jakob had killed himself. The story of Mausi Graf was no less tragic.

Anna Freud saw Mausi for the last time in the summer of 1922. Mausi was having a difficult time with her widowed mother, Rosa, who still mourned the loss of her other child, Hermann: in 1917, when he was only twenty, Hermann had been killed on the Italian front. But Mausi was also remote and less like a sister for Anna Freud because she had become entangled, at the age of twenty-three, in a love affair. On August 16 she went to Vienna, leaving her cousins behind at their grandmother's. Her intention was to commit suicide. Pregnant and forlorn, she took Veronal and wrote her mother a poignant letter while she lost consciousness from the drug. The letter asks her mother's forgiveness and (changing addressee in the middle) absolves her lover, whom she calls simply "Bub" ("Boy"), of responsibility: "You know that you also made me very happy. We saw many beautiful things together, and I thank you. I wanted too much from you."[61] Two days later she died.

Anna Freud had not been aware that her cousin was pregnant— she found that out only many years later from Jones's biography of Freud[62]—but she was aware that Mausi was unhappy in her love affair, and she regretted deeply having been unable to do anything. Mausi had left her a note, too, but by the time she found it her cousin had gone to Vienna. Mausi's note to Anna Freud, her "dear little bird," was loving and concluded with a catalog of thoughtful arrangements—"the savings bank account will be in order, and the house, too, someone can just lock it as it is"—but it also contained a charge that must have been horrifying to Anna Freud: "Do become really happy, Annerl, don't let this get to you—and you'll now have an easier time being with the boys."

It is not clear from Mausi's note just how Anna Freud was supposed to benefit "with the boys," but it is clear from Anna Freud's reflections on her cousin's death that she wished she could have been as helpful as were the male characters in the "nice stories" she had shared with Mausi: "Now I know what I should have said to her concerning the 'other' boys in order to give her confidence, but it is too late." She told the same friend: "She withdrew from me during the last half a year, and I let her. It would be understandable if I had not liked her, but I did like her very much, though that did not help her. So I realize how great is the difference between what I would like to be and how I really am. I had a dream that contained all this."[63]

There is no indication in Anna Freud's correspondence that Lampl was directly involved in Mausi's death except insofar as he too failed to understand her desperation. He had, however, managed to distance himself further from the Freuds on another count just half a year before. Ernst Freud had married a Berliner named Lucie Brasch and they were living in Berlin with the first of their three sons. During a brief period of alienation in their marriage, Lampl became involved as a mediator and also prevented Sigmund and Martha Freud from knowing that there had been any trouble. The episode passed, but not undetected. Freud, blaming Lucie and lamenting how few women know how to love their men, expected the worst—quite wrongly, as the couple's reconciliation was permanent. Lampl had an interview with Freud in which he was called upon to state his version of the events, and Freud believed him, "rehabilitated him" as Freud put the matter to Eitingon.[64] Anna Freud gave Eitingon a rather less resolved image: "Lampl's interview with Papa unfortunately had the effect you would have liked to prevent. But Lampl probably could not do otherwise. Papa himself requires that when one speaks with him one does not stop after telling only half of the information. Only I was very sorry for Papa's sake."[65]

The Freuds continued to be friendly with Lampl after all these events, and Lampl was one of the few outside of the family who were allowed to visit during the summer after Freud's first cancer operations. He acted as a courier between Vienna and Berlin while he was a trainee at Eitingon's Berlin Policlinic, and as aide-de-camp for the Vienna Society in the meetings of the Berlin Society. But as far as Anna Freud was concerned, Lampl had definitely become only a friend. She never changed her original practice of addressing him with the formal "Sie" rather than "Du," and when he announced his engagement in 1925 to Jeanne de Groot, a Dutch trainee of Freud's, Anna Freud was relieved. She could even find it amusing when a Viennese newspaper gossip columnist commented on her great delight of the year 1925, a gift from her father of a black Alsatian dog named Wolf: "Lampl got his Jeanne and Anna got her Wolf." There was a thread of truth to this joke, and Anna Freud was quite aware of it. She had insisted on having a male dog and one big enough to protect her on the summer walks she liked to take without human company in the Semmering.[66] She and her father treated the dog like a child, enjoying the spoiling of him and making Martha Freud furious by feeding him scraps at her meticulous table.

Rumors flew in the Vienna Society to the effect that Anna Freud was, in the meanwhile, in love with Siegfried Bernfeld. This tall, thin, flamboyant character was certainly a more likely candidate than the heavyset, bearded, knickerbockered Lampl, who was talented with people but hardly brilliant. Anna Freud met Bernfeld when he started up a project called the Baumgarten Children's Home to provide food and shelter to Viennese Jewish war orphans and street children. But he was already well known throughout Jewish Vienna for his wartime activities as a Zionist and socialist organizer, and every newspaper reader knew him as the organizer of a huge May 1918 Zionist Youth Rally in Vienna.[67] Martin Buber delivered to this rally his famous "Zion and the Youth" address, and from the solidarity established at the rally came a number of organizations oriented toward the land then called Palestine. Martin Freud was involved with the Zionist community in Vienna, and Ernst in Berlin, but Anna Freud was primarily interested in Bernfeld's youth projects and his lectures to educators.

She had worked in a *Kinderhort*, a day-care center for children of the working class, while she was an apprentice teacher, so she knew some of the Viennese concerned with child welfare. The volunteer work she did for the American Joint Distribution Committee toward the end of the war extended her acquaintance: "The Joint" provided money for getting Jewish children, orphaned or made homeless by the war, properly fed and situated in homes and foster homes. Bernfeld, who had made the need for such funds known with a 1916 piece in Martin Buber's journal *Der Jude*, "The War Orphans," convinced "The Joint" to sponsor the Baumgarten Home and to help educate its children for eventual emigration to Palestine. The educational scheme was the one Bernfeld had outlined in *The Jewish People and Its Youth* (1919): a combination of Montessori methods; socialist conceptions about the importance of trade apprenticeships; the early work on adolescence of Stanley Hall, the American psychologist who had invited Freud to Clark University; and the early work of Freud himself. The project's setting was a dreary former military hospital barracks equipped in a makeshift manner by Zionist volunteers, including a young man named Willi Hoffer, who later took over the direction of the Baumgarten Children's Home. On October 15, 1919, two hundred and forty children came to stay, forty of them under five, a number with various handicaps, and all hungry, undisciplined, and traumatized.[68]

Anna Freud never worked at the Baumgarten Home, but she was quite familiar with its work from Bernfeld's lectures, including those he gave, starting in 1920, at the Vienna Psychoanalytic Society. She admired Bernfeld very much in those first years of their acquaintance, but she felt that his experience with the Baumgarten Home, which closed after less than a year because "The Joint" was not sympathetic to its progressive methods, had left him unreliably cynical. She became convinced of this conclusion in later years when he and his third wife, Suzanne Cassirer Paret, began to collaborate on a series of biographical studies of Sigmund Freud, who had been Frau Bernfeld's analyst. Despite her doubts, Bernfeld and his younger colleague Willi Hoffer were two of the friends with whom Anna Freud met often to discuss education and child physcology.

In the early 1920s Bernfeld and Hoffer came to Berggasse 19 to join Anna Freud for an informal study circle. Their fourth partner was a bit older—seventeen years older than Anna Freud—and much more experienced with children and adolescents. This was August Aichhorn, a man of enormous girth who dressed always in black, smoked his cigarettes with an elegant holder, and looked more like a Montmartre *flâneur* than what he was: the director of a renowned residential institution for delinquent juvenile boys. Aichhorn was at Oberhollabrunn (northwest of Vienna) from 1918 to 1920, and then at another institution for two years more; after that, he worked for the City of Vienna and became a member of the Vienna Psychoanalytic Society.[69] Anna Freud's education about the Viennese social services system came from Aichhorn: "He drags me [on Fridays] to all the most remote regions of the city and shows me institutions and welfare arrangements and we meet the people involved in them. And that is really very interesting, a special and very impressive world."[70]

In 1925, Aichhorn finished a book about his experiences with juveniles, *Wayward Youth*, which established him as one of the leading European authorities on the subject. Sigmund Freud wrote the preface and made in it the gratifying acknowledgment that "children have become the main subject of psychoanalytic research and have thus replaced in importance the neurotics on whom its studies began."[71] Aichhorn discussed his book with Bernfeld, Hoffer, and Anna Freud as it unfolded, and the group was particularly eager to distinguish its conclusions from the very commonly held psychoanalytic view—theoretically argued by Melanie Klein in Berlin—that delinquency is a form of neurosis. But, even more importantly, Aichhorn argued against the nonpsychoanalytic view, dear then to bureaucratic psychiatry, that delinquency is a form of hereditary degeneration.

Anna Freud had wanted Aichhorn to become a friend of the family, and particularly of her father. But Aichhorn was so in awe of Freud, and so self-conscious about his own lack of training as a theorist, that he would only come to Society meetings. Even there he was unwilling to join the conversation, which was renowned for repartee and wit, particularly Jewish wit, which left the Gentile Aichhorn puzzled. He and Anna Freud both grasped the depth of his reserve on the evening when she finally convinced him to come to the Freud apartment for a Saturday-evening game of tarok. Behaving like a textbook example of the psychoanalytic theory of overdetermination that he so admired, Aichhorn managed to fall and break his arm on his way to the party. Neither the very talented rumormongers of Vienna's 1920s nor those since have suggested that August Aichhorn loved Anna Freud. This is not surprising, as August Aichhorn admitted that fact to himself only after the Freuds left Vienna in 1938, and he only admitted it to Anna Freud herself after the Second World War, a year before he died.[72]

When Bernfeld, Hoffer, and Aichhorn came into her world and brought with them their intense concern for children who never made their way into institutions like Anna Freud's Lyceum, she recognized them as the kind of people who would help carry out the mission for psychoanalysis Freud had articulated at the Budapest Congress—that it reach "the wider social strata." But before she was ready to be more than a listener and a spectator as the future of psychoanalysis was determined, she had to finish her training—her psychoanalysis.

3

BEING ANALYZED

No "PROCESS NOTES" for Anna Freud's analysis exist, and Sigmund Freud did not devote an individual case history to her. The main documents for considering the course of her psychoanalysis are those she wrote herself: her poems and "Beating Fantasies and Daydreams." Late in her life, when she became concerned about the inquiries of prospective biographers, Anna Freud several times protected her privacy by declaring that the clinical material for "Beating Fantasies and Daydreams" came from her own analytic practice.[1] But the paper was actually written some six months before Anna Freud saw her first patient, and the occasion for it was her desire to attend the September 1922 International Congress in Berlin as a member of a psychoanalytic society. She wrote to Max Eitingon, head of the Berlin Society, in April 1922 to ask for his advice.

There is something that I would like to discuss with you in Berlin. If it were possible, I would like very much to become a member of a psychoanalytic association before this year's Congress. This would be hard to do in Vienna, and I would fail anyway because I have not yet done enough to give a lecture. But, just recently my translation of the Varendonck book has appeared, and this is a work for psychoanalysis, if only a minor one.

Would the Berlin Society accept me on the basis of this work?
I will get the answer myself when I am with you.[2]

Their decision clearly was that she should prepare a lecture for
the Vienna Society, despite the hypercriticalness she expected from
her father's sharp-tongued, competitive colleagues. The fact that
she did so in six weeks, for delivery in May 31, makes it almost
certain that the patient whose case is discussed was herself—the one
patient she knew intimately. In the written version of her lecture,
she simply noted that the patient, whose story is reconstructed to
the age of fifteen, had been the subject of "a rather thoroughgoing
analysis," she did not say by whom.

In Sigmund Freud's " 'A Child Is Being Beaten,' " the 1919
essay that was Anna Freud's starting point for "Beating Fantasies
and Daydreams," six cases are mentioned, two males and four females. He gave brief notes about five of these cases: three were obsessional neurotics of varying degrees of severity, one was a hysteric,
the fifth "had come to be analyzed merely on account of indecisiveness in life, [and] would not have been classified at all by
coarse clinical diagnosis, or would have been dismissed as 'psychasthenic.' "[3] This fifth patient sounds very much like Anna Freud, who
was trying in 1919 to decide whether to be a psychoanalytically informed teacher or a psychoanalyst. But the sixth patient is not directly described at all, and this may signal that Freud protected his
daughter's privacy with silence.

The exact extent to which either Sigmund Freud or Anna Freud
used Anna Freud's analysis in their essays is not, finally, determinable. But it is at least clear from her various correspondences that
"Beating Fantasies and Daydreams" was modeled—in general, if
not in complete detail—on her own case, and her essay's descriptive
framework is identical with the one that applies to two of the female
cases in Freud's essay.

In the three parts of her essay, Anna Freud presented three
stages in the development of her subject's beating fantasy. The first
was the creation of the beating fantasy, which was itself a substitute
for an incestuous father-daughter love scene that "distorted by repression and regression to the anal-sadistic phase finds expression as
a beating scene," the climax of which coincided with masturbatory

gratification.[4] These fantasies appeared before the girl entered school, between her fifth and sixth years, and they continued until—between her eighth and tenth years—they were replaced by what she called "nice stories." The "nice stories" seemed to the girl to have no connection with the beating fantasies, though she did admit to her analyst that the beating fantasies occasionally rose up to interrupt the "nice stories" and that she then punished herself by temporarily renouncing the "nice stories."

The analyst pointed out to the girl that the beating fantasies and the nice stories had a similar structure. The nice stories invariably opened with a weak young man committing an infraction and being put at the mercy of a strong older man. In scenes of increasing tension, the young man is threatened with punishments until he is, finally, pardoned in a scene of reconciliation and harmony.

In the beating fantasy, too [Anna Freud wrote], the protagonists are strong and weak persons who, in the clearest delineation, oppose each other as adults and children. There, too, it is regularly a matter of a misdeed, even though the latter is left as indefinite as the acting figures. There, too, we find a period of mounting fear and tension. The decisive difference between the two rests in their solution, which in the fantasy is brought about by beating, and in the daydream by forgiveness and reconciliation.[5]

The patient came to understand this structural similarity and, then, to admit that the nice stories could occasionally not only fail to keep the beating fantasies out of consciousness, but revert into them.

During difficult periods, i.e., at times of increased external demands or diminished internal capabilities, the nice stories no longer succeeded in fulfilling their task. And then it frequently happened that at the conclusion and climax of a fantasized beautiful scene the pleasurable and pleasing love scene was suddenly replaced by the old beating situation together with the sexual gratification [masturbation] associated with it, which then led to a full discharge of the accumulated excitement. But such incidents were quickly forgotten, excluded from memory, and consequently treated as though they had never happened.[6]

Even though the nice stories did sometimes give way to their predecessors, they were a kind of advance—a sublimation.

In the beating fantasy, the direct sexual drives are satisfied, whereas in the nice stories the aim-inhibited drives, as Freud called them, find gratification. Just as in the development of a child's relations to his parents, the originally undivided current of love becomes separated into repressed sensual strivings (here expressed in the beating fantasy) and into a sublimated affectionate tie (represented by the nice stories).[7]

Several years after she had produced the most elaborate and complete of her nice stories, the girl Anna Freud portrayed began to write short stories. These had quite a different structure: they were not so episodic, with scene after scene of mounting tension, and they had no single climactic scene of either beating or reconciliation. In Anna Freud's own life, this was probably the period when she began to write poems and to envision her novel. But she also, in August 1919, about five months after her father finished his essay " 'A Child Is Being Beaten,' " told him by letter that she had written down for the first time what she called "the great childhood story," which may have been the medieval tale of Egon referred to in her poems.[8] In "Beating Fantasies and Daydreams" she remarked on her subject's artistic activity: "She had sought to create a kind of independent existence for the protagonists that had become all too vivid [in the nice stories], in the hope that they would no longer dominate her life."[9]

When she moved from nice-story daydreams to short stories, Anna Freud's subject had finally achieved "communication addressed to others." She concluded that

> in the course of this [final] transformation regard for the personal needs of the daydreamer is replaced by regard for the prospective reader. The pleasure derived directly from the content of the story can be dispensed with, because the process of writing by satisfying the ambitious strivings [originating in the ego] indirectly produces pleasure in the author. . . . By renouncing her private pleasure in favor of making an impression on others, the author has accomplished an important developmental step: the transformation of an autistic into a social activity.[10]

The writing activity that Anna Freud described took her young patient one step beyond two of the cases Freud had presented in " 'A Child Is Being Beaten.' " He had noted that

in two of my female cases an elaborate superstructure of day-dreams, which was of great significance for the life of the person concerned, had grown up over the masochistic beating fantasy. The function of this superstructure was to make possible a feel-ing of satisfied excitation, even though the masturbatory act was refrained from. In one of these cases, the content—being beaten by the father—was allowed to venture again into consciousness, so long as the subject's own ego was made unrecognizable by a thin disguise. . . . In both the cases of daydreaming—one of which rose to the level of a work of art—the heroes were always young men; indeed, women used not to come into these creations at all, and only made their first appearance after many years, and then in minor parts.[11]

Freud noted the "masculinity complex" in these two cases and concluded that "when they turn away from their incestuous love for their father, with its genital significance, they easily abandon their feminine role." Freud did not connect the female patients' assump-tion of a masculine role in the fantasies and daydreams with mascu-linized behavior or homosexuality. On the contrary, he saw it as an escape from sexuality: "the girl escapes from the demands of the erotic side of her life altogether. She turns herself in fantasy into a man, without herself becoming active in a masculine way, and is no longer anything but a spectator at the event which has the place of a sexual act."[12] This much was also implied in Anna Freud's pa-per, but she went on to show that the spectator who communicates, who writes down what she understands, enjoys a form of pleasure—not masturbatory pleasure, not sexual pleasure, but the social pleasure of praise.

Insofar as it focused on beating fantasies and daydreaming as inhibitors of work and career decisions, Anna Freud's analysis of nearly four years—quite long by the then current standards—was a successful one. By the terms she herself set, it allowed her to transform fantasy activity and daydreaming into the social activity of writing. Anna Freud's paper is both a study of sublimation and an act of sublimation.

For her analyst and father, Anna Freud's paper was a source of great pride, for he certainly knew the degree to which her fantasy life was susceptible to regression and her intellectual energies to inhibition. But his joy was also in proportion to his anxiety. When he had learned that she planned to prepare and deliver a membership paper, the founder of psychoanalysis and the president of the Vienna Society compared himself to Lucius Junius Brutus, the legendary founder of the Roman Republic and the chief judge in its first tribunals. "Anna returned from Goettingen," he wrote to Max Eitingon, "with a plan for a test lecture in the Society. I will try to arrange for the lecture at tonight's meeting. Then, on Wednesday the 31st of this month, I will feel like Junius Brutus the elder when he had to judge his own son. Perhaps she is going to make a decisive step."[13]

Junius Brutus's son—so the legend has it—was executed after his father had ruled against him in the Roman tribunal. Things went rather differently at Anna Freud's trial. She spoke from notes, lucidly and authoritatively, and was received well, if a little enviously. Only Siegfried Bernfeld made a truly constructive comment— about how the story writer might have chosen her story material for the enlargement of her ego. After Bernfeld spoke, one of Freud's colleagues induced a momentary panic by suggesting that the girl she had written about was "a totally abnormal person whose incompetence and inferiority would absolutely emerge in real life." Anna Freud was shocked into silence, but her father came to her rescue: "Fortunately Papa answered him and defended my little girl."[14] The evening thus turned into a "nice story" of redemption by the father even while it was a success for the daughter.

Anna Freud and her father both associated her decisive career step with her masculinity, however, so that they could never be unambivalently pleased. The price of her success as a sublimator was her continued asceticism. In her life, she stood where both she and her father had left their female patients at the ends of their respective essays—that is, at the point of escape from the erotic side of life, from femininity. As she put the matter: "The sublimation of [the girl's] sensual love [for her father] into tender friendship is of course greatly facilitated by the fact that already in the early stages of the beating fantasy the girl abandoned the differences of the sexes and is invariably represented as a boy."[15] Both the writing of stories and the achievement of tender friendship with her father were linked to this abandoning of the differences of the sexes and the consequent asceticism. For Freud, however, asceticism did not have to be the final result: "the beating fantasy and other analogous perverse fixations would also be only precipitations of the Oedipus complex, scars, so to say, left behind after the process has ended, just as the notorious 'sense of inferiority' corresponds to a narcissistic scar of the same sort."[16] Anna Freud's paper, on the other hand, ended without any hopeful anticipation of the form her patient's sexual life might take; there is only the sigh of relief that praiseworthy social activity has been achieved.

BOTH Freud and his daughter located the origin of post-Oedipal beating fantasies in repression of the "love fantasy" a child has for his or her father: "all the sexual drives were concentrated on the first love object, the father," as Anna Freud wrote of her female patient.[17] Even though Freud's " 'A Child Is Being Beaten' " was his first step toward revising his idea that girls and boys undergo parallel developments until they are distinguished by their choices of objects, he did not reflect upon the role of the mother in his female patients' lives. He did not note that a girl, as he later said, changes objects, switches from mother-love to father-love. And the mother of the girl Anna Freud studied is not so much as mentioned.

At the time of Anna Freud's analysis, Freud was just beginning to see the importance of the mother, and of the first years of life, later given the name "pre-Oedipal," in a child's development. He had, of course, noted the early developmental stages, oral and anal, and he had clearly stated in 1914 that "those persons who have to do with the feeding, care and protection of the child become his earliest sexual objects: that is to say, in the first instance the mother or her substitute."[18] But, as long as he thought primarily in terms of male development, the question of why and how this first sexual object is given up did not seriously arise—for the male does not give up his first object. Freud had, however, become aware that, particularly for female patients who had regressed to that first bond, a female analyst might be needed to remove resistances stemming from intense disappointment in and hostility toward the father.

This had been his suggestion, for example, in the 1920 essay "The Psychogenesis of a Case of Homosexuality in a Woman," where the subject had taken her mother as her love object after her father had disappointed her love of him. But in this case, the woman's love of her mother was understood entirely as a derivative of her disappointment, not as a revival of her oldest love lost.

One of the first suggestions that Freud had received about the importance of the mother in early childhood had come from his friend Lou Andreas-Salomé, a brilliant Russian-born writer, companion to Nietzsche and Rilke, who had come to Vienna in 1912 to study psychoanalysis and then started a practice. In a 1919 letter, she had pointed out that neither Freud's speculative work *Totem and Taboo* (1912) nor his 1918 return to it in "The Taboo of Virginity" had taken into account the possibility that patriarchal societies might have been preceded by matriarchal societies, and that male "precautionary measures" to check female power might have originated in a period when females had not yet been reduced to the "private property" of males.[19] But this suggestion was not translated into clinical work with the present-day legatees of the history Freud and Lou Andreas-Salomé speculated about. Nor did Freud then connect this train of thought with the contemporary essay on female sexuality he most admired, Karl Abraham's 1919 "Manifestations of the Female Castration Complex," though Abraham's work may have been percolating behind the remarks on female mother-love in Freud's 1920 case study of the female homosexual.

In 1921, Freud invited Lou Andreas-Salomé to make an extended visit to his home in Vienna. She came for a brief stay in September and then for six weeks at the end of the year. Freud told Max Eitingon:

> My wife and my sister-in-law are very affectionate with her, and enough is left over of her to occupy Anna, for whom I mainly invited her. Anna has an understandable thirst for friendship with women because the English Loe [Kann Jones], the Hungarian Katá [Levy], and your Mirra [Eitingon] have all departed due to various influences. Otherwise, I am glad to see [Anna] blooming and in good spirits, and I only wish she would soon

find some reason to exchange her attachment to her old father for some more lasting one.[20]

In this nonanalytic remark, Freud did not indicate that Lou Andreas-Salomé was invited for analytic purposes. But whether or not this was his intention, it was the result.

Anna Freud reported her initial response to Max Eitingon: "Frau Lou Salomé has been our guest for three weeks now, and I have gotten more out of her presence than I had expected. We are discussing a very interesting topic in psychoanalysis, from which a paper may be written sometime in the future. I see again how much closer one comes to all these things if one discusses them rather than trying to swallow them down by reading."[21] Despite the obliqueness of her report, the "I see again" phrase does signal that Anna Freud accepted Lou Andreas-Salomé as her second teacher if not exactly her second analyst. And the implication that she was being fed slowly and well signals that the childless Frau Lou had entered into the line of succession to Anna Freud's good mother, the adoring *Kinderfrau*, Josefine, for whom she had been an only child.

The interesting topic, beating fantasies and daydreams, was taken up again when Anna Freud spent ten days in the spring of 1922 at her mentor's home, Loufried, near Goettingen. The Vienna Society paper was emerging at just that time, and Lou Andreas-Salomé played midwife to it. When she was alone, Anna Freud told her father, she did not know as much as she knew when she was with Frau Lou, talking, trying to keep up with the sixty-one-year-old's astonishing "thought tempo."[22] Frau Lou's sympathetic ear and lively example helped Anna Freud overcome her fear of not just public speaking but public theorizing. Two years after Frau Lou's first December 1921 visit, Anna Freud reminisced to her: "Before you were here, it was still very difficult for me to talk to others about theory—I learned it first with you. . . . Now I find it a great pleasure to take part in such talks if they occur, and I am no longer afraid to say something."[23]

Neither in Vienna nor in Loufried was the quasi-analytic relationship a matter of on-the-couch analysis; it was a discussion and consultation relationship—with, as often as not, Lou Andreas-Salomé stretched out on a divan meditating aloud and Anna Freud seated at her feet. Later in her life, whenever the rumor reached her that Lou Andreas-Salomé had been her analyst, Anna Freud always claimed that the idea persisted because people were scandalized by the thought that her father had filled that role. But her father, on the other hand, registered the significance he thought Lou Andreas-Salomé's presence had had by playfully exchanging epistolary confidences with Lou about their shared "Daughter-Anna." Frau Lou, exactly the same age as Martha Freud, was the mother-analyst. And later, in the dark days he suffered through with the combined effects of his first surgery and the loss of a little grandson to tuberculosis, Freud told his partner: "Anna is splendid and self-assured, and I often think how much she probably owes to you."[24]

Lou Andreas-Salomé brought to her talks with Anna Freud nearly a decade of experience as an analyst and a long-standing interest in the topic of anal eroticism, which was obviously important to Anna Freud's essay. The second paper that Lou had submitted to Freud's journal *Imago* was called "Anal and Sexual" (1914), and in response to his " 'A Child Is Being Beaten,' " she had reiterated a central notion of that paper: "The persistence of anal eroticism within mature sexuality has always struck me particularly in the case of the female sex."[25] She had noted that in women anal eroticism is, for anatomical reasons, much more closely associated than in men with masturbation and with fantasies—like beating fantasies—that disguise masturbatory pleasure.

Freud's appreciation for Lou Andreas-Salomé's contributions led him to suggest that the Vienna Society honor her—and itself—by offering her membership. After her own paper had been delivered and approved, Anna Freud helped to secure Lou's admission to the Society. She was accepted without the required membership paper, a breach of the Society's rules, and was delighted when she received the news that this exception had been made for her.

> Anna's night letter has just reached me with the news that I have really and truly become a full member of the Vienna Psychoanalytical Society: as in a dream, so to speak, and as otherwise only happens in childhood, when one suddenly finds lying on one's bed the present one has wished for in one's dream. For

what Daughter-Anna succeeded in reality in doing, i.e., in giving the lecture required for membership, I should never have achieved successfully. . . . I thank you from my heart for this breach of the rules![26]

One can imagine that Freud found this reaction amusing, for his letters to Lou reveal that he had always thought of her as a woman who expected exceptions to be made for her, who had never felt the need to compete for approval. Frau Lou had grown up idolized by not just her elderly father but six older brothers, and Freud had admiringly portrayed the result of this loving abundance in his 1914 essay on narcissism. Lou was of the "fascinating," "purely feminine" type, one of those women who "especially if they grow up with good looks, develop a certain self-contentment."[27]

Frau Lou was not the sort of woman to question Anna Freud's adoration of (or identification with) her father; on the contrary, she promoted Anna Freud's desire to stay at home and dedicate herself to her father and to psychoanalysis. For Lou's sanction, Anna Freud was deeply grateful, because, as she told her in December of 1924, without it she "would have been made insecure by those who feared for my future and would have liked to send me away from [home]." These unnamed people did not know that "I, without any [plans for the] future, have so much here, more than many people get altogether, in a whole life."[28] Lou understood this kind of self-surrendering dedication; she had even extolled it as the quintessence of feminine love in her psychoanalytic essay on femininity, "Zum Typus Weib" (1914). On the other hand, as an exemplary figure Lou represented an important synthetic possibility: she was a "purely feminine" type, but also an intellectual, a thinker and a writer with a "masculine" (in her own terms) bent for sweeping syntheses, bold conjectures, poetic leaps.

Anna Freud paid a number of visits to Frau Lou in Goettingen before and after her membership paper had been successfully delivered, and the two corresponded frequently. Lou also wrote to Freud of her continued pleasure in Anna's company, and added her reflections on Anna's development. On one visit, a young member of the Hamburg Bernays family, the mathematician Paul Bernays, escorted Anna Freud back from a party and then shocked her—and made her angry—by trying to kiss her good night.[29] Frau Lou told Freud with completely nonjudgmental amusement that Anna's asceticism remained: "Altogether Anna has stirred up quite a storm of passion here, as she will tell you, but nevertheless returns home totally unseared by these flames. Nor should I be at all surprised if this sequence of events were to be constantly repeated, so much does she enjoy every homecoming."[30]

THIS last remark—quite prophetic—raises the question that would be obvious to anyone who considered the complexities of a father's analysis of his own daughter. Freud himself counted the analysis a success. In a well-known letter that he wrote in 1935 to Edoardo Weiss, who was contemplating analyzing his son, Freud remarked: "Concerning the analysis of your hopeful son, that is certainly a ticklish business. With a younger, promising brother it might be done more easily. With [my] own daughter I succeeded well. There are special difficulties and doubts with a son."[31] Having issued this warning, Freud said that he had no right to forbid Weiss the trial—but Weiss decided against it.

Even in 1935, the psychoanalytic community was not as concerned as it later became with regulating analytic work—with stipulating, for example, that analysts refrain from analyzing not just family members but friends and associates. When the psychoanalytic community was very small, analyses that crossed family and friendship lines were common, and the demands upon analytic discretion were, thus, very great. But, even given the unregulated state of psychoanalysis, it is obvious that Freud and his circle consistently saw less difficulty for women than for men—for daughters than for sons—in extra-analytic closeness. Freud himself, for examples, analyzed both of his friend Oscar Rie's daughters, Margarethe and Marianne, his friend Sandor Ferenczi's future stepdaughter, and his friend Anton von Freund's sister Katá Levy. Before the first World War, both Carl Jung and Karl Abraham had worked analytically with their young daughters and written essays based on their observations.[32] Freud's assumption at the time of his daughter's analysis was that boys would—like "Little Hans"—feel hostile and rivalrous toward a father-analyst but girls, who were not in competition for the mother, would not.

Apart from the technical psychoanalytic issues, Freud's decision to analyze his own daughter involved a number of practical considerations. Among them was the fact that Anna Freud was employed as a teacher in Vienna while the analysts whom Freud trusted were located in either Budapest or Berlin. When his third child, the middle son of his three sons, Oliver, wanted to be analyzed, the situation was simpler: Oliver was living in Berlin, and could consult one of the younger analysts there of whom Freud thought highly. Max Eitingon did not take Oliver because of his closeness to the family, so the analysis was arranged with the Hungarian Franz Alexander.[33] Oliver, whose first wartime marriage had ended unhappily, lived in Berlin with his brother Ernst until his analysis was completed; then he married the daughter of a Berlin physician, Henny Fuchs, and set up independently. Anna Freud went to Oliver's wedding on April 10, 1923, and was, like the rest of the family, very impressed—and relieved—to find him so well and happy.

Oliver's analysis, which seems to have started in 1921 or 1922, apparently did not raise daunting problems of trust with the Freud family's privacy. Freud did not summon his son home for an experiment with analyzing a "younger, promising brother." But this was not a potential training analysis: it was a therapeutic analysis for an obsessional neurosis. And Freud was also well aware of his own feelings of anxiety and hurt over Oliver's condition: "It is particularly hard for me to be objective in this case," he told Eitingon, "for he was my pride and my secret hope for a long time, until his anal-masochistic organization appeared clearly. . . . I suffer very much with my feelings of helplessness."[34] Oliver, on the other hand, whose relationship with his father was difficult, probably did not desire what his sister had accepted—or desired.

The second important practical consideration was that when Anna Freud started her analysis in the fall of 1918 the Freud family's financial situation was precarious. Anna's salary from the Cottage Lyceum was part of the family budget. Freud's practice was considerably reduced because of the wartime conditions—and, though this meant less money, it also meant more time. Freud started the fall with a training analysand, Helene Deutsch, Katá Levy, and a few paying therapeutic cases. That fall, he had a regular hour for his daughter six days a week—while, later, he saw her after his full schedule, at ten o'clock in the evening.

In Freud's statement to Edoardo Weiss, the emphasis is upon the relatively unproblematic nature of a father's analysis of his daughter. He started off, at least, in a completely confident frame of mind: "Anna's analysis will be very elegant," he told Ferenczi in the fall of 1918.[35] But Freud was certainly aware that his daughter's adoration of him was not an unproblematic affair. He knew the extent of her idealization of him, and he revealed it—sometimes in jest and sometimes somberly—in his letters. In December 1919, after Max Eitingon had sent Freud a sum of money to tide him over during the continuing financial difficulties, Freud wrote him a description of how the Freud family had reacted to the letter announcing this largess: "As I was busy with four analyses in the morning, I had no time to think about it, and read the letter out loud at luncheon during which, apart from my wife, three sons and our young daughter (whom you know) were present. It had a strange effect: the three boys seemed satisfied, but the two women were up in arms and my daughter declared—evidently she can't stand the demolition of her father complex—that as a punishment (!) she wouldn't go to Berlin for Christmas."[36] Anna Freud's feeling that her father should not need money from his friends was transferred later to Lou Andreas-Salomé, to whom Freud sent money in the 1920s. With one of his donations, Freud sent a comment on Anna's attitude: "Anna was, it is true, of the opinion that you would not accept it, but she doesn't realize how sensible you are, and believes you capable of everything possible and impossible, e.g., of living on air and cocoa."[37]

It is not clear from Freud's report about Eitingon's money gift who it was that Anna Freud intended to punish—her father the receiver or Eitingon the giver—by not going to the Eitingons' for Christmas. But there is a fateful formula in her reaction: feeling that her father was diminished or made less than completely magnificent by his lack of funds, she declared that she would stay at home. Staying at home and leaving home had been for years the crucial possibilities in the father-daughter relationship, and they became bound up with the most problematic dimensions of the analytic relationship: the nature of resistance in it, and the manner of resolving the transference, leaving the analyst.

Freud was aware, as a father, that he had difficulty in their day-to-day lives realizing how much he wanted his daughter to stay always at home, as his youngest sister, Dolfi, had with their parents. This was so even though he could, when he focused his attention on their dilemma, state it clearly from his own point of view: "Anna is in excellent shape," he told Eitingon in 1921, "she is gay, industrious and inspired. I would like just as well to keep her at home as to know her in a home of her own—if it would only be the same for her!"[38] Toward the end of Anna Freud's formal analysis, as she was on her way to visit Eitingon in Berlin and then the Halberstadt children in Hamburg, Freud made another very candid statement to Lou:

> I too very much miss Daughter-Anna. She set off for Berlin and Hamburg on March the second. I have long felt sorry for her for still being at home with us old folks [. . .], but on the other hand, if she really were to go away, I should feel myself as deprived as I do now, and as I should do if I had to give up smoking! As long as we are all together, one doesn't realize it clearly, or at least we do not. And therefore in view of all these insoluble conflicts it is good that life comes to an end sometime or other.[39]

In this remark, Freud indicated that the "solution" to their insoluble conflicts would be, precisely, his death. He was, in a sense, addicted to her staying at home, to her presence, as he was to his cigars; and he himself had analyzed very astutely the psychic level at which the pleasure of smoking and the pleasure of female adoration coincided—the level at which an adult remains, as it were, at the maternal breast. Freud had forecast what he told Lou Andreas-Salomé very clearly in his essay of a decade earlier on "The Theme of the Three Caskets": "the doomed man is not willing to renounce the love of women; he insists on hearing how much he is loved. . . . But it is in vain that an old man yearns for the love of woman as he had it first from his mother."[40]

   Soon after the trip to Berlin that occasioned Freud's remark to Lou Andreas-Salomé, Anna Freud was again in Berlin, discussing with Eitingon the possibility that she might seek membership in the Berlin Psychoanalytic Society. Apparently, the possibility of a future practice in Berlin was also discussed, for a year later, when Anna Freud already had her first two analytic patients, she could write wistfully to Eitingon: "This is what I have waited for so long, and now it has finally come—even if not at the Berlin Policlinic."[41] Eitingon may have been one of the people who promoted the idea that Anna Freud should leave home; and she seems to have been more receptive than her letters to Lou Andreas-Salomé indicate. But only a month later, in April 1923, whatever fantasies she may have entertained about practicing in Berlin were delivered a definitive blow. Sigmund Freud had the first of a long series of operations on his jaw, and the possibility that he had imagined as a "solution" to their insoluble conflicts—"life comes to an end sometime or other"— was ominously evoked.

When her father was shown to be vulnerable not by a mere lack of funds but by the far more frightening specter of a mortal illness, the "demolition of her father complex," which Freud had jokingly noted as under way in 1919, came to a complicated pass. Sigmund Freud's illness reinforced his desire to have his daughter with him, and hers to stay at home. Anna Freud and her chief confidante and counselor, Lou Andreas-Salomé, were completely in agreement about what the illness meant for Anna: "You are right," she wrote to Lou, "I would not leave him now under any circumstances."[42] For a start on her new life, she was the one in the family who helped him through the surgery, which turned out to be much more dangerous than his surgeon, Hajek, an unreliable man, expected. Anna's "splendid self-assurance" in the adversity of surgery made its first appearances that spring of 1923—and then it went on for sixteen operations under anesthesia in as many years.

On June 19, only about two months after Freud's operation, Sophie Freud Halberstadt's youngest boy, Heinz Rudolf, called Heinerle, who had been informally adopted by Mathilde and Robert Hollitscher, died of miliary tuberculosis. Mathilde was heartbroken and Freud's grief was profound—he had adored this charming, good-natured child. And Anna Freud too was exhausted from a two-week stay with her sister as they tried to nurse the child, grieved by the loss, and worried about what it would mean for the other Halberstadt boy, Ernst. Ernst had been her protégé: as though he were a version of herself, she had defended him and protected him in circumstances where his little brother's beauty and precocity had been threatening to him. She argued that Ernst's quarrelsome manner belied his substance: "In reality, he is such a nice and highly decent person that I would not wish my own son to be any different."[43]

From her own experience, Anna Freud knew how dreadful it could be to survive the sibling in whose shadow jealousy had always grown like a mold. As she once said of one of her young patients who lost a sibling, it is not easy "to live in comparison with the family's little angel." She herself responded to her father's grief at the loss of Sophie's little boy by an angelic suppression of her annual summer jealousy of Tante Minna, who was to be her father's companion at Bad Gastein. Instead, she was glad that Minna, who was ill herself and had not been in Vienna during Heinerle's illness, and was not, thus, emotionally exhausted by the pathos of the situation, would be in Gastein to comfort her father. She also went to Hamburg and behaved angelically toward Max Halberstadt and little Ernst, as she had the year before when she told Lou: "I live here beyond my means being virtuous and well behaved, even though analysis teaches you that it will come out somewhere as hostility."[44]

Freud's physician, Felix Deutsch, was also concerned about the effect on Freud of the death of Heinerle, coming, as it did, so soon after Freud's surgery. Wishing to spare his patient more anxiety and to allow a planned trip to Rome with Anna at the end of the summer to go forward undimmed by the prospect of more surgery, Deutsch decided not to tell Freud that the first surgery had revealed a malignancy. Anna Freud suspected Deutsch's deception and confronted him with it by suggesting that she and her father might stay longer than they had planned in Rome. Deutsch urged her against this, and she knew, then, that he had further treatment planned. She did not guess that behind Felix Deutsch's solicitous motivations lay a fear that Freud, if he knew how radical the next surgery needed to be, would prefer a Stoic suicide; nor did she know that Deutsch had discussed his fear with Freud's friends, Ferenczi, Abraham, Eitingon, Jones, Rank, and Sachs. When she and her father discovered the true motive of Deutsch's deception, they admonished him for making a decision that was not his to make, and he was dismissed as Freud's physician—though not as Anna's. That his Committee had collectively collaborated in Deutsch's deception incensed Freud when he learned of it—fifteen years later.[45]

Even though neither the analyst friends nor Deutsch spoke

truthfully to Freud before he and Anna left for Rome, both father and daughter understood that an ordeal awaited their return to Vienna: "we both threw coins into the [Trevi] fountain hoping to return, which, because of his impending operation, was a very uncertain matter."[46] "We wanted to see so many things," Anna Freud later told Eitingon, "or, rather, Papa wanted to show me many things and I wanted to share his seeing them again with him; and we were not entirely up to the occasions, for there was still a good deal of anxiety and unrest [about his illness], feelings of 'not being supposed to' and 'having to leave,' a mixture of farewells with our reunions. Depsite this, it would have been hard to have a more wonderful trip."[47] Anna Freud proved herself a delightful companion and an excellent nurse as they dealt with a startling episode of profuse bleeding from Freud's mouth. He asked of her that she be straightforward and unsentimental with him, and she obliged him. Freud wrote to Lou Andreas-Salomé from Rome: "I realize here [in Rome] for the first time what good company my little daughter is."[48]

Out of the months of uncertainty and grief came a new level of closeness. They had suffered together and they had gone together to the city that represented to Freud his own achievements, his imperial command in the realm of science, his fulfilled ambitions. They faced a very uncertain future in partnership: she became his liaison to the psychoanalytic movement, his ambassador, his amanuensis—as he said later, his Antigone.

ALL THROUGH the fall of 1923, Anna Freud sent almost daily medical bulletins to Freud's colleagues, particularly Eitingon, and to their common friend Lou Andreas-Salomé. She chronicled every phase of two major operations on his jaw, the construction of a constantly painful prosthesis, his laborious effort to recover his speech and his ability to chew, the many complicating bronchial infections and coughs—the entire horrendous ordeal. Her own feelings she seldom mentioned except to say how hard it was for her to see him suffer so. The reactions of her mother and her Tante Minna were not mentioned at all, though it is clear in the letters that the entire

household was in a state of suspension for two months until Freud
went back to work with patients in the beginning of January 1924.
He was weak, but lively enough to be writing in the evenings on an
apt topic for a man in constant pain—"The Economic Problem of
Masochism."

By that January, Anna Freud was exhausted from her vigil, particularly as she combined it with her first three analytic patients and
her translating and editorial work with the psychoanalytic press in
Vienna. A New Year's visit from her still eager suitor Hans Lampl
left her unmoved: "he has no luck with me. I can be with him in a
friendly way very well, but I am not suitable for marriage. I am not
suitable at all for Lampl, but also, for the moment, I am no better
[for] a table, or a sofa, or even my own rocking chair."[49]

When she wrote that unhappy report, Anna Freud was trying to
fend off a recurrence of the serial daydreams, the "nice stories,"
which she had been relieved of for nearly two years by her analysis.
Her relapse was aggravated by an irony: her second patient was a
young woman so much like herself that she was constantly amazed.
She told Lou Andreas-Salomé:

> Although I am pretty busy right now . . . in the last week my
> "nice stories" all the sudden surfaced again and rampaged for
> days as they have not for a long while. Now they are asleep
> again, but I was impressed by how unchangeable and forceful
> and alluring such a daydream is, even if it has been—like my
> poor one—pulled apart, analyzed, published, and in every way
> mishandled and mistreated. I know that it is really shameful—
> especially when I do it between patients—but it was again very
> beautiful and gave me great pleasure.[50]

The daydreams seem to have been dormant again while Anna
Freud began attending the morning ward rounds at Wagner-Jauregg's
University of Vienna psychiatric clinic. This privilege had been extended by Wagner-Jauregg's first assistant, Paul Schilder, who was an
associate of the Vienna Psychoanalytic Society and one of the few
Viennese psychiatrists who taught Freud's works at the university.
Schilder's influence over the second assistant, Heinz Hartmann, was
strong, and Hartmann, too, joined the psychoanalytic ranks after an
analysis with Freud. Anna Freud often stayed on after the rounds

to have lunch with Hartmann and another medical colleague, Erwin Stengel, who continued her education in what she called "the symptomology of psychiatry."[51]

Years later, Anna Freud described her experience at the clinic: "We all listened spellbound to the revelations made by the patients, their dreams, delusions, fantastic systems, which the analytically trained among us fitted into a scheme. We also had a chance to witness the first results of [malaria serum] fever therapy, initiated then by Wagner-Jauregg" (and later recognized with the only Nobel Prize ever given to a psychiatrist).[52] In two letters written to a student in 1946 and 1948, she gave a more personal account:

> A first visit to a madhouse is always a shock. . . . When this shock is overcome, then everything becomes interesting, and in the end you forget how wretched the condition of the mentally ill really is. . . . I remember well my student year in the psychiatric clinic in Vienna. What I saw there has remained with me, influencing enormously all of my later analytic work, for you understand the neuroses entirely differently when you consider them against the background of the psychoses.[53]

During the year when she attended Schilder's rounds at the clinic, Anna Freud did learn a great deal, but initially the rounds caused her difficulty: they contributed to another resurgence in her production of compensatory "nice stories." She even felt, as she reported to Lou Andreas-Salomé, "stupid" during the times when the daydreams were "wild" and plagued her.[54]

Her father did not feel well enough to attend the International Psychoanalytic Congress at Salzburg during the Easter holiday, but shortly after the Congress his winter bout with bronchitis ended and he suggested to his daughter that they take up their analytic work again. She accepted gratefully. "The reason for continuing," she explained to Frau Lou in a formal, self-mocking tone, "was the not entirely orderly behavior of my honorable inner life: occasional unseemly intrusions of the daydreams combined with an increasing intolerance—sometimes physical as well as mental—of the beating fantasies and of their consequences [i.e., masturbation] which I could not do without."[55]

In this renewed analytic work, taken up after a two-year pause, she worked "very seriously and thoroughly, with great steps forward and less resistance than in earlier years."[56] She was—particularly as a practicing analyst herself—much more aware of the complexity of her analytic situation. She acknowledged "the absence of the third person, the one onto whom the transference advances, and with whom one acts out and finishes off the conflicts." Anna Freud and her father were working hard, but the analyst who was supposed to be a neutral party, a "blank screen," was, in the nature of the case, missing. And, further, she understood clearly that what she called her "extra-analytical closeness" to her father produced "difficulties and temptations to untruthfulness" in the analysis.[57]

The problematical nature of the tranference was part of the renewed analysis, as it does not really seem to have been of the first. And, at the same time, Anna Freud confronted in her own work what she called "the management of the transference," the part of the analytic work to which she—like most young analysts—had to give the most thought. After her renewed analysis had run for about nine months, she discussed with Lou Andreas-Salomé the transference management in her practice: "I always do it somehow, but now I have to deal with the why and the is-it-right? Above all, I want to handle the transference more freely, as you do."[58]

Judging from Anna Freud's surviving correspondences and from the papers that she and her father wrote in 1924 and 1925, two topics in addition to that of transference emerged as central to the renewed analysis. One was the "masculinity complex" and its precipitate, jealousy, and the other was "goodness," or, as Anna Freud would later call it, "altruism."

Freud's illness brought about not just a deepening of the bonds between father and daughter, but a "reedition" of the old difficulties—the old jealous rivalry—that Anna Freud had had with her mother. Martha Freud felt herself displaced, as, to a lesser extent, did Tante Minna. With the combined stress of her husband's illness and the death of her grandson, Martha Freud suffered through a number of stomach problems and migraine headaches; Minna spent the better part of a year in sanatoria with a heart condition. The day-to-day consideration and civility that was always characteristic of the household was not disturbed, but unhappy currents ran under it.

Anna Freud recognized that she expected a great deal in return for her loyalty and self-sacrificing care, and she analyzed her needs quite clearly—insofar as they related to her father. She told Eitingon, for example, that her father had traveled to Berlin to spend Christmas 1926 with the Ernst and Oliver Freud families—including three grandchildren whom Freud had not yet met—while she stayed at home with an injured foot. "It seems to me now that I was angry that Papa traveled without me. For so long now I have undertaken nothing in order not to leave him behind, and then he suddenly became adventurous and went away precisely when I was not able to move about. That is no fair [as one of my child patients says]. But because he came back in such good condition, everything is fine again."[59]

She did not mention, however, that this trip, his first in three years, was undertaken with Martha Freud, who cared for her husband quite well without help from either the chief nurse, Anna, or her oldest, Mathilde. In fact, the struggle between Anna Freud and her mother over how their desires to care for Freud would be satisfied had only gone underground to irrupt later. For example, in 1929, when Freud was planning a two-week stay at the Tegel sanatorium in Berlin, Anna Freud went to great trouble to arrange her patient schedule so that she could accompany him: "At first Mama wanted to go in my place, but I did not want that at all."[60] Her "place" was hers, and she kept it that way, regardless of her mother's feelings.

Feminine jealousy and rivalry were recurrent topics in Freud's work in the years immediately following his major surgery, as they were the topic of the first paper that Anna Freud delivered after her renewed analysis in 1924–25. Her brief communication to the Vienna Society meeting in December 1925 was called "Jealousy and the Desire for Masculinity," and it was based largely upon two analyses she had conducted simultaneously, one of a girl and one of the woman who resembled herself. The two analyses, she told Eitingon, often ran parallel: "both struggle with the same problems, the masculinity wish and envy of siblings, so similarly that often on the same day they say the same things almost verbatim. I tell Papa many such things."[61]

These reports would have confirmed her Papa's own recently revised view, which he arrived at during his daughter's second analysis. Although Freud had made important remarks on the topic of jealousy in "The Economic Problem of Masochism" (1924) and "The Dissolution of the Oedipus Complex" (1924), his main statement came in a paper called "Some Psychical Consequences of the Anatomical Distinction Between the Sexes," a piece he started early in 1925 and finished in August while his daughter and Lou Andreas-Salomé were with him on vacation to discuss it. He also read a version to Sandor Ferenczi, who visited later in August, around the time Freud agreed to let Anna read the paper, as his representative, at the Bad Homburg Congress in September.

Neither of the Freuds' correspondences gives direct proof to support the claim that his 1925 paper is to his daughter's second analysis what " 'A Child Is Being Beaten' " was to her first—that is, a partial report, set in a larger frame—but the evidence of the paper itself is very compelling. In "Some Psychical Consequences of the Anatomical Distinction Between the Sexes," Freud elaborated on the developmental differences between girls and boys that he had first suggested in " 'A Child Is Being Beaten.' " But he emphasized that a young woman's "masculinity complex," or envy for the penis, disturbs her relations with her mother and, indirectly, her siblings. "Even after penis-envy has abandoned its true object, it continues to exist: by an easy displacement, it persists in the character-trait of jealousy." This development, Freud notes, was not apparent to him when he wrote " 'A Child Is Being Beaten.' "[62] Then he had not seen that a female child holds her mother responsible for her lack of a penis; that she can feel jealous "of another child on the ground that her mother is fonder of it than of her" (and this child can be transformed into one of the anonymous boys beaten in her beating fantasy); and that the mother herself can be an object of jealousy when the female child comes to hope for a child—a "penis-child"—by her father.

The little girl's transition to love of her father from love of her mother was Freud's focus in the essay.

> She gives up her wish for a penis and puts in place of it a wish for a child: and with that purpose in view she takes her father as a love object. Her mother becomes the object of her jealousy. The girl has turned into a little woman. If I am to credit a single analytic instance, this new situation can give rise to physical

sensations which would have to be regarded as a premature awakening of her female genital apparatus. When the girl's attachment to her father comes to grief later on and has to be abandoned, it may give place to an identification with him and the girl may thus return to her masculinity complex and perhaps remain fixated in it.[63]

In these passages from Freud's essay, many of the themes of Anna Freud's "honorable inner life" (as she jokingly called it) are adumbrated: her envy of her brothers and her father; her anger at her mother, who was fonder of Sophie; the early-awakened genital sensations related to masturbation; her jealousy of her mother and Tante Minna as objects of her father's love; and her identification with her father. Freud's hypothesis that a jealous girl will retreat into an identification with her father states in another way the conclusion of " 'A Child Is Being Beaten,' " where Freud had noted that the female takes a male role in her fantasies, relating to her father in that way, and continues in the role as an ascetic or a spectator at quasi-sexual scenes. His emphasis on jealousy as a consequence of the "masculinity complex" restates the problem that Anna Freud left her subject with at the end of "Beating Fantasies and Daydreams." The girl who, through sublimation, became a writer was a person who needed praise as a reward for renouncing the masturbation she had taken up in her transition from wishing for a penis to wishing for a child. But the social activity of writing and the social pleasure of praise are difficult to dissociate from the original maternal and sibling rivalries. As praise is notorious for not appearing of its own accord, when it is desired, needing it induces revivals of old competitions.

Anna Freud herself admitted to Eitingon, and many years later to Ernest Jones, that she was troubled by jealousy of her father's female training analysands—the female "siblings" who appeared for analysis in 1922 or so and were present when she had her moment of renewed rivalry with her mother and Tante Minna. With years of experience as an analyst and her own second analysis behind her, Anna Freud described the situation lucidly: "Candidates of one and the same training analyst behave in the transference as if they were real siblings; they compare themselves with each other; they compete;

they envy each other in view of alleged parental preference; they combine forces occasionally to fight the parent, etc."[64]

The American Ruth Mack Brunswick came to Freud for analysis in 1922, as did the Dutch physician Jeanne de Groot, who later married Anna Freud's friend Hans Lampl, and Joan Riviere, one of Freud's future English translators.[65] Anna Freud felt jealous of each of these women, but she did "work through" her feelings, and became friends with the two—Jeanne Lampl-de Groot and Ruth Mack Brunswick—who stayed close to her father. These two were also, with Helene Deutsch and later Marie Bonaparte, the Freud trainees who contributed most importantly in the late 1920s and early 1930s to the psychoanalytic discussions of female sexuality. Indeed, Anna Freud was one of the few female analysts who did not write essays on female sexuality per se—though, of course, she considered it in all her analytic writings. She tended, also, to use male cases for illustrations in her writings, except when she was specifically considering females who were close to her in psychic constitution. After her brief communication on "Jealousy and the Desire for Masculinity," which she never prepared as a written text, Anna Freud also left the topic of jealousy to her father and the female trainees; in her first book, published in 1927, she discussed jealousy only in male children, and only in relation to the father. It was not until her experience with mothers and their infants broadened during her early years in London that Anna Freud's range as a psychoanalytic theoretician reached the dimensions of female psychology she personally found most difficult.

ABOUT *Gutseins* (being good), the other topic of her renewed analysis, Anna Freud eventually had a great deal to say in publications. But her published reflections had their origin in a shift that came about during her renewed analysis. She marked the shift with a 1924 letter to Lou Andreas-Salomé: "The value of being good is not as great as I thought for a long time. There has to be something else involved, which alone makes being good valuable for other people: perhaps it is to be without internal conflict, to be clear about oneself, but also to be able to endure something."[66] By this last capacity, she meant, she said, "coming to terms with the inevitable harshness" of

people and events and not escaping into saintly hopefulness that all
would turn out well in the end.[67] At that time she thought that
Eitingon was an "effeminate" denier of harsh realities, and she also
found him lacking in insight about what she called his "overgoodness," a mechanism for negating "bad" desires that ended up, nonetheless, negating itself and producing bad actions. August Aichhorn
too seemed to her someone so committed to his altruism that he
underestimated his hostilities. She later revised her views of both
Aichhorn and Eitingon, but not of overgoodness, which she found
in herself and gave the name "altruistic surrender."

One of the most intriguing chapters of Anna Freud's 1936 work
The Ego and the Mechanisms of Defense is devoted to altruistic
surrender. By that time, she understood overgoodness, or altruistic
surrender, as projection of forbidden or dangerous wishes onto other
people. Someone who thus disposes of wishes can take great pleasure
in promoting and supporting the fulfillment of them by proxies, but
may also feel as empty as that lonely figure Rilke described in one
of Anna Freud's favorite poems, "Der Dichter" ("The Poet"):

> *Ich habe keine Geliebte, kein Haus,*
> *keine Stelle auf der ich lebe.*
> *Alle Dinge, an die ich mich gebe,*
> *werden reich und geben mich aus.*
>
> *I have no beloved or place for home,*
> *no circle where I am at center.*
> *The things to which I give myself*
> *grow rich—while I'm impoverished.*

The chief exemplar of altruistic surrender in *The Ego and the
Mechanisms of Defense* is a governess who has lived an uneventful
life entirely dedicated to other peoples' needs: "She lived in the lives
of other people, instead of having any experiences of her own."[68]
This woman, Anna Freud wrote,

displaced her ambitious fantasies onto her men friends and her
libidinal wishes onto her women friends. The former succeeded
to her affection for her father and her big brother, both of whom
had been the object of her penis envy, while the latter represented the sister upon whom, at a rather later period of child-

hood, the envy was displaced in the form of envy of her beauty. The patient felt that the fact that she was a girl prevented her from achieving her ambitions and, at the same time, that she was not even a pretty enough girl really to be attractive to men. In her disappointment with herself she displaced her wishes onto objects who she felt were better qualified to fulfill them.[69]

In her portrait of the governess, Anna Freud combined her insights into the origins of jealousy and sibling rivalry with her meditations on overgoodness. Her remarkably clear and simple description shows her developed ability to step back reflectively and theoretically from the kind of self-understanding she had reached in 1925. Then she had been able to combine her two analytic themes, but not to present the combination theoretically.

For example, she had reacted with a self-portrait to a short story Lou Andreas-Salomé had written after hearing Freud's "Some Psychical Consequences of the Anatomical Distinction Between the Sexes" on the Semmering vacation in 1925. She, her father, and Frau Lou were all in search of the mechanisms of female jealousy toward women and envy of men.

I certainly recognized the character of the beloved, but you had changed a great deal, and she is more beautiful. Surely the story is no longer the complement to Papa's lecture for the Congress about which we talked then? What I mean is that only your Mathilde is good as a woman and has a right to be glad that she is. If one can dance as she does, then it makes sense. But if one looks like Dina, or like me, one only feels envy—in two directions: the one that shows how one might be achieving like a man, and the one that shows dancing and being generous like Mathilde. One would like to be able to do both, and does find oneself to be a little of both, but neither becomes real.

Anna Freud continued with a statement that shows how deeply she—like her father—associated public or professional achievement with masculinity and how much her conscious desire lay in the other direction, toward what she associated with femininity.

I feel like I carry a double load now, and it is especially so because I am required to do a man's tasks in the Vienna Society, in its training program, in negotiations, in complicated situations, even in making money (for the moment). I am pleased to be acquiring a degree of independence in the eyes of other people (not before Papa); but otherwise I would prefer to give and to serve than to acquire and to demand. . . . And once in my life I would like to be allowed to be like your Mathilde. Only it is most likely too late for that, as one does not become like her, one just is like her.[70]

There is an indication in Anna Freud's ability to surpass her jealousies of siblings past and present that the second phase of her analysis, in 1924–25, was very helpful to her. But that the topic was still difficult is signaled by her avoidance of it, and particularly of any direct consideration of female jealousy of the mother, in the medium of her sublimations—writing for others to read. In *The Ego and the Mechanisms of Defense*, Anna Freud did not say whether the altruistically surrendering governess's analysis allowed her to seek the fulfillment of her wishes in her own life rather than through others' lives, but it is clear that Anna Freud's analysis did have such an effect. The effect was, however, slow in coming, and complicated. As it came, she felt both the need to address further her desire for approval and praise and the need to analyze further her altruism. The occasion for her needs was specific, and the analyst she chose was not her father.

ANNA FREUD had been practicing as an analyst of children and adults for nearly three years—the three exhausting first years of her father's illness—when she reluctantly slipped into one of her letters to Max Eitingon a discouraged, depressed remark:

But I think that precisely the great involvement with the children is responsible for the fact that much that should give me peace does not. I could say many things about this, and so it is better, once again, that I not get started. But one more thing anyway: I run across the fact that I do not succeed in doing something to or for others without also immediately wanting to have something for myself (and not just money, which is still supposedly the easiest thing to get). In the long run, however, this is a stupid way to live.[71]

She was signaling to the friend she had previously charged with overgoodness that her own struggle on that front was not finished. Max Eitingon, who had for years been Anna Freud's favorite among her father's colleagues, who had received her often in Berlin for talks, sent her chocolates, looked after her literary education with gifts of books—been in almost every way the perfect uncle—took her last sentence very seriously and wrote a concerned reply. Fortunately, his reply came during a period in their friendship when they had resolved in conversations the distance that had come between them in the first year of Freud's illness. Eitingon had retreated from the Freuds, for his own reason of ill health and his wife's desire not to share him so much with the psychoanalytic movement, and also because he had doubts about how he and the Committee had reacted to Freud's illness. Anna Freud had charged this retreat to the inevitable collapse of his overgoodness. But Eitingon had, by the fall of 1925, returned, and Anna Freud had turned her attention from his overgoodness to her own.

She was grateful to Eitingon for his thoughtfulness: "I thank you very much for everything that you wrote as an answer to that one sentence in my letter. But that which I complained about in myself is, unfortunately, some layers deeper than you imagine, and still further away from Papa's secure independence. Because how one can live without being able to judge oneself, criticize what one has accomplished, and still enjoy what one does, is unimaginable to me."[72] She wanted Eitingon to understand that she was not, really, referring to the high standard for self-reflection that Freud set and that she accepted as a matter of course. What she had in mind was rather different.

. . . what I have always wanted for myself, from the beginning, without much change over time, is much more primitive, and it can be said quite honestly. It is probably nothing more than the affection of the people with whom I am in contact, and also their good opinion of me. It is not just that I myself should say that something [I have done] is good; there must be others who say the same and confirm me. Now in a curiously self-evident way I have always been able not to make such a demand on my patients; in dealing with them I have never felt such human needs. Thus working has become remarkably easy for me in recent years.

But, she told Eitingon, with the children she had in analysis at that particular time, she did feel a very human need for more than good analytic work.

These children were Bob and Mabbie Burlingham and their little friends Adelaide and Harold Sweetzer—all Americans. Dorothy Tiffany Burlingham had brought her asthmatic oldest son, Bob, aged ten, to Vienna in the fall of 1925, seeking help for the psychological problems that had accrued to her son's illness. When Anna Freud agreed to take Bob, Dorothy Burlingham moved to Vienna with her other three children—Mary (Mabbie), Katrina (Tinky), and Michael (Mikey). The Sweetzers also came, and shared a house with the Burlinghams, so that their children could be treated. Dorothy Burlingham then established herself in analysis with Theodor Reik—having been too shy to seek out Sigmund Freud—and eventually arranged for Anna Freud to treat her younger children, starting with Mabbie.

The situation that had caused such need for analysis in this family was complicated and chronic. Dorothy Burlingham's husband, Robert, a surgeon, suffered from a mental illness that had been not so much treated as contained in several American mental institutions. He eventually followed his wife to Europe and consulted with Ferenczi, but he was quite opposed to psychoanalysis and never found any other kind of help for his manic-depressive syndrome.[73] Dorothy Burlingham, distraught over the effects her husband's illness and episodic institutionalizations had had on their children, wanted to keep them away from him. But she had to contend with his continuing hope that the family would be reunited, and with efforts by his father, Charles Cult Burlingham, a prominent New York lawyer and political figure, to draw the children away from Dorothy, from psychoanalysis, and from the Jewish Freuds. Dorothy Burlingham's twin older sisters, Julia and Comfort, two stepsiblings, Charles and Mary, and her father, Louis Comfort Tiffany, the interior decorator and glass designer, lived in New York, so in Vienna she depended on servants for help with her household and on her American friends the Sweetzers for companionship. The Freuds, when she met them, offered a context and comfort as well as psychoanalysis.

Anna Freud told Eitingon that thoughts of Mabbie and Bob Burlingham filled her mind. More than she wished, she had "thoughts which go along with my work but do not have a proper place in it."[74] She put her problem simply: "I think sometimes that I want not only to make them healthy but also, at the same time, to have them, or at least have something of them, for myself. Temporarily, of course, this desire is useful for my work, but sometime or another it really will disturb them, and so, on the whole, I really cannot call my need other than 'stupid.' " Having admitted this much, Anna Freud went on: "Towards the mother of the children it is not very different with me." Her confession ended with: "Curiously enough, though, I am very much ashamed of all these things, especially in front of Papa, and therefore I tell him nothing about it. This [about the Burlinghams, children and mother] is only a small illustration, but actually I have this dependency [Abhängigkeit], this wanting-to-have-something [Etwas-Haben-Wollen]—even leaving my profession aside— in every nook and cranny of my life."

Anna Freud's desire to have in some way the Burlingham children and their mother, like the larger problem that she thought the desire reflected—her dependency, her need for something for herself—marked the limit of her analytic relationship with her father. She also told Eitingon that she had tried, unsuccessfully, to discuss her desire for confirmation from others and for "something" for herself with Lou Andreas-Salomé: "I once spoke with Lou about this years ago. She herself is so enormously distanced from it, though, that we finally both had to laugh about our mutual—not to be overcome by psychoanalytic knowledge—and complete inability to understand each other."

Anna Freud had last seen Frau Lou in the summer of 1925, for a lovely visit that ended a two-year separation. She had longed for the visit, but her father's constantly uncertain condition had made her reluctant to leave him, even for a few days. But after the visit, and after the Burlingham children started their analyses with her, Anna Freud's letters to Lou are less self-revealing: although they are warm and appreciative, they contain more external than internal news, and there is no mention in them of the topics from Anna Freud's analysis that had been so important earlier. Anna Freud was fully—more than fully—occupied with her practice and her responsibilities in the Vienna Society, so she had less time for the correspondence. But the change seems more a matter of Anna Freud's psyche than her schedule: when she kept from her father her feelings about the Burlinghams, she also kept them from Frau Lou.

Anna Freud was not in analysis with her father in the fall of 1925, so her silence was not a breach of the "fundamental rule" for an analysand—to speak what comes to mind without censoring. But it did mean that she felt constrained by her peculiar analytic situation. Under the circumstances, she did the analytically logical thing: she turned to Eitingon, and created a quasi-analytic situation in which she could try to overcome the dilemma of having had her father as her analyst. She could deal with someone who shared her difficulties—as her father and Lou did not. "With me," she had tried to explain to Frau Lou, "everything became so problematic because of two basic faults: from a discontent or insatiability with myself that makes me look for affection from others, and then from actually sticking with the others once I've found them. [The first] is just what you and Papa cannot understand."[75]

Once Eitingon had accepted her confession—and, tacitly, the role she had cast him in—she felt free to tell him in detail about Dorothy Burlingham. "Being together with Mrs. Burlingham is a great joy for me, and I am very happy that you also have such a good impression of her," she wrote to Eitingon after his first meeting with her friend.[76] "I am often very sorry that she is not in analysis with you," said Anna Freud, who might have been speaking of herself. "This is not being very nice towards Reik. I think he has helped her a great deal. But still she would have received something with you which he probably cannot give, and which she certainly seeks."

Anna Freud knew that Dorothy Burlingham, a youngest child like herself, had had a very tense, difficult relationship with her father, who was severe and demanding with his children. His artistic talent had obviously impressed his children—and Dorothy Burlingham identified with it, fostering it in her own children—but his domineering manner and his drinking had been much more influential. Dorothy's mother, Tiffany's second wife, had died when her youngest daughter was thirteen. She had been a model of intelligent, liberal—quite feminist—concern, but she had also been depressed during Dorothy's childhood by the loss of another girl, two years Dorothy's senior, to scarlet fever. As a child, Dorothy Burlingham had felt, as Anna Freud had, like an unwanted hanger-on in her household, a little one who was a bore and a nuisance to the older ones.

At the same time that she was writing to Eitingon about her new friend Dorothy Burlingham, Anna Freud adopted another young mother with a family. Eva Rosenfeld, who was a niece of the chanteuse Yvette Guilbert, whom Freud adored and corresponded with, had also borne four children. But her fortune with them had been dreadful: two boys had died in a diphtheria epidemic, and a teenage daughter had died in a mountan-walking accident. When they became friends, Anna Freud offered Eva Rosenfeld solace as she mourned the loss of her daughter and she got in return Eva Rosenfeld's warm sympathy for the suffering her father's illness and pain brought her. Eva understood what each visit to Tegel sanatorium for surgery on her father's jaw did to Anna Freud: "I have headaches now very often, almost every day, and I somehow never get over the fear that something could turn out badly."[77] She confided to Eva that when her father was being treated she was cast back into her adolescent condition, before her analysis: "These two weeks I have lived as I did in the time before I became an analyst and before you and Dorothy knew me, with the poetry of Rilke and daydreams and weaving. That, too, is an Anna, but without any Interpreter."[78] Like Anna Freud, Eva Rosenfeld needed children, and Anna Freud convinced her to start up a little pensione or temporary foster-care home for several child analytic patients who needed a period of separation from their parents.

In her reports about how she was helping Dorothy Burlingham set up a new apartment in the Freuds' building, Berggasse 19, and consulting with Eva Rosenfeld about her remaining child, Victor, and her husband, Walter, Anna Freud revealed to Eitingon how she was struggling with the conflict between her role as analyst and her *Etwas-Haben-Wollen*, her wanting-to-have-something. "There is not a lot to say about me; it is already in what I have told you, in Eva's child and Dorothy's house. Both of these things belong to me, even if sometimes I feel I must go away for them instead of coming home to them."[79]

Anna Freud's letters to Eitingon do not indicate whether she ever did speak forthrightly with her father about her feelings. But it is clear that Freud accepted the path that Anna Freud found out of her conflict: she did "have" the Burlingham children and their mother as her family—and she did this by merging the Burlingham and Freud families. Freud noted the result in a January 1929 letter: "Our symbiosis with an American family (husbandless), whose children my daughter is bringing up analytically with a firm hand, is growing continually stronger, so that we share with them our needs for the summer."[80] The Burlinghams moved into the apartment above the Freuds'; they had summer houses next door to the Freuds' summer houses; Dorothy transported everyone in her automobile; the children played with the Freud grandchildren, especially Ernstl Halberstadt, who spent much of his adolescence with the Freuds and became Bob Burlingham's best friend. Starting in 1927, Dorothy Burlingham and Anna Freud took vacation trips together, leaving their families to keep each other company; and in 1930 they bought a cottage in the Semmering together so that any of the families' members who wished could join in for country weekends. This cottage, named Hochroterd (High Red Earth), was the physical place where there was no need to keep a distance in order to be at home.

The friendship with Eva Rosenfeld also grew deeper, and Anna Freud characterized the altruistic surrender in it as a kind of twinship. As she said to Eva in a letter: "You are me and I am you and everything of mine that you could use you should take, because it is rightfully yours."[81] Eva Rosenfeld realized that Anna Freud's friendship with Dorothy Burlingham was becoming the most important of her relationships and felt some jealousy about it. But she also formed a friendship with Dorothy Burlingham herself, and later offered her back garden as the location for a little schoolhouse that Dorothy equipped and staffed for the education of her own children, Eva's son, and several of the children who boarded in Eva's home.

After they had known each other for about three years, Anna Freud arranged for Dorothy Burlingham to begin a second analysis—not with Max Eitingon, who was too far away from the happy new life, but with Sigmund Freud. Unlike Theodor Reik, Freud was sympathetic to Dorothy Burlingham's desire to train as a psycho-analyst, and he conducted the analysis as a training analysis while Dorothy Burlingham also attended seminars—including Anna Freud's seminar—at the Vienna Institute. Anna Freud's and Dorothy Bur-lingham's growing friendship was revealed in an analysis to the father-analyst—but not by his daughter.

Anna Freud did find her way to having her own desires rather than displacing them onto others and living vicariously; after her fashion, she had a rich and full family life, though she did not, in the 1920s or afterward, have a sexual relationship, with Dorothy Burlingham or with anyone else. She remained a "vestal"—to use the apt word Marie Bonaparte later chose to signal both Anna Freud's virginity and her role as the chief keeper of her father's person and his science, psychoanalysis.

WHILE he praised his daughter's intellectual and professional achieve-ments, Sigmund Freud was not untroubled by the course her life took. He had written to Lou Andreas-Salomé in 1935: "she is truly independent of me; at the most I serve as a catalyst. You will enjoy reading her most recent writings. Of course there are certain worries; she takes things too seriously. What will she do when she has lost me? Will she lead a life of ascetic austerity?"[82]

Anna Freud's life was ascetic; and her father's death, when it came, brought no change. But "the erotic side of her life"—to use Freud's phrase from " 'A Child Is Being Beaten' "—was restored to her, in a very particular sense: the femininity she had denied herself, in herself, came to her in the persons of the two mothers, Dorothy Burlingham and (to a lesser extent) Eva Rosenfeld. These women also seem to have compensated for her troubled relations with her own mother and Tante Minna and replaced her sister Sophie, the mother whose son Anna Freud had come to think of as her adopted son; they could be loved altruistically and from them she could receive maternal love and sisterly appreciation. As Dorothy Burling-ham became more and more important, Anna Freud could oversee and altruistically support Dorothy's interests in men, as long as these remained Platonic and did not threaten their friendship. But she seems also to have found in her friend a version of the youngest child in need of a perfect father and angry toward a distracted, overburdened mother that she knew in herself. They mirrored each other.

Anna Freud came to trust that her friendship was for her friend—as Dorothy later told her—"the most precious relationship [Dorothy] ever had."[83] She did not have to compete for Dorothy's love after she had won it. Many in her psychoanalytic circles, who knew enough to discount the persistent rumor that the friends were lesbians, but who realized that Anna Freud's life partnership was chaste and her "family" surrogate, found her situation poignant or sad. She, on the other hand, felt she had satisfied her *Etwas-Haben-Wollen*, and avoided the fate that Rilke had etched in a stanza of his "Herbsttag" ("Autumn Day"), a poem that she knew by heart for all her life.

> *Wer jetzt kein Haus hat, baut sich keines mehr,*
> *Wer jetzt allein ist, wird es lange bleiben,*
> *wird wachen, lesen, lange Briefe schreiben*
> *und wird in den Alleen hin und her*
> *unruhig wandern, wenn die Blätter treiben.*
>
> *Who has no house now will not have one.*
> *Who is now alone will so remain:*
> *sitting, reading, writing long letters;*
> *restlessly wandering the avenues,*
> *back and forth, while brown leaves blow.*

There is no evidence that Anna Freud ever felt unfulfilled or regretful in her new family, although maintaining for the Burlingham children the dual role of stepparent and psychoanalyst was always problematic—for her and for them.

In one of her most incisive and important clinical contributions, Anna Freud noted that sexuality repressed or denied can be recovered symbolically or vicariously in a relationship of complementarity. She made the point in a lecture on male homosexuality, as she described a male patient's effort to recover his own split-off masculinity in his male partner's virility.[84] But this analytic concept of complementarity is certainly applicable to relationships of many sorts, whether overtly sexual or not. Dorothy Burlingham, whose older sisters were twins, wrote touchingly about how siblings of twins often invent a twin, a complementary self: "A further element in many daydreams of having a twin is that of the imaginary twin being a complement to the daydreamer. The latter endows his twin with all the qualities and talents that he misses in himself and desires for himself. The twin thus represents an ideal of himself, his super-ego."[85] In later letters that they exchanged, Dorothy Burlingham and Anna Freud agreed that they were each other's twins, or twins for each other, in their "ideal friendship." "I had such pleasure in your letter about the identical twins," Dorothy wrote. "It makes me happy and proud that we have such a bond."[86]

4

PSYCHOANALYSIS
AND POLITICS

During the years of her first analysis, from 1918 to 1922, Anna Freud also received her introductory course in psychoanalytic politics. She was still a neophyte in 1924 when she found herself quite suddenly a member of the Committee of her father's closest advisers; and she was still a very new analyst in 1925 when she joined the executive board of the Vienna Psychoanalytic Institute and started work as a training analyst. But her father's illness, which dictated his withdrawal from active participation in meetings and conferences, and the complex relations among the first- and second-generation analysts combined to command political understanding and institutional involvement from the reticent Anna Freud.

At the end of the First World War, Sigmund Freud's circle of psychoanalytic colleagues expanded and became more organized. Many of the first-generation analysts had left their practices for war service. When they returned in the winter of 1918–19, they faced daunting economic turmoil and daily struggle for the ingredients of physical survival. In Vienna, as in most of Germany and urban Hungary, peoples' lives were dominated by intricate arrangements with black marketeers, links to the countryside where coal and wood could be secured, measures to protect malnourished families from pneumonia and the periodic influenza epidemics, and services to keep children from running wild. The number of people in need of psychoanalysis who could either afford it or find sufficient peace to sustain it emotionally was small—though the need was greater than ever. At the September 1918 Congress in Budapest, questions about how to treat war neurotics had predominated in the clinical discussions, and Ernst Simmel's pioneering efforts with "shell shock" victims had been greeted as crucial adaptions of psychoanalytic methods to war-related illnesses. In Vienna, Anna Freud's friend August Aichhorn was developing methods for applying psychoanalytic insights to the treatment of juvenile delinquents and children from disrupted families. But, to bring former soldiers as well as civilians from "the wider social strata" into psychoanalytic treatment proper, Freud and his colleagues realized that they needed outpatient clinics and various means—lecture courses, publications—for educating a wide public about psychoanalysis. Also, to expand their numbers and keep their scientific progress steady, they needed formalized training programs. The first-generation analysts had to provide not just the personal analyses for trainees that had been proposed at the Budapest Congress, but seminars in psychoanalytic theory and technique.

Freud himself had been the informal director of patient referrals in Vienna, so that his less well known and younger colleagues were often quite dependent upon him for their analysands—a situation that he knew fostered competition for his favor. He was also the chief "training analyst"—to use the designation that emerged after training analyses were mandated in 1926—for his followers and the main propagandist for psychoanalysis through writings and lectures. The Vienna Psychoanalytic Society was a society, a group, but it was completely organized around its founder.

Freud did not have in Vienna the senior and trusted allies he had elsewhere, particularly in Budapest and Berlin, and he had not very much altered the opinion he had expressed to Jung back in 1911: "None of these Viennese will ever amount to anything; the only one with a future is little Rank, who is both intelligent and decent."[1] At the end of the First World War, Freud's plan was to begin the consolidation of psychoanalysis where conditions were best, and then to let the organizational momentum transfer to other locales as they became ready. The organizational effort was to be concentrated in Europe, but Jones was an important link to both England and America for what Freud, sounding like a League of Nations enthusiast, called "our new orientation towards the west."[2] The European hopes fell first upon Budapest. Before his death, Freud's friend and patron Anton von Freund had created a fund to sustain a psychoanalytic publishing house in Budapest, and ministers in the Hungarian government, impressed by the success of the Budapest Congress, wanted to aid the founding of a psychoanalytic institute and sponsor a department at the university for psychoanalytic educational projects. Otto Rank, who was then Freud's editorial and secretarial assistant, went to Budapest to work on the publishing venture with von Freund and Sandor Ferenczi, the senior Hungarian colleague and Freud's closest friend among the Committee members.

But the publishing house was the only one of the Hungarian plans that survived the breakup of the Austro-Hungarian Empire in the fall of 1918; and it had to be removed to Vienna during the complicated months when Béla Kun's revolutionary government, which was sympathetic to psychoanalysis, was unable to sustain itself against a reactionary and very anti-Semitic tide backed by occupying forces from Romania, which swept away all forms of Hungarian progressivism, including psychoanalysis. Many of Ferenczi's younger Jewish colleagues emigrated—chiefly to Berlin—and left him with the task of building up his Society all over again.

Because Ferenczi was virtually incommunicado during the Hungarian tumult, the presidency of the International Psychoanalytic Association, which he held, was transferred to Ernest Jones. The organizational and scientific leadership that Freud had hoped to establish in Budapest was established, instead, in Berlin, where Karl Abraham and Max Eitingon were joined by Hanns Sachs, who moved there from Switzerland, and by two younger analysts from Hungary, Sandor Rado and Franz Alexander. These men together with Theodor Reik, who moved from Vienna, made the Training Institute that was established in Berlin in 1920 a model of its kind. They also made the first psychoanalytic clinic, the Berlin Policlinic, founded and financed by Max Eitingon, the most important treatment and research center for psychoanalysis.

The first International Congress held after the peace treaty was scheduled for September 1920 in The Hague, because travel to Holland would be relatively free of the complicated visa policies that kept former enemies and former allies from crossing one another's borders. This decision perturbed the Germans, who wanted the Congress in Berlin, which was as far as their deflated, nearly worthless currency would take them. The English, in turn, were not willing either to make themselves vulnerable to the English press opinion that psychoanalysis was a "German science" or to travel to the capital city of their recent enemies. This debate, which reveals clearly how difficult international cooperation of any sort was in the crosscurrents of Europe's postwar political turmoil, was resolved by the Dutch analytic group, which generously paid the travel expenses of the Germans, the Austrians, and the Hungarians. The Congress, too, despite the organizational problems, was encouraging to all the participants; the scientific level of the contributions was high, and the language of psychoanalysis spoke beyond the nationalistic fervors that each group knew at home.

ANNA Freud attended the Hague Congress—her second Congress—with her father. She was one of the fifty-seven guests who joined the sixty-two members present for four days of papers and meetings. Between the meetings, she and her father toured the town. Her father bought her new dresses and both went to restaurants, where they ate enthusiastically but cautiously in order not to disturb stomachs accustomed to war rations. They also developed a political parable out of one restaurant experience. Thinking that the full prix fixe menu at their hotel would be too expensive for them, they ordered dinner à la carte—and ended up paying almost twice the prix fixe for it. Ever after, Freud declared that they should never fight for the fundamental principles of psychoanalysis à la carte but only as a full menu.

With her father, Anna Freud was also a special guest at a luncheon organized by the British delegation: "she pleased her father and us," her former English tutor and tour-guide Ernest Jones reported in his Freud biography, "by making a graceful little speech in very good English." When he was writing the Freud biography, Anna Freud had had to remonstrate with Ernest Jones about that little speech, for his memory, always troubled on the topic of the father of psychoanalysis's daughter, told him that Sigmund Freud himself had been the speaker. She insisted: "It was I who made the 'graceful little speech' at the luncheon. I did it to please [Papa] and it was my first effort in English. He was very pleased with it. Don't you remember? You praised it, too."[3]

The problem may very well have been that Jones's memory had also registered more strongly than usual the mixture of Anna Freud's feelings toward him because she was so eager to have Loe Kann Jones and her husband, Jones the Second, at the luncheon. Freud had urged them to come to Holland, and Loe had responded with one of her delightful, bantering letters.

. . . it would be grand being together, like in old times. Except that Anna might make me jealous. Ernest tells me (over the telephone) that she has grown into a wonderfully interesting woman, and a beauty to boot. I'm sure you agree from the bottom of your heart? She always was interesting and very attractive, and I thought she had a pleasing and charming face. Beauties look so dull as a rule, but if she is beautiful on top of all the other things . . . Well, I'll have to keep an eye on Davy [Herbert Jones]. You remember they took to each other like ducks to water?[4]

Loe's letter, of course, had made its way into Anna Freud's hands; she was appropriately flattered by it—and more entranced than ever by Loe. But the reunion in Holland did not take place, and Anna Freud had to endure the further disappointment of not being granted the visa that would have allowed her to go to England for a visit with the Joneses there. She and her father had planned to make this expedition together, but they had to settle for a tour of Holland with several Dutch analysts as their guides.

It is not clear from the surviving correspondences why Loe and Davy Jones decided against their Holland plan. Loe's light-spirited acceptance letter, which had gone on to gossip in the former-mistress manner about Ernest Jones, that "incorrigible fibber," who had told his father and sisters that his new wife, Katharina Jokl, was an intimate of the Freud family, when in fact she had never met them, showed from start to finish Loe's relief at having gotten out of her system an earlier letter. The predecessor had contained many painful pages about what the war had done to Loe's feelings about Germans and Austrians.

She could not take the perspective Freud had offered her: he thought that, as he said, "we country-less Jews" could meet again after such a war without nationalistic animosities. But, for herself, Loe replied: "my Jewishness disappeared to all practical purposes . . . and both of us felt more anti-German than we could ever have dreamt of." She found it appalling that during the years they had spent driving an ambulance, ferrying wounded soldiers and bombed-out civilians, she had come to think of even Freud's sons as "the enemy." "Always we had hated Germany, hated its military brutality, and—fools that we were—laughed at it. And that country was able to force its enemies to play her beastly military game for four years and four months, mocking decency and showing what brutality can still force men to do. And because we have been forced to feel and act in a way that we hoped was impossible, we cannot so easily forget who made us do it." If she came to Vienna, she said with remarkable candor, "I would see in your sons the men who would have killed Davy, had chance been favorable."[5]

Sigmund Freud, "of no country, but of much wisdom" (as Loe wrote, exempting him from her anger), had not pressed the Joneses to visit Vienna; he had accepted their feelings and hoped to see them in Holland. To his daughter, he later confided that he thought Loe's feelings were influenced by Davy Jones's "Christian German-hatred."[6] But Anna Freud nonetheless felt deeply betrayed, though several years later she could acknowledge to Lou Andreas-Salomé, Loe Kann's successor, that she had been hypersensitive: "every 'faithlessness' made my goal, possession of the other person, impossible; and with that my whole past relationship to the person seemed without value, even if I had liked the person so very much, as with . . . Loe Kann Jones, the end always destroyed the whole past, too."[7]

Freud had tried hard at the end of the war to restore his good relations with the Joneses both because he—and Anna— loved them and their company and because he thought of England as a potential refuge. His English had improved, and Anna's had become graceful, because he had taken the precaution in 1919 of hiring an Englishwoman to tutor them and make them linguistically fit for emigration should the economic situation in Vienna become too difficult. In moments of great weariness, Freud often wrote to his friends about how he, like his two stepbrothers, might find himself buried in English soil. He could, in the meanwhile, conduct analyses in English for the fees in stable currencies paid by American and English candidates seeking training. Anna Freud had used her improved skills in the publishing house's English department, where she eventually graduated from translator into German to translator of German into English.

IT was in the Verlag that Anna Freud became directly acquainted with the day-to-day business of keeping an international institution afloat in economic bad times. At the Hague Congress, arrangements for a branch of the Verlag in London were made by Otto Rank, the manager of the Verlag in Vienna, and Ernest Jones. The London operation was to include a bookstore specializing in psychoanalytic publications; a book series, which was to publish translations of German works; and an English-language journal, *The International Journal of Psychoanalysis*. The coexistence of the Verlag's German journals and the English journal meant a constant traffic of manuscripts and translations between Vienna and London. But even the installation of an English assistant, Eric Hiller, in Vienna did not do much to help the tensions over traffic direction that developed between Otto Rank and Ernest Jones—with ultimately disastrous consequences.

In Vienna itself, the situation was difficult enough. Anna Freud's letters to Max Eitingon report enormous energy devoted to elementary questions, like where to house the Verlag, which, given the economic conditions, meant clearing spaces in private apartments. There was never enough paper, enough ink at the printers', enough money to pay the printers; the telephone and telegraph offices were closed intermittently with strikes; the office work was sometimes too much for Rank and Hiller, who had not a typewriter between them. Anna Freud was sometimes pressed into secretarial service, but "after three days I declared a strike. I find the real office work so terribly boring that I cannot endure it. I do not know if this is very bad of me. But I have instead started to translate a book by Dr. Varendonck from Ghent that interests me very much."[8]

The poor working relationship between Otto Rank and Ernest Jones was resolved in September 1922 at the Congress in Berlin, the first Congress that Anna Freud attended as a member. Eric Hiller, finding Otto Rank impossible to work with, had resigned, so it seemed obvious that the English and German publishing enterprises should simply be severed. By the time this decision was reached, Anna Freud had begun her analytic practice and had less daily contact with Rank. As an editorial assistant, her time went into two projects: the German edition of her father's *Gesammelte Schriften*, which was completed in 1924, and the English translation, *Collected Writings*, for which she acted as consultant to James and Alix Strachey, the chief translators. But, like the Committee members, she was preoccupied through the summer and fall of 1923 not with present projects but with the unknown future represented by the first operations on her father's jaw.

ONE of the clearest signs that Freud's illness would deeply complicate the future of psychoanalysis came from within the Committee itself. A struggle for originality and independence became entwined with what was, in effect, another succession crisis. But in this crisis, unlike the one that had resulted in Jung's departure, there was no single prince and Freud did not—could not—take up the crown again. He was more of a Lear than he had been in 1913.

In the fall of 1923, Rank and Sandor Ferenczi published together a book called *The Development of Psychoanalysis*. This book provoked a great deal of puzzlement because, in addition to advocating the technique of analyzing patients' tendencies to "live out" in action their unconscious wishes—a technique that Freud approved—the authors seemed to suggest that this kind of analysis alone, without the traditional reconstruction of the childhood sources of unconscious wishes, might be sufficient for a psychoanalytic therapy. Such a suggestion was explicit in a book that Rank published toward the end of the year, *The Trauma of Birth*, in which he argued that psychoanalytic technique should—in a relatively brief period—bring a patient to relive in the analytic transference the experience of being born, the ultimate source and prototype of all anxiety experiences.

Through 1924, Freud labored to sort out his reactions to his colleagues' work. He vacillated between finding Rank's birth-trauma theory reductionistic and applauding him for his boldness and originality. He praised the coauthored work for its emphasis on acting out or repetition in analyses and its openness to technical experimentation, but he faulted Rank and Ferenczi for their desire to shorten and simplify analyses. Anna Freud detested Rank's book but tried to follow her father's example of waiting patiently for discussions among the Committee members either to confirm or to mollify the opinion, held with particular force by Abraham, that Rank, if not Ferenczi, was headed for the role of chief dissident played so dramatically in 1913 by Carl Jung. Freud's patience was half rewarded when Ferenczi, after meeting with his Committee colleagues at the Easter 1924 Congress in Salzburg, which Freud could not attend, regained a good working alliance with his critics. Rank, on the other hand, was stormy and remote; he held to his conclusion that the Committee should disband as firmly as he held to the more extreme therapeutic consequences of his theorizing. Abraham and Jones were both convinced that Rank's theory was the product of a manic-depressive syndrome, and they warned Freud that he should speak out firmly against it. Freud, in turn, warned them that their attitude toward Rank, their quick judgments and ad hominem arguments, were making Rank's situation worse.

Anna Freud apparently accepted her father's charitable hope that Rank would return to his senses, and thus was completely shocked when Rank, toward the end of the trip he had made to America to proselytize for his theory, wrote her father an openly hostile letter, a collection of reproaches for Freud's failure to accept the birth-trauma theory. Anna Freud made a copy of the letter for Eitingon, and sent a distraught letter of her own with it.

I no longer believe that Rank will suddenly wake up and be the old Rank; maybe he never was at all the Rank we took him to be these many years? I really do not know. But either that which allowed him to write this letter was always in him, and we did not notice it, or it must have suddenly entered into him. If either of these alternatives is possible, though, how can one know anything at all about people, if they can be either way? And why do we go around acting as though everything was friendship and reliability when basically everything everywhere is full of sudden hate and ugliness. I copied the letter for you, and, while doing so, committed it to memory very well. The most incomprehensible thing about it is that even though there is so much said openly, he is still full of hidden, cheap malice—this becomes clear if you know that the psychoanalyzed patients he speaks of are all former patients of Papa's. I cannot understand any of this. But in any case, Rank is very advanced compared to all of us in his understanding that human relations exist for the sole purpose of being ruined. When one knows this with a certainty like his, then one does not need to initiate any relations at all.[9]

In her rage at how faithless Rank had been to her father, Anna Freud felt her confidence in the faithfulness of *anyone* shaken, and she adopted a cynical tone to contain the damage. But she also felt that she had to control her anger for her father's sake, because he had decided to work for a reconciliation with Rank by inviting Eitingon and Ferenczi to Vienna to meet with him in October. Anna Freud acknowledged the practicality of this approach: "I know very well that the question of whether Rank can be checked is the question of whether the publishing house and the magazines will continue to exist."[10] Controlling her anger was not, however, simple, and her father reported that "Anna spits fire when the name Rank is pronounced."[11] But after Rank appeared in Vienna, she met with him, as her father wished, and declared—without anger—that she just had no idea how to understand him. "It is very good that you are coming," she wrote to Eitingon, "so that you can help us figure it out."[12]

Neither Eitingon nor Ferenczi could reach Rank, and his last visit with Freud before departing again for America was inconclusive personally, though it did result in an arrangement to turn Rank's journal editorships over to Sandor Rado and some of his secretarial duties over to Anna Freud. She wrote to Eitingon after Rank had left Vienna at the end of November 1924:

From Papa's report [on the last visit], I got an impression like the one I had when Rank had just returned home; namely, that if one could grab him firmly and shake him very strongly (not just his body, of course), then everything would come out—maybe with much vulgarity and a lot of bitterness, but honestly and truly nonetheless. Papa and I did not try this method because I thought that you and Ferenczi might achieve the same end more easily. But to do so, perhaps, required more warmth and affection than any of us had left for Rank after what had already gone on before. At any rate, it is sad that after such a long acquaintance not even enough of a relationship remains to permit us—even while angry—to come close to each other.[13]

For Anna Freud, the immediate consequence of Rank's departure from Vienna and from his various institutional responsibilities was an invitation from the remaining five Committee members. Prompted by a suggestion from Sandor Ferenczi, they requested that she take Rank's place as their sixth member. The Committee's letter announcing its decision came in time for Anna Freud's twenty-ninth birthday. She wrote to Eitingon:

It came just before my birthday, and I take its news as a very beautiful birthday present: that the Committee wants not only to tolerate me as an accessory but to accept me into its ranks as a member. Naturally I know that on my own merits I have no right at all to this, but I am no longer like I used to be, when I would see to it very carefully that everything I received was earned and thus justified. Sometimes the most beautiful thing is precisely the one that comes unexpectedly and unearned, hence something given truly as a present. Most beautiful, moreover, if it is for Papa's sake. The both of us were pleased together about it, he no less than I.[14]

The woman who had once suspected that all attentions paid to her were really destined for her father, who had thought of herself as like an heiress being courted for her money and not for herself, simply accepted this honor.[15] She even felt that if the Committee had invited her in order to please her father, or for his sake, that was all to the good. A conviction of her own worth stands behind this shift, and also behind the apparently modest claim that her own merits were not at issue. Throughout the Rank dissension, Freud had set very exacting standards for patience and open-mindedness—standards so exacting that they had about them a little of the rigidity that often attends suppression of resentment or disappoinment—and he had asked his daughter to live up to them. She had, and she was rewarded. She replaced the youngest of her father's filial order of six—she was once again the youngest of six, but by election, not by fate; and her acceptance in this group of knights, which was a form of her youthful "nice story" daydream come true, pleased her father as much as it pleased her.

The next act in this drama was peculiar. The resolution, unhappy but at least clear, that Rank's departure had brought was undone abruptly only a few weeks after he left Vienna for Paris. In Paris, Rank fell into a deep depression and reconsidered the break from Freud that his intransigent attitude had led to. He decided to return to Vienna and confess to Freud his Parisian second thoughts, his analysis of what had been moving him for the last year. Freud received Rank and concluded from his confession that Rank had been through what his own theory specified—a "living out" episode that had wrought a cure. Anna Freud reported the end of December 1924 state of affairs:

> . . . now he looks very miserable, as if he had a great number of evil thoughts in him. One can have no doubts that what he now shows is honest. Papa, who knows everything that went on—which we can hardly find out—down to the last detail, has no doubts. In any case, it seems clear that the external and practical motives he had could not have sufficed to cause in anybody what apparently happened to him. Maybe something has actually shaken him the way we wanted to shake him and that which possessed him has as a result let go of him.[16]

Anna Freud leaned in the direction, again, of her father's tolerance, but she found the position very difficult.

> I also made my peace with him, without even a great deal of trouble. But afterwards something about this caused me a special effort anyway. Now, whenever he comes close to Papa in any sort of way, or whenever I come nearer to him—for example, when I recently saw him spending evenings with Papa—there rise up in me, despite my conscious intention, completely wild feelings of (probably) jealousy, as though I felt that he had finally lost the right to any closeness. Papa thinks otherwise about it. Even though he also believed before that we were completely finished with Rank, the change in Rank was a great joy and satisfaction to him anyway.

Having agreed with the conclusion her father finally reached, that Rank was really suffering from some form of mental illness, Anna Freud renewed her efforts to control her anger—and jealousy. She gave up one of her hypotheses: that Rank had been cast by her father's illness into a distorting practical anxiety about making a living or maintaining the style of living to which he and his ambitious wife, Beata Tola Mincer, were accustomed. She tried to believe that the Ranks would not abuse her father's trust over money. But her attitude toward both Rank and his wife continued to be informed by just the kind of jealousy she was considering with her father in the renewal of her analysis, which had begun at the spring of 1924. The project was difficult, and Anna Freud never did give up her feeling that Frau Rank was scheming and ambitious. "Frau Rank was present at the last meeting of the Society. Because I had really done her a great injustice in my thoughts, I wanted to make a new attempt to find her pleasant. It did not do any good: I think once and for all that I just cannot stand her."[17]

In the spring of 1925, Freud took Rank into what Anna Freud described as "a sort of analysis" in an effort to help him, finally, out of his miserable, confused state.[18] Rank did come to an equilibrium and went on another trip to America, after which he wanted, so he said, to reinstate himself in the Vienna Society. But his behavior during the winter of 1925–26, when this reinstatement was supposed to come about, was aloof and cold. Freud finally had to admit, after Rank again left Vienna—this time for good—in April 1926, that his hopeful prognosis had been ill founded, that Rank had gone slowly in precisely the direction his first tumult had presaged: away from Freud. Freud had to deal with this final disappointment just as Karl Abraham, who had been ill for almost six months, became weaker and weaker. A strain came into Abraham's correspondence with Freud, not just over the Rank affair but over a proposed film about psychoanalysis that Abraham supported and Freud opposed. As much as he respected Abraham, Freud always felt alienated from him when Abraham sounded self-righteous and know-it-all, a tone that was all the harder to bear because Abraham had excellent judgment and usually was right. No other colleague had his maturity as a clinician and a scientific writer. To Freud's deep distress, his loyal friend, only forty-eight years old, died on Christmas 1925, leaving a heartbroken widow and two children. In one year, two of the most trusted and gifted organizers and leaders in the psychoanalytic movement were gone.

The standards for behavior under stress that Anna Freud learned from her father's dealings with Rank became for her a kind of code of conduct in psychoanalytic politics. Fifty years later, when one of her own colleagues had to accept a lost alliance, she sent off her own lesson in lieu of direct advice:

> I also remember something my father used to say when friendship or support of this kind came to an end. He said that there is no reason to expect that somebody would go on forever with his positive actions because he had begun them; that one should be grateful for what had happened and not resentful that it is not going on happening. I remember this conversation with him very vividly. It was about Otto Rank's defection, which made me very angry. He wanted me to think of all the years when Rank had given such faithful service instead.[19]

THE YEAR OF Otto Rank's wandering away, 1924, and then the next year, 1925, when he reappeared in Vienna, managed his temporary reconciliation with Freud and then disappeared again, were chaotic years for the Vienna Psychoanalytic Society. Rank had been the Society's vice president, the one who should have taken over during Freud's illness. The vice presidency went, instead, to Paul Federn, who, along with Eduard Hitschmann and Helene Deutsch, had been one of the enthusiasts in Vienna for the idea of a psychoanalytic outpatient clinic, or Ambulatorium. Freud himself had not favored this plan, being painfully aware of the attitude toward psychoanalysis in Vienna's medical and psychiatric circles. But he had simply stood to the side while such a clinic was founded and opened in May 1922 under Hitschmann's direction, and he continued to stay in the background while Federn ran the Society and coordinated its activities with the Ambulatorium. For a time, Freud and Ferenczi had entertained the idea that Ferenczi might move to Vienna from Budapest and take over direction of the clinic, but when this proved financially impossible for Ferenczi, Freud retired into his skepticism about what the Viennese might accomplish on their own.

Toward the end of 1925, Helene Deutsch proposed that a Vienna Psychoanalytic Institute be founded, on the model of the Berlin Institute, to provide a training program for young analysts. This project, unlike the clinic, which demanded medical qualification, was one Anna Freud could support, and she was eventually made its secretary. Helene Deutsch was the Institute's first director, and her second-in-command was Siegfried Bernfeld. Helene Deutsch was forty-one in 1925, just Rank's age, and Bernfeld was thirty-three, only three years older than Anna Freud. But in generational terms, Deutsch and Bernfeld, like Anna Freud and Heinz Hartmann, her partner from the time of her ward rounds at Wagner-Jauregg's clinic, were the middle ground between Federn, Hitschmann, and Freud's other older colleagues—people in their fifties—and the trainees who attended the newly established Training Institute.

Generational differences played a great role in the complicated project of getting a training institute finally founded. Helene Deutsch was on the point of withdrawing in the face of opposition from Federn over her plans and her use of the Berlin program as a model when Anna Freud intervened and insisted that the feuding Vienna Society members meet to air their views with her father. She thought that the Vienna Society had, like the Committee of six during the Rank dissension, a constitutional problem. She described it to Eitingon: "I think that approximately the same thing goes on in the Viennese group as went on between individual members of the Committee—and which does not go on in the Berlin Society. You know what I mean: the common, group interest vanishes when the question of who will take over the leadership of the group arises. If it continues like this, there will in the future be various people ready to lead in Vienna, but nothing left in common to lead."[20] Her impulse was to call back the old leader, her father, as an adviser and to summon the Training Institute's would-be leaders to the waiting room at the Berggasse apartment, the historical beginning place.

The effect was a very strange one [Anna Freud noted a little ruefully to Eitingon]. Suddenly we were a Training Institute with only nice, nearly unified, serious human beings interested in our subject, and it was possible to organize, to discuss, and to clarify a huge number of topics. Frau Deutsch's withdrawing from the group did not happen to get mentioned. . . . The matters given particular consideration were: the question of lay analysis; the question of partial training, especially for foreigners; the appointment of teaching analysts and the training of instructors. [And she concluded] yesterday it was quite clear: there is not a lack of people of goodwill here, but only a lack of one person able to maintain the others' goodwill.[21]

Anna Freud set out to follow her father's example as a mobilizer of goodwill. This meant that she tried to avoid favoritism and to maintain her independence. The task was not easy, as she explained once to A. A. Brill, the leader of the New York Psychoanalytic Society: "Federn thinks I am under Helene Deutsch's influence, and H.D. thinks I am under Federn's. And I am not, I can assure you of that. I am only under my father's influence, and for the rest I try to think of myself as an independent person and to figure things out for myself. . . . I would never believe in anybody who judges a situation with a lot of emotion and all from one side."[22]

In her first years of working with the Vienna Society, its Institute, and its training program, Anna Freud reached conclusions about how groups do and do not work that she retained for the rest of her life. First and foremost, she came to think of leadership as commitment to bringing out the best in everyone by making sure that everyone gave the group's goal—the maintenance and continuance of psychoanalysis—priority over their individual goals. "My interest is not in the individual people but in the analytic movement as a whole," she said quite frankly.[23] Second, she came to think that people should hold positions of responsibility on the basis of their abilities to work without arousing mistrust or producing friction in the group; their abilities as individuals, independently of the group, were of less consequence. For leadership positions, she never favored the brilliant but self-important or exhibitionistic types over the team players. All the institutions that eventually bore her stamp had very strong internal bonds but sometimes had to be recharged from without—or by Anna Freud's own efforts as one of the rare people combining group mindedness and brilliance. As she put her emergent principle in 1925: "The selection of the leadership must follow practical considerations, namely: in terms of relations [within the group], who would manage best? and who would the group allow to work with the least amount of resistance? . . . Maybe I look at things too pessimistically?"[24]

Anna Freud was convinced that she had to dedicate herself to bringing out the best in the people with whom she worked, a conviction that was based on the unflattering, if not truly pessimistic, assumption that any other approach would simply allow the worst in people to do what it was wont to do—come forth. In this, she was certainly her father's daughter. She learned her lesson from observing the course of the Rank affair and from participating in the Vienna Society's postwar reorganization, but she also learned it from noting frankly her own behavior. She wrote to Eitingon after she had lost her temper during one particularly exhausting meeting of the factious Vienna group:

> I already know, Herr Doktor, why I always have a bad conscience when I am irrational. Because Papa always makes it clear that he would like to know me as much more rational and lucid than the girls and women he gets to know during his analytic hours, with all their moods, dissatisfactions and passionate idiosyncrasies. Thus I, too, would really like to be as he sees fit, first out of love for him, and second because I myself know that it is the only chance that one has to be somewhat useful and not a burden and a concern for others.[25]

Anna Freud was so concerned with being "better than all the girls," as she told Lou Andreas-Salomé, that she would not even permit herself the "small depressions" that sometimes accompanied her menstrual periods: "I know that it is so regularly with some women, but it shouldn't be so with me."[26]

Her father was her model for group leadership and for triumph over moods, and he was her interior model, her standard setter, her ego ideal; rationality and lucidity were her goals for both inner and outer domains, and they were her counters to anger, jealousy, rivalry. For herself, Anna Freud interpreted her father's standards as: be above factions, and be above typical femininity.

A group of young University of Vienna medical students came to the Vienna Society's meetings in the early 1920s, worked in the

Ambulatorium, and enrolled in the Training Institute once it was established. Wilhelm Reich, Edward Bibring, Grete Lehner Bibring, and Otto Fenichel had met in their medical school classes and started among themselves a little seminar on topics—like sexuality—ignored in their curriculum. They brought to the Vienna Society their energy and their socialist concern for Vienna's lower classes—to whom the Ambulatorium's services were available without charge.

Within this group, Wilhelm Reich's rise to prominence in the Vienna Society was the most swift: he started practicing as an analyst in 1920, when he was only twenty-three and still a medical student, and two years later he was named first assistant to Hitschmann, the director of the Ambulatorium. Reich, a year and a half younger than Anna Freud, was the youngest instructor at the Training Institute, where his classes on psychoanalytic technique, later presented in a book called *Character Analysis*, were crucial to his whole group of contemporaries.[27]

This younger medical group joined Anna Freud, Heinz Hartmann, and Reich in an informal study group that had started before the Training Institute was founded and continued during its existence as a forum for discussion of theoretical issues and clinical or therapeutic topics. Jeanne Lampl-de Groot also attended the study group, as did Wilhelm ("Willi") Hoffer, Robert Waelder, Jenny Pollak Waelder, Richard Sterba, and René Spitz. Known because of the youth of its membership as the *Kinderseminar*, the group was sometimes attended by Helene Deutsch and Hermann Nunberg. But Helene Deutsch also rather pointedly, perhaps jealously, organized a discussion group of her own for the psychoanalytic married couples—she and her husband, Felix, the Bibrings, Hoffers, Hartmanns, Waelders, and later Marianne and Ernst Kris—while Freud's older, prewar colleagues tended to look upon the *Kinderseminar*—and particularly upon its most precocious members, like Reich—as rather upstart.[28]

On the other hand, the younger people did not have great confidence in the older ones as analysts, and many of the Vienna candidates went to Berlin for their personal analyses. Freud, who decided to prevent competition for his hours by refusing to act as a training analyst except for Americans planning to return to America, fostered the migration to Berlin by referring, for examples, Anny Rosenberg

Angel and Marianne Rie Kris, the daughters of his pediatrician friends, to Theodor Reik and Franz Alexander, respectively. (Analysands like Dorothy Burlingham and Princess Marie Bonaparte, who started with Freud for therapeutic analyses and later decided to study at the Institute did not fall under this rule, for which there was also an occasional exception, like Heinz Hartmann.) As the Institute in Vienna became more established, the younger instructors did more of the training analyses, and Anna Freud's practice by the later 1920s was about two-thirds with children and a third with trainees. She, like the other instructors, also did supervisions of trainees' cases. In 1929, to choose a year for which records have survived, she had five candidates for supervision in child analysis: Dorothy Burlingham; a Dr. Finesinger; two American physicians, Dr. Julia Deming (later of Boston) and Dr. Edith Jackson (later of New Haven); and Dr. Ernst Kris, an art historian who had followed his wife, Marianne Rie Kris, into psychoanalysis while he retained his position as assistant curator at the Vienna Kunsthistorisches Museum.[29]

The three-year program that candidates of the Vienna Training Institute followed was described by Anna Freud retrospectively, in one of the many letters she had to write for lay analysts facing stringent certification requirements in America after the Second World War.

> The first year was devoted to a detailed survey of the literature and the developmental aspects of psychoanalysis, concerning the various parts of the human personality. The second year was devoted to clinical studies of the neuroses, psychoses, perversions, etc. The third year summarized the theoretical and clinical teaching under the heading of psychoanalytic metapsychology. To this teaching were added during the second and third years separate courses on child analysis, the analysis of delinquency and criminality and a course in the application of psychoanalysis to social sciences, art, religion, etc.[30]

Anna Freud taught the child analysis seminar, called *Zur Technik der Kinderanalyse*, while her friend August Aichhorn taught the seminar on analysis of delinquency and criminality, assisted by one of his finest American students, Helen Ross, later the director of the child analysis program at the Chicago Institute. Anna Freud, August

Aichhorn, Siegfried Bernfeld, and Willi Hoffer also continued their weekly conversational group by offering an applied analysis course in Psychoanalytic Pedagogy, which was available not just to candidates but to Viennese schoolteachers and social workers. In conjunction with this course, they worked on a journal, the *Zeitschrift für Psychoanalytische Pädagogik*, which was their means of reaching out both to teacher-training programs and to child analysis programs at other institutes. The journal had been under the editorship of its founder, a Swiss colleague named Ernst Schneider, but then it "did not represent a progressive line within the psychoanalytic movement," as Anna Freud noted.[31] When Willi Hoffer gained the editorship and the journal moved from Switzerland to Vienna, it improved enormously. Until it was closed down in 1938, the *Zeitschrift* was of central importance to the development of child analysis—and it continued to be so in its postwar Anglo-American reincarnation, *The Psychoanalytic Study of the Child*.

In both her seminar on the technique of child analysis and in her course on psychoanalytic pedagogy, Anna Freud made her students familiar with this history—quite a brief one—of child analysis.[32] The founding theoretical text was her father's *Three Essays on the Theory of Sexuality*, first published in 1905, and the key clinical text was her father's 1909 case study of a five-year-old, called "Little Hans," who suffered from a phobia. This study was the inspiration for a number of child observations conducted by analysts with the children nearest by—that is, their own. The informality of these parental efforts is obvious in works like Carl Jung's "Psychic Conflicts in a Child," which Jung discussed with Freud while they were on their 1909 America trip. The paper was based on Jung's four-year-old daughter, Agathali, and her younger sister, Gretl, although, curiously, the girls appear in Jung's paper as Anna and Sophie, which seems to be a joking way of indicating that Sophie Freud greeted Anna Freud's entry into the world with jealousy and rage comparable to that directed at Gretl by Agathali.[33]

Of Freud's close associates, the one who contributed earliest and most rigorously to both child analysis and psychoanalytic pedagogy was Sandor Ferenczi. He lectured on psychoanalysis and education at the first International Psychoanalytic Congress in Salzburg, 1908, and over the years he gave a great deal of his attention to questions about how a child's instinctual life could be helped rather than hindered by education. Ferenczi promoted analysis of children in Budapest, and his colleague Sigmund Pfeiffer wrote one of the foundational works on play therapy. Two Ferenczi trainees, Ada Schott and Melanie Klein, made Berlin the first important center for child analysis after their emigrations there. In Berlin, Karl Abraham fostered the work of the émigrés from Hungary and also of the German Josefine Müller. Anna Freud's only predecessor in Vienna was Hermine von Hug-Hellmuth, who was a retired elementary-school teacher with a Ph.D. in philosophy from the University of Vienna. Hug-Hellmuth had updated her prewar work on play therapy with an extended paper at the 1920 Hague Congress, which Anna Freud had heard. She also reported to the Vienna Society on her play sessions with children, usually in their homes; but it was left to Melanie Klein and Anna Freud to turn this play technique into a properly psychoanalytic method.

From Jung's work too a strand of child analytic work went out: the most important of his followers for the Freudians was a Protestant pastor, Oskar Pfister, who incorporated psychoanalytic teachings into his counseling work with children and adolescents. Pfister, in turn, influenced Ernst Schneider, director of the Teachers' Seminary in Bern, and Heinrich Meng, a young analyst who had joined Schneider in work on the pedagogical *Zeitschrift*. Hans Zulliger, who applied psychoanalytic educational ideas in the Swiss state school system, provided model programs for the Viennese Education Ministry in the late 1920s.[34]

When his early followers began to treat children, Freud discussed with them the peculiar technical conditions of their work. Jung told him of a six-year-old he had seen at the Burghölzli, and Freud, commenting on the case, recapitulated one of his own key discoveries.

In your six-year-old girl, you must surely have discovered in the meantime that the attack [or seduction] is a fantasy that has become conscious, something which is regularly disclosed in analysis and which misled me into assuming the existence of generalized traumas in childhood. The therapeutic task consists in demonstrating the sources from which the child derives its sex-

Annerl, alias "Black Devil," age three

The Freud family: Anna and Sophie (in front row), Oliver, Martha Freud, Minna Bernays and Ernst (in middle), Martin and Sigmund Freud (in rear). Mathilde, the oldest child, was absent.

Sophie and Anna Freud

Anna Freud as a schoolgirl: 1909, age thirteen about six months after her appendectomy

Oliver, Sophie, Minna Bernays, Martha Freud, an unidentified young woman, Anna (about age fifteen), Martin and Ernst, with a photograph of Sigmund Freud on the table

Bottom, A postcard sent to the Freud household in 1912: Sophie, Martin, Hans Lampl (standing in the middle), and Ernst with friends

Anna Freud (about age sixteen)

Above left, Loe Kann before her marriage to Herbert ("Davy") Jones

Above right, Anna Freud in 1914 (age eighteen), from a travel permit issued in London

Below left, Ernest Jones, 1914

Below right, Lou Andreas-Salomé, who came in December 1921 for a six-week visit to Berggasse 19

Anna Freud with her students on a visit to Hungary, 1918

Anna and Sigmund Freud at The Hague, International Psychoanalytic Congress, 1920

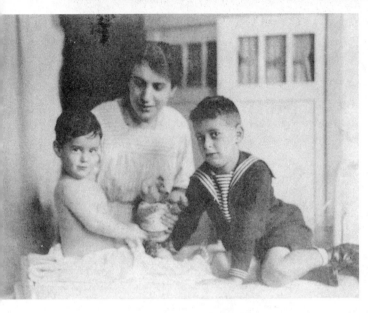

Anna Freud with her nephews Heinerle and Ernst Halberstadt, 1922

Freud with his Committee in 1922: Ferenczi and Sachs (in front), Rank, Abraham, Eitingon and Jones (left to right, behind)

Top, Dorothy Burlingham and Anna Freud on a trip to the Semmering in Dorothy's car

Above, Anna Freud with her dog Wolf and some of the children who attended the Burlingham school (including Tinky Burlingham, center, with short blond hair)

Middle right, Dorothy Burlingham had arrived in Vienna with her four children in 1925.

Right, Anna Freud with Michael Burlingham (circa 1928)

Left, Anna Freud at the weekend cottage Hochroterd

Below, A picnic at Hochroterd with the Burlingham teenagers and friends (Anna Freud's back is to the camera)

Bottom, Ernstl Halberstadt and Anna Freud playing together at Hochroterd

Anna Freud in the Jackson Nursery
Garden, 1937

Dorothy Burlingham helping out
with the Jackson Nursery feeding
experiment

The Jackson Nursery pediatrician
Josefine Stross

Anna Freud and Sigmund Freud leaving Vienna, 1938

Anna Freud and Sigmund Freud in the back garden of 20 Maresfield Gardens, London, 1938

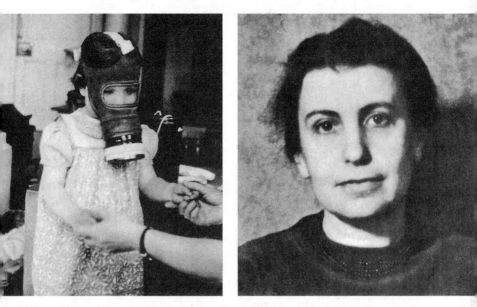

A child in the Hampstead War Nursery learns to wear a gas mask

Anna Freud after her 1946 illness

Anna Freud with August Aichhorn in 1949—a photograph of herself that pleased her

Anna Freud with Dorothy Burlingham—a vacation in Suffolk, 1949

Anna Freud with the Princess Marie Bonaparte in St. Tropez (circa

A ceremony in front of 20 Maresfield Gardens to celebrate the Freud Centenary and dedicate a historical plaque, 1956

Martha Freud shortly before her death in 1951

Anna, Ernst, Mathilde, and Martin Freud at the Freud Centenary celebration

Anna Freud, Josefine Stross, Ilse Hellmann, Willi Hoffer and other Hampstead staff members at a case conference

Anna Freud with one of Dorothy Burlingham's grandchildren, Annie Heller

Anna Freud with Ralph and Hildi Greenson in California, 1959

Dorothy Burlingham at eighty

Albert Solnit, Anna Freud, Dorothy Burlingham, and Joseph Goldstein in Ireland for a working session on *Beyond the Best Interests of the Child*

Anna Freud at eighty-five with her puppy Jo-Fi

ual knowledge. As a rule children provide little information but confirm what we have guessed when we tell them. Questioning of the families [is] indispensable. . . . Another reason why the child fails to talk is that, as your observation shows, she enters immediately and fully into the transference.[35]

In such discussions—and Freud had similar ones by letter with Lou Andreas-Salomé—he had come to see the key technical problems of child analysis: the lack of verbal free associations, the need to seek extra-analytic information and support for the analysis, and the quick transference reactions. But this was as far as child analysis got before the First World War induced a four-year hiatus in its growth.

When Anne Freud, Melanie Klein, and their colleagues in Austria, Germany, Hungary, Holland, and England began to practice after the war, no organized exchanges about their branch of psychoanalysis had taken place, and the very interesting Russian experiments with psychoanalytically based "progressive education" by Vera Schmidt and others had disappeared from view in the Bolshevik Revolution. The field of child analysis grew up in the 1920s. And it matured just as Freud was formulating a new theory, known as the structural theory, which denominated psychic functions as id, ego, and superego, as well as a controversial hypothesis that there are two fundamental instincts called Eros and the death instinct.

As a teacher, Anna Freud had to introduce her students to the history of their field, a history of its infancy, at the same time as she worked out an integration of that history with her father's structural theory and his dual-instinct hypothesis. She was hesitant in this integrative project, for reasons that she explained many years later to one of her contemporaries, Lawrence Kubie.

I [grew up], as you did, with the working concepts of the division of the mind into unconscious, preconscious, and conscious. I felt on familiar ground there, and, like you, I experienced some hesitations and difficulties when my father introduced the new division into id, ego, and superego. My argument was at the time that the gain accomplished by recognition of the unconscious parts of the ego did not make up for the loss in the essential distinctions with regard to consciousness and unconsciousness. Looking back now, I believe that I felt halfhearted about the matter and that—even where I used the structural terms in writing and talking—I continued still to visualize matters for myself in thinking by means of the older topical terms. Then the turning point came for me when my father wrote the *Outline* [in the last years of his life], which is one of my favorite essays in psychoanalysis. Somehow things fell into place for my understanding in a new way. It seemed right to me to divide the mind according to aims and functions, id, ego, and superego each pursuing their aim in life to the best of their possibility. This gave me a real sense for the purpose of life, or rather for the conflicting purposes in human life which are inevitable, once a higher development of the personality is attempted and reached. . . . From then onward, I found it natural to base my thinking on the "structure of the mind." To think of unconscious, preconscious, and conscious as qualities now instead of as topical areas did not seem to give them second place; on the contrary, these qualitative factors seem to offer the only real explanation for the struggle between the parts of the mind being such a muddle— as if they were not only at cross-purposes with each other but also speaking different languages and acting out their intentions in a totally different medium.[36]

Anna Freud's cautious adoption of the structural terms was matched by an equally cautious reaction to the much more controversial death-instinct proposition of Freud's *Beyond the Pleasure Principle* (1920). She never did use this term, "death instinct," but the instinct theory that it presented was definitely included in her metapsychological view. Clinically, she spoke of aggression, on the assumption that the death instinct is not necessarily in a direct way the source for or cause of aggression: the nature of the relation between the two being mysterious, she preferred to speak of aggression independently, without reference to the death instinct. Nonetheless, her early work, although it was clinically as attentive to aggression as to libido, was also theoretically reticent about aggression. In this, she differed from other theorists, like Melanie Klein, who did assume that aggression was a direct manifestation of a biological death instinct, and who stressed aggression in early infancy even more than libido.

Anna Freud's first lectures on child analysis proceeded as though she had taken the Training Institute's curriculum as her guide: she started with general theoretical points and clinical investigations, arriving at metapsychology only in her third year. But she worked toward her third year all along, and particularly in her in-house seminars with her father, where she concentrated on a view of transference in child analysis that ran counter to the expectations he had noted earlier to Jung. While she prepared her first lectures, Anna Freud took all her amendments of his views to Freud for his opinion, and he was impressed by her independence. In November 1926, Freud noted to Max Eitingon:

The most enjoyable event right now is Anna's course on child analytic technique. I suppose that she communicates with you about it. But it is really the general opinion that she knows how to hold the attention of her audience. She tells me the content of each lesson on the evening before, and I am especially gratified that she does not, like a student, simply apply what she has learned elsewhere; she is unconstrained as she deals with the subject, she judges for herself and knows how to assert the particularities of this kind of analysis. Compared to the opinions of Klein, hers are conservative, one might even say reactionary, but it looks as if she is right.[37]

Anna Freud's own assessment of her progress was a little more restrained and more complicated in its portrait of how she stood in relation to her colleagues at the Institute. She wrote to Lou Andreas-Salomé in 1928:

You know, when I am analyzing or when I imagine something in my own mind, then it appears to me as totally clear and, if not "simple," then at least transparent. But if I listen to others in the Society then things look more complicated and difficult, as if I myself wanted to see a simplicity where there is none. This probably comes from the fact that the others understand things better when they distance themselves from the human beings and put things in coldly theoretical terms. And with me understanding just disappears very easily when it is detached from the human being. I feel this strongly during my supervisory hours, which make up the greater part of instruction at the Institute. Dr. Deutsch, for example, always gives the students whom she

supervises a perspective on the total picture of the relevant neurosis. But I always stay—because I cannot imagine it otherwise—
with the momentary situation between patient and analyst and
all the consequent complications for the analyst's attitude. My
way is totally practical, but I would like to learn the other too.
Papa thinks it will come with more experience.[38]

Anna Freud did not doubt her approach to child analysis; she
only questioned her ability to translate it into theory and to teach
it on a level of great generality. Her hesitancy did stand her in good
stead, however, as she and her father compared notes on their continuing reactions to Rank's theory of the birth trauma. They agreed
that any single element of psychoanalytic theory, if taken à la carte
and pushed to its logical extreme, removed from clinical experience
and offered as the key to all mysteries, was bound to be wrong. In
his version of their agreement, contained in his *Inhibitions, Symptoms and Anxiety*, Freud took what he thought was worthwhile from
Rank's theory and abandoned the rest—trying as he did to leave aside
his views on the state of Rank's mental health. Freud clearly set
himself apart from the notion that any cause—birth trauma or any
other—would ever turn out to be demonstrable as "a single, tangible
'ultimate cause' of neurotic illness."[39] Reaffirmed in this conviction,
Freud was not ready to be convinced that intrapsychic conflict with
a superego of great severity was the one cause of neurotic illness.
This was Melanie Klein's "revolutionary" view.

D URING THE months when Otto Rank had published *The Trauma
of Birth*, gone to America, and then returned to Vienna preceded
by his shocking letter to Freud, the Berlin child analyst Melanie
Klein, Karl Abraham's analysand and protégée, had presented two
challenging papers. The first was a general statement about the
technique of "early analysis" (for children aged two to five), delivered to the April 1924 International Congress in Salzburg, and
the second was a case study of a six-year-old obsessional girl, Erna,
presented to the First Conference of German Psychoanalysts that
fall at Würzburg. Klein was invited to lecture before the Vienna

Society in December, and, as it turned out, her visit came just after Otto Rank's depressed, repentant return from Paris to seek Freud's understanding and forgiveness. The coincidence of Melanie Klein's emergence as a theorist to be reckoned with and Otto Rank's dramatic upheaval and eventual departure was fateful. Particularly because Klein's work so clearly echoed Rank's universalizing claims about the role a primal anxiety experience has in the course of a child's Oedipal relations, there was a predisposition toward skepticism in Vienna. But, on the other hand, Anna Freud's recent lessons in her father's school of tolerance had taught her to hold back her response to new ideas until she had had time to let them settle in her mind and—more importantly—to test them in practice.

Anna Freud was cautious about Melanie Klein's child analytic theory and technique in 1924, and she had discussed it often with her friends Bernfeld, Hoffer, and Aichhorn, who all felt that Melanie Klein was mistaken in her equation of dissociality (or delinquency) and neurosis. But she did not publish any critical statements until 1927, after she had had a chance to expand her own practice, face the trial run of her first lecture course at the Training Institute, and—most importantly—consider a case comparable to Melanie Klein's six-year-old obsessional Erna. Anna Freud's case, the six-year-old Adelaide Sweetzer, who was an American friend of the Burlingham children, figured very prominently in her *Introduction to the Technique of Child Analysis*, the book that she made from her lecture notes and used to bring the differences between her own approach and Melanie Klein's into very stark light.[40] The book obviously had a didactic function: it was developed as a teaching manual at the Training Institute, and it advertised clearly what kind of child analysis was practiced in Vienna—in what came to be known as the Vienna School. The published volume, and Anna Freud's later lectures based upon it in Berlin and Budapest, attracted to Vienna the cadre of child analysts who eventually made Anna Freud's techniques the dominant ones in Continental Europe and America.

Melanie Klein, feeling that her work was not appreciated in Berlin, particularly after Karl Abraham's death in December 1925, responded to the interest she had generated on a lecture tour in England and emigrated there in September 1926.[41] She was then forty-four years old—Anna Frend's senior by thirteen years—and an imaginative, contentious, and ambitious theorist. Ernest Jones, who had engaged her to analyze both his two young children and his wife, Katharine, gave Melanie Klein his support in many ways, including the sponsorship of a symposium in May 1927 at which Klein and a number of her English supporters replied to the criticism Anna Freud had published in her *Introduction to the Technique of Child Analysis*. When this symposium was published in the *International Journal of Psychoanalysis*, which Jones edited, the distinguishing features of both child analytic camps were clear, and over the remaining fifty-five years of Anna Freud's life, even as the controversy was thickened with layers of new issues, the initial terms of confrontation remained. There were peace treaties but no fundamental reconciliation.

AT the center of the debate between Anna Freud and Melanie Klein lay Klein's most challenging theoretical innovation: she held that a child's superego develops very early into an "immutable" structure, a "highly resistant product, at heart unalterable."[42] Very often (if not always) the superego is "fantastically severe" in its strictures, and interpsychic conflict with this superego is the inceptor of infantile neuroses. The superego does not, as Freud held, develop with the dissolution of the Oedipus complex, as the legacy or residue of the child's abandoned desires, as the replacement by identifications with the parents for these unfulfilled and unfulfillable Oedipal desires. Rather, Klein held, the superego develops with the Oedipus complex, which "ensues upon the deprivation experience of weaning, that is, at the end of the first year or the beginning of the second year of life." The superego derives from the child's own cannibalistic and sadistic impulses, not from any identifications with parents. Although "imagoes" of the parents are present in the child's mind as the Oedipus complex ensues, the superego, Klein said, "differs fundamentally from those objects [i.e., parents] which really initiated its development. Of course, children (but also adults) will set up all kinds of ego-ideals, installing various 'superegos,' but this surely takes place in the more superficial strata and is at bottom determined by that one superego which is firmly rooted in the child and whose nature is immutable." Like Otto Rank, Melanie Klein looked to an anxiety experience—hers was weaning accompanied by oral aggressiveness or sadism—that analysis could reactivate and relieve. But, most crucially, she challenged Freud's theories both about the timing of the Oedipus complex—putting both its upsurge and its peak (age three) earlier—and about the relation of the Oedipus complex to the superego.

The immediate practical consequence of this theoretical position was that Melanie Klein, assuming no essential difference between the child's and the adult's superego, advocated minimizing the differences between child analysis and adult analysis. Anna Freud, on the other hand, because she felt that the child's superego is, unlike the adult's, dependent on external (parental) influences, emphasized the ways in which child analysis must and should differ from adult analysis. Melanie Klein acknowledged—as all child analysts do—that children do not free-associate verbally as adults do; but she considered the actions of children's play in analytic sessions to be equivalent to verbal free associations, and she interpreted them as such. But, except for the difference in medium of communication, she felt that a child analysis should be conducted like an adult analysis. By contrast, because Anna Freud stressed the child's continued connection—psychically and in reality—to its familial surroundings, she recommended a period of nonanalytic preparation for analysis. She also devised methods for keeping in close touch with a child's parents, and advocated measures for adding to the analytic work a dimension of education or pedagogy to help the child fit the analytic work and its results into life at home and in school. Anna Freud also stressed the importance of working from a detailed life history of the child patient and accounting, in the analysis, for "reality factors." All of these recommendations seemed to Melanie Klein both unnecessary and corrupting to the analytic process.

Within the analytic work itself, the techniques advocated by Anna Freud and Melanie Klein were dramatically different. Klein suggested that, from the very start of the analytic sessions, deep interpretations of the child's play actions should be offered to the child. When a child rammed two little cars together in his or her play, Melanie Klein would tell the child that this represented parental intercourse. Her interpretations inevitably headed toward the child's experience with or knowledge of a "primal scene" of parental intercourse, which Klein assumed "generally occupies the foreground of the picture in early analysis."[43]

A typical instance of Klein's procedure appears in her case study of the obsessional Erna: "Erna used very often to play at being mother. I was to be the child, and one of my greatest faults was thumb-sucking. The first thing which I was supposed to put in my mouth was an engine. She had already much admired its guilded lamps, saying, 'They're so lovely, all red and burning,' and at once put them into her mouth and sucked them. They stood for her mother's breast and her father's penis."[44] In Anna Freud's technique, such interpretations, if they had been suggested by a great deal of material, would come later in the analysis; the child had to be prepared analytically, by cultivation of the positive transference and analysis of resistances, to receive them without extremes of withdrawal or aggressive rage. Anna Freud's presentation of her six-year-old obsessional girl emphasized the girl's slow struggle to control her aggressions, which she had split off into a "devil" self, once the analysis had carefully granted her both knowledge of them and permission to express them in the analytic session.

Melanie Klein's early "deep" interpretations presumed that transference (both positive and negative) is established immediately by child patients (as well as by adults) and that it should, thus, be interpreted in its ubiquity from the beginning. The analyst actively offers interpretations from the start, so that Ernest Jones's little daughter's description of Kleinian analysis always struck Anna Freud as perfect: "While children play, women talk."[45] In Klein's technique, success depends upon the correct content of the deep interpretations, not upon the preparation for them, the timing of them, the analytic and extra-analytic contexts of them—not, in short, upon any means of reaching the depths from the surface of consciousness. Anna Freud, on the other hand, held that children do quickly form transference reactions but that they do not produce a "transference neurosis," a relation with the analyst that recapitulates the early parental relations. She noted that "a child is not ready to produce a new edition of his love relationships because, as one might say, the old edition is not yet exhausted. His original objects, the parents, are still real and present as love objects, not only in fantasy as with the adult neurotic.[46] Because she did not assume a "transference neurosis," Anna Freud did not read a child's relation to her as an image of the child's relation to its parents and interpret accordingly.

To Melanie Klein, Anna Freud's circuitous methods seemed to slow the development of child analysis, the extension of Sigmund Freud's insights into early childhood development. She could—and often did—claim that Sigmund Freud's account of "Little Hans's" analysis provided the prototype of a child analysis conducted on the same principles as an adult analysis.[47] Why, then, should Anna Freud, such an echoer of her father's theoretical views, modify adult analytic technique when she turned to children? The answer that Melanie Klein and her English supporters gave to this perfectly legitimate question was that Anna Freud unconsciously resisted the revelations of strictly conducted, deep child analysis; her technical modifications were manifestations of her resistances. As Joan Riviere, one of Freud's translators and a former analysand, put the matter at the May 1927 London symposium:

> Psychoanalysis is Freud's discovery of what goes on in the imagination of a child—and it still provokes great opposition from all of us; this "childishness," these unconscious fantasies are abhorred and dreaded—and unwittingly longed for—by us even yet; and this is why even analysts still hesitate to probe these depths. But analysis has no concern with anything else; it is not concerned with the real world, nor with the child's nor the adult's adaptation to the real world, nor with sickness nor health, nor virtue nor vice. It is concerned simply and solely with the imaginings of the childish mind, the fantasied pleasures and the dreaded retributions.[48]

The messages of this passage were two: first, as Freud noted in a letter to Ernest Jones, Riviere's propositions opened "the way to the removal of analysis from the sphere of reality," and, second, they opened the way to the charge that Anna Freud feared to probe the depths to which Kleinian analysis led.[49]

The second of Joan Riviere's messages was the public version of the claim Ernest Jones had made much more directly in a private letter to Freud.

It is a pain to me that I cannot agree with some of the tendencies in Anna's book, and I cannot help thinking that they must
be due in part to some imperfectly analyzed resistances; in fact
I think it is possible to prove this in detail. It is a pity she published the book so soon after her first lectures, but I hope she
may prove as amenable as her father to further experience. This
hope is strengthened by my admiration for all her other qualities—also analytic ones.[50]

Freud replied to this letter, so patronizing toward his daughter and
so critical of his own ability as her analyst, by reiterating his intention to stay out of the controversy. But he also restated his opinion
that "the view of Mrs. Klein about the behavior of the ego ideal [or
superego] in children appears to me completely impossible and stands
in contradiction to all my basic assumptions." Freud did not complain specifically about Jones's most personal challenge, he simply
admonished Jones with the general lesson he had also tried to teach
when Otto Rank's views were being debated:

When two analysts are of different opinions on one point, the
assumption that the erroneous view of one may originate in the
fact that he is not completely analyzed, so that he allows himself to be influenced by his complexes at a cost of science, may
in some cases be completely justified. But in practical polemics
I consider such an argument is not admissible, because each
party can make use of this argument and it does not help to
come to a judgment as to which party is in error. It has therefore been generally agreed to remove the use of such arguments
and where there is a difference of opinion to let further experience bring enlightenment.[51]

The exchange between Freud and Jones continued, and Freud continued to hold firmly, though privately, to his convictions: "I would
like to contradict Mrs. Klein in this point, that she regards the superego of the children [to be] as independent as that of adults while
it appears to me that Anna is right in emphasizing that the infantile superego is still under the direct influence of the parents."[52]

Until the London symposium was published, Freud stayed on
this high road of gentlemanly disagreement. Anna Freud even had
trouble getting him to interrupt his vacation rest for a look at the

London symposium papers when they arrived in Vienna during September 1927. But, with the help of Ferenczi, who was visiting, she convinced Freud to read what Melanie Klein, Joan Riviere, Ernest Jones himself, and three other British analysts had written in criticism of her book. Freud was furious and sent off a sharp letter to Jones, whom he held responsible for "organizing a veritable campaign against Anna's child analysis" and for allowing Klein to advance a claim that Freud thought willfully misinterpretive.[53] Arguing from a passage in Anna Freud's book, Klein had stated that Anna Freud did not analyze children's Oedipus complexes. This view was, Freud realized, a buttress to Jones's own claim that Anna Freud's "imperfectly analyzed resistances" kept her from deep analysis. Jones wrote a measured, thorough reply to Freud's angry letter, but he did not—in his reply or ever—address the challenge Freud cast at him: "Who, then, has ever been sufficiently analyzed?" I can assure you that Anna has been more deeply and thoroughly analyzed than, for instance, yourself."[54]

With his daughter, Freud tried to contain the anger he felt toward Jones, just as she had tried to contain her anger toward Rank when her father's feelings were being hurt. With his friends, Freud was less restrained. To Eitingon, he wrote:

This angers me much more than I want to show Anna. I did not conceal anything towards Jones [in the letter] and condemned severely the frivolity, the bad intentions, and the incredible theoretical nonsense that appeared [in the symposium]. Among other things, I got personal and told him that Anna certainly was analyzed for a longer time and more profoundly than he. The result of this cold water treatment has to be awaited. As you are now specializing in making peace, I can take over the aggression. Together, then, we will represent the typical father figure.[55]

When Jones's reply to the cold water treatment arrived, Freud was aroused to a more biting reflection: "I don't believe that Jones is consciously ill-intentioned; but he is a disagreeable person, who wants to display himself in ruling, angering and agitating, and for this his Welsh dishonesty ('the Liar from Wales') serves him well. Riviere claims that he chased her into her position, congratulated her on the telephone for her theoretical propositions, and then betrayed her when he told me that he had tried unsuccessfully to tone her down."[56]

Even though he never again corresponded with Freud on the topic, Jones continued, privately, to maintain that Anna Freud, still under the influence of her father and in the throes of her undissolved Oedipus complex, was projecting that psychic state of affairs into the technique of child analysis she advocated. He also made no secret of his opinion about Freud's bias in the controversy, and he stated that opinion quite baldly in his biography of Freud: "In a long discussion with Freud I defended Melanie Klein's work, but it was not to be expected that at a time when he was so dependent on his daughter's ministrations and affections he could be quite open-minded in the matter."[57]

Freud never offered his correspondents a private opinion about Melanie Klein, nor did he tell Jones directly his interpretation of Jones's fascination with Klein's views. But, when he was writing to Eitingon and Ferenczi, Freud made it quite clear that he thought Jones's hostility to Anna was revenge for Anna's having refused in 1914 to let Jones court her.[58] More generally, Freud thought that Jones was using Klein's work to achieve the originality he had never been capable of in his own work: "Since his very first work about rationalization, he has not had any original ideas, and his application of my ideas has stayed on a schoolboy level. Therefore his sensitivity. I am a piece of his superego, which is dissatisfied with his ego. He fears to discover this dissatisfaction in me, and, as a by-product of his pathological displacement, he has to take care that I have reason to be dissatisfied."[59]

Freud and Ferenczi also had political hypotheses. They speculated that Jones, who had had difficulty in 1925 with a palace rebellion against his leadership of the London Society, had brought on Melanie Klein to recharge the Londoners' enthusiasm for his intellectual command. Ferenczi paid a visit to London in June of 1927, on his way home from an American lecture tour, and made an effort to warn the London analysts to be careful about Melanie Klein's influence on them and also not to accept uncritically her or Jones's accounts of the kind of opposition her work had aroused in Berlin.[60] Freud and Eitingon also discussed the possibility that Jones wanted to foment the child analysis controversy in order to have a reason to separate from Freud, and to establish an Anglo-American psychoanalytic realm under his own hegemony. But Freud could do little, he often said, about these speculations or about the controversy itself because he felt that he had no way to defend himself against the charge of nepotism. "We have not only to avoid nepotism but any semblance of it."[61]

FREUD, Eitingon, and Ferenczi, who became a little circle within the circle of the Committee after Rank's departure and Abraham's death, had all found Jones's support for Melanie Klein's views as well as his tyrannical ways in the London Society distasteful.[62] But they linked forces against Jones on quite another issue, the one that preoccupied Freud in 1926 and 1927 far more than the child analysis debate. Jones had refused to adopt Freud's unqualified support for the practice of psychoanalysis by nonmedical people. He viewed himself as a mediating figure between Freud's view that psychoanalysts should avoid medical education and its complete opposite, the view of a majority of American psychoanalysts that nonmedical people should not be allowed to practice. To Freud and Ferenczi, if not to Eitingon, who was somewhat closer to Jones on the topic, Jones's middle ground was nothing but a corrupting compromise: Jones wanted medical education strongly recommended but not required.

The prospect that Jones might win the presidency of the International Psychoanalytic Association in 1927 and swing it toward his compromise made Freud very anxious. Ferenczi was Freud's choice for the office, but, when it became clear that Ferenczi would meet strong opposition from Jones, Freud persuaded Eitingon, who had wanted to step down from the presidency, to let himself be a candidate again. When Eitingon agreed, Anna Freud let herself be nominated for general secretary of the International Association, for she too felt protected from Jones's hostility.[63] She was elected, and 1927 marked the beginning of her roles in the International Association as the one who corresponded with everyone else, the one on the executive board who both stood for lay analysis and was a lay analyst, and the one who represented Freud.

The debate over lay analysis and the debate over child analysis overlapped in important ways. Ostensibly, the opponents of lay analysis were most worried about how nonmedical people could work without being able to diagnose organic illnesses and psychoses, the provinces of medicine and psychiatry. But they were also worried about the effects of analysis on children, and wanted this specialty to be attached to pediatrics. In America, child analysis was originally thought to be a relatively easy matter, not requiring medical training; but as the number of lay analysts working with children increased, the medical practitioners felt their dominance threatened. Many European child analysts, including both Melanie Klein and Anna Freud, were lay analysts, and many of the nonmedical students who came to the institutes in Vienna and Berlin for instruction were interested in child analysis. Both institutes had training programs for educators and school administrators, and these people too, even though they did not intend to practice as analysts, were nonmedical.

Freud tried to proselytize for his position on lay analysis by writing *The Question of Lay Analysis* (1926). The book was immediately translated for an American edition, for which Ferenczi wrote a preface, and a symposium for reactions to it was organized as a joint project of Jones's *International Journal of Psychoanalysis* and the *Zeitschrift für Psychoanalyse*, edited by Sandor Rado. Jones published the lay analysis symposium in the same volume with the symposium on child analysis, and he also made a strong statement in his own contribution that linked the two issues: Freud's publication was, Jones wrote, "obviously biased"—and many readers then and since have construed that phrase to mean biased by Freud's interest in his daughter's career.[64]

Anna Freud made an indirect contribution to the lay analysis debate by allowing an American contact of Ferenczi's, Pierce Clark, to prepare an edition of her *Introduction to the Technique of Child Analysis* for publication through the Nervous and Mental Disease Publishing Company, a medical house. But her book did not have an English edition until 1946, because Ernest Jones refused to publish it through the International Library, which he controlled. Anna Freud was not surprised by this rejection, as she had become quite familiar with Jones's attitude toward her work, but she decided not to seek an alternative publisher in Jones's dominion. To mollify her, Jones explained, disingenuously, that the British analyst Barbara Low had prepared an extensive summary of Anna Freud's work for the non-German-speaking British before the May 1927 symposium at which it was the focus of criticism. But he did not try to hedge on his reasons for rejecting the book: he simply thought it ill founded, premature, and detrimental to the progress of analysis.[65]

Jones's editorial high-handedness had the consequence that Sandor Rado, who edited both of the German psychoanalytic journals, *Imago* and the *Zeitschrift*, turned down a German edition of the London symposium on child analysis. This kind of trading of insults, in combination with the behind-the-scenes maneuvering over the Association's presidency and the very in-front-of-the-scenes disputes over lay analysis, made the amosphere at the 1927 Innsbruck International Congress very tense. The American medical analysts who opposed lay analysis came to the meeting in small numbers but with the powerful dicta of a recently passed resolution in the New York Society condemning lay analysis and a bill before the New York legislature for making it illegal. Anna Freud made herself the heroine of the meeting when a heated debate broke out over a resolution that would have given the Association's International Training Commission authority to draw up obligatory regulations governing candidates trained in a country other than their own. This resolution would, in effect, have abrogated the autonomy the Americans had recently claimed for themselves. Anna Freud offered, over the fray, a show-stopping charge: "Meine Herren, ich glaube wir thun ein Unrecht" ("Gentlemen, I think we are committing an injustice"). She explained that the Americans should not be told what to do when they had only three voting members at the meeting, a representation not at all proportionate to their numbers. This intervention had the result that the entire dispute was suspended until the next Congress, at Oxford in 1929, where it was again left unresolved.[66]

Anna Freud's less dramatic contributions to the lay analysis debate were educational. Her seminar at the Training Institute brought many nonmedical students—including Dorothy Burlingham—into child analysis as a subspecialty of analysis; her classes for nursery and primary-school teachers in Vienna spread concern for child development psychoanalytically viewed into the Viennese school system;

a series of public lectures invited by the Viennese Board of Edu-
~~~on gave her, for the first time, a forum for interesting school administrators in psychoanalysis.[67]

THE increase in child analytic practice in Vienna, Berlin, and Budapest also brought Anna Freud new experiences to confirm or dis-
confirm the theoretical and technical positions she had taken in her
first book. Slowly, over a number of years, she modified several of
her technical recommendations. As psychoanalysis for children became more familiar, she felt that analysts no longer needed to expend
as much effort on preparing a child for analysis and maintaining
educational contact with both the child patient and the parents.
She and her colleagues began to treat children younger than the
latency-period six-to-ten-year-olds with whom she had first worked.
They saw children down to the age of two, and thus of the same
age as Melanie Klein's youngest patients. Much of the stimulus for
these changes came, however, not from Klein but from Berta Bornstein, a Berlin-based child analyst who worked in Vienna during
1929. Bornstein was also the analyst in Anna Freud's circle who contributed most to the direction that both their latency and their
"early analysis" efforts took: toward analysis of defenses. It was
Bornstein's work in this direction that convinced Anna Freud to
give up the introductory or preparatory nonanalytic phase of a child
analysis. As their techniques for defense analysis developed, the Viennese combined them with the methods August Aichhorn had originated, added some of the technical ideas from Reich's *Character
Analysis*, and began to treat older children, into early and late adolescence. The experience her group gained with prelatency and post-
latency children then helped Anna Freud toward one of the key
hypotheses of her second book, *The Ego and the Mechanisms of
Defense* (1936): that the order in which a small child has developed
various defenses can be seen in the order in which that child recapitulates the early defenses in puberty and adolescence.

But, even though many of Anna Freud's ideas about extra-
analytic preparation and education shifted, her own work and that
of her colleagues convinced her of the essential correctness of her
views on superego development and on the consequence of superego
development for analysis, that is, the absence in child analysis of

the kind of transference neurosis that is central to adult analysis. In a lecture delivered at the International Congress in Innsbruck, Anna Freud presented a case vignette that illustrated her view very clearly. She noted a communication published by the first analyst to practice in Russia, Moshe Wulff, about a little girl of 1½ whose parents had tried to enforce their toilet-training demands too early. The child "could not come up to their requirements and became upset, fearing that she would be sent away. Her anxiety became acute in the dark or when there were unfamiliar sounds, for example, when someone knocked at the door. She constantly asked whether she was good, and kept repeating the plea not to be sent away." When the parents, following Wulff's advice, relaxed their demands and reassured their child each time she soiled herself that they loved her, her anxiety disappeared and she was calm again. "If the child's anxiety had been due to excessive superego development," Anna Freud concluded, "the parents' reassurances would not have had any influence on the symptom. If, however, the cause of her anxiety was fear of the displeasure of her real, living parents, and not of their internalized images, then it is easy to understand that the symptom would have been removed." For Anna Freud, such episodes showed the accessibility of the child's developing superego to influence, and set the contrast between children and adults clearly: for an adult neurotic, "the freer the surroundings into which he is transplanted, the stronger the fears of his drives, his neurotic defense reactions, and his symptoms. The demands which his superego makes upon him are no longer open to influence from his surroundings."[68]

The difference in theoretical and technical views that such examples highlighted were of enormous interest to Anna Freud's followers for social and political reasons as well as for strictly psychoanalytic ones. To socialist activists like Bernfeld and to graduates of the socialist youth movement like the members of the *Kinderseminar*, some form of the belief that altering environments can improve the psychic condition of children was crucial. The Vienna School of child anlysis was, from its inception, linked with efforts to help juvenile delinquents (Aichhorn's specialty), to give working-class children educations appropriate to their situations (the goal of Bernfeld's Baumgarten Children's Home), and child guidance centers for young children (like the Vienna Society's center, directed by

Sterba). Anna Freud herself was not a socialist and had not ʌe kinds of experience in the youth movements familiar to of her colleagues, but her sympathies clearly went in the socialist direction, for scientific if not for political questions.

On the other hand, the English supporters of Melanie Klein, like Melanie Klein herself, were not given to founding institutions for the furtherance or the testing of their work, and their upper-class traditions of cultural radicalism and political conservatism set them in great contrast to the Viennese. Only one of Melanie Klein's English supporters was involved with education: Susan Isaacs, a Cambridge graduate, was the first principal of the Malting House School in Cambridge, which had been founded by Geoffrey Pyke, an educational visionary who stressed the importance of fantasy in a child's mental development.[69]

ANNA Freud's first independent educational experiment was a practical extension of her view that children in analysis needed a psychoanalytically informed school environment to help them fit their analytic work into their daily social lives. She also thought that they needed means by which their parents could be kept in touch with the analytic work and educated to help it. Dorothy Burlingham's four children were the immediate concern: they were being privately tutored by a young man named Peter Blos, who in his later life as an émigré in America was one of the leading psychoanalytic writers on adolescence. But in such a situation the children did not have school friends or a life beyond the family circle. With their friend Eva Rosenfeld, Anna Freud and Dorothy Burlingham organized a school, which was housed first in the Rosenfelds' home and then in a little building in their back garden. The Burlingham children, the Sweetzer children, and a number of other seven- to thirteen-year-olds who were either in analysis themselves or had parents in analysis attended the school to be taught by Peter Blos and his assistant, an artist named Erik Homburger Erikson—later one of the most famous of Anna Freud's trainees in child analysis.

Blos and Erikson taught by what was known as the "project method," which Anna Freud had used when she was a teacher. The method was an outgrowth of John Dewey's theory that children learn best when their interest is fully engaged and centered. "The whole school," Erikson later recalled, "would for a time become, for example, the world of the Eskimos. All subjects were then related to Eskimo life—geography, history, science, math and, of course, reading and writing. This called for an ingenious combination of playful new experience, careful experiment and free discussion, while it provided a sense of contextuality for all the details provided." The students went on trips throughout the city to visit museums and attend concerts, always following out a theme. One Chrismas the theme was Old England, and at the Burlinghams' apartment everyone assembled for "a Yule log, carols, acrobats, dancers, and a boar's head and mistletoe"—with Sigmund Freud as a special guest.[70]

The school also gave Anna Freud an opportunity to be helpful to analytic colleagues whose children needed special attention. One of these was Reinhard Simmel, the son of Ernst Simmel, the physician who had worked with war neurotics in Berlin and later established a sanatorium, Schloss Tegel, where Freud stayed when he was being treated by his Berlin oral surgeon. Early in the spring of 1927, Simmel asked Anna Freud if she would take his son into analysis, for the boy had become "vulnerable, thinner, even more nervous."[71] Reinhard had been in analysis with Melanie Klein after Simmel and his wife divorced, and he had improved, but Simmel thought he was relapsing. Arrangements were made for Reinhard to stay with Eva Rosenfeld and to attend the school, so that his analysis could begin in September 1927. He arrived, that is, just in time to be (as Anna Freud noted) "an illustration of the English controversy" on display in the London symposium papers.[72]

Reinhard Simmel was Anna Freud's first direct acquaintance with the results of a Kleinian analysis, though she had given a consultation at about the same time to the relatives of a "fifteen-year-old aggressive boy, who during his analysis with Miss Searl [an English Kleinian] nearly destroyed his family."[73] (This boy she referred to August Aichhorn.) Her task was, as she told Simmel, complicated: "Frau Klein has revealed to him the deepest layer of his problems; the surface area was not even touched, so I have to work with him in a remarkably roundabout way, detouring from bottom to top, to end up where I usually start out. The trump card, which I usually play to persuade a patient, is in his hand already."[74] This succinct tarok-party simile for her usual analytic route—from surface slowly down through the defenses or resistances to the bottom, to the secret of the defense structure, the trump—summarized Anna Freud's conviction that a quick interpretation might be deep, but could not be lastingly therapeutic.

Anna Freud was certainly aware that her practical or technical methods looked very conservative, even superficial from the Kleinian perspective; but from her own point of view, Anna Freud feared that her methods might look—in comparison to the accepted techniques of Freudian adult analysis—"wild" and unanalytic. She put a great deal of effort into clarifying and justifying her methods theoretically. She had written at the conclusion of her *Introduction to the Technique of Child Analysis*:

> I am prepared for the practicing analysts among you to say, after what [you] have heard here, that my methods with children are so different that they cannot be called real analysis at all, but are a form of "wild" analysis which has borrowed all its tools from analysis but in no way conforms to strict analytic principles. But consider: if an adult neurotic came to your consulting room to ask for treatment, and on closer examination proved as impulsive, as undeveloped intellectually, and as deeply dependent on his environment as are my child patients, you would probably say, "Freudian analysis is a fine method, but it is not designed for such people." And you would treat the patient by a mixed method, giving him as much pure analysis as he can stand and for the rest child analysis—because, owing to his infantile nature, he would merit nothing else.[75]

THE controversy between Anna Freud, who thought of her work as "wild" and was accused of ultraorthodoxy, and Melanie Klein, who thought of herself as the true Freudian and was accused of being "wild," had one more public upsurge before both women drew back in the 1930s to expound their visions—and revisions—in more ranging books. The occasion was the 1929 International Psychoanalytic Congress—the first Congress to be held on English soil.

Anna Freud went to England with two documents in hand. One was a public letter from Freud that she was to read at the formal celebration of Ernest Jones's fiftieth birthday, which was six months after the actual birthday, but two days before the Congress. Freud had complained bitterly to Eitingon about how little he wanted to say anything in praise of Jones and how badly he played the role of diplomat; but Eitingon and Anna Freud had convinced him that, for the sake of peace, the letter should be written. Freud complied and even sent Jones a private letter minimizing the recent "family quarrel."[76]

But Anna Freud also took with her a paper for the Congress, where she joined Melanie Klein, Nina Searl, and David Eder, all of the British Society, on a child analysis panel. This paper, "A Counterpart to the Animal Phobias of Children," only made the family quarrel worse—as did, from the other direction, Melanie Klein's "The Importance of Symbol Formation in the Development of the Ego."[77] Anna Freud's paper was hotly contested by Melanie Klein, but neither their debate nor Anna Freud's paper, which was published only in German, made their ways into the *International Journal of Psychoanalysis*, which Jones still edited with his firm hand. Anna Freud's reports to her father were sent in daily telegrams. "Anna is having rather a hard time in Oxford," Freud told Lou Andreas-Salomé; "by this evening she will have given her paper and will then, I hope, take things more easily. As to the accommodation, she writes, as one might expect: 'More tradition than comfort.' I expect you know that the English, having created the notion of comfort, then refused to have anything more to do with it. Like Wolf, I can hardly wait for her return. I write, and he spends half the day lying apathetically in his basket."[78]

Anna Freud certainly knew that her paper would be contested, but she had written it without the anti-Kleinian polemical cast of her *Introduction to the Technique of Child Analysis*. Rather, the paper offered a critical revision of a segment of her father's 1926 work *Inhibitions, Symptoms and Anxiety*. This book had been finished before Anna Freud's *Introduction*, but she had not taken account of it there. Her Oxford paper, on the other hand, shows a very careful study of it. And her Oxford paper was, also, her first step in the direction of *The Ego and the Mechanisms of Defense*, which was framed by and suffused with ideas from *Inhibitions, Symptoms and Anxiety*—some of which she adopted and some of which she revised.

In "A Counterpart to the Animal Phobias of Children," Anna Freud used two of her child cases to question an assertion that her father had made as he reviewed his own early case study of "Little Hans," the five-year-old with a horse phobia.[79] What distinguished Little Hans with his neurosis from a normal boy with typical Oedipal mother-love and father-fear was, Freud claimed, "the replacement of his father by a horse." Anna Freud protested this formulation by comparing to Little Hans a seven-year-old patient of hers who had, like Little Hans, hated and feared his father as a real rival in relation to his mother. This boy, however, had produced not a phobia but a fantasy in which he had a tame lion—a substitute for his father—which loved him and frightened everybody else. Another boy, ten years old, had not just a tame lion but an entire circus of animals that he had trained to be good to one another and not to attack humans. In this circus master's fantasy, the father was turned into the animals, and their tamed and appropriated strength protected him against any renewal of his anxiety about his father. If fantasies such as these are successful in denying reality, Anna Freud argued, the ego has no need "to resort to defensive measures against its instinctual impulses and to the formation of a neurosis."

Freud's formulation—"the replacement of his father by a horse"—had, Anna Freud argued, covered up a key difference between normal and neurotic displacements. Her argument represented her first step in the direction of one of the most important areas of her later research—normal developmental psychology—but it also represented a generalization from her own experience. She was a fantasizer, a daydreamer who had satisfied her "father loves only me" wishes masochistically but not necessarily neurotically. Beating fantasies and lion fantasies both fit the conclusion Anna Freud drew in her paper:

> The efforts of the infantile ego to avoid unpleasure by directly resisting external impressions belong to the sphere of normal psychology. Their consequences may be momentous for the formation of the ego and of character, but they are not pathogenic. When this particular ego function [i.e., avoiding unpleasure] is referred to in clinical analytic writings, it is never treated as the main object of investigation, but merely as a by-product of observation.

Freud himself had not made two of Little Hans's fantasies the main object of his investigation. After he had been cured of his horse phobia, Hans fantasized that he had a number of children whom he cared for. Then he fantasized that a plumber, who had taken away his buttocks and penis, fitted him with bigger ones. These fantasies, Anna Freud argued, were means of denying two crucial realities of his life: that his mother took care of his much-resented little sister, and that his father had buttocks and a penis much larger than his own—two intractable givens. All children, not just neurotic ones, need ways of dealing with their littleness and their objective reasons for envy and jealousy—as Anna Freud herself certainly knew.

Although he was revising her father's analysis of Little Hans's case, Anna Freud was doing so in the spirit of his book. In *Inhibitions, Symptoms and Anxiety*, Freud had made a relentless effort at posing very basic questions: why does one person develop a neurosis and another not? why one kind of neurosis rather than another? why one type of symptoms rather than another? These questions were designed to distinguish the secure areas of psychoanalytic knowledge from the mysteries, and to highlight the significance of Freud's new theory of anxiety. His book was structured like a labyrinth: in each chapter he raised a question and gave it an answer, which he would then, turning to another chapter, another question, show to be insufficient or confusing. Many readers of the work declared that Freud was sinking into pessimism—deeper pessimism—because he found so little secure ground. Anna Freud had the opposite reaction, which she expressed to Eitingon: "The remarkable thing is that Papa—unlike all the others—continually emphasizes how much remains unexplained and uncertain about these questions, so that one gets the feeling of being surrounded by the completely questionable, the unknown, where one can only here and there see the first clues. With the other psychoanalytic writers, everything is always so known and fixed, so well tidied up, that one really has to become suspicious."[80]

In the context of the Klein debate, the general perspective of *Inhibitions, Symptoms and Anxiety* was also very important. Freud admitted that in *The Ego and the Id* (1923) he had made the ego look like a beleaguered garrison, always fending off assaults from the id, the superego, and the outside world. This image, he noted, had neglected the bonds and reciprocities among the id, its former other half (the ego), and its offshoot (the superego). The new theory of anxiety advanced in the book, which situated anxiety in the ego and claimed that anxiety dictates repression in response to dangers, rather than arising as a consequence of repression, made Freud caution against "overestimating the part played in repression by the superego." He noted: "The earliest outbreaks of anxiety, which are of a very intense kind, occur before the superego has been differentiated. It is highly probable that the immediate precipitating causes of primal repressions are quantitative factors such as an excessive degree of excitation and the breaking through of the protective shield against stimuli."[81] Such statements about the superego were supportive of the stand that Anna Freud had taken in her debate with Melanie Klein, and her revision of the "Little Hans" case was, she thought, in perfect accord with them.

While Anna Freud kept her attention on the relations between the child's inner world and its outer one, and between pathology and normality, Melanie Klein made a further step in her declared direction: into the depths. At Oxford she too offered an amendment to Freud's *Inhibitions, Symptoms and Anxiety*. She declared that "the early stages of the Oedipus conflict are dominated by sadism" and went on to put aggression even more firmly at the center of early childhood development than she had in her previous work.[82] Both Melanie Klein and Anna Freud turned, after the Oxford confrontation, to elaborating theories of psychic defense—but these elaborations only set them further apart.

5

MECHANISMS OF DEFENSE

THERE WAS, as both Sigmund and Anna Freud undoubtedly knew, a kernel of truth in the charge that Ernest Jones had leveled at *Introduction to the Technique of Child Analysis*. Freud protested his daughter's independence, and she stressed how different her technique for child analysis was from the technique her father had developed for adult analysis. She had no hesitation about questioning his "Little Hans" analysis. But what was at issue was not whether Anna Freud did or did not adhere to her father's theoretical or technical views, which were at any rate still evolving, but whether her innovations reflected limitations in her own self-knowledge—"unanalyzed resistances" as Ernest Jones had put it. Such limitations are reflected in any psychoanalytic contribution, of course. What time and testing by other analysts reveal is the meaning of the limitations for the truth or falsity of the contribution. Freud had carefully weighed Rank's birth trauma theory, for example, and noted in *Inhibitions, Symptoms and Anxiety* where he located the borders of its truth. Other analysts did the same.

The two elements of her first technical recommendations that Anna Freud later withdrew were the most obvious manifestations of her unresolved father-complex. Child analysis does not, she eventually decided, require a preliminary nonanalytic period of preparation in which the child's trust is won and a positive transference established as the major artery for future transference traffic. Secondly, the analyst does not have to perform pedagogical functions during the analysis if the analysis itself can obviate the need for pedagogy. Anna Freud's cautiousness about providing preparation and pedagogy had its merit for controlling and containing children's aggression and destructiveness. But, on the other hand, it stood in the way of analytic exploration of aggression and of negative transference.

Anna Freud was quite well aware that she was inhibited about revealing to her own father-analyst the persistence in her life of her "unreasonable" need for praise and admiration. She had turned to Max Eitingon with her analyses of how much she wanted to be judged by her father as more reasonable than the girls and women he had in analysis, and with her efforts to understand the need for appreciation and the vague "wanting-to-have-something" feeling that the Burlingham children and their mother aroused. But she expressed to Eitingon nothing negative about her father, except on the occasion of his Christmas 1926 trip to Berlin without her—and with her mother. Even then, her anger was quickly covered over with pleasure in her father's enthusiasm and good health. With Eitingon himself, however, when he was in the role of correspondence-analyst, she was often contentious and complaining: he did not write often enough, he did not send the proper birthday letter, he did not take precisely the right positions on political issues, he insisted on making peace—particularly with Ernest Jones—when she was attacked. Behind the adoration of Freud that she expressed to all her correspondents, there was a prickliness that came forth only to a substitute, like Eitingon. "People who harbor fantasies of this kind," Freud had written in 1919 of the "a child is being beaten" patients, "develop a special sensitiveness and irritability towards anyone whom they can include in the class of fathers."[1]

A distance gradually grew between Anna Freud and Eitingon, which by 1930 was a gulf: "between him and me things are no longer as they were," she told Lou Andreas-Salomé.[2] The surviving correspondences do not make the situation quite clear, but it seems that Eitingon had wanted Anna Freud to detach herself more from her father—perhaps more available for his friendship—and she had refused. Anna Freud lamented that the friendship was "sunken," but she was furious that Eitingon seemed so unaffected by the change: "I think what humiliates me so is not his loss, but that he takes my loss so lightly, that he gives me up so easily."[3] There was a negative transference, but displaced onto Eitingon, the quasi-analyst.

In her emphasis on positive transference in child analysis, Anna Freud's own reluctance to express negative feelings toward her father was crucial. But the other side of the story was that she wanted for herself, as an analyst, the love and admiration not of all her patients, adult or child, but specifically of the ones who became like children of her own—the Burlingham children and, to a lesser extent, Adelaide Sweetzer and her brother, Harold. Anna Freud had been candid with Eitingon about wanting more than just to make the children healthy; she wanted, also, "to have them, or at least to have something from them, for myself." Her desire was, she noted, useful for her work—temporarily. But she did not say how the temporarily useful pursuit of the children's love and admiration was to be halted or converted into something else—and this was equivalent to the technical question of how preparation for analysis and establishment of a positive transference could allow, eventually, expression of negative feelings. When she wrote *Introduction to the Technique of Child Analysis*, Anna Freud had all six of the American children in analysis, which meant that they were two-thirds of the cases on which she had based her technical recommendations.

It is on the technical or therapeutic level that Anna Freud's unresolved father-complex is most obvious in her early work. She focused her theoretical attention on the Oedipal period, on the progress and dissolution of the Oedipus complex, and did not follow the direction her father had indicated in his "Some Psychical Consequences of the Anatomical Distinction Between the Sexes." That is, she did not—like most of Freud's female trainees—turn her attention to early childhood, the pre-Oedipal period, and to the role of the mother in children's lives. Neither female psychology nor the topic of gender differentiation were taken up in any terms except those focused on male castration anxiety and female penis-envy. The father was the main character in the psychic stories Anna Freud told.

The presence in Vienna of coworkers like Berta Bornstein, who had begun to develop "defense analysis" as a method that made both nonanalytic preparation for analysis and the emphasis on positive transference unnecessary, challenged Anna Freud far more effectively than the broadsides from Melanie Klein and her followers in London. But the difference between the views she expressed in *Introduction to the Technique of Child Analysis* and those in her Oxford paper, the shift from battling with Klein to extending the reach of her father's "ego psychology" into the domain of normal development, relates directly to a shift in her attention toward Dorothy Burlingham and toward the Burlingham children as they entered puberty and adolescence. She did not give up any of the duties she had assumed as her father's nurse, secretary, and companion, but, as Freud himself noted in an October 1927 letter to Eitingon, "Anna . . . geht ganz in der Freundschaft auf"—she was totally absorbed in her friendship with Dorothy Burlingham.[4] Both Sigmund Freud and Martha Freud worried that their thirty-two-year-old daughter was further than ever from any thought of marriage, but both loved Dorothy. Martha Freud found it easier to be affectionate with her—signing her letters to "my dearest Dorothy" with "a hug"—than with her daughter.[5]

Two things changed deeply in the late 1920s. Anna Freud's father-complex was no longer conflictive for her, both because of her analysis and because she had so securely won her father's admiration and so gratifyingly become his companion. On the other hand, she had balanced her need for him with her new friendship and her family life.

THE two women left Dorothy's children with their nanny and made a first vacation trip together in 1927. They toured the northern Italian lake district, traveling by motor launches from island to island, staying in small pensiones with balconies where they could sit sunning, enjoying the mountains, and—in Anna Freud's case—writing home. This was her first vacation away from her father since the onset of his illness, since their excursion to Rome together in 1923, and she was very apprehensive. She requested a daily letter from Freud, who was at the Cottage Sanatorium recuperating from one of the many operations on his jaw, and she sent him letters, postcards, and a daily telegram announcing her address and immediate travel plans. As the scheduled end of the trip approached, Anna

Freud made a small but, for her, momentous decision: she tele-
grammed her father and asked whether she was urgently needed,
for, if not, she and Dorothy were considering extending their holiday.
Freud immediately replied that he hoped they would stay on, and
she was delighted, without apparently feeling that her contributions
to his comfort had been slighted.[6]

Both the taking of an independent vacation and the extending
of it were breaks with Anna Freud's traditions and contrary to her
reputation. Her father often characterized her in letters to his friends
as someone who took things too seriously and worked too hard.
"She works really well," he told Ferenczi in 1927, "but, like all
women, she is always fanatical and makes herself very tired."[7] And
to Eitingon in 1928: "Anna works quite well, but she is a female
[Frauenzimmer] and does not husband her strength."[8] These characterizations, with their easy assimilation of his daughter's behavior to
an unexplained universal feminine condition, would have been understood by his colleagues as references to his views on "feminine
masochism." Freud held that the masochist's basic desire is "to be
treated like a small and helpless child, but particularly like a naughty
child," and he categorized the desire as feminine (whether in men
or in women) because it is accompanied by fantasies representing
typically female situations, "being castrated, or copulated with, or
giving birth to a baby."[9]

Overworking can be an active, ascetic, internalized version of
collaborating with a punishing parental fantasy figure: it is not just
that exhaustion and illness come along as punishments, but the feeling of being beleaguered, beaten down, spreads into every part of
life, demanding more and more good—though never good enough—
behavior. As Anna Freud wrote to Eitingon after a particularly
strenuous week of her regular work plus a lecture in Berlin:

> After this I was very run-down, and really did take a two-day
> weekend, though it was not very profitable. In the meantime,
> though, the headaches I have had for so long went away. Now
> I only become tired much too easily, and I don't know what I
> should do about this. Sometimes I have a terrible desire to take
> a little vacation, to see and hear only lovely things, and not to
> do anything. There is the matter of sleep, which never tallies up
> to the proper amount at the end of the week; but there is also

much more to this condition. People with whom one would like to speak but cannot; things one would like to acquire; affairs one would like to keep in order; letters and all sorts of other possibilities. Sometimes, also, the complications in which my patients and even my colleagues are caught seem so great to me that the amount of courage required to join up with their struggles is frightening. I know that in my own life I am simply spared from so many complications. Maybe because of this I do not know well enough how difficult it is for the others?[10]

But, as she became closer to Dorothy Burlingham, Anna Freud both gave herself the vacations that broke her overwork routine and acquired some of the complications that made her less a creature apart. Robert Burlingham and his father, C. C. Burlingham, appeared in Vienna several times during 1928, and the upheaval these visits caused Anna Freud's child patients and their frail mother, who was "worn down by the constant torment" of her husband's behavior, was dramatic.[11] Both Anna Freud and Sigmund Freud became involved in complex negotiations: Burlingham was in the care of an American psychoanalyst named Amsden, in Budapest, and the Freuds pressured both Amsden and Ferenczi to do their best to keep Burlingham in Budapest and to convince him not to sue for custody of his children after Dorothy Burlingham finally gave up any hope of his cure. The Freuds then negotiated Dorothy's change of analysts, from Reik to Freud, by carefully engaging Eitingon as the mediator, so that they would not be directly involved. "Dorothy's disgruntlements"—as Anna Freud called her friend's tumult during her first analysis—were part of Anna Freud's lesson in domestic patience and care. Being convinced of the inadequacies of Reik's treatment and having, at the same time, to wait until Dorothy was ready to change was not easy: "Understandably, I always tolerate her disgruntlements rather poorly," she wrote to Eitingon.[12]

When Dorothy's situation became less fraught, and her analysis with Freud had begun to release what Lou Andreas-Salomé referred to as Dorothy's "strong productive capacity"[13] for analytic work and writing, Anna Freud too was more able to enjoy their retreats and recreations. She was even converted to the American two-day weekend—though hers ran from Saturday noon to Monday noon—in her new venue.

The next step was the purchase of their country place in the Semmering. The ramshackle cottage was slowly restored, on plans Ernst Freud drew up, by contractors and troops of Burlinghams and Freuds. Neighbors named Fadenberger, a couple with two children, kept the cow and watched over the property. Anna Freud and Dorothy Burlingham made the forty-five-minute drive out on Wednesday afternoons to keep the house and garden in order and to bring fresh milk and vegetables back to Vienna for their families. Then, for the weekends, they took children and friends for the picnics, berry picking, horseback riding, and genteel farming. The Fadenberger's younger child, a blond-haired, open-faced girl called Annerl, after Anna Freud, and called "our child" by Anna Freud, joined the parties and posed for dozens of photographs with her unusual friends. Anna Freud also made a photographic record of the cottage in all stages of its renovation, and she sent albums of these, with commentaries in verse, to the two people she wanted most as visitors—her father and Lou Andreas-Salomé.

The life that developed after the 1927 vacation trip and especially after the purchase of the cottage was in the starkest contrast to the one that Anna Freud had described to Eitingon in October 1926, about a year after the Burlinghams had arrived in Vienna: "Psychoanalysis is a good occupation, but now and then one would also like to set up a house, or merely to help someone do so, or simply to have free time. But, then, it is always either/or and not simultaneously, which would after all be much nicer."[14] Then she had felt drained by the people around her: "because one is useful, one will be carried off piece by piece during the daytime; no one takes much interest in the unusable bit that is left by the evening—though, strangely enough, that unusable portion is the real self."[15]

It was Anna Freud's unexploitable self—or the self that did not desire to be exploited—that flourished in Dorothy Burlingham's company and at the cottage called Hochroterd. A kind of retroactive nonanalytic cure for her childhood unsociability went on: "It is funny," Anna Freud told Lou in 1928, "but only last year and this did I really enjoy my birthday. Until then there were too many mixed feelings, and now everything is much simpler: only beautiful. I even had a big afternoon children's party."[16]

Dorothy Burlingham had the remarkably generous ability to

understand and accept that Anna Freud's strongest and most important feeling would always be for her father; their friendship and family life always came second. But that order of things did not mean that the friendship was not the balance, the expansion of horizons, a lesson in love. Nor did it mean that any lesser degree of loyalty was involved. Anna Freud had initially expected a repetition of her rupture with Loe Kann Jones, or a version of her father's long-ago break with Fliess. "Do you remember in the Semmering the way you said friendships only last a certain length of time, then change?" Dorothy asked after they had known each other for fourteen years. "How that upset me. As a matter of fact, it is generally true—certainly the friendships I used to have [in America] are no more. . . . [But] if you made friends with me as I was, I don't see why you should not keep me as I am. . . . Your faith in me has always done more for me than anything else."[17] Dorothy Burlingham thought of herself as the one who had been redeemed, by Anna Freud and by Sigmund Freud; but she was also the one who kept Anna Freud from staying entirely in the shelter of her father's sure affection, tied there with the lesson she had drawn from observing all the complications of other peoples' lives: "As far as I can see," Anna Freud had confided to Dorothy, "being in love is never really enjoyable."[18]

Anna Freud's growing up came late in relation to the developmental line psychoanalysis had established: her adolescent turn outside of her family for friendship and love was still in course when she was faced with her father's illness in 1923. She was almost twenty-eight then, and almost thirty when the Burlinghams arrived. Her analytic practice, her membership on her father's Committee, and her responsibilities at the Vienna Training Institute had suddenly filled her days and taught her a great deal in a short time about human beings and their complexities. She could not be "a hermit" (as she had once described herself to Lou Andreas-Salomé) whose only pleasures were knitting, weaving, reading Rilke, and taking solitary walks. "So much is no different from me," she told Lou in 1927, "and I can understand things that I simply could not understand earlier. I don't know if it is the result of analyzing or just getting older?"[19]

•

WHILE she was successfully entering into her career, the other Freud children were also settling. Ernst's architectural practice flourished, and he had the honor in 1926 of traveling to Palestine to build a house for Chaim Weizmann, a leading Zionist political figure and later the first president of Israel. Oliver's marriage in 1923 was very good for him, and he was delighted with the birth in 1924 of his first (and only) child, Eva, a charming, lively girl. Martin used his law degree in banking, and, although his marriage was not a harmonious one, his two children, Anton Walter (named after Anton von Freund) and Sophie (named after her aunt), were a pleasure. Mathilde slowly recovered from the terrible disappointment of losing Sophie's little Heinerle in 1923. One of her consolations was that she and Anna had grown closer as they knitted and made dresses together for weeks after the boy's death. Anna got Mathilde involved in one of her largest knitting projects: a veritable wardrobe of sweaters and dresses for Lou Andreas-Salomé, who lived on a small income from her practice. As Mathilde came through her mourning, she was able to appreciate one of their father's favorite little jokes about Anna: "If the day comes when there is no more psychoanalysis, you can be a seamstress in Tel Aviv."

Mathilde and Anna saw another disaster through together in 1931. Robert Hollitscher's niece, Edith Rischavy, who had left her mother's pensione in Merano to seek analytic treatment with Lou Andreas-Salomé, then moved to Vienna to be near her Uncle Robert and Aunt Mathilde. But she had a severe episode of mental illness, was hospitalized, and took up an analysis with Freud's colleague Hermann Nunberg. When a wound in her hand became infected and the infection spread, she was in such a weak state that she died.[20] At the same time Rosi Winternitz was in a sanatorium after a relapse into schizophrenia. She had become pregnant by a young poet named Ernst Waldinger and married him in 1923 at a ceremony in the Freuds' apartment, despite his lack of a job or prospects, and their impoverished, chaotic married life had been too much for her.[21] These episodes came soon after the suicides of Tom and Jakob Seidmann, so the extended Freud family was in constant need of support—emotionally, and also financially. Dorothy Burlingham had even tried to convince Anna Freud that they should find a way to adopt together the Seidmanns' little girl, Angela (who eventually went to relatives in Haifa).

Her cousin Rosi's condition was particularly distressing to Anna Freud. In a tone that indicates how clearly she had become an elder in the family, she told Frau Lou that Rosi "was always my problem child (*Sorgenkind*), and I had hoped to be able to protect her." But Rosi's institutionalization had coincided with one of the most frightening and prolonged installments of Freud's illness, one that involved nearly seven months of sanatoria, doctors, surgery, and secondary pneumonias. "Do you still remember," Anna Freud asked Lou in January 1931, "what you said at the time of the Japanese earthquake? One thinks oneself so secure and then a shrug of the Great Mother's shoulder comes and everything collapses. I thought of that when Papa had pneumonia and now with Rosi."[22]

Through the time of these family troubles, Anna Freud acquired the reputation among those who knew her well of having a very high tolerance for stress. She very seldom retreated into her fantasy world, her nice stories, and she no longer behaved as jealously and angrily as she had toward Otto Rank when people troubled Freud or strained his trust. When Sandor Ferenczi began to show signs of leaving Freud's circle in the late 1920s, she suspended judgment and awaited developments. Ferenczi had begun to advocate a therapeutic technique that involved supplying good mothering and tender caresses to compensate patients who had missed out on love in their childhoods. Anna Freud felt about this, as she said in 1931 to Lou Andreas-Salomé: "it is not troubling as long as this method is confined to Ferenczi, for he has the necessary restraint for it. But others should not do it. I am very much afraid that Ferenczi will draw back from us and close himself off."[23] Ferenczi, the Freuds knew, suffered from pernicious anemia; he was under the care of their friend Lajos Levy in Budapest, who kept them posted. But no one found it simple to assess what caused Ferenczi's retreat from Freud and his touchiness when Freud questioned his psychoanalytic innovations.

In his biography of Freud, Ernest Jones claimed that Ferenczi had had psychotic episodes in his last years, but his jealousy over Ferenczi's closeness to Freud certainly influenced his judgment, which angered Ferenczi's many friends, including Lajos Levy.[24] Anna

Freud never came to a conclusion or a diagnosis. When Ferenczi, sixty years old, died on May 24, 1933, the anemia having affected his spine and brain, the Freuds were grieved for him and his widow, Gisella, but their attention was overshadowed by events in Germany. The anti-Semitic measures Hitler enacted on becoming chancellor threatened the psychoanalytic institutes and immediately deprived Eitingon of his role in the Berlin Policlinic. No Jews were allowed to head scientific organizations. Eitingon was contemplating emigration to Palestine, and that possibility meant that of the original six Committee members only Ernest Jones would be in Europe to work for the cause. Anna Freud had to assume the Continental secretarial duties of the Committee in addition to her other responsibilities.

EVEN friends who did not see Anna Freud that often noticed the change in her after she became involved with her Burlingham family, her practice, and one organizational position after another. Katá Levy, while she was sorting through her papers in 1952 and preparing to emigrate from Hungary to England, read through her correspondence from Anna Freud and summarized—with the benefit of hindsight—what had changed. Her story started in 1918.

> From the start I was much older. I was "dear old Katá," and you asked once in a postscript whether you were to me a daughter or a sister. For a while, you were only concerned with being grown-up, something that I—apparently—already was. Then for a time we were like sisters, with all the accompanying jealousy. I was a "straight little oak tree" and certainly not [illegible] enough and you seem to have felt at that time like the rich girl who, on account of her money, fears to be loved or, more precisely, to get married. You seem to have felt, for example, that my interest in you was really an interest in your father. . . . But then you started to march forward in seven-mile-a-step magical boots: you were in the Society, you worked for the publishing house, you became grown-up, learned a great deal of scientific thinking (from Lou Andreas-Salomé, too). During our summer visits, then, I always had the feeling that I was superfluous. And we didn't notice it at all when it came: you became the *older* sister. Via detours through social work and sculpting, I finally did find my profession in psychoanalysis; and I had a great deal to learn about it from you.[25]

To her father's friends Anna Freud was no longer "the little daughter," and to her own older friends she was a peer. She no longer automatically transferred to new situations her complicated feelings about being the littlest one in her own family and not able to be her father's companion. She did not issue laments like the one she had written in 1922 to Lou Andreas-Salomé: "I regret that I was not born 30 or 40 years earlier, then I would not have to be such a belated hanger-on to you and Papa."[26] Even Lou Andreas-Salomé suggested in 1928 that Anna Freud had changed so much that she should give up being "Daughter-Anna" and become a sister. "I am glad that I should be your sister," Anna Freud told Frau Lou, "but I always look way up when I look at you."[27] Their agreement on sisterhood, however, came only after Anna Freud had had a period of nervous reaction to her friend's feeling that she had changed. "When we first met, I was so happy that you liked me the way I am and did not, like most others, expect something in me which I didn't have. Can't you do that anymore? I think I haven't changed as much as you think. Or did Edith [Rischavy] tell you a lot of stupid things about me?"[28]

Anna Freud was annoyed at being the subject of gossip, either on her own or as Dorothy Burlingham's companion, and eager not to have her new life misconstrued or labeled homosexual. She disliked it when less intimate friends remarked on her new contentment and she completely quashed any suggestion that Dorothy Burlingham, much less Dorothy Burlingham's wealth, had made a difference in her own life. But when Ernst Simmel asked if he could give her a gift to thank her for what she had done for his son in analysis, he was quite surprised to learn that she had no wishes—a condition no psychoanalyst would find plausible. She explained: "That I am so without wishes is an old complaint and not connected solely with Dorothy Burlingham, as Eva Rosenfeld thinks. I believe that it comes from the fact that, with me, all my wishes have always been met with fulfillments and that I really do have so many more possessions than other people."[29] Anyone who had known her as a little girl renowned for the number and insatiability of her wishes would have found this an amusing rewriting of personal history; but it did serve the purpose of covering her new contentment with an old cause. To a friend like Max Eitingon, she could be more honest: "That I never have wishes, not even so that you can fulfill them, is an old story. The cause of it, as we have jokingly noted in the old Berlin times, is my immodesty, which makes the wishes so high in the beginning that reality can never reach up to satisfy them."[30]

Behind all the changes, though, was the fact that Anna Freud always had to worry about her father, as he went from one episode of trouble—with his heart, his lungs, his sinuses, his bowels—to another, and from one operation on his jaw to another. He had shown such patience and equanimity that she was buoyed by him: "Papa is very calm and in a good frame of mind and not afraid—I try to catch some of this from him."[31] But she became able to support him in turn, drawing more on her own strength and less on his as the years passed. As she said in 1933: "It is good that I react so slowly, for that way I am functioning when it is needed most. Somewhere [each operation] takes a piece of me. But that is just the way it is. One cannot ask for the raisins without the surrounding bun. I understand that."[32] But she was, on the other hand, fortunate that her achievement of a kind of inner peace came in a period of relative social peace and prosperity. Her material wishes were, if not entirely fulfilled, as she claimed, at least fulfillable.

AFTER the founding of the Austrian Republic in 1920, there was nearly a decade during which neither Austrian politics nor world politics impinged drastically on either the Freuds or psychoanalysis. In Austria, there was constant contention between the Social Democrats and their opponents, the Christian Socialists, which was made very sinister by the growth on both sides of private armies. But Vienna itself, known to the Christian Socialists as "Red Vienna," was securely in Social Democratic hands and became a model for the period of progressive socialist municipal governance. The municipal government's offer to the Vienna Psychoanalytic Society in 1927 of a parcel of city land for its headquarters was the most remarkable sign of political understanding that the Society had ever received. And the offer was all the more important because it came soon after the Socialists had suffered through a tense time when riots and arson at the Palace of Justice seemed to augur civil war.

The chief friend of psychoanalysis in the municipal government was Hugo Breitner, the financial councillor whose ambitious projects

included taxing the Viennese wealthy to provide the Viennese prole-
tariat with affordable housing and adequate schooling. He was very
interested in the kind of training for the city's schoolteachers that
Anna Freud, August Aichhorn, Siegfried Bernfeld, and Willi Hoffer
wanted to offer through the Training Institute. And it was he, along
with the inspector of schools, Anton Tesarek, who arranged for
Anna Freud to give a series of four lectures—later entitled *Psychoanalysis for Teachers and Parents*—to the staff of the city Hort, or
working-class day-care system.[33] This same Hugo Breitner miracu-
lously stayed in office even after 1933, when the national leader of
the Christian Socialists' army, the Heimwehr, stood on the steps of
the Town Hall and prophesied to a wildly enthusiastic crowd that
Breitner's Jewish head would soon roll in the dust.

It was just as the wave of extended family troubles hit the
Freuds that the relative peace in Austria began to end. The 1929
financial disaster in America percolated through Europe, and by
June 1931 the main Austrian bank, the Creditanstalt, which had in
its charge most of Austrian industry and also the psychoanalytic
publishing house's small estate, crashed. The Verlag was able to
stumble on with help from its subscribers, consolidation, and very
capable negotiations with its creditors by Martin Freud, who had
lost his job in the crash and soon after had taken up financial direction of the house.

In the wider world of Austrian politics, there was less resiliency.
With the banking crisis went the very possibility of coalition politics
in the national government and any independence Austria had enjoyed from the backers of its nation-state status—France, England,
and, most important, Mussolini's Italy. Into the chancellorship from
the obscurity of the Agriculture Ministry came Engelbert Dollfuss,
and in short order Austria was, with Mussolini's urging, an authoritarian, corporatist state, fervently Catholic and fervently anti-Socialist
and anti-Semitic. Dollfuss pledged his government to two tasks: independence from Germany and liberation from the internal sabotage
of Social Democracy. At first, he had little success in "Red Vienna,"
but as the unemployment rate reached one-third of the population,
and as the threat of a Nazi takeover, an *Anschluss*, grew stronger,
Engelbert Dollfuss came to be viewed as a necessarily strong-armed
patriot even by those who shunned his domestic politics and his

bigotry. Sigmund Freud, whose hatred of Germany had intensified with Hitler's successes, often alluded in his correspondences to a celebration in August 1933 of the 250th anniversary of Vienna's victory over its would-be Turkish conquerors, and he shared the hope of Dollfuss's government that the current aspiring conquerors would also be stopped at the city's gates.

But domestic tension ran very high, and in February 1934, after Dollfuss ordered sweeping arrests of the Social Democratic leadership, the country plunged into a brief and fruitless civil war. Anna Freud, sounding quite like her father, remarked: "Our one wish is for peace and quietness. But reality is not very eager to fulfill our wishes just now."[34] The fighting taught Anna Freud a lesson: "What is true for today can become nonsense in no time at all. So one lives just in the present and must get used to it."[35] The Freud family adopted this idea with more or less success: "Papa is not doing badly and he always remains the calmest of us all," Anna reported, while her father, who often marveled at her strength and calm, admitted that "even Anna [gets] depressed."[36] (Neither reported Martha Freud's or Tante Minna's feelings.)

The Dollfuss regime, on the other hand, was not at all calm after order was restored. It became even more authoritarian, and wrote itself a new constitution to legitimate its excesses. But the Nazis in Germany and their counterparts in Austria were not pleased with Dollfuss's ability to deny Nazi participation in the government by his one-party dictatorship. They replied with an attack at the Chancellery on July 25, in the course of which Dollfuss was shot. For Hitler, the putsch in Austria was, however, not the step toward *Anschluss* that he had anticipated. It was a temporary setback, for it brought Mussolini even more strongly to the support of Austrian independence, and it resulted in a new chancellor, Kurt von Schuschnigg, who was Dollfuss all over again politically even though he was less ingratiating and less adroit.

For most of the socialist-leaning Jewish psychoanalysts in Vienna, the suppression of the Social Democrats and the installation of a Catholic one-party dictatorship marked the end of their hopes. The Berlin Jewish analysts had begun to flee after the 1933 anti-Semitic legislation; by 1934, German psychoanalysis was an "Aryan" business. New societies sprang up on the edges of Europe—in Czechoslovakia, Scandinavia—and old ones expanded to accommodate the Germans. The English and the Dutch were particularly helpful to refugees, and Ernest Jones's unstinting efforts in London both amazed Anna Freud and made it possible for her to work very closely with him after she had to take up the position of second vice president (and actual leader) of the Vienna Society in 1933. Because Paul Federn, the first vice president, was so given to holding up business over petty details and worrying excessively about questions of power, Anna Freud was challenged to run the Society without appearing to do so and to turn it at the same time into a refugee placement agency.[37]

When Eitingon, who had lost most of his family fortune in the American economic upheaval of 1929 and the European banking crisis of 1931, resigned his presidency of the International and decided to emigrate to Palestine, the Freuds were astonished and disappointed. Anna Freud particularly felt that Eitingon should have moved to Vienna. "Shouldn't we build up a new center for psychoanalysis, make the center here once again? I think that we will be allowed to work here. The manpower would be here to do it."[38] But Eitingon was convinced that he could make a life in Palestine for himself, for his wife, who sometimes resented his commitment to the Freuds, and for psychoanalysis. He did found a Society and bring a talented, dedicated group of pioneers to the land, but his health, which had declined after a thrombosis in 1932, never allowed him the new beginning he had hoped for.

Ernst Freud and his family prepared to leave Berlin for London as soon as Hitler's chancellorship was a fact. Oliver and his family, without Ernst's professional prospects, moved to Vienna. Oli was without a job, and he eventually decided to try his luck in Paris. Hermann Nunberg and his wife, Anna Freud's friend Margarethe Rie, stayed in Philadelphia, where they had gone for a year in 1932. Hanns Sachs took a position in Boston, where Franz Alexander had started out after leaving Berlin, and in 1934 the Boston Society also welcomed three Viennese: Helene and Felix Deutsch and Otto Rank's ex-wife, Beata, who had become a protégée of Helene Deutsch's. The Berlin emigration wave also brought to Vienna the Lampls, Theodor Reik, and Berta Bornstein—temporarily.

Among the younger Viennese, several aligned themselves with a group that grew up after the February 1934 fighting, the Revolutionary Socialists (R.S.), an underground resistance organization. The group was led by Otto Bauer, a militant Social Democrat, but its daily operations were directed by a workingman named Josef Buttinger. Buttinger formed an alliance—later a love affair, and still later a marriage—with an American psychoanalytic trainee named Muriel Gardiner, and she brought into his conspiracy her friend Edith Jackson.[39] After finishing her analysis with Anna Freud, Anny Rosenberg, who had divorced her first husband, Otto Angel, in 1928, worked for the resistance group as a courier and messenger. (She continued her anti-Nazi work in Holland after she emigrated there with her ten-year-old son in 1936, and she and her second husband, Maurits Katan, were active in the wartime Dutch Resistance.)

Even though they only expected the Austrian situation to get worse, many of the Vienna Society's younger members wanted to help keep the Society and its Institute, its Ambulatorium, its child guidance center going as long as possible. This was the goal that Sigmund and Anna Freud both articulated often and forcefully, although they were realistic enough to cultivate their influence in safer territories, for the future. Anna Freud, for example, joined the editorial board of the American journal *Psychoanalytic Quarterly* and produced for it in 1935 a Child Analysis issue dedicated to the work in Vienna.

Marianne and Ernst Kris, Grete and Edward Bibring, Willi Hoffer and his wife, Hedwig, all of whom later worked with Anna Freud in England, and Editha and Richard Sterba, and Jenny and Robert Waelder stayed on in Vienna as long as they could. Ernst Kris became Anna Freud's consultant on questions of scholarship—he supplied her with all her bibliographic references, and worked with her on organizing and clarifying her manuscripts—and Robert Waelder became her chief theoretical ambassador, undertaking a mission to England in 1935 for a scientific debate with the Kleinians.[40]

Ernst Kris and Robert Waelder also shared the editorship of *Imago* after 1932, while Paul Federn and Eduard Hitschmann took over the *Zeitschrift*. Freud made these appointments carefully, to keep both the journals headquartered for practicality's sake in Vienna, and to keep both the older and the younger generations involved in the fortunes of the Verlag. He was sorry not to be more confident in Otto Fenichel, whom he esteemed deeply for his erudition and the power of his intellect, but he worried that Fenichel's medical school friendship with Wilhelm Reich was still strong. Reich had fallen completely out of favor, in part because of his Bolshevism and in greater part because the Freuds felt that he had become quite unstable. As Anna Freud explained to Jones, when they were considering how to deal with Reich's membership in the International: "I could always get along with him a little longer than the others because I tried to treat him well instead of offending him. It helps a little way and would help more if he were a sane person, which he is not."[41]

Freud presented his desire to stay on in Vienna in terms of political assessments. He felt that the Austrian Nazis were incapable of the ruthlessness and organization of their German counterparts. The good old Viennese *Schlamperei* (careless ineptitude) would mark the majority of the Austrian Nazis, he felt sure. This opinion was not proved to be unrealistic until after the spring of 1935, an interlude when international criticism greeted Hitler's introduction of conscription in Germany. But, as the Führer became more and more assertive, Freud realized both that the Austrians would make fine partners for the German Nazis, and that Mussolini, who first embarked on his campaign in Abyssinia and then intervened to support Franco in Spain, was quite prepared to hand Austria over to Hitler. He wrote to Jones in March 1937:

> The political situation seems to be becoming ever more somber. There is probably no holding up the Nazi invasion, with its baleful consequences for psychoanalysis as well as the rest. My only hope is that I shall not live to see it. It is a similar situation to that in 1681 when the Turks were besieging Vienna. . . . If our town falls the Prussian barbarians will flood over Europe. Unfortunately the only protector we have had hitherto, Mussolini, seems now to be giving Germany a free hand. I should like to live in England like Ernst and travel to Rome as you are doing.[42]

Anna Freud's reactions were considerably less detached than those of her eighty-year-old father. She said again and again that she did not want to leave Vienna, to leave her house in the country, all that she had helped to build up at the Institute. She told Ernest Jones that only one thing could induce her to emigrate: "the idea that my father might be subject to any indignities like a house search, etc."[43] Her reaction to the deteriorating situation in 1936 and 1937 was to spend enormous energy on the equipping, opening, and running of a small nursery for Viennese working-class children. But, for her, this was rest after the years 1934 to 1936, when she had spent most of her spare time writing a book—a kind of labor she found much more taxing and unsociable than organizing colleagues and playing with twelve interesting babies.

WHEN ANNA FREUD began to contemplate writing a book-length manuscript to gather together what she had learned since her *Introduction to the Technique of Child Analysis*, she focused her attention on puberty, that period of instinctual "second efflorescence" that precedes the trials and tribulations of adolescence. Most of the children in the little Burlingham school had then reached adolescence and some had moved on to other schools. The Burlinghams themselves after a decade in Vienna were quite cosmopolitan, but still Americanly individualistic and upper-classly amateur-artistic. They made friends with, for example, Bob's and Mabbie's fellow students at the Vienna Kunstgewerbe Schule, where they studied crafts and architecture, and all were alluring with their sketchbooks, cameras, film projectors, and their automobile, with chauffeur. "I felt extremely lucky," Bob Burlingham wrote to Anna Freud of those years in a December, 1946 letter, "as I guess all of us Burlingham children are. . . . So much of this is due to you."

Anna Freud told Max Eitingon in October 1934 that the work she was considering would be called "On Defense Mechanisms" and that it would be "a sort of theoretical base for the thoughts on puberty" she had presented in recent lectures. "It is really the first time that I am writing something slowly and gradually and this is a very strange experience. Perhaps I will learn how to do that now. In any case, it is high time that I did." By December, she was making notes so that she could "work it all out when the vacation time comes along."[44] Apparently, she thought that she could—like her father—write a book over a short vacation, for she reported to Lou Andreas-

Salomé: "I think something in me got freed, so that I can start writing. At Christmas I want to complete my first serious work about defense mechanisms, really a kind of ego psychology. I am looking forward to it and now I have new ideas all the time, which was not the case earlier."[45] She noted in the same letter that this book, rather than her exhausting work in "the outer world," was close to being of, by, and for her true self: "This is really close to being 'I.' Then nearby there is Dorothy and Hochroterd, where everything is well."

The writing took much longer than Anna Freud had anticipated, however. The Christmas vacation passed, and then she found it impossible to write systematically while she was analyzing—sometimes up to ten hours a day—teaching at the Institute, and carrying out her various organizational and familial responsibilities. During her next vacation, she sat with her notes, but she also needed to recuperate, to rest. A working draft of the book did finally get produced, but not until the end of the summer in 1935. The senior Freuds had started that vacation at a villa in the suburb of Grinzing in April because Sigmund Freud was so unwell after two operations. His condition kept his daughter in a state of suspense, but he nudged her forward. "As first I could not commit myself to getting started again, but now it goes better than I expected," Anna Freud told Frau Lou. "Naturally, I would not have started if Papa had not urged me to."[46]

Freud was very eager about his daughter's work, and he often told his friends that she and her growing abilities were his great solace in the deteriorating political situation. "She has grown into a capable, independent person, who has been blessed with insight into matters that merely confuse others. To be sure, for her sake I would like—but she must learn to do without me, and fear of losing vital parts of my still intact personality through old age is an accelerating factor in my wish."[47]

FREUD had also engaged himself in a project for which his daughter's work on the defense mechanisms was invaluable. His book was not easy to write either; he spent more time over it than over any single work since *The Interpretation of Dreams*. The political turmoil in Germany and Austria had precipitated his book, and each wave of Jewish suffering and emigration made it harder to finish. Freud was not only forced to stand helplessly by while his colleagues and his science were persecuted, but he did not even feel at liberty in the Christian Socialists' Austria to publish his book, *Moses and Monotheism*, for fear that its content would bring more wrath upon psychoanalysts and psychoanalysis.

The first draft Freud made of this book, which he originally subtitled "a historical novel," was completed in the summer of 1934—just at the time Anna Freud was starting to write her book. Freud then worked over its three parts for nearly four years, and only after his emigration to England did he see the whole work into press with de Lange Verlag in Amsterdam. But in its various versions, the book continued to have the same central question, a question of and for the times: How can anti-Semitism's strange persistence through the centuries be explained? Just as difficult, and even more important, were the corollary questions: How can it be that the Jews have survived? What is the source—from the past, for the future—of Jewish strength?

Like Freud's previous writings on religion, *Moses and Monotheism* rests on an analogy "between neurotic processes and religious events." The key formula for this parallel went: "early trauma—defense—latency—outbreak of neurotic illness—partial return of the repressed."[48] Religions, Freud argued, have childhoods in which a trauma takes place, a series of what his daughter called "defense mechanisms," a period of instinctual quiescence called latency, a puberty of instinctual "second efflorescence," and a battle with repressions returning.

The religious story he told was this: Moses was not a Hebrew but a nobly born Egyptian, a religious leader who chose a group of followers and set them apart from their countrypeople by converting them to his belief in the unpopular monotheistic proclamations of Akhenaton—the first monotheism. Moses endured many revolts against his authority and the challenging purity of his beliefs until, in the course of one such revolt, Moses the Father, who spoke for God the Father, was killed. In their remorse, Moses's guilty followers eschewed any memory of him—though, at the same time, they hoped for a Messiah. The traumatic murder was repressed and it stayed repressed through generations of Yahwehistic pseudomonotheistic worship, until the defenses the followers had erected against the

memory of Moses failed them. The religious equivalent of an outbreak of neurosis in puberty was the reestablishment by the prophets
of the Mosaic religion, the original and true Judaism; and the return
of the repressed was another murder, this time of a Jew named Jesus,
a son, not a father.

Freud's history of the Jews was, in effect, a history of a defense
mechanism that was undone not by therapy but by a group process:
the group's memory of the patricide would not stay repressed. But,
on the other hand, the neurotic outbreak allowed the Jews to realize
that Moses had created them as a people, as Jews; he had chosen
them to be his followers, to be the worshipers of the One God.
Moses had delivered to them a moral code far superior to that of any
of the surrounding polytheists and barbarians, including those polytheists and barbarians whose customs so corrupted the sequel to Judaism, Christianity, which Freud viewed as a quasi-Judaism, a kind
of fake Judaism.

The message of this story could not have been clearer, and
Freud drew it starkly: anti-Semitism has historically had many sources
and particular conditions, but its deepest source is the resentment felt
for a people that comes to know or rediscover itself as a chosen people. Similarly, the deepest source of the chosen people's strength is
precisely their chosen-ness, or their father's favoritism. Among peoples, as among siblings, there is rivalry and competition; the people
that wins—even if at great, though never lethal, physical cost—is the
people that has won in its own eyes the paternal favor. The more
purely and strictly such people restore or revert to the father's original vision, and their sense of specialness, the more they will be hated.
Being "The Chosen People" is both the great liability and the great
strength of the Jews. Or, to put the same matter in other terms: the
strength of the Jews, for which they will always be hated, is their
greatly defended against and greatly realized father-complex.

It is certainly possible to read *Moses and Monotheism* as not
only a fascinating historical speculation but also as Freud's expression
in his old age of a childhood wish for his father's uncomplicated love
or for loving his father uncomplicatedly. For a boy who had grown
up to be a father, and even to be the father of a science, a scientific
movement, the difference between such a childhood wish and a wish
for his own children's uncomplicated love is very slight. That the

two sides of this one wishing coin were on Freud's mind in 1936, the year of his eightieth birthday, is apparent in one of his most beautiful short essays, an autobiographical rumination called "A Disturbance of Memory on the Acropolis."

This piece, a contribution to the celebration of the French writer Romain Rolland's seventieth birthday, offered an analysis of an uneasiness and sadness that Freud had felt in 1904, when he and his brother, Alexander, had made what should have been a joyful journey to Athens. They had had some hesitation, which neither understood, about making their first voyage to Greece; upon analysis, Freud realized that the good fortune of their trip signified to them that they had "gone a long way," surpassing their father, leaving their father behind. "Our father had been in business, he had had no secondary education, and Athens could not have meant much to him. Thus what interfered with our enjoyment of the journey to Athens was a feeling of filial piety. And now you will no longer wonder that the recollection of this incident on the Acropolis should have troubled me so often since I myself have grown old and stand in need of forbearance and can travel no more."[49]

Freud wondered, in his old age, if his would-be "sons," the heirs of his science, the psychoanalysts, would feel filial piety. He had, of course, wondered about the future when Adler and Jung and Rank departed, but the question was acute when he felt so frail, when psychoanalytic books were being burned in Berlin and psychoanalysts were being chased out of Germany, and when the old filial order was being so diminished with Eitingon's departure and Ferenczi's death. In this wondering, he was the father, he was the Moses who had made a people, given them a creed and a purpose that could lift them out of the ordinary run of human purposes.

With his daughter, he had been wondering aloud for years about how his people would survive. She told Lou Andreas-Salomé:

> The other day while we were talking, Papa and I agreed that analysis is not a business for mere humans, but that one needs to be something much better—who knows what! It is not the analytical work that is so difficult, for one can accomplish that with some human reason, it is the everlasting dealing with human fates. That comes even more to the fore if one is not dealing with real pathology. It is curious how the concepts deteriorate

in the younger analysts after they have worked for a period. For instance, the other day I talked with Reik about a man whose authoritarian, imposing, somewhat brutal manners toward all women outrage me. And Reik said: "What do you want? These are the truly masculine traits, all the rest is only superstructure." This "only superstructure" Reik spoke about is an analytical concept, of course, but used in a wrong sense. It impressed Papa very much when I told him about it.[50]

What filial piety meant to the daughter was not so much preserving an orthodoxy of theory and technique as preserving the father's humanity, which she held to be more than merely human, and the humaneness of his science. Her survival strength, too, was a once greatly defended against and then greatly realized father-complex.

Freud's appreciation in his old age of his daughter's loyalty, when he stood in need of forbearance and could travel no more—at least not to Athens—was expressed in his "A Disturbance of Memory on the Acropolis." He allowed himself to make his first remark for publication about his daughter's work.

There are an extraordinarily large number of methods (or mechanisms, as we say) used by our ego in the discharge of its defensive functions. An investigation is at the moment being carried on close at hand which is devoted to the study of these methods of defense: my daughter, the child analyst, is writing a book upon them. The most primitive and thoroughgoing of these methods, "repression," was the starting point of the whole of our deeper understanding of psychopathology.[51]

The Ego and the Mechanisms of Defense was carefully divided into four parts made up of twelve chapters, but it really had three main movements, which served its three main purposes. Anna Freud wanted, first, to review generally the technical and theoretical developments that had taught analysts how to give equal consideration clinically to id, ego, and superego—and specifically to balance Freud's original procedure of "id-analysis" with "ego-analysis." Secondly, she wanted to review all of the defense mechanisms that her father and his colleagues had isolated and described—to make a *summa* of them. She did this not by presenting them in their chronological or developmental sequence of appearance, but by correlating them to the three sources of anxiety her father had outlined in *Inhibitions, Symptoms and Anxiety*—objective anxiety, instinctual anxiety, and superego anxiety. The question of chronology had to be left unanswered, she argued, because the answers to it proposed by her camp and by the Kleinians were so at odds that only more research could determine the true sequence. Her catalogue *raisonné* contained ten defenses: repression, reaction-formation, projection, introjection, regression, sublimation, isolation, undoing, reversal, and turning against the self. Finally, she wanted to add to her list of ten mechanisms several that she thought had not been previously described.

The second two purposes in Anna Freud's book were both served by the many case vignettes in which she correlated types of anxiety and types of defense mechanisms to produce a rough map of defenses in normal development. But she also showed how different correlations are bound up with different psychopathological symptoms or illnesses. Her procedure presented vividly the intricacies and layerings of psychic formation. She noted, for example, that a girl suffering from penis-envy and the ambivalence toward her mother that accompanies such envy might try to project the hatred side of her ambivalence onto other females; then, when this defense proved inadequate, she might turn some of the hatred on herself; and, finally, still disturbed, she might feel the hatred she had projected onto other females as directed at herself from them. This constellation of projection and turning-on-the-self defenses could be constructed without pathology. But a girl who repressed her mother-hatred might find the hatred aggressively expressed in bodily symptoms or a phobia—some form of hysterical illness. And a girl who repressed her mother-hatred and then maintained the repression with the defense called "reaction-formation"—covering the repressed hatred with sweetly loving conscious ideas and behavior, for example—or who combined reaction-formations with rituals to control aggression and strict moral codes to control sexuality, might end up with a full-scale obsessional illness. With analyses of defense structures like these, Anna Freud viewed the neuroses that her father had first described—hysterical and obsessional neuroses—from the viewpoint of ego-activity, not just id-activity. In other words, she looked not just at the unconscious wishes or id-contents defended against but at the ways the ego has of doing its defensive work.

The third part of *The Ego and the Mechanisms of Defense* is the most original and powerful one. It is also the one most clearly connected to Anna Freud's clinical work with latency and puberty patients—including the Burlinghams—and to her ongoing analysis of herself, both as her father's supervisee and in "self-analysis." This section—roughly the last six chapters—contains her autobiographical case study of the governess who practiced "altruistic surrender," which was the first thorough description of a defense her father had called "retiring in favor of another" and presented only in male cases.[52] But the one defense that she presented in this section for which there was no existing literature was called "identification with the aggressor."

One of the most powerful ways the ego has to deal with external threats or objective anxiety is to imitate the threat, to become like the threatener. A little paient who got accidentally knocked in the head by one of his teachers during a school game came to his next analytic session, for example, in full armor, wielding both a toy pistol and a wooden sword. He thus made himself big, powerful, manly, and capable of doing unto others as had been done unto him. Such behavior is quite normal, and also "a by no means uncommon stage in the normal development of the superego."[53] Identification with the aggressor as a stage of superego development is equivalent to internalizing criticism from parents or other authorities, and it is usually combined with projection, which allows the criticism to be aggressively taken out on others, not felt as self-criticism. A child who is punished, then, both internalizes the punishment and also gets angry toward someone else or punishes someone else, often someone smaller. "True morality begins when the internalized criticism, now embodied in the standard exacted by the superego, coincides with the ego's perception of its own fault. From that moment, the severity of the superego is turned inward instead of outward and the subject becomes less intolerant of other people."[54] Those who do not make their way to "true morality," however, remain peculiarly aggressive toward others; and those who go too far and become peculiarly aggressive toward themselves are melancholic or depressive.

The child cases Anna Freud and her colleagues treated presented many variations on the theme of "identification with the aggressor." But Anna Freud seems also to have come to her formulation by reflecting on herself. When she was considering her "sunken" friendship with Eitingon, for example, she compared her humiliation in being rejected with his lack of affect and set the comparison in an older context: "This dates back to a time when I was very little, and I think I know exactly when it started. From then on, I always sought out children who gave me up, and it always had the same effect as now. It is as though I looked at myself with the others' eyes and was of just as little worth to myself as I was to them. Now it is almost alright, because I know it. Only this time [with Eitingon], I did not make it [i.e., did not seek out a rejecter]."[55] As a child, she had identified with the aggressors, although in her description she skipped over the step of projecting the rejection outward as intolerance of others and went right to the step of accepting the criticism as self-criticism. In effect, she was noting that she had a tendency to go too far and become peculiarly aggressive toward herself or depressive. She was telling the story of being the littlest child, of being only a bore and a nuisance to the older ones and only a rival to Sophie, as a story of coming to feel self-critically like nothing much.

That she had always had difficulty in projecting outward the aggression she had felt and identified with, she was very aware. In the early 1930s, she often noted how she felt the "aggression" of her father's surgeons as keenly as if they had been operating on her own jaw. But she did not behave like a little patient of hers who, after he had been to the dentist, went about furiously cutting up pieces of string and sharpening pencils. Rather, she had a dream: "Tonight I dreamt that I killed our cook Anna. I cut off her head and cut her to pieces and had no feelings of guilt, which was very peculiar. Now I know why: because her name is Anna, and that means me."[56] She identified with the aggression and then turned it on herself—or at least refused to acknowledge that there might be any other "Anna" than herself.

Even over the concept of "identification with the aggressor," Anna Freud anticipated a bit of aggression—specifically, a bit of rejection from her peers in the Vienna Society. And she was not entirely mistaken. Otto Fenichel's criticism that her contributions always seemed to stop just at the point where they became interesting haunted her.[57] She obviously felt "identification with the aggressor" to be a common and important defense, not a minor one, but she would not put it on the main list of ten in her book. Many years later, reflecting on her book, she explained: "I didn't list it here because I thought only of the recognized defense mechanisms, and I felt modest about this new one. I didn't think it had a claim to be introduced yet."[58] But, on the other hand, she noted that over the years it was "only identification with the aggressor which is a newcomer to the aristocracy" of the univerally recognized defenses.

Several factors helped the recognition of her contribution. Within the psychoanalytic community, it became clear that the concept represented a key counter to Melanie Klein's emphasis on aggression as a manifestation of the death instinct, an internally arising force. Aggression in the child's environment is not, Anna Freud argued, to be left out of account. Reflecting back on her book's discussion of identification with the aggressor, she noted:

> You know, in wartime, when we discussed the Hampstead Nursery children, we had the question very often in mind of how we could teach them to control their aggression when they saw everyone around them being aggressive. . . . Children don't really differentiate between the big aggression in the outside world and the small aggression in themselves. I remember one of our children passing a house in one of the streets that had been completely bombed. He looked at the bombed house and said "naughty, naughty." There was no difference for him between what he broke to pieces and what they broke.[59]

Anna Freud eventually took the child's identification with external aggression, the big aggression of parents, siblings, or the world, so seriously that she was prepared to make it the crux of superego formation: "If you want to make a very sweeping statement, you could say, "What else is the superego than identification with the aggressor?"[60]

This way of conceptualizing superego formation was an extension of Anna Freud's earlier quarrel with Melanie Klein over developmental chronology. The third part of her book, even though it passes by the complicated question of the developmental order of the defenses, does present a developmental order for the anxieties as motives for defense: objective anxiety, she claimed, appears first, before anxiety over the strength of the instincts or superego anxiety (the doman of identification with the aggressor). "The child learns how to defend against stimuli that come from the internal world on the basis of his dealings with the external world. . . . The first clashes in the child's life are between the instinctual wishes and impulses on the one hand and the frustrating agencies and powers of the external world, on the other. And only later does this become an internalized process and an internalized conflict."[61] This claim was, when it was made in 1936 and thereafter, a source of contention not just with the Kleinians, but with all analysts who drew their concepts from the early work of Freud, before the structural theory of the 1920s.

"The idea that fear of the external world could, at any time of life, cause similar results as the fear of internal agencies, was a more or less heretical revolutionary idea," Anna Freud noted retrospectively.[62] But the most active supporter of the idea was close to hand, and he summarized it well in a 1937 essay called "Analysis Terminable and Interminable." This was Freud's theoretical review of the implications his daughter's work had for assessing therapeutic results.

> Under the influence of its upbringing, the child's ego accustoms itself to shift the scene of the battle from outside to inside and to master the inner danger before it becomes external. Probably it is generally right in so doing. In this battle on two fronts— later there is a third front as well [the superego]—the ego makes use of various methods of fulfilling its task, i.e., to put it in general terms, of avoiding anxiety, danger and unpleasure. We call these devices defense mechanisms. Our knowledge of them is as yet incomplete. Anna Freud's book (1936) has given us our first insight into their multiplicity and their manifold significance.[63]

Both the importance of her work in the context of the Klein debate and her father's support of it assured that Anna Freud's innovation, "identification with the aggressor," would be taken seriously by analysts. But the factor that most strongly recommended the concept was of quite another order: it simply presented a necessary truth in a mendacious, brutal time. External aggression was, in the years after Anna Freud published *The Ego and the Mechanisms of Defense*, everywhere available to be identified with: hardly a child, hardly an adult, escaped encounters with "the big aggression in the outside world." Sigmund Freud and Albert Einstein exchanged letters in 1932 over the question "Why War?" and the question echoed through the Continent's civil wars, assassinations, internments, invasions, and revolutions until the Second World War actually—after seven years of strained suspense—began.

Anna Freud was not a political thinker, and she avoided the kind of historical-cultural speculation her father presented in his "Why War?" letter or in works like *Moses and Monotheism*. But it was very clear to her that children who grow up in violent familial and social environments are well prepared eventually to make violent sociopolitical environments as they project onto others what they have identified with themselves. Depressives or melancholics, who have gone past projection to the point of turning aggression upon themselves, do not generally make wars; but those who stop short of "true morality," who are arrested at the stage of identifying with the aggressor and projecting aggression onto others, are ready for battle.

With her conceptualization, Anna Freud had, in effect, written a complement to the thesis of *Moses and Monotheism*. Freud had indicated how a people that feels itself specially favored or chosen by its One God through His earthly representatives has a special strength and also a special destiny as maximally resented. The nature of the bond between the people and the leaders had been the subject of Freud's earlier work, *Group Psychology and the Analysis of the Ego* (1921). There he had stressed that members of a church, like soldiers in an army, feel that their commander in chief is like a father who loves all of them equally—they are as a group his "chosen people." As they do not compete for their father's love, they love one another without sibling rivalry. Aggression is reserved for the enemy or, in the case of the church, the nonbelievers, the infidels, those outside the circle of equalitarian love. Freud's explanation of the source of this outwardly directed aggression points to a mystery:

In the undisguised antipathies and aversions which people feel towards strangers with whom they have to do we may recognize the expression of self-love—of narcissism. This self-love works for the preservation of the individual, and behaves as though the occurrence of any divergence from his own particular lines of development involved a criticism of them and a demand for their alteration. We do not know why such sensitiveness should have been directed to just these details of differentiation; but it is unmistakable that in this whole connection men give evidence of a readiness for hatred, an aggressiveness, the source of which is unknown, and to which one is tempted to ascribe an elementary character.[64]

Freud alluded, of course, to his death instinct theory with this "elementary character."

Her father had presented a line of thought to which Anna Freud was psychically predisposed to agree. She once said of *Group Psychology and the Analysis of the Ego* that she had found herself in it: "everything was in there, my old daydreams and all I wanted."[65] She had only wanted to be a beloved believer in her father's organization, a soldier in his company, a sibling loved as much as (if not more than) the other siblings. But she could also add to her father's line of thought the idea that true believers and foot soldiers are bound to their parental figures not just by love but also by "identification with the aggressor." They are aggressive to their parents' enemies, having earlier identified with their parents' aggression. It may be that people draw on an instinct of an "elementary character" as they defend aggressively their self-definition, their difference. And it is easy to see that they need the leader's love to preserve their internal group cohesion. But Anna Freud was aware that there is also something like a group superego rooted in shared "identification with the aggressor."

That people in groups, as well as individually, derive great strength in adversity from the mechanism of defense called "identification with the aggressor" was Anna Freud's insight. But she was also very alert to how dangerous it is for individuals and groups to remain arrested at this stage, this source of strength, which falls quite short of "true morality." She later put the problem succinctly in an essay called "Notes on Aggression" (1948):

Aggressive urges . . . may become redirected from the child's main love objects (the parents) to people of lesser importance in the child's life. This relieves the intimate family relationships of their negative admixture. But the gain is offset by the emergence of an excessively negative and hostile attitude toward people outside the family circle (such as complete strangers, casual acquaintances, servants, foreigners).

Attitudes such as these are not reversible by experience, since they are not rooted in a real assessment of the hated persons, but arise from the necessity to prevent the hate reactions from reverting to the original, ambivalently loved objects.

Projection and displacement of aggression are responsible for much of the strain, suspiciousness, and intolerance in the relationships between individuals and nations.[66]

Anna Freud presented a first edition of *The Ego and the Mechanisms of Defense* to her father for his eightieth birthday. The publisher's deadline had caused her much exhaustion, and Freud had been suffering from heart trouble in April, just as she finally brought the book to a close. Their evening exchanges over its organization and content came to an end, and they were replaced with conferences about how to prevent the birthday celebration from getting out of hand. Freud managed to bar many of the proposed expressions of esteem from his followers, but he could not control the international traffic of bouquets, letters, and visitors. "One can tolerate endless amounts of praise," Freud was honest enough to admit,[67] and the attentions paid him by his most distinguished contemporaries, like Thomas Mann's famous lecture "Freud and the Future," gratified him. But the two months that it took him and his daughter-secretary to thank everyone by mail were tiring nonetheless.

Her book was the first birthday present that Anna Freud had felt was adequate to her feelings. In many of her adult years, she had come forward on May 6 with jokes or pieces of self-mockery, viewing herself as a kind of clownish Cordelia among the euphemizers. On May 6, 1925, the spring before the Burlinghams arrived, for example, she could still revert to the insecure, jealous mode of her first-analysis era: "I did not give Papa a present for his birthday because there is no present suitable for the occasion; I brought only a picture of Wolf that I had made as a joke, because I always assert that he transferred his whole interest in me onto Wolf. He was very pleased with it."[68]

It was for far deeper reasons that Freud was pleased with his 1936 gift. He—in his analytic voice—praised it to Eitingon as her "uninhibited achievement."[69] Because Lou Andreas-Salomé was so familiar with his daughter's years of uncertainty and with how difficult writing was for her, he knew Lou would feel as he did: "It is surprising, too, how sharp, clear and unflinching she is in her mastery of the subject."[70] Freud paid his daughter an obeisance in return when he next had a volume of his own to present to her. In 1939, he gave her, inscribed, a copy of *Der Mann Moses und Die Monotheistische Religion*. This was the first time that he had ever given her one of his books as a gift, and, until the end of her life, she kept it, carefully wrapped, among her most precious possessions.

The late spring of 1936, the two-month-long wake of the birthday, was a hiatus for Anna Freud, a moment of comparative privacy and pleasure in her achievement. She learned that her book was to be the subject of a very weighty critical symposium in the *International Journal of Psychoanalysis*, a collection of essays by Ernst Kris, Otto Fenichel, and even an admiring one from Ernest Jones, who had moderated his criticism of her views during the recent years when he and Anna Freud had become, as he said in a metaphor quite typical of his sense of himself, "the pillars of Eastern and Western Europe" for psychoanalysis.[71] The tone of the book's public reception was the opposite of what she had endured with *Introduction to the Technique of Child Analysis* in 1927. Even when the work was criticized, it was respected.

But two painful operations on her father's jaw in July brought Anna Freud's peace to an end. For the first time since 1923, the tissue under his prosthesis was unmistakably malignant. The return of his cancer marked a new stage in Freud's long battle. The next operation, in December, was excruciating and resulted in a temporary locking of his jaw that made eating solid foods and speaking impossible. Anna Freud, in her characteristic way, controlled her own pain by launching into a new and exhausting project.

EDITH Jackson, who had been analyzed by Sigmund Freud and trained in child analysis at the Vienna Institute by Anna Freud, offered in gratitude a sum of money from her family's fortune—and thus became the first of a long list of American sponsors for Anna Freud's projects. With the money, Anna Freud wanted to establish a nursery for children under the age of two. A nursery for such young children was unheard of at the time, but that was the only sense in which Anna Freud wanted her nursery to be designated "experimental." In a set of rough notes prepared for the nursery's first—and last—annual report, Anna Freud's project was described *via negativa*:

> The Jackson Nursery [Krippe] is neither an experiment in pedagogy nor an experimental psychology laboratory. It is also not connected to the type of research conducted by Vera Schmidt [in Russia], which was concerned with whether, how, and when children can achieve control of their instincts without accessory educational measures. Research at the Jackson Nursery was not even designed to see how children react to a predetermined, specifically organized environment. The purpose was different, and less harmful [than "experiments" sometimes are]. We know something about infants from developmental studies, from adults' retrospective reconstructions, and from child analysis with its microscopic view of the infant's inner life. What we need to see now are the actual experiences of the first years of life, from the outside, as they present themselves. Thorough knowledge of infancy is the goal.

Many years later, in an obituary for Edith Jackson, Anna Freud recalled that their desire had been "to gather direct information about . . . earlier ages, particularly the second year of life, which we deemed all-important for the child's essential advance from primary to secondary process functioning; for the establishment of feeding and sleeping habits; for acquiring the rudiments of superego development and impulse control [and] for the establishment of object ties to peers."[72]

As Anna Freud noted in another retrospective on the nursery:

Since these toddlers are of prenursery school age and access to their families cannot be gained, our solution was to create a separate organization for a group of them, something between a crèche and a nursery school. . . . We choose toddlers from the poorest families in Vienna, their fathers being on the dole and begging in the streets, their mothers at best doing some work as charwomen. Prerequisite for acceptance was a measure of independent movement, crawling in some cases rather than walking. . . . Their parents were delighted with their good care; the children thrived and, on their part, recompensed us by providing knowledge about a child's first steps out of the biological unity between infant and mother."[73]

This bargain was well and easily made—particularly in comparison to the bargain that had brought the nursery into being.

While Edith Jackson was still in Vienna finishing her studies and involving herself in a number of clandestine operations for Viennese Jews trying to emigrate and socialists trying to aid their beleaguered comrades in Germany, she was Anna Freud's liaison to officials in the city government. The plan that was presented to officials made no mention of Anna Freud, so that it would not be thwarted because she was a Jew, and it also carefully linked the nursery to a respected institution, the Haus der Kinder, a school run by the Montessori Society of Vienna, so that it would not be thwarted by opponents of projects to serve the working class. When Edith Jackson returned to America, the diplomatic mission was undertaken by Dorothy Burlingham, who also contributed to the budget when extra funds were needed. Dorothy Burlingham was acquainted with the American ambassador to Austria, George Messersmith, and his influence was brought to bear on the mayor of Vienna: "the Bürgermeister evidently decided it was not worth being impolite to an American ambassador," Anna Freud reported to Edith Jackson in her laconic style.[74] The Viennese city officials were mollified with the kind of flattery that they expected from petitioners: the American ladies, they were told, thought "that the pedagogical work in Vienna in general and Vienna Montessori work in special is so excellent that such a [nursery] scheme seems more tempting than an undertaking of the same kind in America."

When the necessary permits had been secured, Anna Freud set about adapting the space she had rented from the Montessori Society, which was about a third of their Haus der Kinder on Rudolfsplatz and a portion of the garden. This sharing arrangement, so helpful to the Montessorians, who were foundering financially, as well as to Anna Freud, who would have had to pay much more to rent and fix up an apartment, also brought Anna Freud the expertise of Hilde Fischer, a teacher in the Montessori kindergarten, who worked three half days a week in the nursery. Hilde Fischer collaborated with the nursery's main director, Hertha Fuchs-Wertheim, and her assistant Mizzi Milberger, whose acquaintance Anna Freud had made while she was nurse to Peter Schur, the son of Sigmund Freud's physician. One of Anna Freud's trainees in child analysis at the Institute, Dr. Julia Deming, another American, was in charge of feeding arrangements at the nursery, and the pediatrician was Anna Freud's friend Josefine Stross, who was not an analyst but who had completed the course work at the Vienna Institute for the sake of her practice in pediatrics.

To be admitted to the nursery, a child had to be needy by Anna Freud's standards, and healthy by Josefine Stross's. Any child with an infectious disease was refused. Reporting to Edith Jackson on February 7, 1937, Anna Freud sent the profiles she had written up on the twelve children accepted:

> But I am sorry to say we had to give up Hanne-Lore in the meantime, so it makes eleven now. . . . Her Pirquet test [for tuberculosis] was positive, and since she is hardly over a year Fiffi Stross says it is too dangerous for the other children. It is very sad, because the child is very sweet and the mother is heartbroken about it. . . . We will see that Hannele goes to Franz Josef Hospital, where they keep children like that for several months in open air and try to cure them.[75]

All kinds of precautions had to be taken to prevent the spread of disease, since the children came from families that could hardly afford to feed them, much less secure proper medical care. Each morning, after they arrived at the nursery and had a little time to acclimatize themselves, the children were examined by Josefine Stross, who kept careful daily records. The children's mothers stayed through these exams, so that Dr. Stross could report any problems to them and hear from them how the children were at home. The children were bathed each morning, and then diapered and dressed in clean clothes provided by the nursery. All during the rest of their day, the children's adult companions took notes on small cards about their behavior. These notes were recopied and filed thematically in a wooden file box at the end of the day, and then they were used as the source material for discussions. This simple indexing system was later elaborated into one of Anna Freud's and Dorothy Burlingham's most important scientific contributions: the Hampstead Index.

Anna Freud equipped the nursery with characteristic attention to detail. A list of her purchases (in English, more or less) and an accounting down to the schillings went off to Edith Jackson. "150 diapers (150 more ordered), 25 towels, 31 bath towels, 30 rubber trousers but not tight ones, 48 bibs . . . 30 washcloths . . . 15 training *Anzüge* . . . 10 meters rubber sheeting, 10 most attractive wooden beds with big wheels so we can wheel them out onto the terrace, 2 *Gehschulen*, I've forgotten my English, 14 blankets . . . etc. The wash goes out every day and is returned the next day—it amounts to about 4 schillings a day."[76] She and Dorothy Burlingham went to the nursery for at least an hour a day and spent many additional hours meeting with the staff, collecting information, writing reports, solving problems as they came up, and, later, helping the neighboring Montessori nursery school keep financially afloat.

The opening of the nursery in February 1937 was exhausting for everybody, including the children. "After a week the children seem to have made themselves much at home, there is very little crying, much activity, they eat much better, and they now have stools— the first week I think not a child had a stool. I am sure that is a sign that they now feel at home. However, they do not look well, probably a result of strain the adaptation meant for them."[77]

She herself did not look well either, and her family chided her about overworking while they teased her: "they laugh at me at home, because I think and talk of babies continually and because I lead a sort of double life at the moment."[78] To her lives as analyst and nursery school director, she then added nurse to Dorothy Burlingham. Dorothy, whose family tree was dotted with cases of asthma and tuberculosis, developed a persistent fatiguing cough that was diagnosed as tuberculosis. Her maid, who was susceptible to infection, had to leave the apartment. When Dorothy's condition proved too severe for home treatment, she went to a Swiss sanatorium for a time. For Anna Freud and the Burlingham children, the worry was incessant. Bob and Tinky, who were in America at college, wanted to come back to Vienna as soon as they could. But Robert Burlingham had the opposite idea, and, not wanting his estranged wife's condition to endanger the children, he eventually traveled to Vienna and arranged for Mickey to return to America for a tutorial course that prepared him for college. Robert Burlingham's visit was exhausting for everyone, and it propelled Mabbie Burlingham forward in her effort to win the affection of a young Viennese architect named Simon Schmiderer, her future husband. Martha Freud was not able to help her daughter with her parenting responsibilities because Martha had her own patient to care for. Tante Minna, who had a weak heart, underwent surgery for cataracts and then was confined to her bed for months.

Freud was also not well during the months when Dorothy's tuberculosis was first diagnosed, and Anna Freud was concerned enough about him to want to keep from him the news that their old friend Lou Andreas-Salomé had died of a uremic infection at the age of seventy-six. Frau Lou had been failing physically—though not at all mentally—for several years, with a heart condition, deteriorating vision, and finally a mastectomy to endure. Freud saw an announcement of her death in the newspaper—and mustered his strength to write a lovely farewell piece about her for his *Zeitschrift.* "Those who were closer to her," he said, "had the strongest impression of the genuineness and harmony of her nature and could discover with astonishment that all feminine frailties, and perhaps most human frailties, were foreign to her or had been conquered by her in the course of her life."[79] That was the Lou Andreas-Salomé who was his daughter's ego ideal and whom his daughter described (privately) in similar terms: "The unusual thing about her was what ought actually to be quite usual in a human being—honesty, directness, absence of any weakness, self-assertion without selfishness."[80]

When she and Dorothy had first vacationed together, Anna Freud had written Frau Lou long letters full of their plans and their adventures. Dorothy had accompanied Anna Freud to Goettingen in 1929 for what seems to have been her last visit with Frau Lou. Not all of Anna Freud's letters after that reunion have survived, but it is clear from Frau Lou's letters to Freud that *The Ego and the Mechanisms of Defense* was one of the last books she, nearly blind, had read aloud to her. For both women, the lack of visits meant, necessarily, a distancing; as Frau Lou noted realistically to Freud, it is almost impossible to write deeply "without having the personal contact we used to have years ago."[81] But when Anna Freud lost Lou Andreas-Salomé, nonetheless, she lost the most loyal and constant friend of her early adulthood. Although Marie Bonaparte later took up parts of the large role Frau Lou had played, there was no true successor.

AT her nursery, Anna Freud flung herself into work. She and her staff puzzled over how to handle the meals for children who could feed themselves, and for the littlest ones who could not. On the principle that the environment should be as close to the children's home life as possible—that is, that it should not be experimental or utopian—the children were, at first, given a midday meal in courses while they sat around two little tables. Of the eleven children, only four had any interest in their food. So another method was tried. An American researcher named Clara Davis had reported that children given an assortment of dishes on a tray and allowed to choose what they wanted would provide themselves with a balanced diet. The Jackson Nursery staff decided to use this method, but they used it for asking a question that went beyond the American pragmatism about eating well. Their question was: Would an active attitude toward food—rather than the usual passive one—increase the desire to eat? They were concerned with the conditions for pleasure.

Dr. Julia Deming kept an intricate notebook in which each child's food choices at each meal were recorded. The result was that all the children ate more and gained weight when they could choose from the little tray buffets than when they were simply presented with first soup, then a main course, then dessert. Some of the children had crazes for certain foods that went on for a few days, but over the course of a week they would achieve a nutritional balance in toto. As their desire to eat increased, less disciplinary energy had to be expended on keeping them from playing rather than eating or from playing with their food: "when children once begin to play, they do not eat; the pleasure in playing seems to be greater than the desire to eat."[82]

For playing, the children had the simple, unpainted wooden toys that Maria Montessori advocated. Lili Roubicek Peller, who directed the Montessori school for children under six, was particularly interested in children's play, and wrote articles that combined her observations with those of the Jackson Nursery staff. Other workers with particular interests also came to the nursery to observe the children. Dorothy Burlingham, who had established contact with a Jewish residential home for blind children in Vienna, observed the educational methods at the institution and formed a plan for enrolling a blind child in the nursery. Because time ran out on them in Vienna, the Jackson Nursery did not include a handicapped child, but in all the English institutions that Dorothy Burlingham and Anna Freud organized together, admission of handicapped children was always emphasized—for the sake of the handicapped children, and for the sake of letting the nonhandicapped learn early basic lessons in tolerance and understanding under analytic eyes.[83]

AROUND the little oasis of cooperation that was the Jackson Nursery, political chaos brewed. For the Freuds, the summer and fall of 1937 were relatively peaceful. A major operation under general anesthesia that Freud had undergone in April stemmed the recurrence of his cancer. But Freud, his physician Max Schur, his surgeon Pichler, and his family knew that it was only a matter of time before the cancer would reappear. In January 1938, yet another incision revealed, once again, cancerous tissue. At the same time, it became apparent to everyone in Austria that an invasion from Germany was imminent.

Adolf Hitler summoned the Austrian chancellor, Schuschnigg, to Berchtesgaden in February. In the quiet resort town where Sigmund Freud had vacationed peacefully with his family and completed his *The Interpretation of Dreams*, Schuschnigg received the Führer's ultimatum. One month later the Germans marched unopposed over the northern border. The Austrian chancellor felt he had no choice but to resign: he saw his defeat coming and preferred not to be a party to it. When Vienna was occupied on March 12, Freud, who had lived on a fantasy that the barbarians would be stopped at the city's gates, wrote in his daily log a summary of the story: "Finis Austriae."[84]

The end of Austria was the beginning of an agonizing period. Martin Freud's office was broken into the next day, the thirteenth, by a gang of Viennese ruffians, little imitation Nazis, who wanted an occasion for strutting about and whatever money he had. While Martin was trying to handle this crisis, and Anna Freud was on her way to join him, Berggasee 19 was visited by another group, a unit under a more disciplined leader, who simply relieved the senior Freuds of some six thousand schillings and departed. Martha Freud won her children's respect by calmly and shrewdly treating the raiders as though they were decent guests who deserved her usual hospitality. They were so disconcerted by her behavior and by Freud's entry with (as Ernest Jones recalled) "blazing eyes that any Old Testament prophet might have envied," they they took the cash and departed without thoroughly searching the apartment.[85] Freud's wry comment about this house call was typical of him: "I have never taken so much for a single visit."

Ernest Jones journeyed to Vienna from London, and Princess Marie Bonaparte from Paris. Jones took on the task of persuading Freud to leave Vienna, and then went home to negotiate permission for him and his family to live in England. The Princess visited the Berggasse every day to provide her protective royal presence and to help the Freuds prepare to leave. A house telephone connected the Freud apartment to Dorothy Burlingham's apartment one floor above, and whenever trouble threatened, Dorothy called the American Embassy, where the ambassador to France, William Bullitt, had insisted that the consul general, Mr. Wiley, be on call. Bullitt, a former patient of Freud's who had earlier collaborated with Freud on a study of Woodrow Wilson, also set in motion the complicated negotiations that guaranteed the Freuds their safety and eventually their exit permit. For once, Freud's frailty served him well. Because he could not leave his apartment, he missed meeting the thugs who attacked another elderly Herr Freud after mistaking him for the famous Jewish professor.[86]

The board of the Vienna Psychoanalytic Society had met on

March 13 and taken two decisions: that all the members should flee the country as soon as possible, and that the future headquarters of the Society would be wherever Sigmund Freud was. Jones later reported Freud's comment: "After the destruction of the Temple in Jerusalem by Titus, Rabbi Jochanan ben Sakkai asked for permission to open a school at Jabneh for the study of the Torah. We are going to do the same. We are, after all, used to persecution by our history, tradition and some of us by personal experience."[87] The non-Jewish members of the Vienna Society either joined their Jewish colleagues in exile, as Richard and Editha Sterba did, or went into a kind of internal emigration, as August Aichhorn did. The Vienna Society did not, like the German Society, continue in non-Jewish hands and under Nazi regulation. Freud's true followers preferred Exodus—and so gave the parable of *Moses and Monotheism* the historical particularity he had anticipated for it.

On March 22, the Nazis paid the Berggasse apartment another visit, to complete their search. Martin Freud remembered two scenes from that day vividly.

> The first was the view I had from the window of Anna being driven off in an open car escorted by four heavily armed S.S. men. Her situation was perilous; but far from showing fear, or even much interest, she sat in the car as a woman might sit in a taxi on her way to enjoy a shopping expedition. . . . The second scene, quite as clearly outlined, is of mother, highly indignant with an S.S. man who, on his way through a passage, paused at a large cupboard, pulled upon its doors and began roughly dragging out her piles of beautifully laundered linen all efficiently arranged in the way dear to her housewifely heart, each package held together by colored ribbons. . . . Without showing the slightest fear, mother joined the fellow and in highly indignant tones told him precisely what she thought of his shocking behavior in a lady's house, and ordered him to stop at once.[88]

Martha Freud's self-possession once again produced the desired result—the searcher withdrew. Anna Freud's manner also saved her, but the result was delayed enough to unnerve her father completely.

Freud did not know that his daughter and his son Martin,

anticipating that they would be picked up for questioning, had visited Max Schur, Freud's physician, and requested from him sufficient amounts of Veronal to be able to choose suicide over torture or internment camps. Schur was also asked to pledge himself to care for their father as long as possible. They shared their father's defiance—but they chose to interpret it in their own fashion: Anna had asked Freud, soon after the Nazi invasion, "Wouldn't it be better if we all killed ourselves?" To this her father had replied, "Why? Because they would like us to?" She had taken his meaning, but she had no intention of being tortured.[89]

The Gestapo took Anna Freud in at noon to question her about the psychoanalytic publishing house. She was left waiting in a corridor. Realizing that if she languished in that corridor she might simply be taken away at closing time to disappear, she managed to get herself transferred to a room where some prisoners were being questioned. The Gestapo men were trying to track a group—probably quite imaginary—of Jewish terrorists. When she was questioned about her organization, Anna Freud gave her captors a description of the International Psychoanalytic Association's scientific activities, which seemed to them innocuous enough. By seven o'clock in the evening, she returned home.

Freud had spent the day pacing the apartment and smoking one cigar after another. "I'll never forget," Dorothy Burlingham remembered in 1939, "the time you were . . . with the Gestapo and he was so dreadfully worried—the only time I ever saw him like that—I realized then fully what you meant to him."[90] The others who were present saw this too, but they followed the family dictates about discretion in their roles as biographers. "Freud, who was rarely demonstrative in his affection, showed his feelings to some extent that evening," wrote Max Schur laboriously. Jones was a bit more direct in reporting what he had been told: "When she returned at seven o'clock that evening, [his emotions] were no longer to be restrained."[91] Among themselves, the family and friends could express their amazement when Sigmund Freud—so stoical, so controlled—wept and declared that he wanted them all to flee Vienna at once.

All through April and into May, past Freud's eighty-second birthday, the family waited. Both the analyst Freuds continued to see a few patients, and in the evenings they worked on translations, including one into German of Marie Bonaparte's charming memoir of her chow, Topsy, who had, like Freud, struggled with a cancer of the jaw. Pichler—a non-Jew of great integrity—came as usual to care for his patient. With help from his daughter and the Princess, Freud went through his papers, deciding what to keep and what to destroy. Anna Freud did the same for the Vienna Society's archives. Paul Federn had been entrusted with the Society's early Minutes, which included so many pages in Otto Rank's meticulous, conscientious hand, and those bundles of manuscript made their way to New York.

When it began to seem likely that they would be able to escape, Anna Freud also turned her attention to how she might rescue her own work and her own house, Hochroterd. Dorothy Burlingham, still weak and convalescing, decided to move temporarily to Switzerland, where she could spend her money freely to help fleeing Viennese and also arrange with Anna Freud for the evacuation of their common property. The friends hoped to be able eventually to find in England both a way to re-create the Jackson Nursery and a replacement cottage. Dorothy negotiated for the Hochroterd furniture—rustic, peasant pieces in painted wood—to be shipped to America for storage until the world again became a place in which vacation cottages were thinkable. The Jackson Nursery equipment was packed and sent, with help from the Princess, to England. The Viennese cots, the little tables and chairs, the feeding experiment trays, and the wooden Montessori toys were unpacked in 1940 to furnish the Hampstead War Nursery—and they have remained in use to this day.

AFTER Ernest Jones was successful in getting English entry and work permits for the Freud family and a group of followers, Anna Freud spent her days making Kafkaesque visits to government offices and trying to obtain exit visas and tax clearances. Minna Bernays's permit came through first, and on May 5 Dorothy Burlingham, returning briefly from Switzerland, escorted her—nearly blind and very weak—to London. Martin and Mathilde and their families also left safely in May. "Our clan is melting down," Freud wrote to Minna. "We wouldn't be needing an extra train but only a sleeping car." The days inched by. "But when will the tax clearance come? We are waiting for it as we waited twenty years ago for the enemy."[92]

"Anna is working with great skill and good humor to get us clear," Freud reported. "She is managing a lot better than Martin did. She also gets on well with people, is liked by them, and gains influence over them. It is said that when the fox gets caught in a trap he bites one of his legs off and limps away on three. We shall follow his example, and I hope we will get free, though limping." The daughter Freud called "St. Anna" obviously took it as her duty to make the suspense tolerable: "Anna tries to make the present bearable by saying that we now have a much needed rest between the exertions here and the tasks we have to face."

On June 4, Sigmund, Martha, and Anna Freud, with Josefine Stross accompanying them to act as physician, set out for their next tasks. Their train to freedom took them first to Paris, where Princess Marie Bonaparte, her husband, Prince George, and Ernst Freud received them. The Princess gave Freud two important items she had ingeniously smuggled out of Vienna: a receipt for a stash of gold money that she had shipped to Greece and thence to London, and one of his favorite antiquities, a statuette of Athena. After a day's rest, the Freuds went on to London. "The one day in your house in Paris restored our good mood and sense of dignity," Freud wrote to his friend; "after being surrounded by love for twelve hours we left proud and rich under the protection of Athena."[93]

Marie Bonaparte's loyalty and generosity were apparent throughout the Freud's last days in Vienna. When the Gestapo had taken Anna Freud in on March 22, the Princess had even tried to get them to arrest her too. But, as Martin noted, "the Gestapo in Austria had not then enough courage, if it may be called courage, to risk trouble by arresting one with a royal passport."[94] The Princess had not, as she herself knew quite well, overcome "all feminine frailties, and perhaps most human frailties," but she, like Lou Andreas-Salomé, knew how to be grateful, and she fulfilled splendidly her role as the chief patroness of psychoanalysis. And for Anna Freud she filled a role that Lou Andreas-Salomé had played for many years: she was the older woman to whom Anna Freud could, without any feeling of rivalry, tell of her love for her father. With Dorothy

Burlingham, Anna Freud could and did talk about her father, but she also needed a maternal correspondent-confessor. And she needed a woman who could accept unquestioningly the view of life to which Lou Andreas-Salomé had once given words that Anna Freud never forgot. "I cannot tell you how often I think of a sentence you spoke to me once," she had written to Lou back in 1932, "that it does not matter what fate one has if one only really lives it."[95]

PART TWO

LONDON

6

ANOTHER LIFE

W<small>HEN</small> E<small>RNEST</small> J<small>ONES</small> was writing his biography of Freud, he read through the letters that Freud and Martha Bernays had exchanged during their painfully long engagement, and he was very impressed— by both of them. To their youngest daughter, he wrote an admiring letter: "What parents you had! You have inherited his depth of feeling together with her firmness and intactness. Now I have understood more fully your father's remark to me in 1938 in Vienna—"Anna ist stärker wie ich!" ("Anna is stronger than I am!").[1]

As he wrote her father's biography, Jones came to understand a good deal about Anna Freud, and much of his old ambivalence toward her disappeared. But the source of her strength in 1938, as she herself understood it, was not the inheritance from her parents that he proposed. In the chapter on "A Form of Altruism" in *The Ego and the Mechanisms of Defense*, Anna Freud gave her most succinct description of her type of strength.

> In conclusion, we may for a moment study the notion of altruistic surrender from another angle, namely, in its relation to the fear of death. Anyone who has very largely projected his instinctual impulses onto other people knows nothing of this fear. In the moment of danger his ego is not really concerned with his

own life. He experiences instead excessive concern and anxiety for the lives of his love objects. Observation shows that these objects, whose safety is so vital to him, are the vicarious figures upon whom he has displaced his instinctual wishes. . . . Analysis shows that both the anxiety [about others] and the absence of anxiety [about himself] are due rather to the subject's feeling that his own life is worth living and preserving only insofar as there is opportunity in it for the gratification of his instincts. When his impulses have been surrendered in favor of other people, their lives become precious rather than his own.[2]

As they were waiting to leave Vienna, and during their first months in England, Anna Freud worked tirelessly to help arrange escapes for those to whom she had surrendered her impulses—her family members, friends, and colleagues—and she was a calm in the middle of the Nazi storm. More than ever, also, she dedicated herself to her father's care and comfort. He was the chief recipient of her vicariousness, and he recognized her service even more fully than he had when he wrote to Lou Andreas-Salomé in 1935 that he was reminded of Mephistopheles in Goethe's *Faust*, who claimed that " 'In the end we all depend / On creatures we ourselves have made.' In any case," he added, "it was very wise to have made her."[3]

Anna Freud and Max Schur, in the absence of their trusted helper Pichler, divided between themselves the full responsibility for Freud's care as his cancer battle continued in London. She was on twenty-four-hour call, and during the last six of Freud's fifteen months that meant rising several times in the night to apply Orthoform to his jaw as well as helping him each time he removed his prosthesis for cleaning or for examinations. She saw patients, usually six or seven a day, sometimes as many as nine, but her world narrowed drastically. She had no desire to write. Caring for her father in what she knew was the approach of his death—even though she did not expect that it would come as quickly as it did—became her life. Years later, when she read an account of Sigmund Freud's "last chapter" that Max Schur had written, she said of it: "There is contained my whole biography."[4]

WHILE Anna Freud assumed the role of chief nurse, the other family members looked after the domestic arrangements. Ernst Freud, who conducted the search for a permanent residence, had provided a temporary furnished rental house at 39 Elsworthy Road. He and Ernest Jones took Freud and Martha Freud there after they arrived to a crowd of journalists and well-wishers in Victoria Station. Martha Freud and Mathilde Hollitscher took on the household management. They were helped by Paula Fichtl, the maid who had accompanied the family from Vienna. Mathilde and her husband stayed in the house until they found quarters of their own around the corner at 2 Maresfield Gardens, where Dorothy Burlingham and her younger daughter, Katrina, acquired a flat. Minna Bernays, still convalescing from her cataract operation, was confined to her bed on the second floor in Elsworthy Road, so that Freud, who was too frail to climb the stairs, could not even visit her.

Freud, apprehensive about his own ability to keep working, and depressed by Tante Minna's condition, felt an unexpected nostalgia for "the prison from which I have been released." Four of his elderly sisters remained in that prison, well provided for financially, but—as he could judge only from newspapers, in the absence of mail—not well protected from either the German or the Austrian Nazis. But, even though he was worried, Freud was gratified, as he reported to Eitingon:

> . . . all the children, our own as well as the adopted ones, are charming. Mathilde is as efficient here as Anna was in Vienna; Ernst is really like his name, "a tower of strength," and Lux and the children live up to him; the two men, Martin and Robert, who lost their heads a little under the pressure of the Nazis, are holding them high again. Am I to be the only one who doesn't cooperate and disappoints those who belong to him? My wife, moreover, has remained healthy and is undaunted.[5]

Freud's spirits were helped by summer visits from his half brother's son Samuel Freud of Manchester, and from his brother, Alexander, with his wife, Sophie, and son, Harry, who were on their way to a new home in Canada. A troupe of friends and distinguished cultural figures also came, and on June 23 a delegation from the Royal Society brought him the official Charter Book of the Society, so that he could add his signature to a collection that included—he was proud to note—two of his heroes, Newton and Darwin. By the be-

ginning of August, Freud was well enough so that Anna could undertake a brief journey to Paris for the International Psychoanalytic
Congress, the last Congress for nearly a decade.

But the end of the first summer in England brought the beginning of the "last chapter." Freud's cancer made a strong reappearance, and on September 8 he had to go into a London clinic for the
most severe surgery since the fall of 1923. The radical excision was
to be followed in a few weeks, his surgeon hoped, by removal of a
bone sequestrum; but the stubborn bone chip refused to surface,
and Freud spent the entire fall, in pain and fatigued, waiting for it.
The consolation was that the fall was also spent at 20 Maresfield
Gardens, the lovely three-story brick house with an enclosed rear
garden that is now the Freud Museum. And this house became, for
Freud himself, the museum for his antiquities collection, which
arrived there just before he was released from the clinic. Ernst Freud
designed his father's study to hold the collection, and Ernst Kris
helped arrange the treasures in just their Berggasse 19 order. Freud
and Anna Freud both saw patients in the house, he on the first
floor and she in her quarters on the third. In the evenings they discussed his last great effort to summarize his science for its practitioners, the never completed *Outline of Psychoanalysis*. They also
considered an essay criticizing Melanie Klein and her British Society
followers, an essay that was drafted but neither completed nor ever
published because the Freuds did not wish to cause trouble in the
psychoanalytic society that had given them refuge.[6] Life went on,
day by day.

IN February 1939, the cancer, back in force, was pronounced for the
first time inoperable. Schur and Anna Freud, so long familiar with
the enemy, had had difficulty convincing the English physician,
Dr. Trotter, of its severity, but Marie Bonaparte's friend Dr. Lacas-
sagne of the Institut Curie in Paris had come and confirmed their
judgment. Radiotherapy was prescribed, and for several weeks Freud
made exhausting daily visits to the offices of an English radiologist,
Dr. Finzi, and then endured less frequent further visits. The treatment, though it produced terrible pain and dizziness, helped—temporarily. Anna Freud was able to take a weekend at the end of May
for a vacation in Holland, where she visited the Lampls and gave her

encouragement to the struggling Dutch psychoanalytic group. The vacation helped her, but she labored under the feeling she described to Ernst Simmel, whom she had aided on his way to safety in Los Angeles: "sometimes I seem to myself as though I were at least a thousand years old and already had several lifetimes behind me."[7]

By June it was obvious that the radiotherapy was not going to stop the cancer's progress. The remnant of Freud's jaw was necrotic; as Schur reported, "The foetor became more and more unbearable, and could not be controlled with any kind of mouth hygiene."[8] Even Freud's chow dog, Lun, released from her quarantine to rejoin her master, shied away from his sickroom. Toward the end of July, Freud made the difficult decision to stop seeing his few patients. He dictated case reports on them to Anna Freud, and she arranged for them to see other analysts. A month-long visit from Oliver's lovely fifteen-year-old daughter Eva, who came from her new home in Nice, and one—the last—from Marie Bonaparte lightened the grayness of the August days, but nothing relieved Freud's incessant pain, which he chose to endure—for the sake of retaining his mental clarity— without opiates.

The beginning of the Second World War surprised no one in the household, but it did make everything more complicated. Freud's bed was moved toward the center of the house, away from the garden windows, in anticipation of air raids. The Freuds and their circle began to look for means to send children and nonworking spouses away from London. And, worst for Anna Freud, Dorothy Burlingham decided that she and her daughter Katrina would sail to New York, while sailing was unrestricted, so that they could be there when the older daughter, Mabbie, gave birth to her first child. Dorothy's plan was to return after helping Mabbie with the baby, checking that Katrina and Mikey would be well looked after by relatives in New York while they finished college, and seeing that Bob and the Norwegian woman he had married, Mossik, were settled so that Bob could take up an urban-planning program at Columbia. Both Katrina and Bob had been in renewed analyses with Anna Freud in London, and Dorothy hoped to arrange for other analysts among the New York émigré circle. All the young Burlinghams were still dealing with their grief over their father's suicide in May 1938, shortly after Mabbie's wedding.

The Burlinghams had been getting from Anna Freud the kind
of mixture of parental and analytic understanding that Dorothy herself had gotten then from Sigmund Freud. He had written her a
warm, somber letter.

> Maybe even the most intimate of friends, whose lives are indis-
> solubly linked with yours, should keep their distance at this time
> and leave it up to you to take hold of your emotions and mem-
> ories and to conquer them. But I am beset with worry that you
> may cause yourself pain, unjustifiably so, by an understandable
> effort on your part to grant your love (which never died) one
> last expression. Therefore, someone outside the family should be
> allowed to remind you of how little guilt, in the ordinary sense,
> there was in your relationship with your husband, but instead
> how overpowering was the influence of his illness, which made it
> impossible to have a satisfactory relationship, and which has to
> be accepted as yet another of those acts of fate that fall upon us
> human beings and cannot be changed by any brooding or self-
> analysis.[9]

When she left England for New York, Dorothy fully expected to
return in a few weeks and find her kind protector still alive. Confident in her plans, she departed on August 25 for a trip that ended
up, because of restrictions on American civilian travel, lasting seven
and-a-half agonizing months. On the day that Dorothy left and his
granddaughter Eva set out to rejoin her parents in Nice, Freud made
his last entry in his daily logbook: "Kriegspanik" ("war panic").[10]

On September 1, Max Schur, whose wife and children had been
evacuated to the English countryside, pending the whole family's
eventual emigration to New York, moved into 20 Maresfield Gardens. Freud grew weaker and weaker; eating was difficult; sleep was
nearly impossible. "He could hardly leave his bed and gradually
became cachectic," Schur noted.[11] Anna Freud was with him constantly, as her patients were on their two-month summer break until
the first week of October. She kept her vigil, and waited for Dorothy's
letters. "No, I don't worry about the war," Dorothy assured her,
"because I know that to you it is so unimportant in comparison to
your father. . . . I keep imagining you, your life and your difficulties
and problems—I am really with you most of the time."[12]

Sigmund Freud asked Max Schur on the twenty-first of September to relieve his pain with morphine. They had agreed in 1929, as Schur became his physician, that if a moment came when Freud felt himself to be suffering needlessly, *in extremis*, that Schur would administer morphine. When Freud said, "Now it's nothing but torture and makes no sense any more," Schur assured him that the promise was not forgotten. In his biography of Freud, Schur described their last conversation: "He sighed with relief, held my hand for a moment longer, and said: 'Ich danke Ihnen' ('I thank you'), and after a moment of hesitation he added: 'Sagen Sie es der Anna' ('Tell Anna about this')."[13] What Schur did was to ask Anna Freud to agree to her father's decision, which she did, reluctantly.

Hard as it was to know that the end was near, Anna Freud was grateful that her father was himself until he actually lost consciousness. His dying was as gentlemanly, stoical, and lucid as his life had been. "I believe that there is nothing worse than to see the people nearest to one lose the very qualities for which one loves them," she later told a friend whose husband was deteriorating. "I was spared that with my father, who was himself to the last minute."[14]

The vigil continued until three o'clock in the morning of September 23, 1939. Freud, peaceful, without pain, had lapsed into a coma from which he did not awake.

On the morning of September 26, the Freud family and a large group of mourners gathered at Golders Green, where Freud's body was cremated and his ashes committed to a Greek vase, a gift from Marie Bonaparte. The Princess came from Paris, but the war kept most of Freud's surviving friends and colleagues at their homes abroad, their old ones or—much more frequently—their émigré ones. Jones eulogized his colleague of thirty years in English, Stefan Zweig in German, and both the speeches pleased Anna Freud, as she wrote to Dorothy after the service. Dorothy had been afraid that her friend would be beyond such comfort: "You have gone through so terribly much—nothing will ever seem of great importance to you again, for the greatest has happened to you that will ever happen to you." But Anna Freud assured her that the profound loneliness she felt did not have a desperate quality to it. "I am so glad that life does not seem empty to you," Dorothy replied. "I had thought it would, but can understand that your father filled your life with so much meaning that it cannot be empty now."[15]

Martha Freud was, as always, gracious, concerned for others, and as strictly correct as she expected everyone else to be. She kept her poise through many weeks of worrying over her sister Minna's health, trying to reorganize the household when Paula Fichtl was interned on the Isle of Man as an "enemy alien," and thanking people for their condolences. Margarethe Rie Nunberg, in New York, for example, received a printed card on which Martha Freud had written a note that was characteristically full of commonplaces and also quite uncommon. In her grief, Martha Freud did not feel sustained by a transcendent meaning.

> I thank you from my heart for your good, warm words! I know that you loved our dear departed one, but he also loved you! Now we must continue to live without all of his goodness and wisdom, and you can judge what that means! Not even once may I beg, even if it could be granted to me, to be allowed to empower him with more than one human life span and the possibility that he continue to relieve the misery of our everyday life. Perhaps missing him is all the greater because of this. And even if the children surround me with touching love, and from all over the world written proofs of loyalty and devotion fly to me, my life still has lost its sense and meaning! Of you, my dear child, and of your dear children, one would like to hear something, but unfortunately we must get used to the fact that you are not one who likes to report on things! Isn't it remarkable that you are not liked any the less for it? Along with your dear husband, receive the most intimate greetings from your old friend Martha Freud.[16]

Five days after her father's funeral, Anna Freud went back to work with nine patients; she added a tenth in November. Freud had left the earnings from his books to his grandchildren, and that money was spent on their schooling, but Anna Freud had to act on her own resources as the family loan agency while her siblings tried to re-establish themselves financially. The hard work, she told her correspondents, was good for her. She always recommended work to mourners: "There really is nothing else and the worst at such times of mourning is to be idle, which only means to be sad or worse. I remember times in the middle of work when for minutes at least I could really forget what had happened."[17] And the work in which she could forget more easily was the work she added to her analytic hours: she wrote to all her father's friends and asked them to return his letters, made files for his notes and manuscripts, and generally put his literary remains in order. When she was sitting at her father's desk reading his handwriting, she felt him near.

Learning to live with her grief was a long ordeal; learning to control her anger, her feeling that her father's death—in his eighty-fourth year—was linked to Dr. Trotter's break with Dr. Pichler's treatment plan was a more pressing project. Even to people who were not close to her personally, she filled her letters with angry "ifs" and regrets as well as with her longing. As she wrote to A. A. Brill, the leader of the New York Psychoanalytic Society, for example, the two emotions filled her first two paragraphs.

> I was very glad to have your letter and I thought it was very good of you to write to me as you did. It makes it easier for me to realize what my father's not being alive any more means to friends of old, as you are. Because then it seems all the more natural that it means to me what it does mean. Besides the idea of his being there which you are missing, I miss the daily contact with him, the interchange of thought, the need he had for me, quite apart from all I needed from him. He had such a way to reduce every occurrence to its right proportions, whether it was just some daily difficulty or a disappointment or a big loss, like that of home and work and security as it occurred before our emigration. There was nothing that could throw him off his balance. It is much more difficult to see things in their right light without his help.
>
> It is really not so that we had known for a long time that he would die. He was very ill, but then he had been very ill many times before. It was just that the operations always saved his life again for a period, and the radium failed to do so. If the radium had cured the cancer, his own strength would still have been enough to carry him along. But the cancer had evidently become more malignant in these last two years. If we had stayed near his old surgeon, he might have kept him alive longer—but life under those conditions would not have been worth prolonging for him. He suffered greatly in the end, otherwise he was un-

changed. I do not think he worried in the least how we would carry on without him. I think he thought we should have learned enough by now to manage alone.[18]

Anna Freud was not feeling at one with a united, if dispersed, group of survivors when she wrote to A. A. Brill; she was feeling detached. Life seemed to her—so she told Dorothy—a farm that she was just visiting, on holiday.[19] This idea was a variation on an image she had once shared with Lou Andreas-Salomé: she was an "itinerant Indian monk" sojourning for a time in this world but really of another—except that the other world was now quite specific, it was with her father.[20] She dreamed of being with him, and she fantasized that she had always been with him, sharing all his troubles: "I am always sorry that I was not with him in the earlier days of his work and his difficult times with the world around. I should have liked to help him then. I really only came in when most of his battles were fought and won already."[21] Her interior balance was kept by her work and by anticipation of Dorothy's return. But, at the same time, she wondered anxiously what the quite this-worldly separation from Dorothy Burlingham, which she endured perforce, would mean. In the end, the separation was clarifying, but in its course it was ambiguous and fraught with complications.

IN New York, Dorothy Burlingham came to understand that for her, as for the whole circle of Vienna émigrés, Anna Freud was the intellectual center of gravity. One by one, their Viennese friends let Dorothy know how much they depended upon Anna Freud. Berta Bornstein said of herself that she was capable of "digesting and reusing what she had learned" in the Vienna child analysis seminar, but not of creative work on her own.[22] (This seems quite an act of self-underestimation, but it is true that Berta Bornstein had great difficulties in writing—if not in thinking.) The émigrés reconfirmed the lesson that Anna Freud had first learned when the newly founded Vienna Institute nearly foundered for lack of someone who could mobilize goodwill and inspire dedication to a common goal. "All are working with you in mind," Dorothy noted. "They all want a leader, but not one of them is ready to take the help they could from each other. Jealousy, fear of *Konkurrenz* [competition] keeps them all apart and hate is growing among them."[23] At one point, Anna Freud considered responding to the pleas her colleagues sent and making a trip to New York, but she was deterred by both the British travel restrictions and the possibility that her ship and Dorothy's might—after all their waiting—pass on the Atlantic.

Dorothy was also not convinced that America, for a visit or for an eventual emigration, would be good for her friend. Everything, she felt, would be available to Anna Freud: group seminars, patients, a revival of the Jackson Nursery. But, Dorothy wrote: "Somehow all these things would make original work very difficult, and that is what seems to me all important. I want you to carry on that part of your father's work." Dorothy disapproved of the "big business" mentality of the Americans, and she also found oppressive the infighting and jostling for position and prestige among the émigré analysts: "it is all so sad that people are not so strong and steady as they want and try to be." Summarizing a view with which Anna Freud had been familiar since her father's trip to America in 1909, Dorothy concluded: "I am not sure that you [would be] strong enough to change the current if you were here—I suppose that is what your father felt when he was here, that American life is not favorable to the growth of analysis."[24]

When Dorothy imagined Anna Freud sitting in London dutifully answering the boxes of condolence messages that had accumulated in the weeks after Freud's death, she realized that the demands that would be made upon her friend's time and energy in America would be much greater than those in the little world of English psychoanalysis. "You have often told me I exaggerate people's friendliness and [dependability]. 'One should not expect anything from anybody.' Do you remember you also told me that by not answering all letters you would be blamed and criticized, and I felt that people could only understand the tremendous correspondence you have. . . . But each one does feel you should have time for them, even if it is just a line."[25] In England, the friends agreed, things would be calmer—even taking into account the opposition of the Melanie Klein circle and the ongoing controversy over the theory and practice of child analysis.

Dorothy's professional commitment to life in England with Anna Freud was never seriously in doubt. But the resolution that was most important to her came on another front. She thought, for a time, that she was in love with Walter Langer, an American clinical psychologist with a Harvard doctorate who had trained with Anna Freud in Vienna from 1936 to 1938, and then in London through 1938. He had earned the Freud family's gratitude for his helpfulness during their migration and many Viennese owed him their safety because he had been so active in securing the American affidavits that made their emigrations possible. Langer was eight years Dorothy Burlingham's junior, not in good health, because he had been gassed as a First World War infantryman, and without much in the way of prospects because, as a nonmedical analyst, he was barred entry to the New York Institute. Dorothy was not deterred, however, until Anna Freud wrote to suggest that she be careful. Langer himself had revealed to Dorothy that his repetitious pattern of loving women and then suffering a sudden change of heart was what had taken him into analysis; he kept his distance. She was the one who had wanted his attentions. "Was it really just to make this separation easier?" she asked Anna Freud. "Was it to spoil something, to make complications? To produce again America versus Europe? Was it fantasy? Was it to take him away from Berta Bornstein?—but there was in reality no such relationship [with Bornstein]."[26]

Dorothy could not answer her own questions, and she feared that she had hurt Anna Freud by writing about her dilemma. When no telegram arrived on January 1, 1940, to bring Anna Freud's expected New Year's greetings, Dorothy—in her guilt and confusion—assumed that her candor had cost her Anna Freud's friendship. She was frantic, and by the time the telegram—delayed on the wires—arrived, Dorothy was completely clear in her mind that nothing in life mattered more to her than her friendship with Anna Freud. "Someone else did come into my life but it did not force you out—you were always there in my thoughts, and even there you tried to help me. You know from my letters that I was afraid—afraid of complications, afraid of being forced apart—but it was only now that I was shocked into realizing that I might really lose you—and that the consequences might ruin my life and ours together." Anna Freud's reassurances calmed Dorothy, who was then able to write: "Life has a sense again, perhaps I can still make it worthwhile, so long as you help me—for, Anna, it is always you who have to help."[27]

Anna Freud, for her part, felt an anxiety all too familiar: she did not want Dorothy to return because she felt sorry for her, or because she felt guilty about hurting her. Being treated as an inadequate littlest child or as a woman with no life of her own was not a condition Anna Freud wanted revived in any form; she wanted Dorothy to make her choice freely. Dorothy's reassurances were just as clear as the ones she had received: "You need not worry I never could come back to you out of a sense of guilt or being sorry for you—that is something the experience of January 1st showed me forever—if that is what you mean by freedom in my relationship to you, then I understand—for there I was not divided. I knew definitely just how I felt about you and what my relationship to you meant."[28]

When she was separated from Anna Freud, Dorothy Burlingham had identified with her—almost as though she had been mourning for Anna Freud rather than for Sigmund Freud. Like a mourner, she surmounted her loss with identification. What she chiefly identified with was Anna Freud's detachment, her feeling of being a visitor in life; and this condition was very different from Dorothy's previous dependence on people—particularly her children—for company and support. "I think I have tried to identify myself not only with your father but with you—which shows in the absolute indifference I have to life. It's a very strange contrast to the way I used to be, but it has its advantages." Writing as though she had lived through Anna Freud's chapter on "altruistic surrender," Dorothy reflected: "It is so curious how different it makes the world if you lose the fear of death or do not hang onto life. One really only cares about the other [person]. I know life without you would be quite without sense— just to live out and nothing more—I am quite sure there would be no more development." Dorothy Burlingham became convinced that her own intellectual inhibitions, her insecurities, and her unresolved phobia about noise would paralyze her if she turned away from the central source of meaning in her life—Anna Freud.[29]

A<small>T THE END</small> of March 1940, Dorothy Burlingham was finally able to set out for England. She sailed on the *Conte di Savoia* to Genoa and then went by train through Italy and France to arrive in London on April 10—just about six months after she had planned. Even though she and Anna Freud had become surer in their relationship, they decided not to live together while Minna Bernays was still an invalid in the house and in need of a full-time live-in nurse. Anna Freud wanted to keep her father's part of their house just as it had been, as a memorial to him, and there were not enough other rooms to provide Dorothy with a suite that could include a consulting room. Until Minna's death in 1941, Dorothy stayed in her flat at 2 Maresfield Gardens and maintained another small place there so that she could put up visitors and provide temporary quarters to émigrés. Her children were unable to visit until 1946.

In America, Dorothy had made an important set of contacts. Bettina Warburg in New York sent money that was used to support émigrés to England. William Bullitt, the former American ambassador to France, helped with visas, and when Joseph Kennedy was installed as American ambassador to the Court of St. James's, he helped those members of Anna Freud's circle who wanted to leave the English and air raids behind and move to America—particularly Edward and Grete Bibring and, later, Ernst and Marianne Kris. But the most important contact for the future of the Freud-Burlingham partnership was the American Foster Parents' Plan for War Children. Dorothy had visited this organization in New York hoping to get back to England by offering her services to its offices in France. That effort, like so many others she made, had been fruitless, but a year later American Foster Parents' did become the chief funding agency for the Hampstead War Nursery.

Anna Freud had made a number of acquaintances among English philanthropists concerned with child welfare and specifically with children whose families had been broken up in one way or another by the war. The Duchess of Kent, Marie Bonaparte's niece, Lady Lyons, whose husband was the governor of the Isle of Wight, Lady Clarke, and William Gilchrist, an analysand of Anna Freud's, all at various junctures helped Anna Freud fund her wartime projects. The first venture, planned in October 1940, was a temporary shelter for bombed-out families. But the need for such a shelter turned out to be less than the need for a residence designed particularly for children who were "billeting problems," that is, who could not be evacuated without their mothers or who had developed difficulties in foster care situations. In January 1941, the Children's Rest Center at 13 Wedderburn Road was opened in a house loaned for the purpose and furnished with donations from a Swedish Committee and imports from the Jackson Nursery, Vienna. Gifts from Dorothy's American sources and from the British War Relief Society helped keep the Children's Rest Center going on its small scale. Most of the ten to twelve children came—a few with their mothers—from the East End of London, which had been reduced to rubble and chaos in the first Blitz.

Then, early in 1941, the American Foster Parents' Plan increased its contribution so that the number of children at Wedderburn Road rose to thirty and, by the summer of 1941, two additional buildings were equipped and opened: a Babies' Rest Center at 5 Netherhall Gardens in Hampstead, and a country house called New Barn in Essex, an evacuation residence for older children. After a financial crisis in February 1942, the original Wedderburn Road house was used only as a nursery school, not as a residence, so that the Foster Parents' Plan money could be focused for maximum effect in just two buildings.

The Netherhall Gardens and New Barn buildings allowed Anna Freud to address her two most urgent concerns: to have an evacuation residence organized and ready to receive children from the London homes, and to be able to care for babies, including newborns, the most vulnerable population. When the three buildings were all working at capacity in 1941, 120 children were being cared for in them. Anna Freud and Dorothy Burlingham supervised the London centers, but New Barn was in the charge of a Berliner, Alice Goldberger, who was requisitioned from a nursery school that she had established on the Isle of Man for children whose "enemy alien" families were awaiting residence permits. Anna Freud came to know of her work as she was trying to negotiate release for her nephew Ernst Halberstadt and her maid, Paula Fichtl, who were both interned on the Isle of Man.[30]

Alice Goldberger was one of the most important people who came into Anna Freud's circle during the war. But there were many others, the majority of whom were German and Austrian Jewish refugees and noncitizen émigrés who could not, by government decree, leave London for evacuation areas. Martha Herzberg, who had worked as a volunteer in the Jackson Nursery, donated her services as the chief matron for the London homes. A prominent Viennese salon hostess, Frau Herzberg was adroit at reconciling conflicts that arose between departments—and among classes—in the various homes, and she completely relieved Anna Freud of such diplomatic responsibilities. She also made a friend for the homes of the English poet Stephen Spender. In his capacity as air-raid warden in Hampstead, Spender objected to the fact that the Children's Rest Center had only a heavy curtain for a front door. Frau Herzberg convinced him that if each person in need of assistance for a child had knocked on a wooden front door, the children already getting assistance would be unable to take their naps. She also convinced skeptical parents that in the basement air-raid-shelter bunks their children should sleep behind rope nets, where they looked like caged animals but were at least safe from getting tossed onto the floor when bombs shook the house. Anna Freud and her staff wove the nets themselves.

Josefine Stross, the pediatrician for the Jackson Nursery, acted as the doctor for children and staff at both the London centers and also, in emergencies, at the Essex center. Finding medical supplies, particularly vaccines, to administer to the children was a constant problem, and finding ways to isolate children with contagious diseases while keeping them within the centers—and thus avoiding traumatic hospital stays—was just the kind of logistical challenge that someone raised in a large family as Anna Freud was could appreciate. Whooping cough, scarlet fever, measles, and flu came and went in the homes, but there was only one death in the War Nursery's five-year existence—a baby already weakened by starting off his little life in a subway-station shelter.

When one of the epidemics of flu hit the Hampstead staff, Ilse Hellman, who had trained as a psychologist with Charlotte Bühler at the University of Vienna, went to help out for a day. Anna Freud observed the volunteer on the floor playing with a group of children, and later asked her if she would take the post of superintendent for 5 Netherhall Gardens, which was about to open. This fortunate hiring brought Anna Freud someone who was well trained in empirical psychology and could teach, for example, the Bühler-Hetzer Scale, which was a general developmental test for preschool children. Ilse

Hellman, and later another Charlotte Bühler trainee, Liselotte Frankl, supplied a balance of empirical methods to the predominantly psychoanalytic training the Hampstead staff received.

Many of the young women who worked and trained in the Hampstead War Nursery came to it because they had heard of its unique psychoanalytic approach. Some had experience in child welfare or nursing, some were beginners; some stayed for relatively brief periods, and some stayed for the entire five years. Six of the trainees used their Nursery experience as the basis for later psychoanalytic training under Anna Freud's supervision: Joanna Kohler (later Benekendorf), Lizzy Wallentin (later Rolnick), Sara Kut (later Rosenfeld), Hanna Engl (later Kennedy), Alice Goldberger, and Anneliese Schurmann. Sophie Dann, a nurse who had worked for the Freud family caring for Tante Minna, headed up the baby department in Netherhall Gardens; her sister Gertrud, who gained her experience on the spot, was in charge of the toddlers. Both the Danns remained associated with Anna Freud's work even after Anna Freud's death, in part bec use of the family feeling they found at the Hampstead War Nursery. When their younger sister married in 1944, Anna Freud arranged for a family party in the Netherhall Gardens house. "Her mother lent a lace tablecloth, china, silver cutlery, roses: everything came from 20 Maresfield Gardens," Sophie Dann remembered. "The Nursery provided the dinner, cooked by the kitchen staff. It was a lovely present for us three sisters."[31] The Danns' parents were—luckily enough—in Palestine, so the young women were in the same condition as many of the Hampstead children: their parents were alive but away.

UNLIKE the typical British residential nurseries of the wartime, the Hampstead War Nursery made a point of involving the absent parents as much as possible in their children's lives. Mothers of newborns were encouraged to live in and work as housekeepers so that they could nurse their babies; a number of sibling groups were accepted together so that the sibling bonds would not, like so much else, be disrupted and so that their parents would be visiting in just one place. The London buildings were open to visiting at all hours, and transport to the Essex farmhouse was provided as often as finances, air raids, quarantines, and gasoline rationing permitted—

usually about once a month. With the help of her secretary and bookkeeper, Jula Weiss, who had worked for Sigmund Freud in Vienna, Anna Freud maintained an enormous correspondence with fathers serving overseas in the British forces and mothers working at military agencies and munitions plants in London. Cards and letters and parcels came to the children when the parents could not. The Nursery's social worker, James Robertson, then a conscientious objector and later a prominent psychoanalyst, made every kind of effort to help the children's families stay together and stay in touch with the Nursery.

The theory behind this practice came from August Aichhorn's work with delinquent and dissocial children in Vienna. Aichhorn had described the differences between "institutional children" and children raised in families—even in tumultuous families—in general terms that stressed the importance of early mothering for character development. Anna Freud and Dorothy Burlingham elaborated on his description in their 1942 booklet *Young Children in War-Time: A Year's Work in a Residential War Nursery* and in a more extensive book published in 1944, *Infants Without Families: The Case For and Against Residential Nurseries*. Both of these works were developed from lectures Anna Freud gave to the Nursery Schools Association of Great Britain, like her 1941 "The Need of the Small Child to Be Mothered," and from pieces of the reports that Anna Freud wrote for the American Foster Parents' Plan. The monthly and year-end reports often felt like a terrible burden: writing was never easy for Anna Freud, and writing during long nights of air raids after long days of administrative struggle to keep the Nursery in good order was extremely difficult. She even had to write within the bounds of the wartime mail censorship, which forbade details about the air-raid conditions. But the reports were, on the other hand, a valuable incentive to record and formulate the research dimension of the Nursery work. Dorothy Burlingham, whose tuberculosis made it impossible for her to work as consistently as Anna Freud, supplied to the joint writing endeavor her skill with analyzing their case records and her interest in charting the children's eating, sleeping, and playing patterns.

Aichhorn had noted clearly the advantageous and disadvantageous results of institutional upbringing as he saw them in teenagers, including teenagers who had been children during the First World War. What Anna Freud and Dorothy Burlingham did was to note the effects of institutional life at each developmental stage. Their general conclusion was simple: "Advantages and disadvantages [of institutional life] vary to an astonishing degree according to the periods of development." But to get to this conclusion they had to make elaborate observations and adapt the psychoanalytic theory of oral, anal, and phallic-genital stages for use in the extreme wartime conditions.

> Babies between birth and about five months of age, when not breast-fed under either condition, develop better in our Nursery than in the average low-income household. . . . The reasons are not difficult to find: more carefully prepared food, with variation in the food formulas whenever necessary; plenty of air in outdoor life, whenever the weather permits; less economy in laundry; skilled and regular handling and removal from the disturbances of a crowded household in restricted conditions.

After five months, and up to about twelve months, the advantage for a baby's intellectual and emotional development shifts to the family context, though a nursery may retain the advantage for physical development. The emotional interplay and resulting intellectual stimulation between a mothering figure and a child cannot be duplicated in a nursery, when any one child receives individual attention only for feeding, bathing, changing, and whichever activities the staff has time for. Children between one and two years of age, on the other hand, thrive in nurseries where they have the space to do what they most love to do: move. But, for all the advantage a nursery presents for developing muscular coordination, it is at a disadvantage with one- to two-year-olds in other areas—particularly language learning and toilet training, both of which depend upon an ongoing emotional bond with a mothering figure. A child's pleasure in eating can be cultivated adequately in a carefully organized nursery setting, as the Jackson Nursery feeding experiments had confirmed earlier. But to the Jackson Nursery results a new dimension of understanding was added: a child "shows every inclination to treat food given by the mother as he treats the mother, which means that all the possible disturbances of the child-mother relationship turn easily into eating disturbances."[32] A nursery child, uncomplicated by the identification of mother and food, eats according to appetite rather than for love or hate of the mother or desire to please or annoy her.

The carefully delineated balance sheet that Anna Freud and Dorothy Burlingham offered was lucidly summarized: "The institutional child in the first two years has advantages in all those spheres of life which are independent of the emotional side of his nature; he is at a disadvantage wherever the emotional tie to the mother or to the family is the mainspring of development."[33] The Hampstead War Nursery was organized, in all its departments, to minimize the institutional children's disadvantages. Involving the children's parents was crucial, but insufficient. After the Nursery had been running for a year, Anna Freud and Dorothy Burlingham, in consultation with the staff, decided to reorganize their nursery population into familylike groups of four or five children and a "mother." The groups were formed according to the preferences of both the children and the young staff members, and the children looked to their mother-substitute for all the needs that had been supplied previously by whichever staff member happened to be on duty or available.

The organizers of this revolution were astonished by its immediate result. "The need for individual attachment [and] with [it] the feelings which had been lying dormant came out in a rush and in the course of one week all six families were completely and firmly established."[34] Along with the children's joy went tremendous anxiety about loss—for they had all experienced painful separations from their own mothers—and also riotous jealousy of both their newly created siblings and their neighboring groups. Each child expected his or her mother's exclusive dedication within the group and tolerated no attentions given to neighbors. The commotion from frustrations and fights was tremendous—for two or three weeks; and then the frenzy subsided and something like normal family life appeared, with all the anticipated benefits for the children's emotional lives.

There were not enough male staff to provide the groups with substitute fathers as well. But James Robertson, Willi Hoffer and the various air-raid wardens and firemen in the neighborhood were encouraged to visit as much as possible. Anna Freud herself took on one traditionally male role: at Christmas, she played Father Christmas for the children. When the New Barn residence was operating at full capacity, she and Dorothy Burlingham took the opportunity to affirm their shared image of what they meant to each other. They both dressed up as Father Christmas. "There are so many people here," Anna Freud explained to the children, "that I had to bring my twin brother along."[35]

In the process of establishing the familylike groups, the Hampstead staff had an opportunity to reexamine one of the key conclusions that Anna Freud had advanced in her first year of work. She had argued that it was not simply their separations from their own mothers that had traumatized the Nursery children; it was the manner of their separations. Gradual separations, involving visits from the mothers and careful introduction of a substitute mother figure, allowed children to keep their feelings directed toward others; they did not turn their love or their rage on themselves. With a system of substitute mothering to offer new admissions to the Nursery, there were no cases like the three-year-old named Billie who had been abruptly left at the door in 1941. The child had mourned for his mother ceaselessly, by nodding and repeating over and over his hope that she would come back and take him home. His ritual incantation was slowly condensed into a mumble and a series of gestures that represented putting on an overcoat, zipping it up—getting ready to go home. "While the other children were mostly busy with their toys, playing games, making music, etc., Billie, totally uninterested, would stand somewhere in a corner, moving his hands and lips with an absolutely tragic expression on his face. . . . We were shocked to see an apparently healthy child develop a compulsive tic under our very eyes." When Billie's mother was able to return after an illness, the tic disappeared; when she was persuaded to visit him as often as she could, "Billie became a member of the nursery like any other child."[36]

In November 1941, after the Nursery had been in operation for about nine months, Anna Freud and Dorothy Burlingham decided to offer the twenty young staff members an informal training course. The staff used their rest hours to attend a series of courses prepared by the older staff members and heads of departments, many of whom had some prewar teaching experience. They also agreed to rotate from department to department in the Nursery, so that they could learn to handle babies, junior toddlers, nursery children, and ill children in the infirmary. Their rotations also gave them experience with the kitchens, housekeeping operations, and administration. As Anna Freud told them: "My father often said, a good woman is able to do everything."

Josefine Stross gave an initial course of thirty lectures on anatomy, first aid, nutrition, hygiene, and children's diseases. Later Sophie Dann took hygiene as a separate topic, and nutrition was taught in its practical aspects by the Nursery's chief cook, Sofie Wutsch, a lady who had the miraculous ability to turn out meals for sixty to eighty people as though shortages and rationing were not problems. Sister Claire Nettl taught courses in gymnastics for babies and for toddlers, and the head nursery-school teacher, Hedy Schwarz, introduced students to the Montessori Method as she had learned it in the Vienna Montessori school. Mental Development and Testing were both taught by Ilse Hellman.[37]

Anna Freud and Dorothy Burlingham also brought to the training program several psychoanalyst colleagues. Hedwig Hoffer, Willi Hoffer's wife, joined Dorothy Burlingham for a two-part course on Freud's writings. This was Dorothy Burlingham's first try at teaching, and the experience was as valuable for her as for her students: she used the classes to do for herself what she had suggested in 1940 that Anna Freud do for her—"Someday you will have to help me with theory."[38] Consulting with Hedwig Hoffer and teaching helped prepare Dorothy Burlingham for the role of training analyst that she later assumed when the Nursery training scheme evolved into a full-scale, certified psychoanalytic course.

Throughout the war, Anna Freud conducted a Wednesday-evening seminar for analysts, modeled on the famous Wednesday evenings of the Vienna Psychoanalytic Society. Her old friend Eva Rosenfeld and several analysts trained at Eitingon's Berlin Policlinik came to the seminar, and Anna Freud recruited from among them for the Nursery training scheme. Dr. Kate Misch Friedlander, who had emigrated to England in 1933 with Ernest Jones's help, prepared a course called "Fundamental Concepts of Psychoanalysis" for the Nursery staff. Anna Freud came to respect Kate Friedlander's theoretical ability highly, and she also admired the work she was doing in child guidance and with juvenile delinquents—a continuation in England of August Aichhorn's Vienna work.[39] Kate Friedlander and her close friend Dr. Barbara Lantos, a Hungarian-born analyst, were instrumental after the war in convincing Anna Freud to organize the Hampstead Child Therapy Clinic and Course, in which they both served as teachers and training analysts. They both also gave to Anna Freud's seminar continuity with the socialist political leanings of the Berlin Policlinik and of the first generation of trainees at the Vienna Psychoanalytic Institute: they, like Anna Freud herself, were dedicated to making sure that psychoanalysis was not a therapy for the rich and that its applications were tied to progressive educational and child guidance institutions.

The training that was offered at the Hampstead War Nursery solved a practical problem: "The Nursery never lacked working students; vacancies were in constant demand, and applicants frequently had to be refused or placed on a waiting list."[40] In fact, the training was such an allure that the students joined the older staff in working without wages during a month-long financial crisis in 1942. But they were well rewarded, both by the training itself and by Anna Freud's dedicated efforts to find them placements after the war in hospitals and child guidance centers, in England and in America.

Anna Freud considered herself well rewarded too. "So far as the organizers of the Nursery were concerned, their interest in the training scheme went far beyond its practical wartime value. For them it created an opportunity to realize and thereby put to the test certain ideas concerning an all-round training for workers with children, i.e., a training which does not unduly stress either the bodily or the mental side of the development of children, but is based on an understanding of the interaction of the two sides." The teaching staff was able to implement a principle that was crucial to all of Anna Freud's later educational work: "All theoretical teaching was given in close connection with the practical work of the students in the various departments, and constantly illustrated with living examples which the rich case material of the Nurseries provided. Advanced students were put in individual charge of problem children and received guidance in the handling of their difficulties."

The interplay of practical work, theoretical instruction, and supervision depended on the same simple technique that Anna Freud had introduced in the Jackson Nursery: everybody took notes on index cards. "Observations were recorded in all departments and furnished the basis for teaching and discussion." Out of the index-card files they built up developmental charts and histories for each child that focused on key areas: feeding, sleep, bodily development, intellectual development, and formation of relationships (or "object relations"). To the index-card record they also added photographs and films made by Willi Hoffer, whose work inspired James Robertson to make an influential series of postwar films of children in hospitals, foster placements, and other situations of stress.

BECAUSE the Nursery staff had so carefully cultivated contacts with their children's chief "objects," their parents, the end of the war did not mean another time of traumatic separation. Of the one hundred children who were at Netherhall Gardens or in Essex at New Barn when the war ended, only sixteen were not returned to a parent or parents. Three homeless children were placed in one of the Foster Parents' Plan for War Children residences; an orphan and a handicapped child went to special homes; several children who had been sent by charitable institutions were taken in charge by those institutions. A brother and sister whose expectant mother was divorcing and planning to remarry were the only ones completely estranged from their parents. The rate of restoration to families was remarkable, since, of the 191 children who had been admitted to the Nursery, 101 had stayed for between a year and five years. Ten of the children had spent five full years away from their families.

For Anna Freud, who, with her staff, had virtually raised the long-timers, they were "our children." With both social work and research goals in mind, she organized an After Care Scheme to follow them out into the world after the war, but she also kept track of many of them in the way she found most familiar—she corresponded with them and sent gifts. The Foster Parents' Plan, she told a friend in 1954, "still gives us 25 pounds a month to spend on our former nursery children, and we use this to help with education or clothing, and for keeping in touch with the children through little gifts on their birthdays or at Christmas time."[41] Holidays brought a deluge of cards for Miss Freud. She replied to each. Important dates in the children's later lives were conveyed to her in the form of graduation invitations, wedding and birth announcements, notices of prizes, performances, and career plans. Several of the children, in-

cluding one boy who went on to become a well-known member of
the National Theatre Company, kept in touch to the extent of sending their own children to Anna Freud's later nursery school. Not all
the families were pleased with their family news, however. The
mother of one of the Nursery children was reluctant to admit that
her daughter had (as she put it) "slipped up" and married six
months' pregnant; but this first report that a Nursery child had had
a child met with the same calm, concerned, familial response from
Miss Freud that the mother herself had known during the war. "I
was really delighted that we have a grandchild, and I only hope that
the young people will not have too difficult a time."[42]

In the fall of 1938, while Sigmund Freud was still alive, Anna
Freud gave a series of three public lectures on psychoanalysis. The
invitation to speak came from John C. Hill, head of the East London
school district from which a number of the Hampstead War Nursery
children later came. Hill, a Scotsman whose interest in Freud had
informed his pedagogical leadership for almost fifteen years, had first
approached Ernst Freud to ask whether Freud himself might be able
to lecture, but he accepted Ernst's suggestion that Anna Freud be
asked instead because their father was too frail. Hill's openness to
this suggestion brought him a friendship he treasured for the rest
of his long life, and Anna Freud found in him the only friend in
England for whom she agreed to be "Anna" rather than "Miss
Freud."

Hill, ten years Anna's senior, always remained "Mr. Hill." But
his later invitations for dinner at the Trocadero and evenings at the
theater or the cinema were accepted gladly—when Anna Freud's
schedule permitted—and his rather fatherly attentions, graciously
supported by his wife, gave Anna Freud great pleasure. Like August
Aichhorn, Hill was just the kind of ardent admirer of her father
whom Anna Freud most enjoyed: he was largely self-educated,
tenaciously independent-minded, unpretentious, wry, and commonsensical. The tenets of psychoanalysis seemed to him self-evidently
true—he saw them illustrated every day in his schoolchildren and in

the behavior of his three sons. What he observed in school he recorded in a remarkable book, *Teaching and the Unconscious Mind*;
what he observed at home he reported to Anna Freud anecdotally,
complete with the relevant quotations from her father's writings, in
charming letters.

The excitement that J. C. Hill felt at Anna Freud's fall 1938
lectures was shared by an audience of London educators—many of
them from East London—and émigré analysts. She presented a version of her 1930 publication *Psychoanalysis for Teachers and Parents*,
and, as had happened in Vienna, she used her lectures to build a
bridge from the analytic community to the school system. Hill later
incorporated what she had to say into his work with the "special
classes" for East London children he organized during the war. But
the effect of the lectures on the émigré analysts was, for the immediate moment, even more important. Rudolf Ekstein, one of the
younger Viennese émigrés, later the coordinator for training and research at the Reiss-Davis Clinic for Child Guidance in Los Angeles,
reminded her "how solidified all of us felt after the debacle in
Austria, when we came to listen to you."[43] The lectures were the
first gathering of the Freudian clan after the Freuds' emigration, and
what they meant was: psychoanalysis will survive. Analysts of Anna
Freud's own generation and of the next generation, which she had
helped train in Vienna and in Berlin, and even several of her former
elementary-school students who were studying social work in London, listened to her as to the future.

But the solidarity that Anna Freud cultivated at her lectures,
and kept on cultivating in her Wednesday private seminars and her
Hampstead War Nursery training scheme, was difficult to maintain in
the face of the opposing psychoanalytic camp: Melanie Klein and her
followers in the British Psychoanalytical Society. Even while Freud
was still alive, the disagreements between Anna Freud's group and
Melanie Klein's group had been strenuous enough to prompt Freud
to work on his never published critique of Klein. During the war,
as everyone's nerves grew more and more strained, the disagreements
became more vehement and more personal. No one inside the British
Society could be as uncomplicated a Freudian as J. C. Hill was, and
certainly no one could put their convictions into the kind of statements he loved to pen: "Every cat knows much about bringing up

kittens, and every parent knows much about bringing up children, if one can reduce the anger, anxiety and daft ideas which get in the way of their wisdom."[44]

ANGER, anxiety and daft ideas were in great supply in the British Psychoanalytical Society, where an odd situation had developed. Ernest Jones, who had ruled the British Psychoanalytical Society since he founded it after the First World War, worked heroically to bring to England as many of the persecuted Continental analysts as he could. Most of the people he helped, however, were professionally opposed to Melanie Klein, whose cause he had championed for more than a decade. The influx of opponents had made Melanie Klein so furious that any consideration she might have felt for the fate that her opponents would have suffered without Jones's help was overwhelmed. She charged Jones with having "done much harm to psychoanalysis" by providing the Freuds and their circle with a refuge.[45] Jones stooped to defend himself by reminding Melanie Klein that the entire Council of the British Society had reviewed the Viennese applications for membership, and then he attempted to placate her by denigrating Anna Freud; "She is certainly a tough, and perhaps indigestible morsel. She has probably gone as far in analysis as she can and she has no pioneering originality." Klein seems to have accepted Jones's explanations, but she tried to keep his tether short: "Some of the Viennese who since went to the USA have very soon volunteered the information to me and to others that they had every possibility to go to America and would have done so had you not invited and encouraged them to come to England."

Caught between his desire to aid the Freuds and keep their good—if not warm—opinion and his desire to promote Melanie Klein's work, Jones had little room to maneuver. When the war began, he saw that the opportunity to retreat from the psychoanalytic fray and the opportunity to save himself from the Blitz were one and the same. By retiring to his country home in Sussex, he left most of the practical administration of the Society to Sylvia Payne, who was sympathetic to Klein but not a Kleinian, and Edward Glover, once an advocate of Klein's views but since 1935 an opponent. Glover, in alliance with Melanie Klein's daughter, Melitta

Schmideberg, who was in analysis with him, had been actively criticizing Klein's work at the British Society meetings even before the
Viennese emigration. The British analysts had had to struggle with
both a split in their own ranks and the terrible spectacle of a
daughter, aided by her analyst, attacking her mother in public. When
the Viennese began to attend the meetings, and hold positions on
the research and training committees, the internecine struggle in the
Society began to look like the political macrocosm: the two critical
factions, Glover's and Anna Freud's, could hardly understand each
other, but they were perceived as a united front; both professed to
find Klein's work since the mid-1930s incomprehensible, but for different reasons. Anna Freud admired Edward Glover, but did not
want an alliance, particularly as she found Melitta Schmideberg "too
asocial to cooperate with."[46] The Kleinians, quite reasonably from
their point of view, wanted an end to Glover's de facto leadership,
and they felt that Ernest Jones was further betraying them by maintaining that Glover was the only member qualified to be his successor. Jones, having worked himself into an increasingly untenable
position, decided that the period of his "aristocratic leadership"
should, indeed, end.[47] But everyone concerned knew that an experiment with democracy in the Society would accentuate the controversies among the factions, for they would have to fight for power, not
just for the ear of their old czar.

Ernest Jones, who was always capable of playing any side of
any court as the need arose, assured Anna Freud that his support of
Melanie Klein implied no disrespect for Freud's work. He appreciated her awkward position in London as a latecomer, instructed by
her father not to intrude on the affairs of the British Society and
always to remain grateful for her English refuge. In the winter of
1942, when she felt that the dissension in the Society had become
intolerable, Jones conceded that Melanie Klein's contributions, valuable as they were, came from a mind "neither scientific nor orderly."
He went on, placating Anna Freud in the same denigratory tone he
had used earlier to Melanie Klein: "her presentations are lamentable.
She is also in many ways neurotic and has a tendency, which she is
trying to check, to become '*verrannt*' [obstinate]. It would not be
surprising, further, that the danger would exist in such a person to
distort the objective reality by emphasizing certain aspects at the

expense of others."[48] Anna Freud certainly knew from her own experience that Jones was quick to charge others with neurotic distortions of "objective reality," and she must have found it curious for Jones to be noting that Klein might underestimate "the Oedipus complex and the part played by the father," since she was familiar with Jones's arguments for Klein's view of the Oedipus complex, which he had been making since the 1934 International Congress in Lucerne.

THAT Congress had provided the prologue for the second major phase of the controversy between the Freudians and the Kleinians, the phase in which the old theoretical differences grew to new depth and the new factor of forced emigrations altered the old political-theoretical alliances. All the main actors in the London-based second phase had been present at the Congress, each in search of his or her role. Melitta Schmideberg, who had left her mother's camp temporarily in 1929 to study with Anna Freud in Vienna, delivered a paper that was so intemperately critical of Anna Freud that Paul Federn of the *Zeitschrift* and Jones of the *International Journal* had refused to publish it until it was revised.[49] But this was her last pro-Kleinian effort, and her future publications dealt out criticism of the same tone to her mother.

Melanie Klein's own Congress paper, "A Contribution to the Psychogenesis of Manic-Depressive States," had been a new departure. It was her first major effort since the publication of her summary volume, *The Psychoanalysis of Children*, in 1932, and it was also, personally, an important part of her mourning for the death in April 1934 of the oldest of her two sons in a climbing accident. In the paper, as in a sequel that contained a thinly veiled, very touching self-analysis of her own mourning for her son, Klein introduced and elaborated her concept of "the infantile depressive position."[50] This concept was the centerpiece of the controversy in the 1930s and 1940s.

Jones, aware of the incomprehension with which Klein's Congress paper would be greeted by the Viennese, wrote a paper of his own, "Early Female Sexuality," which he delivered in Vienna for the purpose of furthering the debate launched in Lucerne about what happens in the first year of a child's psychic life. Jones's scientific mission to Vienna was the first of three discussions: Joan Riviere also lectured to the Vienna Society, and Robert Waelder responded to her paper with a visit to the British Society. Anna Freud heard both the Vienna lectures, but she did not wish to participate in the exchange as a lecturer, both because she wanted to avoid direct theoretical polemics and because she was preoccupied with and worn out by the chaos of the psychoanalytic organizations.

The Lucerne Congress, the first after Hitler's ascension to power in Germany, had also been politically tumultuous—and not just because the question of Wilhelm Reich's membership in the international was so volatile. A few German émigré analysts had taken up residence in England and America in 1933; they sought hospital positions and established private practices that drew heavily on the limited pool of analytic patients. The economic uncertainty caused by the emigration made everyone nervous about their livelihoods; nonmedical analysts heading for America, which was so illiberal on "the question of lay analysis," were particularly worried. At Lucerne, Eitingon had introduced a resolution allowing members severed from their own psychoanalytic societies for political reasons to be accepted directly as members of the International Association. This humane resolution met with isolationist rigidity from the American Psychoanalytic Association, which subsequently demanded that such "free floating membership" be withdrawn from analysts settling in America.[51] The American obsession with keeping lay analysts from corrupting psychoanalysis grew more rather than less severe during the international crisis.

Anna Freud had found the combination of theoretical and political struggles exhausting, and the Lucerne Congress had marked, for her, the beginning of an effort, which became even stronger in England, both to let others take over the theoretical battles and to relinquish some of her official responsibilities. With great relief, she gave up the position of Central Secretary of the International to Edward Glover, who at the time was still an ally of Klein's—a fact that mattered not at all to Anna Freud, who always took his theoretical work quite seriously. "Do you know what they call *Viehsarbeit* [swinish labor] in Vienna?" Anna Freud asked Ernst Simmel. "Well, that was the Lucerne Congress. I am now able to imagine what it must be like to be a politician, since it proves so hard to hold together and manage even our handful of people. . . . From now on, if people complain that the blackboard is not washed clean after class, it is no longer my fault; I have already played the maid-of-all-work for too long."[52] After her father's death, her patience for politics in the psychoanalytic world was even slighter.

In the wake of the Lucerne Congress, while the implications of Melanie Klein's paper were percolating through discussions and commentaries, the ranks of the Kleinians in England shrank—to expand again later with a younger generation. Ella Sharpe, who had had Melitta Schmideberg in analysis for a year before Glover took her over, turned away from the Kleinian camp as Glover did. Nina Searl resigned from the British Society for personal reasons; John Bowlby, particularly as he became more involved with psychiatry in the British Army, took an independent path; and John Rickman, though he was Kleininan in orientation, refused to be a party person, a camp follower. Klein's strong, and very capable, adherents at the time of Anna Freud's arrival in England were Susan Isaacs, Joan Riviere, Clifford Scott, David Matthew, Donald Winnicott, and a Polish émigré, Paula Heimann. James and Alix Strachey, who had been Melanie Klein's original English promoters, stayed aloof. Summarizing with the clarity of caricature the exaggerations that marked both sides as the controversy entered the war years, James Strachey noted: "My own view is that Mrs. K. has made some highly important contributions to [psychoanalysis], but that it's absurd to make out (a) that they cover the whole subject or (b) that their validity is axiomatic. On the other hand, I think it is equally ludicrous for Miss F. to maintain that [psychoanalysis] is a Game Reserve belonging to the F. family and that Mrs. K.'s ideas are fatally subversive."[53]

MELANIE Klein took as axiomatic in the second phase of the controversy what she had argued for so strenuously in the 1920s: that a child's superego comes into ferocious, implacable being during the child's first months of life and that it is made up of "part objects": "The imagos of his mother's breast and of his father's penis are established within his ego [by introjection] and form the nucleus of his superego."[54] This conception of the superego, she acknowledged, was not compatible with Freud's: ". . . as regards the nature of the superego and the history of its individual development, my conclusions differ from those of Freud." The divergence was viewed as an opportunity: "An understanding of this complex inner world [of the child's first months] enables the analyst to find and resolve a variety of early anxiety-situations which were formerly unknown, and is therefore theoretically and therapeutically of an importance so great that it cannot yet be fully estimated."[55]

Assuming the superego she had postulated, Melanie Klein went on to argue that the determinative period in a child's life is its second six months, and not—as Freud had argued—the Oedipal period, not even the Oedipal period moved back from the third to fifth years into infancy. The six-month-old child is entering into mourning in "the depressive position."

> The object which is mourned is the mother's breast and all that the breast and milk have come to stand for in the infant's mind: namely, love, goodness and security. All these are felt by the baby to be lost, and lost as a result of his own uncontrollable greedy and destructive fantasies and impulses against his mother's breasts. . . . The sorrow and concern about the feared loss of the "good" objects, that is to say, the depressive position, is, in my experience, the deepest source of the painful conflicts in the Oedipus situation, as well as in the child's relations to people in general.[56]

Every infant, Melanie Klein argued, experiences anxieties that are psychotic in content, and these are rooted in his or her own aggression, which flows from the death instinct in its initial intensity. A child who is unable to overcome the depressive position by making reparations for his or her destructive fantasies and impulses against the mother's breast is headed for psychopathology; he or she is failing at the crucial developmental task: "we may say that every step in emotional, intellectual and physical growth is used by the ego as a means of overcoming the depressive position."[57]

With this concept, "the depressive position," Melanie Klein had proposed a theory that was quite un-Freudian. It eliminated the Freudian theory of libidinal stages—surges of the life instinct—starting with a primary narcissistic and autoerotic stage. It also posited infantile anxiety-situations involving elaborate and aggressive fantasies, while Freud had assumed that the child's first-object relations were rudimentary and under the sway of the pleasure principle, that is, of need and gratifications of need. But Klein was nevertheless sincerely convinced and very eager to assert that her theory was Freudian, quintessentially Freudian, more Freudian than Freud—certainly than Anna Freud. She differed, in this respect, from the earlier Freudians who had struck out on independent paths. Adler, Stekel, Jung, Rank, Reich—each had been first a dissident, then a heretic, and finally a schismatic founder of a new path, not called psychoanalysis. But these male analysts had contended with Freud while he was still alive and while he was able to respond without fear of being perceived as his daughter's advocate and protector. Now the sons had departed and the would-be daughter fought in-house, in order to possess the father. Anna Freud, of course, did the same, and the quality of sisterly rivalry is palpable in Klein's work and submerged in Anna Freud's.

After Freud's death, Melanie Klein could advance her theories in conjunction with both a retrospective judgment on his place in the history of psychoanalysis and her claim to inheritance of his scientific estate. She often did this quite forcefully, but nowhere in her published works as candidly as in a private letter to Ernest Jones.

> Freud himself after having reached his climax in *Inhibitions, Symptoms and Anxieties* not only did not go further, but rather regressed. In his later contributions to theory some of his great findings were weakened or left aside, and he certainly did not draw the full conclusions from his own work. That might have had many reasons in himself, such as age, his illness, and the fact that there might be a point beyond which no person, no matter how great a genius, can go with his own discoveries. I am convinced though that Anna's influence was one of the factors that held him back. . . . It is tragic that his daughter, who thinks that she must defend him against me, does not realize that I am serving him better than she.[58]

THE more strenuously the Kleinians pressed the claim of merited inheritance, the more Anna Freud behaved—to use Strachey's image—like a Game Reserve keeper. It was just as intolerable to her in the years after her father's death to think of any rearrangement of his theoretical house as it was to think of rearranging his study. This reaction did pass by the late 1940s, but it was in full force during the war, and it gave a core of steely inflexibility to her very reasonable desire to preserve Freudian analysis as she understood it. Klein, so dedicated to considering mourning as the central experience of not just the infantile but the human condition generally, had remarked very astutely that an increase in obsessional mechanisms is characteristic of mourners: "Some people in mourning tidy the house."[59] But she does not seem to have felt any more sympathy for Anna Freud, who was in mourning, than Anna Freud felt for her.

If Klein had, like the earlier dissidents, taken her followers out of the Freudian house and into a separate group or society, Anna Freud would have been delighted, but she could hardly argue for such a solution when she was herself an émigré to the British Society. And Klein realized quite clearly that such a split would be construed as an admission that she was the dissident, not the true daughter. Anna Freud was inhibited from forming a group of her own by the same feeling that the Society should not be left in enemy hands, and she also knew that the daily demands of her work at the Hampstead War Nursery would leave her group with no energy for a secession. So the two remained tied to each other and to the Society.

By the end of 1941, the British Society members were convinced that their potentially explosive theoretical and political differences required a public catharsis, so they scheduled a series of Extraordinary Meetings. These began early in 1942. In May, Melanie Klein telephoned Anna Freud to suggest that a concurrent series of private meetings to discuss scientific questions might be helpful. Anna Freud agreed, but these meetings did not come off because Marjorie Brierley, a respectful critic of Klein's, argued successfully that any scientific discussions should be open to the full Society membership. But Brierley also drew up an armistice agreement, which eliminated much of the personal attack and bickering that had made meetings so taxing. She also hammered out an arrangement for the open scientific forum that came to be known as the Controversial Discussions.[60]

The Controversial Discussions proposal met with Anna Freud's approval and accorded with her policy of not agreeing to any reorganization of the British Society's political structure or its training programs until the scientific controversy had been addressed. She argued that altering the rules before settling the scientific differences would be "like renovating the house before we know who wants to live in it."[61]

Anna Freud also successfully argued that the burden of scientific argument should fall upon the Kleinians; they were challenged to show both how their theories had developed from Freud's work and that they were fundamentally compatible with it. Melanie Klein accepted this proposal gladly, for she hoped that the work which she, Susan Isaacs, and Paula Heimann intended to do would lay to rest once and for all the charge of heresy and, further, establish that she was the great Freudian innovator she claimed to be. Each of the four papers presented and discussed between March 1943 and May 1944 began with a survey of Freudian concepts—and each of the discussions began with a claim from the oppositional audience that the Freudian concepts had been misunderstood, cited out of context, or distorted.

To the tug-of-war over who was truly Freudian, the Controversial Discussions gave no respite. Both sides strained mightily, but the rope stood still. What did come from the discussions, however, was clarity about the territory in dispute. This clarity was greatest in the discussions dedicated to Susan Isaacs' strongly argued first paper on "The Nature and Function of Fantasy," which attributed to innately rooted unconscious fantasies pervasive influence on an infant's mental life and development. Against this view, the Anna Freudians argued for an interplay of innate and environmental factors in development and for an interplay of bodily and mental factors, which meant keeping in view the importance of instinct gratification (and the pleasure principle as *the* crucial principle in the unconscious). The Kleinians set the focus on first-year-of-life mother-infant interactions, which were also the focus of a great deal of the Hampstead Nursery research, but they referred entirely to mother-infant interactions as they exist in the infant's internal representations. The Anna Freudians continued to stress infants' primary narcissism and autoeroticism, for which the real mother plays a key role by providing satisfaction or dissatisfaction.

It became obvious in the discussions that Klein's work had challenged Anna Freud and her coworkers to reconsider their views about how the psychic life of very young children is articulated, and it was also apparent that Anna Freud's conception of the stages of development and their timing had loosened over the years of her controversies with Melanie Klein. Klein tried to present Anna Freud's evolution as a victory for her own camp, but Anna Freud rejected any such insinuation and the two women adhered to their basically irreconcilable positions implacably. Unlike the exchanges between Freud and the men who had eventually dissented from him, however, these discussions were between one group and another. They cannot be seen as reflecting personality differences between the two main protagonists unless those differences are, in turn, viewed as refracted through the groups.

Klein's followers, like Klein, believed in direct, aggressive attack and defense. They wielded their views more or less provocatively depending on their strategic assessments of different occasions. Anna Freud preferred to avoid direct engagement: she put her efforts into research over which she had undisputed control and waited for the truth of her views to prevail, first among receptive groups—these turned out eventually to be located in America—and then among the convertible opponents. She exerted control by being the most lucid, iron-willed, and conscientiously devoted person in her group, while Melanie Klein inspired her group with her imaginative verve, her ambition, and her startlingly uninhibited egoism. Anna Freud was a cautious and circumspect leader, but her group knew her as an adventurer in her plans and fantasies. Melanie Klein presented herself as an adventurer, but had to rely on others—chiefly Joan Riviere—for bucking up when she was tempted to be cautious.[62] Neither of the leaders of the largely female groups was stereotypically or conventionally feminine, and each could appeal to her followers in both masculine and feminine ways. But the general structure of their groups was as different as a hierarchical convent is from a charismatic cult. Collectively, the Kleinians thought of themselves as crusaders and tended to view the Anna Freudians as authoritarians unwilling to hear challenging views, while the Anna Freudians thought of themselves as the bastion of reasoned science and looked on the Klenians as power seekers and manipulators, subversives whose claim to be the truly "deep" theoreticians was a Trojan horse in psychoanalysis. The battle was protracted for group psychol-

ogy reasons as well as for the theoretical and clinical reasons both
sides announced so adamantly.

As the Controversial Discussions were in process, a report com-
missioned by the British Society's Training Committee, which consisted of Anna Freud, Melanie Klein, Edward Glover, Sylvia Payne,
Marjorie Brierley, James Strachey, John Rickman, and Ella Sharpe,
was drafted and presented. The full committee had rejected an
earlier draft, prepared by a subcommittee, because it had failed to
address frankly the complicated issues involved when one institution, consisting of two opposed camps and a "middle group" of independents, was trying to train young analysts. The revised version,
presented in January 1944, made recommendations for keeping ideological tendencies and persons out of the training process while letting candidates become acquainted with all the different "sections
of opinion in the Society, including the most extreme." Anna Freud
inquired of the presenter, James Strachey, whether she and her work
were being located at an extreme, and when it appeared that this
was so, she declared that she intended to resign from the Training
Committee. The other members prevailed upon her to change her
mind, but she would agree only to review her mind.

Edward Glover then declared his intention to resign from not
only the Training Committee but the Society. This announcement
caused a storm of astonishment, but no one tried to stop Glover,
who had, at any rate, prepared for his action in advance by ascer-
taining that his membership in the Swiss Society would keep him
a member of the International even if he departed his national society. Glover had been simmering for months over a political maneuver that had deprived him of much of his power as president of the
Society, but he took the high road and emphasized his theoretical
differences with the Kleinians as his reason for resigning.[63]

Anna Freud stayed away from the Training Committee and
from the Society for almost two years after the resignation episode.
And she herself took the precaution of obtaining membership in the
Swiss Society, so that if no acceptable venue was ever reached in the
British Society, she could resign without losing her membership in
the International. When Jones wanted to appoint her Central Secre-

tary of the International at the end of 1944, however, she accepted. Even though she was replacing Glover, whose International membership Jones was contesting by arguing that it required presidential (that is, Jones's own) approval, she felt that she could, on the International Executive, protect Glover, influence Jones, and preserve the principle of International membership for political and doctrinal refugees.

Anna Freud also did what she could, via the unreliable airmail, to lend support to a venture that Ernst Kris was organizing in New York, a yearly journal to be called *The Psychoanalytic Study of the Child*, for this looked like a forum, off British soil, for presenting the research that she had launched at the Hampstead War Nursery. Kris, along with Heinz Hartmann, Marie Bonaparte, and Otto Fenichel, was also exploring publishing possibilities for an English edition of Sigmund Freud's collected works. Because she considered these activities so much more heartening and important for the future than the English debate, Anna Freud was reluctant to cooperate when a newly elected Training Committee approached her to suggest one more try at cooperation. But she did make a last-ditch effort and submitted a proposal outlining the kind of collaborative training arrangement she considered reasonable.

The educational principle embodied in Anna Freud's proposal was "separate but equal"—a principle often invoked in school systems, of course, but seldom without the result that one group is or becomes more equal than the other. She suggested that there be two training programs, one at the Institute and one under her auspices, which would have a third-year curriculum in common. This proposal underwent nearly six months of negotiations until a compromise was hammered out in the Training Committee, chaired by John Bowlby, which won the agreement of all parties—Freudians, Kleinians, and "Middle Groupers." The compromise called for a Course A at the Institute with two parallel tracks, one Kleinian and one taught by analysts of all persuasions, and a Course B taught by analysts allied to Anna Freud. The details of the scheme, and means for selecting candidates' training analysts, were to be worked out by a representative committee. To Bowlby's surprise, a block of seven Kleinian members voted against this proposal at a meeting called specifically to consider it. They had given no prior notice of their intention, and Bowlby had, up to the day of the meeting, been under the impression that a much-desired unanimity was, finally, at hand. To his astonishment, the Kleinians argued for a single course in which all viewpoints could be represented—an argument which, had it been successful, would have sent the whole training controversy back to square one and Anna Freud into resignation.[64]

THE compromise that brought into being the most complicated and conflicting training program in the history of psychoanalysis was acceptable to Anna Freud, but she placed her hopes for the future of psychoanalysis elsewhere. Through the fall of 1945, before and after the Training Committee requested her proposal, she had been meeting regularly with her closest supporters to consider their situation. Ernst Kris was included by correspondence in these discussions, because he was hoping to return soon to England, with his family, to work with Anna Freud and to complete an analysis he had started with her in 1938. The Hampstead War Nursery was closing down, and arrangements were being made both to do follow-up work with the children and to provide training for the young staff members who wanted it. But the group's discussions ranged beyond the immediate practical problems. They sensed that psychoanalysis in the world after the war would be different, and they were trying to judge their local situation in the light of their broadest hopes for the future.

Ernst Kris galvanized the ongoing discussion with a document dated November 21, 1945: "MEMORANDUM—Free Associations to the Topic What to Do Next?" His main contention in the memorandum was that all available energy for the immediate future should be given over to writing. Since 1936, none of the clinical or theoretical advances in the Anna Freud circle had been committed to paper, and the Hampstead War Nursery findings had not been integrated into existing knowledge. "Nothing is, at the present time, as important as authoritative statements of what we believe to be 'true Freudian psychoanalysis.'"[65] In effect, he invited the group to produce for their own cause the kind of fundamental papers the Kleinians had produced for the Controversial Discussions.

Training should follow, Kris argued, the project of theoretical and clinical formulation and not be dependent on existing Institutes. From the large numbers of people—including many former military psychiatrists—wanting training, those with the best credentials should be selected and educated in the "the Freudian heritage." If you find outstanding individuals, train them without consideration of whether or not the Society will recognize them. . . . Who will care ten years from now whether the 1945 conditions in the British Society did, at the time, permit the recognition of a trainee." He suggested, bluntly: "The Kleinians are hopeless. Don't bother with them or their candidates."

Kris was just as pointed on his next topic, the International Psychoanalytic Association: "Briefly, forget about it, as it is an organization with other than purely scientific purposes." The International had orginally been created to secure recognition for psychoanalysis; but now psychoanalysis, recognized but very seldom understood, needed to secure its identity. "It is essential to convince people that not everyone who has recognized the basic truths of psychoanalysis knows anything about it or is in a position to improve upon Freud." Kris clearly realized that the two main institutional problems of postwar analysis would be to keep political power from consuming more interest than scientific progress and to keep the heirs' natural drive for matching the founder's originality and innovation from expressing itself at the expense of truth.

On December 12, after she had considered Kris's memorandum with Dorothy Burlingham, the Hoffers, Kate Friedlander, Barbara Lantos, and Josefine Stross, and after she had discussed it by telephone with Marie Bonaparte, Anna Freud sent Kris five single-spaced typed pages of point-by-point reply prefaced with an overview.

> You know what it invariably means when one is under the impression that somebody else has said or written something exceedingly clever and satisfactory: that that is exactly what one thinks oneself, and that for some reason one has so far not been successful in putting it into plain words. That is my case here. What you have put down is exactly what goes around in my head for the last year or two. Though I have said things like that here or there, to Dorothy, to the Princess, to the Hoffers, I have never succeeded in putting them together. It is not too difficult for me to know why. Essentially your attitude means a break with the past tradition of the International Association. And, though I fully realize that the time for such a break has

come, I have so far played with it in thought rather than decided to put it into action. To me it is still very vivid how the whole building up of the International Association was done, what plans and hopes went into it, etc. With some parts of it, i.e., in the I.U.K., I was very intimately connected. That gives the habit of continuing to think in terms of it. But, in reality, I have realized that those times are over, and that all which one could bring into life again would be an empty framework, and the impotent shadow of what was once a very real and living structure and organism.[66]

With the priority Kris gave to writing, she was in complete accord, and she noted that her attitude had begun to shift as the War Nursery work began to conclude: "I now long to write certain things, while before I used to avoid the opportunities. Others seem to feel the same urge." *The Psychoanalytic Study of the Child* could be the forum, but even more would be needed to promote the creation of a new literature. Among other ideas, Anna Freud wanted to make Maresfield Gardens a study center, with a seminar for reviewing works in progress and a reference library. "The Princess has bought Eitingon's library and is very ready to give it to me for a purpose of this kind." She also wanted the new literature to be grounded in the new English edition of Freud's collected works—and she urged Kris himself to be the editor in chief of that project.

Kris's feeling that there were many people who wanted psychoanalytic training seemed right to Anna Freud, but she was very skeptical about whether they should train any army psychiatrists. The military psychiatrists she had gotten to know in the British Society struck her as ill suited for psychoanalysis. "What these people do is based on their power over other human beings, their results are largely influenced by their official standing in relation to their patients and they have to deal with such large numbers that the individual becomes more or less insignificant. . . . The question is whether somebody who has been an army psychiatrist can still acquire the respect for the individual, the patience and the submission to facts as they emerge which is the ideal analytic attitude. I think it is highly significant that with some people the analytic technique has returned to its dramatic cathartic beginnings"—complete with expectation for quick and miraculous cures, even for the psychoses.

The schisms and discord in psychoanalytic institutions made them, Anna Freud agreed, unlikely sources of good training.

> I also do not believe that it is possible at present to establish a new Institute, or central place, which can be a stronghold of teaching in the [old] sense. . . . I suppose training has to be dispersed again, as it used to be in the beginnings. People have to go here and there, to find the analysis they want, to pick out the lecturers who have something to offer. . . . My own work still goes back to the times when diffuse training was done, and I know all the disadvantages of it. But if I have to choose between organized distortions of analysis and unorganized ones, I prefer the latter. There is good hope that a better situation will emerge again, if a sufficient number of good people are on the job.

About the situation in the British Society, Anna Freud was calmly resigned.

> I know that the Kleinians are hopeless. My proposal to the Society here was not based on the idea that it might be possible to cooperate with them, but on the fact that there is still a fairly strong "middle group" whose cooperation it is a pity to lose forever. My sole aim was to provide for just enough independence to enable our small group to do some intensive but "diffuse" training for a few individuals who might be worthwhile, while avoiding all the fuss and upheaval of forming a new society, which is desired by some people but which to me at the present seems completely out of place. I do not want to form a new society at just the moment when I have lost faith in the function of societies.

Ernst Kris's memorandum brought Anna Freud's group to a clearer focus, and it agreed to stay as independent as it could of the British Society and of the political dimensions of the International Association. For Kate Friedlander, this policy implied that they should prepare to launch not just a course—Course B—but eventually a clinic for child psychoanalysis. Her idea took three years to mature: the three years in which Anna Freud gave up her rigid defense of her father's ideas and entered into the most fruitful period of her working life; three years of a "dark night of the soul" followed by an awakening.

In late December 1945, as Anna Freud was finishing a Final Report for the Hampstead War Nursery's benefactors in New York and contemplating Friedlander's idea, she came down with a bad attack of flu. By January, the flu had given way to pneumonia. The First World War had ended with a raging Continent-wide influenza epidemic—the epidemic that took Sophie Freud's life in January 1920—and the Second World War did the same. Penicillin was available but so rare that prescriptions had to be renewed every other day; there was hardly any more fuel or food. Anna Freud lay in her bed on the third floor of 20 Maresfield Gardens and, in the freezing cold of January, grew more and more seriously ill with viral pneumonia affecting both lungs. She did not lose her concern with the future as she lay day after day in a fever, but she was swept over— as by a wave—with images of the past. The grief she had kept under control since September 1939 pulled at her.

When Sigmund Freud had lost his father—and begun to fear the loss of his friend Fliess—he had worked through to a new equilibrium by a self-analysis, and by writing *The Interpretation of Dreams*. Psychoanalysis was born of his grief in combination with his genius. His daughter, never without his life in which to seek her precedents, spent many hours during her illness considering her dreams and writing them down, with interpretations, for Marie Bonaparte. She came very close to death in January 1946, while she was mourning, and from her experience came not a monumental book but a collection of dreams and eventually an essay—the first chapter in the second half of her life.

7

ON LOSING
AND BEING LOST

WHEN A NOVEMBER 1945 letter from August Aichhorn, covered with official stamps from the Allied military censor, made its way to London in the suitcase of an American soldier, Anna Freud was amazed. Even more amazing was Aichhorn's news: he was planning to reopen the Vienna Psychoanalytic Society as soon as possible.[1] During the war, while he was living in the comparative safety of the countryside just south of Vienna, he had managed to train several young psychiatrists, and this little cadre was, Aichhorn hoped, going to help him restore psychoanalysis to Austria, its first home. The war had been terrible for Aichhorn—his wife, who had become ill in 1938, never recovered her health, his apartment in Vienna was bombed out, one of his two sons spent time in a Nazi concentration camp for his political activities. And Austria in the fall of 1945 seemed hardly any better as far as daily life was concerned. Aichhorn faced a more chaotic version of the situation that had led him to his work with delinquent boys at Oberhollabrunn after the First World War. The Viennese city government was, however, receptive to Aichhorn's plans.

It sounds almost like an irony of fate [Anna Freud remarked] that the Viennese authorities, who made nothing but difficulties for my father during the long years of his work, have now finally gotten to the point where they view positively the Psychoanalytic Institute and the fruits of his work. Imagine what we might have accomplished between 1908 and 1938 under supportive conditions. With our large teaching staff and the possibilities in Vienna, our Institute would have become the world center for all the psychoanalytic Institutes. But, despite all this progress, building an Institute will still be a difficult task for you to accomplish.[2]

At Aichhorn's request, Anna Freud wrote a formal letter of greeting and encouragement for the opening ceremony of the new Vienna Psychoanalytic Society. The letter arrived in time—but just barely. She sent it off with an apology: "I am terribly sorry if it is too late by this time, but the delay was not my fault; it was unavoidable. After I made it through the whole war without being sick for a day, suddenly five weeks ago I went to bed with the 'flu, hoping that after three days I might be up and about." Five weeks of incapacity with the penumonia that followed was "a new experience for me, because, as you know, I have never been sick and never had to interrupt my work. Everyone probably has to learn to do this at some time or another, but I am not very good at it. I am constantly promised that if I am reasonable about it now and don't rush about much, the disease will not leave behind any permanent damage."[3] Sophie Dann, who had nursed Tante Minna before her death in 1941, came to care for Anna Freud, and to try to keep her from returning to work too soon.

In March 1946, Anna Freud and Dorothy Burlingham went to the Norfolk Hotel in Brighton for a vacation by the sea, and after that Anna Freud began to feel something like herself again, even though she was suffering, as she knew, from five solid years of wartime nerves and overwork. She told Richard and Editha Sterba in Detroit: "In a way [I have had] a feeling similar to that after an examination: something is gone that you were keyed up for the whole time, but instead of feeling merely relieved, you begin to realize how strenuous the time has been."[4] Her recovery was slow, and she was not as reasonable about it as she should have been, to her later regret. The pneumonia left her vulnerable to infections for the rest of her life; each winter she had a bout, more or less severe, of bronchitis. As she said jokingly: "I am so used to doing things thoroughly that I went into pneumonia very thoroughly also."[5] She did not, however, go as thoroughly into winter illnesses as Dorothy Burlingham, though they were twins in their susceptibility to bronchitis. Dorothy's tuberculosis, which had plagued her throughout the war, was particularly severe in 1945 and 1946, and it was not really controlled until a new generation of drugs became available in the mid 1950s.

During the months of her illness and recuperation, Anna Freud had much time for thinking. "While I was so ill," she told Max Schur, "I thought nearly the whole time about the past and my father's illnesses and all the medical details which I had learned from you."[6] She was obviously identified with her father, but other losses also reinforced her sense that his death and the precarious condition of psychoanalysis were linked. In January 1946, Otto Fenichel, who had been involved with Ernst Kris in plans to publish Freud's collected works in English, died of a coronary at the age of forty-eight. He had decided to get a California medical license by doing an internship at Cedars of Lebanon Hospital in Los Angeles, but keeping an intern's hours while maintaining an analytic practice to support his family was too much for him. "One of his friends wrote me: He was an institute of psychoanalysis in himself, and that is certainly true," Anna Freud reflected. "What will happen to psychoanalysis if his generation of teachers dies out?"[7]

Only a few days after she learned of Fenichel's death, Anna Freud heard that Ruth Mack Brunswick, only two years her junior, had died in New York. Brunswick had been ill for several weeks with a stomach ailment and unable to attend a reunion dinner with Marie Bonaparte. But the Princess had visited her after the dinner and found her lively and alert, much better than in her Vienna days, when she had developed a morphine dependency. "As always since her divorce, she was in excellent psychological condition and free of all narcotics," Ernst Kris reported. "The Princess left her after midnight. One assumed that she would sleep late the next morning. She must have gotten up around noon, and it is unknown whether she collapsed due to a sudden heart failure or, still sleepy, took a fall and died of the fractured skull she got hitting the door. The only certainty is that it was not suicide." Judgments by friends like Kris about Ruth Brunswick's psychological condition were questioned later by detractors who had never met her—"she died of too many opiates" a biographer announced without evidence—but the analysts in her circle felt her death as a tragic discontinuation of a recovery.[8]

Anna Freud had never felt an intellectual kinship with Ruth Mack Brunswick, for she questioned her objectivity. As she had told A. A. Brill in 1934, after Ruth had made a report on conditions in the American Psychoanalytic Association: "We like Ruth and we had hoped she would bring back a clear picture of the situation and tell us more than one can in letters. My father and I saw immediately that she only gave us a personal view of it and took it as such."[9] But Anna Freud knew that Ruth Brunswick had made important scientific contributions, particularly in her explorations of the psychoses and their possible roots in pre-Oedipal mother-child relations and in her work on the pre-Oedipal period in females. When one of Brunswick's papers had been rebuffed at the *International Journal of Psychoanalysis* by Ernest Jones, who found it in ignorance of Melanie Klein's work, Anna Freud had protested through the agency of Max Eitingon.[10] The Freuds also appreciated how attentive Ruth had been to the complicated business of securing affidavits for analysts fleeing Austria after the *Anschluss*, and how helpful she had been to Oliver and Henny Freud when they arrived in America from France in 1943.

That Oliver and Henny had managed to escape from France and get to America was one of the few joyful pieces of news that came during the war. But neither they nor their family in England knew until the winter of 1946 that their daughter, Eva, who had stayed in Nice with her French fiancé, had died of influenza—another Freud family influenza victim. This news came to London just before a letter from the Red Cross about Sigmund Freud's four elderly sisters. "We have now had the first report about the aunts, and it is the worst possible," Anna Freud wrote to Katá Levy in March 1946.[11] To the best of anyone's knowledge, this horrible Red Cross letter declared, Freud's sisters had all been killed in 1942 by the Nazis, Marie in the Theresienstadt camp, and Dolfi, Rosa, and Pauline in the camps to which they had been shipped after Theresi-

enstadt. (Only years later did records surface indicating that Rosa
had died in Auschwitz, her two sisters in Treblinka.) A gloom de-
scended over the extended Freud family. Marie's two surviving
daughters, Lilly Marlé (in London) and Margarethe Magnus (in
Copenhagen) consoled each other as best they could; Pauline's
daughter, Rosi Winternitz Waldinger, renewed an analysis with Paul
Federn in New York, which Anna Freud paid for indirectly by never
claiming a debt Federn owed to her. For the bereft cousins, Martha
Freud made 20 Maresfield Gardens home, and it was some solace to
her to be able to help them as she was still grieving herself over her
husband and her sister.

THE professional losses and the family losses, all reported within
two months, had very different meanings even though they merged
in a dark time. For the aunts' deaths, Anna Freud felt very guilty—
on her own and on her father's behalf. Her father and her Uncle
Alexander had made the decision to leave their sisters behind, financially well provided for and in their own apartments. In 1938, no one
would have imagined that four old ladies, with no political connections, would be in danger of deportation.

As Anna Freud's psychological understanding of the Nazis was
always quite bound to her aunts' fates. A friend once asked her if
she could in any way comprehend how the Nazis could do something
like send four helpless old women to their deaths, and she replied
with the same terrifying view that Hannah Arendt summarized with
the phrase "banality of evil": "The Nazis wanted their apartments."[12]

As Anna Freud read more and heard more—particularly from
Aichhorn—about what the Nazi occupation of Austria had been like
she became even firmer in her resolve never to set foot in Austria—
or in Germany—again. She supported the efforts Aichhorn and others
made to restore psychoanalysis to the German-speaking countries,
but she took no part in them herself. She had no affection for the
German colleagues who—unlike the Viennese—had decided to keep
psychoanalytic institutes open under Nazi auspices, but she also said
that she could not realistically have asked that they "be heroes" and
sacrifice themselves or their private work to the Nazis.[13] She did,

however, hope that postwar German psychoanalysis would have the chance to be truly Freudian, and to that end she spent many hours of her recuperation translating into German her *Infants Without Families*.

The professional deaths made her uneasy for the future. As Ernst Kris noted, Ruth Mack Brunswick was "the first close friend in our analytic generation, and the first from Freud's own circle" to die.[14] Fenichel was the first of the group trained at the Berlin Policlinik and representing psychoanalysis in its socialist-sympathetic form. Anna Freud felt these losses as her father would have. "Being ill in bed gives me plenty of time to think about psychoanalysis, the psychoanalytic movement and its difficulties and the great need we have just for people like Fenichel with his inexhaustible knowledge of psychoanalysis and his inimitable way of organizing and presenting his facts."[15] Thinking of him, she plotted papers she would like to write herself, as fulfillment of Kris's charge that their group should make writing a priority and as a release for ideas she had had brewing for years. The first paper she outlined was "The Psychoanalytic Study of Infantile Feeding Disturbances," a piece that drew on the studies made in the Jackson Nursery and the Hampstead war nurseries of how children do—or do not—take pleasure in eating. This, like most of her papers for the next thirty years, went to *The Psychoanalytic Study of the Child*, the first issue of which had appeared just as Anna Freud became ill.

She also thought again and again as she lay in bed of the analysts and their families who had physically suffered or died at Nazi hands. In the hiatus between the International Congress in 1938 and the one in 1949, the membership of the International dropped by sixty-four, and most of those people were Nazi victims.[16] On the anniversary of Karl Landauer's death, she recalled his years as the president of the German Psychoanalytic Society, and wrote to his daughter, who later trained with her in London: "You don't know how often I have thought during this illness of mine about you and your family and your experiences of the last several years. It has been very hard being ill even with the best nursing and accommodations available to reach ones health again. I always think: you had to endure a similar illness in the concentration camp, and you, and your mother,

got through it."[17] She suggested to Eva Landauer that she read
Freud's "Mourning and Melancholia"—a suggestion Anna Freud had
given herself many times—for the text's solace and for the praise of
Karl Landauer's work it contained.

She kept in touch with her scattered friends by dictating letters
to Dorothy Burlingham, and then did herself the very great kindness
of hiring as a corresponding secretary Jula Weiss, her father's former
secretary and the Hampstead War Nursery administrative assistant.
With this secretarial help, Anna Freud could make long-distance
efforts to keep up the morale of the émigrés in America. She consoled
Hanns Sachs in Boston when he wrote her an annoyed letter about
Theodor Reik's latest book. His opinion about Reik's ceaseless self-
promotion and denigration of Freud was succinct: "a great cause will
produce megalomania in a mind that is not great enough for it and
unable to subordinate itself to greatness."[18] That was the kind of
loyalty with which Anna Freud could gratefully concur, and it lent
her some detachment for receiving Sach's news about the officers
elected to lead the American Psychoanalytic Association: "The APA
has crowned its work by electing a president [Leo Bartemeier] who is
entirely innocent of psychoanalysis," Sachs reported.[19] The consolation she sent to a letter from Hermann Nunberg about the general
swell of pseudopsychoanalytic literature in America, of which the
Reik book was just a wavelet, was a little more wry: "I hear often
how difficult it is in America for true psychoanalysis, but can it be
any harder than here in England?"[20]

But the other side of this critical coin was that, since Ernst
Kris's bracing memorandum, Anna Freud had felt less need to contend with the complexities of the English psychoanalytic world.
When she received an invitation from the Menninger Foundation
in Topeka, Kansas, to join the renowned research and training staff
there, the prospect was not alluring: "I have always hated the idea
of emigration, and I would dislike it now almost as much as I did in
1938," she explained to Robert Waelder.[21] England had become
dear to her, and she waited impatiently for her naturalization to be
completed in the spring of 1946. "Please do not think that I spend
my time here trying to counteract Melanie Klein's influence," she
said to Waelder. "That would indeed be a hopeless task."

THERE WERE many dimensions to Anna Freud's bedridden review of psychoanalysis, but being ill also meant, most deeply, a time for self-reflection, self-analysis. She was preoccupied with a self-analytic effort on May 6, 1946, when her group gathered in London to celebrate what would have been Freud's ninetieth birthday. Ironically enough, Marie Bonaparte came from Paris bearing the collection of Freud's letters that she had purchased just before the war—the letters to Wilhelm Fliess, the most elaborate record of Freud's own self-analysis outside of *The Interpretation of Dreams*. In the winter, the Princess had discussed the possibility of publishing the letters with Ernst Kris and Heinz Hartmann in New York. But she had waited through Anna Freud's illness for her judgment—which did not come quickly. Anna Freud started to read the letters immediately, and by May 10 wrote to Ernst Kris that "the material is indescribably interesting."[22] Like the Princess, she was quite sure that the letters were of enormous historical significance; but she was not at all sure she could ignore to any degree her father's explicit injunction that the letters never be published, indeed that they be destroyed. She tracked back and forth over the reasons for and against publication even after the letters actually were published—in an abridged version— with a detailed commentary by Ernst Kris. Her filial disobedience, for the sake of the history of her father's science, caused her great turmoil, as did the example of his self-analysis, there in page after dense page of the Fliess letters.

One of the immediate results of the intertwining of the father's and the daughter's self-analyses was her resort to a male correspondence-friend—a humane, sympathetic Fliess. Marie Bonaparte continued as a crucial recipient of Anna Freud's self-analytical letters, but August Aichhorn provided adoration and something like fraternal devotion. She was willing to respond in kind when Aichhorn defied the military censor and his own internal censor, his enormous discretion and self-consciousness, to tell Anna Freud how much he missed her: "I will reveal only one thing to you: after you left, I came by the Berggasse often, deliberately. On every anniversary of your departure, I am there."[23] She replied:

I have missed everything we had between us whenever we met and went places together or worked together. I was completely certain that this could not have come to an end, and now I am happy because you have confirmed that it is still alive. . . . I would like so much for once to tell you of my father's last weeks and days, and what it means for me to live without him. I would also like to tell you what leaving Vienna has meant to me and how strange it is to carry a past within oneself which can no longer be built upon. With this experience, I have come to a new understanding of the process involved in repression and infantile amnesia.[24]

She opened this venue for retrospective reporting to Aichhorn just a year after the onset of her illness. During the illness itself, the self-analytical work she did consisted mostly of dream analyses, which she produced while she was still in a dependent state, the kind of childlike condition quite conducive to regression. "During my illness, I felt that the most difficult thing about it was that I had to let so much be done for me by others, and becoming healthy really meant that I had to manage for myself again. I am always surprised that people forget to consider how much a child must suffer from the fact that it needs so much help."[25] And in the same vein: "during my pneumonia in 1946, it took a good long while before my confidence in my ability to work returned. Regaining my confidence took longer than regaining my capacity to work."[26] Even in the manifest content of her dreams, she was often a child or childlike, vulnerable and at the mercy of surrounding adults.

Many of the dreams were sent to Marie Bonaparte; some were written on miscellaneous pieces of paper and kept in a folder. On two pages, she made herself the following handwritten memorandum (originally in German) about two dreams involving the mechanism of projection.[27]

Dreams from the illness, Jan.–Feb. 1946
Dream from the time of breathing difficulty (dyspnoea) during the afternoon nap.
I. Old man Hammerschlag died. (Strong feeling of reality.) Interpretation: Emil Hammerschlag [Freud's Hebrew teacher, father of Anna Hammerschlag, after whom Anna Freud was named] is suffering from breathing difficulty because of infir-

mity. One always meets him on the street [in Vienna] gasping. Therefore *he* has breathing difficulties, not I; *he* dies, not I. *He* is old and has to die anyway, I still want to live. The fulfillment of the wish is clear.

II. I have a baby. Someone throws it (for reasons unknown) onto the ground from above, again and again. Therefore it suddenly is dead. I weep full of despair and suddenly say or think reproachfully: you people have killed it by dropping it.

Associations and interpretation: In the pressure gauge of my oxygen tank there is a marker in the form of a tiny man, who rises and falls. Tiny marksman (?)—[the homonucleus in] *Faust*—in the bottle—artificial baby—the illness instead of pregnancy—which I spared myself—but without consequence, one comes out [of illness] empty-handed—like a stillborn child (Marianne [Kris], who almost lost [her daughter] Annerl from bleeding after birth—dead Annerl—myself.

I obviously lament my own death, again as projected onto someone else.

On another single page, she wrote (also in German) another memorandum, but this time without interpretations. The ambience in these dreams is maternal, and the common theme seems to be that a child is not properly taken care of by forgetful or more actively neglectful, self-absorbed women.

Two dreams in the same night during convalescence
February, 1946

I. It is my birthday. Dorothy forgets all about it, and I am so hurt that I weep.

II. My cousin Rose [Winternitz Waldinger] is ill and is put into Mama's bed in the Berggasse. In order that Tante Minna does not disturb her by walking through, [Minna's] bed is made up in the wicker recliner in the bathroom. But [Minna] is so hurt and insulted by this (I am also sure that she will not accept it), that, as always, she gets her own way and sleeps in her own room in spite of the situation.

Anna Freud kept these two memoranda together with a set of notes, dated December 27, 1942, which she wrote in German but entitled in English "About Losing and Being Lost." The notes were the first step toward an essay with a similar title that she drafted in

1948, delivered as a lecture in 1953, but did not publish until 1967. Like the later essay, the notes center on Sigmund Freud's death—the archetypical events of losing—and how it was represented in Anna Freud's dreams.

About Losing and Being Lost
Concerning last night's dream:
I dream, as I have often done, that he is here again. All of these recent dreams have the same character: the main role is played not by my longing for him but rather by his longing for me. The main scene in the dreams are always of his tenderness to me, which always takes the form of my own, earlier tenderness. In reality he never showed either [i.e., tenderness in his form or her own] with the exception of one or two times, which always remained in my memory. The reversal can be simply the fulfillment of my wish [for tenderness], but it is probably also something else. In the first dream of this kind he openly said: "I have always longed for you so."

The main feeling in yesterday's dream is that he is wandering about (on top of mountains, hills) while I am doing other things. At the same time, I have an inner restlessness, a feeling that I should stop whatever I am doing and go walking with him. Eventually he calls me to him and demands this himself. I am very relieved and lean myself against him, crying in a way that is very familiar to both of us. Tenderness. My thoughts are troubled: he should not have called me, it is as if a renunciation or a form of progress had been undone because he called. I am puzzled. In the dream the feeling is very strong that he is wandering around alone and "lost." Sympathy and bad conscience.

Associations: The poem by Albrecht Schaeffer, "You strong and dear wayfarer . . .":

> I was with you at each step of the way—
> there was no victory I did not also win—
> no sorrow I did not suffer beside you,
> you strong and you dear wanderer . . .

Odysseus—even if he is unfaithful—homeless—a servant in the distant lands.
Odysseus is truly lost, and cannot find his way to his homeland.
Rest of the day: Inquiry from Kag [Kagran] whether he [Freud]

is returning to Vienna. I answer: never. Wanderer, emigrant, eternal Jew.[28]
The reproach is: he is unfaithful to me on his travels, in spite of my faithfulness; like Odysseus toward Penelope.
The self-reproach which is projected in this reproach: I am unfaithful to him; which shows in the feeling in the dream. Whether it concerns this house, which I want to leave (?) for one with which he is not familiar. "Mumm's seen it." Thought: "How then shall he find me in my dreams?"—The woman in "On [sic] Which We Serve" who does not leave the house so that her husband on holiday is able to find her, and who dies. Another layer of meaning: "I am surprised that he calls me to him." He never wished that I would die as a result of his death.

Anna Freud's illness in the winter of 1946 reactivated the recurrent "losing and being lost" dreams. For some two years after the illness, such dreams made their appearance whenever she felt that she was, in any way, going against her father's wishes or when one of her wishes became fused with a wish that had been Freud's and the joint wish was threatened with frustration. An example of both these feelings in one dream was sent off in a letter to Marie Bonaparte dated August 6, 1946. At the time, Anna Freud was impatiently waiting for a cottage in Walberswick to come up for auction. Ernst Freud had purchased a weekend home in this little Suffolk town to replace one on Hiddensee, an island in the Baltic, that he had lost when Hitler came to power in Germany; Anna Freud and Dorothy Burlingham were hoping to replace their lost Hochroterd. While Freud and his daughter-secretary were still in Vienna, Freud had dictated a letter about the Suffolk cottage to Ernst: "My best wishes for the opening of Hidden House! It is typically Jewish not to renounce anything and to replace what has been lost. Moses, who in my opinion left a lasting imprint on the Jewish character, was the first to set an example."[29] Both the sanction for repetition and the historical generalization linger in Anna Freud's dream.

I must tell you a dream which I had in my last night in Walberswick. I was very depressed that night and I only slept a very little. But in that short time I dreamt: I was in Palestine and it was all very interesting. I visited all sorts of places and met many people whom I half seemed to know. A woman invited me to eat goose with them. I cried apparently and she asked me whether I was ill. I said "no, but I have been ill." I saw a modern school and looked at the faces of the pupils, who looked very alert, etc. And there was one very disturbing factor throughout the whole dream. I could not understand a word of anybody's language and they could not understand me.

When I woke up I was very interested by the vividness of the dream, though I had no idea what it meant. Then the interpretation flashed through my mind: Palestine is the "Promised Land," as Walberswick had become the place of my wishes. But I was afraid that we would not succeed in buying the cottage there which will come up for auction on the 16th of August. In that case, I would not want ever to return to Walberswick, I would be like Moses who had been shown the promised land from the top of the mountain (there are wonderful views in W. from the hilltops), but had never succeeded in entering it. Therefore my depression.

The difficulty of language goes even a step further. It reminds me of the fact that in dreams not being able to talk is a symbol for death. That means that my "paradise" will only come after death (the peace and quiet which I am always longing for now), it is only the young people, the pupils in the school there, who will find it on earth. I am too old, or it is too late. The reference to the illness means that I should have died then, for convenience.

The only reference which I do not understand is the eating of the goose. It has something to do with being killed, perhaps with my father's sisters who have been killed. The woman was rather like them. It is, after all, our fault that we left them to be killed.

I wonder where all this self-pity and lack of self-confidence has suddenly come from. Whether it has something to do with the Fliess letters? Or with the naturalization, which I wanted so much but have not got? I suppose I shall have a wish-dream to find out. But I thought I would tell you.

In her dreams Anna Freud again and again found variations on the idea that any redirection of her libido would constitute a betrayal of her father and of her love for him, a love that she presents as frankly like a wife's for her husband. The betrayal theme and the image of her father as a wanderer, "lost," were joined in a dream she had in Walberswick in August 1947.

> I had a further dream about my father, a curious double (one might say halfhearted) one. It was actually in two parts, running alongside. In Part I, I was to marry a man, rather indistinct, youngish, a doctor (I was very unwilling). In Part II, my father and mother had got lost in a dark place (in a city, Paris? Vienna?) and I was looking for them with search parties. My mother was found after a while but not my father and I was quite desperate. I urged the people to search more and more, but it seemed quite hopeless.
>
> Half awake, I interpreted to myself "I lost my father through marriage with another man." But that seemed too glib to me to be true. Anyway, I was glad to be awake again.

WHEN Anna Freud told August Aichhorn that her experiences of mourning for her father and for her lost home in Vienna had brought her to a new understanding of repression and infantile amnesia, she was summarizing one of the key themes of her essay "On Losing and Being Lost."[30] The first of the essay's two parts deals with the interpretations of losing that Freud had proposed and other analysts had elaborated. She surveyed the accepted dynamic interpretation of how mental conflict between an unconscious desire and a conscious desire can detach us from our possessions; then she considered the economic interpretation of how quantitative or qualitative changes in our investments of libido (or aggression) in people or things cause us to hold on to them, misplace them, lose them, or find them. But these preliminaries were to make a context for exploring a new topic: typical reactions to losing and being lost.

Anna Freud stressed how losers become identified with the thing or person they have lost, by means of projection or what Melanie Klein had called "projective identification."[31] She noted: "In our work with separated children during wartime, we had many occasions to observe those who experienced not their own, very real separation distress but the imagined distress, loneliness, and longing of the mother whom they had left behind. 'I have to telephone my Mummy, she will feel so lonely,' was a frequent wish, expressed especially in the evening." Comparable displacements occur in analytic treatment: "It is not difficult in analysis to understand and interpret such displacements of feeling. When traced back to their source, they reveal themselves as based on early [or earlier] childhood events when the loser was himself 'lost,' that is, felt deserted, rejected, alone, and experienced in full force as his own all the painful emotions which he later ascribes to the objects lost by him." Children whose early experiences are such that they are unable to love or form object ties, very often get lost or become chronic losers. These are the children who regularly play hooky or whose books and jackets and money never make it to school with them. With chronic losers too there is an identification process: "they live out a double identification, passively with the lost objects which symbolize themselves, and actively with the parents whom they experience to be as neglectful, indifferent and unconcerned toward them as they themselves are toward their possessions."

This discussion of identification prepared the way for the second part of the essay, which compared losing and being lost experiences to mourning. Again, identification is the central topic, but this time identification is explored as the means by which a mourner overcomes mourning, gets through "the later stages of mourning" to its end. The second part of the essay is based on the 1946 dream analyses and the 1942 notes, but it presents a richer, more complex working through of the autobiographical or self-analytical material.

. . . We assume that the process of mourning for a loved person will last while the emotions of the mourner are concentrated on the loss, as well as on the necessity of withdrawing feeling from the inner image of the dead. So far as this means withdrawing from the external world, the task of mourning interferes with life itself. So far as it signifies a reunion with the dead by means of reviving and reliving the memories concerning him, mourning is known to be as absorbing and fulfilling as it is painful.

In analysis we have occasion to notice that in some persons the later stages of mourning are characterized by a series of typical dreams, the latent content of which is fairly easy to interpret. In these dreams the dead person appears, either manifestly or slightly disguised, and makes every effort to bring himself to the notice of the survivor. He searches for him [sic], or pleads with him or beseeches him to come and stay; he expresses long-ing, or complains about being alone and deserted. The dreamer feels in the grip of conflicting emotions and alternates between pure joy about the reunion and remorse and guilt for having stayed away from the dead one, neglected him, etc. He wakes up, usually with anxiety and finds it difficult to realize that the whole experience has "only been a dream."

It seems to me that the latent content of these dreams has much in common with the mental processes ascribed [in the first section of the essay] to the person who loses a material pos-session. Here too a part is played by the interference of two op-posite tendencies with each other, the simultaneous wishes to retain and to discard being replaced in this instance by the si-multaneous urges to remain loyal to the dead and to turn toward new ties with the living. Here, as in the former examples, the survivor's desolation, longing and loneliness are not acknowl-edged as his own feelings, but displaced onto a dream image of the dead, where they are experienced in identification with the dead. As above, it can be shown here, when the dream is sub-mitted to interpretation, that identification with the "lost ob-ject," the deserted person, is derived from specific infantile ex-periences when the dreamer, as a child, felt unloved, rejected and neglected.

There is no doubt about the dream wish here, of course, since its fulfillment is brought about openly by the reappearance of the dead and accompanied by the positive emotions which characterized the lost relationship. The painful accusations, re-grets, etc., in the manifest content correspond to the dreamer's realization that he is on the point of becoming disloyal to the dead and his guilt about this. The anxiety which interrupts the dream corresponds to the defense against the opposite wish: to yield to the dream image's invitation, turn away from life alto-gether, and follow the lost object into death.

After she had presented the typical dream—her own recurrent dream—Anna Freud noted that often in fairy tales and myths and folk stories awesome images or ghosts of the dead appear to com-mand the living or to haunt them with a version of the living's own ambivalence. The physical appearance of the dead is connected to the survivor's feelings about the dead. On the other hand, "lost souls" wandering abroad at night, unable to rest in peace are, she wrote,

> pitiable rather than threatening and uncanny rather than outrightly frightening. They are "poor" since they symbolize the emotional impoverishment felt by the survivor. They are "lost" as symbols of object loss. That they are compelled to "wander" reflects the wandering and searching of the survivor's libidinal strivings, which have been rendered aimless, i.e., deprived of their former goal. And, finally, we understand that their "eternal rest" can be achieved only after the survivors have performed the difficult task of dealing with their bereavement and of detaching their hopes, demands and expectations from the image of the dead.

These descriptions of how feelings are displaced onto the lost loved one and then recaptured in an experience of identification, and of how this process is linked to early experiences of rejection, which may also have been projected onto lost objects, were the fruit of Anna Freud's self-analysis. But they were also her answer to a question raised by her father's "Mourning and Melancholia." He had provided the crucial dynamic and economic descriptions of mourning, but then he had admitted that he did not understand how the work of mourning was completed. His conjecture had been quite simple: "Each single one of the memories and situations of expectancy which demonstrate the libido's attachment to the lost object is [reviewed and] met by the verdict of reality that the object no longer exists; and the ego, confronted as it were with the question whether it shall share this fate, is persuaded by the sum of narcissistic satisfactions it derives from being alive to sever its attachment to the object that has been abolished."[32] This is a picture of slow severance—memory by memory. Anna Freud portrayed displaced feelings recaptured in an experience of identification; not a severance, but a form of perpetual oneness or assimilation of the lost one into the loser's psychic structure, a form of sublimation.

Nonpsychoanalytic, folkloric, or religious versions of Anna Freud's portrait usually take the form of images of reunion with the lost loved one in an afterlife. Mourning is not so much completed as transcended with expectation of shared eternal life. Anna Freud, completely irreligious, did not theorize this way. But she also could not feel this way because of the premise from which she drew her own portrait: that is, that the displacement-identification process is linked to childhood experiences of rejection, being lost. Childhood experiences are neither undone nor transcended with images of the future—they are only reflected in them. Her premise is very obvious—and poignant—in a dream she reported to Marie Bonaparte in April 1948. This dream came several days after she had had dreams in which she was looking for women—Dorothy, Marie Bonaparte—whom she could not find, and it also came as she prepared herself for the annual celebration of her father's birthday on May 6.

After I had written to you, something became clearer in my mind and I feel better. I had a dream in the following night, and I believe I understood most of it. I dreamed: "there was a big road, going up in a serpentine fashion (like the Semmering road). But people were rebuilding it or changing it. I saw the very wide road and felt activity going on. Instead of going on the road, people (I too) were going straight up, cutting out the curves. But it was like going up through one house after another, in and out of windows, not doors. I thought, all the walls will be spoilt by their doing that. At last I arrived at the highest point, and there in a room, very quietly and peacefully sitting were Mama and Tante Minna. Tante Minna was sewing and Mama was mending something (a doormat?). There was a feeling that my father was present all through. That ending was a curious anticlimax. I felt, in the dream, after all that commotion and activity, this peaceful household scene."

I was puzzled at first and then I had two associations which put me on the track. (1) the first line of the poem which I like: "Does the road wind uphill all the way?" It is the road to heaven, death, on which I take destructive shortcuts (Dorothy had reproached me the day before that I was self-destructive [for working too hard]). (2) I had dreamt part of the same dream before in my big illness [in 1946] and had been very influenced by it. Namely, that I could not reach my father in death because Tante Minna was there before me [i.e., she had died in 1941]. This time Mama and Tante Minna were there as they had been in life. That is the anticlimax: after all my efforts I find exactly the same situation which aroused my jealousy in life. So death is not much good either.

W HEN ANNA FREUD shared her dreams and her self-analysis with Marie Bonaparte, she assumed that her friend would understand her out of their similar psychic constitutions and experiences. The Princess sent Anna Freud parts of her own memoirs, and these got woven into Anna Freud's dreams.

> I had another of my recurrent dreams. They become ever more insistent. After reading the part in your memoirs where your father complains that you loved Mimam [a nursemaid] more than him, and him not enough, I dreamed: "He [Freud] was in a sanatorium and I was not with him. (I was actually in Walberswick on weekend.) He asked whether I could not at least visit him next day and I desperately went through my whole program for the Monday, every hour filled from arrival in London at midday. Then it suddenly struck me with enormous relief that one patient had called off, and I said: yes, I can come between 5 and 6 (or 7?). He said that he was busy at just that time and I felt quite desperate. He was busy when I was free and only free when I was busy, so we could not get together." I woke up and it took me quite a time to realize that it was a dream and not true. That was a relief. I remembered, somehow with astonishment, that I had never left him in a sanatorium, and had always stayed with him. (Not quite true: when he was in the Cottage Sanatorium, I used to come home to work in daytimes, also after operations, while my mother or Tante Minna were with him. I often worked [with patients at the sanatoria], and after operations I never left him, not even for a walk as nurses do.) [33]
>
> Do you remember, when I read your papers on your father, and your son, how I said you describe it so well how the generations never really get together? In reality, you said, not even lovers of the same generation get together completely. That feeling of impotent longing was in the dream.

As daughters who viewed their lives chiefly in relation to fathers—and for Marie Bonaparte, Freud was also a father—with whom they could not get together completely, the friends had similar "impotent longings." By their own interpretations, they had in common their jealousies of powerful older female rivals for their fathers; their feelings of having been rejected, which at a deep level defied consolation; and their envies for the masculinities of their fathers and other males. But Marie Bonaparte thought of her organizational work for psychoanalysis and of her writings as her potency: when she was using her head she was male, and she fantasized that her head was male. Anna Freud thought of her identification with her father, her assimilation of him into her psychic life as her power and her potentiality for continuing and complementing his work. This difference was crucial. Marie Bonaparte did not have an identification with Freud, and she related to Anna Freud's identification in a very literal way: "you have replaced your father for me, in my love for you," she told Anna Freud.[34] For Anna Freud, there was no replacement. This great difference between them was starkly reflected in their attitudes toward the Freud-Fliess letters.

Marie Bonaparte wanted to publish Freud's letters without any abridgment that would detract from their historical and biographical value—despite the objections Freud had spoken and written to her after she recovered the letters in 1937. Anna Freud found this attitude incomprehensible. For her, a betrayal of her father's wishes was a self-betrayal, as an exposure of his private life was a self-exposure. She accepted only disguised self-presentations, like his in *The Interpretation of Dreams* or her own in "Beating Fantasies and Daydreams" and in "On Losing and Being Lost."

> You probably know me well enough [she noted to Heinz Hartmann in 1947] to know that I, if it were up to me, would absolutely not publish the letters. To me any betrayal of personal details, as far as it concerns my father, goes against my convictions, and I cannot even summon up the feeling that we owe it to the external world to do such a thing. I heard him say so often that he thought that he had revealed enough to the world, and that the rest was his personal property. On the other hand, I understand that others are of a different opinion and will not allow me the right to exercise my own belief. . . . It is definitely true that neither before nor after Fliess did my father have a similar relationship with a friend; in other correspondences he shared his scientific experiences in a manner that only approached the like of this. The letters from a later time are letters to pupils and avoid any sort of intimacy.[35]

Hartmann, like Ernst Kris, stood halfway between Anna Freud and Marie Bonaparte on this issue, though both men felt reluctant to find in themselves any of what Kris called the "peeping qualities" of those, like the Princess, with a lust for biography. He knew, as they all did, that the letters might be—probably would be—misunderstood and misused. As Hartmann noted, problems would arise precisely because of that element in the letters that was "at the same time largely responsible for the greatness of the letters: the story of the creation of psychoanalysis is at the same time the story of the creator's crisis. This certainly does not surprise us; it would surprise us if this were not the case. But to the public these things are little known and somewhat incredible." To Anna Freud's personal argument for privacy, he countered: "I am of the opinion that today, more than before, human historical consciousness has a right to knowledge of its few great men, and, further, that people cannot take away this right even if they wanted to. There will be biographies of Freud. The question is only whether among these biographies there will be a work which one can accept."[36]

American publishing inadvertently weighed into the debate on Anna Freud's side. Two American biographies of Freud appeared in 1946 and 1947, one by Emil Ludwig, who had been very successful with popular lives-made-simple in Germany and had continued to write prolifically after his emigration to America, and one by Helen Puner, a journalist. Both books bristled with factual errors and presented psychoanalytic concepts in terms fit for fools. Ludwig's book was, in Anna Freud's quite accurate characterization, a "labor of hate."[37] In addition to whatever other reasons Ludwig may have had to hate Freud, there was the fact that Freud had once told him that his biographies were superficial because they did not take their subjects' childhood experiences into account.[38] The sources of Helen Puner's hostility were as unknown as she was to anyone in the Viennese group. Her contention that Freud had been apologetic for his Jewishness and secretly enamored of Catholicism astonished and enraged the Freud family, particularly Martin and Ernst, the Zionists among the Freud children. Martin took the Puner book as evidence that the Fliess letters would be exploited by unscrupulous biographers and he became even more adamantly opposed to their publication than his sister was.

Martin's objections reinforced Anna Freud's doubts—but not quite in the way Martin intended. He had argued that the material in the Fliess letters that Freud himself had called "Dreckologie," his effort to analyze his own anal and phallic libidinal stages, was not of value for the history of Freud's early discoveries.

> What do I have to say to that? [Anna Freud asked Ernst Kris]. I think he is right. . . . We were already in agreement not to include everything from the period in which the perverse fantasies appear as the forerunner of the infantile sexuality theory. But we probably did leave in a bit too much. . . . Anyway, we should avoid diverting the reader's interest from the development of his thought to the sensational. The amazing thing is—as I notice from my siblings—that perversion is still regarded as a sensation.[39]

She reasoned, logically, if not very psychoanalytically, that if Martin and Ernst, who was in charge of Freud's copyrights, found their father's perverse fantasies sensational, readers who had not grown up in an enlightened—or at least an enlightener's—household certainly would.

THE person who not only shared Anna Freud's opinion about the letters to Fliess but held it on the same principles was Aichhorn. She was as relieved by Aichhorn's understanding on this particular matter as she was touched by the attention he gave to all her concerns. As they exchanged letters, both looked forward with great anticipation to a reunion during the Easter vacation, 1948, at a conference in Lausanne, Switzerland. Afterward, she thanked him tenderly for the time they had spent together.

> I think you really did spoil me too much in Lausanne. I now notice that it is quite true that I had gotten out of the habit of expecting people to care for me, or, more accurately, to worry about me. And there is something else I have not told you: namely, that I never speak about my father the way I did with you. I never do it because I really cannot. It comes from too deeply within and forces too much to the surface. But it was very beautiful to do it.—He has been dead now for eight and a half years. But when I let myself go, then it always seems as if

his death had been only yesterday. That's probably also the reason why I don't let myself go.[40]

Aichhorn responded to this letter by asking if they might use the
familiar pronoun *Du* in their letters, even if not in public, so that he
could more freely write his mind and his heart. Then he added:

> That you told me so much about your father came as no sur-
> prise. He is my father, too. You alone know of the depth of my
> love for him, and you probably have known it for a long while,
> despite the pains I took to keep it completely to myself.
>   He lives on in me and will continue to do so always. I don't
> know if you also have realized that since you left Vienna and I
> stayed on alone, all of my activities were dedicated only to him.
> I don't know how great the significance of these activities is, but
> I do know that they are my single task.
>   When I congratulated him on his eightieth birthday, he
> wrote a single sentence in reply: "I credit you also to my suc-
> cesses." Here he gave me acknowledgment that I am his creation,
> his son. You may hold it against me that I am proud of it, or
> think that I feel too deeply that I also, along with you, belong
> to him; his death doesn't change this at all.
>   You say that I spoiled you too much while we were in Lau-
> sanne. That was nothing in comparison to the way I would like
> to care for you. I am angered that your social environment of-
> fers no compassion, and I really am worried about you. The
> coughing, the exhaustion after the serious pneumonia, and your
> self-abnegation make me worried.[41]

To Aichhorn's great joy, Anna Freud suggested that she call him
"Aichhorn" and that he call her "Anna," but she did not want to try
to cross the line that marked the difference between her family—
including Dorothy—and all others. "I would not like to use *Du* with
you, because I know from experience that I could not get used to it.
It would then have the reverse effect and not bring me closer to you.
So, if it suits you, we will make it 'Aichhorn' and 'Anna,' both when
we meet alone *and also* in the company of others."[42] This carefully
circumscribed gift and her letter of thanks gave Aichhorn the confidence to tell her—using *Du* himself—how much time he spent with
her in his daydreams, and how he loved and cared for her there.

Anna Freud did not wish to respond to the erotic dimension of Aichhorn's solicitude, though she had, since he first made her aware of his love, consistently accepted his desire while she was at the same time delimiting it: "Your letter from Bad Gastein did not startle me," she had said the first time he ventured a declaration of his feelings, "I already knew some of the things in it and guessed others. And good friendship is, as we know, always put together with every possible ingredient. The most important thing remains that the resulting mixture is true friendship and closeness. And it certainly is."[43] What she wanted—and got—was a kind of extension of her identification with her father, company in it, which was company of quite a different kind than she got from Dorothy, much less from her uncompassionate "social environment."

The complex merging of "Anna" and "Aichhorn" and their shared absent father is apparent in a letter she wrote after receiving Aichhorn's description of a sudden faintness he had experienced—the prelude to the cerebral thrombosis that ended his life. In her reaction, written two days before the ninth anniversary of her father's death, the three of them were at one in an experience of illness, fragility, loss of speech.

> Your description strangely reminded me of how my father complained when he had what he called "flicker migraines" that words escaped him or distorted themselves. Usually this lasted for a few hours. But yours must have been sharper and more concentrated than his were.
>
> I can imagine very well how frightening it was. The worst of it is the sudden insight that everything you are hangs by a single thread, something minimal, mechanical, over which you have no power, though you are completely in the palm of its hand. When I received your letter, it was suddenly as if I myself were the sick one, and I found it difficult to speak.[44]

Earlier, when Aichhorn was celebrating his seventieth birthday in July 1948, Anna Freud pleaded with him: "I really don't want you to get any older, I would gladly overlook all round, impressive numbers concerning you, and don't want to be reminded that you are older than I am. Much more pleasant to me than your seventieth birthday would be a promise that you will always remain the same, stay healthy, that your heart behaves itself—and that you remain my friend."[45] But Aichhorn's health and his heart did not obey. He suffered with chest pains and a number of small strokes. She encouraged him to spare himself: "Maybe we have all learned how to work too well and done rather poorly in learning to loaf."[46] But easing his schedule did not help, and they had to miss seeing each other again in Zurich, at the first postwar International Congress in August 1949.

Then they were left with a dilemma, for Aichhorn could not travel and Anna Freud would not visit Vienna: "the humiliation of having to emigrate from Vienna has still not been overcome. I was admittedly only too happy to be a Viennese—the opposite of my father, who had never liked Vienna. . . . There is the entire past, and it even feels as if one could enter into it one more time."[47] They hoped his condition would stabilize. But on October 17, just three weeks after he and Anna Freud had exchanged letters about the tenth anniversary of Freud's death, Aichhorn died.

DURING THE three years that she worked with Ernst Kris and Marie Bonaparte to select and abridge her father's letters to Fliess, Anna Freud had often told inquiring publishers, colleagues, and friends that she would never write a biographical word about her father. "A serious biography needs not only knowledge but detachment and objectivity, two attitudes which one can hardly expect to combine with a close personal relationship."[48] But she set out soon after Aichhorn's death to write his obituary for the *International Journal of Psychoanalysis*, of which their mutual friend Willi Hoffer had become the editor. This was her biography project, and it was many-faceted.

In part, she simply wanted to honor her friend's life and work, fulfilling as she did the terms of a joke they had shared. Aichhorn had told her how his enjoyment of his seventieth-birthday celebration, which included bestowal of the title Professor by the University of Vienna, was marred by how hard he had had to work to prepare a lecture—always a task Aichhorn dreaded.

I must recall for you a funny story I read one time in Vienna about Mother's Day [Anna Freud had written]. A family went on an excursion in honor of the day, and in preparation the worthy mother had to wash, iron, and starch the children's clothing, bake a cake, pack up the food basket, etc. etc. etc, until, in honor of herself she was completely exhausted. This is the way you are treated, it is the way my father was treated, and I myself am often treated this way. In the end, the obituary is the only thing one doesn't have to do for onself.[49]

Aichhorn's death seemed to her the most important marker in the history of psychoanalysis since her father's death: "Aichhorn's death is again a kind of full stop at the end of a great chapter in analysis and in all our lives," she wrote to Richard Sterba. "I had corresponded with him a good deal in the last years, and I can hardly say how I will miss his letters."[50] The obituary was meant to give Aichhorn his historical due, while it was an act of gratitude for his work, his concern, his letters, his existence. But it was also—displaced—a biography of Freud and an autobiography. The theme of her three-way depiction was the one that Heinz Hartmann had formulated in his letter about publishing the Fliess correspondence: "the story of the creation of psychoanalysis is at the same time the story of the creator's crisis."

Early in his own analysis [she wrote], Aichhorn had realized that he owed his interest in delinquency, and probably his therapeutic successes with young offenders, to an unstable phase in his own adolescence when he had narrowly missed becoming delinquent himself. Since then, the re-educator's double allegiance and identification, with society on the one hand and the world of the delinquent on the other, remained for him a fascinating problem. Discussing the role of the superego in social behavior in *Wayward Youth*, he wrote: "We cannot imagine a person who is unsocial as a worker in this field." But, in contrast, he wrote several years later (1948): "Whoever wants to work successfully with young delinquents has to be capable of stepping out of his own secure position in the social community, to identify himself with the offender, and thereby to become receptive to and understanding of the intricacies of the delinquent's char-

acter structure." . . . Unsuitability for the work he characterized as follows: "People who cannot escape from their own superego demands and invariably remain identified with society
fail to win the confidence of the delinquent or to understand the
workings of his mind."[51]

The crisis of the creator of psychoanalytic study of juvenile delinquency was the crisis of a man who felt that he was less talented
and less favored than his twin brother—a brother who had died in
1898, when they were twenty. He and Anna Freud had in common
the loss of their sibling companion-rivals soon after they had started
on careers as elementary-school teachers. Both also took their disliked first names as signs of all that was not right in their childhood
worlds: "I don't like my first name either," Aichhorn wrote when he
and Anna Freud were discussing how to address each other, "and I
have a particular reason for this dislike. No one ever used it in an
abbreviated form. My twin brother was called by a nickname, something I always wished would happen to me. Because of this I felt
that I wasn't loved as much; I don't know whether this was really
true."[52]

Anna Freud stressed Aichhorn's ability to use his own crisis in
order to identify with his delinquent students and patients, and
finally to admit theoretically that such an identification was necessary. From his insider's view came the careful distinctions he drew
between neurotic symptoms and delinquent behavior, with corollary
distinctions between psychoanalytic therapy and the therapy appropriate to delinquency, which chiefly involved the therapist's ability
to win the delinquent's identification. "The stronger his attachment
to me and his identification with me," Aichhorn said of his con-
quests, "the more he loosens his hold on 'delinquency' and inciden-
tally becomes social. . . . This strikes me as an excellent method for
building up a criminal gang for myself—if my inclinations went that
way."[53]

AICHHORN did build up quite a gang anyway—"not only personal
friends . . . but hundreds of pupils and admirers in all parts of the
world," as Anna Freud noted. Her biographical obituary was directed
to them, and it was constructed to allow Aichhorn to speak in his

own words as much as possible, to interpret himself. She wrote to Margaret Mahler in New York: "Since you belong to those of us who were Aichhorn's best friends, I should be very glad to know whether you think that I got his picture right."[54] This was just the attitude she wanted from a Freud biographer: desire to get her father's life and work "right," which meant respectful of his own point of view. She also wanted awareness of the identifications that had informed the views of each member of the gang who had known Freud—including herself—for she had become quite aware that each psychoanalyst has his or her own particular inner image of Freud.

Ernst Kris was the one she trusted to write the biographical commentary for the Fliess letters, although she must have realized what a complex situation was created when he began his introduction in the summer of 1946, because he was also in analysis with her. (Both the analysis and their work on the letters continued for three summers.) Kris was the most accomplished historian of ideas in their group, and he had, in addition, a great desire to work cooperatively, as he worked with Heinz Hartmann and Rudolph Loewenstein, his coauthors on psychoanalytic essays. Siegfried Bernfeld, who had emigrated to San Francisco, was also working on several long articles about Freud's early career; Kris benefited from Bernfeld's careful archival research and gave him, in turn, access to some of the Fliess letters.

Over particular biographical questions, Kris and Anna Freud compared notes by airmail. For example, they discussed at length Freud's physical ailments in 1894, and whether he suffered from a myocarditis or a nicotine hypersensitivity with psychosomatic dimensions—the condition Breuer diagnosed or the one Fliess diagnosed. She proposed: "As there is no final word to be spoken in this matter, wouldn't it be better to let it remain as [Freud] presents it to the reader, that is, as vacillation between two different possibilities, and not to attempt interpretation? For me, Max Schur's conclusion about the episode has lost any value because he has changed his mind so often . . . and Felix Deutsch is, as you know, hardly unbiased."[55] This was the general tendency of Anna Freud's critical collaboration in Kris's work: she argued for staying as close as possible to the conclusions of her father's own analysis, letting his autobiography be his biography, as she herself had done for Aichhorn in the obituary.

I realize [she noted on another point] that what you intended to show was to what extent my father analyzed and understood his own friendships with Breuer and Fliess as offshoots of his father-relation [*Vaterverhältnis*]. I now remember well that this was your intention, but strangely enough this idea has been superseded by another impression, which grew clearer to me as I read and reread the introduction: namely, that that is how you analyze it, not how he analyzed it.[56]

True to her policy of letting her father speak as much as possible for himself and mediating by abridgment rather than by interpretation, Anna Freud was very frank with Kris about his first draft.

One notices in all the parts about the self-analysis that you are still stuck in an internal conflict. There is too much explanation and too many apologies, and these will give the reader a feeling you do not want him to have, namely, that his curiosity has brought him onto forbidden ground. I think we have to solve the matter of conscience before you give this paragraph its final form. If we decide that it is not right to include certain things, then we have to leave them out. If we decide the opposite, then there is no need to apologize, and the more naturally you as the author of the introduction present these things, the more natural it will seem to the reader that he is getting to know them.[57]

In his essay on Leonardo da Vinci, Freud himself had warned prospective biographers about the dangers of idealization or ideal father-figure creation (of male subjects). Kris was very aware of the warning, and stopped himself well short of writing out his most idealizing thesis, which was that Freud had brought on the crisis in his life for the purpose of making himself into a properly neurotic object of analytic inquiry. Kris told Anna Freud in the privacy of their correspondence:

I believe that Freud's change after the self-analysis was so great because his neurosis had become a research instrument. Sometimes I think he allowed himself the neurosis in order to solve it, like a riddle. But I know full well that one cannot say such a thing, and I view it as my private version of hero worship, which I otherwise avoid. This thought is not new to me, though, and it fits with my long-running series of speculations about "regression in the service of the ego" in the creative process.[58]

There is, of course, a great difference between making a crisis in order to study it and having the curiosity and endurance to study a crisis that defies such management. Anna Freud understood her father's crisis to be of the second sort; she saw Aichhorn's as similar; and she had treated her own youthful crisis as a story to be told in "Beating Fantasies and Daydreams." When she again found herself in a crisis, made acute by her illness but more deeply shaped by her mourning, she had renewed her analysis as a self-analysis, and had written "On Losing and Being Lost." But her shift from self-analysis to thoughts about biographical analysis and to the actual practice of writing Aichhorn's obituary brought Anna Freud to a new attitude. She became convinced that the words—her father's, Aichhorn's, her own—that told the story of a crisis worked through analytically would ultimately be stronger than any words of incomprehension, exploitation, or detraction directed at them. So she could write to Siegfried Bernfeld in 1950: "The Fliess letters should appear soon now. Their publication takes as long as things do in England. I agree with you that misunderstanding and distortion will follow them. But I do not think that it matters very much."[59] She never ceased to be annoyed, sometimes infuriated, by the library of biographical articles and books about Freud that grew up over the years, but she was convinced that only those in which Freud had, as it were, converted the authors would ever matter very much.

EXTERNAL evidence for the come-what-may attitude she had reached internally came from Anna Freud's old ambivalent friend Ernest Jones. In 1946, Leon Shimkin, president of the American publishing house Simon and Schuster, approached Jones and suggested that he write Sigmund Freud's biography. Jones was interested, but not sure that he had the strength for such an undertaking. When Shimkin asked her for her advice, Anna Freud suggested Kris, or Kris and Bernfeld in collaboration, so that Jones would be "restricted to supplying material."[60] She reported to Kris: "Jones is not averse to looking for coworkers, since he is probably not able to do it alone in his present state of health. He himself thought of Bernfeld, which is not a bad idea if the work can be divided up. He also turned to me, but naturally I declined due to reasons already known to you."[61] Jones's seniority eventually prevailed, and, even though she was not in favor of the biography idea at all, Anna Freud decided not to protest for strategic reasons: "I don't want to lose all influence in this matter." About Jones as the biographer, she was cool—"he is not the worst"—but she reminded herself that he had given a beautiful eulogy for her father in 1939. "Jones's negative attitude [toward Freud], as it revealed itself to you," she noted to Bernfeld, "is no secret and is only too well known to me. But I believe it was mainly the result of jealousy and a feeling that he was not appreciated enough, and it probably has diminished greatly since my father's death."[62]

Such optimism was short-lived: May 1947 brought a panic. Jones wrote a preface for a special edition of Freud's *The Question of Lay Analysis*. Apparently quite pleased with his effort, he sent Anna Freud a copy. She was appalled by the whole piece but particularly by Jones's characterization of Freud's "antimedical bias." However, she summoned up a restrained letter to Jones: "I think your remark, especially that the author never did achieve a medical or even biological outlook is too condemning for the prospective reader."[63] Without strategic politeness, she sent her copy along to Kris: "Your work with the Fliess letters will make it easy for you to judge the attached preface in its entire arrogance and miserableness."[64] At her request, Kris had a word with the publishers about the preface, and it was modified, but Anna Freud was left deeply worried about a future biography. "I discussed with Ernst [Freud] the question: should I now write to Shimkin and withdraw my agreement to the choice of Jones as the biographer." The wry English civil servant who had translated Freud's text for the special edition brought the only moment of comic relief during the Freud family's biography debate. Nancy Procter-Gregg remarked that if Ernest Jones was any indication of what psychoanalysis can do for someone, she herself would rather make her way through life unaided by it and relying only on "lots and lots of bottles of gin."[65]

No decision about the biography seems to have been made in 1947. Anna Freud and Ernst Kris hoped that Bernfeld would just keep working along on his articles and that they would grow into a biography, which would discourage Jones. To all other prospective biographers, she simply indicated that Freud's letters to Fliess and other collections of letters—the basic ingredients for a biography— were being slowly prepared for publication. To other projects, like a historical novel proposed by Irving Stone and a film envisioned by Anatole Litvak, she simply said no—again and again. In a slightly different class were memoirs by Freud's colleagues, and she looked with friendly eyes on a lovely book Hanns Sachs published shortly before he died and on one called "Friendship with Freud" that Arnold Zweig worked on intermittently for many years but did not live to complete.[66] These were manuscripts in which her feeling that her father's story would work—as it were—therapeutically upon worthy authors was reconfirmed.

Kris did not want to do a full-scale biography because he had projects of his own and in collaboration with Hartmann and Loewenstein that compelled his attention. He was, also, not well, and the early indications of the heart condition that caused his death in 1957 appeared in 1949. Bernfeld, too, became ill, and he died in 1953, while he and his wife were still at work on studies of Freud's first psychoanalytic discoveries. Ironically enough, Jones, whose health had seemed an obstacle, decided to go ahead on his own, and the Freud family decided that they trusted him more than anyone else. They waited, however, until they had seen his drafts on Freud's boyhood and youth before they began to release documents to him, including the letters exchanged between Sigmund and Martha Freud during their engagement—letters that none of the children had read. Anna Freud could hardly believe her eyes: "I have read the first chapter, and I am simply amazed at his objective, factual and scientific approach to the whole topic."[67] She watched, reading draft upon draft, chapter by chapter, as Jones absorbed Freud's own enthusiasm and conviction—another kind of identification. "In the beginning he approached the task with some hesitancy, or even fear. However, this changed quickly and made itself felt as an intense and pleasurable preoccupation."[68] As Jones became more and more engaged, she encouraged him to do just what she and the family wanted done: "it should be your role to silence the other 'biographers' who have to invent half their facts."

•

WHILE Kris, the Bernfelds, and then Jones began the work that Jones alone completed, Martha Freud found a new role in the family: repository of memories. The biographers came to ask her questions and she assembled facts and genealogies of her family and Freud's for them—though she never even considered making her letters or those of her sister available. Since Minna's death in 1941, she had often been lonely, despite the attentions paid her by her children, the maid, and the large circle of family friends. She tried to maintain her dominance over the domestic arrangements at 20 Maresfield Gardens by supervising the gardener and walking out to do a daily shopping. Anyone who accompanied her on her expeditions had to be a true friend, though, because Martha Freud marched imperiously past any traffic sign or light, expecting to be deferred to. But she was also frail and susceptible to illnesses, particularly in the winters—like both Anna Freud and Dorothy Burlingham. In July of 1948, when she had been celebrating her eighty-seventh birthday and August Aichhorn had been celebrating his seventieth, Frau Freud wrote him a letter very characteristic of her conscious feeling about herself in the last years of her life.

> What difference does it make if such an old grandmama still toddles around between children and children's children? You will agree when I say that the merciful gift of a high old age should be granted above all to those who are capable of accomplishing something worthwhile and even irreplaceable for humanity. And with this thought in mind, let me wish that you may be granted yet many years of sprightly creativity, to the joy of your many, many friends, among whom the old mother Freud very unobtrusively counts herself.[69]

Martha Freud enjoyed writing little poems for family events and the Jewish holidays, which she celebrated more after her husband's death. She received visitors, did her handiwork, and wrote to old friends from Vienna who had emigrated to America or Palestine. To Anna Freud's mind, her mother was too controlling in the household, much too interested in the patients who came to the third-floor consulting room, and much too inclined to gossip about them with the maid. The adult patients interested her much more than the children who had come in Vienna; about them she had just been skeptical in her characteristic way. Noting how many plates of cookies and skeins of knitting wool were dedicated to the children's treatments, she had remarked: "Sie lasst sich's was kosten, die Kinderanalyse!" ("You'd be amazed what it costs, this child analysis!") [70]

Martha Freud's remarks about Anna Freud's plainness and drab clothes and unattractive flat shoes were a source of tension, and Anna Freud had little patience with her mother's dedication to elegant dresses, coiffures, and cosmetics. Rouging her cheeks a little in the weeks after her winter colds was as far as Anna Freud would go in the direction of her mother's vision of femininity, although she did wear proudly the necklaces her father had given her as birthday presents. But between mother and daughter there did reign a peace, not always an easy one, but a well-delineated one. Mathilde helped make the treaty workable by coming often to take their mother out, and Anna Freud helped the Hollitscher's in turn by providing them with a loan through a period of financial trouble in 1949 and 1950.

The cottage in Walberswick was Anna Freud's refuge for many weekends and all holidays, including the two months of August and September that had been the traditional Viennese analytic vacation months. There she felt free of the efforts of both Martha Freud and Paula Fichtl to make rules and take over, and there she shared her life with Dorothy Burlingham. After 1946, the Burlingham children vacationed in cottages in Walberswick, too. Those times were not always peaceful, because the Burlinghams were disconcerted by having their mother both so preoccupied with Anna Freud and so restricted from physical contact by her illness. But the playfulness of the Hochroterd years did return. And Anna Freud could play out her adventurer fantasies as well—as she did, for example, during the harvests when the farmer neighbors needed an extra hand to drive their tractor and she volunteered, to her own great joy. The Krises, the Katans, sometimes the Bibrings, and other Viennese friends took cottages and inn rooms nearby for reunions and informal workshops— in psychoanalysis for the analysts, crafts for the others. Anna Freud and Anny Katan eventually bought horses and went riding together on the beach; Dorothy Burlingham took up watercolor painting.

In the summer of 1951, Anna Freud had to be in London much of the time to care for her mother. Martha Freud had become very feeble in her ninetieth year, and finally she needed home nursing, which Sophie Dann, who had been working with a program for war orphans since 1945, graciously and capably provided. Then, on the second of November in 1951, after weeks of being unable to leave her bed, Martha Freud died. Her last weeks had been lived in the past. She had told Sophie Dann so often about her daughter Sophie and how deeply she had mourned her ever since 1920 that when she called out "Sophie, Sophie" as she was dying, no one knew whether she wanted her daughter or her nurse.

When her mother died, Anna Freud once again was in the role of the family correspondent: condolences came from all over the world, and Anna Freud answered each one with a letter. In the letters that went outside of her intimate circle, Anna Freud was detached, treating her mother as a historical figure, the one who had had the privilge of being her father's *Lebensgefährtin*, his life's companion. Letters about her mother's death to intimates have not survived or are not available, but people around the household remember very vividly that Anna Freud, always so controlled, particularly with her mother, wept openly when she died. She called one of her analysands to cancel a session and wept over the telephone—to his complete surprise.

The year had been particularly strenuous: Dorothy Burlingham had been in bed with a recurrence of her tuberculosis all through the fall; Anna Freud had started the year with a severe bronchitis and then been frantic in June when she injured a cyclist (not severely, as it turned out) with her automobile. Ernst and Mathilde had both had bronchitis in the spring; and both Marie Bonaparte and her husband, Prince George, had had heart trouble, his requiring surgery in America. The Princess, realizing how tired and distressed Anna Freud was, came for a two-week visit after Martha Freud's death—and probably heard Anna Freud's effort to understand her tears. Without intimate knowledge of Anna Freud's troubled relationship with her mother, but with good psychoanalytic instincts, Helen Ross wrote the appropriate condolence from Chicago, where she had gone after training with Anna Freud and Aichhorn in Vienna: "to give up a mother is to be no longer a child, and that is hard even for those we call mature."[71]

·

WHEN her mother died, Anna Freud lost her chief rival along with her being-a-child. But she also lost her *mother*—hard as it was for her to admit that she in any way needed her mother. The dreams she had had during her 1946 illness were—in her interpretations—of losing her father and of his being lost as a projection of her own being lost; the dreams of a manifestly maternal cast were not interpreted. Even those in which Dorothy, who in waking life was often ill and thus not available, played the role of the neglectful mother were not interpreted. Further, in all of her reflection on identification in the late 1940s, Anna Freud did not consider her own identification with her mother, despite the fact that she had opened her mind and her research through the years of the Hampstead War Nursery to facets of the mother-child relation she had not considered before.

In the spring after her mother's death, she read for the first time the *Brautbriefe*, the letters her parents had exchanged during their engagement. "They give me an enormous longing for the past, and, on top of that a remote past which has never been my own," she told Ernest Jones.[72] But she interpreted her feelings—and her dreams—in her characteristic fashion: she was a child (of unspecified gender) longing for her father's past, not for a past her parents had shared. She had thought of herself as desiring her mother's (and Tante Minna's) place, but not as loving her mother, not even in and through her identification with her father. Her father was always at the center of her longing, and her mother at the center of her jealousy: "I dream of apartments of the past and happenings which never existed or took place. I believe that I really dream of my father's past and not of mine. Like most children, I have always been jealous of his past that I did not share, and your descriptions bring it home to me what a long and full life he had before my time, that I really only appeared somewhere in the middle as a very insignificant item."[73]

Her mother's death gave Anna Freud this acquaintance, through her mother and father's engagement correspondence, with their past, and she was so caught up in it that the positive feelings she had had for her mother also surfaced. She took to reiterating to the Burlingham daughters and granddaughters how sturdy her mother had been through the emigration. "I often think what you said about your mother," Mabbie Schmiderer wrote, "and how she adjusted herself to all demands."[74] She repeated to Mabbie as she had to her Hampstead staff her father's often announced high standard for his household: "a good woman must be able to do everything." Martha Freud's death certainly did not end the old grievances, which surged forth out of memory for the rest of Anna Freud's life, but it did bring a balance of expressed appreciation.

Her mother's death also gave Anna Freud's life a new domestic structure for the future—the end of her own long period of waiting for a shared life. There was room in 20 Maresfield Gardens for Dorothy to invite her children and grandchildren to visit there. The friends also bought together a larger cottage in Walberswick, so that they could have Dorothy's family as visitors in their house there as well. For the first time in her adult life, Anna Freud, fifty-six years old, was a partner in her own household, not responsible for taking care of either of her parents, free to travel, free for what she and Dorothy called "the adventures" of their vacations.

JONES's first volume, which tracked Freud's life up to 1900, pleased Anna Freud enormously, and its reception made her feel that the book really could convey her father's life and work to a nonanalytic audience and also silence the biographer-pretenders. She was even willing to give over parts of her precious weekends to become the volume's translator into German. Working with Ernest Jones's wife, Katherine, she translated about half the volume, but then the publisher's tight schedule and token payment discouraged her, as did the copy editor's opinion that her German prose was archaic and too formal.

Being Ernest Jones's translator was also a rather peculiar role, both because it took her back to the period of her analysis, when she had been the underadmired translator of his psychoanalytic articles, and because the job confirmed her in a second-place status she had noted in a letter to Jones praising his first volume: "I thought that I knew my father better than anybody else, but I do not think it any more."[75] These themes came together in a dream that she reported to the biographer: "I had a most curious dream about you last night. We were both trying to decipher a passage in my father's handwriting, the transcription of which you had queried. You were right, it did not say what the typing person had put down, but we could not make it out. Suddenly I caught it; it said 'mirabile dictu.' I felt very proud, but also it was felt in the dream to be your achievement, not mine, since you had spotted the mistake."[76]

Although it was strange to have Jones on such intimate terms with her father, Anna Freud did more than just tolerate it; she gave Jones a place—limited, but a place—in the circle of men who kept her company in her father identification. Many people remarked on the mellowing of Ernest Jones in the last decade of his life, and Anna Freud was not alone in thinking that he had been changed by writing her father's life, that his feeling of being unappreciated and his jealousy of his peers had truly diminished. But she was the one in the position to grant him the affection he had felt denied by her father and, earlier, by herself. When Jones gave her a necklace for her sixtieth birthday in 1955, she thanked him: "When my father died, I thought that this was also the end of my collection of jewelry, to which he contributed every year."[77] She felt that Ernest Jones had been, as a biographer, tender toward her father—and tender toward her father was what she most desired to be herself, as strongly as she had desired his tenderness. Ernst Kris expressed clearly their feeling about the second volume of the biography: "As a whole the volume is naturally weaker than volume I, but everything human and personal is treated wisely and almost with tenderness. Only the thinker Freud, the man in battle with his task, was not sufficiently done. The solitary greatness does not emerge; the struggle for psychoanalysis is almost lost from view."[78] She saw a curious reversal: Ernest Jones, renowned as an untender fighter, was tender but missed the fight.

Ernest Jones had come to know the young Freud better than anyone, Anna Freud conceded, but about her father's later years and his later struggle to keep psychoanalysis on a truthful path, she remained the expert, the eyewitness. Volume three of Jones's work was her territory, and it is interesting to note that in none of the available correspondences did she comment on his survey of this territory. She also simply accepted without comment Jones's decision about how to tell—or how not to tell—her own story in the third volume, and particularly in its last chapter: "Not a word about your noble devotion—I felt you would prefer that, and it is between the lines in any case."[79] She did not say that Jones's strategy involved presumption or preemption. By the time the biographer presented her with his version of Freud's death, Anna Freud was on the other side of her mourning. She had wondered whether she would find it "harrowing" to read the story; but she did not. She had finished telling the story to herself.

In a biography, a life is held as it were in suspension, to be contemplated as a whole, with any records that might remain of the subject's self-understanding giving the only clues to what the life might have been like in the living, moment by moment. What Anna Freud discovered for herself and described for psychoanalytic theory in the years just after the Second World War was the one way that human beings have to preserve a life, a life story, in a true dynamism. This way, by identification, is not a matter of history writing and it lacks the supposed objectivity of history, although capacity for identification is surely as influential in the course of events as ability to immortalize in words. Anna Freud wove the weft of insights about identification through the woof of her essay "On Losing and Being Lost," but she was able, years after her essay had helped her through her mourning, to put the insights quite directly, in two sentences. These she wrote in a letter of condolence sent to her American friend Ralph Greenson, who was mourning the death of his analyst and colleague Max Schur, Sigmund Freud's physician. She reached out to comfort a friend who had written her about his own discovery of the identification process: "I agree that mourning is a terrible task, surely the most difficult of all. And it is only made bearable by the moments, which you also describe so well, when one feels fleetingly that the lost person has entered into one and that there is a gain somewhere which denies death."[80]

8

CREATIVITY
AND SCIENCE

Aɴɴᴀ Fʀᴇᴜᴅ's ᴘᴀᴛʜ away from her illness and from her mourning
was—like the path in her anticlimactic dream—serpentine. At the
end of 1947, she was in such a manic state that she several times
asked Ernst and Marianne Kris to send her shipments of the American fountain pens she liked for writing: "A strange change has come
over me, I am writing one article after another and I'm even enjoying
it. But naturally it's strenuous for the fountain pens." To another
friend she later confessed: "As you know, I am addicted to pencils
and can never have enough."[1] Anny Rosenberg Katan and her Dutch
husband, Maurits, who had moved from Amsterdam to Cleveland,
were the paper suppliers for this writing upsurge, and the nutrition
supplements came from one of Aichhorn's students in New York,
Kurt Eissler, who regularly sent coffee and sausages—the former for
her mind's alertness, Anna Freud noted, and the latter for her body's
strength. But, even well supported, the manic stage could not last.
In the spring of 1948, after her winter colds had passed, she was still
weak.

Sometimes a relapse into exhaustion occurs, and then I begin to
calculate how I could make my life easier and more comfort-

able. Then the exhaustion passes, and I begin to make plans of just the opposite sort. I would like to write a lengthy book about psychoanalysis and education, for which I have already assembled most of the material needed; or perhaps I should write a book about the latency period, for which I also already have the material, and in which I have always been so interested. But then my daily work always gets in between these projects and nothing comes of them. Sometimes I reflect on this exhaustion: I ask whether it is really my body which rebels, or whether it's more likely that I myself rebel against the busy engagement of my work. I don't know the answer, but I am trying to find it out.[2]

This body of hers, which she spoke of as though it was not part of "myself," was rebellious, but it was also despised for its prior rebellions. Anna Freud often complained to her medical friends about the aftereffects of her illness and the program of medications it had required: her hair became thin and limp, her fingernails were (as she said) "quite sick," she gained weight and also become so stooped that she looked many more than her fifty-two years.[3] Before she had set out in 1948 for her last reunion with August Aichhorn, she had warned him again and again that he should not mistake her changed appearance for any deeper change, that the decade between forty and fifty was a difficult one for women, that he should not be surprised to find her looking so old. When they met, he had responded in his characteristic fashion by insisting that they be photographed together so that she could see how well she looked while he was taking care of her. His experiment was a success, and she ordered many copies of the photographs: "We must really be very good friends," she had written to him, "because everyone here notes that I have never looked upon a photograph with such friendliness as upon yours. Everyone is completely enthusiastic about the likeness, and I even look good to myself, which usually is not the case. Indeed, the opposite: I am always angry when I see myself in a picture."[4]

Her appearance made Anna Freud feel reluctant about attending meetings and conferences. Dorothy Burlingham and Marie Bonaparte, who had become quite friendly, collaborated in urging her, while they also took the opportunity of her vanity to convince her, to take more vacations in the fresh air. By 1948, the Princess was even successful in getting Anna Freud to fly to Greece and spend

Christmas in the Aegean sun. But business travel left her uneasy. After a trip in the spring of 1947 to lecture in Amsterdam and Paris, she noted her reaction in a letter to the family wit, her brother Martin: "Paris and Amsterdam look much more beautiful than London; the difference is about as great as that between a really elegant woman and myself."[5]

The 1947 trip was too taxing. It had been harder for her than a shorter one she had made to Paris six months earlier, in November 1946, when she had been buoyed up by her great relief over being in "an unbombed-out place" and "spoiled" by the luxury the Princess provided.[6] The 1946 trip also brought her some hope that her research in the Hampstead War Nursery might play a social role in the reconsruction of Europe. She addressed a meeting of UNESCO, which invited her through Stephen Spender to talk on children in wartime, and the American Joint Distribution Committee, which met informally at the home of the Baroness de Rothschild. Her contacts with "The Joint" were later helpful for securing assistance for Jewish analysts, like Katá and Lajos Levy in Budapest, who had survived the war only to face new dangers from Stalinism. But in a more general sense, the reconstruction of Europe went on with little influence from the insights of child analysis.

Both the limitations that came from her illness and her self-consciousness about her changed appearance—a wound to her narcissism, in analytic terms—required from Anna Freud increases in the quite conscious efforts at sublimation she made to finish her mourning. She made these in the mode she had learned as a child and modified during her analysis—fantasizing, daydreaming, and writing—and she accompanied them with characteristic self-reflection—a paper about sublimation. "Sublimation as a Factor in Upbringing" was a popular lecture, which she delivered as part of her contribution to the 1947 Durham Summer School for social and health workers and then wrote up for the *Health Education Journal*.[7]

Anna Freud noted in this paper that neither a restrictive upbringing in which prohibitions corral children's libidinal and aggressive instincts nor a "progressive" upbringing in which the instincts are allowed to run free is good for children. Neurotic disturbances or social maladjustment result at the extremes. However, a freer, less restrictive upbringing is definitely advantageous in two areas.

Such a regime has proved helpful where eating is concerned: infants and small children have shown surprising powers of self-regulation when left free to choose their own food according to kind and quality. A less exacting demand for good manners has also done much to decrease the incidence of eating disturbances. And a more tolerant attitude to dirtiness, and the postponement of [toilet] training to the second year of life has had beneficial results for the child's character formation.

With the sexual and aggressive urges of childhood, Anna Freud argued, the middle path between extremes is best, provided that it is paved with imaginative substitute gratifications.

So long as the child is not made afraid of his own desires and not estranged from them through repression, the instinctive energy with which they are invested can be displaced and outlets found which are acceptable to the instinct as well as to the environment. Where, for instance, training for cleanliness is carried out without producing excessive disgust, the young child can easily be induced to turn to the substitute pleasures of smearing and modeling with paint and plasticine instead of handling his own feces. Children who have not been made too ashamed of their exhibitionistic tendencies are eager to show off their skills and mental accomplishments instead of their bodies, or will turn to acting and dancing as acceptable ways of gaining admiration. Sexual curiosity, if not severely repressed is especially productive of substitute wishes; it gives rise to the general attitude of wanting to know—about the origin of things (based on curiosity about the birth of babies); about the working of engines and cars (based on curiosity about the functioning of the penis, especially the phenomenon of erection); about big animals (as representatives of the powerful parents) etc. The aggressive urges, if handled wisely, accept many similar compromises. When displaced onto activities such as cutting, hammering, handling efficient tools, the tendencies to tear open, to break, to hurt, can be tempted to serve constructive rather than destructive aims. The wishes for self-assertion and for fighting others may be turned from people to material difficulties and to the overcoming of obstacles, and finally displaced to the fight with the dangers and difficulties of life conditions.

After she had discussed how sublimation can be aided—though neither taught nor commandeered—by providing a child with the right opportunities at the right moment, Anna Freud turned her attention to sublimation in adult life.

Sublimation is, thus, more than a mere mode of behavior which can be adopted at will in adult life when external circumstances, such as absence or other inaccessibility of the sexual partner, imprisonment, illness, etc. make the satisfaction of sexual or aggressive wishes difficult or impossible. It consists of an actual, far-reaching modification of the instinctive processes themselves, as far as their fixation to particular aims is concerned. Where the ability to sublimate has developed in early childhood, the instinctive wishes become less inexorable in their claims, more ready to accept substitute gratifications and therefore more adaptable to the circumstances of life.

One of her readers, Dr. Robert Sutherland, wrote asking for clarification about these brief remarks on adult sublimation. Can a person who is without a sexual partner in adulthood learn to sublimate? She replied with a statement of what she had learned from her own chaste life as much as from her research: "The answer to the unmarried adult who wants to sublimate is, of course, that he cannot do so unless the ability to sublimate has been acquired in childhood. But I thought it was rather unkind to say that; I hope it emerges from the article."[8] In her recovery years she had become surer and surer of the echo in her present life of her own childhood virtuosity in sublimation.

One result was quite specific: she began to think of her writing as a child, as she had earlier thought of the Jackson Nursery and the Hampstead War Nursery as her children. But her writing was a gendered child—a boy child, or as her father and she in their professional mode would have phrased it, a penis-child. In nonbusiness correspondences, she referred to her papers with masculine pronouns, in English and in German. Often the writings pleased her immediately, but sometimes she was tentative: "I am sorry I have been so niggardly about lending you the bits of my book which you wanted to read," she wrote to a colleague. "My only excuse is that I feel towards them as a good mother feels toward her infant who is by no means ready to meet the world unaccompanied."[9] The more general result of her sublimation efforts was that she took comfort from her lifework as a whole, not just from individual facets of it with particular sublimation functions. As she noted to Max Schiller, who had lost his wife, the singer Yvette Guilbert Schiller, and was doing some counseling work to console himself: "I am so glad that you have begun to be a bit of a psychoanalyst. There is no time or age limit to the pleasure and benefit one gains from looking at oneself and at other people that way. So far it is the only thing I know which makes this difficult life easy."[10]

THE pleasure in writing that came as Anna Freud recovered from her illness and went through the last stages of her mourning coincided with one of the most challenging therapeutic and research opportunities she had ever had. In his *Wayward Youth* and in his later papers, August Aichhorn had produced the seminal psychoanalytic descriptions of youth gangs; this work had inspired other descriptions of gangs, including Dorothy Burlingham's first paper on twins, "Twins—A Gang in Miniature."[11] But nodoby had seen, much less treated, a gang like the one that arrived in England in August 1945: six children who had been together since they were between six months and a year old, when they were left in the Ward for Motherless Children at the concentration camp Theresienstadt. Before they were liberated by the Russians and housed for a month in a Czech castle, these children spent nearly three years in the camp, being cared for by many different overworked and undernourished prisoners. They eventually became part of a project that brought a thousand concentration camp children and adolescents to a reception center on Lake Windemere in England, which Alice Goldberger, Anna Freud's Hampstead Nursery colleague, ran with Oscar Friedmann, a social worker who also trained as an analyst. From this center, all one thousand of the young survivors were eventually placed in homes, hostels, or training centers throughout England.

Their inseparability having been recognized and respected, the six children from Theresienstadt were kept together: "It was evident that they cared greatly for each other and not at all for anybody or anything else."[12] A Sussex home called Bulldogs Bank was donated for their residence by Lady Betty Clarke and their care was financed by the Foster Parents' Plan in New York. Anna Freud's Hampstead colleagues Sophie and Gertrud Dann, with several helpers, were hired to manage the little gang, and they kept index cards of their observations as they had been trained to do in the War Nursery. Sophie Dann made a rough draft of a paper on the children, Alice Goldberger acted as a consultant, and then Anna Freud converted the draft into "An Experiment in Group Upbringing" (1951), one of the most unusual and fascinating papers in the history of psychoanalysis.

The terrible "experiment" provided by Nazi totalitarianism produced six children who were like a sibling group without parents.

> Siblings are normally accessories to the parents, the relations to them being governed by attitudes of rivalry, envy, jealousy, and competition for the love of the parents. Aggression, which is inhibited toward the parents, is expressed freely toward brothers and sisters; sexual wishes, which cannot become manifest in the Oedipal relationship, are lived out, passively or actively, with elder or younger brothers and sisters. The underlying relationship with siblings is thus a negative one (dating from infancy when all siblings are merely rivals for the mother's love), with an overlay of positive feelings when siblings are used for the discharge of libidinal trends deflected from the parents.

The parentless Theresienstadt children loved one another quite directly, not through the mediation of their parental loves or of their negative, rivalrous sibling feelings: "the feelings of the six children toward each other show a warmth and spontaneity that are unheard of in ordinary relations between young contemporaries."

According to the assumptions of Melanie Klein's prewar work and to those of John Bowlby, who had recently written about "separation anxiety" and children's responses to a "rejecting mother," the kind of deprivations the Theresienstadt children had endured should have been massively pathogenic. But, Anna Freud noted, although the children were unusually given to autoerotic pleasures, showed some incipient neurotic symptoms, and were "restless, aggressive, difficult to handle," they were "neither deficient, delinquent, nor psychotic." "They had found an alternative placement for their libido and, on the strength of this, had mastered some of their anxieties and developed social attitudes. That they were able to acquire a new language in the midst of their upheavals bears witness to a basically unharmed contact with their environment."

These children offered Anna Freud confirmation of both the theory and the therapy she had developed for the Hampstead war nurseries children who were both without their parents and abnormally aggressive. By providing the children with a staff member substitute mother, she was able to achieve a reign of peace unattainable by admonishments or punishments. "The results confirmed that with the development of good object relationships, aggression became bound and its manifestations reduced to normal quantities. It proved possible, as it were, to effect therapeutic results by bringing about the necessary fusion" of the libidinal and aggressive drives.[13] Because their libinal development, even though so group-related, was strong enough to bind their aggression, the Theresienstadt children had not suffered from a failed fusion or a splitting of their instinctual drives.

WHILE Anna Freud's London group was still considering the results of the Dann sisters' year of work with their six charges, she herself had two opportunities to present papers on aggression. The first was an invitation from the Psychiatry Section of the Royal Society of Medicine, which she addressed on December 7, 1947, and the second was an international conference on child psychiatry set for August 1948 in London. The Congress on Mental Hygiene, as the second was called, had as its central theme the role of aggression in normal and abnormal child development. Anna Freud took the opportunity of this Congress to present a lucid review of theories of aggression, a catalog of "controversies and problems," and a summary statement of the conclusions about fused and unfused drives that she had reached at the war nurseries and then seen confirmed in work with the concentration camp children.[14]

In a nonpolemical tone, she distinguished her understanding of aggression from Melanie Klein's and John Bowlby's. Bowlby, she noted, operated with Freud's first theory of aggression, which classified aggression as an "ego instinct" directed toward the preservation of life. He considered increases in aggression to be due to frustration of instinctual wishes.[15] Freud had abandoned this theory in 1920, and replaced it with the theory of life and death instincts, in which aggression is considered necessary and normal in fusion with the sexual instincts, the representatives of the life instinct. Freud argued that psychopathology is present when repression or inhibition of aggression makes sexuality ineffective, or when aggression unfused with sexual urges manifests itself in destructive or criminal behavior. But Freud's dual instinct theory left unanswered the key question about how and when the instincts conflict, a question that divided the main English groups of adherents to the dual instinct theory: the Melanie Kleinians and the Anna Freudians.

In order to state Klein's current theory as accurately as possible, Anna Freud contacted Klein's rather independent colleague Donald Winnicott, a well-known pediatrician and a capable popularizer of psychoanalytic child-care recommendations. Winnicott sent a page summarizing Klein's views on "the depressive position" and a letter reflecting his own views. Anna Freud then used his summary to indicate that Klein assumed a necessary conflict of the life and death instincts in every child. Every child recognizes that a loved object is in danger of being attacked and destroyed precisely because it is so loved. "When the loved object is no longer merely a part of the other person from which satisfaction is gained (such as the mother's breast), the infant feels guilt with regard to its destructive fantasies. This produces feelings of depression which are lessened only when reparative and restitutive ideas appear and bring relief."[16] By contrast, Anna Frued held that the two instincts could peacefully coexist in early infancy. "The mental representatives of the two organic forces remain unrelated to each other so long as no central point of awareness is established in the personality. It is only the growth of this focal point (the ego) which results in the gradual integration of all instinctual strivings, and during this process may lead to clashes and realization of incompatibility between them." When the aggressive urges are felt as incompatible, the ego represses or eliminates them with the same defense mechanisms it uses for dangerous pregenital sexual urges.

Melanie Klein had always claimed that she was a pioneer in emphasizing aggression, the more theoretically neglected of the two instinctual representatives. This was a reasonable claim, and Anna

Freud acknowledged it by indicating generally that "in recent years, aggression, destruction, their expressions and their development have assumed central interest for workers in the field of education, child psychology and child therapy." But she was quite unwilling to concede that psychopathology originated in an inevitable battle of the instincts or in aggression itself. In her view, the root of psychopathology was on the libidinal side, or, more precisely, in a lack of fusion between libidinal (erotic) urges and aggressive ones. If erotic or emotional development is held up through adverse external or internal conditions, such as "the absence of love objects, lack of emotional response from the adult environment, breaking of emotional ties as soon as they are formed, deficiency of emotional development for innate reasons," then "the aggressive urges are not brought into fusion and thereby bound and partially neutralized, but remain free and seek expression in life in the form of pure, unadulterated, independent destructiveness."[17] Anna Freud never—as many commentators have claimed—rejected her father's death instinct theory, she simply argued for the primacy of Eros.

The mental health Congress was itself threatened by an outbreak of unfused aggression on the international scale as the bonds that had held the Soviet Union to its European allies deteriorated. In the summer of 1948, while Eastern Europe was being dragged into the Soviet's orbit, there were dire predictions that another world war would ensue. Earlier in the year, from his new home in America, René Spitz wrote Anna Freud his doubts about the reunion in London which all the Viennese analysts looked forward to so much: "by that time the world situation can easily have deteroriated to a point where the Congress will either not take place or will be a last opportunity to meet old friends before Armageddon; but I must not be too pessimistic."[18] Anna Freud, never one to expect anything of the political realm, concentrated her attention on plans for surviving what she called "Der Monster-Kongress," the impending arrival of some twenty-five hundred delegates from forty-two countries for ten days of meetings.[19]

When the Viennese gathered in London for the Congress, they found Anna Freud looking very frail, but when she rose to address the multitudes she seemed to grow in stature and gain in health. She was in her public mode: representing her father, carrying on the work of psychoanalysis, inspiring her troops, enjoying the limelight. She was also sure that she was bringing to the Congress a fundamental insight with her paper on aggression. As she had said in the understated style she used for corresponding with Heinz Hartmann, a peer she considered more than her equal: "The last year here was not uninteresting, even if very strenuous. But somehow it has left me with the impression that I have learned something really new."[20]

ANOTHER new branch in Anna Freud's research grew by chance. In the years after the war she had in analysis four male homosexuals, and their analyses led her to reflect both on the therapeutic problems posed by male passivity and on the theoretical issues involved in purely internal conflicts between activity and passivity—as opposed to conflicts derived from the Oedipus complex, or from traumatic experiences, or conflicts among the personality's structures, like those from guilt feelings sent out by the superego. She reviewed the psychoanalytic literature on homosexuality, and particularly her father's 1922 paper "Some Neurotic Mechanisms in Jealousy, Paranoia and Homosexuality," but her own approach to her patients depended on an equation that was not, as such, part of the literature. She put this very simply in a lecture: "the active male partner, whom these men were seeking, represents to them their lost masculinity, which they enjoy in identification with him. This implies that these apparently passive men are active according to their fantasy, while they are passive only so far as their behavior is concerned."[21]

Even though the four patients had developed very differently, they all fit this equation and reacted to the analytic situation as though it were a castration threat, a threat to deprive them of their masculinity in the form of their masculine partners. When the analytic situation did bring about in them interest in heterosexual relationships, they required of their female partners unending admiration of their phallic potency: "narcissistically they loved their own genital, just as in childhood they had wanted someone [usually the mother] to admire it or to share their own admiration of it with them." As Anna Freud remarked in a rare public moment of irony: "They were once more like boys five years old, but boys five years old are not very good lovers, in spite of the Oedipus complex."

In a lecture prepared for the 1951 International Congress in

Amsterdam, Anna Freud again took up these men who had been therapeutically restored to "phallic potency" but remained "emotionally impotent" or negativistic. She had become more generally interested in negativism or disturbance of the capacity for object love. Noting that such a disturbance is often attributed to insufficiencies in a child's relationship with its mother or to its rejection by its mother, she reminded her audience that overstimulation (or seduction) by the mother may also produce negativism, as may withdrawal of love from an object and focus of it on the self or on the genital (as in the phallic narcissism of the homosexual patients). Anna Freud questioned, however, why libido withdrawn from an object and focused narcissistically is not later outwardly redirected onto new objects or old objects newly encountered. Her analyses of homosexuals and impotent males suggested an answer: "Such persons see the relation to a love object exclusively in passive terms. To love means: to be maltreated, kicked about, impoverished, tormented, possessed. . . . Paradoxically, then, for these patients the symptom of impotence in intercourse serves the preservation of their masculinity." Being physically or emotionally impotent meant avoiding love, with its threat of maltreatment or further loss.

This interpretation, with further analytic work, led to another: an ego-psychological explanation of why these men feared passivity. "The passive surrender to the love object may signify a return from object love proper to its forerunner in the emotional development of the infant, i.e., to primary identification with the love object. This is a regressive step which implies a threat to the intactness of the ego, i.e., a loss of personal characteristics which are merged with the characteristics of the love object." Rejecting love objects to preserve his ego may be the dominant mode of a person who, at other times, actually does emotionally surrender himself to the love object or put himself in bondage (*Hörigkeit*); the less frequent behavior is a clue to the dominant one.

Anna Freud saw this avenue of explanation, and the therapeutic successes that came with it, as very encouraging for psychoanalytic work with male homosexuals. She also took the position that a homosexual's contentment with his sexual preference was a great obstacle to psychoanalytic therapy—no matter whether the therapy was undertaken to cure homosexuality or for other reasons. That refusal to question a preferenc :—*any* preference—puts obstacles in a therapeutic path is an obvious truth. But Anna Freud was particularly and unusually irritable about the resistance she had described in libidinal terms as fear of passivity and in ego-psychological terms as fear of regression to a primary identification. She was, further, convinced that homosexuality is invariably a condition to be cured.

In 1935, Sigmund Freud had written a very comforting reply to an American woman who had asked for advice about her son. He had offered to try to cure the son, but he also said clearly: "Homosexuality is assuredly no advantage, but it is nothing to be ashamed of, no vice, no degradation, it cannot be classified as an illness; we consider it to be a variation of the sexual function produced by a certain arrest of sexual development. Many highly respectable individuals of ancient and modern times have been homosexuals, several of the greatest men among them (Plato, Michelangelo, Leonardo da Vinci, etc.)."[22] But in 1956 Anna Freud recommended to Nancy Procter-Gregg, who was writing a popular article on psychoanalysis for the London newspaper *The Observer*, that she not quote this letter of Freud's. "There are several reasons for this, one being that nowadays we can cure many more homosexuals than was thought possible in the beginning. The other reason is that readers may take this as a confirmation that all that analysis can do is to convince patients that their defects or 'immoralities' do not matter and that they should be happy with them. That would be unfortunate."[23] She maintained this attitude and reiterated it later: "a feeling that their perverse practices are completely normal, natural and even 'good' " had kept a number of her manifest homosexual patients, she said, from making much use of therapy.[24]

Anna Freud's attitude that homosexuality was there for curing was no different than that of most analysts of her generation, although she did, later in her life, shift to the uncommon position that a homosexual could be accepted for psychoanalytic training—uncured—if his or her character and credentials were suitable.[25] Her contribution to the theory of homosexual development, which does fit many cases, has been subsumed in work done in a more tolerant era than the 1950s.[26] From a biographical point of view, however, the lectures on homosexuality are very important. They extended Anna Freud's "on losing and being lost" reflections, and they connected these with earlier threads in her work and in her self-analysis.

She was studying, once again, something lost—masculinity, the phallus—and then found by way of identification or projective identification. She held that a homosexual does not relinquish either his normal youthful identification with his father's masculinity or any adolescent identification with hero's exploits he may have: "The abnormal development of these patients corresponds to an arrest at or a regression to this particular phase of normal development." Then actual impotence in heterosexual intercourse maintains the homosexual's identificatory phallic potency—he cannot lose what he has found by identifying with his father if he does not do as his father does.

This step in her analysis, as a number of her colleagues pointed out in correspondence, connected with her earlier understanding of altruistic surrender. Robert Waelder noted: "That the passive homosexual submits to a strong man in the hope thereby of becoming a big man himself, was common knowledge; but that the virility with which he is in love had once been his own and was at one point lost or given up, is the new twist, and this concept reminds me somewhat of the concept of *altruistische Abtretung*."[27] Neither Waelder nor Anna Freud herself asked in their correspondence whether the theory had applications for females like the autobiographically based case who had been Anna Freud's chief example of altruistic surrender in *The Ego and the Mechanisms of Defense*.

But it does seem that Anna Freud's theory belongs in the small but centrally important collection of her self-analytical results. That she was so interested in patients whose potency was constituted by their identifications with the masculinities of their fathers (and later lovers) is not surprising. In her earliest essay, "Beating Fantasies and Daydreams," she had noted that the female patient adopted a masculine role—identified with her father—in order to avoid forbidden father-daughter incestuous desires. The girl also constructed thereby the all-male love-world of her beating fantasies, where love meant either being maltreated or kicked about or watching such scenes of punishment. The girl, in effect, made herself emotionally into a male homosexual but avoided *any* kind of sexual involvement.

The "losing and being lost," the altruistic surrender, and the "beating fantasies and daydreams" themes of Anna Freud's analysis and self-analysis all echoed in the male homosexuality studies. But it was the last step in this work that was really new to Anna Freud. When she conceptualized fear of losing potency and fear of passivity as fear of self-dissolution, ego-dissolution, she was on novel territory. Later she met this conceptualization in the young English analyst Marion Milner's remarkable book on psychic creativity, called *On Not Being Able to Paint*, and was so impressed that she agreed to write a preface for the book's 1957 second edition, despite the threads in it of Kleinian formulation with which she was unsympathetic. In Milner's book, Anna Freud noted in her preface, there is

> a highly interesting treatise on negativistic attitudes toward psychic creativity in which certain inhibitions to create are ascribed to fear of regression to an undifferentiated state in which the boundaries between id and ego, self and object become blurred. Owing to this anxiety, no "language of love," i.e., no medium, can be found in which to "symbolize the individual's pregenital and genital orgiastic experiences." These views coincide in a welcome manner with certain clinical observations of my own concerning states of affective negativism, in which the patient's ability to express object love is blocked by the fear of an all too complete emotional surrender. Future studies of this kind will owe much to Marion Milner's lucid explanation of this "unconscious hankering to return to the blissful surrender, this all-out body giving of infancy."[28]

Anna Freud quoted the passage on "all-out body giving of infancy" from a section of Milner's book that discusses not phallic potency but "the anal aspect" of psychic creativity. Milner had noted that "for patients whose fixation point is at this stage, the surrender of the consciously planning deliberative mind to the spontaneous creative force can be felt as a very dangerous undertaking," not just because of the surrender itself but because of the messiness, lack of sphincter control, it may entail.[29] In the anal stage, the connection between fear of passivity or ego-surrender and the mother who handles and cleans a child is even more obvious than the connection between the fear and the mother in the phallic stage. Longing for passivity with the mother was a domain of feeling that Anna Freud herself found very difficult to consider, although she had obviously considered it often in relation to her father. In her lectures on male homosexuality and her preface to Milner's book, Anna Freud did, however, approach the child-to-mother surrender, and it is probably significant that she set out in this direction in the year of her own mother's death. What she implied is that behind such mechanisms as altruistic surrender lies fear of emotional surrender to the mother or a mothering figure like the *Kinderfrau* Josefine. This is a layer of feeling deeper, more archaic, than the wishes that the altruistic governess had feared and deemed unacceptable: the wish for a penis, the "feminine wish for children and the desire to display herself, naked or in beautiful clothes, to her father"—wishes of the phallic stage, in relation to the father.[30]

In the two most personal pieces of her immediate postwar work, the papers on aggression stemming from the concentration camp children observations and the lectures on male homosexuality and passivity, Anna Freud made crucial progress toward the two topics that had been most obviously missing from her writings of the Vienna period. As her Kleinian critics never tired of pointing out, she had not written about aggression (except as identification with the aggressor) and she had not written theoretically about pre-Oedipal mother-child bonds (although she had presented them descriptively in her Hampstead War Nursery reports and her work on feeding disturbances). Before she even had another research unit, a successor to the Jackson Nursery and the Hampstead War Nursery, in which to extend her work, Anna Freud had renewed her readiness for new experience. And she had done so by taking up two areas of her father's science that needed elaboration, not protection from those she thought were heretics. She had moved forward as she characteristically did, by examining herself as she examined patients. Two kinds of human experiences unknown to her had compelled her: siblings spontaneously and unambivalently loving siblings and adults emotionally in thrall to their mothers—the first new to her because it was the product of novel horrors and the second because infantile amnesia lays claim to it in the pasts of adults and keeps it from consciousness.

AFTER THE June 1946 resolution of the British Psychoanalytical Society's long debate over training, Kate Friedlander convinced Anna Freud that they should go ahead with plans for a full training program of their own. They could train people independently of the Society as long as they agreed that only graduates of the two-course program sponsored by the Society would officially be recognized as psychoanalysts, that is, they could train "child experts" (as they decided to call their trainees). Friedlander had established three clinics for the West Sussex Child Guidance Service at the end of the war, and she could thus provide trainees with a clinical setting while they took seminars in Hampstead. They had a similar arrangement with the East London Child Guidance Clinic directed by Dr. Augusta Bonnard, who became a teacher in the program as well. Anna Freud was hesitant about the responsibilities a training course would entail, but she agreed on the condition that she would be the head teacher while Kate Friedlander, seven years her junior and so full of energy and drive, handled the administration. Meanwhile, Anna Freud represented her group on the British Psychoanalytical Society Training Committee.

It was to a joint meeting of this Training Committee and the board of the Society that Anna Freud introduced the memorandum on their training scheme that Kate Friedlander had drawn up. John Bowlby, the Training Committee secretary, and, after some persuading, Sylvia Payne were supportive, but Anna Freud was more than a little annoyed when Donald Winnicott and another board member worried on about how the program might lower the standards of analysis in England. The debate dragged on unpleasantly, and Anna Freud grew very weary of it. As she wrote to Kate Friedlander in September 1947: "The Training Committee is, so far, more disagreeable than ever. If I were not the only representative from our side in it, I would look for the first opportunity to withdraw."[31] She was diplomatic, but, with Friedlander's support, she did not refrain from criticism for the sake of the program. When John Rickman sent copies of a paper he planned to deliver at the Society on October 14, 1947, she wrote to Friedlander: "He said to me that he would welcome criticism and I think he should get it. It seems to me an awful *Machwerk* [botched job]. . . . I quickly decided to take up the point that he represents guilt as an occurrence between the individual and an object and not as a result of a conflict between the various parts of the apparatus of the mind, that is, as anxiety felt by the ego with regard to the superego."[32] The terms of the ongoing Kleinian debate had not changed at all.

As she worked toward the establishment of her own training program, Anna Freud was careful to cultivate support outside of Great Britain. She and Kate Friedlander had gone together to the Easter 1948 meeting in Lausanne where Anna Freud and Aichhorn had had their last reunion. They met with the Swiss Psychoanalytic Society, of which Anna Freud was an honorary member, and also gave a short course in the fundamentals of psychoanalytic therapy for a group of Swiss child guidance workers. This was a trial run for ideas they had about affiliating English child guidance workers with their training program. Through Marie Bonaparte, Anna Freud kept up her contacts in the Paris Society, where she was elected an honorary member. Several French candidates came to London for brief periods of analytic work with Anna Freud, and her scientific links to Paris were strong until the mid-1950s when the French analysts entered into a period of civil war. The Dutch Society, too, both sent her students and received her advice regularly after they reopened their Institute in October 1947.

Six former Hampstead War Nursery workers and a seventh student, Lily Neurath, who had worked for the psychoanalytic publishing house in Vienna before the war, were accepted for the first class and the training program developed as well as the British conditions permitted until the fall of 1948. Then Anna Freud had to reflect that "it is not very pleasant to suddenly begin to feel in this way that fate toys with us human beings."[33] Kate Friedlander was diagnosed as having an inoperable brain tumor. She died in February 1949 at the age of forty-seven.

> There is a great deal that is sad and depressing about this death [Anna Freud wrote to a friend], even apart from the horrible illness itself—for example, the metastases in the brain, which left her weeks of time to be conscious of her condition. She had not had a happy life; a marriage full of torment, then the emigra-

tion, a hard start in England, the war years, only animosity from the local psychological association, and no field of work for her vigor and her ambition. Her work [in West Sussex] with child guidance and delinquency was a positive turn for her, and she had just begun to find her way, to assemble a group of coworkers, and to make a name for herself. She did a little follow-up analysis with me [in 1938], and I think this helped her.[34]

Kate Friedlander's death left Anna Freud at a crossroads: if she went forward with the training program, she would have to take on its administration. After hesitating again, she decided that she could go ahead with help from her veteran associates, and in partnership with Dorothy Burlingham. One newcomer was also secured: Liselotte Frankl, who had both a medical degree and a Ph.D. in psychology from the University of Vienna, agreed to be "Psychiatrist in Charge" for the course and later for the clinic, which meant being both administrative second-in-command and medical cover for the lay analysts and candidates.

But there were several further conditions that had to be met. First and foremost, Anna Freud's time had to be reorganized. She noted at the end of December 1948:

I have not reduced the number of patients, but I have reduced my working days to five and Dorothy and I now regularly spend Saturday and Sunday in Walberswick. Dr. Hoffer has this year taken my place on the Training Committee and I have instead joined the Board. Last year I did both, which was too much. I have retained my weekly lecture to first-year candidates on "Principles of Psychoanalysis." I have done this for several years now and I am slowly getting a better grasp of the material.[35]

Secondly, there had to be money. The training program started without classrooms—the classes met in the lecturers' homes—a library or a clinic of its own. A building was needed to make the biggest step, toward having a clinic for children; and the clinic was needed to employ the students who were being trained so that they did not have to spend time working at other clinics "where they learn nothing, or are taught the opposite of what we are teaching them." The clinic idea was a reedition of an unfulfilled Vienna Society wish.

Do you remember [Anna Freud asked Grete Bibring] how helpful it was in Vienna that the Ambulatorium could employ at
least a few of the candidates in training in part-time posts? I had
then always dreamed of extending this scheme to all the candidates, but we were very far from realizing that idea. This is, of
course, more of a training ambition than a research ambition,
but at the same time it would create the possibility of having a
great variety of cases under treatment.[36]

Salvation came from America, at first in the form of donations
from Viennese friends, and then in the person of Helen Ross, who
was in the process of establishing a child therapy program in the
Chicago Institute. Helen Ross had become acquainted with the
philanthropist Marshall Field and she volunteered to act as Anna
Freud's emissary to the administrator of his foundation, Maxwell
Hahn. Mr. Hahn sent a letter asking for more information after he
had favorably reviewed the preliminary inquiry. Anna Freud was
skeptical, as she explained to Helen Ross:

If I had to answer the questions in Mr. Maxwell Hahn's letter,
all the answers would sound very negative to him: there would
be no university linked with such a clinic as ours, except that
our course itself, like other courses of this kind, may receive university status in time.
    There would be nothing unique about such a clinic, except
that it would be an attempt to apply our particular kind of analytic knowledge to child guidance work. So far as our [training]
course is valuable, it would be a point in our favor that a clinic
of this kind would make it more efficient and more valuable.
On the other hand, the clinic would benefit from the close cooperation with the lecturers and students of the course. But
again such co-operation has happened in other places and I do
not see why a Foundation should be especially enthusiastic about
ours.[37]

Fortunately, the initial grant getting was in Helen Ross's steady,
enormously capable hands, and Anna Freud's diffidence did not
influence it. It was very clear to her friends that Anna Freud was—
as she put it—very good at saying "thank you," but not at all adept
at "please." Over the years her grant proposals became masterpieces

of clarity and order, but ingratiation eluded her, despite many shrewd explanations from the Viennese, assimilated to America, about how things work in foundations. "I will take to heart what you say about one's behavior with Foundations, and I feel that you are right," she said to Grete Bibring, who had raised money for many research projects in Boston. "How far I am really able to change myself is another matter."[38]

It took until 1952 to complete the complicated process of winning the Field Foundation funding, routing it through the Chicago Institute for tax purposes, and using it to run a clinic set up in 1951 at 21 Maresfield Gardens. But, in the meanwhile, other sources of help had appeared. The Foundations' Fund for Research in Psychiatry, in New Haven, made a renewable grant and Anna Freud made the very valuable acquaintance of Dr. Milton Senn of Yale, who was working with Ernst and Marianne Kris on various child observation projects at the institution that came to be called the Yale Child Study Center. Then Kurt Eissler, who had become one of Anna Freud's most attentive supporters, made plans to establish the Anna Freud Foundation in America. This allowed individual American donors to the Hampstead Course and Clinic to make tax-exempt contributions, and it provided a mechanism for organizing donations from American psychoanalytic societies. All the Clinic's needs got Anna Freud's meticulous attention, and her American friends got requests that reflected her thoroughness—for example, to send packages of tea and sugar so that mothers bringing their children long distances for analysis could have a cup of tea while they sat in the waiting room. "You see," she explained to a patient supplier, "as soon as one gets a new problem child, as I have gotten with this clinic, one gets full of wishes."[39] She wrote this request just a few weeks after her mother's death, which came during the week when the first Clinic building was finally purchased.

THE house at 21 Maresfield Gardens had six treatment rooms, a playroom, offices, and a small library and classroom for the training candidates. Before the building was even ready, there was a waiting list of children to treat, and also a list from which Anna Freud could draw "mother and child couples" for simultaneous analyses, a project Dorothy Burlingham supervised. Before the Hampstead Clinic focused attention on the research possibilities of simultaneous mother-child analyses, there had been a few such analyses in private practice, but no clear recorded data on how a mother's neurosis can influence a child's neurosis (or other disturbance). Dorothy Burlingham, who had a particular interest in techniques of scientific reporting, and who had used many of them in her book on twins, published in 1952, was Anna Freud's close collaborator in developing the Clinic's research methods.

Dorothy Burlingham also formulated a new way to use the simple record keeping that Anna Freud had originated in the Jackson Nursery and the Hampstead War Nursery: she converted the old procedure of filing handwritten index cards under developmental topics into the Index. In the Index, material gathered in child analysis (not just from observation) was put on cards and filed under topics that were directly related to the analytic context and what children reveal there. The new topics were, for examples, unconscious contents, anxieties, defenses, character traits, symptoms, object relations, transference manifestations. By 1955, there were sixty children in analysis at the Clinic, and materials from all these cases were combined in the Index, so they could be compared, cross-referenced, and composited. The idea was to make available to the Clinic's analysts many more cases and courses of treatment than any one analyst would ever see and to produce shareable data in two forms: extracts of case histories and topic files.

While Dorothy Burlingham supervised the indexing of cases and chaired a committee organized to evaluate the Index and write papers on the basis of it, Anna Freud devoted much of her scientific attention to a related project. She developed a procedure—what might be called a depth psychological questionnaire—for formulating diagnoses by categorizing and collating data gathered in diagnostic interviews with children and their families. She wanted to see if a preliminary diagnosis could get behind a child's manifest syndrome to the underlying disorder before any analytic work began. "This technique promises to increase the reliability of child analysis and to enable child analysts to institute therapeutic measures much earlier than it was possible up to now." Here again, the research goal was generality: "This new approach toward the diagnostic interview requires testing a large number of cases in order to establish its general validity."[40] As the analyses of children who had been assessed with the diagnostic technique unfolded, the results were compared against the original diagnosis, for confirmation or disconfirmation, and also for assessing the questions and categories of the diagnostic interviews.

The Index and the diagnostic technique, which was later published as the Diagnostic Profile, were the two Hampstead projects that involved the entire clinical staff—for producing or for recording data. In 1954, when the Clinic's operations had become widely known and respected in London, a contact Dorothy Burlingham had made with the Royal National Institute for the Blind resulted in a remarkable opportunity. The Institute asked the Clinic to diagnose and treat a small number of totally blind children under the age of five who had proved uneducable in the Institute's facilities. Dorothy Burlingham thus had a chance to fulfill a hope she had had since the Jackson Nursery days—to have a blind child in analysis; but the scale was greater, and the cooperation of the Institute meant that the analytic results could be compared with established educational methods. In theoretical terms, Dorothy Burlingham set out to learn as much as possible about the role of visual perception in the building up of children's personalities. In broader practical terms, she wanted to set up an advisory service for the parents of blind babies, one that could include home visits for observing the babies with their parents. The services were coordinated with Mr. Colborne Brown of the Royal National Institute for the Blind—though funded from America. The final phase of Dorothy Burlingham's favorite project was put in place after she had trained younger colleagues and established the reputations of the initial services: a small nursery school for blind children. The school was located in a special little cabin, designed by Ernst Freud to be safe and convenient for the sightless, which was built in the back garden at 21 Maresfield Gardens.

As the Clinic's services for neurotic or disturbed children, sighted and blind, grew, the analysts felt the need for two extensions of the Clinic's work: more contact, for comparative observational purposes, with normal children; and more educational work with parents, to be combined with observational study. The two needs were eventually met with overlapping projects. A Well-Baby Clinic was established to advise young mothers about how to handle their babies' physical and emotional needs. This work was under Josefine Stross's supervision, and she acted as head pediatrician. Then a group for mothers with toddlers was organized for morning play sessions. Mothers who had graduated from the Well-Baby Clinic could bring their children. In the mothers-and-toddlers group, where the old Montessori school toys from Vienna got another workout, the Clinic staff could make longitudinal observations, that is, follow children whom they had met in the Well-Baby Clinic into their crawling and walking years. The obvious sequel, established on a small and informal scale at first, was a nursery group. This provided the toddlers with a setting for their next developmental step, but it also provided a protective, analytically supervised school context for children who were in analysis at the Clinic—and the possibility of observing these disturbed children in such a context, interacting with more normal children.

In 1956, Anna Freud set out to secure funding to make the nursery group into a Nursery School. Her effort was made in coordination with a fund-raising campaign to purchase 12 Maresfield Gardens, where the Nursery School could have the full lower floor and the enclosed yard for outdoor play while the upper floors provided office space and consulting rooms. The New-Land Foundation, sponsored by Muriel Gardiner, who had affiliated herself with the Philadelphia Psychoanalytic Society after her years in Austria, helped Anna Freud buy and refurbish the second building. Another foundation came forward for the Nursery School, and Anna Freud, delighted, wrote immediately to Anny Hermann, who had followed her work for the Vienna Montessori school and the Jackson Nursery with years of organizing and teaching work for the New York Child Development Center. "I should like it very much if you could come and help us to set up the scheme and to carry on with it for a while before you can hand it on to somebody else."[41] The somebody else was standing by, with six years of nursery work experience but no psychoanalytic preparation. She was Manna Friedmann, an émigré from Germany by way of Palestine, recently married to Alice Goldberger's colleague Oscar Friedmann. Manna Friedmann felt ready to head the school after Anny Hermann launched it, and she stayed there—with outstanding success—from 1957 until her retirement in 1978, when she became a consultant emeritus.

EACH project and department in the Clinic generated research ideas, and the production of papers and books that started in the early 1950s grew as the Clinic itself grew. The original commitment of the institution never varied: it was to provide therapy in combination with support for families; treatment for disturbed or handicapped children in the context of education for children of all constitutions, problems, backgrounds, income levels; and training for the candidates that was as multifaceted and balanced as it could be on such a scale. Anna Freud's institutions were always—like her—modest in appearance and style, but ambitious in function, and she was always adjusting them to find the right measures of immediate, practical tasks and long-term, innovatory challenges. Her patrons helped her strike a balance, as she freely admitted to Kurt Eissler on the fifth anniversary of his fund-raising efforts.

> Please do not be astonished that among all the uses which I make of you the superego use is included. Sometimes I feel that the demands made on me by the Clinic necessitate support to all parts of my person. I know you believe that I am very careful and even restrictive where the use of money is concerned. But I can assure you that this is only a thin surface layer. In the next layer I am an adventurer, always branching out in more directions and always ready to spend large sums of money. This leads to the need for restrictive conscience agencies.[42]

All of Anna Freud's imported restrictive conscience agencies were male; they took in charge—more or less—the adventurer in her. The careful, cautious nurturer in her was supported by the many women she assembled around her at the Clinic, but also by the Clinic's founding patroness, Helen Ross. In 1959, she assumed her maternal voice to report to Miss Ross, who had remained faithfully at her fund-raising post, that the Clinic was behaving like a very well fed child. As usual, her metaphor extended as far as her fantasy that the Clinic, like her writing projects but on a grander scale, was a child—her child. "Perhaps it will tell you a great deal if I say that we spent this year altogether 50,000 pounds, which is exactly ten times as much as in our beginning year. It makes one think of the babies who have to double, treble, and further multiply their birth weight in their first years. Every baby at some time reaches the state of affairs when it does not multiply further except by producing offsprings. I wonder when we will reach this stage."[43]

Neither to the male financial authorities nor to the female helpers, however, did Anna Freud show the deepest layer of her identifications with her Clinic. This came out to strangers, who would have no motive to interpret it or use it; and it was expressed in the old never completely abandoned *Etwas-Haben-Wollen* terms of the altruistic woman who wanted something for herself when she was so busy doing things for other people. Or, to put the matter in the terms her 1950s work on affective negativism had furnished: her Clinic was a creative expression that assuaged her fear of passivity or ego-dissolving regression to an earlier stage. In her Clinic, Anna Freud could imagine herself as a child—one might guess: a messy, naughty child—who was going to give herself over to the care of psychoanalysts. This was Anna Freud allowing herself a loosening of her ego boundaries, emotional surrender. "It is a most pleasant place," she wrote to a business contact, "it looks so gay and charming that one regrets not being a problem child oneself."[44]

THE INITIAL American support for Anna Freud's Clinic was a direct result of an echo from the past. Clark University, where Freud, Jung, Ferenczi, and Jones had visited in 1909, invited Anna Freud to lecture and receive an honorary degree as the university celebrated its sixtieth anniversary. "I had always postponed this visit to America, but this seemed a beginning that appealed to me." She was contacted by mail in October 1949, and the date for her visit was fixed for April 20, 1950, during her Easter holiday. The prospect was thrilling. But it was also immediately problematic, in a familiar way. The Americans wanted their ceremony large and well publicized; Anna Freud wanted it small and unpublicized. Compromises were reached over everything but the question of newspaper interviews and the presence of reporters at the lecture. Anna Freud was adamant. "All my life," she told the bewildered Mr. John E. Bell of Clark, "I have been an enemy of any kind of publicity, and I may well have 'inherited' this attitude from my father, who has felt the same throughout his life. I feel very much that I am a private individual and that I have nothing to say to a newspaperman which could be of interest to him."[45]

The influence of her New York cousin Edward Bernays, a founder of the field called public relations, was applied for the sake of there being no public relations. But the matter was still unresolved when Anna Freud, in order to make the journey in a style acceptable to Dorothy Burlingham, who dreaded the noise and the danger of airplanes, made reservations on the *Queen Elizabeth*. "If I really knew that things like that [news conferences] were inevitable, I would give up or jump into the sea from the *Queen Elizabeth* and drown myself," Anna Freud announced with great drama to Grete Bibring, who was also trying from Boston to explain her old friend's peculiarities to the Clark officials.[46] The situation got worse with the explanations, and Anna Freud had to appeal again to Grete Bibring, whom she had come to view as a kind of security service.

I had a letter from President Jefferson [of Clark], written on March 6th, of which I send you a copy. Do you think from reading it that they are very cross with me already? Or do you think that they only feel they have a "problem child" on their hands and do not know exactly how do deal with it? Anyway, I do not want to play the "problem child," and I am certainly under an obligation to Clark University, since they spend so much money on me. (I somehow feel as if they had bought me, and that is never a feeling I enjoy.) As you see from Jefferson's letter, your diagnosis was quite right: he says quite openly that they are indebted to the press and that they should be in a very awkward position if they had to stand out against them.

At her Clinic, she could enjoy imagining herself as a problem child; elsewhere, she resisted adamantly. But, with some persuading from Grete Bibring, she agreed to concede, and then she did a little psychotherapy on herself: "Anyway, I have decided beforehand to take all the unavoidable worries and irritations lightly and to enjoy the good sides as much as possible."[47]

Enjoying the good sides was not easy in anticipation. She had taken on a subject, at Clark's request, that was strange: "The Contribution of Psychoanalysis to Genetic Psychology." After she had beseeched all her émigré friends to mail her bibliographical introductions to the unfamiliar terrain of "academic psychology," particularly in its American version, she undertook to read a small library. "I have done more reading in academic psychology in the last two months than in all my other life put together."[48] But it is obvious that her brief but intense immersion in "academic psychology" did have an important effect on Anna Freud's conceptualization of her "genetic" (i.e., developmental) research projects when she founded the Hampstead Clinic.

In her lecture, Anna Freud noted that while her father and his colleagues were still trying to work out the basic tenets of psychoanalysis, their contacts with academic psychology were not extensive. The rapprochement came from the academic side, and psychoanalysis became widely and deeply incorporated into academic theory and research, particularly in America. Only in the 1940s did psychoanalysts begin to make sustained efforts to use academically approved experimental and statistical techniques. They tried to meet charges laid at their doors by psychologists like Robert Sears of Harvard, who had noted in 1943 that psychoanalysis "relies upon techniques that do not admit of the repetition of observation, that have no self-evident or denotative validity, and that are tinctured to an unknown degree with the observer's own suggestions."[49] As examples of psychoanalytic research, she cited David Levy's comparative studies of infants and animals, Margaret Ribble's infant observation work, René Spitz's work on early childhood and mothering, which was related to John Bowlby's research in England, and Margaret Fries's longitudinal studies of child development. And as examples of attempts to reformulate psychoanalytic theory in terms linked to academic developmental psychology, she referred to articles by Hartmann, Kris, and Loewenstein as well as to David Rapaport's *Emotions and Memory* (1942). Having been diplomatic over the cooperation between the two fields, Anna Freud then tracked down a number of academic misunderstandings of psychoanalytic methods and concepts that, she felt, marred efforts to test and validate or disprove psychoanalytic findings. And she warned psychoanalysts that if they were to continue as the innovatory spirits in psychology, the ones producing hypotheses and theories for others to work on as Freud had, they would have to do so on the basis of their own technique. Unlike so many other analysts, particularly in America, she refused to be defensive about the persistent idea that psychoanalysis is "not *good* science," as Sears had charged, speaking in the paltry spirit of positivistic philosophy of science.

With her lecture finally prepared, Anna Freud felt more secure about her first American trip. But while she was preparing it, she allowed her trip to be scheduled so extensively that she had to create an hour-by-hour, day-by-day chart for organizing the engagements, the meetings with individuals, and the travel arrangements—a very scientific-looking document. Radcliffe College asked her to be the first woman to act as guest lecturer, and she complied, particularly as she wanted to keep good relations with the faculty at Harvard, where she had been invited by the sociologist Talcott Parsons to take up a teaching appointment in 1948. At that time, she had had a dream that confirmed her negative decision, and she had written it out for Marie Bonaparte.

I must tell you a dream which I had shortly after saying No to the Harvard invitation. I was in Paris (or St. Tropez?) in your house, but in your absence (you were probably in Greece, as you really are). Everything was very formal and elaborate, especially entering the house. One had to sign in at an office or reception room where secretaries sat. (Somewhat like the American Embassy in Vienna or a Ministry.) Then I entered the drawing room where members of your family were, and other people who belonged, and there was a general conversation. I felt dreadfully uncomfortable, though people tried to be nice to me because of you, they knew as well as I that I did not belong and should not be there. I woke up in a great discomfort.

I was astonished about the dream at first, but then I understood it. The royal and aristocratic circle to which I do not belong is the academic world for which I am in no way fitted, neither by my type of mind nor by my analytic upbringing. You,

absent in Greece, represent my father, absent. The people are
nice to me, with me, because of him, his name (that is my very
natural suspicion [in waking life] of course). Still, I do not fit.
The elaborate entrance refers to the very humiliating procedures
emigrants had to undergo in the American Consulate in Vienna.
I have often said I would never undergo that. It had reminded
me of the way one had to enter and leave the Gestapo headquarters in Vienna, in the Hotel Metropole, where I often was. (I
had said to Dorothy that I would feel in an academic life as if
I were in prison.)[50]

The themes of this 1948 dream about the invitation to join the
Harvard faculty recurred one by one and in a network as Anna Freud
accepted first the Radcliffe invitation, then one from Douglas Bond,
an associate of the Katans at Western Reserve in Cleveland, then
one from Richard and Editha Sterba of the Detroit Psychoanalytic
Society, then another from her friends in the New York Psychoanalytic Society, and, finally and most elaborately, one from the Boston
Psychoanalytic Society for a weekend-long meeting and reunion of
émigré analysts at the Austen Riggs Center in Stockbridge, Massachusetts. Only invitations from would-be hosts and hostesses of parties were turned down unceremoniously. "I am not better at parties
now than I was in Vienna, rather worse if anything," she admitted.[51]
In her six stops, she would give nine prepared lectures, many informal discussion presentations, and the one dreaded Worcester press
conference—all in a little over two weeks.

"It nearly seems to me as if in their imaginations people felt that
it was my father who is coming," she said nervously, as the marathon
approached, "but in reality it will be only me."[52] That she was going
to sail off in regal style on the *Queen Elizabeth* to the fulfillment of
wishes for praise, admiration, adoration—quite forbidden exhibitionistic wishes—made her fall back on her "altruistic surrender" strategy: the wishes should be fulfilled by someone else, her father. But
she was sailing off nonetheless as her father's representative, if not as
her father. Her anxieties got so entangled that her identification with
her father, which usually gave her such strength, weighed heavily in
the fantasies she generated to defend herself from other people's
disappointment. She wrote to Ernst Kris:

I am only sorry that you have so much trouble and expense with [the Stockbridge weekend], and somehow the whole expenditure does not seem altogether justifiable. It strongly reminds me of little Adelaide Sweetzer—you perhaps remember that she was in analysis with me when she was six years old in Vienna. She once criticized the Burlingham children for always speaking of their absent father with such enthusiasm and interest; she couldn't understand that and said "my father is right here, and I don't think he is so especially wonderful." It's the same with me. Here in England, where I live, nobody finds me "so especially wonderful," and I'm afraid that I wouldn't seem so in America either.[53]

Her anxiety was a bit contagious, and Ernst Kris got entangled himself as he tried to reassure her: "Everyone will be at your feet. Not because you are Freud's daughter, but nonetheless in a sense because you are: if you prefer, you may assume that the positive aspect of their ambivalence toward him is intended for you."[54] But, even though she expected the worst and had to lecture herself about enjoying whatever the best might turn out to be, she did not lose either her identity or her sense of humor. In an article subtitled "The Model Woman Scientist," a Worcester journalist described Miss Freud posing for the press photographers at the Clark University gymnasium (which doubled as an auditorium): " 'You know,' she said, 'we had two little girls at our school, one with a small mouth and the other with a large one. Whenever they had to pose for pictures, the one with the small mouth was urged to say "cheese" so that she could present a big mouth to the camera, while the other had to say "soup" in order that her mouth would remain small.' She added, 'I should say "soup." ' But she smiled instead!"[55]

Anna Freud could hardly believe that the public was informed in the women's pages that "her two-piece navy blue and white polka dot silk dress had a small V-shaped insert of lace in the front of the jacket" or that she wore "a double strand of small pearls, knotted in front," but, in general the press was reasonably accurate, sympathetic, and willing to concede that child analysis did not have to be reported to women only, in Home-and-Fashion language. "Miss Anna Freud of London, psychoanalyst daughter of Sigmund Freud, founder of psychoanalysis, held her first press conference in the United States today and for an hour answered or parried questions on psychiatric matters from the value of demand feeding of infants to the effectiveness of prefrontal lobotomies," read a typical lead paragraph.[56]

How her lectures and remarks, as reported, were greeted by newspaper readers is indeterminable, but their impact on the student groups she addressed—at Radcliffe, and in the analytic training programs in Cleveland and Detroit—was powerful and immediate. The Radcliffe students were so enthusiastic that plans sprang up there for a return engagement in the form of a short seminar on child development—and that came about in 1952. In Cleveland, Douglas Bond and his psychiatry students were convinced that Anna Freud would have to come back to help with the establishment of a full psychoanalytic training program in affiliation with the Medical School at Western Reserve. This too came about in 1952, and it helped Anna Freud establish a contact, through Bond's father, with the Grant Foundation, later the chief supporter of her nursery school.

One of the many thoughtful individual responses she received came from a student in Detroit, who had heard a lecture on psychoanalytic technique.

> I expected to hear an impassioned plea urging no deviation from the technique which is so frequently called orthodox, particularly by its opponents. . . . Needless to say, instead of the emotionally charged paper I expected, we heard a paper which was remarkable for its lack of biased attitude, and in addition to the historical background contained in it, only asked for a return to the scientific method; namely, we should have a theoretical substructure explaining the application of any particular technique. I was both surprised and moved by your logical and yet simple approach to the problem. A little reflection reveals that while one is in a struggle with his own resistances, he can easily be caught in the meshes of a group reaction in which one group is calling the other "rigid orthodoxy" and is receiving the answer "resistance" in return. Further, your objective intellectual analysis brought clearly to my attention the fact that these differences in theory and technique will undoubtedly always be present. I am hopeful that there will also always be people of sufficient stature and objectivity to constantly point out the scientific method to us.[57]

For the American and émigré senior analysts, the meetings in New York, where she gave her lecture on male homosexuality, and at the Riggs Center in Stockbridge were the most significant. Her Stockbridge paper, "Observations on Child Development," finally fulfilled a challenge issued in Ernst Kris's 1946 memorandum: she reviewed the results of her wartime observations and indicated in what ways they "helped to swell the body of existing analytic knowledge, even though . . . they did not break new ground."[58] She emphasized the importance of corroborating insights gained in the analytic treatment setting with data from "experimental" settings like the Hampstead War Nursery—the same point she had made at Clark to her predominantly "academic psychology" audience.

In Stockbridge, Dorothy Burlingham also emerged from the background and gave a paper that was very well received by her peers, even though it went quite unmentioned in the press report, which simply noted that Dorothy Burlingham had accompanied Anna Freud to a dinner given by the conference host, Dr. Robert Knight. She reported on some of her work with the mothers of young children in analysis. Clinton McCord of Albany, who had trained with Freud, had not seen Dorothy Burlingham for twenty years, and he was amazed, as he wrote to Anna Freud: "It was good to see Mrs. Burlingham after these many years; she has deepened and developed in marvelous fashion and must be a source of great satisfaction to you."[59] He was not alone in remarking on the maturity of Dorothy Burlingham's work in the period after her collaboration on the Hampstead War Nursery reports. But old friends also noticed that Dorothy's health was not good, and a transatlantic round-robin medical consultation began, which, by 1954, after the advent of streptomycin-enhancing drugs, finally yielded a regime of diet and medications that gave her both relief from her tuberculosis symptoms and less susceptibility to colds and bronchial infections. Her father-in-law, C. C. Burlingham, received her and Anna Freud at his Long Island home and was his usual difficult self, but he did reassure her of his intention to continue his benevolence toward his son's children and a growing tribe of grandchildren.

Anna Freud found time to visit with the Burlinghams who were in New York—Bob, Mabbie, and Tinky, who had married and had a daughter. Michael, who was working as a mechanical engineer, lived in Connecticut. Anna Freud also took two days to make a visit to her brother Oliver and his wife, Henny, in Philadelphia. No one in the London family had seen the Oliver Freuds in their American home or visited with them since the collapse into legal problems of a plan they had tried to execute in 1949: the adoption of one of the young German-speaking concentration camp survivors—a girl, like their lost Eva—living in a home run by Alice Goldberger. In New York, Anna Freud also saw briefly her Tante Anna, the only survivor of Freud's five sisters; her cousin Rosi Winternitz Waldinger; her cousin Harry Freud, Uncle Alexander's son; and two of her Bernays cousins, Edward Bernays and Judith Bernays Heller.

At Helen Ross's suggestion, Anna Freud also met for lunch with Marshall Field and discussed in person the grant proposal that eventually founded the Hampstead Clinic. When she returned to America in 1952, Anna Freud came as the director of the Hampstead Clinic, and was careful to make time to attend a meeting of the Field Foundation board in New York. Most of her three-week return visit was spent in Boston, where she gave seminars at Harvard and lived in a Radcliffe dormitory—an experience she was not eager to repeat. On two weekends, she flew to Cleveland and helped plan the Western Reserve training program, despite her reservations, which eventually proved so well founded, about directly affiliating a psychoanalytic training program with a university and a medical school. She had intended to refuse all other speaking engagements, but, as usual, she did not succeed, for neither the Hanns Sachs Memorial Lecture at the Harvard Medical School nor a lecture at Grete Bibring's hospital, the Beth Israel, nor a discussion at the Boston Society could be refused. The stir in the press was very much less for the return visit, and Anna Freud found that—at least consciously—a great improvement.

AFTER the two wearing visits in 1950 and 1952, Anna Freud engaged external superegos, "restrictive conscience agencies," explicitly for the purpose of controlling her adventurer-lecturer self. And when the senior members of the New York Psychoanalytic Institute, especially Ernst Kris, volunteered themselves for the task, she accepted immediately. They made their offer through their president, Ruth

Loveland, who wrote to Anna Freud on March 3, 1953, inviting her to give the 1954 Freud Anniversary Lecture. "While we ourselves do not wish to impose on your energy too much, we are also determined to prevent others from doing so. We therefore would like to stipulate that the terms of this invitation include that you do not address any other audience or body in New York." "I was very touched by the consideration for me which is expressed in your letter," she replied.[60] The contractual obligation clause seemed the perfect protection, though the New Yorkers could not restrain themselves from planning not just a single lecture but a weekend symposium on Problems of Infantile Neurosis at Arden House on the Hudson, and Anna Freud promptly acquiesed when Robert Waelder asked her to address the Philadelphia Association for Psychoanalysis and Marshall Field requested an address to the Child Welfare League of America, meeting in Atlantic City, New Jersey. But both of these acceptances were connected to fund raising for the Clinic: she owed Marshall Field her gratitude, and she wanted Muriel Gardiner's goodwill.

Anna Freud did not write up her 1954 presentations after she returned to England; she published her Freud Lecture only in abstract, and had transcripts made of her Arden House discussion remarks. In abbreviated forms, the work later entered into *The Writings of Anna Freud*, a project that was proposed by International Universities Press and Lottie Newman, who became her editor, on the third American trip. Anna Freud let the lecture material sit, and went on to several major research and theory innovations in the late 1950s. This was because, with nearly a decade of work at the Hampstead Child Therapy Course and Clinic behind her, and with the stimulation of her first three American journeys, she was ready for a new synthetic scientific effort—for the book that eventually appeared under the title *Normality and Pathology in Childhood*.

9

THE DIRECTOR

As May 6, 1956, the centenary of Freud's birth, approached, Anna Freud was putting her affairs in order on almost every front, from the most mundane to the most metapsychological. She could not prepare a book for her father's birthday, as she had in 1936, but she did prepare a series of lectures that constituted a first draft of her 1965 work *Normality and Pathology in Childhood*. She gave these lectures at a number of different celebratory occasions, as promissory notes on the major work she was contemplating. But her primary concern in 1955 and 1956 was to be sure that the birthday was recognized as she thought it should be.

With paint and polish and intensive gardening, she readied 20 Maresfield Gardens for the psychoanalytic visitors—the true pilgrims—who would come for a conference at the Clinic, and for the press, who would come for the installation of a London County Council blue plaque to designate the house as a historical monument. A second housekeeper was hired in 1955 to aid Paula Fichtl; a pension application went off on Anna Freud's sixtieth birthday; and one of Dorothy Burlingham's American nephews, a banker, was consulted about investments to secure her own and Dorothy's retirements; the fur coats that her mother and Tante Minna had worn were, at last, sold; and Sigmund Freud's *Lodenmantel*, his long wool winter coat, was refurbished and carefully stored away in her own closet. Ernstl Halberstadt, who had changed his name to E. W. Freud, married, studied psychology, and finished a training analysis with Willi Hoffer, was encouraged to prepare and present—successfully—a membership paper to the British Psychoanalytical Society. Anna Freud's pleasure in her nephew's "excellent development in recent years" was compounded when he announced that his wife, Irene Freud, was pregnant.[1] Anna Freud's joy when Colin Freud was born in her own father's centennial year was marked with grandmotherly notes to all the family members abroad about his beauty, Ernstl's pride, and Irene's good mothering. About her own child, the Clinic, she wrote happy letters announcing that the Nursery School would be opened in time for the Freud birthday celebrations.

Ernst Freud also opened another house in Walberswick, so that Anna Freud and Dorothy could invite to the Freud compound in Suffolk their old friends and the American family to share refuge hospitality after the public events. Robert Hollitscher was very ill, and Mathilde had to suffer through many months of his decline and eventual death, but she too joined Anna, Ernst, and Martin in the formidable task of deciding how to respond to the deluge of celebration proposals. Ernst was put in charge of dealing with the press after Anna Freud declared firmly that she had nothing to say publicly about their father's last months in England: "I just cannot bring myself to talking about it."[2] Martin, for his part, decided to write a family memoir, *Glory Reflected*, in the hours he had off from running a tobacco and candy shop in London. His little sister's attitude toward this project was characteristically negative, but for his sake she held back her criticism: "it would have been preferable to me if the book had never been written. But I forced myself to say nothing about it and to be pleased with the parts that are charming and humorous. Martin does not have an easy life, and the book means a sort of ray of hope in it."[3]

The Freud children were of one mind about what they considered the most important long-term goal of any celebration. They wanted to assure that the right Centenary spirit informed future efforts to make their father's work permanently and properly available. James Strachey, with his wife Alix's help, was steadily advancing on the completion of his huge translation project, *The Complete Psychological Works of Sigmund Freud*—the so-called *Standard Edition.* Anna Freud spent countless hours reading and checking every one of Strachey's twenty-three volumes and supplying him with detailed commentaries and suggestions. Ernst, as the head of Sigmund Freud Copyrights, Ltd., did all of the copyright footwork that released Freud's works from earlier English-language contracts.

In New York, Kurt Eissler had proposed that an organization called Sigmund Freud Archives be charged with the project of gathering and preserving Freud's letters and documents pertinent to his life and work, a project that Ernst and Anna Freud had been conducting informally since their father's death. The family council kept in their own hands, however, arrangements for eventual publication of Freud's correspondences. Ernst started editing a selection of the letters, which was published in 1960. This volume was, he told its publisher, "my personal reaction to the publication of the [Jones] biography. Why not for once let my father speak for himself?"[4] In the same spirit, he arranged for the publication of a collection of the Freud/Karl Abraham letters, which was coedited by Hilda Abraham, like Anna Freud a psychoanalyst daughter. The Freud/Lou Andreas-Salomé correspondence was edited after Anna Freud had assured herself that nothing compromising to her own privacy would appear in the volume. Negotiations also got slowly under way with Carl Jung and his family about a Freud/Jung collection. For each of the correspondence collections, Anna Freud acted as the checker of translations. "It seems to be my fate," she declared at one of the many weary moments this role produced.[5]

Outside the family council, Anna Freud's Centenary decisions strictly followed a single principle: nothing was to happen that Freud would have disapproved. Maxwell Gitelson, newly elected president of the American Psychoanalytic Association, wrote in January of 1956 to say that *Time* magazine wanted to mark the celebration with a "cover story." He asked Anna Freud if she would consent to be interviewed and have her picture on the cover of the magazine, for the sake of the good publicity the story would give to psychoanalysis and to the Hampstead Clinic's fund-raising efforts.[6] He got a firm no, which put him on general alert about Anna Freud's way of doing things—a clarification that helped establish their very good relationship during the years when Gitelson gave American psychoanalysis his excellent, thoughtful leadership. When he eventually declared himself in favor of admitting lay analysts to the American Psychoanalytic Association, she marveled at his courage. It was a rare pleasure for her to read in a 1964 issue of the American Psychoanalytic Association's own journal his bold claim:

> While there may have been valid reasons in the late thirties for American psychoanalysis to declare its exclusive adhesion to medicine as its parent discipline, the question must be raised whether these reasons retain their cogency today. . . . I think the time has come for psychoanalysis to accept its identity as a separate scientific discipline whose practitioners can be various kinds of intellectually qualified persons who are humanly qualified for the human experiment which is the psychoanalytic situation.[7]

At the beginning of 1955, Anna Freud had already declined an invitation from Gitelson's predecessor, Ives Hendrick, who had suggested that she address a joint spring 1956 meeting of the American Psychoanalytic Association and the American Psychiatric Association. Very carefully, she replied: "If I went to the United States at that time it would more or less cancel all possibilities for a celebration at my father's last home. I hope you will understand this and not feel that I act ungratefully or unappreciatively towards the members of the Planning Committee and the Executive Council of the American Psychoanalytic Association. I do feel grateful as well as appreciative."[8] Linking herself with the American psychiatric establishment, which was just as opposed to lay analysis as Hendrick himself, in Dallas, Texas, a place with no connection whatsoever to the history of psychoanalysis, was beyond contemplating. Fortunately, Ernest Jones was willing, despite a series of illnesses and a cancer that had weakened him, and he included Dallas on a veritable grand tour of celebrations in various American cities. The Freud Centenary was a triumphal moment for Freud's biographer—the highlight of the last two years of his long life. Anna Freud was truly grateful to Jones, and grateful too for his fine speech at the Centenary in London. Many of the Viennese were annoyed by the way Jones wore his biographer's mantle—like Max Schur, who complained of the pride with which Jones had told him of his cancer: "it is as though he had said 'now I am really like Freud' "[9]—but Anna Freud simply felt that the consoling processes of identification in Jones would continue to support contributions to Freud's memory.

Even though the American Psychoanalytic Association plans activated her negative feelings, and she was relieved that Jones and not she was going to be involved, Anna Freud also summoned up her best diplomatic response for a positive reason. She was keenly aware that America, even though so hostile to lay analysis, was the most important site of psychoanalytic activity, the banner-carrying nation of the international movement. So she wrote a brief address of praise to be read on her behalf at various meetings.

> There seems to be good reason why so many people, otherwise respectful of my father's ideas and attitude to life, disregard lightheartedly on this occasion his well-known abhorrence of ceremonies and formal celebrations. While honoring his person, every psychoanalytic group, Society or Association reviews, in fact, their own achievement in taking up, pursuing, deepening and spreading the science, practice and application of psychoanalysis. In some parts of Europe analysts will assess today their slow uphill work with transitory successes and disastrous setbacks; in other parts the societies can feel secure in the consciousness of steady growth and progress with increasing respect and recognition now from the scientific and lay public. In the United States the American Psychoanalytic Association has the unique privilege of looking back on the development of psychoanalytic teachings from hard beginnings in a predominantly hostile environment to their triumphant entry into the cultural atmosphere of an enormous community with significant repercussions on science, ethics, literature and, above all, education. It is this brilliant and spectacular success which lends today's festive meetings their specific color and, incidentally, doubles my regret for not taking part in them.[10]

Anna Freud wrote in general terms, but she had very specific European developments in mind when she congratulated the Americans. With a group of Hungarian-born émigrés, she and Eva Rosenfeld worked to raise money for the little analytic community in Budapest, which, during the events that culminated in the Soviet invasion, was in great danger. Katá and Lajos Levy were able to emigrate with English funds and the promise, for Katá, of employment at the Hampstead Clinic, where she eventually did important work on the simultaneous mother-child analyses project.

In Paris, the political problem was not external. The Paris Society had split in 1953, and the dissenting group, the Société Française de Psychanalyse, unofficially led by Jacques Lacan, made Marie Bonaparte despair of the work she had done over so many years for French psychoanalysis. Anna Freud's opposition to the Lacan group was firm, even though she did not have much sympathy for Lacan's chief enemy in the Paris Society, Sacha Nacht, who was a strong opponent of lay analysis (which Lacan favored). "It is an indubitable fact," she told Heinz Hartmann, "that Lacan trained his candidates by analyses of less than an hour a week and then forced their acceptance, which will certainly mean the ruin of a future psychoanalytic society [with such members]. If the IPA covers the situation up in any way, then it will have ruined all attempts in Europe to create order in the methods of training."[11] This view, which Hartmann, the IPA president fully shared, prevailed and the Lacan group was not extended IPA membership. In 1963, the IPA made it clear that the group would never be recognized unless Lacan—and his training methods—were barred. The anti-Lacan group within the Société Française de Psychanalyse dropped Lacan and, under the name Association Psychanalytique de France, received admission to the IPA. Lacan responded with a new group of his own, the École Freudienne de Paris.[12]

The turmoil in Paris also spilled over into the four-member Egyptian group, which included Ishak Ramzy, who had been in a supervisory analysis with Anna Freud and attended courses at Hampstead. Ramzy, unjustly held responsible by a Lacan-trained colleague for a patient's violent rampage, but unable to get Sacha Nacht and the Paris Society to censure his enemy, left Cairo for the Menninger Clinic. Anna Freud gave Ramzy all the support she could muster, but neither she nor Marie Bonaparte could help him vindicate himself. All that she could do was to visit and encourage him and his family at the Menningers', and to keep her distance completely from all the factions in France.

The Centenary celebrations around the world emphasized both

how widespread the influence of the psychoanalytic community was and how internally strained both the national and the International groups were. Anna Freud had felt since the war that the International Association had wrongly abdicated its role as the standard setter for training. The Americans, by far the majority population, had turned the International itself into an organization dominated by American views about training—and as long as the International was so politicized, Anna Freud refused to take the leadership. As she noted in 1977: "I never tried to get the presidency of the International, though I could certainly in earlier years have had it. I have always had the feeling that a person who does not carry the imprimatur could have more influence than one whose hands were tied by an official position."[13] She was a member of the Executive Council of the IPA reluctantly throughout the 1950s and early 1960s, but her interest was only truly engaged there in the mid-1960s—when the future of child analytic training came on the Congress agendas.

In the wake of the Centenary, the American genius for publicity continued to be a blessing—not entirely unmixed—for the cause, and a personal trial. The celebrations had resurrected many American hopes that various films made of Freud during his lifetime by Ruth Mack Brunswick's former husband, Mark, and others would be released from private hands into public distribution. Mark Brunswick had the idea that he could finance his then current psychoanalysis with proceeds from the sale of his home movie to the Sigmund Freud Archives. Anna and Ernst Freud stood firm in their opposition to these plans, even though they found Brunswick's situation pathetic, and they enlisted the whole rank of the Viennese analysts in America to back their refusal.

Nothing, however, stopped the professionals in Hollywood. John Huston, allied with various producers, took over the feature film idea that had arisen a decade earlier and marched on with it through protest after protest. Anna Freud spoke with many of the Americans who came to London for the Centenary about her opposition to the film idea, but met with little sympathy. "It did not shake my conviction but it made me feel a bit lonely with it," she admitted to Ralph Greenson, who was one of the colleagues who respected her wishes and set out to help her from his base in Los Angeles.[14] Various anti-film strategies were debated, and a decision was reached to stay in quiet legal channels rather than to follow the course proposed by the novelist Leo Rosten, a friend of Greenson's and an acquaintance of Kurt Eissler's. "I think what I did not like about Mr. Rosten's [plan] was the idea that the best way to fight a big noise is to make a bigger noise oneself. Of course, I see his point that thereby certain legal rights will be protected. On the other hand, the probable outcome would be that we [sic] have to make a film because we do not want a film to be made."[15] Reflecting further, she added: "After all, one has to disregard a good many things one does not like, and this may be one of them." The family's attention then shifted to means for making it clear that the film was not authorized.

When John Huston officially announced his plans, he was greeted with letters of protest from Anna Freud's solicitor, a solicitor employed by Ernst for Sigmund Freud Copyrights, and one representing Ernest Jones. Through his lawyers, he replied that the film would be a serious one and a benefit to psychoanalysis. "He seems to be in French Equatorial Africa at present," Anna Freud told Greenson, "and I feel it would be nice if he stayed there."[16] When Huston actually began to shoot his film in Vienna, with Montgomery Clift in the role of the young Freud of the Fliess friendship period, he received further protests, but did not reply. At the suggestion of her friend David Astor, editor of The Observer, Anna Freud later received the paper's film critic, Penelope Gilliatt, for an interview and asked her to make it clear that the film was going forward without Freud family sanction. That a film by such a respected director might not be the worst that Hollywood could present had seemed irrelevant: "I know that many people don't agree with me, but I still feel that a bad unauthorized film is much preferable to a better but authorized one."[17] This was, again, her theory that stupidities about Freud would quickly sink away without a trace, and that anything produced outside of the real atmosphere of Freud's greatness would eventually follow such stupidities into oblivion.

Anna Freud decided to trust her theory, but the waiting was painful. She was furious that her rescue fantasy would not translate directly into reality: "not to be able to protect one's own father against becoming a film hero."[18] When there was a pause between the film's production and its distribution, she hoped that her waiting period was going to be short: "I have heard nothing about the film in the meantime, not even a remote whisper. Somehow it makes me hopeful that they are all dead."[19] But even such direct, uncensored death wishes did not hasten the film's demise. It had to go the whole circuit of fanfare followed by dismal reviews before it did, in fact, sink under its own artistic heavy-handedness.

ANNA Freud viewed the Freud Centenary at Hampstead as a delightful confirmation that a proper celebration of her father's memory could still bring out the best in his followers. Her pleasure in the whole series of events was enormous: "The celebrations in May were very satisfactory indeed. They had the nature of a Congress but a very special one, reminding the older ones among us of former times when all the meetings of analysts brought forth the best efforts of everybody and were a high point in everybody's life."[20]

She had been careful to arrange different types of events, so that her own group and its Clinic would come away with renewed dedication. The British Psychoanalytical Society hosted a private reception for seventy psychoanalysts visiting from fourteen countries and sponsored a series of public lectures on general topics of "applied psychoanalysis" deftly scheduled by Sylvia Payne so that all the British theoretical persuasions received equal time. Isle Hellman represented Anna Freud's group with a talk on "Psychoanalysis and the Teacher." On May 6, the London County Council sponsored the plaque unveiling ceremony and a lecture by Ernest Jones, who was introduced by Heinz Hartmann in his capacity as president of the International Psychoanalytic Association. But for her own group and its students, Anna Freud arranged an "unofficial program" of old friends at her Clinic: Heinz Hartmann, Rudi Loewenstein, Elisabeth Geleerd Loewenstein, Ernst Kris, and Jeanne Lampl-de Groot. The result was just what she had hoped. Her group enjoyed both the rare lack of tension among the British Psychoanalytical Society members at the public events and the special quality of the Clinic meetings. As Ruth Thomas, the Clinic's director of student training, noted:

It seemed as if after all we found our one point of agreement in veneration of Freud. I have never before experienced this sense of togetherness amongst analysts and am convinced that it does not have to disappear from a mature life. There was no doubt that the occasion at the Clinic had a warmth and pleasure for us all that was very special. You were quite right. We did feel it as a more personal celebration, which it was a special honor to take part in. . . . Please accept my most grateful thanks for what was certainly the happiest occasion and for your inclusion of us all in so personal a way.

And from the visitors came the mutual admiration: "It was a great joy to me," Heinz Hartmann wrote, "to experience the enthusiasm of your coworkers."[21]

Building on the momentum of the Centenary, Anna Freud inspired her Clinic coworkers to an extraordinary burst of collective creativity: she introduced them to the guiding themes that ended their infancy as a research organization and set them on their way to the decade of their maturity. The Centenary had given her an occasion for historical reflection, and she had formulated for herself quite explicitly a conviction with which she had been working implicitly for years. Her father had, she understood, aimed at a *general* psychology, and this meant that he had rejected any effort from his followers to treat any single theoretical or practical element of his science as the crucial one, the key to all the mysteries. He stood firm against reductionism, whether it took the form of permanently substituting a part for the whole, or ignoring one end of a complementary series (like the series linking external and internal factors in psychopathology), or overemphasizing—temporarily, in the heat of discovery—one specific focus of research at the expense of all others. Every time Freud himself had opened a new path or taken up a new theoretical approach, he had carefully reviewed his entire creation and tried—with more or less success—to restore it to consistency and to keep the novelty in its perspective. No discovery was either elevated above others or abandoned; each found its circumscribed place in a larger scheme as the goal of generality came closer. Anna Freud had understood that it was possible to be systematic without aiming for a fixed system when she read *Inhibitions, Symptoms and Anxiety* in 1926, but she became aware of what such an intent implied for her own generation's research only after his death.

The history of psychoanalysis since her father's death appeared to Anna Freud as weighted down with examples of all three forms of reductionism. With reference to the history of child analysis, she noted:

> In [the psychoanalysts'] own activity of fact finding, one element of the human mind after another moved into the center of attention and naturally received prominence in publications: infantile sexuality and the sequence of libidi..al stages; repression and the unconscious mind; the division of the personality into various agencies and the conflicts between them; the Oedipus and castration complexes; the role of anxiety; aggression as an independent drive; the relationship between mother and infant and the consequences of early interruptions of the mother-child relationship. Yet, no single one of these factors was ever meant to be considered the only or even the foremost pathogenic agent, as happens all too frequently in clinical evaluations and publications.[22]

What Anna Freud herself wanted was constant intellectual mobility, the ability to see from all angles and to work carefully toward a synthesizing view, and she wanted her Clinic coworkers to translate this ideal into both their diagnostic and therapeutic practice and their research. In effect, the whole dynamic history of psychoanalysis was to be brought to bear on every case and in every research project.

The use each therapist made of the historical vision Anna Freud articulated depended, of course, on his or her individual translation of it. But for the Clinic training candidates, examples of how the history of psychoanalysis could be fruitfully tapped for present use were important. And to that end, Anna Freud sponsored a study group at the Clinic—called the Concept Group—that spent six years producing four volumes of brief articles on the "basic psychoanalytic concepts" making up Freud's metapsychology, libido theory, theory of dreams, instincts, conflicts, anxiety, and so forth. These volumes were also her answer to the question often debated in psychoanalytic training institutes about whether to teach psychoanalysis historically— by beginning with Freud and working forward through the literature—or topically. Her answer was: try to do both at once; and the volumes were her Clinic's encyclopedia-like record of its try.[23]

ANNA FREUD's comprehensive historical vision was a true product of the ambitious adventurer lurking just below the cautious Miss Freud surface, but the method to which it led was more innovatory. To her father's method of working from explorations of psychopathology to conclusions about normality, she added one for working from a complex description of normal development to assessments of psychopathology and techniques for treatment.

> We have broken with the tradition according to which every mental difficulty is seen and explained by comparison with severe pathological patterns, and, instead, try to see it against the background of the norm, expectable for the particular child's age, and to measure its distance from that.[24]

With his approach, Freud had discovered what he called "the infantile neurosis." With her method of measuring against normality, Anna Freud added a novelty to psychoanalytical theory: "beyond the infantile neurosis" (as she titled a paper, echoing her father's *Beyond the Pleasure Principle*) she found "developmental pathology." This phrase summarized a wide range of developmental irregularities or complete arrests producing not psychic conflict but defects in a child's psychic structure and personality.

Anna Freud's break with tradition and her new focus on developmental pathology were spurred not by theoretical reflection but by reflection on the Hampstead War Nursery children and on the cases she and her coworkers had encountered in the Clinic's first four years. The Clinic staff had seen children with classic infantile neuroses precipitated by Oedipal conflicts: the hysterias, obsessional syndromes, and phobias that had been familiar since the early years of child analysis. But they had also seen many "nontypical" cases—like Dorothy Burlingham's little blind patients—and many "borderline cases." Anna Freud used the term "borderline" not just for children who were psychically on the border between neurosis and psychosis, but for those on the border of autism, of mental deficiency, of delinquency, of perversion, and so forth. That is, at the Clinic the term was used for all evolving states with mixed features that were unclassifiable by the traditional standards. Indeed, the very wide range and variety of these cases made Anna Freud and her coworkers question generally the applicability of the traditional diagnostic standards.

In a paper prepared for the Dutch Society's Freud Centenary celebration and in one presented on a fall, 1956 return visit to the Cleveland Society, Anna Freud made the theme that emerged from her clinical reflections very clear.[25] Her father, she argued, had developed his therapeutic and theoretical science by concentrating his attention on adults' psychopathological symptoms: "symptoms give us our bearings when we make our diagnosis," he said.[26] But children's symptoms, Anna Freud noted, are not the same as those of adults. They are related to particular developmental stages and they are—often—transitory. Children are in process; the nucleus of an adult's pathology is not. Because taking analytic bearings from a child's symptoms can be very misleading, Anna Freud simply and startlingly suggested that this traditional method not be applied to children. "Once we decide to disregard the diagnostic categories derived from descriptive psychiatry for adult psychopathology and to play down the importance of symptomatology as such, we can hope to be alerted more vigorously to . . . other aspects of the patient's personality. Where children are concerned, these will be mostly developmental ones."[27]

With the collaboration of her Clinic staff, Anna Freud set out to convert the diagnostic interview technique she had introduced when the Clinic was founded into something much more sweeping and comprehensive: a Developmental Profile, a diagnostic method for assessing both normality and abnormality in a given case. The Profile combined basically two types of descriptions. The first was a composite consisting of specific assessments of the structural, dynamic, economic, and genetic aspects of a patient's psychic functioning. Each assessment was sketched from one of the different types of metapsychological viewpoints Freud had mapped through the historical course of his work and Anna Freud had taken over—in their historical completeness. The second was a composite made by considering a child's achievements and arrests and regressions along a number of different "lines of development." Compositely, the developmental lines made up what is known in the social sciences (following Max Weber) as an "ideal type," a hypothetical norm for development.[28]

The prototypical development line, the one that wove through most of the more specific ones Anna Freud detailed, was given the title "from dependency to emotional self-reliance and adult object relationships." The libido stages Freud had cataloged—oral, anal, phallic—are the maturational base, the general growing-up program for any child's procession from being bound in a biological unity with its mother to living independently and directing its instinctual, emotional, and intellectual attention outside of its own family. The steps along this procession had been noted many times in the analytic literature, so Anna Freud offered her catalog of them as a *summa* and went on to chart other well-known but less thoroughly described lines.[29] "Body independence," she noted, involves lines leading from sucking to rational eating, from wetting and soiling to bladder and bowel control, from irresponsibility to responsibility in body management. Two other lines were of particular importance: one tracing emergence from egocentricity (or primary narcissism) to companionship with others as "partners and objects in their own right," and one tracing a child's play with its body (autoerotism) and its mother's body to play with "transitional objects" (the phrase was Winnicott's) and toys to that play-transforming activity that is work. This last line, from play to work, was a particularly original contribution: others, including Anna Freud's associate from the Montessori school in Vienna, Lili Peller, had presented psychoanalytic approaches to play, but Anna Freud's scheme was more encompassing and detailed. And it supplied her with another way to think of her own first psychoanalytic interest in daydreams: "When toys and the activities connected with them fade into the background, the wishes formerly put into action with the help of material objects, i.e., fulfilled in play, can be spun out imaginatively in the form of conscious daydreams, a fantasy activity which may persist until adolescence, and far beyond it."[30]

At the Clinic, Developmental Profiles built up from information gleaned in diagnostic interviews and compared with information obtained from parents, teachers, and medical, guidance, or social workers were made as initial diagnostic indicators—to recommend one form of treatment or another. Later they were compared with other Profiles drawn up in the course of treatment and after treatment. Such comparisons yielded crucial data about what the treatment had achieved and not achieved and why it had taken the course it had taken; about how psychoanalytic and other kinds of therapies actually work—the nature of their curative powers; about how different factors of endowment and environment interact in a given child and a given psychic configuration.[31] Before Anna Freud constructed the Developmental Profile (and she and others extended it, to babies and to adults), diagnosis was not an area given much attention by psychoanalysts. Analysts took their bearings from symptoms, as Freud suggested, and then got on to the real work of therapy, in which the manifest symptoms were not of significance except as signposts indicating deeper problems. Anna Freud wanted to know whether a diagnosis focused more widely and aimed more deeply could, before therapy, give a much more accurate picture of a patient than psychiatric labeling. But, further, she was very well aware as a clinic director that not every child with a problem is a child who should be in psychoanalytic therapy. Unlike adults, children do not present themselves at a psychoanalytic clinic with at least some insight into their problems and some sense that such a method of treatment may help them. Correct therapeutic recommendations for children depend on differential diagnosis, not on the kinds of information and commitment an adult has.

Combining their metapsychological and developmental lines descriptions allowed the Hampstead analysts to go "beyond the infantile neurosis." The metapsychological descriptions were oriented toward diagnosis of the structural, dynamic, economic, and genetic factors that combine in hysterias, obsessional syndromes, and phobias. In diagnosing these infantile neuroses, the analyst looks for signs of trauma and of conflict between the psychic agencies followed by anxiety, defense, and compromise (or symptom) formation. The developmental lines were oriented toward "developmental psychopathology," which can be seen clearly when there is unevenness in development along the different lines. The manifestations are psychosomatic symptoms, backwardness, and the atypical and borderline states, and Anna Freud assessed these according to a scale that ranged between variations of normality and complete cessation of progressive development.

The two types of psychopathology are different in origin, but just as intermeshed in a child's life as are the two types of description in the Developmental Profile. As always, Anna Freud refused even when directly discussing the origins of the two forms of psychopathology, to reduce one to the role of primary causal agent.

It would be convenient to take the point of view that success or failure on the developmental lines primarily shapes the personalities which secondarily become involved in internal conflict. But any statement of this kind would be a gross falsification once the infant ceases to be an undifferentiated, unstructured being. It would ignore the temporal relations between the two processes which occur simultaneously, not subsequent to each other. Progress on the lines is interfered with constantly by conflict, repression and consequent regression, while the conflicts themselves and quite especially the methods available for their solution are wholly dependent on the shape and level of the personal development which has been reached.[32]

Before she formulated the notion of developmental psychopathology, with its base in a multilinear concept of normal development, Anna Freud had been unable to address positively the Kleinian genetic emphasis on interpsychic events in the first year of life. She had only been able to say something negative: there is no way to prove the correctness of reconstructions of such internal events—or alleged events—as "the depressive position," much less to say that it is critically pathogenic. Her positive alternative was to focus on the many types of observable developmental steps in the first year, and to make assessments from these, rather than to focus on what cannot ever be reconstructed with certainty—the object relations of the preverbal infant. Melanie Klein did not, unfortunately, live long enough to address, if she had wished to, this addition to Anna Freud's evolving work: she died in 1960, at the age of seventy-eight. Willi Hoffer, who had become the president of the British Psychoanalytical Society in 1959, wrote Klein's obituary for the *International Journal of Psychoanalysis* while Anna Freud lamented the loss of her debate partner more personally: "There is no one to fight it through." She also knew that when Klein was not there to restrain her followers the controversy would grow worse, just as Klein's own controversy with Sigmund Freud had grown worse after Freud died.

"I hear that the Kleinians here maintain that the whole controversy is based on a personal rivalry between Melanie Klein and myself!" Anna Freud complained in 1969. "The world does not change."[33]

For her conception of developmental psychopathology, Anna Freud drew on the notion of "basic faults" formulated by Michael Balint in England and on research done in America by Augusta Alpert and Peter Neubauer. In her reorientation toward the first year of life, she had more extensive debts, particularly to the work of two Viennese émigrés to America who also published through *The Psychoanalytic Study of the Child*. Margaret Mahler, Aichhorn's protégée, had established an observational research project at the Masters Children's Center in New York in which she indicated the stages of children's "psychological birth," their separation out of the original symbiotic mother-child union in the second year of life.[34] Anna Freud kept in touch with this research and the two women exchanged views at length in 1961, when Margaret Mahler paid a two-week visit to Hampstead. René Spitz's research was older—it had begun in Vienna and then been adapted in his Swiss and American locations—but it was also under the influence of Aichhorn's work with children who had suffered early deprivations. His summary volume, *The First Year of Life* (1965), discussed the functions, affects, and attitudes normal and abnormal infants can develop and gave detailed descriptions of the interrelationships between their id impulses, ego growth, and changes in their relationships with their mothers. Spitz's work also inspired Anna Freud to return to a fascinating series of papers that her friend Willi Hoffer had written while he was working at the Hampstead War Nursery and taking photographs of the children there—the first papers from the Hampstead group that seriously took up the challenge of Melanie Klein's speculations about the first year of life.[35]

Both Mahler's contributions and Spitz's were, however, from Anna Freud's perspective, too narrow as causal theories. She did build their results into her developmental lines—as she built in what she thought was useful in Melanie Klein's object relations approach, the notion of "part objects." But she refused to follow either of her colleagues—or anyone else—in attributing to any particular period or any particular developmental process the role of chief pathogenic agent. The history of child analysis is, she noted, as replete with causal reductions as with any other kind: "theory as to the causation of pathology [has] veered, rather wildly, from the Oedipal period as the responsible constellation to the mother-infant relationship at the beginning of life; to the separation-individuation phase (Margaret Mahler); to the disturbances of narcissism (Kohut); to the developmental frustrations and interferences (Nagera)."[36]

It is a clear indication of how serious Anna Freud was about avoiding any kind of disbalanced or reductionistic view that she ended this list (one of her many historical lists) with a reference to Humberto Nagera's *Early Childhood Disturbances, the Infantile Neurosis, and the Adulthood Disturbances* (1966). Nagera, a Cuban, had joined the staff at Hampstead just before the Cuban Revolution, while Anna Freud was offering her staff preliminary formulations of the Developmental Profile, and he had emerged as the Profile's most eager champion. In the Profile, Nagera saw the psychoanalytic equivalent of basic diagnostic procedure in medicine—the construction of a syndrome by combining different types of data, anatomical, anatomicopathological, physiological, physiopathological, and so forth—and he joined Anna Freud in her conviction that the scientific rigor of psychoanalysis depended on innovations like the Profile. But Nagera, in her judgment, eventually tipped the balance of the interplay of developmental psychopathology and infantile neurosis too much to the former, so she added him to her list, despite the fact that his book was so clearly a grandchild.

In the decade after the Freud Centenary, the decade during which the Developmental Profile was formulated, revised, tried on an expanding range of cases, and revised again, Anna Freud was fortunate to add to her staff a fine younger group of newly qualified Hampstead graduates and some newcomers like Humberto Nagera. What Nagera was to the Profile research and to the Concept Group as it did its historical research on key psychoanalytic concepts, Joseph Sandler, Hanna Engl Kennedy, and Sara Kut Rosenfeld were to the other branch of the original research projects, Dorothy Burlingham's Index. The Clinic staff kept building up its Index, and there was a good deal of cross-referencing between the Index project and the Profile project. Both tracks of the metapsychologically geared research, as well as Dorothy Burlingham's two clinical areas, the work with blind children and the simultaneous analyses of mother (later also father) and child couples, began to produce the stream of publications that turned about half of every issue of *The Psychoanalytic Study of the Child* into a report from London. In the late 1950s, almost every publication passed under Anna Freud's remarkable editorial pen and came out much the clearer for it, but as the researchers gathered experience and momentum, she simply reported to the managing editor of the journal, Ruth Eissler, what was coming for each issue.

The Psychoanalytic Study of the Child was the Hampstead Clinic's main forum, but it was also Anna Freud's *in memoriam* for Ernst Kris. When Kris died at the age of fifty-six in February 1957—suddenly, but after years of heart trouble—Anna Freud rearranged her schedule and went to New York to deliver a lecture that acknowledged in personally reserved, completely scientific terms the debt she owed to his work and his encouragement. "Child Observation and Prediction of Development" was a continuation of discussions she had had with Kris for years about how psychoanalysts should make use of observation, but it also forecast the importance observation was going to assume at the Clinic, not just in confirming analytic results but in suggesting new areas of research and new hypotheses.[37]

Anna Freud gladly acknowledged her debt to Ernst Kris's scientific cast of mind and his willingness to make psychoanalysis a partly observational science, but she did not say that she had lost the one of her contemporaries who was most important to her work. Just as she refused to engage in polemics that singled out opponents, she refused to create jealousies with praise. To Marianne Kris, on the other hand, she and Dorothy immediately sent word that they expected her in London and in Walberswick that summer—and the invitation signaled a closeness among the three women that grew ever stronger over the years. "You are the *one* person with whom I need to be now," Marianne wrote, "and I fantasize all the time that you are here. I am so grateful to you and Dorothy for 'my' room in Far End and mine at home in Maresfield Gardens. Even though I cannot right at the moment be there, it did something very good

for me to know it."[38] To the Kris children, Anna—her namesake—
and Anton, who both became psychiatrists and then psychoanalysts,
Anna Freud also extended her hospitality and friendship. Tony was
invited to use the familiar Du with Anna Freud, as his father never
had been——though Marianne, as a childhood friend, had of course
always been Du. Anna Kris Wolff received a summary of Anna
Freud's vision of mourning and identification: "As you know, I am
an expert in 'good fathers,' and even in losing a good father. The
saving thing is that one never really loses them in spirit if they have
been good enough. And anyway, one has something to live up to."[39]

Heinz Hartmann, who had lost in Ernst Kris his most important
"thinking friend," was consoled by Anna Freud's messages to him,
but they hardly had time to exchange the letters that made them
much better thinking partners for each other before they both lost
another close friend. Hans and Jeanne Lampl were involved in a
dreadful automobile accident; Jeanne Lampl was hospitalized in very
serious condition, though she did eventually make a full recovery,
but Hans Lampl was killed immediately. With him went a large
piece of Anna Freud's youth: he had come into her life as Martin
Freud's friend, but he had slowly become something like an auxiliary older brother. In the last two years of his life, partly as a result
of reading Jones's biography of Freud and partly because he felt his
health deteriorating, Lampl had shifted their correspondence—long,
sentimental letters from him and cooler, shorter ones from her—into
the mode of reminiscence. When Anna Freud cared to express her
nostalgia for Vienna, for her father, for the past, Lampl had been
there. After his death, Jeanne Lampl became a frequent visitor to
Maresfield Gardens and to Walberswick. Anna Freud never thought
of her as an intimate friend, but she was an old one and, after 1958,
a needy one.

In the late 1950s summers, Anna Freud and Dorothy Burlingham ran what they jokingly called "the girls' boarding school" for
their widowed friends.[40] Anny and Maurits Katan also eventually
bought a summer house in Walberswick, so the Vienna circle continued supportively, even though sadly diminished. Marie Bonaparte
visited after she too lost her husband, Prince George, in 1957. The
Princess was then both very happy with the attentions paid her by
an admirer, a Parisian physician twenty years her junior, and dis-

traught over the situation in the Paris Society. But as her health failed, she became more and more difficult, and less and less available to Anna Freud as a confidante. In 1960, she made a trip to California to argue with Governor Brown about the death penalty, hoping to win a stay of execution for Caryl Chessman; both the trip and her obsession with Chessman's case were disastrous for her health. While Anna Freud was visiting Ishak Ramzy and lecturing at the Menninger Clinic in 1962, the Princess died, defeated by leukemia.

Anna Freud, who had always admired Marie Bonaparte's honesty, her straightforwardness, and her capacity for self-analysis, paid her the tribute at a July 1963 memorial service in Paris of the only nonscientific public eulogy she ever wrote. She honored her friend's memory as her father had honored Lou Andreas-Salomé's by saying of Marie Bonaparte's unpublished memoir:

> As a book it is a wholly unusual and perfect blending of literary and scientific values; of emotional subjectivity and analytical objectivity; of feminine charm, intuition and longings with the relentless sharpness of a masculine intellect; of abandon and submission to the present and the actual with a sense of detachment and appreciation of historical development. If the value of psychoanalysis for autobiographical studies was ever in question, her example of turning the searchlight of analytic insight towards the self should be able to dispel such doubts forever.[41]

In retrospect, Anna Freud could see that Ernst Kris's death was also the beginning of a slow changing of the guard in her life and her extended friendship circle. With the exception of the Princess, it was the ranks of the men she had known and cared for in Vienna—often, like Kris, as analysands—that thinned dramatically in the next decade and a half. Only a year after Lampl's death in 1958, Edward Bibring came to the end of an agonizing illness, and Anna Freud again rearranged a trip to America so that she could speak at his memorial service in Boston. Grete Bibring was in a very distraught state, drained by her husband's last months of incapacity and psychological disorientation, which she had labored to keep disguised from his many students and colleagues, and she turned to Anna Freud for a correspondence-analysis: "Dearest Anna, thank you for your gentle friendship and for your understanding, which means more to me and gave me more help than I can express. Let me tell you, and only you, what really happened. . . ."[42]

Very directly, Edward Bibring's death brought Anna Freud one of his training analysands, Joseph Michaels, and increased her closeness with his student Arthur Valenstein, who had been referred to her earlier and had, during his time in London, met and married Dorothy Burlingham's younger daughter, Katrina, whose first marriage had ended in divorce. Ernst Kris's position on the editorial board of *The Psychoanalytic Study of the Child* was taken by Marianne Kris, who eventually brought to the board and to Anna Freud's acquaintance Albert J. Solnit and Seymour Lustman, two of the Kris's young protégés at Yale. When Anna Freud returned to New York in 1960 to deliver four lectures—the first draft of her *Normality and Pathology in Childhood*—Solnit and Lustman attended, along with three of their New Haven colleagues, Samuel Ritvo, Jay Katz, and Joseph Goldstein, a group that welcomed Anna Freud to Yale for a number of extended stays in the 1960s. These younger Americans, along with the Hampstead graduates working in Cleveland, at the Menninger Clinic, and in New York, were Anna Freud's new world. They joined Douglas Bond of Cleveland and Ralph Greenson of Los Angeles, who was a decade their senior, in the role of external courtiers.

From these men, Anna Freud received echoes of the kind of attention that had helped her to flourish as a young woman in Vienna, attention of the kind Aichhorn, Hoffer, Hartmann, Kris, Waelder, and Bibring had paid her. She rose to such attention and gave her best in its light. When Greenson sent her some photographs he had taken of her, she responded just as she had to Aichhorn in 1948. Usually, she told him, "I look like some sort of sick animal, but I find myself very human in yours."[43] Ralph Greenson was a hard-living man of passionate enthusiasm and even flamboyance, a man for whom psychoanalysis was—as Anna Freud thought it should be, and as it was for her entire friendship circle—a way of life. When he was suffering over the death of Max Schur, he wrote—like Aichhorn before him—to ask her if he might use her first name. Her reply shows what a difference familiarity had come to assume for her as she was feeling the loss, one by one, of her friends and as she was placing her hopes for the future more and more on Greenson and his peers. She prepared him to think of her as she thought of her father: "I am willing to call you Romi, and you can call me Anna, under one condition: that you promise not to rage against fate, God (?), and the world when my time comes to disappear. My father used to call that 'not to kick.' One kicks against fate, but, as you describe it, one only hurts oneself, and through hurting oneself, those who are nearest to one. I would not like to think that some day I shall give you such a cause."[44]

THE admiration and support that came from the younger men in America were crucial to Anna Freud for her work at the Clinic. Her old "altruistic surrender" tendency to displace ambitious wishes onto younger men reached into a new generation, to men of the right age to be sons. Albert Solnit's mother and Anna Freud were, she discovered on one of her Yale visits, exactly the same age: "You could be my son," she told him with rare openness.

America was a better location for her displaced wishes than the Clinic, where—she knew—there was enough built-in, siblinglike competitiveness. At the Clinic, she tried hard to minimize the kind of politicization, greediness, and free play of individual ambitions that wreaked havoc in many psychoanalytic institutes. "I know all the difficulties concerning our present-day type of colleagues," she wrote to a Vienna trainee, Lydia Dawes of Boston, "but I am really luckier than other people in this respect. The Hampstead Clinic has made it possible for me to create at least a semblance of the past by trying to bring up young people with the right type of human attitude and interest in analysis. I know that this is only an island within an ocean of different circumstances, but life on that island is rather pleasant."[45]

Anna Freud was sixty-five in 1960, five years past the age that she had often announced, to general disbelief, would find her retired in Walberswick for a life of weaving, gentry farming, and horseback riding. But the 1960s, the decade of her most remarkable creativity—at her writing desk and in her role as inspirer and director of the Clinic—was also the decade in which she had to struggle to bring about even the possibility of retirement. She worked to assure her Clinic's future, which, as always, meant its financial future. But

the Clinic's leadership future was just as important, and more difficult to secure. Unlike her father, she did not have an Anna Freud
to rely on. And, on the other hand, any successor would have her
awesome intellectual and organizational example to live both with
and up to.

In America and on vacations in Walberswick, she could discuss
with her old friends, particularly Marianne Kris and Heinz Hartmann, and with her new ones, particularly Romi Greenson, her
succession problem. After she made a wonderful trip to California
in 1959 and enjoyed the hospitality extended by Greenson and his
Swiss-born wife, Hildi—"I find it quite difficult to imagine Los Angeles without me in it," she wrote in grateful exuberance—she resolved to take more and more exciting vacations and to delegate
more responsibility at the Clinic.[46] Eventually Anna Freud and Dorothy Burlingham added quite a catalog of islands-visited to their vacation fantasy—the Scilly Isles, Puerto Rico, Ireland, among them—
but the immediate result of their resolve was to make a model of
their September 1958 trip. They had rented a motorized canal boat
and spent five days steering it about the Norfolk Broads. This lark,
"one of the highlights of recent years . . . made us feel very young
and adventuresome."[47] Their spirits renewed, they returned to the
Clinic resolved to deal with its internal stresses and strains. "The
work would not be too difficult if people were not difficult sometimes."[48]

One of the first moves they made was to give their experienced
staff more opportunity for recognition, so that the Hampstead Clinic
would eventually become less identified with Anna Freud herself.
Psychiatrist-in-Charge Liselotte Frankl was, accordingly, invited to
Los Angeles, where she gave a very successful series of seminars. With
Romi Greenson, Anna Freud reflected by letter on her second-in-
command's situation and gave, in the process, a rare self-description.

> She is an absolutely sound person with solid knowledge, secure
> in her factual clinical and theoretical ability. But she lacks self-
> confidence and the courage to put herself over, also she lacks
> the decisive spark or step in imagination which pulls data to-
> gether and makes a unified whole of them. She does not paint
> pictures (as we more daring people do), she builds with bricks
> (which is probably much less pleasure). She is a very good

teacher when she is alone with the students and, I believe, the
Clinic feels that her need for solid structures serves as a very
good counterweight against my quicker flights of imagination.
Sometimes I wonder whether the close cooperation with me is
very hard on her and whether she feels it as too demanding. So
far as I am concerned, I value her very much as a coworker.[49]

In 1963, when Liselotte Frankl was scheduled for another lecture trip and Anna Freud herself was scheduled for a month-long
stay in New Haven, the moment seemed right to bring in another
leader, someone to share with Frankl the administrative responsibilities under Anna Freud's continued directorship. Willi Hoffer,
whose wife, Hedwig, had died in 1961, was ill, and could not as
effectively keep up his roles as the senior male presence and the
main link to the British Psychoanalytical Society and the *International Journal of Psychoanalysis*, which he continued to edit and
where he sadly oversaw the steady production of obituaries for his
Viennese colleagues. The old guard's choice fell upon John Bolland,
who was a member of the B-group—Anna Freud's sector—in the
British Psychoanalytical Society but not so much of an insider at
the Clinic as to lack "breath of fresh air" quality.

After a year in his post, John Bolland was nursing an ulcer, and
by May of 1966, three years after his acceptance, he resigned, worn-
out and well aware that his administrative style was not that of the
Clinic. He was more impatient with the intricate web of study and
research groups than Liselotte Frankl, and considerably less inspiring
than Anna Freud. Bolland did not have Anna Freud's rare ability to
be strictly and implacably in charge while also being available to
anyone who needed help, apprised of every case in the Clinic, close
to every facet of the clinical and clerical staffs' work. As his main
contribution Bolland left not any organizational mark but a volume
he coedited called *The Hampstead Psychoanalytic Index*.[50]

Humberto Nagera, who had been so capable in his role as prime
mover of the Profile research, was Anna Freud's next hope. But he
felt that he had to seek a better-paying, larger-scale operation in
order to support his growing family, and he departed, regretfully, for
the University of Michigan. Fortunately, there was a very capable
alternative, Clifford Yorke, a Yorkshireman who was both sensitive
to the complexities of the Clinic personalities and disinclined to

force his own ideas on them. He stood for growth with continuity, and he—like Bolland—represented the Clinic to the outside world as what it largely was not—he was male, non-Jewish, native British, and equipped with British medical and psychiatric degrees. In the 1960s, Anna Freud had taken care with her hiring to assure that the Clinic was not isolated from the community or the London mental health community by remaining a largely female, Jewish émigré enclave, with thickly accented "Hampstead English" as the predominant language.

Clifford Yorke was well enough acclimatized to the Clinic to be able, in 1967, to assume Liselotte Frankl's work as well as his own. She suffered from a depressive episode and took a leave from the Clinic to seek treatment with Anna Freud's colleague from the Wagner-Jauregg Clinic in Vienna, Dr. Erwin Stengl, who worked in Sheffield. After her recovery, she did not want to take up administration again. Anna Freud decided that her next effort had to be more definitive; at the age of seventy-two, she wanted to hand over her directorship and put a leadership combination in place that would last. Clifford Yorke could be part of the team, but the leadership had to come, she felt, from someone with training in child analysis.

"You had better be prepared for it," she wrote to Romi Greenson while she was considering the dirctorship problem, "old age consists above all in an insatiable desire for holidays."[51] Her desire for a permanent holiday was gaining on her desire to follow her father's example and work up to the very end. As always, she balanced her desires and compromised in the direction of duty by buying a house in Ireland with Dorothy and arranging for longer, more remote and adventurous holidays—without giving up the dirctorship.

This decision came about for external as well as internal reasons, however. Her fear for the Clinic's future became acute in May of 1967, when Willi Hoffer died. She missed his friendship and counsel deeply, and she was apprehensive about how his work for the Clinic's training program would be continued. In 1956, as part of the Centenary celebrations, Hoffer had helped establish the Centenary Fund, which raised money from private English sources—mostly former patients—to support candidates while they did their course work and training analyses. His ability to size up prospective students and to help them on their way had been extraordinary, and he had left no successor on his committee. Convinced that she had to act quickly, Anna Freud offered the directorship to an American—and was refused.

During her stays in New Haven, she had found in Seymour Lustman the man she considered the perfect heir. Although he was not renowned for his administrative abilities, Lustman was a fine clinician, experienced in many facets of the research project Ernst and Marianne Kris had established at the Yale Child Study Center, and respected among the board members of *The Psychoanalytic Study of the Child* and in the American Psychoanalytic Association. At Yale, he was beloved as a teacher—a man of passionate enthusiasm both for psychoanalysis and for transmitting it to students. He and Anna Freud had taught a course together, and she felt that he was undaunted—admiring, but not idealizing—in his relationship with her. His response to her work had impressed her deeply: "I had never realized until that visit [to Hampstead] what a superb grasp you had of the formal characteristics of theory and how consistent was your theoretical orientation and development. It seemed to me that we are not aware of your skills as a methodologist and epistemological conceptualizer primarily because you just did it and did not talk about it."[52]

Seymour Lustman was torn—and took three months to make his decision. Finally, he said that although the invitation was "the highest compliment I have ever experienced," he could not accept. "What I have come to feel—with a sense of the deepest regret—is that my roots are so deep that I fear the burden of leaving my children and the United States would severely compromise my effectiveness in my work."[53] What he did suggest was that they work toward a formal connection between the Yale Child Study Center and Hampstead so that he might spend some time in London, as Marianne Kris put it, "to do whatever he could to keep the level up and stimulate with whatever he has to give."[54]

While Anna Freud was waiting as patiently as she could for Lustman's decision, Robert Waelder died in Philadelphia, and then Martin Freud, who had been suffering for months with various illnesses, died in the little south England town to which he had retired with his second wife. The loss of her oldest brother was very hard for

Anna Freud, and her grief was aggravated by her anxiety about Ernst, who had recovered—but not completely—from a coronary in 1963. Often in those months she fell back on an old Jewish saying that her father was fond of: "Es soll einem nicht zukommen, was man aushaltern kann" ("What one is able to bear is seldom what one must bear"). Heinz Hartmann, ill himself but still able to sign his name with a shaky script to one of his laboriously typed letters, caught the mood they shared thinking about Willi Hoffer and Robert Waelder and Martin Freud: "Of the participants in those lovely intimate evenings with your father, only you and I are living still."[55]

AFTER Seymour Lustman made his difficult decision, there was a pause, a time for reconsideration. The Clinic's developmental line from poverty to large-scale patronage meshed with the story of its organizational vicissitudes to produce a new set of goals.

The enormous expansion of research horizons that had given rise to the Diagnostic Profile and the publications connected with it and the Index had been supported by a redeployment of grant-getting energy in 1960. The early years of the Clinic, from its opening in 1952 through the Centenary addition of the new building and the nursery, had been funded by the relatively short-term and specific grants channeled through the Anna Freud Foundation in New York. The Clinic director had marveled often in the spirit of an October 17, 1955 letter to Kurt Eissler and Dora Hartmann, who acted as the Foundation's treasurer: "I feel great admiration for the Anna Freud Foundation, which is so much better at money collecting than the person it is named after has ever been." But this method of funding was, as all its organizers knew, too precarious to allow the Clinic to expand safely. Stable funding had to be found—most probably in America, as English efforts had never been successful except for Willi Hoffer's Centenary Fund, which had the loyal support of Lord and Lady Normanby.

In the spring of 1960, Anna Freud had almost reached the end of her ability to generate dozens of grant proposals yearly. Mathilde Freud Hollitscher was then in the hospital for a gallbladder operation, Ernst Freud was beset with puzzling migraines, and Bob Burlingham, suffering from a depression with extreme agitation and fears, was in London needing Anna Freud's help while he started an analysis with one of her most respected colleagues, Max Goldblatt. She was exhausted, and could not—for once—use her vacation time in Walberswick to meet a deadline: "for a few weeks my mind would not function willingly and insisted on 'time off.' Tomorrow I return to London and to work."[56] The Clinic staff was functioning well and efficiently, collecting material and keeping nearly fifty children in analysis, but Anna Freud's presence and attention were needed everywhere. "The enthusiasm of the people working at the Clinic tends to lag especially in your absence," her staff informed her, "and personal problems come to the fore. It might be a great help if you told them about your reception in America and how other people view what we try to do here."[57] Anna Freud had just returned from her September 1960 lectures in New York—the "normality and pathology in childhood" preview—and a visit to the Menninger Clinic in Kansas; both visits had generated great interest in the Clinic's work, and that interest did need relaying.

Anna Freud reported on her trip and also let the staff know about a possibility she had discussed with the Anna Freud Foundation officers in New York: large-scale and renewable grants from the National Institute of Mental Health in Washington. The staff rallied for an application to support the Diagnostic Profile research; an NIMH investigatory group came from Washington; and then there was a long wait. Anna Freud was very nervous, especially because the investigatory group had included several members not renowned for their love of psychoanalysis: "The trouble is that I am no good with 'doubters,' and certainly no good at selling myself," she lamented to Helen Ross.[58] The doubters were, however, impressed, and July 1962 brought notification of the Clinic's success. Both the staff and the secretaries, who had been paid wages that constantly taxed their remarkable loyalty to Anna Freud and to her work, were given pay increases that brought them at least into the vicinity of comparable workers elsewhere.

The success, then, as such successes do, brought more successes. The Grant Foundation came through with support for Services to Other Institutions, a project that brought to the Clinic five severely disturbed children from High Wick Hospital. These were the most difficult "borderline" cases the staff had ever seen. Another research group, on adolescents, was also renewed with several new foundation grants, and a major decision was reached about the Nursery School. Influenced by the methods and results of the Chicago Institute for Early Childhood Education where Maria Piers was directing work for Project Head Start and gathering material on Head Start's schools in rural Mississippi, Anna Freud decided to change the Hampstead nursery's population. By 1966, the nursery children were predominantly poor, underprivileged, and often from homes of recent immigrants, particularly from Jamaica. Observation of these children was indebted to the book Maria Piers and her collaborator, Robert Coles, dedicated to Anna Freud, *The Wages of Neglect*. Erik Erikson, Anna Freud's student from the Vienna days, was associated with the Chicago work, and Anna Freud's position as a correspondent-consultant there also brought them back in touch with each other.[59]

By 1965, the Clinic had forty-three therapists (most of them part-time at the Clinic) and thirty secretaries, receptionists, nursery teachers, and psychiatric social workers crowded into its two buildings. The staff had been able to do ninety-six diagnostic interviews in 1960, but only forty-three in 1965 because of the Clinic policy of not interviewing children for whom there were no possible treatment vacancies.[60] To keep up the number of diagnostic interviews, which meant increasing the number of therapists, there had to be more room. Romi Greenson, who had organized a fund for psychoanalytic research in Los Angeles, was able to find the solution to the space problem. His chief donor, Lita Annenberg Hazen, supplied money for another house, and when 14 Maresfield Gardens was put up for sale, the Clinic was able to acquire it. By February 1968, the house was refurbished according to Ernst Freud's specifications and ready for use. Both the Hampstead therapists and the three-typewriters-to-a-room secretarial staff rejoiced at an opening party.

It was just then, in early 1968, when Seymour Lustman declined the directorship. And it was also just then that the United States Congress, swirling in debate over the Vietnam War and the fate of Lyndon Johnson's presidency, began to scale back budget allocations for such agencies as the National Institute of Mental Health. War, as Anna Freud had learned when she directed the Hampstead War Nursery, is as hard on mental health institutions as it is on mental health. The Clinic's budget shortfall for 1968 was sixty thousand dollars. Lustman, as the head of the Robert Knight Research Fund, immediately supplied half the money, and Romi Greenson's fund came up with matching funds. But the situation was grave, and there seemed only three ways out of it: permanently linking the Clinic with an endowed American institution; finding new large partons; or retrenchment. The question of how to organize the Clinic's leadership for the future hung on the decision.

If THERE WAS one thing, other than the constant companionship and support Dorothy Burlingham provided, that kept Anna Freud from being slowed down by her extraordinary work load and her worries about the Clinic, it was her capacity for fantasy. On the developmental line from play to work, she was very advanced indeed; but she also could regress creatively, enjoying what Ernst Kris called "regression in the service of the ego." This ability served her well when she was with children, who always know a big child when they meet one. The nursery children knew her as one of them, particularly as she got older and more bent over—closer to them. They even offered their solicitude. One of the children asked her once, for example, why she wore such a long skirt. She replied: "It gets longer as I get older." The child was sure that this meant imminent death, but one of his friends reassured him: "It's all right, it hasn't touched the ground yet." Another one asked her where she lived. Knowing that the children adored her dog, Coco, she said, "I live at Coco's house." Alarmed, the girl asked tenderly, "Haven't you got a home of your own?"

Adults who, like herself, let the child in themselves act freely, got to know the fantasizer in her. Romi and Hildi Greenson gave her a souvenir of California, an Indian maiden doll in buckskins. "I play with the doll sometimes," she told them, "but at other times only looking at her and imagining she is my heathen goddess."[61] Adults who did boring things like economizing over Christmas presents got somewhat petulant responses: "I accept your ruling about Christmas, of course. You are right; it does not fit with the times. Actually, most pleasures do not if looked at closely."[62] In another case, she was not annoyed: "I feel just a little sad about the cancellation of the Christmas presents . . . but I realize it is sensible and that you are right. We have all ceased to be children by now and thoughts become more important than material things. So we shall leave it at that. At least for the present time."[63] The future was left open, in case this sad friend, Ernest Jones's widow, Kitty, could be playful again.

Adults who suffered from awe in the presence of the venerable Miss Freud, on the other hand, got lessons about her from their children. One such five-year-old daughter of an American psychoanalyst received elaborate instructions about what her best behavior should consist of while Miss Freud was visiting her house. But when Miss Freud came through the door with a retinue of psychoanalysts on their best behavior, the little girl snapped her tether, galloped up to the famous guest, tugged at her skirt, and asked, "How many children do you have?" Miss Freud knelt down to give her a hug and quietly told her a truth: "I have many, many children."

The adult daughter of another American psychoanalyst came to Hampstead for a visit and stumbled across the most treasured of Miss Freud's fantasies. She thanked her hostess for the tour she had been given of Sigmund Freud's study, still completely unchanged on the first floor of 20 Maresfield Gardens. Anna Freud shook her hand and said warmly, "Have a good trip home and please say hello from me to my father." There was a pause while each registered exactly what had been said, and then they laughed, in unison. The daughters of psychoanalysts do have a quite particular link with Anna Freud, one that was clear to Nadia Ramzy, who received a gift from Anna Freud—a fountain pen, not surprisingly—and summoned up her best school English to write a thank-you from Cairo: "At home in Daddy's library Daddy has many books which you and your father have written. Do you know that since I was three years old very often I am used to hear the name of 'Sigmund Freud' very much indeed. I think you are very lucky to have a father who is very much liked and admired."[64] What this link felt like to Anna Freud is apparent in a note she sent to an eleven-year-old autograph collector: "Thank you for your nice letter. Since we are both daughters of psychoanalysts, we are almost sisters. I hope you enjoy having such a father as much as I did."[65]

As a fantasizer, Anna Freud specialized in reversals, in making the absent present, the lost found, the past current. But she could also make the undone done, or—even more valuable—doable. When she was tired and faced with a stack of letters to answer, for example, she would simply set her pen down on a blank page and scurry it along, making quick mountain ranges of scribble. Then she would sign her name under the rows of scribble in her characteristic way, as one flourishing word: ANNAFREUD. Having thus written a letter in fantasy with complete ease, she wrote a real letter helped by the sense that the task was accomplished already. Her lectures were composed in the same way. First she lectured in her imagination, enjoying the thunderous applause, and then she made an outline of what she had said, adjusting it if she needed to for greater simplicity and coherence. Later, with her outline in hand, she would give the lecture extempore. The method—if it can be called that—also supplemented her pleasure in sprints of thought. Intellectually she was, as she noted in comparing herself to Liselotte Frankl, a quick sketcher.

Dorothy Burlingham too had something of a whimsical quality for the refreshment of her spirit, though what she liked most was slowing herself down, reducing strain on her health. She cultivated her step-by step enjoyment in her hobby, watercolor painting, and she brought it to the planning of their vacations. After she and Anna Freud had returned from an American visit by luxurious ship, she wrote to the Greensons: "It is amazing how many hours it is possible to sleep in such a situation. Too bad we cannot bottle it up for future use." Their best holidays were, as Anna Freud said, "just for rest and thinking." "I talk too much and I write too little. Everybody agrees as to the latter, while people are too polite to mention the former." "Anna and I often wonder," Dorothy Burlingham mused, "how to get anywhere in the world . . . without an Anna Freud lecture. That would be refreshing. Does that sound very unfaithful to Anna? I do like her lectures, but times without them would be heavenly."[66]

THE ability to imagine—and bottle up imaginatively—the Blessed Isles of vacation can serve simple escapism, but when it filters into work it is a great leavener. Anna Freud helped herself deal with the complex and taxing realities of her Clinic by imagining them in the suffused light of her Ideal Clinic—just as she helped her own psychoanalytic writing by imagining it as recorded conversations with her Ideal Reader, her "ego ideal," her father. In the product of her second habit, *The Writings of Anna Freud*, the product of her first one resides, in Volume VII; it is a lecture called "The Ideal Psychoanalytic Institute: A Utopia," which she delivered in 1966, on Heinz Kohut's invitation, at the Chicaco Institute.

The utopian institute Anna Freud described was very like the Hampstead Child Therapy Course and Clinic, gracefully relieved of all its interior stress and problems of exterior support, and already arrived at a destination toward which she had just begun to steer it: the addition of training in adult analysis.

> Unlike the present institutes, the Ideal Institute provides equally
> for work with adults and with children. Since we now possess a
> technique of child analysis which is not merely a derivative of
> adult technique, but equivalent to it, it is no longer necessary to
> relegate child analysis to the end of training after the candidate
> has familiarized himself with the classical technique. . . . [Candidates] will be trained in both and may specialize in either in
> the future.[67]

All the official institutes existing in the world trained for adult analysis and had child analysis as an appendage; Anna Freud's Course and Clinic was headed in the opposite direction. She had a fantasy that the addition of adult analysis to the program at Hampstead might someday win it—by a backward route—the status of an institute, recognized by the International Association, if never directly by the British Society. In the light of this fantasy, the issues of Hampstead's future leadership and financing slowly turned into issues to be approached in a much broader context. Their solutions required waiting for reality to catch up with wishes.

Behind the Institute fantasy there was another one, concocted in coordination with projects launched by Marianne Kris and Helen Ross. These two friends saw two different ways to point out to the American Psychoanalytic Association that the second-class citizenship accorded institutionally to child analysts and their specialty should cease. This demonstration would, they knew, eventually be connected to the old "question of lay analysis," since many child analysts were nonmedical. But that vexed question was not strategically their focus. Anna Freud saw in her friends' ideas a circuitous pathway to her hopes for Hampstead.

Helen Ross had kept Anna Freud apprised since the Freud Centenary year of 1956 about the project she had codirected with Bertram Lewin: an investigation of training in America, which had been mandated by the American Psychoanalytic Association. The book that Ross and Lewin produced after two years of visiting and revisiting all fourteen American institutes (and three training centers) was an astonishingly thorough presentation of information about and reflection on psychoanalytic trainees and trainers, curriculae, institute research projects, offices, buildings, libraries, journals— everything comprising, as their title put it, *Psychoanalytic Education in the United States.*

In a section of the book on child analysis, Ross and Lewin indicated how, in America, "child analysis became a veritable stepchild of the institutes" during the prewar years when much child analytic attention went outside of the institutes, to child guidance centers.[68] They noted that a 1948 Committee on Child Analysis, chaired by Erik Erikson, had tried to address questions about what child analytic training should consist of and how standards for qualification should be formulated. "At this time they brought up the question of training nonmedical persons as child analysts but deferred the discussion, which was again delayed in 1951 and has continued up to the present to be relegated to future consideration." A series of 1958 APA reports had recommended that a child analysis course be required at every institute, but this recommendation had come up against a complete lack of consensus in the various institutes. Nonetheless, a recommendation has been made, and Ross and Lewin, after citing the work of Anna Freud in England, closed their chapter with the hope that the next stage—active encouragement for child analysis and even for the training of nonmedical practitioners—would begin.

Helen Ross put the project of such encouragement at the center of her life, and her own personal next step was an official visit to Hampstead to produce a report on it for the American Psychoanalytic Association. She and Anna Freud were in complete agreement about what was at stake: "You are right," Helen Ross wrote, "there is grave danger that child analysis will be diluted more and more."[69] Anna

Freud looked to the American Psychoanalytic Association's concern for the broader future: "I can only repeat that a revised training for child analysis is really a very serious matter and that the whole future of child analysis within the International Association will depend on it. If we could do something to remedy matters, it would be just wonderful."[70]

In-house, what Anna Freud did was to encourage a group under Joseph Sandler's direction in their production of a 1967 manual based on Index material, "Treatment Situation and Technique," a book that supplied an obvious lack in the child analytic training literature.[71] At the same time, in the mid-1960s she poured energy into the preparation of her own *Writings*, a project that its dedicated editor, Lottie Newman, coordinated. Anna Freud did not want to be without both a model training scheme, her own, or a training compendium should the wonderful remedy suddenly be at hand. And she knew that her *Writings* were as important for inspiring the acceptance of child analysis in the institutes as her father's *Gesammelte Schriften*, which she had helped edit, had been for the founding of institutes after the First World War.

But she also knew that reform within big institutions very seldom comes about without vigorous pushing from a smaller, strategically placed special interest group. It was an initiative from Marianne Kris that spoke to this need. She had called together a group of child analysts in 1962 and suggested that they incorporate themselves within but independently of the American Association. Some of the group had been anxious about whether such a move would be perceived as a lay analytic conspiracy, but the activists had prevailed. "At the American Association the rumor of our Association spread and got very excited negative reactions from some quarters and very positive from others," Marianne Kris reported to Anna Freud in her delightfully approximate English. "This was one of the most exhausting weeks I went through but by now I have recovered from it."[72] The old friends and students from the Vienna days—Anny Katan, Helen Ross, Peter Blos, and Jenny Waelder-Hall among them—and some of the new ones—Albert Solnit, Samuel Ritvo, Peter Neubauer—were in the league. Grete Bibring was chief among the American Psychoanalytic Association officers who wanted to meet the group halfway and open "a real child division in the

American."[73] By 1964, a regular forum on child analysis in the American Association's yearly meeting program had been accepted, as had
a provision for making nonmedical training or supervising analysts
regular members of the APA. Marianne Kris registered this progress,
and introduced Anna Freud to her next wish: "I have to find whether
it would be possible for the International Psychoanalytic to incorporate this association. It would be very nice if we were part of the
International."[74] To help the group keep its momentum, Anna Freud
agreed to chair its first scientific forum in April 1966, at the Menninger Clinic in Topeka.

While she was waiting to see what would come of Helen Ross's
work and Marianne Kris's Association, Anna Freud got an opportunity to contribute to the reform of child analytic training in another way. In 1966, she was approached through Jeanne Lampl-de
Groot by the Dutch Analytic Society, which wanted to establish a
child analytic training scheme. An arrangement was worked out for
a number of Hampstead analysts to fly regularly to Holland to supply
the scheme with the instructors the Dutch did not have within their
own ranks. This seemed a wonderful remedy in and of itself, and it
was well launched before it hit a formidable obstacle: because only
graduates of the Institute of Psychoanalysis had official standing in
Britain, and thus with the International, Hampstead graduates could
not be training analysts for Dutch candidates. The solution was
either recognition for the Hampstead program directly from the
International—something Anna Freud had always hoped would be
offered—or acceptance at an International Congress of the principle
of direct training for child analysis. Meanwhile, the Dutch initiative
could proceed only with help from Hampstead analysts who had
British Society membership—and that it did.

The result of the Dutch Society's initiative was the first child
analytic training program that aspired to make its graduates members
of a Society recognized by the International, and thus eligible for
membership in the International. Such an innovation was, of course,
widely—sometimes wildly—discussed before it reached the forum that
had to deal with it. That was the 1969 International Congress in
Rome, a Congress that Anna Freud had decided not to attend on
the grounds that the late July heat in Rome was not something a
seventy-three-year-old woman should have to endure. She had pre-

cious memories of the only other time she had tried Rome in August—1923, when she traveled with her father before his first major surgery—but those memories did not include comfortable temperatures.

The discussion in Rome was itself rather heated. All the speakers at the business meeting diplomatically stressed their confidence in the Dutch Society's program before they raised their objections. Michael Balint of the British Society expressed the most general fear: "What they have done and are proposing to do is to achieve a split inside analysis, distinguishing children from adults, distinguishing the psychoanalysis of children from the psychoanalysis of adults."[75] This position fit the Kleinian emphasis on the similarity of adult and child techniques, but it was held by a segment of the analytic population that went beyond Kleinian borders. Among the British, the fear connected with another, frankly articulated by Masud Khan: "If this precedent is set up, I see no reason why Miss Freud's . . . people trained at Hampstead should not qualify immediately. Should that happen, it would create such an imbalance in the British Society that it would be unmanageable." After the discussion had gone on for quite a time, it was clear that the majority favored a suggestion made by Michael Balint to the effect that the whole matter be the subject of a report for the next meeting.

Another decision crucial for the future of child analysis was made at the Rome meeting. The International's Executive had consulted with Anna Freud before the meeting to ask whether if the next meeting, in 1971, were to be held in Vienna she would attend. She had agreed, particularly because she had anticipated that action on the Dutch Society's initiative would be postponed. Looming on the horizon, she realized, was a historical coincidence fit for one of her father's old Jewish jokes: Vienna, where Anna Freud had begun her work as a child analyst, the lost home to which she had refused to return for more than thirty years, could be the place where the organizational fate of child analysis was to be decided. Romi Greenson said the concluding words to the Rome Congress debate about whether to have the next Congress in Paris, Mexico City, or Vienna: "I think as analysts who have any feeling of continuity with the origins of psychoanalysis, we ought to respect this very important historical and emotional factor." The vote was unanimous. And with

that vote, the fantasies shared in Anna Freud's circle since the Freud
Centenary, and the enormous efforts she and her friends and colleagues had made for the reality of recognized child analytic training, converged upon the "origins of psychoanalysis" and the birthplace, Vienna.

10

IN THE FACE
OF ENEMY FORCES

In the two years between the Rome Congress and the Congress scheduled for the end of July 1971 in Vienna, Anna Freud and her colleagues at Hampstead and in America worked intensely to make their shared wish come true: to gain for child analysis official recognition in proportion to the contribution they thought it had made to psychoanalytic theory and practice. Anna Freud had hoped for nearly forty years that child analysis would achieve the "triumphant career we had envisaged for it,"[1] and she knew that if her own authority were ever to contribute to a triumph over the attitude among the majority of adult analysts, she would have to give up her strategy of working only behind the scenes politically. As she was preparing for the Vienna Congress, she sent fair warning of her intentions to Leo Rangell, who had been elected president of the International Psychoanalytic Association in Rome: "There are many members who take the issue of child analysis very seriously . . . and who feel that the whole matter has been turned from a scientific issue into a political one. . . . On the occasion of former Congresses I have often acted as peacemaker, but I do not feel that I shall be able to take that role this time. I feel myself rather strongly about the issue and militant concerning it."[2]

Littlest children who are anxious to grow up fast and be as big as the bigger ones, as Anna Freud herself had been, do succeed in the course of things—even if they carry the traces of their fervent frustrations always in their unconsciousness. With the youngest sub-specialty of analysis, the matter was different. The majority of adult analysts had not sponsored its growth—and Anna Freud was realistic enough to realize that child analysis was far less likely to be success-ful in winning the love of adult analysts than she had been in win-ning her father's love for herself and for her work. As science in general threatens to disturb human illusions, the particular psycho-analytic science of child development threatened to disturb the illu-sions of unenlightened analysts. Carefully but firmly, Anna Freud charged: "It was difficult not to suspect that most analysts preferred the childhood images which emerged from their [analytic] interpre-tations to the real children [studied through child analysis and ob-servation] in whom they remained uninterested."[3] In this combative frame of mind, Anna Freud accepted the invitation of the Vienna Congress Planning Committee to give the plenary presentation and she prepared a brilliant scientific framework for the Congress's theme, aggression. But in this framework she showed that the vexed topic of aggression requires for its elucidation the insights of child analysis and observation—so the political point was forcefully made, and in the service of science as Anna Freud thought it should be. A further point was made as well. In her paper, Anna Freud never once men-tioned her own postwar writings on aggression, particularly on what the six little concentration camp survivors had taught her. But she drew upon this material and made it plain to those who could hear that adult analysis had contributed nothing in nearly thirty years to the exploration of the central questions she had posed after the war about how the aggressive and sexual instinctual drives interact, fusing and defusing.[4]

In addition to the authority she had as the key commentator at the Congress, as Sigmund Freud's daughter, as the training analyst of the most influential child analysts from Vienna, as the cofounder of the Hampstead Clinic, and as the author of one book univer-sally regarded as a classic and a *Writings* full of seminal papers, Anna Freud could deploy the authority she had as the person re-garded in Europe and America, by majorities of both psychiatrists and psychoanalysts, as their outstanding colleague.[5] She was still constrained by the Kleinian hostility within the British Society, by the medical prejudice against lay analysts, and by the adult analytic prejudice against child analysts, but her influence outside these psychoanalytic battlegrounds was without parallel. By the late 1960s, she had also gathered to her name enormous academic and popular recognition: she could sign herself, when she wished to impress her correspondents, as "Anna Freud, LL.D., Sc.D., CBE." The last initials referred to her appointment in 1967 as a Commander of the Order of the British Empire, an award that had never before been given to a psychoanalyst. Her title sounded like exactly what she needed to gain control over the British Psychoanalytical Society, but she contented herself with joking about the possibilities: "I am not yet used to my new rank and on the whole it seems safer not to try out the commanding. But all our friends are very pleased, especially about the official mention of psychoanalysis."[6]

Her policy of refusing interviews with newspaper, radio, or television journalists helped keep Anna Freud from having the fame that W. H. Auden had tartly disparaged as "public faces in private places"; and as she grew older—more stooped, frail, and wizened—she looked less and less obviously like a person with her worldwide renown. Once, standing at an American occasion with her old Vienna friends Grete Bibring and Jenny Waelder-Hall, she was enormously amused as her American host, who had never met her, twice guessed wrong about which of them was Miss Freud. Having met her, however, most people were deeply impressed. In 1966 she had arrived, for example, at the Topeka Psychoanalytic Society's Twentieth Anniversary celebration still bruised after an automobile accident in New Haven, but nonetheless amazed the young Kansas candidates: "None of us will ever forget the enthusiasm, vigor and diligence which you exemplified, despite the unfortunate accident prior to your arrival. The most prominent memory of your visit with us, however, remains the scope and depth of the psychoanalytic insights which you brought to bear on papers, discussions, case material, research projects, present problems and future plans which we were privileged to be able to discuss with you."[7]

Since the early 1950s, Anna Freud had traveled to America at least once every two years, each time making dozens of new acquaintances while she renewed her old associations. She occasionally attended meetings in Europe—usually in Holland—and kept apprised of developments within the European Psychoanalytical Federation, of which she became honorary president at the 1966 meeting in Geneva. Many younger analysts from both Europe and America had come to meet her at the Hampstead Clinic, which became the most important center for intellectual and spiritual renewal and for learning psychoanalytic research methods. Her presentations at the International Congresses were always among the highlights of the programs, especially as the programs grew in the 1960s to Gargantuan proportions. In an effort to bring some order to the agenda for Amsterdam, 1965, Robert Knight of Austen Riggs and his committee decided to focus on a single clinical topic, obsessional neurosis, and to have the contributions surveyed or summarized by one individual. For this role, the most respected discussant in the profession was chosen—Anna Freud— and her "Obsessional Neurosis: A Summary of Psychoanalytic Views" was so masterful that many felt compelled to thank her for it in writing. Anna Maenchen reported from San Francisco: "Everyone who was in Amsterdam speaks or writes in a letter how magnificent your concluding presentation was. In fact, they appreciated the papers they had listened to only after they had heard you place them into the proper context in the development of the history of psychoanalysis."[8] Heinz Hartmann noted more trenchantly that the entire Congress had, in an hour, been elevated from "the kindergarten of psychoanalysis" into a "postgraduate course."[9]

The enormously successful Amsterdam Congress, which to some degree restored the Viennese psychoanalytic elders' faith in the scientific usefulness of international meetings, was also the model for the Vienna Congress focus on aggression. Another echo from Amsterdam was the prominence of Dr. Samuel Ritvo of New Haven. In Amsterdam, Ritvo had presented a case study of a man who had been analyzed as a child by Berta Bornstein. His paper, in combination with a comment Bornstein prepared for Amsterdam, formed a ground for comparison with Sigmund Freud's famous case study of an obsessional neurotic, the so-called "Rat Man."[10] This core of the 1965 program had brilliantly exemplified how the insights of adult analysis and child analysis can and should complement each other. Ritvo took the exemplification a step further in Vienna. He headed the committee that had been mandated at the Rome Congress to present a report in Vienna on the current status and future possibilities of child analytic training.

While the Ritvo Committee was working to prepare its report, Anna Freud took the opportunity of a meeting convened by the European Psychoanalytic Federation to prepare a manifesto—a call for child analytic workers of the world to unite because they had nothing to lose but the institutional regulations that bound them. She pointed out that psychoanalysis, entering upon its sixth decade as an organized movement, was lively with theoretical controversies over almost all of its basic tenets and techniques. But, at the same time, the psychoanalytic institutes were trapped in the past.

> Whatever changes have occurred during the growth and development of our training institutions, they are not changes toward greater freedom or toward the introduction of new teaching methods. . . . Thus while there is revolution and almost anarchy in the field of theory and technique, there is rigidity, conservatism, and bureaucracy on the organizational side. The two may, in fact, not be unconnected. The more the scientific bonds between members and societies are falling apart in the absence of shared convictions and mutual understanding, the greater efforts are made, locally and internationally, to hold the membership together by means of increasing the number of rules and regulations.[11]

This situation, Anna Freud argued, was as detrimental to child analysis as to psychoanalysis in general. Like all other theoretical and technical innovations added to psychoanalysis as Freud had originally envisioned it, child analysis had supplied new knowledge to the parent science; but it was unique in that it had permitted verification or:

> checking up on the correctness of reconstructions in adult analysis. . . . Now, for the first time, with the direct application of psychoanalytic treatment to young children, what had been merely guessed at and inferred became a living, visible and demonstrable reality. . . . I think there was every justification to expect that all analysts of adults not only would be highly interested in these findings, but that they would also be eager to

share the experience of having direct analytic contact with children of all ages, and to compare what emerges in child analysis with their reconstructions—in short, to undergo a training in child analysis, additional to the training for adults which they have received, and to apply it, at least in a number of selected cases.

Surprisingly enough, this development failed to occur, in spite of its being the only logical consequence of the situation. The analysts of adults remained more or less aloof from child analysis, almost as if it were an inferior type of professional occupation.

In an era of organizational rigidification, this attitude became institutionalized so that the paucity of child training curricula or programs remained. Hampstead and the Tavistock Institute in London, the Katans' program in Cleveland, and Peter Neubauer's Child Development Center in New York existed as best they could and drew hope from Marianne Kris's Association for Child Psychoanalysis, but the Dutch Society's experiment stood out as the only one challenging the institutional inertia. In order for child analysts to flourish and also to gain adult analytic training—and for adult analysts to remedy the incompleteness of their own training—Institutes everywhere needed what Anna Freud called, simply but powerfully, "revolutionary overhaul."

This public manifesto ended on an optimistic note, but Anna Freud was not optimistic. The tides of the times were pulling against her cause, in spite of her personal prestige. Like the other papers given at the Geneva meeting of the European Psychoanalytic Federation, Anna Freud's manifesto had been designed as a provocation to thought before the Vienna Congress. The papers were to be published in French, English, and German prior to the Congress. But they did not appear, and a telephone call to the *International Journal* in London produced the information that the English versions would not appear until eighteen months after the Congress. In a cool letter to Mme. Evelyne Kestemberg, secretary of the Federation, Anna Freud asked for an explanation about this "matter which I find quite a bit upsetting."[12] After exchanges of politesse and profuse apologies, the French versions did appear a month before the Congress. Then Anna Freud's paper was prepared as a special reprint of the *International* so that it could be distributed in Vienna, just barely better late than never.

The Geneva debacle was followed by another. A First Conference of English-Speaking Psychoanalysts was scheduled for London by the British Society so that the relationship of adult and child analysis could be discussed. Originally, Anna Freud had declined to attend because the invitation reflected the condescending attitude toward Hampstead that still prevailed among certain of the Kleinians.[13] She was also still irritated from an episode in May 1970 when the Clinic Administration protested a series of remarks made during a British Society meeting about how the British Society was the only source of child analytic training in England.[14] This protest had received a curt little memo from the Society's Council that cited chapter and verse in the Society's Handbook to reassert that there was only one *official* training scheme in the United Kingdom.[15] Michael Balint, the Society's president, realized that Anna Freud had reason to be suspicious of the London conference given his Society's resort to legalisms, so he intervened to propose that the Hampstead analysts be given half the weekend's program and a mixed group of adult analysts the other.

Anna Freud was so astonished by this rare display of equity that she consented to participate. The program was then rearranged so that her group was given a mere two hours of the weekend conference for both her prepared talk and general discussion. In October 1970, at the conference itself, the two hours shrank to a bit more than one—just time for Anna Freud's talk and a brief, futile discussion. Balint wrote a letter full of rationalizations and regrets, to which she replied:

> I am also sorry things happened at the Conference as they did. I must say that for once I had really made an effort to cooperate with the [British] Society and it would have been nice if it had come out all right. . . . You are quite right that I should have objected when I received the program giving us 2 hours. . . . I hate to fight for the right to be included, especially when I feel that the other side is not too eager or willing. Perhaps it would have been better to do so in this case.[16]

This coolness was characteristic of Anna Freud, but when the International Association's newsletter did not mention her participation in its report of the conference the temperature of her response passed from cool to icy. She told the International's secretary, Frances Gitelson, "Of course I knew that it was the report from London which was responsible."[17]

The next British Society slight was produced by William Gillespie. As chair of the International Association's Committee on Constitution and By-Laws, he sent out a questionnaire to members asking for their assessments of the Dutch Society's initiative to secure membership in the International for graduates of its child analytic program. "I found the questionnaire so wrong that I did not even answer it," Anna Freud noted in a tired tone.[18] Because Gillespie was so obviously biased against the Dutch position, Jeanne Lampl-de Groot fired off a letter, with copies to everyone on the International's Executive, to make the displeasure of the Dutch plain to him. She then sent one to Leo Rangell, the president, asking him to consider that the International was about to debate not just the Dutch initiative but the future of Anna Freud's Hampstead Clinic. She asked why the International had never extended formal recognition to Hampstead, and proposed that it do so.[19]

When Anna Freud received copies of Jeanne Lampl-de Groot's barrage of epistles, she wrote directly to Rangell.

> I suppose that you would like to know what I feel about [Jeanne Lampl-de Groot's] proposal. I agree that I would have expected the I.P.A. to take some notice of my Clinic during the last twenty years, i.e., to welcome it at least officially as the pilot study in training which it represents. That in time it might become a nucleus of a new Society is not wholly impossible, though it may be premature to consider that possibility. What it really needs at present is the possibility to extend its activities in the direction outlined by Dr. Ritvo in his excellent report, i.e., to add to the training of our candidates two adult cases, so as to round off their training in child analysis. This, of course, would meet with strong opposition from the British Society. Is there any possibility that the American Psychoanalytical Association could give their backing to such a step? It will not surprise me very much if you say there is no such possibility in existence.

But that, especially if Dr. Ritvo's report is accepted by the [International] membership as it should be, leaves me and my co-workers again as complete outsiders.[20]

Both the International's rules as they stood and the agreement Anna Freud had reached after the war with the British Society made it impossible for her to offer her candidates adult analytic training at Hampstead. As she said to Ritvo: "Actually, if we were in the position to add adult training to what we are doing now in the Hampstead Clinic, we would come up to exactly the level of training which you outline in your report."[21]

WHILE she was urging forward the friends of child analysis and trying to disarm the foes, Anna Freud also gave a great deal of attention to the mise-en-scène of the drama that was to unfold. For some four years she had been in close communication with a group in Vienna, organized by Baron Musulin and aided by a Viennese émigré to America, Fredrick Hacker of the Hacker Clinic in Beverly Hills, that wanted to make a study center and museum out of the Freuds' old apartment, Berggasse 19. This project, which had support from the mayor of Vienna and from the Austrian chancellor, had initially given Anna Freud pause. She had consistently refused any public connection with Germany or Austria. When the Kultur-Referent of Munich wrote in 1964 to announce that the city—without informing her in advance—was bestowing on her its cultural prize and 15,000 German marks, she was very annoyed. But, in order not to make an issue of her refusal "for reasons obvious to me" to accept a German prize, she proposed a compromise: declining the prize in her own name, she asked that the money go to the International Psychoanalytic Association "for help with the reconstruction of psychoanalysis in Germany."[22] About proposals that the Hampstead Clinic make applications for German grants, she was uncompromisingly negative, even in the Clinic's darkest financial days. But the plan from Vienna connected with an old wish, wrapped in layers of nostalgia: that Vienna be a center for psychoanalysis.

Her only reservation was that the proposed Sigmund Freud Gesellschaft be coordinated with, and in no way in competition with, the small, struggling Vienna Psychoanalytic Society. Reassurances on this point came from all the plan's initiators. After consultation with her brothers, Ernst and Oliver, and with her sister, Mathilde, Anna Freud wrote a letter at once childlike and full of double meanings to the mayor of Vienna.

Sehr geehrter Herr Buergermeister,
Dass die Stadt Wien die Absicht hat, das Andenken meines Vaters zu ehren, ist mir eine grosse Freude und Genugtuung. Ich moechte Ihnen meinen herzlichen Dank dafuer aussprechen.[23]

That Vienna had the intention of honoring the memory of her father gave Anna Freud great joy and *Genugtuung*—a word that means simply satisfaction, but also compensation or reparation.

When the Freuds sanctioned the Gesellschaft plan, they also agreed to supply the museum with family books and art objects to prepare for the July 1971 opening. When Sigmund Freud and Ernst Kris had installed Freud's collection of antiquities in Maresfield Gardens, they had dispatched to the basement a box of odd or slightly damaged pieces; this *"salon des refusees,"* as Anna Freud called it, went to Vienna. Mathilde made provisions for the museum in her will. And while the Freuds were sorting out their testaments, they agreed to time their donation of a huge bundle of some 2,500 of their father's letters to Kurt Eissler's Sigmund Freud Archives for announcement at the Vienna Congress. Oliver did not live, however, to ratify this decision, and Ernst did not live to see it carried out.

After Martin's death in 1967, health troubles came to the older Freuds one after another. "What kind of a family have we become!" Mathilde lamented. "On which patient should one think first?"[24] Oliver and his wife had retired to Williamstown, Massachusetts, from their home in Philadelphia, but neither was well. Ernst continued to suffer from the aftereffects of his coronary and from his mysterious migraine headaches, which Romi Greenson was finally able to help with tranquilizers. Mathilde herself battled neuralgia and a heart condition that later required a pacemaker insertion.

When Oliver died in January 1969, Anna Freud went to Massachusetts, representing the family, and was forced to put Oliver's widow in a nursing home, where she died two years later. The entire trip was exhausting and made the family's exile and diaspora once again agonizing. Back in England, Anna Freud tried, to no avail, to help Dorothy's son Bob Burlingham survive an onslaught of heart disease and his recurrent asthma that threatened the balance he had tried to achieve through psychoanalytic work and antidepressant drugs. But after a painful, suicidal period, he died of his illnesses and his exhaustion at the end of February, leaving his second wife widowed and his first wife with their teenage children to look after. Dorothy Burlingham was in despair.

Anna Freud was again on the wrong side of the ocean when Ernst died in April 1970. Leaving her seminars at Yale, she flew to England for two days—but with a guilty heart: "I came too late. His widow is ill and confused, which made it a nightmare." Fortunately, Dorothy Burlingham was with her in New Haven, so that she could share her grief; but otherwise she kept it stoically to herself. "My brother Ernst died three days ago, with me here far away. I do not tell anybody [at Yale], since that makes it easier to work. He was my last brother. Now only my eldest sister and I are left. But that is how it is."[25]

Ernst's death marked the end of an era in the family for Anna Freud, for he was not only her favorite, but her collaborator, the one who had given as much care to their father's work as she had. Ernst's wife, Lucie, took his place on the board of Sigmund Freud Copyrights and worked feverishly to finish the project to which Ernst had dedicated his last years—a biography in pictures of their father, a complement to his edition of Freud's letters—but there was no one else in the family who could really share with Anna Freud their loyalty.[26] Except for Ernst Halberstadt-Freud, who had joined the staff at Hampstead, the Freud grandchildren in England were not interested in psychoanalysis. Sophie Freud Lowenstein, Martin's daughter in America, who had a degree in social work and taught in Boston, was interested but geographically distant. Sigmund Freud Copyrights was turned over to a literary agent, Mark Paterson, with oversight from a board of directors. Masud Khan, an aristocratic, Pakistan-born analyst, who had studied at Hampstead and been helpful to Anna Freud in his capacity as head of the Institute of Psychoanalysis Library, acted as her conscience on the Copyrights board.

Six weeks after Ernst's death, Heinz Hartmann died in New York after a long struggle with a failing heart. And then for more than a year the death toll went on and on, in the family and among

Anna Freud's colleagues: her old Hungarian friend Katá Levy, her analysand Elisabeth Geleerd Loewenstein, Max Schur, Hermann Nunberg; her cousin Rosi Waldinger's daughter Ruth, and then Rosi herself, then her cousin Harry Freud, Uncle Alexander's son, a spirited, generous family-minded man who had been for years a faithful correspondent from New York and a liaison to the Burlingham children.

In her mid-seventies, Anna Freud's letters contained, more and more frequently, reflections on aging and illness, on ways of living out one's decades and ways of dying. Only two years before his death, she had sent Max Schur a marvelous letter, to be read at the celebration of his seventieth birthday, in which the pendulum of her meditations swung back and forth, reckoning up the pleasures and the pains of old age.

> . . . Not all I have to say will make pleasant reading. When my father reached the figure of 80, and later my mother that of 90, people used to say to me: "What a wonderful age!" But, is old age in reality so wonderful? Is this not rather a myth, parallel to the "happiness of childhood," which is rare enough, or the "innocence of childhood," which, as we know, does not exist at all? Are not these rather exaggerated congratulations and felicitations of one's friends their way of denying the awe and fear of their own oncoming old age, or of hiding their contentment that this is still remote? . . .

> It would be dishonest to promise the entrant into the new decade that all will be smooth going; that there will be no illness; no gradual decrease in the spirit of adventure; that he will not, perhaps, find his daily work more of a strain; traveling more uncomfortable; his longing for holidays increasing; that his friends will not observe him surreptitiously for signs of bodily or—worse still—mental decline and that he himself will not watch his body and mind with the same suspicions.

> There will also be compensations, of course. People who, throughout their younger years, have suffered from shyness, or inhibitions, or lack of self-confidence find that, to their surprise, after 70 they begin to like themselves better, to be more content with themselves and tolerant towards the way they are, sometimes in addition to and sometimes instead of becoming from year to year more amenable and tolerant towards the ways of

others. Disharmonies and quarrels seem to matter less after 70; sometimes even disappointments and frustrations are survived more quickly.

Further—and this is not to be despised—after 70 it seems easier to find a seat in a crowded room, or to be listened to with some respect—or even to have one's parcels and luggage carried. by a younger person.

With such a mixture of good and bad experiences ahead, is it suprising that a 70th birthday is envisaged with mixed feelings? On the other hand, a 70th birthday (and, in fact, any other) is not a matter of choice. It happens and it is lived through like other happenings. . . .

I remember an occasion after one of my father's bigger operations when his younger brother [Alexander] presented him ceremoniously with a gold piece, inscribed like the medallions with which Austrian soldiers were decorated for bravery in battle. This impressed me then and comes to my mind again today. I think, if we, as his friends, celebrate Max Schur tonight ceremoniously, we should do so not only because he is seventy but because he has known how to weather storms, and we could do it with the words inscribed on that medal: "For Courageous Deportment in the Face of Enemy Forces."[27]

Max Schur was both too much associated with Sigmund Freud's illness and too problematically engaged in the writing of a biography of Sigmund Freud that Anna Freud disapproved of to receive the kind of light-handed, whimsical tribute Anna Freud sent to Helen Ross on her eightieth birthday.[28] She composed her letter for Helen Ross in late February 1970, in the midst of her family worries and also of a crucial set of grant proposals for the Clinic. With her powerful fantasy, Anna Freud transformed Helen Ross into not only the perfect director of the Hampstead Clinic, the solution to all its difficulties, but also the paragon of health and longevity.

. . . I do not really approve of the reason for this celebration. Watching myself as well as those nearest to me in recent years, I have learned to distrust the 70ies and 80ies, not to speak of the 90ies, as figures which stand for restriction, deprivation and frustration rather than for adventure, achievement and fulfillment. It is the latter, not the former, which I want for you and with which your image is connected in my mind.[29]

She then proceeded to imagine what Helen Ross might have been like at twenty, at thirty, at forty, and to play with the idea that it was, indeed, Helen Ross's fortieth and not her eightieth birthday that was being celebrated.

> I have a much better idea: I wish you to be 40 tonight, with at least a decade of hard analytic work behind you. On the strength of that, I invite you now to join the governing body of the Hampstead Child-Therapy Course and Clinic: to devise our plans with us; to set up our applications; to guide the disposal of our grants; to solve our staff problems; to write our annual reports; in short, to be not only our Founder (as you are in reality) but quite undisputed our Administrator-in-Charge. I hope you will accept. And if you do, I look forward to 40 more years of amicable, pleasurable, profitable and untroubled cooperation with you.
>
> Since even the most enjoyable excursion into wishful thinking will come to an end, I wake up from mine and return to the sober fact that this is your 80th birthday. It strikes me that what I have offered you are 40 additional years of active life and that, by doing so, I have behaved, without realizing it, on the basis of an ancient Jewish tradition. No orthodox Jew will ever mention the age of anybody dear to him without adding the pious, even though wholly unrealistic wish-formula: "Until 120!"
>
> With love, yours, Anna Freud.

WHEN she and Dorothy Burlingham arrived for the Congress, and checked in at the Hotel Regina, where psychoanalytic colleagues had always stayed when they came to visit her father in Vienna, Anna Freud brought both her grief and her whimsy with her. She escaped the hour-by-hour schedule Kurt Eissler had prepared for her in his self-appointed role as her manager—a role she did not want him to assume but which she could not bring herself to refuse him—and went to the museum with Lottie Newman, her editor, and Lottie's husband, Richard Newman, an analyst, for a quiet, unpublicized preview before her official scheduled visit. Berggasse 19 as a museum seemed to her something for the future, not of the past. Like the statue of Freud by Oscar Nemon that had recently been installed in a small park near the Hampstead Clinic, it provided, she had said, "a presence and image of him of greater permanancy than either nature or fate can bestow on human beings."[30] From the statue unveiling ceremony too, Martin and Oliver and Ernst were absent, so living memory seemed especially impermanent. Anna Freud had very pointedly made sure that her children from the Hampstead Nursery School did attend, and then she sent pictures of them looking up at her father's presence and image to all of her friends and colleagues.

The museum was for posterity, for duty, while for adventure there was a private performance, arranged especially for her, at Vienna's famed Spanish Riding School, where four white Lippizaner stallions and their red-coated handler appeared like creatures of her own youthful fantasy life. She told one of her Viennese contemporaries that it made her feel like a head of state to be given such a gift, to which he replied with proper Viennese gallantry in typical Viennese English: "I too love the Spanische Reitschule and certainly it is quite an extraordinary event to have a special performance, but, I think you are wrong when you say that it made you feel as if you were a head of state, because you are only of a different type of state and one that causes more good than bad, as many others do not."[31]

Anna Freud and Dorothy Burlingham visited in Vienna with old schoolmates of Anna Freud's and with members of the Austrian Ministry of Education; with members of Sigmund Freud's B'Nai B'Rith lodge, who asked Anna Freud to address a special meeting; and with émigré friends from Europe and America, many of whom were, like them, making their first return to the city from which they had fled. None of these activities was reported in the newspapers, where journalists competed in the game of making a legend out of what Anna Maenchen had called, in a letter to Anna Freud, "the sentimental journey of psychoanalysis."[32] Instead it was reported— and the report was then broadcast around the world—that during the City of Vienna's official reception for the 2,316 registrants of the International Psychoanalytic Congress, a lavish affair at the Rathaus, Anna Freud had danced a waltz. "In her youth," a typical story went on, "only the Kaiser and his guests could dance in these enormous rooms, beneath the huge crystal chandeliers and the ornate ceilings, between the baroque pillars and statues of Hapsburgs and their servitors."[33] Anna Freud, who had not attended the reception, much less danced a waltz, began on the second day of the Congress to retreat to a greater psychic distance.

More than she usually did, she had allowed herself to enjoy the
panoply of the public events, where she was everywhere applauded
and photographed and mythologized. The occasion had legitimized
a loosening of her tightly controlled pleasure in being the center of
attention, but she was just bemused when the analysts encouraged
the journalists in the mythmaking by piously presenting her with a
medallion inset with an ancient Greek coin picturing Pallas Athene,
Goddess of Wisdom. "The whole thing was not as bad or as difficult
as I expected it to be," she noted to Grete Bibring. "Naturally there
was a feeling of estrangement about it all, but perhaps it was this
which made it easier."[34] She was then in accord with the ambivalence of a dream she had had several months before the Congress:
"The anticipation of Vienna has brought me so far one curious
dream, reintroducing two Vienna streets which lead to Berggasse,
but in the dream never arrived there."[35]

MOST OF THE analysts who found the Vienna Congress so moving
and so mythologically exciting had no idea that their Pallas Athene,
while she joined them in celebrating a historical triumph for her father's creation, felt personally betrayed. The Ritvo Committee's report, which was ready in time for distribution at the Vienna Congress but not in time for a pre-Congress mailing, was the subject of
an intense exchange in a preparatory meeting of the International's
Executive Council. Anna Freud very much wanted the report to be
debated at the Congress in the business meeting; Leo Rangell very
much wanted open discussion of the report to be postponed until
the 1973 Congress, on the grounds that such a sensitive issue should
not be forced forward. He wanted—as he had been telling Anna
Freud by letter for many months—a peaceful Congress.

There was no peace in the closed session of the Executive Council. When Rangell announced to the open business meeting that
"the recommendation is for this report to be taken back by all members . . . for study, discussion and the rendering of an opinion in
a leisurely way in the next period of time" he was announcing his
own victory at the Executive Council meeting preceding. "[The re-

port] will also be open for discussion now," he went on, and there was a dead silence.[36] Anna Freud had decided to say nothing, just as she said nothing when Rangell announced that the Executive Council had accepted an application from the Hampstead Child Therapy Course and Clinic for "study group" status. This application marked a deal of last resort. Since no recognition of her Clinic had been forthcoming from the IPA, and discussion of training and membership in the IPA for child analysts was being so obviously blocked, Anna Freud had decided to set in motion the only alternative: a study group could, after some years, apply for the status of a component society, a regular training unit. Her application for study group status was a way to exert pressure and force her Clinic to the attention of the reluctant IPA. Not one of the journalistic reports on the Congress even mentioned that Hampstead's future and the future of child analysis had been at issue in Vienna.

Anna Freud's tactical retreat was, of course, deeply distressing to the majority of the British Society, for it meant that Hampstead might eventually become a second society in Britain, a rival. To prevent such a split, the British Society came forward after the Congress, for the first time since 1938, with a plan of reconciliation. The impetus for this plan came from the British Independents, or Middle Groupers, who feared that if the Anna Freudians had their own society the British Society would become the province of its Kleinians. Anna Freud reported the resulting agreement to Romi Greenson.

You will be interested to know that the British Society has made its peace with the Hampstead Clinic now. Largely to avoid our becoming a second Psychoanalytical Society in London, they have made very sensible advances to us and together we have worked out a compromise according to which the Society accepts a Hampstead Training Course in child analysis as their second official training course. They will also create better facilities for our graduates to take their adult training at the Institute. A document referring to this has been signed last week by Dr. Gillespie and myself, and both the Society and the Clinic are pleased. Following it I have withdrawn my application for Study Group status with the International and, as you know, I never wanted to be a study group anyway. What I had wanted originally was International recognition for the Hampstead Clinic's total organization, but since that proved impossible what is happening now is probably a good way out.[37]

The second deal represented a combination of Anna Freud's desires for independence and for affiliation. "The main point for me," she said to Kurt Eissler, "is that it leaves our organization intact and untouched, while securing for us the benefit of having an affiliation with the International."[38] The unspoken corollary was that Anna Freud's own group would not be torn internally by disagreements between those with sole loyalty to Hampstead and those with close ties to the British Society.

By the time she reported her news to Greenson, Anna Freud had made an effort to put her disappointment at the outcome of the Vienna Congress behind her and to go on to her next milestone, an international symposium to celebrate the twentieth anniversary of her Clinic. But she never lost her bitterness or revised her attitude toward the IPA. She offered her resignation from the Executive Council, but was kept from making even this much of a public protest by Leo Rangell, who proposed instead that she allow herself to be nominated as the successor to Ernest Jones and Heinz Hartmann in the position of honorary president of the organization. She acquiesced for the sake of whatever historical weight the honor might give to her cause. "You did not hear everything that went on in Vienna between me and the board of the International," she noted to Greenson. "But if you knew you would not be surprised that I have had enough of them."[39] To indicate her remove quite clearly, she refused to attend the 1973 Congress, which took place in Paris, where she was elected honorary president *in absentia*. So the postponed debate on the Ritvo report unfolded without her, and took exactly the course she had anticipated but had no power to influence.

The deal between the Hampstead Clinic and the British Society was invoked along with the Dutch training scheme in the Paris discussion. The general sense of that meeting was that such experiments in training were welcome. But the specific sense of the meeting, reflected in a vote, was that the Ritvo report was not acceptable. The vote of 118 to 71 indicated that child analysts with training in a component society's program would not, as members of the component society, automatically become members of the IPA. The status of child analysts was left just as it had always been, and there was no deal to resolve the matter—as there has been none since.

ONCE Anna Freud knew clearly how her cause stood in the International and in relation to the British Society, she went forward with plans to make sure that her Clinic suffered no infirmities of age in its third decade. She consolidated the Clinic's achievements of the 1960s and saw to it that a series of new initiatives kept the Clinic in its position of scientific leadership. Colleagues like Leo Rangell did not fail to register the critique her self-sufficiency implied, but they were never able to acknowledge it without disparagement. His public statements never disguised his attitude: "At one Hampstead Symposium," he noted, "Anna Freud stated, with somewhat less than complete objectivity, that the IPA and other organizations concentrate in their scientific programs on what is already known, while the Hampstead Clinic centers on the advance edge into the unknown."[40]

Disregarding such condescension, Anna Freud declared repeatedly after the Vienna Congress that the great unknown of psychoanalytic theory and practice was normal development. "When you come to London again," she told an American colleague, "I think you will be very interested in the Clinic's present work. Our interest, and especially mine, has veered quite markedly from psychopathology to normal development, and according to my feeling, that is the real field where child analysis should prove its worth."[41] Her basic idea was to push forward in the direction she had charted in *Normality and Pathology in Childhood* by studying child cases where the obstacles to normal development were particularly clear. She then wanted to apply the results of this work in two specific areas: childrearing practices and the emerging field of child and family law. Her hope was to indicate how consistently differences between adults' and children's experiences and views of the world are ignored in psychoanalysis itself and in the ways families and societies consider children. "I am reminded of something my father once said," she noted while explaining her concerns. "He spoke of how we bring up our children: . . . we supply them with a map of the Italian lakes and then send them off to the North Pole."[42]

But Anna Freud and her coworkers also knew full well that normal child development is no abstraction and no prescriptive program to be followed; it is for specific children in real social contexts. The social context of the late 1960s and 1970s presented challenges full of echoes of the 1930s, when the Jackson Nursery children had come from poor, often broken homes, where violence and addictions were common, and appropriate emotional and intellectual stimulation almost unknown. A majority of the Hampstead nursery children of the 1970s came from emigrant families making wrenching cultural and linguistic adjustments and from single-parent households. The adolescents studied by the Adolescent Research Group had severe eating disorders, including anorexia, and drug addictions. To serve these children, the Clinical Concept Research Group and their spin-off subgroups focused on language, acquisition, learning disturbances, problems of delinquency, promiscuity, and transvestism, on guilt and shame, lying, aggression turned against the self, and sadomasochistic behaviors. In the late 1970s new study groups responded to Anna Freud's interest in psychoanalysis and the law's child placement provisions by reviewing the Clinic's Index material on adopted children and trying to describe "the inner world of the adopted child." Both the Index Group and the Diagnostic Services unit responded to these evolving topical concerns by accumulating and sorting the relevant data in their charge. Many reports were published through a new journal designed to present the ongoing research—the *Bulletin of the Hampstead Clinic*, under Joseph Sandler's editorship.

Clinic papers continued to go off regularly to *The Psychoanalytic Study of the Child*, but the *Bulletin* was there for work in progress and for student papers. The student training was also reorganized so that each candidate could study and work at the Clinic full-time for the first three of the four-year course and then, in the fourth year, take the kinds of community service agency and hospital positions that had previously been offered to first-year students. Keeping the students in-house at the start of their training allowed the senior staff to make better use of the unique Hampstead teaching techniques: the candidates learned how to Index their cases and work with the Diagnostic Profile; and they attended the case conferences at which Anna Freud regularly made her memorable contributions. Her acumen was preserved in anecdotes that passed from generation to generation: all the students knew her comment about a child whose harassed, frenetic mother was pressing for Clinic help, "It is not quite clear yet whether the child needs analysis or the mother needs a housekeeper."

The Hampstead trainees of the 1970s also gathered a great deal of experience in projects designed to pursue Anna Freud's notion that "developmental pathology" should be distinguished from infantile neuroses. As observers in the nursery school, they could see physically handicapped children interacting with the emigrant children and with a few children from stable, two-parent middle-class homes who were important contributors to the often chaotic adjustments of the other children. The trainees could also participate in the program developed with High Wick Hospital to treat children so severely disturbed that the Clinic's psychoanalytic methods had to be carefully, experimentally adapted for them. To the existing research groups on atypical and borderline children were added groups focused on various kinds of psychosomatic disturbances and on the problems of children with diabetes. Finally, to explore differences between child and adult syndromes, the Clinic took on comparative analyses: a blind adult's analysis was compared to the results from analyses of blind children; two adult overeaters were compared with children who had been treated for eating disturbancees. Another group of adult cases used for comparative purposes came from hospital work directed by a Hampstead graduate, Thomas Freeman, with psychotics and heroin addicts.

Anna Freud and Dorothy Burlingham brought to the weekly case conferences, nursery meetings, and diagnostic discussions the impressions they had gathered in bimonthly meetings with a group of English pediatricians who presented their problematic cases for the psychoanalysts' comments and advice. But they also developed a program within the Clinic for providing the wider mental health community with lectures, visits, short courses, and consultations. Two of the Hampstead senior members, Mary Mason and Bianca Gordon, represented the Clinic and its research to any organization requesting information or instruction, while James and Joyce Robertson took films that they had made of children in hospitals on English and American tours to instruct doctors and nurses. The Clinic never obtained much in the way of British financial support, but it did achieve very great influence on the practical day-to-day work of hospitals and child welfare agencies. Anna Freud's emphasis on the importance of allowing parents to be with their children during the children's hospital stays, for example, had a great impact on changes made in English hospital policies that had allowed only brief visits. Similarly, a little book called *Children in the Hospital*, co-authored with a Vienna trainee, Thesi Bergmann, contributed to a psychoanalytic revolution in both English and American treatment protocols for children requiring long-term hospital care.[43] Again and again, Anna Freud's theme was, simply, that children should not be approached as small adults with mature abilities to comprehend surgery, invasions of their bodies, confinements, or separations.

There may have been an element of redress for the wrong she had suffered as an adolescent led off to an appendectomy without forewarning from her parents in Anna Freud's advocacy for psychoanalytic understanding applied to pediatrics. But Anna Freud's reformism was far more general, and it extended right to the heart of medical disregard for patients as persons in their own rights. "Miss Freud's comment in 1970, that medical work with children's health and ill-health was 'untouched by insight into the complicating emotional factors,' was salutary and largely true," one of the pediatricians noted appreciatively.[44] The group learned her lesson well and delighted in her forthright approach. One of her colleagues remembered, for example, a meeting during which a well-meaning specialist announced that he was going to discuss the case of a thirteeen-year-old girl with "hysterical aphonia manifested by expressive aphasia as a conversion symptom." Anna Freud stopped the presentation at that point to ask quietly but directly: "Why don't you say simply that this is a thirteen-year-old who developed an inability to speak?"[45]

THROUGHOUT the drama of the Vienna Congress and the new venue achieved between the Clinic and the British Society, Clifford Yorke both continued to serve as the psychiatrist-in-charge at the Clinic and undertook training as a child analyst. With his child analytic credential, he was, Anna Freud and Dorothy Burlingham decided, the right person to direct the Clinic in its third decade. They wanted stability and continuity—particularly after their great young

American hope, Seymour Lustman, died tragically in a 1971 boating accident and the possibility of a direct link with Yale's Child Study Center languished. But they also accepted Yorke's suggestion that Hansi Kennedy, a member of the Clinic's first graduating class and a therapist with twenty-five years of experience in every facet of the Clinic's work, should be codirector. This partnership was formalized in 1976, and Anna Freud took the opportunity to announce her retirement from the financial helm. Everyone on the staff knew this was a serious announcement when she also allowed herself the luxury of part-time secretarial help for her private correspondence and scientific writing. Gina Bon, the secretary, became a crucial internal support of the administration with the other half of her time.

The Clinic also got the local external support it needed in the form of Mr. G. G. Bunzl, a man with so many responsibilities that he rivaled Anna Freud herself in exemplifying his unusually commonsensical advice: "If you want something done, give it to a busy person." A few years before the Vienna Congress, this wealthy Austrian émigré businessman and philanthropist in Jewish causes had offered his services as a fund-raiser. During the 1970s he emerged as Kurt Eissler's counterpart in Britain, second superego, and formally took on the title Treasurer for the Clinic's board of directors, which then consisted of just the two founders, Dorothy Burlingham and Anna Freud. They gave Bunzl many practical problems large and small to solve, and were grateful too for the help he gave Anna Freud with investing her savings, which were limited because she had never accepted any salary for directing the Clinic. She came to trust Mr. Bunzl's advice and patronage as her father had once trusted Anton von Freund's, especially because he did not have Kurt Eissler's tendency to overstep his role.

G. G. Bunzl could not, however, do a thing about the international oil crisis of the mid-1970s and the inflation it brought to England and America. Anna Freud had hoped that the end of the Vietnam War would help her cause in America: "I really thought that there would be such a surplus of NIMH funds that what the Hampstead Clinic needs would only be a drop in the ocean. But that was optimistic."[46] In 1973, she did secure National Institute of Mental Health funding for two more years, but the money was not allocated with inflation in mind. Belts were tightened in every department of the Clinic. "I wonder what you hear or read about London at present," she asked an American friend. "We are in trouble in various ways, with heat, light, strikes, bombs and similar matters. Sometimes I think it is only the experience of the two world wars that I have behind me which makes me look at such occurrences as if they were an ordinary part of life."[47] She did not, however, sit in her Clinic office writing a sequel to *Civilization and Its Discontents:* "If you could look inside my head now," she wrote to Eissler, the provider, "you would find nothing neither clinical nor metapsychological data, merely figures."[48]

But, true to her psyche's old habits, beside the columns of figures there was a fantasy, and she wrote it down for G. G. Bunzl, who was on his way to a meeting in New York with Eissler.

> If you want to discuss not only facts with Dr. Eissler but also New Year's wishes, or new year's wishful thinking, utopias and pipe dreams, then I would say the following: could we not ever find in America three real millionaires who would endow the Clinic in a way which would diminish almost all of Dr. Eissler's and all of my money concerns for it, so that one could really foresee a future, at least one of ten or twenty years? Not that I wish or intend to hold out so long, but it would be so nice to know that the Clinic will. Dr. Eissler knows that at the time of the Vienna Congress I had cherished the hope that the International Psychoanalytical Association would somehow adopt the Clinic as one of its important concerns and help therefore to keep it alive. But nothing could have been further from the truth. So the whole burden is now really on Dr. Eissler and I cannot do much to share it or make it easier for him.[49]

No millionaires materialized, but, ironically enough, the Clinic did get a sizable portion of the tardily settled estate of Marilyn Monroe. The actress made the bequest to her New York analyst, Marianne Kris, in a will she had made while she was with her Los Angeles analyst, Romi Greenson, who had had to live with the fact of her suicide. Dr. Kris was instructed to give the money to the charity of her choice, and she chose the Hampstead Clinic. Greenson had turned in the same direction for comfort, and Anna Freud had given it by return mail.

I am terribly sorry about Marilyn Monroe. I know exactly how you feel because I had exactly the same thing happen with a patient of mine who took cyanide two days before I came back from America a few years ago. One goes over and over in one's head to find out where one could have done better and it leaves one with a terrible sense of being defeated. But, you know, I think in these cases we are really defeated by something which is stronger than we are and for which analysis, with all its powers, is too weak a weapon.[50]

MARILYN MONROE's bequest came to the Hampstead Clinic just while the Clinic was adjusting to the tremendously influential work that Anna Freud had undertaken outside the Clinic—work in which the plight of children, like the young Marilyn Monroe, who had been bounced from one foster home to another, was central.

In the 1960s Anna Freud had been offered a position at Yale University's Law School where two professors, Joseph Goldstein and Jay Katz, were teaching courses in family law and producing two volumes, *The Family and the Law* and *Psychoanalysis, Psychiatry and Law*, that helped make their area a standard one in American law schools. Jay Katz, the only practicing psychoanalyst in America with a law school appointment, and Joseph Goldstein, Professor of Law and a research graduate of the Western New England Institute for Psychoanalysis in New Haven, wanted Anna Freud to share their seminars for a month every other year and give their students the benefit of her clinical expertise and her knowledge of child development. Eugene Rostow, dean of the Law School, sent a formal invitation; Anna Freud accepted and then, during her stays, also accepted a characteristically long list of other invitations—even one to help in the preparation of a pamphlet, *Sex and the College Student*. Her energy left her hosts weary trying to keep up with her and to supply her constant demands for "more homework."

In her first visits, Anna Freud was more delighted with her student role than with her teaching one. Joining classes in criminal law, she considered cases of murder, treason, arson, rape, and armed robbery—exactly the kind of cases that had fascinated her old friend

Marie Bonaparte. Class after class of Yalies started out dismayed that their famous guest looked like a frail, wrinkled great-grand-mother and ended up humbled by how easily she outraced them mentally. For her part, she loved being with the young American men after they got used to her, for they flattered her by treating her as a normal mortal, someone who might like to go out for a pizza, ride a motorcycle, be presented with a Yale sweatshirt. The defer-ence that came her way in her own Clinic was something she toler-ated for the sake of not provoking jealousies, but did not enjoy; at Yale, she was freer, more like her vacation self.

What she learned in criminal law surprised her. She had two distinct impressions, which she sketched in a memorandum to her colleagues, a memorandum that shows clearly the way in which, for thirty years, Anna Freud had inspired the psychoanalytic research and application projects of her Clinic staff. She started off by indi-cating that psychoanalysts would approach criminals and delinquents with the assumption that their acts against the law could be under-stood as the outcome of an "internal constellation" acquired in child-hood. Criminal law brought this assumption up for questioning.

> When following the case histories of criminals brought to court in the Yale seminars, my impression was a very different one. In many of the instances scrutinized, one feels that the commit-ment of the actual criminal act is unnecessary, almost fortuitous, i.e., that there is usually a moment when the sequence of events could have been altered and deflected decisively by compara-tively minor intervention. That is, the tension which finds its outlet in the criminal act could either have been reduced (through human or therapeutic contact) or released through a different channel (mental conflict, neurotic symptom formation, depres-sion, etc.). This would not reduce the suffering of the individual necessarily, but might drastically reduce the actual commitment of acts which have to be brought before a court.
>
> This hypothesis rests on the assumption that there is, actu-ally, in a large number of cases such a point at which the con-stellation within the individual is not only favorable for inter-vention but also where there are manifest signs to betray this possibility. If this is true, a new system of "crime prevention" could be based on it, comparable to the existing schemes for the detection of the earliest signs of cancer and tuberculosis.[51]

The hypothesis Anna Freud outlined in this memorandum, in which she was also *inter linea* invoking the doctors who had made timely interventions to help her father's cancer and Dorothy's tuberculosis, was not the research focus the Yale colleagues eventually decided on. Albert Solnit and Seymour Lustman helped swing the balance of her interests back to her home ground, child development, and in the late 1960s her appointments at Yale were cosponsored by the Child Study Center and by Davenport College, where Lustman was the master. While she was witnessing nonviolent protest preparations for Yale's May 1970 anti-Vietnam War demonstrations, she prepared seminars on "The Child and the Law" and discussed with her colleagues a collection of essays that might focus on how courts construe cases involving the criterion "in the best interests of the child." The book possibility went through many transformations and finally, after Lustman's death, turned into an adventure in co-authorship with Goldstein and Solnit. They produced what she called "our common child," *Beyond the Best Interests of the Child*.[52]

The co-authors did their preparatory work at Yale and then via airmail exchanged case materials and legal papers, newspaper articles, and social welfare agency reports. To prepare for their writing meetings—about a dozen between 1969 and 1973—Anna Freud did her homework with her usual conscientiousness and sent off short papers full of simply expressed psychoanalytic definitions and reflections on cases. The three authors represented their main competencies—law, pediatrics, and psychoanalysis—while they shared the psychoanalytic perspective. But they found that they had to invent a persona when they wanted to speak in unison. So they created Judge Baltimore, named after the small Irish town near the Freud-Burlingham country house, where they often met to argue themselves into agreement. The common child, then, had not only its two young fathers but, importantly for Anna Freud, an older father who lived in fantasy.

Dorothy Burlingham not only participated in all the Irish discussions but provided a preface, which she sent off to the Yale partners with a wry remark: "Anna has worked on it and taken out some of the less serious bits that I had put into it."[53] So, everyone had his or her role, and the arrangement was so satisfying that two siblings followed: *Before the Best Interests of the Child* and *In the Best Interests of the Child*.

Her collaboration with Goldstein and Solnit was one of the great joys of Anna Freud's last years. They were fun, informal, and fell naturally into the first-name familiarity that others before them had felt compelled to request. She sometimes felt too tired and over-burdened to do much writing without what she called "the prompting" of their energy, their materials, and their drafts.[54] While her vitality when she was with them amazed them, she felt she had to keep being frank: "the book and I have a sort of competition: who will finish first?"[55]

THE first of the three joint volumes was the one that had the most sustained impact on American, and later (to a lesser extent) British, legislators, lawyers, judges, and social service agencies. It was, as one American reviewer claimed, "certainly the most discussed book on law and family ever published in this country," and this was so not just because it was a simply and powerfully argued book but because it came at the right moment.[56] The perspective it presented was slowly beginning to emerge as part of the social and political upheaval of the 1960s.

That perspective, put briefly, was that children's not parents' needs must be primary in any decisions made to resolve contests over their placements. Children's needs should be satisfied by their "psychological parents," the one or ones who truly want and value them, and with whom they feel truly wanted and valued, whether or not the "psychological parents" are the biological parents. "The law must make the child's needs paramount" was not a new premise, but the coauthors sustained it by arguments and examples against decisions in which adults' interests had, in fact, been made paramount. They argued for replacing the vague "in the best interests of the child" criterion with "the least detrimental available alternative for safeguarding the child's growth and development," a formulation designed to convey that a child being considered by a court is already at risk, already a victim, and that no decision fashioned upon competing adult claims about what is in the child's best interests can truly focus on the child's immediate and long-term physical and especially emotional needs.

Beyond the Best Interests of the Child reflected one of the key themes of Anna Freud's research at the Hampstead Clinic: a child's needs and feeling about his or her situation must not be judged by the standards of adult experience; the difference between adult and child psychology must be taken into account for the child's sake. A child's sense of time, for example, cannot compass a postponed decision or a year of probation in an adoption or a month away from a "psychological parent." A child's need for continuity can mean that a series of temporary foster placements ruins the child's capacity for forming strong bonds. Custody decisions that divide the child between warring adults or undermine the designated custodian's authority can completely confuse a child, whose notions of presence and absence, acceptance and rejection are not the same as an adult's.

The attacks that *Beyond the Best Interests of the Child* made on such sacred items as the "natural" rights of biological parents, and such cherished experiments as joint custody and court-mandated visiting rights for noncustodial parents, were strong and in several instances much too swift. The book's aim was legal reform (it includes a Model Child Placement Statute) and it made no pretense to consideration of a variety of cases; but its illustrative cases did not cover all its claims, and some of its most provocative recommendations came in bare, clipped legalistic paragraphs in which Anna Freud's usual psychoanalytic circumspection was at a minimum. So many reviewers singled out for criticism the recommendation that a parent granted custody have the right to control visitation by the noncustodial parent that the authors added a discussion of the proposition in a second edition of their book. But this statement too was very terse, even for readers who granted the claim that a parent's authority is undermined who is not able to make crucial decisions about his or her child's welfare. Nonetheless, the book's general perspective was clear and persuasive, which was quite enough to give it tremendous influence.[57]

The two succeeding volumes had different agendas. *Before the Best Interests of the Child* discussed questions that arise before a child ends up the subject of a placement decision. Its theme was that state intervention to remove children from established relationships with their psychological parents should be strictly limited to "gross failures of parental care." The authors tried to delineate specifically the kinds of abandonment, violence, and insane or criminal behavior over which state intervention is necessary, and also the kinds of parental behavior that, even if questionable or troubling, should not be grounds for intervention. Steering a middle course between too little and too much intervention and trying to map "the muddled and badly defined situation," they recommend intervention "if and only if it provides the child in jeopardy with a less detrimental alternative." This stance required, as they noted, an emphatic attempt "to place ourselves in the position of children of different ages, of different developmental phases, and of different backgrounds," and to consider from these vantage points the problems of intervention, adjudication, and placement. The difficulties— many and agonizing—that anyone involved professionally in a contested child placement decision will encounter were the subject of *In the Best Interests of the Child*. This third volume of the trilogy is like a field manual for lawyers, judges, social agency workers, child psychiatrists, and expert witnesses, but it aims beyond the kind of questions and dilemmas that arise in placement processes to the psychology of decision makers. This larger, deeper aim is not just a matter of reemphasizing the differences between adult's views and children's needs. The book speaks frankly about how often personal views color professional decisions, how rescue fantasies carry professionals into overestimations of their competences and their roles, which they can confuse with the parental role. In simple terms, the authors make a plea for professional modesty, which means a plea for self-knowledge and a constant recognition that the science of child development is not a panacea.

ANNA FREUD was able to dedicate herself to the collaborative work with Joseph Goldstein and Albert Solnit (and, for the last volume, with Sonja Goldstein) because she and Dorothy Burlingham had worked to shift their administrative responsibilities at the Hampstead Clinic to their successors. With her coworkers beginning to take the administrative and financial reins, Anna Freud felt able to greet 1975 and the start of her ninth decade with feelings less mixed with anxiety about the Clinic than she had expected. But she vacillated between wanting to retire even more thoroughly and wanting to stay on as the director; between wanting unending peaceful holidays and wanting to keep her unchallengeable control; between wanting to continue trying to secure the Clinic's perpetuity come what may and wanting the Clinic to last only as long as it could last after her generation ceased to animate it with their fervor and their loyalty. When Manna Friedmann declared that she was going to retire as head of the nursery at the unthinkably young age of sixty, Anna Freud thought of closing the little school. Overseeing a transition to a new teacher after twenty-one years seemed too much to undertake. But then she reconsidered, hired a splendidly capable young American named Nancy Brenner, and urged her favorite project into a renewed life. On the one hand, she frankly envied Manna Friedmann her freedom; on the other hand, she talked about following the advice her father had garnered out of Shakespeare's *Macbeth*—she would "die in harness" and forgo premature division of her kingdom.

In her old age, Anna Freud had the "age appropriate" reedition of her youthful ambivalences: she could move along cautiously or she could be an adventurer to the last; she could make herself lovable with superconscientious dedication, or she could retreat to an island of fantasy and handicrafts. But in her youth she had never been able to find her way by humor out of the tension these possibilities generated. In her old age she joked about how to produce inner reconciliation: she and Dorothy would move to their country house in Ireland and found there the County Cork Psychoanalytical Society, a brilliant scientific initiative, limited to two members but welcoming selected visitors. She also viewed it as something of a joke that she took more and more of her adventures lying down: she read late into the night almost every night, devouring one mystery novel after another, not always preferring psychological subtlety over exotic locales and sheer mayhem. Not even a series of novels featuring a female detective rather than the male ones with whom Anna Freud found it easy to identify diminished her enjoyment. Dorothy did not share "the detective story addiction," but she devotedly visited secondhand bookshops and bought thrillers by the stack to supply her friend's habit.[58]

But even as they joked, the old partners felt increasingly vulnerable. As they drove back to London from their Walberswick fantasy house one rainy, foggy weekend at the end of October 1973, a car came sliding down a slick hillside and rammed them broadside. Dorothy, who was in the passenger seat, was so badly bruised and cut that she had to spend a week in a wheelchair. Anna Freud was jolted, and her back, which had been troublesome the year before because of a slipped disk, gave her months of pain. The friends had come so near to dying together that Anna Freud felt their oneness deeply, and expressed it often: "But we are still in one piece, each of us."[59] She worried that her habitual fast driving had contributed to the accident, and she wondered if they were too old for the escapes to the countryside that had always given them such pleasure. The answer to this question was no, but Anna Freud did not finally deliver it to herself until the police investigator declared that she bore no responsibility for the accident. Being an experienced self-analyzer, Anna Freud had been quite ready to declare that her unconscious had dictated "a child is being beaten." She even joked wryly with long-time colleague Ilse Hellman, who telephoned to offer a sympathy visit: "I am certainly not lonely," she said, "I have my pain." "It helped me a great deal that the police declared me, who was driving, as the nonguilty party," she noted at the end of this episode.[60] Dorothy Burlingham, with only her body's brittleness to lament, recovered slowly but more easily.

That winter, however, brought Dorothy Burlingham a grief from which she never recovered. After her son Bob's death, there had been a period of relative peace in her complex family. She had celebrated her eightieth birthday in 1971 with a gathering of her three remaining children, acknowledgments from the many colleagues who were grateful for her warmth and wisdom, and an edition of her collected essays, *Psychoanalytic Studies of the Sighted and the Blind*. But this happy time had then been overshadowed as she slowly realized that her older daughter, Mabbie, then fifty-seven, was in a deep, dangerous turmoil. Mabbie wrote letters about her marital discord and new versions of her old questions about why she was never able to focus her many talents into a profession. Trying to keep her balance, she analyzed her condition in her letters, sometimes drawing on stories Anna Freud had told her, like the one Sigmund Freud had offered to describe marriage: it is like the endless problem of hedgehogs, when they get too close they prick each other, then they move apart, and then they try again to get close.

Her husband, Simon Schmiderer, had had a heart attack while they were residing in Puerto Rico, which Mabbie had loved as a place to live, and the couple had agreed to return to New York and its medical facilities. Mabbie reworked a recurrent and troubling idea that she might have filled up the empty spaces in her life with another child; her husband assuaged his fears by being rational and in control; the extended family wondered if this was a "menopausal depression." Desperate, Mabbie cried out for help and went to England for three weeks in February 1974 to be with her mother and to work analytically with Anna Freud. Then she was unable to decide whether to continue analysis in New York with Marianne Kris, as Anna Freud suggested. Over the course of nearly twenty-five years, Anna Freud had been trying to convince Mabbie that she would benefit from having an analyst less than an ocean away, but this had only produced in Mabbie the feeling that she was being rejected by "Mother Anna Freud."

Rather than insist, Anna Freud had remained there as Mabbie's part-time analyst during most of their summer reunions; and the arrangement had provoked in Simon Schmiderer a good deal of resentment. The problems of a kind of stepparent analyzing her stepchildren, to which Anna Freud's own experience with her father leant visions of solution, were by no means suppressed in Anna Freud's work with Mabbie Schmiderer, or with Bob Burlingham earlier, before he had agreed to see another analyst. But Mabbie neither freed herself nor was she freed of the fact that Anna Freud was not just her analyst but the person to whom her mother gave unstinting devotion—a figure for deep jealousy—and the beloved person whose houses were in a very elementary way home. Waves of gratitude and waves of anger surged, one after the other, through Mabbie Schmiderer's letters.

In the spring of 1974, Mabbie sent pages of her tumultuous feelings to Anna Freud, made a brief trip to England with her husband, sporadically went to see Marianne Kris in New York, wanted to be with her husband and her grown children, and wanted to be with her mother. She felt herself in the grip of an old battle, an internalized version of the one waged between her psychotic, suicidal father's camp, in America, and her mother's, abroad with the healers, the Freuds. Finally she went back to England just before the August 1974 summer holiday was to begin, so that Anna Freud could see her during the Walberswick month. But while her mother and Anna Freud were still busy closing down the Clinic, she took an overdose of sleeping pills.

Mabbie lay unconscious in a hospital for nearly four days, regained consciousness for three days, and then died. Dorothy Burlingham's younger children, Tinky and Michael, came immediately, and she was grateful; but the suicide of the child she had always favored—who was Anna Freud's favorite too—was just devastating. To all the friends who kindly sent their condolences, she wrote poignant notes, often revealing how much she had loved her daughter's mothering: "It is very hard to imagine life without her caring continually about what I was doing and sharing it with me. Tinky is shattered too, they were very close."[61] Anna Freud summoned her stoicism and also attributed it to her twin, Dorothy: "Dorothy behaves like a stoic, doing what has to be done. But it is a hurt that will never go away."[62] Mathilde Freud Hollitscher went into the hospital for her pacemaker in August; then one of Bob Burlingham's daughters, Lynn, suffered a spinal injury in an accident that September—and a kind of pall fell over 20 Maresfield Gardens.

During the next year, while she was continuing as the scientific chief at the Clinic, working with Goldstein and Solnit, and taking up one editorial task after another on publications of Sigmund Freud's correspondence with Jung and with Lou Andreas-Salomé, Anna Freud began to feel uncharacteristically fatigued and dispirited. Her friend Josefine Stross and a second doctor, Tony Toszeghi, who was Anton von Freund's son, were unable to make a sure diagnosis, but they did effectively treat her with iron tablets for anemia. A medical watch on her hemoglobin level began, and by the summer of 1976 it was declared normal and Toszeghi happily announced to Josefine Stross that "it looks as if Anna's undiagnosed illness was over and finished."[63] When the hemoglobin level took a plunge the next year, they were baffled again. Iron treatments alone proved ineffective, so Anna Freud launched upon an ordeal: periodic blood transfusions requiring hospital stays of a few days to a week. She wrote to Anny Katan in October 1978:

You ask how my blood behaves. Well, I must say it does not behave too well. It was 8 before we went to Ireland, but we did not want to stay home for a transfusion. It was somewhat less when we came back, and then it suddenly dropped quite dramatically to 5½. This meant that I had to go to hospital as an emergency for a transfusion and I did not enjoy that. Now I am home again and the next thing we are trying is iron injections, which seem to work better than anything before. In any case, I have climbed to 8 again.[64]

Anna Freud gave her illness, which bore the name chronic iron deficiency anemia but remained a causal mystery, the same kind of scientific scrutiny her father had given his as she, like him, underwent treatment after treatment to keep it at bay. "There are days when one feels full of energy and able to do almost anything, and other days when all one wants is to be left in peace."[65] Daily planning became very difficult, travel was risky, and humor was hard to come by; she felt displaced from the center of her world. "I just want to tell you how much I enjoyed your small article in *The Observer* about name-dropping," she wrote on a so-so day to Stephen Spender. "What you describe is exactly what happens to me, namely not only that people treat me as a relic, but that they are quite surprised that I am still alive."[66]

Even the honors and public recognitions that had always given her pleasure seemed a mixed blessing. She was careful to bear her trouble with her father's equanimity, and she turned to one of her mother's favorite proverbs for expressing—obliquely—her annoyance: thanking the Foundations' Fund for Research in Psychiatry for an award, she asked, "I wonder whether you know the North German proverb that 'one receives a good soup when one is ill, and a good name when one is dead.' With this in mind, I feel that I am receiving the latter part too early."[67] All that she could do was hope that her mind would not be affected. "So long as body and mind function, age does not matter so much, and even if the body begins to give up, one can still put one's trust in the mind. That is what I am doing at present."[68]

Anna Freud's trust was shaken and her heart wrenched as her sister, Mathilde, declined very rapidly, physically and mentally, following a December 1977 operation. After two months in terrible pain, she died. Anna Freud, who had visited Mathilde daily and spent many hours on the telephone with her companion, Tini, was exhausted and distraught. Her sister's death revived the four sibling deaths that had preceded—all of which had taken place out of Anna Freud's presence—and it made her feel disoriented. "I was always the littlest, and now I am the only child," she told a friend. Her own illness she had to face without the comfort of her sister's steadiness and reasonableness; and she knew she would die as the only child.

Hard as it was for Anna Freud to endure a disease that sapped her legendary energy and made her dependent on hospital stays and transfusions, she committed herself to being as stoical as her father had been in his last years. And she took over one of his favorite stories to say how she intended to keep herself from wishful thinking if she began to lose her battle despite her courageous deportment in the face of enemy forces. This is how she told "Death in Ispahan" to a friend:

There lived a man in Persia who, one day when walking in the street, saw Death walking on the other side. Death waved to him. That gave him a terrible shock, and he ran to a friend and said, "Please, can you lend me your fastest horse, so that I can ride away to Ispahan and hide there. I met Death today in the street, he waved to me, and that must have meant he is coming for me. Perhaps I can escape."

So the friend lent him the horse, and he rode away to Ispahan. But in the evening there Death came for him. He was terrified and said: "I thought I had escaped you. Why did you wave to me today?" And Death said: "I did not wave. I made a gesture of astonishment, since I had received orders to fetch you in the evening in Ispahan, and there you were in the morning, still so far away from the place."[69]

11

FUTURE AND PAST

During the years when she was so disappointed by the outcome of the 1971 Vienna Congress and so concerned with protecting her Clinic's independence and self-sufficiency, Anna Freud had the comfort of her father's presence through his letters to Jung, which she was rereading as German and English editions of the Freud/Jung correspondence were being prepared. Since 1955, when she had first read the surviving correspondence, she had been looking forward to its publication. The work William McGuire, the editor, did to help her check Ralph Manheim's Freud translations and to annotate the volume pleased Anna Freud enormously and made the correspondence, as she said, "truly into a history of the beginnings of psychoanalysis, something that was very much needed and is not given anywhere else with the same attention to detail."[1]

Comforting as it was to have the correspondence, its conclusion, in which the relationship between Freud and Jung grew gradually more taut and then snapped, always left Anna Freud pensive. "I can never read the end of this correspondence without getting quite sad and depressed about the turn it takes."[2] She felt her father's disappointment in Jung as her own, and she also connected her own struggle of her father's pre–World War I years. The lesson of the correspondence was not to expect too much of the next generation, not to put too much pressure on the "heirs." Reading in the correspondence how much hope her father had placed on Jung's personal charm and great talents, Anna Freud was reconfirmed in her personal policy: "not to make public pronouncements about the past or future of psychoanalytic work and other people's part in it. As a subject, it is much too complex and too many opinions of the positive or negative kind are vented about it anyway."[3]

Privately, she was not so restrained. When Harold Blum, the editor of the *Journal of the American Psychoanalytic Association*, sent her his critical assessment of the 1975 International Congress, which was held in London, she replied frankly:

> My attitude towards the opinions expressed there were even more negative than yours. Where you still give them the benefit of the doubt, I am afraid I am already fully convinced that most of the avenues of thought presented to us do not lead to anything constructive. I think that instead of further developing psychoanalytic thought there is a definite tendency to destroy the gains and advances which have been made already, and to substitute for them something less valuable. The difficulty which you as well as I meet in discussion is of course that all these so-called advances are made under the flag of progress, and that threfore anybody who does not welcome them is looked at as "orthodox" and "conservative," which I believe neither you nor I are.[4]

What Blum and Anna Freud were chiefly agreeing about was the appearance in psychoanalytic discourse of what he called "mysticism and obscurity," just the characteristics Freud had deplored in Jung's work. But she also objected to the enormous attention paid to psychoanalysts themselves, not just in the analytic context, but in general. After the London Congress, she was invited to a symposium convened in Surrey by the International Executive, the members of which felt that the low level of the London Congress called for a review and an effort at consensus for the future. "I had hesitated at first whether to come to Haslemere . . . but then I read the prepublished papers, and I saw that there is no sense in it for me. I have nothing to add to the question of the identity of the psycho-

analyst, because for me that is self-evident and whoever puts all these
queries and arguments evidently has lost his satisfaction in analysis
already."[5]

But Anna Freud's rejection of her colleagues' personalized quest
for identity was just a part of her hope that questions about the identity of psychoanalysis itself would be properly framed. She recognized
that the key site of controversy in the 1970s among analysts of adults
was, at bottom, technical. Analysts who were making efforts to treat
borderline patients and psychotics psychoanalytically were constantly
faced with a decision: to modify the theory and technique or to
acknowledge that the theory could comprehend more than the technique could cure. In her own work, Anna Freud had for more than
a decade been giving careful attention to developmental pathologies,
a domain quite different from that of the infantile neuroses that her
father had explored. She admitted, however, that while the developmental pathologies could be mapped or reconstructed with extrapo-
lations from classical psychoanalytic theory—chiefly, with her own
concept of developmental lines—they could very seldom be cured
with standard child analytic techniques. She and her coworkers experimented with modifications of technique, but they never felt that
these modifications cast the original child analytic techniques in
question. Techniques that can cure an infantile neurosis and techniques that have some effect on a developmental pathology work in
different ways. Other analysts "doubt the value of our psychoanalytic
tenets if therapeutically they prove to be applicable only to a restricted field." These analysts, for whom André Green of Paris was
the spokesperson at the London Congress, saw that "a positive future
of psychoanalysis was dependent on therapeutic ambition and expansion."[6] Many of these analysts found the Kleinian methods appealing
because they assumed a direct relationship between early infant
psychic states and adult psychoses, and some, like Green, suggested
methods similar to those Sandor Ferenczi had tried toward the end
of his life: re-creations of mother-child relations in the analytic situation, complete with overt displays of affection designed to repair
retroactively early childhood deprivations or experiences of abuse.

When the Hebrew University in Jerusalem decided to establish
a chair in psychoanalysis to be inaugurated at the time of the 1977
International Congress, set for Jerusalem, Anna Freud reiterated her

annoyance with the would-be innovators in psychoanalysis. "Of course everybody is curious who the elected man will be," she wrote to Rafael Moses, head of the committee charged with filling the position. "If it had been 30 or 40 years earlier, I suppose I would have applied," she added in her own rather masculine adventurer mode. "Now I shall be content if it is a recognized and hard-working psychoanalyst who will teach and build on the basic and indispensable principles and elements of psychoanalysis and not only propagate some latest theories of his own. This is unfortunately what has happened here in a similarly donated psychoanalytic lectureship that has been established at London University."[7] Anna Freud agreed with the assessment her old friend J. C. Hill, in his nineties but as clear as ever in his convictions, rendered after he had been to hear one of the London University lectures that Lord David Astor had endowed: "I have no patience with this post-Freudian psychology, which usually consists of Freud's psychology with all the difficult parts left out."[8]

Anna Freud found a constructive outlet for her own lack of patience in a project proposed by Fischer Verlag in Germany. The publishing house wanted to bring out a two-volume edition of Freud's papers, selected and introduced by Anna Freud. In 1977, when she was eighty-two, she wrote her introduction, "A Study Guide to Freud's Writings," one of her most lucid educational efforts, a summation of the way in which she had, earlier in her career, guided class after class of candidates to her father's work. In this piece, Anna Freud also addressed one of the main extramural sources for questions about the theory and therapy of psychoanalysis—namely, feminism. "Representatives of this movement experience [Freud's] theory as an affront and a depreciation, very similar to how formerly the representatives of the ideal of 'innocent childhood' reacted to the theory of infantile sexuality."[9]

With this brief introduction, Anna Freud set out to explicate, stressing its developmental basis, the main tenet of Freud's theory of sexual difference and to compare it to her understanding of feminist theory.

In fact, psychoanalysis and the women's movement differ in their essential propositions. On the one hand, Freud stressed the bisexual disposition of all human beings; on the other, he was convinced that anatomy determined whether predominantly male or female qualities would be developed and prepare the individual for his or her differing future life tasks. As little as the sexual manifestations of boys and girls differ from each other in the oral and anal phases, as significant is the marked dissimilarity in the phallic phase during which the anatomical equipment of the female child puts her at a disadvantage in relations to the possessor of the phallus, as far as masturbatory and exhibitionistic pleasures are concerned. While the boy who highly values his sexual organ is exposed to castration anxiety, the girl in turn develops penis envy and the wish for a substitute for what has been withheld from her, a wish that ultimately culminates in the wish to have a child.

The pre-stages of the female sexuality which Freud reconstructed, piece by piece, on the basis of data gained in the analysis of female patients, are simply brushed aside by liberated women, who deem them the result of male chauvinistic prejudice. They deny the existence of any inherited difference between man and woman and explain the appearance of early unlikeness as the exclusive result of social influences on upbringing which push the girl to play with dolls and propel the boy toward interest in motors, soldiers, and war games. The anatomical difference between penis and vagina, between impregnation and giving birth, and its decisive impact on psychic development are pushed aside in the passionate efforts to free women from the subjugation in which they have in fact been held for centuries and to put women in a position that in every respect equals that of their male partners.

Denial of inherited difference was, of course, only one version—and not the predominant one—of the feminist critique of Freud that began after the Second World War and gathered great momentum in the 1970s. Anna Freud's presentation of the critique is a great simplification. It both underplays the main feminist complaint—quite legitimate—that male development has often served psychoanalytic theory as the paradigm of development, and shows no awareness that female psychology was, as Freud himself had admitted, an area in need of clinical and theoretical exploration, particularly by female analysts. But she also did not indicate that her explanation of why girls feel disadvantaged—because of the "masturbatory and exhibitionistic pleasures" provided boys by their penises—was quite differently focused than her father's emphasis on the girl's feeling that she is castrated. The girl's "phallic stage" had been the topic of many discussions in the Clinic, culminating in two fine papers by Rose Edgcumbe and Marion Burgner, and Anna Freud was echoing the staff's important, shared revisionist conclusions.[10]

On the other hand, she did state clearly the one area of her father's theorizing about women that was, she felt, obsolete, a product of his historical context: "Some of Freud's remarks relating to the attitude of women to cultural tasks are a consequence of the exclusion of women from the professional life of men in his times and as a description are no longer valid in our times when all possible professional activities, in business, medicine, the law, or as a head of state, are open to women." How the equality women had enjoyed from her own generation forward as Freud's collaborators and in psychoanalytic institutes squared with Freud's remarks on the attitude of women to cultural tasks, Anna Freud did not indicate. The professional success of women analysts—including Anna Freud herself—had never been taken by Freud as reason to recant his general remarks, just as he had never advanced the hope that women analysts would be a vanguard of cultural change.

The challenges posed within psychoanalysis by its would-be innovators and those that came extramurally from, for example, feminism, were both, Anna Freud thought, versions of challenges psychoanalysis had always faced. "It is characteristic of the resistances to and attacks on psychoanalysis that in the course of time their rationalizations and place of origin change, while the intensity and passionateness of the antagonism remain more or less the same." She did not say so publicly, but she also thought, however, that a new type of challenge faced psychoanalysis while it, as a scientific movement, surpassed its three score and ten on this earth. The more history a scientific movement (or any other) has accumulated, the more history there is to be misunderstood or misrepresented by both participant-historians and external historians. In the 1970s, psychoanalysis reached a threshold for distortion, and many weary remarks on the forms this distortion took went back and forth through the mails among the few survivors of Anna Freud's Vienna seminars.

With Muriel Gardiner, Anna Freud was in accord about the general state of historical writing about psyhcoanalysis: "I think you are quite right not to enter into polemics with anybody who writes disagreeable books. Their number now, about subjects which we both know intimately, is so endless that the only method is to shut one's eyes to them. One can do nothing else otherwise."[11] But when Muriel Gardiner decided to defend herself in print against a personal attack, Anna Freud understood both her anger at the challenger and her need to write: "I am not surprised, after having experience with all the malicious things written recently about my father, at the absolute disregard of historical truth. . . . I can imagine that it was not easy to write, because you evidently feel about polemic as I do, namely, that it is very unprofitable. But sometimes it has to be done and then it is very nice when it is done right."[12]

Anna Freud never replied to the "malicious things" written in the late 1960s and 1970s about her father, but she did entertain a fantasy about an informal committee, like the Committee of six her father had convened before the First World War, that might be readied for combat. After a book by the French scholar Marthe Robert, *From Oedipus to Moses: Freud's Jewish Identity* (1974; trans. 1976), appeared, Anna Freud wrote to Masud Khan:

> Don't you think it is about time to create something like a "Defense League," namely a few people who are ready to defend accuracy and truth as far as my father's life is concerned? Up to now only Kurt Eissler had this role and it really cannot be fulfilled by one person who then becomes known as the "defender" and is not believed any more. I would not mind these inaccurate descriptions if they were not quoted by the next writer as if they were gospel truth, and thus the distortions are dragged on through the literature.
>
> The best example from the efforts of Marthe Robert is the following: she describes my father's father as an authoritarian figure, orthodox Jewish and in every respect the kind of father against whom a son revolts. The true facts are that he was a freethinker, a mild, indulgent and rather passive man, just the opposite. Etc.[13]

Nothing came of the committee idea, as Anna Freud herself realized that truth is no better served by "Defense Leagues" than it is by offense leagues. So she contended herself with surrendering her retaliatory wishes to those who wanted to go to battle for their own reasons—and she sent them for their provisions lists of factual and malicious errors. Kurt Eissler remained the chief among her proxies, and chief among Kurt Eissler's targets was a Harvard-trained historian named Paul Roazen, who had once been recommended to the confidences of Anna Freud and Eissler by Helene Deutsch. In 1969, Roazen published a sloppy, superficial book about Victor Tausk, one of Freud's early colleagues, who had ended his own life in 1919. Onto this little book Eissler heaped a huge volume of defense, *Talent and Genius*, and then went on to prepare another, *Victor Tausk's Suicide*.[14] Unfortunately, Eissler never could give up the role of the "defender" to attempt an accurate biography of Freud; he just collected materials in the Sigmund Freud Archives and used his authority to rebut other's biographical excursions. He could not complete Anna Freud's "developmental line" for Freud biographers because he could not, like Ernest Jones, start out a worthy person and then be raised to an even higher level by Freud— he started out too rigidly identified with his hero. But Anna Freud also could not get over her need for Eissler, because hard as she tried to ignore the books that came out one after another, she was vulnerable. When a German scholar named Marianne Krüll published *Freud and His Father* (1979; trans. 1986), which included among its many speculations a lengthy one about how Freud had denied his childhood masturbation by inventing a theory about the relationship in males between urination (not masturbation) and ambitious fantasies, Anna Freud was furious—for the biographical allegation and for the theoretical nonsense. Eissler wrote Krüll an overheated thirteen-page, single-spaced letter, for which Anna Freud was grateful: "I like it very much and read it with great pleasure. . . . I do not know why Frau Krüll somehow got under my usually well established defenses against the kind of work she is doing."[15]

Eissler monitored the burgeoning Freud literature, reporting to Anna Freud so that she could choose what she wanted to read, and periodically issued catalogs of its features. Freud, he noted in *Victor Tausk's Suicide*, was not only charged by Roazen with murderous hostility toward Tausk, but he was also described in other biographical studies

> as a plagiarist, as tyrannical and intolerant, as indifferent to his children because he never changed their diapers, as greedy for money, as hating his Jewish origin, as a corruptor of morality and ethics, as not having been original, and as one who created legends about himself. Recently it was even claimed that the goal of his scientific endeavors was not to find the truth but to conceal and obscure it. . . . At one point, an author openly stated that Freud wanted his pupils to be castrated. If one adds the horror one author expressed about Freud's having analyzed one of his daughters, as if this had been an act of incest, one can hardly escape the inference that some biographers look on him as the primal father in the primal horde.[16]

Eissler did keep after Roazen and the other "would-be biographers" in lectures and reviews, but outside of analytic circles he achieved only the reputation Anna Freud had feared for him: he was the man who cried "anti-Freud" so often that no one would listen should a significant anti-Freud come along. He was a publisher's dream—a man who helped book sales by bestowing psychoanalytic concern on hostility to psychoanalysis. Eissler also fueled scholars' desires to go around finding all the secrets that the public defenders of psychoanalysis must, surely, be trying to hide by creating a sealed Archives. Roazen interviewed some associates of the Freud family for his 1975 book, *Freud and His Followers*, and Anna Freud had tense exchanges with her friends as she tried to find out who had discussed with Roazen such matters as her own analysis with her father, which she had consistently refused to discuss when asked about it by historians. Roazen claimed to have interviewed people who insisted that they had refused to be interviewed. Anna Freud's opinion was firm, and she spoke it often: "Even though Roazen professes to have admiration for analysis itself, he is busy trying to dig up whatever negative facts about personalities he can find. This includes my father and me and what he cannot find he invents."[17] Both because the general debunking biographical style of the 1960s and 1970s was so distasteful to them and, specifically, because Roazen was considered "a menace whatever he writes," Eissler and Anna Freud and many of their circle began to protect letters and memories even more carefully than before.[18] They quite rightly interpreted the grain of truth in Roazen's published opinion that "what seems gossip to one generation may be history to the next" as much too small to stop the wholesale conversion of limited perspectives and fallible individual memories into facts.[19]

Anna Freud encouraged the publications of her father's important correspondences on her theory that the only antidote to assaults upon his person and his work was his own voice. Muriel Gardiner became a key figure in this hope, as she both supplied funds for purchasing letters and undertook the editing of Freud's youthful correspondence with a friend named Silberstein. But there was little that Anna Freud could do to influence publications of letters that were, to her mind, poorly presented, translated, or introduced. She urged Masud Khan not to publish through the International Psychoanalytical Library Edoardo Weiss's *Sigmund Freud as a Consultant*, a collection of Freud letters followed by Weiss's memoir. Her reaction to this book was characteristic of her literary and historical sense:

> To my mind it is a worthless book in every respect and not even the [Freud] letters can redeem it. Instead of increasing the interest in publications of my father's correspondence, it may only do the opposite, i.e., make the public tired and slightly contemptuous of it. . . . I think Grotjahn's Foreword is exaggerated, making the letters look more important than they are. Of course, my father wrote letters like that all the time since many people among the analysts asked him for advice and he was very patient and careful in giving it. His attitude to Edoardo Weiss was in no way different from his attitude to many young colleagues to whom he gave encouragement from a distance. . . . You are right about [Weiss's] own contribution, of course. It is ambivalent, ungrateful and somehow mean; but it is also shallow and on a low level intellectually. There is really no reason why readers have to be exposed to it. . . . The translation . . . is sloppy and inexact."[20]

Weiss's production was, certainly, of no particular significance, but it alarmed Anna Freud because it was not just a biographical misrepresentation of Freud, but an appropriation of him, a distortion of his own words.

While she was contending with the scholarly Freud industry of the 1970s, Anna Freud let it be known to her entire circle that she also wanted nothing to do with any biographies or studies of her own life and work. When a young British scholar, Raymond Dyer, and then a German psychiatrist, Uwe Peters, set out on books, she cooperated to the extent of answering their factual queries, but she said many times that she hoped no biography would be published before her death. When Uwe Peters' biography appeared in German in 1979, she sent him a list of fifty-two errors she had found in it—a list that itself contained quite a number of errors—and then she made it clear to her influential friends that she would prefer that the book not find an English publisher until after her death (which it did not). "The real deficit of the book is that it offers little more than dates and places of travel, and somehow it gives me the feeling as if I had been on the move continually, which of course I was not. But after all, it is only the poor man's fault for undertaking it, not for not knowing more."[21]

Anna Freud rather triumphantly kept her life story to herself, as she told Muriel Gardner: "I get letters from strangers from time to time, urging me to write my memoirs, almost as if it were my duty to do it. But, of course, that is the last thing in the world that I would be able to do. I cannot share my feelings with the reading public and there is too much feeling bound up with the past, and above all with the part of the past in which others would be interested. So I allow myself the privilege of taking it all with me." Her attitude toward all the biography projects that were proposed to her was simple: "People should not be so impatient."[22]

Given her attitudes toward Freud scholarship and toward her own privacy and historical place, it is quite remarkable that Anna Freud finally gave into a proposal she detested: she agreed to a reedition of her father's letters to Wilhelm Fliess, one designed to replace the abridged edition she had worked on with Ernst Kris and Marie Bonaparte. The proposal came in 1978 from a young man named Jeffrey Masson, a Sanskritist, an analytic candidate in Toronto, and, most importantly, a protégé of Kurt Eissler's. Eissler personally guaranteed Masson's suitability for the editorship—though it took a number of letters to convince Anna Freud.[23] Then Masson's personal charm and his enthusiasm for the edition impressed even those in London who had sworn that after their experiences with Paul Roazen no Freud scholar would ever again win their trust. Anna Freud admired Masson's intelligence and thoroughness, and she thought that his obvious and annoying tendency to get carried away with his projects and himself could be contained, particularly if he worked with her trusted editor Lottie Newman and William McGuire, the conscientious Freud/Jung editor. "You are quite right of course about Professor Masson," she wrote to a skeptic. "But he is a nice man and I think we will be able to cope with him."[24]

Coping with Masson got increasingly difficult, however, as he got more and more power, thanks to Eissler's desire that he become projects director of the Sigmund Freud Archives and be groomed for assuming Eissler's position as director in 1982. Anna Freud tried hard to quell her doubts because Eissler had done so much over the course of thirty years for her and for the Clinic, but she became irritated by Masson's rambunctious, greedy behavior in her father's library, and by his attempts to appropriate Sigmund Freud's letters. His strategy was to wrap Freud's words in editorial comments that reflected his own, not Freud's, ideas. At one point he planned, for example, to publish the Freud/Fliess material in three volumes: one of Freud's letters with notes, one of auxiliary documents, and one of his own speculations. Anna Freud viewed this projected third volume as unnecessary and grandiose, and she wondered repeatedly why the editing job had to be so elaborate and involve her in such a mass of correspondence with Masson.[25] She noted to Eissler about plans for the Freud letters to Silberstein, which she had transcribed herself: "What I absolutely cannot understand is Masson's crazy idea of dissecting the letters, and looking at them from the point of view of present analytic knowledge of adolescence. That sounds to me almost like sacrilege. However, I know that he means well and is only misguided in his ideas."[26]

It became undeniably clear to Anna Freud that Masson could not be coped with when he declared that Freud had made a great mistake in 1897 by giving up the idea that his patients must have been seduced as children for the idea that all children entertain love fantasies about their parents, Oedipal fantasies, whether they have undergone a seduction or not. Masson even implied that Freud had changed his mind because he could not face the prevalence of child molestation and abuse in Vienna or, possibly, face the example of it in Fliess's household.[27] Anna Freud had known about this idea of Masson's since 1977, when he advanced it in a letter, but then he had presented the idea in a context of praise for Freud and Freud's integrity—so Anna Freud was appeased. But when Masson was foolish—or self-destructive—enough to announce his views without disguise in a lecture at the Western New England Institute for Psychoanalysis, before Anna Freud's Yale friends, trouble started to brew. The whole affair got out of hand completely after Masson was interviewed for an August 1981 article in *The New York Times*.[28] At first, Anna Freud wanted to believe that the *Times* article must have misrepresented Masson. But if his views even resembled those presented in the article, she wondered: "how could he not notice that this is destructive to the whole fabric of psychoanalysis? Quite apart from the fact that it is based on a complete misunderstanding of my father's motives when working."[29]

Masson's many explanations failed to convince his patrons that he was not conducting a frontal assault on Freud's work and Freud's integrity. "One wonders what his understanding of analysis is altogether," Anna Freud lamented to Eissler. "For my part, I could only say one thing: that I am deeply sorry that I ever agreed to the publication of the unabridged Fliess letters."[30] As publicity about what one newspaper chose to call "the Watergate of psychoanalysis" accumulated, and as she began to receive frequent lengthy letters from yet another ambitious young Freud scholar, Peter Swales, who was engaged in a rivalry with Masson for access to materials, Anna Freud grew impatient for all the parties to somehow, by some miracle, exit the scene. She treated all the newspaper articles that came her way as pollutants—and sent them immediately out of her house by airmail to Eissler, the collector, the chagrined source of the problem, whom she still could not bring herself to criticize any more directly. "I can only say that I hate the whole affair," she told Eissler as she sent him a *Time* magazine article that Peter Swales had covered with annotations and sent to her.[31] She, at the age of eighty-six, explained to friends that Eissler was too old to be reprimanded for his poor judgment.

Hoping to prevent future damage and aggravation, Anna Freud simply begged Eissler to see to it that, after the Fliess and Silberstein letters had appeared, further publication of the Freud correspondences would stop for a number of years. But, more immediately, she supported the Archives board's decision not to renew Masson's appointment as projects director, and she was relieved that the Sigmund Freud Copyrights, including Masud Khan, who kindly kept her informed, reconsidered a plan to have Masson join its board. Eissler also, although he could not yet bring himself to a clear admission of how disruptive Masson was, retracted his suggestion that Masson be appointed live-in supervisor of the eventual conversion of 20 Maresfield Gardens into a Freud Museum; but Eissler did not tell Anna Freud that he had given up this plan because, knowing she would never agree to having Masson live in her house, he had not informed her about it. At a stormy November 1981 meeting, the Sigmund Freud Archives relieved Masson of his post—and as a result Masson sued for breach of contract. Muriel Gardiner, who was involved in the suit because her foundation had funded Masson's work, insisted that the suit be settled out of court. She thought that fighting it would destroy her already frail health and use up the resources of her foundation, which were needed elsewhere—including at Anna Freud's Clinic. So Masson was paid a sum equivalent to the yearly budget of a Clinic that offered psychoanalytic help to some fifty children. And work on the Silberstein letters came to a standstill because Muriel Gardiner found that every time she took them up her blood pressure rose dangerously: she could not ignore the debacle and the way in which Masson had, she felt, betrayed her trust in him. "I know I have disappointed you," she wrote to Anna Freud, "by giving up on the Silberstein work, and I am sorry, but I could not do otherwise."[32] "The main thing," Anna Freud wrote sympathetically to her old friend, "is that you keep your health and whatever peace you can have."[33] The cost of the tumult to Anna Freud's own health was not so easily measured—although she wrote to Muriel Gardiner while she was recovering from a stroke.

Aᴌᴛʜᴏᴜɢʜ Aɴɴᴀ Fʀᴇᴜᴅ learned entirely too many lessons about the sad state of psychoanalytic scientific and historical research in the late 1970s, she was nonetheless eager to find ways to keep herself and her Clinic connected to the people who were keeping psychoanalysis alive and well by her standards. In Vienna, she found a sympathetic group, and she went to her home city a number of times after the 1971 Congress—to receive an honorary doctorate in medicine at the university, to inaugurate a May 6 birthday lecture series in honor of her father, to speak at the unveiling of a Freud statue, to meet with the colleagues who founded the Anna Freud Nursery School. She also received doctorates from Columbia University, Harvard University, and the University of Frankfurt. The people who came into her orbit on these occasions were a pleasure too—particularly the ones at Columbia who suggested that she fly to New York on the Concorde, which she viewed as a great adventure. The Harvard trip was a good opportunity to visit with the Kris children (Tony had instigated the degree idea) and to have last visits with her cousin Edward Bernays and with Helene Deutsch, whose state of health and mind made Anna Freud certain that she never wanted to be ninety years old. The Frankfurt officials, who presented her with her degree in London, were the recipients of her decision finally to lift her ban on relations with Germany: "It was a very nice occasion and it helped me to make peace at last with the Germans."[34] But public honors, pleasing as they were, did not do psychoanalysis itself the honor of respect and renewal.

She felt this need for new people and initiatives even more strongly when her old friend Romi Greenson was repeatedly hospitalized with the heart condition from which he died on November 24, 1979. In the years before his death, they had been corresponding about a documentary film on the Hampstead Clinic that Greenson had insisted was necessary for effective fund-raising. Anna Freud and Dorothy Burlingham had reluctantly consented to appear in the film, which they finally did think quite good, and they had high hopes for its future as a money magnet. But Greenson himself did not live to carry through on his generous plan to screen the film throughout California. In the last letter she wrote to him, Anna

Freud had agreed that the work of Heinz Kohut, once a member of their circle, had become antipsychoanalytic, and she had mused: "What will happen to psychoanalysis in the future? and where will its backbone be when our generation is gone?"[35] Missing her friend terribly, she continued on in the same vein through a piece she wrote for his memorial service: "We are raising new generations of psychoanalysts all over the world. Nevertheless, we have not yet discovered the secret of how to raise the real followers of people like Romi Greenson, namely, men and women who make use of psychoanalysis to its very limits: for the understanding of themselves; of their fellow beings; for communicating with the world at large; in short, for a way of living."[36]

Analysts from all over the world came to the Clinic as visitors, and Anna Freud received each one personally, but she felt that both she and the Clinic needed an organized forum—a true Congress, like the kind her generation had been raised with. The Clinic's senior staff shared her views, particularly as they had four students just starting their training who were, they thought, an unusually promising group, capable of really benefiting from a stimulating forum. (One of these, George Moran, an American, was eventually appointed as the long-hoped-for young director of the Hampstead Clinic.) In the same year, 1977, the staff had also just sent off to the National Institute of Mental Health in Washington a volume of papers summing up almost thirteen years of work on the Profile and the Index and all the clinical and theoretical contributions that had flowed from the use of those two methods. So they felt positioned both for learning from outsiders and for a new way to present the Clinic's work to the wider psychoanalytic community.

Arthur Valenstein, on one of the visits in Walberswick that he and his wife, Katrina Burlingham, made each summer, had formulated a proposal that exactly fitted Anna Freud's need. He suggested an annual "Summit meeting" at the Clinic to which a selected group of analysts from different countries would be invited. The annual meetings would each have a topic—on the model of the 1965 Amsterdam Congress—but they would be structured so that all the participants could be actively involved. They would also be arranged so that adult analysts and child analysts could learn effectively from each other; there would be none of the common separation of the two types of analysis—to the detriment of both. Peter Neubauer of New York, who had often been helpful to the Clinic in its grant-getting enterprises, joined Valenstein as coinitiator of the Hampstead Symposia and as a member of the International Advisory Board established to oversee the Symposia. Anna Freud explained the project to Ruth Thomas, who had retired as the Clinic's supervisor of training in 1974:

> If we would be willing to set up a series of yearly symposia with different topics and different invited guests, we could tie these guests gradually closer to the Clinic as a form of corresponding membership, and make them consider the Clinic as a scientific meeting place. . . . This would give us an international connection without the difficulties of bureaucracy and administration, that is, bypassing all the official psychoanalytic organizations who do not want any part of us anyway.[37]

The first symposium was scheduled for November 1979, and its topic was "The Significance of Insight in Psychoanalytic Theory and Practice," a topic that Anna Freud had become quite interested in the year before as she had prepared a lecture to be read on her behalf at an American meeting organized by Humberto Nagera.[38] The Hampstead symposium, formally dedicated to Willi Hoffer's memory, was a very great success. All who attended praised it, and the praise assuaged a great deal of Anna Freud's feeling that she and her Clinic had been left stranded by the International Psychoanalytic Association. The IPA, she very candidly remarked to her guests, had behaved like a parent with no insight into the best interests of its child, much less into its own interests in having the child. "Individuals without parents," she had said, "need friends and siblings; so you are here to adopt us."[39]

Anna Freud also convinced the adopters that insight, as the goal of psychoanalytic therapy, was going to be given by the symposium the theoretical place of honor it had largely lost to transference in the recent psychoanalytic literature. But, in addition to rectifying a misemphasis common in discussions (particularly Kleinian discussions) of what makes a psychoanalysis work, Anna Freud wanted to challenge her guests to think not just about how patients gain insight but about their lack of insight—is lack of insight, she asked,

pathogenic? when? how? Everyone was amused to notice how difficult it was for one after another of the speakers who addressed the
question to get anywhere with it, and most agreed with Robert
Wallerstein of San Francisco, who said: "I think Miss Freud has
again demonstrated her capacity always to set tasks for us that may
be just a bit beyond where we are."[40]

ANNA Freud, who thought of herself as the littlest child, the one
wishing, personally and organizationally, for an adoptive family, was,
to her colleagues, the last member of the founder's family, the
founder's heir, the one who always issued the challenges. To her old
friends Marianne Kris, Anny Katan, and Jeanne Lampl-de Groot,
Anna Maenchen and Muriel Gardiner, who came for the symposium,
she was also able to be what she had always been—the still, steady
center of their circle, now so diminished. Although they missed
Romi Greenson, Anna Freud and Dorothy Burlingham felt that all
their symposium wishes, explicit and implicit, had been fulfilled.

For Dorothy Burlingham, the symposium was a special pleasure
because she had had a very difficult year with one bout of illness
after another, and had not been well enough for the annual September vacation month in Ireland. She was able to attend all the
meetings during the weekend and enjoy lunch each day at 20 Maresfield Gardens with the old Vienna friends. "Agatha Christie would
call us all 'the old pussies,' " Muriel Gardiner joked, using an affectionate term that she knew her fellow mystery-story reader, Anna
Freud, would enjoy.[41] But the weekend was strenuous and soon after
it Dorothy Burlingham was in bed again. She was able to meet once
with Anna Freud, Albert Solnit, and Joseph Goldstein to discuss the
last volume of their trilogy, but she missed their final meetings. And
she was not responding to Josefine Stross's prescriptions.

On the evening of November 19, a Monday, Dorothy died—
with Anna Freud sitting quietly in her room, in their house. Anna
Freud was numb, and spoke in the terms she had used when she lost
her father:

There is very little that one can say, except perhaps to be glad
that she was still there to enjoy the conference and one last session of our book Nr. 3. I still told her what we discussed on the

next two days, and she was interested as usual. Perhaps one should also say that it is a boon to be quite oneself until the very end and to die without being an invalid for a long time. But it is not so easy to be grateful to fate when one really feels the opposite.[42]

Tinky Valenstein and Michael Burlingham came and gave Anna Freud all the comfort they could. There was a memorial service at Golders Green, where Dorothy Burlingham's ashes were placed in the Freud family crypt. Clifford Yorke and Hansi Kennedy eulogized her as a colleague and a friend, and Anna Freud herself spoke briefly and stoically, summoning up the more than fifty years of their companionship. She closed her reflections by telling the mourners that her father had once said of a friend whom he had lost that it would be best to be grateful for the friendship rather than to lament its loss. Unbeknownst to her hearers, Anna Freud was alluding to the lesson her father had taught her in 1925, when Otto Rank's behavior had made her so angry; she was admitting publicly but in a private language what most people do not admit at all when a loved one dies: that the absence feels not just like a blow from fate but like a betrayal, that loneliness feels like abandonment. But she did also follow her own advice and feel gratitude toward her companion for all they had known. Michael Burlingham spoke the gratitude as he had heard his mother say it, for her part: "You were everything to her and she had a most wonderful life with you; how fortunate she was in finding and capturing someone like you. . . . I keep thinking of all the happy times you had with each other, day after day after day."[43]

One of Dorothy's grandsons, Michael John Burlingham, had been in London with his wife a month before her death, and he had taken photographs of her for her eighty-eighth birthday. Anna Freud kept these on her desk. She also comforted herself by wearing Dorothy's sweaters around the house and stroking these representations of the friend whom no one in their acquaintance had ever seen her caress or embrace. Although she was grateful for the generous sympathy of her friends, she retreated. No celebration of her eighty-fourth birthday on December 3 was permitted. As soon as she felt able, she drove alone to Walberswick for a weekend, explaining to Hildi Greenson, for whom November 1979 was also the beginning of being alone: "You ask who goes with me now. The answer is simple: I go alone, since I do not believe in substitute company. I try to learn being alone apart from work."[44] Hildi Greenson shared her own feelings about being a widow: "I feel this awful 'homesickness' for all the wonderful years, including the many times when the four of us were together."[45]

Apart from work, time hung very heavy for Anna Freud. The holidays, which she and Dorothy Burlingham had always looked forward to with such pleasure and so many plans, became "the empty holidays." She only wished them over. Plans were made to sell the house in Ireland, as Anna Freud had no desire to spend an Easter break or a September there without her friend. When the Clinic reopened after Christmas, Anna Freud was glad, and she devoted herself to organizing a memorial meeting there at which she spoke again, this time about Dorothy Burlingham's work in Vienna, her school, her start in child analysis, the Jackson Nursery. Marianne Kris and Jeanne Lampl-de Groot then spent part of the summer holiday in Walberswick, when Anna Freud's need to be alone had abated somewhat. She planned a fall meeting at the Clinic to discuss further Dorothy Burlinghams' school in Vienna. As the next Hampstead Symposium approached, she read and reread the literature on its topic, early development of the superego—a topic that had presented itself for consideration the year before. But, apart from learning to be with friends again and working, the thing that Anna Freud did with the greatest joy in the year after Dorothy's death was to get a chow puppy, Jo-Fi, named after one of the chows Dorothy had given to her father in Vienna. Jo-Fi was also to play the role of her old friend the Alsatian Wolf, who had been her companion in the years before Dorothy Burlingham came to Vienna. Anna Freud even thought of Jo-Fi as, like Wolf, a male: "Er (oder richtiger sie) soll helfen dass das Haus nicht zu leer ist," she wrote to the Fadenbergers, the family that had acted as caretakers for her first country cottage with Dorothy, Hochroterd. "He (or more correctly she) should help keep the house from being too empty."[46]

THE second Hampstead Symposium was as successful as the first, but it ended dreadfully. Marianne Kris, who had participated eagerly and warmly in the symposium, despite her need to keep her unruly heart under control with frequent doses of nitroglycerin, died on the morning after the last day of meetings—in Martha Freud's bedroom, twenty-nine years almost to the day after Martha Freud had died there. Anna Freud came calmly to the lunch table where Jeanne Lampl-de Groot and Muriel Gardiner were seated, waiting, and told them that Marianne had died. Then she insisted that lunch go on. The public stoicism that Anna Freud mustered for the loss of her oldest and most maternal friend, her childhood playmate, was proportionate to the pain she felt—a compounded pain, for she had to bear it without Dorothy Burlingham.

And this loss too was quite unexpected, a complete shock. Marianne Kris had been through torturous operations on her hip and various episodes with her heart, but she had seemed, at the symposium, so lively. With Dorothy, things had been different. She and Anna Freud had known her end was coming, and Anna Freud had even spoken of it to others in the private language of allusion to the past that she developed for communicating obliquely how she felt and what she knew. When Dorothy's grandson Michael John was visiting and taking the last photographs, she had looked out the window and remarked that the autumn leaves, coming down off the trees, reminded her of the last act of *Cyrano de Bergerac*.[47] In her allusion system, this meant that she, who had, like Cyrano, surrendered—altruistically surrendered—her wishes to others, would rather die herself, as Cyrano had in the last act, than to lose the silently loved Roxane.

> . . . *You brought me all that I could know*
> *Of woman's goodness, all of woman's grace!*
> *My mother happened not to like my face.*
> *I never had a sister. Later I*
> *Feared over-much a mistress' mocking eye!*
> *Beloved Roxane, Dearheart, I owe to you*
> *Having a sweet friend in a woman, who*
> *Throughout my life, has brought a woman's touch!*[48]

Anna Kris Wolff and Tony Kris came to London, as the November before Tinky and Michael Burlingham had come. They were at 20 Maresfield Gardens when Anna Freud's own heart "misbehaved." "It looked as if I tried to be the next loss by producing some heart trouble shortly after Marianne's death," she wrote to Hildi Greenson. "It made me spend a fortnight in the hospital, but now it has quieted down again and I am home, and very gradually starting patients. I am told to take it easy, but I do not know for how long."[49] When she got home, weak but not as tired as she sometimes was before her blood transfusions, Anna Freud took up correspondences with old friends of Marianne Kris's who had written to her to say that they did not know what they would do without Marianne's presence, her telephone calls, her gracious, warm understanding. In German she wrote to Miriam Beer-Hofmann-Lens, daughter of the Viennese dramatist Richard Beer-Hofmann: "I can only say that I feel with you everything you say about Marianne, and it is astonishing how many other people, friends, patients, colleagues, students, feel as we do. I often said to Marianne that she spent too much time on the telephone. But now I understand very well what those telephone talks meant to other people."[50]

There were not many left to whom Anna Freud could write, as she did to Miriam Beer-Hofmann-Lens, whom she had not seen since 1939, when they had stood near each other at Sigmund Freud's funeral and admired the German prose of Stefan Zweig's eulogy: "I am, like you, the last in my family and I think we are nearly the same age, I perhaps a little older. Does it seem to you that the Vienna time does not lie so very far in the past? or perhaps this is only so for old age thinking?"

After Marianne Kris's death, Anna Freud was more and more in what she called *Altersgedanken*, old age thinking, which meant— for her—thinking in German and about her childhood, about Vienna. She used her lifelong capacity for sustaining fantasy to good purpose for the present, as when she kept her lost friends close: "I miss her very much," she wrote of Marianne Kris to Edna Mingo, the Kris's housekeeper in New York, a woman who had lavished on the whole circle of Viennese analysts the kind of devotion they had not known since they had had *Kinderfrauen* as children. "Sometimes I pretend that she is still in New York and I only have to wait for the next opportunity to see her."[51] But Anna Freud also needed to use her fantasy capacity—as do all people feeling their losses deeply and feeling their own mortality daily—for the past, for the Vienna time. And she too needed a *Kinderfrau*, a companion who could receive her reminiscences in German and care for her. Her maid, Paula Fichtl, had never been a companion; and Paula, who was seventy-nine in 1981, grew more infirm—given to falls and paranoid spells—and was hardly even able to keep up the house, though she was ferocious if anyone tried to help her or even suggest that she needed help. Paul Fichtl and Anna Freud lived together in 20 Maresfield Gardens, with the chow Jo-Fi, who was a little more than either of them could handle, until help came from the new *Kinderfrauen*—for they were two—Alice Colonna and Manna Friedmann.

ALICE COLONNA, an American analysand of Anna Freud's and a graduate of the Hampstead program, arranged to take a leave of absence from her work at Yale's Child Study Center to become Anna Freud's in-house attendant. Careful plans were made so that this generously self-appointed task would seem to Anna Freud a matter of convenience for her guest. Slowly, Alice Colonna's presence became not just acceptable but enjoyed, for she provided Anna Freud with the basic practicalities—help with the chow, trips to Walberswick, a degree of control over Paula, outings around Hampstead—and she kept the distance appropriate to both Anna Freud's temperament and her mourning.

While Alice Colonna was able to establish herself discreetly as the caretaker *Kinderfrau*, Manna Friedmann, the retired nursery-school teacher, was also accepted as the Jewish mother, the German-speaking *Kinderfrau*, the one with whom Anna Freud could recite German poetry, sing school songs, and share all the handicraft projects, the knitting and the weaving. When Manna Friedmann came around frequently in 1981, the eighty-five-year-old Anna Freud announced joyfully that it was time for her to take up a new profession, as she was really getting too old to take patients: she and Manna Friedmann would produce handwoven goods and market them under the name "Mandanna." In January 1981, Anna Freud had told her weaving friend, "I had a dream: I wanted to go to work and I could not find the Clinic."[52] She did, waking, often go to the Clinic, but she was weak and less sure of herself than before—

and her uncertainty made her withdraw inwardly from her colleagues. She felt no strong bonds with her nieces and nephews in England or with their children, and Ernst Halberstadt-Freud was then too preoccupied with divorcing his wife and wrangling with his coworkers at the Clinic to be any comfort. When she was in the hospital in July 1981 for another transfusion, she was asked to indicate on a form the name of her next of kin. She jokingly—but not so jokingly—wanted to write in the blank: "Jo-Fi."

The year after Marianne Kris's death was, for Anna Freud, a matter of battles with her anemia and with her worries: about what the Clinic would do without G. G. Bunzl, the treasurer and benefactor, who died in February 1981 of cancer; about which Freud scholars would next set out to harass her and defame her father; about whether to trust the people laying complicated plans for turning 20 Maresfield Gardens into a Freud Museum after her death. She was depressed by having so few patients, but she also admitted that she was enthusiastic not so much for psychoanalysis or for writing about it—"I suppose I have written enough"—as for weaving. There was little that she could do for her Clinic scientifically while she was recovering from her transfusions, so she came up with the idea that she would produce a lot of knitting and weaving that could be auctioned off in a benefit for the Clinic. She made plans for a November 1981 auction, and this did—with the cooperation of her English and American friends—net the Clinic some 2,500 pounds.

Anna Freud dreaded November 1981 for months before it arrived. Not just the auction and the third Hampstead Symposium, on pathogenesis, for which she was able to prepare and present a fine brief paper, but also the unexpected culmination of the Sigmund Freud Archives battle with Jeffrey Masson added to her inner strain. "This is a specially difficult month," she wrote to Anna Kris Wolff, "and the names of Dorothy and Marianne are written over it, at least for me and Tinky and you and Tony."[53] But once the taxing November was past, and the awful anniversaries had been endured, things seemed a little smoother. "I had a blood transfusion on December 4th and since then the hemoglobin has not dropped perceptibly. That means I am quite mobile, can go to the Clinic and even plan to go to Walberswick for a weekend in the near future. I even have been to a film once, which hasn't happened for more than two years."[54] Her coauthors Joseph and Sonja Goldstein had arrived in London for a sabbatical semester, and Alice Colonna, "the Savior," as Anna Freud was then calling her, was able to arrange parties and outings for Anna Freud to meet the Goldsteins and a few others socially.

In January and February of 1982, however, Anna Freud's improved mood was quite overcast by yet another bizarre episode in the tragicomedy Kurt Eissler was trying to manage in New York. While Jeffrey Masson was preoccupied with his legal proceedings and with making money from new projects he planned, the mysterious Peter Swales let it be known that he was soon going to make public his theory that Sigmund Freud had had an affair with his sister-in-law Minna Bernays. This absurd theory, for which there was no documentary proof, only an old rumor launched by Carl Jung and Swales's strange construal of one of the dreams Freud had analyzed in *The Interpretation of Dreams*, must have seemed to Anna Freud the most annoying of the many annoying fantasies about her father—for it conjured a liaison that she, who had been so jealous of her Tante Minna, would have been vigilant enough to detect for herself had there been any sign of it. Before Swales himself came forth as a lecturer in America, she and other readers of the London *Sunday Times* were treated to two articles based upon research he had sold to an editor there: "Sex and Cocaine: Freud's Pact with the Devil" and "The Secret Love Life of Sigmund Freud."

There was nothing, Anna Freud knew, that would restrain the imaginations of people like Masson and Swales. And she got further indication when Eissler, who was generating quite a collection of letters to and from Swales, wrote to ask her about a set of notes she had written ten years earlier for an edition of Freud's youthful "Cocaine Papers." She replied that she had written no such notes. Dr. Robert Byck, the editor of the volume, then explained to them that he had received the notes—typewritten on plain paper—from the edition's unscrupulous publisher, whose assistant had then been Peter Swales.[55] Eventually, Mark Paterson of Sigmund Freud Copyrights produced a Xerox copy of five handwritten notes. Anna Freud admitted that "they seem definitely in my handwriting," but she did not recognize the words as her own. In her extremely orderly files, she could find no correspondence over the notes with anyone concerned. "I have always trusted my memory, and I think I had reason to do so. But in this case there is an absolute blank, and I am sorry about this."[56] She had no evidence to call foul play or forgery, but she was worried by the completely uncharacteristic "blank." Eissler wrote to Swales saying that Anna Freud had made a mistake, so that the matter could be closed. She then refused to write any further letters to Swales, or to Masson. "Whatever one does, all it does is give food for new attacks."[57]

The only comfort—and quite cold it was—for a stroke in her cerebellum that Anna Freud suffered on March 1, 1982, was that she no longer had to deal with the scholarly banes of her existence. "Now I can hide behind my illness quite legitimately."[58] Otherwise, she was miserable. Her motor abilities and her speech were immediately affected, although her mind had remained as clear as it had been when she asked Josefine Stross, while she was being taken by ambulance to the hospital, "Is this the end?" Over the next few months, while she struggled valiantly to make herself understood, to focus her eyes for reading a newspaper headline, and to regain enough control over her shaky hands for simple knitting, Anna Freud often wished that her end had really come: "I never knew one could be so miserable." When she was able to do a little knitting, she was more discouraged than pleased, for, as she lamented in the old metaphors of her youthful fantasies: "I feel degraded, like a Captain having to scrub the deck of the ship." Her humor never completely disappeared, but it was all at her own expense: as she and a pretty young nurse were standing before a mirror in which she was to watch herself try to walk, she said frankly, "I'd rather look at you." When her hands refused to knit as she ordered them to, she mocked herself for the good sublimation behavior she had demanded of them when she was young: "Look at what that hand did, it is angry because I controlled it for so long."

Bits of German poetry floated into her mind, and she told Manna Friedmann that for one whole day she had been possessed by the opening of Schiller's *Maria Stuart*, a beautiful passage in which Maria longs for her "land of youth"—"Gruesset mir freundlich mein Jugendland!"—which Anna Freud misremembered as *Heimatland*, homeland. In one of her many nostalgic reenactments of times in her homeland, she had tried to dictate a story about her chow Jo-Fi to

Manna Friedmann, who had a friend, a former patient of Anna Freud's, who wanted to do illustrations to make up a little children's book. This was like working with her father on their translation of Marie Bonaparte's *Topsy, A Goldenhaired Chow* as they waited to leave Vienna for London. In the hospital, she took up the story again, and it was some compensation for the fact that she had to send her delegates, Alice Colonna and Mathilde's companion, Tini, to visit her father's grave on his birthday, May 6, a pilgrimage she had always so faithfully made herself.

After more than three months in the hospital, Anna Freud returned to 20 Maresfield Gardens in June. Nurses were hired and the house was equipped with ramps for her wheelchair, but for the real problem, Paula Fichtl, who would not admit that she was too unsteady to be helpful and so weak as to need a nurse herself, there was no solution, because Anna Freud refused any suggestions. "A home for Paula is out, because she will say that I have used her for fifty years and then thrown her out." Her maid was a terrible burden, but Anna Freud also could never get around the fact that Paula had cared for Sigmund Freud in his last illness with great devotion. Over Paula's wild protests, a very capable, steady daytime housekeeper and cook was added to the staff, but Paula still would not give up her rule in the kitchen.

Through the summer, Anna Freud lived quietly, with help from her new housekeeper, paid nurses, her doctors, Alice Colonna, and Manna Friedmann. She could sometimes dictate letters, laboriously, to Gina Bon; she could sometimes rally herself for a visit with the Goldsteins or her nephew Ernst or her niece from America, Sophie Freud Lowenstein, who tried to make contact with her failing Tante Anna by letters, visits, and presents of knitting wools. Anny Katan and Jeanne Lampl-de Groot came, but Anna Freud did not enjoy greeting them in her incapacitated state. "I am glad Dorothy did not see me like this, she would have minded so." Only with Manna Friedmann did she feel comfortable, and that made it very difficult to give her up for Manna's annual August and September visit to her brother in Philadelphia: "I don't agree with your brother claiming you, I am more ill than he is," she said with all the passion of a little child who wants no rivals for her *Kinderfrau's* attention. The approach of another November, and another Hampstead Symposium, which Anna Freud knew she would never be able to attend, much less grace with a paper like her last one, weighed on her mind: she said that she would prefer to die before a Symposium, rather than after as Dorothy and Marianne had.

Even though she rallied a bit physically, August was a bare month, with the Clinic colleagues on vacation and the Goldsteins returned to America. Her inability to do anything, even produce a little crocheting, wore on her tenacious spirit. But Alice Colonna read many mystery stories out loud, and Anna Freud, her evenly hovering psychoanalytic attention working right through little dozes, never missed a clue or a turn of the plot. Jo-Fi was enrolled in much-needed obedience classes and Anna Freud turned her child development curiosity to the results, even enduring a bit of teasing about how she, despite her principles, had raised a very spoiled child. But she tired very easily, could hardly eat, and despaired over the constant shaking of her head and hands. Alice Colonna went to Freud's grave on the anniversary of his death, September 23, and brought fresh flowers.

By the time Manna Friedmann returned from America at the beginning of October, Anna Freud could hardly speak and had to support her head with the hand she could control, her right one. *"Sehr schlecht,"* she announced "very bad." The shaking became so extreme by the seventh of October that a neurologist who had been consulted before came to the house and prescribed an opiate to quell it. Like her father before her, she had been brought to the limit of her tolerance, and she had said in her halting voice, "I cannot stand it any more." Early in the morning of October 9, she died in her restless sleep.

ANNA Freud's last days were so full of misery that even her strong fantasies were of little help. She had only recent memories for solace—though their roots went deep. During her long hospital stay, Manna Friedmann had often pushed her in a wheelchair to the nearby paths of Hampstead Heath, to the lily pond, where they could throw bread crumbs to the ducks and watch the children sailing toy boats. These happy outings had been like going with Josefine up the Berggasse, over to the Ringstrasse and then down to the Prater and the children's playground with its goldfish pond. While they were planning one of their excursions for the next day, the summer weather was turning cooler. Struggling for words, Anna Freud asked Manna Friedmann to stop by 20 Maresfield Gardens on her way to the hospital: she would find hanging in Anna Freud's bedroom closet the Professor's *Londenmantel*, which had been ritualistically cleaned and refurbished every year since the end of the war. Then, when they went off to the park, the *Kinderfrau* and Anna Freud, she, shrunken to the size of a schoolgirl, sat wrapped inside her father's big wool coat.

POSTSCRIPT

A FTER *The Interpretation of Dreams* was published, there were three generations of analysts who could claim direct affiliation with Freud. The first was Freud's own generation: men and women who came to him between the first meetings of the Vienna Psychoanalytic Society and World War I. The most famous of this group were its defectors—Adler, Stekel, and Jung—and its Committee members—Abraham, Ferenczi, Jones, Rank, Sachs, and later Eitingon. The one who came to Freud with a brilliant reputation already established was Lou Andreas-Salomé; the others achieved their reputations as analysts. The second generation began its training just after World War I. Among Freud's own analysands, the most prominent were his daughter Anna Freud, Helene Deutsch, and Heinz Hartmann. Slightly younger in training terms was a remarkable group of couples: Wilhelm and Annie Reich, Robert and Jenny Waelder, Edward and Grete Bibring, Richard and Editha Sterba, Ernst and Marianne Kris, Wilhelm and Hedwig Hoffer. Among the others were René Spitz, August Aichhorn, Anny Rosenberg Katan, Erik Erikson, Peter Blos, Anna Maenchen, and Dorothy Burlingham, roughly contemporaries in training, as were the associates of the Viennese group who trained in Berlin: Otto Fenichel, Hans and Jeanne Lampl, the sisters Berta and Steff Bornstein, Ernst Simmel.

Of this second generation, it is interesting to note that there was only one defector—Wilhelm Reich; that the number of women is equal to the number of men; that the group was mostly Jewish, like the founders; and that the chief preoccupation of the majority was the field developed by Anna Freud in Vienna, child analysis. After being trained by people in Freud's circle, either in Europe before 1938 or after the second generation had emigrated, a third generation came to prominence, many of them in America. In this third generation there were fewer women, child analysts, and lay analysts, but more psychiatrists (many with military experience); much more diversity of cultural and ethnic backgrounds; and looser connection to Freud and to the traditions of the earlier generations. The fourth and later generations are not easy to characterize as groups except to say that they are both more diverse and more embattled than the third.

In histories of scientific revolutions, it is commonly noted that successive generations work both to stabilize (or make "normal science" out of) the revolution and to distinguish themselves as innovators rather than mere inheritors or epigones. But the history of psychoanalysis is unusual in two important regards: no Einstein challenged the Newton, the genius of the founder has never been equaled and still acts as the standard for the successors; and the generations were tied not just as masters and apprentices, mentors and protégés, but as analysts and analysands—a completely unique form of knowledge transmission and one fraught with difficulties.

Only the second generation of Viennese maintained both an internal group coherence and a relatively stable relationship to Freud. The political events that sent this generation into exile helped many members to maintain the continuity, but these events alone were not enough to hold together the groups in Berlin or Budapest. Many of the Viennese did feel like missionaries in wild territories, bearers of enlightenment where there was none or only an indigenous approximation (like American psychoanalysis). But, more importantly, they felt that Freud's psychoanalysis was both home—the home that Nazism had not been able to destroy—and the only hope for humankind's better future. Their lives were psychoanalysis: their companions or spouses were usually analysts, their children often became analysts; they analyzed one another's family members and friends; there was no division between personal and professional psychoanalysis. Their emotional tie to Freud—and then to Anna Freud—was the center of their familial-professional psychoanalysis, the ballast in their creativity. Anna Freud epitomized this generation; in her their attitudes existed in a pure state, and in her they saw the measure of themselves.

The second generation was also involved in psychoanalytic work when Freud made two out of three of the major reformulations of his own theory. He was alone (although in correspondence with Fliess) when he abandoned the "seduction theory," but this generation came in time to witness his abandonment of two forms of libido (ego and object) for the "dual instinct theory"—the theory of the life and death instinctual drives—and his abandonment of the idea that the ego is all consciousness and not partly unconscious, as he said in outlining the "structural theory." This generation learned firsthand a powerful lesson about the depths from which true revisionism and lucid self-criticism arise. They also lived through enough challenges to psychoanalysis, from within and from without, to know that the sexual instinctual drive theory was always at issue—no matter whether critics wanted to eliminate it, submerge it in a biological theory, or reformulate its stages and ties to gender differentiation.

Some analysts of the fourth generation—Ralph Greenson, for example, trained by Schur and Fenichel, or the Yale group, trained by the Krises—maintained their attitudes in their own contexts. In the late 1960s and 1970s, others needed distance from "orthodoxy" and from what they viewed as obeisance to Freud. They wanted the supposedly legitimizing methods of empirical or medical science (which implied the exclusion of lay analysts), and sought new fields to conquer technically (chiefly, the psychoses) through new methods (including psychopharmacology). Such a shake-up was as predictable as any revolt of the youngsters against the father and the father's court. In the media of biographies and theoretical treatises, Freud was shown by members of this generation to be limited, blinded, rigid in his reactions to dissent, a compromiser in his pursuit of truth—in short, surpassable. In Europe, and then in South America, the revisionist tendency often focused more on the court, the second generation, which was held to have obscured the real Freud and substituted something superficial and Americanized, ego psychology, for his discoveries. Klein's search for the depths of Freud's work was often echoed. Anna Freud, not surprisingly, referred in her private correspondences to "the false generation," and she took a certain pleasure in outliving most of the English "false generation" and a good number of the Americans. But she did not think that their heirs were or would be any different.

She certainly judged those she disapproved of in the younger generations by standards both formidable and—in the richest sense of the word—conservative, conserving of what she and her father valued. Many found her conservatism unreasonable and restrictive. She, on the other hand, found the theory she conserved unendingly exciting and the ones she objected to quite boring. Her suspicion was that her opponents wished to be lulled and mystified rather than excited. Commiserating with her old friend J. C. Hill about a "modern" analyst's lecture, she wrote:

> I think I know what you miss when you hear such reports of my father's work. You miss the essence of it, which is the emphasis on conflict within the individual person, the aims, ideas and ideals battling with the drives to keep the individual within a civilized community. It has become modern to water this down to every individual's longing for perfect unity with his mother, i.e., to be loved only as an infant can be loved. There is an enormous amount that gets lost this way and what you call the excitement about the discoveries goes by the board of course. Psychoanalysis is above all a drive psychology. But for some reason people do not want to have that.[1]

She continually stressed that both the analysts who were interested only in ego developments—who tended toward being cognitive psychologists—and the analysts who were interested only in the unconscious mind missed what was, for her, the real analytic pleasure.

> Looking back into my analytic past [she said in 1979, when she was eighty-three], I realize now why, with regard to children, I have always been more attracted to the latency period than the pre-Oedipal phases. In the latter, the id reveals itself quite unashamedly. But the latency period presents the observer with all the efforts of the ego to deal with the id. This is of course what makes child analysis in the latency period so very difficult, since the patient strenuously opposes the analyst's wish to undo the defenses which he has built up in good faith, and with so much trouble.[2]

Anna Freud's conservatism was, obviously, bound to her love for her father, her veneration of him, and to the fact that conflict was his terrain: he thought in oppositions, dualisms, tensions of two. Her analytic pleasure in the latency period, in the conflicts between id and ego, was also bound to the process of her own analysis, which had revealed her latency so fascinatingly. But her love and her analytic experience might have led her into being a mere continuer and a hagiographer; it is her ability as an innovator that they do not explain.

Phyllis Greenacre, an American contemporary of the Viennese second generation, who, along with Ernst Kris, most interestingly continued the line of thought Freud had opened about creativity—its psychic preconditions and its development—once made a fine generalization about precocious children.[3] They are either born with special potentialities, made temporarily "special" by pushy parents (to later disastrous consequences), or brought to their "remarkable performances [as] the result of neurotic conflict." In cases of the last sort, the "development of special achievement usually [takes place] on a somewhat compulsive basis as part of an effort to overcome or counteract a masturbation addiction which is heavily charged with anal problems." "Such children are erotized early and if subjected to extreme frustration, sickness, or bad handling got readily into states of frenzied masturbation, sometimes of a compulsive sort." In truly gifted individuals of this third sort, Greenacre argued, imagination unfolds initially in connection with masturbation activity, but is liberated from it later—or the creativity fails.

This pattern is the one that appears in Anna Freud's childhood. Her masturbation conflict was early on partially sublimated into fantasies that were progressively more liberated—first beating fantasies, then daydreams, then creative work; and partially controlled with somewhat compulsive substitute physical activities like knitting and weaving. She developed a habit of finding acceptable outlets for unacceptable impulses and wishes, ultimately altruistically surrendering her wishes to others. The processes of sublimating and surrendering did not, of course, mean that her drives were depleted—she had the awesome, somewhat compulsive energy that is characteristic of chaste people with burning faith or compelling causes. Nor were her conflicts eliminated. She was able to have a scientific interest in sexuality, but not to be actively sexual in either a heterosexual or a homosexual mode. The crucial fact for her creative life, however, was that her main defense was sublimation—and this also means: not repression.

The part of this story that must, for lack of information, remain more obscure is the consequence of the complicated mothering. Three women handled Anna Freud as a child—her mother, her Tante Minna, and her *Kinderfrau*, Josefine. The first were rivals for her father's love (as were her two sisters to a lesser extent), while

Josefine was the "good" mother. Josefine was the one for whom Anna was not last in line and littlest; the one whose affection did not have to be won away from siblings, particularly Sophie; and the one who was not a rival for the father. It was Josefine who reappeared most obviously in the form of Manna Friedmann when Anna Freud was childlike in her old age and illness, when she had lost her companion Dorothy Burlingham, and when she could no longer work as a psychoanalyst. But there had been quite a number of important female figures earlier: Loe Kann Jones, Katá Levy, briefly Margarethe Rie's mother, Melanie, most importantly Lou Andreas-Salomé, and then Marie Bonaparte. Later friends were also maternal, like Marianne Kris and Dorothy Burlingham—although Dorothy played many other roles as well: brother/sister twin, mother of the children most nearly Anna Freud's own, admiring tutorial student and utterly loyal partner in work, fellow adventurer. The needs expressed to and through these many women were more complex than the needs to love and be like a man that were filled by Freud and Freud only—even if it is taken into account that identifying with her father, being male, might originally have served to deny the intensity of her daughterly love as well as to satisfy phallic wishes. For Anna Freud herself, the topic of "the mother/daughter relationship" was one of the few within psychoanalysis that she did not take up: it was, she said in response to a query, "not one of my special interests and if it were, and I felt that I have a great deal of knowledge of it, I would probably have written about it myself."[4]

As with any analyst, including the first one, the limits of self-insight and the limits of theory construction coincide. Important contributions to psychoanalytic theory are, as Nietzsche said of great philosophies," involuntary and unconscious autobiography." The progress of psychoanalysis as a science is therefore necessarily a matter of complementarities among clinicians and researchers; only cooperative work can overcome the limitations of individual subjectivities. But for individuals it is true that expansions of theory and expansions of self-insight coincide, and greatness is a matter of growing for and through the work. In Anna Freud's case, there were successive upsurges of creative thinking, registered in more or less autobiographical writings: during her analysis; during the early years of her practice, which were the years of second analysis and her supervisory work with her father; during her mourning for him after the war; and when she formulated her "Studies in Passivity" on the basis of analyses of homosexual men, which she did the year of her mother's death.

But her creativity was also intertwined with her settings, and with the kinds of patients treated in those settings. She was not, like her father in his early days, a solitary worker; she was initially dedicated to proving psychoanalytic hypotheses as much, if not more, than framing them, and this required, she felt, collective work—the process of establishing diverse analytic and observational contexts and pooling results from them. Later she thought of child analysis as not only the main site for testing hypotheses framed from reconstructions in adult analysis but also the main launch for revisions and new syntheses. Anna Freud had two worlds of discovery: the inner one where she was the analysand and the self-analyst; and the outer one where the men and women with whom she worked were her delegates, her proxies, her team, her "family"—her psyche, as it were, turned inside out.

In both her worlds she had the possibility for that "mechanism of production" her father had succinctly described as "the succession of boldly roving fantasy and ruthlessly realistic criticism."[5] The language of her fantasy was, additionally, vivid and often quite anthropomorphic.[6] When she took pleasure in describing intrapsychic conflict, part of the pleasure was in the dramatization: she imagined unconscious and conscious, id and ego, battling, negotiating, striking bargains. In order to placate unplayful methodologists, she would restrain this habit, or indicate that she was just pretending: "To personify the idea of the ego for the moment, it seems to me that the ego doesn't mind where the content comes from that is objected to. What the ego minds is the content becoming conscious."[7]

The simplicity, the clarity, and the originality of Anna Freud's thought were based upon this anthropomorphizing: she explored the structure of psyche as others might explore the class structure of a town or the power relations in a government. While her father had specialized as a thinker and writer in simile and metaphor, making general ideas concrete and immediate, she specialized in personification, making general ideas alive and interactive. His wit, too, tended toward complex comparisons, while hers grew from her capacity for empathy, for seeing things from the points of views of her personifications as she saw them from within the psyches of her patients. One of her colleagues offered a characteristic anecdote about Anna Freud's way of thinking: "A fat little girl said to Miss Freud: 'It is funny, Miss Freud, but I always think in my head.' Miss Freud said: 'With Pamela this really is funny, she ought to think with her tummy.' "

It is tempting to think of Miss Freud's anthropomorphic dramatizing and her empathy as typically feminine, embedded in and concerned with relationships. But this notion of what is typically feminine is probably too simple for any woman who is not a theoretical construct, and certainly in Anna Freud's case what is remarkable is how consistently her thought reflects her bisexual constitution. Her fantasies always had been full of battles and bargains: ego-like men in control and id-like boys on knightly quests, struggling to be recognized, being beaten, being loved. Such fantasies were the ground for brilliant, vivid imagining once the fantasies were liberated from their specific early content and the masturbation activity to which it was connected. And Anna Freud had the habit of following boldly roving fantasy with ruthless criticism from the process of the liberation, analysis, and from the examples of her male and female liberators, her father and Lou Andreas-Salomé.

It has become a commonplace of historical writing that since Freud's death "the most original work done in psychoanalysis has been in and around the area of 'object relations' theory, which traces the origin of the severer neuroses and of the psychoses to disturbances of the relationship between mother and child in the earliest period of life, known as the pre-Oedipal period."[8] Such work is original in the sense that it is taking place in an area that Freud looked into but did not map. Anna Freud's contribution was not original by this criterion. She learned from the "object relations" work, but she had it in a much larger perspective.

Her labor of checking and revising all of her father's maps of psychic life was not original in the sense that it revealed a mapless territory. But it provided her with a survey-making or synthetic sense that was without equal in her generation or the next ones. She was not a specialist in any one area of psychoanalytic work—especially not the earliest period of the mother-infant relationship—and she was leery of any conversion of a specialist part into a whole, the whole. Late in her life, on the basis of many years of collective work and progressively growing capacities for survey and revision, Anna Freud went in quite another direction than the supposedly "most original work in psychoanalysis." Instead of finding the origin of the severer neuroses and psychoses in disturbances of the relationship between mother and child in the earliest period of life, she offered a great number of "developmental lines"—lines of *normal* development—along which and between which disturbances can occur. She argued that pathology is multiple, multilateral, taking forms in childhood and adulthood which are not necessarily directly or simply causally related or even similar.

Unwavering in her opposition to reductionism of any sort, Anna Freud vastly complicated psychoanalysis—and that is neither a popular nor a popularizable thing to have done. It has meant that her influence, more widespread and widely recognized than that of any analyst since Freud, has been piecemeal. Parts of her work, her work on particular topics, have been assimilated, but not—outside of her Clinic—the full ambition or intention of her way of thinking psychoanalytically.

Anna Freud herself tended to the long view, about her own work and about psychoanalysis in general, even in the last years of her life, when she was so disheartened by the vituperative criticisms of her father's person, from within and without the profession. In 1979 a younger analyst sent her a popular American magazine article on the death of psychoanalysis, and out of her lifelong familiarity with conflict, inner and outer, she told him: "to predict the imminent demise of psychoanalysis may be very topical. The only sensible answer is the one that Mark Twain gave when some paper mistakenly brought the announcement of his death: 'Reports of my death are highly exaggerated.' Anyway, you say that the old-timers did not mind, and that is natural since they were always used to attacks. In many ways psychoanalysis does best when under attack."[9]

APPENDIX

Anna Freud and Dorothy Burlingham
at Hempstead
The Origins of Psychoanalytic Parent–Infant Observation

There are many reasons why Sigmund Freud began in the mid-1920's to be more sensitive to the importance of the early mother-child relationship in female and male development. He had been challenged theoretically a decade earlier by Jung's interest in mothering and in the Great Mother, and Lou Andreas-Salomé too, who might be considered the Muse of Freud's science, had reminded him of the theories of matriarchy swirling among anthropologists. Then in 1924 Freud had been challenged again by both Otto Rank's birth trauma theory and Sandor Ferenczi's "theory of genitality" with its emphasis on normal regression to the mother and to the mother's womb in sexual intercourse (regressions that Ferenczi held to be common to men and to women, even though he had difficulty in making his case for women in *Thalassa: Towards a Theory of Genitality*) (Ferenczi, 1933). Freud had also acknowledged that his own reconsideration of the psychodynamics of anxiety, including in the war neuroses, and the new definition of anxiety that he made public in his 1926 work, *Inhibitions, Symptoms and Anxiety*, had led him to question whether anxiety over loss of maternal love was not central to female development, as castration anxiety was to male development. There were also many stirrings of discontent with his views on female psychology among the older of his female followers, such as Helene Deutsch in Vienna and Karen Horney in Berlin. But, to judge from his correspon-

Reprinted with permission from *Annual of Psychoanalysis* 32 (2004): 185–97.

dences, Freud's clinical work in the mid-1920s seems to have stood crucially behind the momentous sentences on preoedipal female development standing at the beginning of the 1931 essay "Female Sexuality."

> It is well known that there are many women who have a strong attach-ment to their father; nor need they be in any way neurotic. It is upon such women that I have made the observations which I propose to re-port here and which have led me to adopt a particular view of female sexuality. I was struck, above all, by two facts. The first was that where the woman's attachment to her father was particularly intense, analysis showed that it had been preceded by a phase of exclusive attachment to her mother. . . . The second fact taught me that the duration of this at-tachment had also been greatly underestimated. . . . [These facts show that] the pre-Oedipus phase in women gains an importance which we have not attributed it to hitherto. . . . Our insight into this early, pre-Oedipus phase in girls comes to us as a surprise, like the discovery, in another field, of the Minoan-Mycenaean civilization behind the civi-lization of Greece [pp. 225–226].

Freud did not hesitate to conclude from the observations summarized in this statement that he should "retract the universality of the dictum that the Oedipus complex is the nucleus of the neuroses" (p. 226), but no sooner had he done so than he reversed himself. If the concept of the Oedipus com-plex were extended to include both parents and if the female's positive Oedi-pus complex were seen as following after a negative Oedipus complex in which the mother was the little girl's love object, he noted with relief, then the nucleus of the neuroses dictum could remain undisturbed in dogmatic slumber as it had been for decades in his theory. The retraction, however, once envisioned, would not fade away.

The story of how Melanie Klein explored in her child analytic work and in her theoretical speculations the domain of the preoedipal is well known. But I would like to explore (in part psychobiographically) in this es-say a less well known path of clinical and theoretical development that leads from Freud's clinical work in the 1920s to the Hampstead Nurseries in the 1940s, where both Dorothy Burlingham and Anna Freud continued the in-vestigations of the first years of life that they had started in their own analytic work with Freud. This is the story of the birth in psychoanalysis of parent-infant observation.

Freud had a number of women with strong father attachments in analysis in the mid-1920s, women who were, in effect, doing "training analyses" with him and preparing themselves for the important roles they would come to play in the psychoanalytic movement. His daughter Anna Freud was one, and it seems that she came in her treatment to appreciate both the strong and passionate early bond she had with a maternal figure, her nanny, Josefine, whose dedication was first and foremost to the youngest of the six Freud children, the one who had to struggle fiercely for recognition and inclusion with the sibling higher ups. She came to explore as well her lack of a close bond with her own controlled and proper mother and her tense, competitive relation with her Aunt Minna, the third woman with caretaking functions in the Freud household. But the analysand with a strong father attachment whose mother relationship was most formidable and long—and tragic—was the youngest daughter of the famous and famously eccentric and difficult American artist in glass Louis Tiffany.

Dorothy Tiffany Burlingham had started an analysis with Theodor Reik, but then transferred to Freud in 1927, after finding that almost two years with Reik had not helped her.[1] At the time, she was herself the mother of four young children—all of whom eventually worked analytically with Anna Freud—and she was very concerned from that perspective with the bonds between mothers and young children. Her first child, a son named Bob, had begun six months after his birth in 1915 to suffer from a series of illnesses. At six months, he developed a severe eczema over his entire body and had to be literally tarred to prevent him from scratching himself. Then an allergy to milk started up and Bob, who stopped eating, had to be force-fed (a case of what would now be called "failure to thrive"). A year after his birth, his parents left him with his paternal grandparents while they arranged their New York apartment, and he had his first intense asthma attack, turning blue and coughing convulsively. At some point during his first year—the chronology is not exactly determinable—Robert Burlingham, the father, had a breakdown, perhaps not the first, that was Dorothy Burlingham's clear signal that her husband was seriously ill. At the age of 23, she was dealing with a highly sensitive baby, whose ability to intuit—and whose capacity to identify with—her own moods and anxiety was acute from the beginning and grew as their troubles grew, and a husband who was eventually diagnosed with manic-depressive psychosis. Following the medical advice of the time, she continued to leave her son with his grandparents or a succession of nannies while she tried to manage her domestic affairs, but each time she did he suffered an asthma attack. Then Bob's asthma attacks also began to correlate with separation from his father at a juncture when his parents were living in different residences. The attacks continued while the father had a second breakdown. When Bob was less than two years old, Burlingham had her second child, a girl named Mary Tiffany; then at two-year intervals a third, Katrina, and a fourth, Michael, arrived. By the time

Bob was a latency boy, he was explosively temperamental, deceitful, and given to petty thefts and delinquencies. To cite the diagnosis indicated in Anna Freud's 1927 *For Lectures on Child Analysis*, where he appears in disguise as one of the cases: "salient features: perversions, very diverse anxieties, semi-delinquent" (p. 11).

Burlingham made the difficult decision to remove herself and the children from her husband and from their New York home in 1925. She then went to Europe, and eventually to Vienna, seeking help from psychoanalysis, which she had learned about from one of Otto Rank's 1924 American lectures and from a relative, Izette de Forest, who, along with another American woman, Clara Thompson, had sought training with Ferenczi in Budapest. (These two later became influential in the development of Budapest School psychoanalysis in Washington and Boston, where, mixed with the work of Sullivan and others, it became known as interpersonalism.) The powerful Burlingham family disapproved completely of Dorothy's decision for Vienna and psychoanalysis, and until Robert Burlingham committed suicide by jumping out of his New York apartment's window in May 1938, Dorothy was constantly involved in complex negotiations about what contact he and his family would have with his children and what form her own marital (including sexual) relationship with him would take.

Meanwhile, in Vienna, the Burlingham and Freud families became progressively more entwined — or, as we would say now, merged — through the late 1920s. In the summers, the families had next-door vacation villas on the Semmering, and then they shared a farm cottage, Hochroterd, that Burlingham and Anna Freud bought together. So Freud was in the day-to-day company of young children, like a grandfather, for the first time since his own children had supplied him with dreams for "The Interpretation of Dreams" (1900) and sexual theories for "Three Essays on the Theory of Sexuality" (1905). Dorothy Burlingham remained in analysis with Freud through her children's teenage years, and up until Freud's death from cancer in 1939 — a 12-year-long analysis, which was, as far as can be told from the evidence available, the longest analysis he ever conducted.

Freud had marked his closeness with Burlingham by making her a gift in the spring of 1926 of a brooch made of variously colored opals set in gold; as he later would give her a ring to mark her membership in the founding circle of his psychoanalytic followers. To her great distress, she lost the brooch only a few days after receiving it. Freud immediately ordered a replacement, and even when the original was found, he wanted her to keep the replacement — perhaps to reassure her that he was the reliable giver of gifts no matter what, as her unreliable father had never been. It is hard not to think that this episode was in Anna Freud's mind when, nearly 30 years later in 1953, after the period of the Hempstead War Nurseries, she wrote her classic essay "About Losing and Being Lost," an essay that, inter linea, shows so many signs of having been talked through with Dorothy Burlingham.

The essay begins with a recapitulation of two chapters in the history of Sigmund Freud's thought, written out in "The Psychopathology of Everyday Life" (1901) and "Introductory Lectures" (1916–1917), about the parapraxis "losing and retaining." Then comes an acknowledgment that "a new chapter" (beyond Freud, she might have said, but did not) had opened when analysts (including herself, she might have said but did not) had begun "to concentrate their attention on the events of the first year of life and the earliest interactions between infants and their mothers" (A. Freud, 1953, p. 304). In the very year that she was writing, she acknowledged that D. W. Winnicott had offered his famous paper on transitional objects, for example.

After she had cataloged with her usual thoroughness the libidinal dynamics of losing, Anna Freud turned her attention to what would now be called an "object relations" perspective on how people identify with the objects they lose, making use in her description of (it is interesting to note, given the heated controversies of that day) one of Melanie Klein's key concepts, "projective identification." The deeper layers of feeling involved, she noted, come to light when something is lost during an analysis or when an episode of losing is revisited in an analysis, for then it can become clear how the child or the adult as a child has felt lost or abandoned by a parent. To illustrate, she used (in disguise) an autobiographical story about herself as a young girl losing her cap on an Alpine walking trip and then sobbing, in identification with her cap as she imagined it "exposed and deserted in the dark solitude of the mountain scenery" (p. 305).

Frequently, she noted, children and adults who are identified with objects that they feel are themselves as lost, displace their painful affect onto their analyst or onto their caretakers, imagining that the analyst misses them while on vacation, or that the mother is pained when they are apart. "In our work with separated children during wartime, we had many occasions to observe those who experienced not their own, very real separation distress, but the imagined distress, loneliness, and longing of the mother whom they had left behind" (p. 310). In summary:

> It is not difficult in analysis to understand and interpret such displacements of feeling. When traced back to their source, they reveal themselves as based on early childhood events when the loser was himself "lost," that is, felt deserted, rejected, alone, and experienced in full force as his own all the painful emotions which he later ascribes to the objects lost by him [p. 310].

While Burlingham was losing her brooch in 1927, she was considering in her analysis the impact of her separation from her husband on herself and her children, the impact of her departure for Vienna on her husband, and the whole history of traumatic separations in her own childhood, starting with her separations from her mother.

The Minoan-Mycenaean civilization of Burlingham's relationship to her mother was hidden behind her painful memories of her mother's agonizing death from bowel cancer when Dorothy was 12 years old (uncannily enough, given the length of her analysis with Freud — 12-years — up to the point of his death from cancer). Her mother had been stepmother to three children from Louis Tiffany's first marriage and to four girls of her own — the third of whom, Annie, had died when Dorothy was six months old. Annie's death plunged her mother into a depression and delivered Dorothy into the care of a neglectful nanny who was partial to the lost Annie. So, at six months, Dorothy had been abandoned to the maltreating nanny and separated from her mother.

Her older sisters, twins, were, she felt, favored by her mother after her mother recovered. Dorothy felt herself to be the least and the least adequate of the siblings: not an exquisite angel like the lost Annie, not beautiful and musically talented and dedicated to each other like the twins, and not the boy she felt her father and mother and Tiffany grandparents (for whom she was the ninth straight granddaughter) had wanted. When her mother was dying, Dorothy — it appears — suffered from a renewal of the feeling she had had as a little child that her presence had disappointed and then harmed her mother. But she also blamed her father, whose enormous and narcissistic energy for creative projects, for real estate acquisition, for travel, for business, and for self-promotion had exhausted both his first wife and his second.

In her analysis, Dorothy Burlingham became aware of the extent to which she had spent her youth guiltily being haunted by her mother's groaning during her painful death; trying to please her mother in the relation Freud called "the negative Oedipus complex"; trying to rescue her mother; identifying with her mother, who was not only a dedicated mother, but a dedicated philanthropist on the Board of the New York Infirmary for Women and Children; marrying a man who was both depressed and a doctor; and hoping to be a mother (as she did become, of four children, like her mother). Dorothy had been as attuned to her mother as her children later became to her.

In the year while Anna Freud was writing *The Ego and the Mechanisms of Defense,* published in 1936 and presented to her father as a present on his 80th birthday, Dorothy Burlingham also produced a gift to recognize the effect her analysis was having on her ability to join the psychoanalytic movement as a productive member. Her gift was two essays, full of observational material — the first of their kind — all about mothering, and very autobiographically about her own experience of mothering and of being mothered, and being in analysis simultaneously with her own children: "Child Analysis and the Mother" and "Empathy between Infant and Mother," both later collected in the volume *Psychoanalytic Studies of the Sighted and the Blind* (Burlingham, 1972).

Empathy emerged in these essays as the key to understanding the complex communications that take place between very young children (especially in the first year of life) and their mothers. In her first essay, Burlingham was inclined to invoke telepathy or thought transference — a capacity that Freud and Sandor Ferenczi had spent much time considering and corresponding over — as the explanation for how preverbal children can be so attuned to their mothers' every action and, especially, every affect and thought, including unconscious affect and thought. "The mother's unconscious is no less vital for the child than what happens in her consciousness. . . . The mother's character, her neurosis, her obsessions, anxieties, symptoms, in short, her affects as well as her repressions have passed from mother to child with lightning speed and power" (p. 5). But she had come around by the second paper to the conviction that it is not telepathy — or, another possibility: inherited shared proclivities — that connects children and their mothers, but the children's own empathic abilities.

> It is my contention that young children have a greater capacity for observation than had been thought previously; that they observe the direct expressions of affect as well as the efforts to deny emotion; that they are especially receptive to those expressions of repressed impulses on which the mother's character is based, are seduced by them, and in turn use them to seduce the mother; and these capacities are lost as the child matures, develops and adapts to the environment. In short, empathy between infant and mother, mysterious and almost uncanny as it used to appear formerly, is here shown as lodged to a large degree in the child's perception [p. 69].

Although Anna Freud had been involved just after the First World War with a project for offering young children from war-disrupted families shelter and therapeutic support, the first work that she did in an institution of her own design was undertaken with Burlingham, and it focused specifically on young children — babies, preoedipal children — from economically deprived backgrounds. The Edith Jackson Project, funded by the wealthy American Edith Jackson, who had a parent-infant observation unit of her own in New Haven, was a krippe or creche for one- and two-year-olds whose mothers were working — a day care center in current parlance, but one with an on-site pediatrician (Josefine Stross, later the pediatrician for the Hempstead Nurseries). The Jackson Project lasted only a year in the turbulent period of the Nazi consolidation of power in Germany, and the dire political situation left no time for the conversion of their meticulous notes into reports or articles.

In their analytic work with children and in the work that they did in schools and in the Jackson nursery, as in their family life, Anna Freud and Burlingham gave leadership in the 1930s to a group of women analysts who began to think about the relations of mothers and young children, and who worked observationally with babies as well as analytically with verbal children. Most of these were women who observed their own babies — except for Anna Freud herself, who was not, of course, a mother, but who shared the mothering of Burlingham's four children and was very involved in the lives of her colleagues. Most of the Viennese women were observing their own children in the contexts of training analyses and psychoanalytic marriages while they were operating as peers in Anna Freud's child analysis seminar in Vienna: Grete Bibring (and Edward), Marianne Kris (and Ernst), Jenny Waelder (and Robert), Annie Reich (and Wilhelm), Editha Sterba (and Richard), Anny Katan (and Mauritis), and Jeanne Lampl (and Hans).[2] The unmarried Bornstein sisters, Berta and Steffi, were part of this circle, as was Margaret Mahler, who came from an initial training in Budapest.

The Viennese child analysts were, in this period closely connected to Budapest (rather than to Berlin, Melanie Klein's base), where Alice Balint (wife of Michael), who wrote one of the first books on *The Early Years of Life* (1931), and Kata Levy, another of Freud's analysands (and wife of the physician-psychoanalyst Lajos), were teaching child analysis, and where the young Therese Benedek was training before her emigration to Chicago, the base from which she continued to produce her series of important psychoanalytic and empirical essays on early mother–child relations.

Little is known about the observations made at the Jackson Nursery, but when Burlingham and Anna Freud established the Hempstead Nurseries in January 1941, they were required by the American funding agency to produce reports, so they trained their staff to keep notes, and they crafted a rich portfolio of observations and then the book *Infants Without Families* (A. Freud, 1941).

The wartime conditions set the terms for their research: they were observing children — babies, toddlers, young schoolchildren — who were both separated from their parents and surrounded by all of the dangers of the Blitz. That is, their "subjects" were deprived in these two major ways; and their "experiment" — "an experimental situation provided by fate for our investigation" (p. xix) — was focused on how to assess the impact of the deprivations at different developmental levels and how to supply what was missing or foster healthy adaptation.

The Hempstead Nurseries experience then set the terms for much of the observational work Anna Freud and Burlingham did over the next 40 years: "that this method of examining a specific environmental or innate agent via its elimination from the situation is a fruitful one is bourne out by the many subsequent studies of deprived or handicapped infants in which the same procedure has been adopted" (p. xix).

Quickly, the nursery workers observed two things — both of which were known already to Burlingham from her analytic retrospection on her son Bob's first year of life and her own childhood. They observed, first, that the "infant's need for emotional closeness to other human beings" cannot be ignored or slighted or met with only "impersonal and professional hygiene, care, and supervision" (p. xix). The need must be met by arranging (if at all possible) that separations from parents be gradual rather than abrupt, and that a substitute mothering caretaker be in place, available in a familylike group — one staff worker to at most five children. Children in a group larger than five could not get the warm attention and nurturing that they needed, and they regressed. "Regression happens while the child passes through the no-man's-land of affection, that is, during the time after the old object has been given up and before the new one has been found" (p. 209).

Second, they observed that children who were in the presence of a calm and attentive adult when air raid warnings sounded or bombs fell did not panic or grow fearful. The father of a six-year-old girl whose home area had been heavily bombed told the staff when he brought her to the nursery that "You would have to drop a bomb down her back before she would notice!" and they understood that it was the transmission of her parents' calm attitude to her that had protected her, enwrapped her. "The situation is different with two of our children who were brought in by excessively nervous mothers . . . These mothers used to pull their children out of bed and stand around trembling; one child stood near his mother all night, unable to leave her" (p. 8).

> Altogether, it is our experience that oversensitiveness to danger has nothing to do with the actual experience of bombing that has gone before. Rather, the children's fears are to a large extent dependent on their parents' anxiety. After separation from these parents, fears either vanish or at least decrease. The anxiety of playmates does not seem to be infectious in the same sense. [p. 12]

As the nurseries developed over the next four years, up to December 1945, with new locations and new tasks, including evacuation to the countryside for some of the children, Anna Freud and Burlingham were able to make longitudinal observations, and to delineate in great detail stages of development in the children's relations with their parents, living and dead, absent or intermittently visiting. They wrote separately about the 25 babies that they had in their Babies Home, and they distinguished children of two and three from children older than three most clearly on the basis of the different children's abilities to keep their absent parents in their minds and feelings. Again quoting *Infants without Families*:

> Most of the children under three will, because of the inner situation described, forget about their parents or at least become apparently indifferent toward them. They shift their attention to the new surroundings, and, after some hesitation, and some loss of valuable development to be described later, will restart normal life on a new basis.
>
> After three years of age, children will not normally forget their parents. Their memories are more stable; change of attitude takes the place of complete repression. It is already easier for the children to find active and conscious expression for their feelings. The image of the parents remains in their mind, especially when helped from the outside by frequent visits, receipt of parcels, and constant talk about the parents. Frequently these parental images undergo great changes and no longer resemble the real parent in the child's past. In fantasy life, the parents seem better, bigger, richer, more generous and more tolerant than they have ever been. It is the negative feelings, as shown above, which undergo repression and create all sorts of moods and problems of behavior, the origin of which remains unknown to child and teacher alike [p. 190].

Five years after the end of the war and the closing of the nurseries, Anna Freud took the occasion of a meeting at the Austen Riggs Center in Stockbridge, Massachusetts, to reflect generally on what can be learned about infant and child development from observation, as distinguished from what can be learned only in psychoanalytic situations. In "Observations on Child Development" (1951) she noted: "As psychoanalysts, we are not interested in behavioristic data for their own sakes. We ask ourselves whether observational work outside the analytic setting can ever lead to new discoveries about underlying trends and processes, and can thereby supplement that data gathered by analyses of adults and children" (p. 144). In her own estimation, the observational data from the Hempstead Nurseries did not "break new ground" for psychoanalysis, but it did "swell the body of existing analytic knowledge" (p. 145), and it did offer some refinements and raise some questions for future investigation. For example, it suggested a refinement of the libido theory as it had come, by that time, to be applied to the Mycenaean-Minoan layers in both boys and girls. Analysts had long stressed that the oral, anal, and phallic libidinal phases were never clearly distinct, but always overlapping and intermixed.

What impressed us particularly was the wide overlapping between the oral and the anal stage. Much of this may have been due in our case to the oral deprivations which many of our children had had to undergo when separated from their mothers. But even those who had been breast fed by their own mothers in the Nursery, and remained in close contact with them, showed a survival of oral wishes, oral greed and oral activities which seemed protracted when compared with our expectations. They kept up thumb sucking as a major oral-erotic gratification, and biting as their main aggressive expression, far into the anal phase, and indulged in these activities alongside of their anal interests. The line of demarcation between anal and phallic interests seemed in comparison to be much sharper.

On the other hand, despite this overlapping of pregenital gratifications, it was possible to distinguish clearly between the libidinal phases on the basis of the child's behavior toward the mother or her substitute: a greedy dependence (oral); a tormenting, harassing possessiveness (anal); and a continual bid for attention and admiration linked with an indulgent protectiveness toward the love object (phallic)—these attitudes were expressed by the children daily, hourly, and from minute to minute in their behavior [p. 150].

Refinements of this sort, discrepancies between analytic knowledge and the Hempstead observational data, experiences with how differently early events look while they are unfolding in comparison to how they look when reconstructed within adult analyses, and instances where analytically informed expectations were not met by the observational data—all these suggested research programs that Anna Freud eventually initiated at the research and training program she founded after the war. And they kept up the intricate study of mothers and children both by working to involve mothers in the analyses of their children (Burlingham wrote technical papers discussing how this could be done) and by arranging for a number of simultaneous analyses of mothers and children reported by a third analyst. The results were sifted over the next 15 years and then issued in Anna Freud's 1965 summa *Normality and Pathology in Childhood*. From there, they were woven into work that Anna Freud did in a wide range of fields, from pediatrics to theory of law, from psychosomatic medicine to adolescent psychiatry.

A book with a title like *Normality and Pathology in Childhood* would not be written today; its emphasis on normativity and its implication that normality and pathology can be clearly distinguished are out of step with contemporary psychoanalysis, and even in parts of the Anna Freud Centre in London. Because this comprehensive work was so grounded in Freud's theory of the instinctual drives, which has been questioned from almost every theoretical direction recently, Anna Freud is now considered a conservative in relation to others of her generation and certainly to the next generation's leading figures, such as Winnicott, Lacan, and Kohut, whose influence has spread widely enough now to be the subject of biographical and historical study.

Similarly, her parent–infant observational work has been overshadowed by the parent–infant observational work that now supports theories that are critical of hers. Looked at from the perspective of historian-psychoanalysts who see the current moment as one "beyond Freud," Anna Freud — and "Ego Psychology" generally — look like the orthodoxy of an era that has faded. But, as I have tried to suggest in this essay, things would look very different if she were being studied, with the present situation in mind, as a progressive, not a conservative. There is a good deal of emphasis now in psychoanalysis on the importance of research. As a researcher Anna Freud was certainly the great model, first in the 1930s, then as the codirector with Dorothy Burlingham of the Hempstead War Nurseries in the 1940s, later the cofounder in the 1950s of the Hempstead Center, which was for decades the most important psychoanalytic research center in the world. In this perspective, it would be obvious how innovatory was her focus, spurred by Burlingham, on what is now called "the mother–child dyad."

A master concept precipitated out of Anna Freud's many institutions and research projects: "developmental lines." And from it eventually came — in the last decade of her life, the 1970s — a whole area of pathology, called the developmental pathologies, and many technical innovations for treating them, including innovations that grew out of Burlingham's supervision of the simultaneous analyses of mothers and children. Because the cliché that Anna Freud was a conservative is so pervasive, this work has not even begun to be studied by psychoanalysts outside of the Anna Freud Centre, although workers like Rose Edgcumbe (2000) at the Centre have written about it for a wider audience.

Anna Freud's methodology of studying diverse subpopulations of children — institutionalized children, evacuee children, handicapped children, émigré children and so forth — whose developments were affected by missing elements, and her creativity in finding means for comparing observational data with clinical data gained from analytic work with them (reported collectively in the Hempstead Index, Dorothy Burlingham's special

interest) has "bourne fruit" (as she liked to say) in theories and clinical practices that will take another generation to elaborate. These two women who
shaped psychoanalysis, Dorothy Burlingham and Anna Freud, did so quietly, by the route Anna Freud called "altruistic surrender," more than by direct assertion or promotion of their conclusions. Their influence cannot be
judged from the headlines of recent psychoanalytic history, for it is to be
found in the wider world where their work has reached every institution
concerned with the welfare of children.

Notes

1. See Burlingham (1989) for further biographical information about Dorothy Burlingham and
her family.
2. Helene Deutsch (married to psychoanalyst Felix, Freud's physician) was ten years older than
Anna Freud but her reflections on mothering postdate the early 1930s work by Anna Freud's
group. Anna Freud (1953) described the situation as "When the knowledge concerning infantile sexuality and its transformations had spread in the circle of psychoanalytic workers, direct
observation of children began. Such observations were carried out first by parents, either under
analysis or analysts themselves, on their own children, and were recorded regularly in special
columns of the psychoanalytic journals of the time" (p. 144).

References

Balint, A. (1931), *The Early Years of Life*. New York: Basic Books, 1954.
Burlingham, D. (1972), *Psychoanalytic Studies of the Sighted and the Blind*.
    New York: International Universities Press.
Burlingham, M. J. (1989), *The Last Tiffany: A Biography of Dorothy Tiffany
    Burlingham*. New York: Atheneum.
Edgecumbe, R. (2000), *Anna Freud: A View of Development, Disturbance and
    Therapeutic Technique*. London: Routledge.
Ferenczi, S. (1933), Thalassa: A theory of genitality. *Psychoanal. Quart.*, 3:361–403.
Freud, A. (1927), *Four Lectures on Child Analysis* (originally titled *Introduction
    to the Technique of Child Analysis*): *The Writings of Anna Freud, Vol. I.*
    New York: International Universities Press.
——— (1936), *The Ego and the Mechanisms of Defense: The Writings of Anna
    Freud, Vol. II.* New York: International Universities Press.
——— (1941), *Infants Without Families: The Writings of Anna Freud, Vol. III.*
    New York: International Universities Press.
——— (1951), Observations on child development. In: *The Writings of Anna
    Freud, Vol. IV.* New York: International Universities Press.
——— (1953), About losing and being lost. In: *The Writings of Anna Freud, Vol.
    IV.* New York: International Universities Press.
——— (1965), *Normality and Pathology in Childhood: The Writings of Anna
    Freud, Vol. VI.* New York: International Universities Press.
Freud, S. (1900), The interpretation of dreams. *Standard Edition*, 4 & 5. Lon-
    don: Hogarth Press, 1953.

—— (1901), The psychopathology of everyday life. *Standard Edition*, 6:1–291. London: Hogarth Press, 1960.

—— (1905), Three essays on the theory of sexuality. *Standard Edition*, 7:136–234. London: Hogarth Press, 1953.

—— (1916–1917), Introductory lectures on psychoanalysis. *Standard Edition*, 15 & 16. London: Hogarth Press, 1963.

—— (1926), Inhibitions, symptoms and anxiety. *Standard Edition*, 87–175. London: Hogarth Press, 1959.

—— (1931), Female sexuality. *Standard Edition*, 21:225–243. London: Hogarth Press, 1961.

NOTES

In the notes below, the following abbreviations will be used for published materials:

Freud, *Letters* = *Letters of Sigmund Freud*. Edited by E. L. Freud. New York: Basic Books, 1960

Freud/Abraham = *The Letters of Sigmund Freud and Karl Abraham*. Edited by H. C. Abraham and E. L. Freud. New York: Basic Books, 1965

Freud/Fliess = *The Complete Letters of Sigmund Freud to Wilhelm Fliess, 1887–1904*. Edited by J. M. Masson. Cambridge: Harvard University Press, 1985

Freud/Jung = *The Freud/Jung Letters: The Correspondence Between Sigmund Freud and C. G. Jung*. Edited by William McGuire. Princeton: Princeton University Press, Bollingen Series, 1974

Freud/Salomé = *Sigmund Freud and Lou Andreas-Salomé Letters*. Edited by Ernst Pfeiffer. New York: Harcourt Brace Jovanovich, 1972

Freud/Zweig = *The Letters of Sigmund Freud and Arnold Zweig*. Edited by E. L. Freud. New York: Harcourt Brace Jovanovich, 1970

IJP = *International Journal of Psychoanalysis*

Jones, I, II, or III = Ernest Jones, *The Life and Work of Sigmund Freud*. New York: Basic Books, 1953, 1955, 1957

Martin Freud = *Sigmund Freud: Man and Father*. New York: Vanguard, 1958 (the English title: *Glory Reflected*)

Pioneers = *Psychoanalytic Pioneers*. Edited by Franz Alexander, Sam-
  uel Eisenstein, and Martin Grotjahn. New York: Basic Books,
  1966
PSC = *Psychoanalytic Study of the Child*
SE = *The Standard Edition of the Complete Psychological Works
  of Sigmund Freud*. Vols. I–XXIV. Edited and translated by
  James Strachey et al. London: Hogarth Press and Institute of
  Psychoanalysis, 1953–74
Writings = *The Writings of Anna Freud*. Vols. I–VIII. New York:
  International Universities Press, 1966–80

Unpublished letters will be cited by author, addressee, and date. Unless otherwise indicated, all letters cited are in the Sigmund Freud Archives; see Acknowledgments and Notes on Sources at the beginning of
this biography.

1: ANNERL

1. Martin Freud, p. 24.
2. Schur, p. 62.
3. Freud/Fliess, p. 69; April 25, 1894. Note: Masson, the editor, inter-
prets the phrase about libido to refer to desire for smoking rather than
sexual desire.
4. Freud/Fliess, p. 74; May 21, 1894.
5. Freud/Fliess, p. 442; June 9, 1901.
6. Freud reported on the Emma Eckstein episode intermittently; see
Freud/Fliess, pp. 106–54.
7. Freud/Fliess, p. 29, May 25, 1895, notes that Fleiss's work on contraception is too late for the Freuds; and p. 147, October 20, 1895, states:
"You will not have any objections to my calling my next son 'Wilhelm.'
If he turns out to be a girl, she will be called 'Anna.' "
8. Manna Friedmann's journal.
9. Freud/Fliess, p. 131; June 12, 1895.
10. Freud/Jung, p. 395; February 17, 1911. The "Irma's injection" dream
is presented in *SE*, IV, 106–20 and 292–95; see also Freud/Fliess, pp.
106–54. The first explication of the Emma Eckstein episode as a referent
of the dream was by Max Schur, "Some Additional 'Day Residues' of
'The Specimen Dream of Psychoanalysis,' " in Loewenstein et al., *Psychoanalysis–A General Psychology*, pp. 45–85.
11. Freud/Abraham, p. 18; January 9, 1908.
12. *SE*, IV, 110, note 1.
13. Freud/Fliess, pp. 148, 151, and 170.
14. Freud/Fliess, p. 154; December 8, 1895.
15. Jones, I, 164–65.
16. An April 7, 1893, letter cited in Masson's introduction to Freud/
Fliess, p. 2: Fliess "is a most unusual person, good nature personified: and
I believe, if it came to it, he would for all his genius be goodness itself.
Therefore his sunlike clarity, his pluck."

17. Anna Freud to Kurt Eissler, July 2, 1973. My assessment of Martha Freud here depends heavily on an interview with Margarethe Rie Nunberg, whose mother was Martha Freud's friend.

18. Jones, I, 119. The following account is based upon Jones's letters to Anna Freud date April 23, and November 18 and 26, 1952.

19. Freud, *Letters*, p. 288; to Max Halberstadt, July 7, 1912.

20. Martin Freud, pp. 34–35.

21. Jones (I, 328) dated the acquisition of the downstairs apartment 1892; Martin's account places it in the fourth year after the family moved to the Berggasse, that is, 1895 or 1896 (pp. 24ff). I am following Martin's story because it seems to involve a clear memory of Anna Freud as an infant, and because it accords with Freud/Fliess, p. 203 (dated November 22, 1896): "The first person to whom I am writing from my new quarters is you. . . ."

22. *Writings*, IV, 311–12.

23. Martin Freud, pp. 35ff.

24. Anna Freud to Max Eitingon, July 22, 1925. Anna Freud to Lou Andreas-Salomé, July 26, 1925: "My old nanny Jo has died. She did not have much left to give any more, but still it is sad to lose such an old relationship." Anna Freud to August Aichhorn, July 17, 1925, indicates that the Freud family arranged Josefine's final hospitalization in the suburb of Lainz; this was typical of the Freuds' generosity toward their former servants.

25. SE, IV, xix–xx (a composition history).

26. SE, IV, xxxii (a 1931 Preface).

27. Cited in Peters, p. 46.

28. A letter to Muriel Gardiner quoted in the *Hampstead Bulletin* 6/1 (1983): 64. Anna Freud to Lou Andreas-Salomé, August 5, 1923, on visiting Lavarone, where the Freuds had vacationed in 1906 and 1907: "We were here twice before. . . . And I rejoice that I am so much older, independent and not at all 'little' anymore."

29. Martin Freud, p. 55.

30. *Writings*, I, 98.

31. *Writings*, VIII, 116–17.

32. Manna Friedmann's journal.

33. Freud/Fliess, p. 300; February 23, 1898.

34. Anna Freud to Ernest Jones, February 27, 1954.

35. Martin Freud, p. 141–42.

36. Martin Freud, p. 28.

37. Freud/Fleiss, p. 358; July 3, 1899. On Oliver's neurosis, see Chapter 3.

38. Anna Freud to Max Eitingon, February 7, 1922.

39. Anna Freud to Ralph Greenson, June 25, 1970.

40. Sigmund Freud to Max Eitingon, December 13, 1920.

41. Jones, III, 8.

42. Freud/Jung, p. 394; February 17, 1911.

43. Anna Freud to Evelyn Weber, September 3, 1980, about Sophie: "I think she was my mother's favorite, but never especially near to my father. The role, if you want to assign it, would go to my elder sister Mathilde, until her marriage."

44. Sigmund Freud to Mathilde Freud, March 19, 1908 (an excerpt of this letter appeared in Freud, *Letters*, p. 272).

45. Freud/Fliess, p. 187; May 17, 1896.

46. Freud/Fliess, p. 357; June 27, 1899.

47. Sachs, *Freud: Master and Friend*, p. 81.

48. Freud/Fliess, p. 322; August 20, 1898.

49. Freud/Fliess, p. 244; May 16, 1897.

50. Martin Freud, p. 9.

51. Anna Freud to Ernest Jones, February 14, 1954.

52. Freud/Jung, p. 394; February 17, 1911; cf. note 42 above.

53. Mathilde's illness is mentioned in *SE*, VI, 169 and again on 180; this account is based on Anna Freud's obituary for her sister, *Sigmund Freud House Bulletin* (Vienna) 2/1 (1978): 2, and Anna Freud to Masud Khan, May 22, 1974.

54. Manna Friedmann's journal.

55. *SE*, XXII, 132.

56. On the name derivations, Jones, I, 163. Anna Freud always denied that her name was from either her father's oldest sister, Anna, or "Anna O.," the fictitious name of a famous patient of Breuer's, Bertha Pappenheim.

57. Anna Freud to Lou Andreas-Salomé, August 12, 1922.

58. Martin Freud, pp. 47 and 25.

59. Freud/Fliess, p. 313; May 1, 1898.

60. Anna Freud to M. and H. Kapit, July 22, 1975.

61. Rilke's "Kindheit" cited from his *Sämtliche Werke (Erster Band)*, Insel-Verlag, 1955. The same edition will be used for further citations below; translations are mine.

62. Manna Friedmann's journal.

63. On Elsa Reiss, see Drucker, "Miss Elsa and Miss Sophy" in *Adventures of a Bystander*.

64. Anna Freud to Eva Rosenfeld, undated, ca. 1929.

65. Manna Friedmann's journal.

66. Anna Freud to Ernest Jones, December 21, 1953.

67. Anna Freud to Herman de Levie, March 9, 1968.

68. Anna Freud to Sigmund Freud, August 2, 1919.

69. Anna Freud to Dora Kail, July 12, 1976.

70. Anna Freud to David Jacobs, March 14, 1974.

71. For a brief review and bibliography, see Friedlander, "Children's Books and Their Function."

72. *Writings*, VII, 73–74.

73. Peters, pp. 16–17, and Manna Friedmann's journal.

74. A collection of Anna Freud's school reports are at the Freud Museum, London.

75. Anna Freud to Mary Lee, February 9, 1950 (and on the porcupine joke, Jones, II, 59).

76. Sigmund Freud to Mathilde Freud, March 26, 1908; Sigmund Freud to Sandor Ferenczi, January 30, 1908, mentions an illness in the family, and this may refer to Anna's subsequent operation. Freud mentioned the appendectomy to Binswanger (in Binswanger, p. 38, dated March 15,

1912). The information about Anna's reaction to the operation is from
Manna Friedmann's journal and Anna Freud to Bertha Plant, December
14, 1981 (cited below).
77. Anna Freud to Sigmund Freud, July 13, 1910.
78. Sigmund Freud to Anna Freud, September 18, 1910.
79. Anna Freud to Sigmund Freud, June 15, 1911.
80. Ibid.
81. Jones, II, 93.
82. Anna Freud to Sigmund Freud, December 9, 1912.
83. Anna Freud to Sigmund Freud, December 16, 1912.
84. Freud, *Letters*, p. 295; December 13, 1912.
85. Anna Freud to Mirjam Stern, April 22, 1954.
86. Freud's letter has not survived; I am inferring its contents from Anna
Freud's reply, cited in full.
87. Sigmund Freud to Anna Freud, February 2, 1913.
88. On the essay as autobiographical, cf. Chapter 3.
89. SE, XII, 239–45 and editor's references.
90. Freud/Jung, p. 240; July 7, 1909.
91. Amalie Freud's illness mentioned in Schur, p. 274; Mathilde's in
Jones, II, 94–95; Binswanger's in his *Sigmund Freud*.
92. Sandor Ferenczi to Sigmund Freud, January 25, 1913.
93. Freud, *Letters*, p. 301; July 9, 1913. It seems likely—but I cannot
verify it—that Freud was also depressed because Sophie had had a therapeutic abortion in spring 1913. The fact that Sophie had an abortion before the birth of her first son is mentioned in Hans Lampl to Anna Freud,
July 27, 1956. Freud mentions in a letter to Ferenczi (July 9, 1913) that
Dr. Kaufmann, who performed so superbly for Sophie, has just diagnosed
a circulatory condition in Loe Kann, on Freud's referral. If the abortion
was in spring 1913, and Freud knew of it, he may have wondered whether
Sophie, like Mathilde, would be childless.
94. Freud, *Letters*, p. 301; July 9, 1913.
95. This and subsequent quotations from SE, XII, 291–301.
96. Sigmund Freud to Sandor Ferenczi, June 8, 1913.
97. Jones, II, 99.
98. Freud, *Letters*, pp. 40–41; July 13, 1883.
99. Sigmund Freud to Sandor Ferenczi, December 21, 1913.
100. Freud/Abraham, p. 165; February 15, 1914.
101. Freud/Salomé, p. 32; July 30, 1915.

2: IN TIMES OF WAR AND DEATH

1. Freud/Abraham, p. 197; September 22, 1914: "Strict upbringing by
an intelligent mother enlightened by Hug-Hellmuth . . ."
2. Anna Freud to Sigmund Freud, January 13, 1913.
3. For information on all the Jones circle, see Brome, Chapter 5.
4. *Writings*, VIII, 347.
5. Sigmund Freud to Anna Freud, July 16, 1914.
6. Sigmund Freud to Sandor Ferenczi, July 17, 1914.

7. Sigmund Freud to Sandor Ferenczi, July 12, 1914.

8. Ernest Jones to Anna Freud, July 5, 1953.

9. Sigmund Freud to Sandor Ferenczi, June 23, 1912; May 13, 1913; and also July 9, 1913.

10. Anna Freud to Sigmund Freud, July 26, 1914.

11. Sigmund Freud to Ernest Jones, March 6, 1917 (with Anna Freud's postscript).

12. Freud quotes Davy Jones (in English) to Sandor Ferenczi, August 23, 1914; Loe Kann Jones to Sigmund Freud, August 13, 1914, gives details about Anna Freud's return to Austria. These letters in Freud Museum, London.

13. Anna Freud to Sigmund Freud, September 21, 1914, mentions the Kipling poems.

14. The prose piece "Am Schiff" (undated) was included in a packet of Anna Freud's literary works (see note 45 below).

15. Jones, II, 179.

16. SE, XIV, 278–79.

17. Sigmund Freud to Sandor Ferenczi, November 9, 1914.

18. Sigmund Freud to Sandor Ferenczi, April 8, 1915.

19. Sigmund Freud to Sandor Ferenczi, July 10, 1915.

20. Sigmund Freud to Sandor Ferenczi, September 7, 1915.

21. Sigmund Freud to Anna Freud, July 1, 1915 (included in the German Freud, Briefe, pp. 324–26).

22. Anna Freud to Sigmund Freud, July 23, 1915.

23. Anna Freud to Sigmund Freud, July 26, 1914.

24. Anna Freud to Sigmund Freud, July 19, 1915.

25. Anna Freud to Sigmund Freud, July 12, 1915.

26. Anna Freud to Sigmund Freud, July 19, 1915.

27. Beatrice Waldinger (née Winternitz) to Anna Freud, April 8, 1948.

28. Anna Freud to Sigmund Freud, July 23, 1916.

29. Anna Freud to Sigmund Freud, July 27, 1915.

30. Anna Freud to Sigmund Freud, August 6, 1915.

31. Anna Freud to Sigmund Freud, July 19, 1915.

32. A document entitled "Zeugnis," dated February 27, 1918, and signed by Dr. Goldman was in Anna Freud's possession in England; Anna Freud to Toni Stolper, March 11, 1981, mentions that she was Dr. Goldman's "secretary and assistant."

33. Richard Tislow, M.D., to Anna Freud, February 20, 1957.

34. Cited in Peters, p. 23.

35. Cited in Collins, p. 77.

36. Manna Friedmann's journal.

37. Walter J. Garre, M.D., to Anna Freud, November 16, 1960.

38. Anna Freud to Ernest Jones, March 3, 1955.

39. Manna Friedmann's journal.

40. Sigmund Freud to Sandor Ferenczi, September 24, 1917.

41. Ibid.

42. Sigmund Freud to Max Eitingon, May 27, 1920.

43. Freud/Abraham, p. 255; August 21, 1917.

44. This quotation and the following from SE, XVII, 166ff.

45. All the poems cited below are from a collection that Anna Freud at some point organized into three files. I will present them (in part) chronologically, as I cannot determine what her organizational principle was. Altogether, there are twenty-four poems (plus a little hand-copied booklet of eleven school exercises); five short prose pieces; and eleven short prose reflections. In literary quality, the work is certainly not outstanding; but it is more than competent and occasionally quite remarkable. The poetic style is somewhat archaic (as was typical at the time) and the diction is inconsistent (colloquialisms mingled with high cultural clichés). I have tried to keep to the literal sense and tone of the poems in my translations, rather than to imitate their style or form. (My thanks to Brigitte Molnar and Hilda Damiata for help in transcribing Anna Freud's Gothic script.)

46. Anna Freud to Lou Andreas-Salomé, May 18, 1922: "For the first time I had a daydream or a story with a female main person in my head, and I thought of it all the time (it was even a love story)."

47. Anna Freud to Sigmund Freud, July 24, 1919.

48. Anna Freud to Sigmund Freud, August 5, 1919.

49. Anna Freud to Margarethe Rie Nunberg, September 7, 1920.

50. Ibid.

51. Sigmund Freud to Sandor Ferenczi, February 4, 1920 (in Freud, Letters, p. 328), and March 15, 1920.

52. Anna Freud to Lou Andreas-Salomé, March 26, 1922.

53. Anna Freud to Lou Andreas-Salomé, August 17, 1923.

54. Sigmund Freud to Anna Freud, July 22, 1921.

55. Anna Freud to Lou Andreas-Salomé, October 26, 1922.

56. Anna Freud to Lou Andreas-Salomé, February 18, 1922.

57. Hans Lampl to Anna Freud, January 3, 1955.

58. Hans Lampl to Anna Freud, October 9, 1956.

59. Anna Freud to Sigmund Freud, July 7, 1921.

60. Anna Freud to Sigmund Freud, November 12, 1920.

61. Caecilie Graf's letter to her mother (August 16, 1922) was kept by Rosa Graf in an album of photographs of Caecilie; the album and a journal of Caecilie's were in Anna Freud's possession in England, as was the letter to Anna Freud cited below, which is marked "Abschrift, Aug. 16." These documents in Freud Museum, London.

62. Anna Freud to Ernest Jones, May 4, 1955.

63. Anna Freud to Lou Andreas-Salomé, September 1, 1922.

64. Sigmund Freud to Max Eitingon, May 19, 1922.

65. Anna Freud to Max Eitingon, May 22, 1922.

66. Anna Freud to Lou Andreas-Salomé, April 14, 1925: "The dog will arrive soon I think. If I had decided to get a female, she would have been here already. I prefer the male incomparably more."

67. On Bernfeld, see Hoffer, pp. 93–145; also Pioneers, 415–29.

68. See Bernfeld, Kinderheim Baumgarten.

69. On Aichhorn, see Paul Federn, "A Biographical Outline," in Eissler et al., Searchlights on Delinquency, pp. ix–xiii; Anna Freud's obituary in Writings, IV, 625–38; and Pioneers, 348–59.

70. Anna Freud to Lou Andreas-Salomé, January 13, 1924.

71. SE, XIX, 273.

72. The correspondence between Anna Freud and August Aichhorn will be discussed in Chapter 7.

3: BEING ANALYZED

1. For example, Dyer, p. 42. See also. Anna Freud to R. Besser, January 16, 1973: "Meine Lehranalyse ging in den Jahren des ersten Weltkriegs vor sich." Anna Freud told Jones (November 7, 1955) that her practice began in 1923, and he reported this in his biography of Sigmund Freud (Jones, III, 291). In her letters to Eitingon, she mentions the possibility of a child patient for the fall of 1922; but perhaps this did not work out. Cf. Sigmund Freud to Lou Andreas-Salomé (Freud/Salomé, p. 122; March 23, 1923): "Anna has now also joined the practicing analysts, but at least she has started off cautiously and still enjoys her work."
2. Anna Freud to Max Eitingon, April 15, 1922.
3. SE, XVII, 183. "Psychasthenia" was a term used primarily by the French psychologist Janet for "lowering of the mental level" or reduced mental functioning. Jung adopted the term: Freud/Jung, p. 63; June 12, 1907. See Chapter 2 (p. 59) referring to SE, XII, 249.
4. Writings, I, 140.
5. Writings, I, 149.
6. Writings, I, 151.
7. Writings, I, 153.
8. Anna Freud to Sigmund Freud, August 9, 1919.
9. Writings, I, 155.
10. Writings, I, 157. Freud had suggested (SE, XVII, 182) that "sublimation arises out of some special process," and this passage summarizes Anna Freud's discussion of that process. The term "autistic activity" in this passage echoes Varendonck's The Psychology of Daydreams, where "austic" and "realistic" are said to be the two types of thinking activity. Anna Freud translated this book into German shortly after its publication.
11. SE, XVII, 190–91 (and Anna Freud's citation of this passage in her essay, Writings, I, 138). See also note 46 to Chapter 2 above.
12. SE, XVII, 199.
13. Sigmund Freud to Max Eitingon, May 19, 1922.
14. Anna Freud to Lou Andreas-Salomé, May 31, 1922.
15. Writings, I, 153.
16. SE, XVII, 193.
17. Writings, I, 152.
18. SE, XIV, 87, but see also Three Essays on the Theory of Sexuality (SE, VII, passim).
19. Freud/Salomé, p. 89; January 30, 1919.
20. Sigmund Freud to Max Eitingon, November 11, 1921.
21. Anna Freud to Max Eitingon, November 29, 1921.
22. Anna Freud to Sigmund Freud, April 27, 1922.
23. Anna Freud to Lou Andreas-Salomé, January 13, 1924.
24. Freud/Salomé, p. 125; August 5, 1923.
25. Freud/Salomé, p. 66; October 19, 1917. Freud offered a summary of

Andreas-Salomé's "Anal and Sexual" in a footnote to his own *Three Essays* . . . (SE, VII, 187).

26. Freud/Salomé, p. 115; June 26, 1922.

27. SE, XIV, 88.

28. Anna Freud to Lou Andreas-Salomé, December 4, 1924.

29. Anna Freud to Ludwig Bernays, September 14, 1981.

30. Freud/Salomé, p. 115; May 6, 1922.

31. Edoardo Weiss, p. 81 (letter dated November 1, 1935).

32. See Abraham, "Little Hilda"; Jung, "Psychic Conflicts in a Child" in his *Collected Works*, Vol. 17.

33. Oliver's emotional difficulties are mentioned in Anna Freud's letters to Max Eitingon throughout 1921 and 1922, but there is no specific information about the analysis in these letters. Anna Freud to Lou Andreas-Salomé, May 15, 1924, indicates that Eitingon had set out to help Oliver find an analyst and then left the project unfulfilled; Hans Lampl took up the task and sent Oliver to Alexander.

34. Sigmund Freud to Max Eitingon, December 13, 1920.

35. Sigmund Freud to Sandor Ferenczi, October 10, 1918.

36. Freud, *Letters*, p. 325; December 2, 1919, to Max Eitingon.

37. Freud/Salomé, p. 118; September 8, 1922.

38. Sigmund Freud to Max Eitingon, September 24, 1921.

39. Freud/Salomé, p. 113; March 13, 1922. It is interesting to note Freud's very similar response later to a separation from his loyal, unambivalently loving chow dog: "I miss her now almost as much as my cigar." (Freud/Salomé, p. 188; May 8, 1930.)

40. SE, XII, 301 (and see Chapter 1 above on this essay).

41. Anna Freud to Max Eitingon, March 23, 1923.

42. Anna Freud to Lou Andreas-Salomé, August 29, 1923.

43. Anna Freud to Sigmund Freud, August 4, 1921. Everyone in the Freud family called little Heinz "Heinerle" except Freud, who called him "Heinele." If this nickname echoed the name of Freud's younger brother Julius, who died as an infant, Freud's extreme grief when Heinele died in 1923 could be explained as, in part, an ancient wound reopening.

44. Anna Freud to Lou Andreas-Salomé, April 9, 1922.

45. Jones reported the events of summer 1923 with Deutsch and the Committee (Jones, III, 93–94) and they are discussed in the Anna Freud/Jones correspondence. But it seems (cf. Anna Freud to Lou Andreas-Salomé, May 15, 1924) that the Freuds did know that at least Eitingon, if not the whole Committee, was aware that Hajek had found a malignancy; that Eitingon chose not to tell Freud was baffling and distressing to Anna Freud, who charged it to his inability to face hard realities (see pp. 127–28).

46. Anna Freud to William McGuire, July 26, 1973.

47. Anna Freud to Max Eitingon, October 12, 1925.

48. Freud/Salomé, p. 126; September 4, 1923.

49. Anna Freud to Lou Andreas-Salomé, January 3, 1924.

50. Anna Freud to Lou Andreas-Salomé, January 25, 1924.

51. In Anna Freud's correspondences with both Eitingon and Lou Andreas-Salomé, her year of ward rounds clearly begins in January 1924.

Her German biographer Uwe Peters suggests—without citing any source—that she was at the clinic "between 1915 and 1918" (Peters, p. 28). Apparently he was led to this dating by a letter Anna Freud wrote to his colleague R. Besser, March 19, 1973. But Paul Schilder, noted by Peters as Anna Freud's instructor, did not join the clinic until 1918, and Hartmann did not arrive until 1920. It seems unlikely that she was at the clinic before 1924. Anna Freud to Heinz Hartmann, May 14, 1958: "wo Sie und Stengel und ich bei Wagner-Jauregg in Wien unser Vormittage verbracht haben."

52. *Writings*, V, 512.

53. Anna Freud to Eva Landauer, March 15, 1946, and November 5, 1948.

54. Anna Freud to Lou Andreas-Salomé, March 15, 1924.

55. Anna Freud to Lou Andreas-Salomé, May 5, 1924.

56. Anna Freud to Lou Andreas-Salomé, June 1, 1924.

57. Anna Freud to Lou Andreas-Salomé, May 15, 1924.

58. Anna Freud to Lou Andreas-Salomé, January 24, 1925.

59. Anna Freud to Max Eitingon, January 3, 1927. The episode is mentioned in Anna Freud to Lou Andreas-Salomé, November 21, 1926; in September 29, 1925, Anna Freud had noted that her mother very much wanted to go to Berlin.

60. Anna Freud to Lou Andreas-Salomé, February 20, 1929.

61. Anna Freud to Max Eitingon, January 3, 1927.

62. SE, XIX, 254.

63. SE, XIX, 256.

64. *Writings*, IV, 418.

65. Anna Freud to Ernest Jones, February 14, 1954 (cited in Roazen, *Freud and His Followers*, pp. 436, 590).

66. Anna Freud to Lou Andreas-Salomé, May 15, 1924. Freud noted (Jones, II, 182): "Analysis makes for *unity*, but not necessarily for *goodness*. I do not agree with Socrates and Putnam that all our faults arise from confusion and ignorance."

67. Anna Freud to Lou Andreas-Salomé, June 1, 1924.

68. *Writings*, II, 125.

69. *Writings*, II, 131.

70. Anna Freud to Lou Andreas-Salomé, undated but written soon after her birthday, December 3, 1925.

71. Anna Freud to Max Eitingon, February 5, 1926.

72. This quotation and the following from Anna Freud to Max Eitingon, February 19, 1926.

73. Sigmund Freud to Sandor Ferenczi, July 11, 1928.

74. Anna Freud to Max Eitingon, February 19, 1926 (cited further below).

75. Anna Freud to Lou Andreas-Salomé, December 16, 1922.

76. Anna Freud to Max Eitingon, July 5, 1926.

77. Anna Freud to Eva Rosenfeld, August 27, 1931.

78. Anna Freud to Eva Rosenfeld, July 21, 1930.

79. Anna Freud to Max Eitingon, October 12, 1927.

80. Binswanger, p. 88.

81. Anna Freud to Eva Rosenfeld, June 1929 (no day).
82. Freud/Salomé, p. 204; January 6, 1935. To others, Freud gave the impression of being less astute about his daughter's love of him and how it bound her to him. Anny Rosenberg Katan remembered an evening when her father came home from an evening of tarok with Freud and Oscar Rie. He reported that Freud, hearing him talk about Anny's engagement to Otto Angel and hearing Oscar Rie talk about Marianne's engagement to Ernst Kris, said, "And when will it be my Anna?" Ludwig Rosenberg, renowned for his caution as a diagnostician—so Freud portrayed him as Leopold in "Irma's injection"—said, "Is it possible he doesn't know?" Anny and her mother, not given to caution, declared: "He denies the extent of Anna's love."
83. Dorothy Burlingham to Anna Freud, December 1, 1939.
84. Anna Freud gave a number of lectures on male homosexuality between 1949 and 1951, but she published only the abstracts that are in Writings, IV, 245–59, apparently for reasons of patient confidentiality. See Chapter 8.
85. Burlingham, Twins, p. 4.
86. Dorothy Burlingham to Anna Freud, November 15, 1939.

4: Psychoanalysis and Politics

1. Freud/Jung, p. 403; March 14, 1911.
2. Freud/Abraham, p. 293; November 2, 1919.
3. Jones, III, 27; Anna Freud to Ernest Jones, March 7, 1955. It is interesting to note that Jones (III, 27), having misattributed Anna Freud's speech to her father, felt compelled to note that Joan Riviere, when she recollected the Hague Congress, misattributed to Freud a speech by Geza Róheim. Biography is a peculiar genre.
4. Loe Kann Jones to Sigmund Freud, no date, ca. summer 1920 (located at the Freud Museum, London).
5. Loe Kann Jones to Sigmund Freud, August 20, 1919.
6. Sigmund Freud to Anna Freud, April 4, 1922.
7. Anna Freud to Lou Andreas-Salomé, December 16, 1922.
8. Anna Freud to Max Eitingon, April 20, 1921.
9. Anna Freud to Max Eitingon, September 16, 1924.
10. Ibid.
11. Sigmund Freud to Max Eitingon, October 7, 1924.
12. Anna Freud to Max Eitingon, October 27, 1924.
13. Anna Freud to Max Eitingon, November 21, 1924.
14. Anna Freud to Max Eitingon, December 4, 1924.
15. Similarly, when she accepted a birthday present from Lou Andreas-Salomé (December 4, 1924): "I am no longer ashamed as I used to be when someone gives me something; do you remember how upset you were with that? But I now realize how lovely things are which are received without being earned, the truly 'donated.'"
16. Anna Freud to Max Eitingon, December 24, 1924 (cited further below).
17. Anna Freud to Max Eitingon, February 14, 1925.

18. Anna Freud to Max Eitingon, June 11, 1925 (Rank comes weekly for "einer Art Analyse").
19. Anna Freud to Ralph Greenson, February 3, 1974.
20. Anna Freud to Max Eitingon, October 2, 1925.
21. Anna Freud to Max Eitingon, October 23, 1925.
22. Anna Freud to A. A. Brill, February 28, 1934 (copy in Freud Museum, London).
23. Ibid.
24. Anna Freud to Max Eitingon, October 2, 1925.
25. Anna Freud to Max Eitingon, November 19, 1925.
26. Anna Freud to Lou Andreas-Salomé, November 24, 1922, and January 23, 1923.
27. In addition to Reich's *Character Analysis*, see also Sharaf's biography of Reich.
28. Deutsch, *Confrontations with Myself*, p. 167.
29. A collection of reports and minutes from meetings at the Training Institute was taken by Anna Freud to London and is now in the Freud Museum.
30. A letter of recommendation for Marie H. Briehl, May 29, 1957.
31. Anna Freud to Ruth Eissler, September 26, 1955.
32. Anna Freud wrote several brief histories of child analysis, e.g., *Writings*, IV, 302–16. See also Ekstein and Motto, Chapter 1: "Psychoanalysis and Education—An Historical Account."
33. See Jung, "Psychic Conflicts in a Child," in his *Collected Works*, vol. 17.
34. Jean Piaget's influential work on children's intellectual/cognitive development was not directly tied to Swiss psychoanalysis, and it only became important to Freudians after WW II. Anna Freud had two Piaget students in her London training program, Anne-Marie Sandler and Agi Bene Moses.
35. Freud/Jung, p. 48; May 23, 1907. Jung introduced Freud to the work of his Polish colleague Mira Gincburg (later Oberholzer), who was one of the first women to treat children psychoanalytically. Jones (III, 291) reported that Rank originally worked entirely with children, but there is no clear evidence for this in Rank's work.
36. Anna Freud to Lawrence Kubie, January 1, 1955.
37. Sigmund Freud to Max Eitingon, November 21, 1926.
38. Anna Freud to Lou Andreas-Salomé, February 16, 1928.
39. *SE*, XX, 152.
40. *Writings*, I, 3–69 (under the title "Four Lectures on Child Analysis").
41. For biographical information, see Grosskurth.
42. "Symposium on Child Analysis," pp. 357, 359 (cited further below).
43. Ibid., passim, and Klein, *The Psychoanalysis of Children*, p. 10.
44. Klein, *The Psychoanalysis of Children*, p. 37.
45. Sandler et al., *The Analysis of Defense*, p. 66.
46. *Writings*, I, 44.
47. Klein tended to ignore the problems raised by the fact that "Little Hans's" analysis was conducted by his own father—and to ignore Freud's discussion of those problems. On Klein's analyses of her own children,

two boys and a girl, cf. Grosskurth, Chapter 2.

48. "Symposium on Child Analysis, p. 376.
49. Sigmund Freud to Ernest Jones, September 23, 1927.
50. Ernest Jones to Sigmund Freud, May 16, 1927.
51. Sigmund Freud to Ernest Jones, May 27, 1927.
52. Sigmund Freud to Ernest Jones, July 6, 1927.
53. Sigmund Freud to Ernest Jones, September 23, 1927. See Anna Freud to her French translator Anne Berman, March 31, 1950: "Das ganze Symposium von 1927 war ein erbitterter Angriff der englischen Gruppe gegen mich, der böse gemeint war und von dem man mich damals vor der Veröffentlichung gar nicht verstandigt hat."
54. Sigmund Freud to Ernest Jones, September 23, 1927.
55. Sigmund Freud to Max Eitingon, September 23, 1927.
56. Sigmund Freud to Max Eitingon, November 27, 1927.
57. Jones, III, 197 (Anna Freud did not contest this claim in her correspondence with Jones about the biography).
58. Sigmund Freud to Max Eitingon, May 30, 1927: "I don't find Jones's behavior very puzzling. For a long time, he has been looking for 'conflicts' or fights that hold the temptation to become independent from Europe and to establish his own Anglo-American realm, something which he cannot very well do before my demise, and he believes he has found a good opportunity in the partial contradiction between Anna and Mrs. Klein. Perhaps one should add to it a partial anger with Anna dating since 1914, when she refused him."
59. Sigmund Freud to Max Eitingon, January 14, 1929.
60. Sandor Ferenczi to Sigmund Freud, June 30, 1927. Ferenczi had reported earlier (July 15, 1925) on the anti-Jones faction in London, but Freud decided to let the storm take its own course and for a split to occur if it was going to: "Jones makes trouble all the time, but we know his worth well enough" (July 18, 1925).
61. Sigmund Freud to Max Eitingon, December 20, 1927. This remark was made in the context of a discussion about whether and how to publish Frau Klein's work: "Perhaps one can get concessions from her, get her to be satisfied with just one not overly hypertrophic volume in view of the poor chances of multivolume works."
62. Sigmund Freud to Max Eitingon, October 25, 1925.
63. Freud to Max Eitingon, July 5, 1927: "As you know, she enjoys Jones's particular enmity; it is not certain that he will not succeed in getting her defeated, and one must spare her that. She knows, too, that she would owe such a position largely to her relationship with me and not to her own merit, and thus it would not be a satisfaction to her."
64. IJP, VIII (1927).
65. Anna Freud to Max Eitingon, February 13, 1927 (dated 1926 in Anna Freud's letter).
66. Jones, III, 295–96.
67. Writings, I, 73–133. Anna Freud also gave Jones a chance to publish her pamphlet "Psychoanalysis for Teachers and Parents," but he turned this down too, and it was published in England by Allen & Unwin in 1931.

68. *Writings*, I, 172–74. On Moshe Wulff, see *Pioneers* (where he is referred to as Woolf), pp. 200–209.
69. As an example of the English class bias, cf. Joan Riviere on working-class morality ("Symposium on Child Analysis," p. 375): ". . . many severe neuroses develop in persons who are very little checked and allowed comparatively to 'run wild' as children, and the comparative absence of moral training of children in the lower classes ought to show us the unimportance of this factor in childish experience."
70. Erik and Joan Erikson, "Dorothy Burlingham's School in Vienna," *Bulletin of the Hampstead Clinic*, 3/2 (1980): 91ff.
71. Anna Freud to Ernst Simmel, May 31, 1927.
72. Anna Freud to Max Eitingon, October 4, 1927.
73. Ibid.
74. Anna Freud to Ernst Simmel, December 27, 1927.
75. *Writings*, I, 69.
76. Sigmund Freud to Max Eitingon, January 14, 1929.
77. Klein, *Contributions to Psychoanalysis*, pp. 236–50.
78. Freud/Salomé, p. 182; July 28, 1929.
79. See *Writings*, II, 71–82 (the lecture was incorporated into *The Ego and the Mechanisms of Defense*).
80. Anna Freud to Max Eitingon, August 20, 1925.
81. SE, XX, 94.
82. Klein, *Contributions to Psychoanalysis*, p. 249.

5: MECHANISMS OF DEFENSE

1. SE, XVII, 195.
2. Anna Freud to Lou Andreas-Salomé, December 10, 1930.
3. Anna Freud to Eva Rosenfeld [Tegel, summer 1930].
4. Sigmund Freud to Max Eitingon, October 11, 1927.
5. Martha Freud to Dorothy Burlingham, postscript to a letter of Freud's, May 1, 1938.
6. Anna Freud to Sigmund Freud, [soon after Easter] 1927.
7. Sigmund Freud to Sandor Ferenczi, March 25, 1927.
8. Sigmund Freud to Max Eitingon, February 4, 1928.
9. SE, XIX, 162.
11. Anna Freud to Max Eitingon, August 16, 1928. Sigmund Freud discussed Robert Burlingham's illness in letters to Ferenczi, July 11 and August 17, 1928.
12. Anna Freud to Max Eitingon, December 19, 1927.
13. Freud/Salomé, p. 201; May 3, 1934.
14. Anna Freud to Max Eitingon, October 10, 1926.
15. Anna Freud to Max Eitingon, March 4, 1927.
16. Anna Freud to Lou Andreas-Salomé, December 12, 1928.
17. Dorothy Burlingham to Anna Freud, December 1, 1939.
18. Dorothy Burlingham to Anna Freud, January 17, 1940.
19. Anna Freud to Lou Andreas-Salomé, February 13, 1927; April 14, 1925: "It seems to me as if last year I was still blind to many things and

only now one after another comes clear, especially with the children, about whom I am always talking to Papa."

20. Anna Freud to Lou Andreas-Salomé, June 11, 1931.
21. Anna Freud to Lou Andreas-Salomé, February 4, 1923.
22. Anna Freud to Lou Andreas-Salomé, January 1, 1931.
23. Anna Freud to Lou Andreas-Salomé, November 29, 1931.
24. When the third volume of Ernest Jones's biography of Freud was published, many of Ferenczi's friends wrote to Anna Freud objecting to Jones's assessment of Ferenczi's condition in his last years. The most important statement came from Lajos Levy in a letter he sent to Robert Waelder, October 18, 1958, with copy to Anna Freud: "Never before his lethal illness, the pernicious anemia, could I perceive in him any kind of paranoid manifestation." In a letter to Anna Freud, September 8, 1958, Levy speculated that Jones got the idea that Ferenczi had had paranoid episodes by misconstruing a note from Gisella Ferenczi attached to Ferenczi's last communication to Freud; otherwise, Levy said, there was no evidence for Jones's contention. Actually, Freud himself gave Jones at least some grounds for his assessment in a letter he wrote to Jones shortly after Ferenczi's death (May 29, 1933); but Jones might also have realized how much Freud's disappointment and grief colored this letter.
25. Katá Levy to Anna Freud, July 19, 1952.
26. Anna Freud to Lou Andreas-Salomé, November 24, 1922.
27. Anna Freud to Lou Andreas-Salomé, November 15, 1928.
88. Anna Freud to Lou Andreas-Salomé, November 30, 1927.
29. Anna Freud to Ernst Simmel, January 11, 1928.
30. Anna Freud to Max Eitingon, November 10, 1925.
31. Anna Freud to Lou Andreas-Salomé, October 10, 1923.
32. Anna Freud to Lou Andreas-Salomé [circa December 1933].
33. Anna Freud to Erik Adam, May 12, 1978.
34. Anna Freud to Ernest Jones, February 23, 1934.
35. Anna Freud to Max Eitingon, February 22, 1934.
36. Ibid.; Freud/Salomé, p. 200; May 14, 1933.
37. See Anna Freud to Ernest Jones, January 1, 1934, for example: "I am sorry that [Federn] always raises questions of that kind that are certainly not vital but make trouble so often."
38. Anna Freud to Max Eitingon, April 16, 1933.
39. See Gardiner's memoirs, *Code Name "Mary."*
40. Waelder's paper (revised) appears in his *Psychoanalysis: Observation, Theory, Application*, pp. 121–88.
41. Anna Freud to Ernest Jones, January 1, 1934.
42. Sigmund Freud to Ernest Jones, March 2, 1937, cited in Jones, III, 213.
43. Anna Freud to Ernest Jones, June 5, 1933.
44. Anna Freud to Max Eitingon, October 4, and December 8, 1934.
45. Anna Freud to Lou Andreas-Salomé, December 6, 1934.
46. Anna Freud to Lou Andreas-Salomé, September 2, 1935.
47. Freud/Zweig, p. 140; April 2, 1937.
48. *SE*, XXIII, 80, 92.
49. *SE*, XXII, 247–48.

50. Anna Freud to Lou Andreas-Salomé, August 19, 1926.

51. *SE*, XXII, 245.

52. Freud discussed "retiring in favor of another" in "The Psychogenesis of a Case of Homosexuality in a Woman" (*SE*, XVIII, 158–60) and in "Some Neurotic Mechanisms in Jealousy, Paranoia and Homosexuality" (*SE*, XVIII, 231). Both of these papers, of course, date from the period of Anna Freud's first analysis. They do not seem to report directly on her case, but they do discuss or allude to many of its features—e.g., "altruistic surrender." Freud also talked about the use of proxies for evil wishes in "Dostoevsky and Parricide" (*SE*, XXI, 190) and commented on the novelist's altruism: "That is not kindly pity alone, it is identification on the basis of similar murderous impulses—in fact, a slightly displaced narcissism."

53. *Writings*, II, 116.

54. *Writings*, II, 119.

55. Anna Freud to Eva Rosenfeld [1930].

56. Anna Freud to Eva Rosenfeld, August 27, 1931.

57. *Journal of the Philadelphia Association for Psychoanalysis* 1/1 (March 1974): 35–42 (a discussion of *The Ego and the Mechanisms of Defense* with Anna Freud).

58. During 1972–73, Anna Freud discussed *The Ego and the Mechanisms of Defense* with a group of her coworkers at the Hampstead Center. Those discussions, transcribed and edited, were published in the *Hampstead Bulletin* and then, later, in book form: Sandler et al., *The Analysis of Defense*, p. 113.

59. Ibid., p. 400.

60. Ibid., p. 404.

61. Ibid., p. 525.

62. Ibid., p. 264.

63. *SE*, XXIII, 235.

64. *SE*, XVIII, 102.

65. Anna Freud to Max Eitingon, February 13, 1927 (dated 1926 in Anna Freud letter).

66. *Writings*, IV, 72. Anna Freud mentioned "group conscience" in Sandler et al., *Analysis of Defense*, p. 418.

67. Jones, III, 204.

68. Anna Freud to Lou Andreas-Salomé, May 18, 1926.

69. Freud, *Letters*, p. 436; February 5, 1937 (where the words "ungehemmte Leistung" are rendered "consistent achievement," but this translation disguises the analytic meaning: she had overcome her inhibitions).

70. Freud/Salomé, p. 204; January 6, 1935.

71. Ernest Jones to Anna Freud, June 13, 1933.

72. A transcript of Anna Freud's "Bemerkungen für einen Jahresbericht der Kinderkrippe" is in the Freud Museum, London; Anna Freud, "In memoriam Edith Jackson," *Journal of the American Academy of Child Psychiatry*, 17 (1978): 731. Other documents from the Jackson Nursery are in the Freud House, Vienna.

73. Anna Freud, "In memoriam Dorothy Burlingham," *PSC* 35 (1980): xiii.

74. Anna Freud to Edith Jackson, January 18, 1937.
75. Anna Freud to Edith Jackson, February 7, 1937.
76. Anna Freud to Edith Jackson, February 8, 1937.
77. Ibid.
78. Anna Freud to Edith Jackson, January 18 and 20, 1937.
79. SE, XXIII, 297.
80. Anna Freud to Ernst Pfeiffer, cited in Livingstone, p. 11.
81. Freud/Salomé, pp. 209–10; May 6, 1936.
82. The food choice notebooks are in the Freud Museum, London, with a report called "Children's Lunches, with trays," (in English).
83. Anna Freud, "In memoriam Dorothy Burlingham," op. cit., p. xii.
84. Martin Freud, p. 205.
85. Jones, III, 219.
86. Gideon Freud to Anna Freud, November 13, 1957.
87. Jones, III, 221 (Freud was quoting himself, see SE, XXIII, p. 115).
88. Martin Freud, p. 212.
89. Schur, pp. 498–99.
90. Dorothy Burlingham to Anna Freud, November 30, 1939.
91. Schur, p. 498; Jones, III, 224.
92. Sigmund Freud to Minna Bernays, May 14, 1938; letters of May 20, 23, 26, 28, and June 2 cited below. These letters are in the Freud Museum, London (transcribed and translated by Michael Molnar). Quoted with the permission of Sigmund Freud Copyrights.
93. Jones, III, 227–28.
94. Martin Freud, p. 214.
95. Anna Freud to Lou Andreas-Salomé, December 11, 1932.

6: Another Life

1. Ernest Jones to Anna Freud, November 26, 1952.
2. Writings, II, pp. 133–34.
3. Freud/Salomé, p. 209; May 16, 1935.
4. Max Schur's 1964 lecture formed the basis of "The Last Chapter" in his Freud: Living and Dying.
5. Freud, Letters, p. 446; June 6, 1938; Schur, 505–6; my translation is based on the unexcerpted original letter.
6. Freud's manuscript on Klein was mentioned to me by Masud Khan, formerly archivist of the Institute of Psychoanalysis; it is also mentioned by Khan in various letters of which he sent copies to Anna Freud; if the manuscript survived, it is presumably in the Sigmund Freud Archives. Many passages in Freud's Outline of Psychoanalysis (1938) are cast in opposition to Klein (SE, 22, 141–205).
7. Anna Freud to Ernst Simmel, March 26, 1939.
8. Schur, p. 526.
9. Sigmund Freud to Dorothy Burlingham, May 29, 1938.
10. Freud's logbook for 1938 and 1939 is being prepared for publication by the Freud Museum, London.
11. Schur, p. 527.

12. Dorothy Burlingham to Anna Freud, September 12, 1939. Anna Freud's side of this correspondence is missing, so my inferences to it below are based on Dorothy Burlingham's side, which is complete.

13. Schur, p. 529. Certain details of Schur's medical care in Freud's last days were altered in his biography of Freud to protect Schur from a charge of euthanasia. Schur informed Anna Freud that he had deposited an exact account in the Sigmund Freud Archives, and he sent her copies of his correspondence in 1957 with Ernest Jones in which a version of the death scene acceptable to Schur had been worked out for Jones's biography. It seems that Anna Freud was very reluctant to let Schur administer the morphine and that she acquiesced only when her father insisted.

14. Anna Freud to Muriel Gardiner, September 15, 1979.

15. Dorothy Burlingham to Anna Freud, October 17 and 29, 1939.

16. Martha Freud to M. Rie Nunberg, October 29, 1939 (kindly made available to me by Ms. Nunberg before her death in July 1986).

17. Anna Freud to Jenny Waelder-Hall, September 7, 1976.

18. Anna Freud to A. A. Brill, December 27, 1939. Anna Freud to Dr. Schavelzon, March 6, 1980: "I believe that the long duration of the course of the illness was due to Dr. Pichler's great care. He had decided to remove every new sign of growth, even if precancerous, immediately and not to wait for full development. When we emigrated to England, the surgeon here [Trotter] changed the method, waited for full development, and that led to a very quick end."

19. Dorothy Burlingham to Anna Freud, October 29, 1939.

20. Anna Freud to Lou Andreas-Salomé, June 1, 1924.

21. Anna Freud to Dr. Jelliffe, in Burnham, p. 283.

22. Dorothy Burlingham to Anna Freud, November 28, 1939.

23. Dorothy Burlingham to Anna Freud, October 3, 1939. Dorothy met with Berta Bornstein, Annie Reich, Walter Langer, Marie Briehl, Paul Federn, Hermann Nunberg, Margaret Ribble, Edith Jackson, and Edith Buxbaum; they were often joined by Robert and Jenny Waelder, Julia Deming, and Lydia Dawes from Boston.

24. Dorothy Burlingham to Anna Freud, October 14 and 22, 1939.

25. Dorothy Burlingham to Anna Freud, November 28, 1939.

26. Dorothy Burlingham to Anna Freud, December 8, 1939. See Walter Langer, "An American Analyst in Vienna During the Anschluss," *Journal of the History of the Behavioral Sciences*, 14 (1978): 37–54.

27. Dorothy Burlingham to Anna Freud, January 3 and 17, 1940.

28. Dorothy Burlingham to Anna Freud, February 20, 1940.

29. Dorothy Burlingham to Anna Freud, February 11, 1940.

30. Information below about the people connected with the Hampstead war nurseries is from my interviews, published obituaries, and a series of questionnaires developed by R. Dyer for his *Her Father's Daughter*, and the doctoral dissertation on which this book was based.

31. Sophie Dann, *Bulletin of the Hampstead Clinic*, 6 (1983): 72.

32. *Writings*, III, 544ff.

33. *Writings*, III, 558.

34. *Writings*, III, 220ff and cf. 356, 586ff.

35. Alice Goldberger, *Bulletin of the Hampstead Clinic*, 6 (1983): 66.

36. *Writings*, III, 20–21.

37. Anna Freud, "To Whom It May Concern" (for F. Hyndman), March 4, 1952.

38. Dorothy Burlingham to Anna Freud, February 20, 1940.

39. See Friedlander, "Psychoanalytic Orientation." There is a portrait of Friedlander in *Pioneers*, pp. 508–18.

40. *Writings*, III, 537–39 (cited further below).

41. Anna Freud to Edward Bibring, January 13, 1954.

42. Anna Freud to James Robertson, September 23, 1955 (it is interesting to note that Anna Freud speaks of her grandchild in a letter written on the anniversary of her father's death).

43. Rudolf Ekstein to Anna Freud, December 22, 1960.

44. J. C. Hill, undated (but 1957) memorandum on the London County Council "special classes" during the war (in Anna Freud's estate).

45. Grosskurth, pp. 253–55.

46. Anna Freud to Ernst Kris, December 12, 1945.

47. Ernest Jones to Anna Freud, January 21, 1942 (cited in full in Grosskurth, pp. 285–286).

48. Ibid.

49. Grosskurth, pp. 218–19; Schmideberg's paper appeared in English in *IJP* 6 (1935): 22–48.

50. Klein, *Contributions to Psychoanalysis*, pp. 282–310 and 311–38.

51. Jones, III, 299–300.

52. Anna Freud to Ernst Simmel, December 13, 1934.

53. Cited in Grosskurth, p. 255. The discussions were published in the *Scientific Bulletin of the British Psychoanalytic Society* (1967).

54. Klein, *Contributions to Psychoanalysis*, p. 379.

55. Ibid., pp. 330–31.

56. Ibid., p. 312.

57. Ibid., p. 320.

58. Grosskurth, p. 386 (no date given, but see p. 287 for a possibly contemporaneous Klein statement).

59. Klein, *Contributions to Psychoanalysis*, p. 323.

60. Grosskurth, Part IV.

61. Ibid., p. 290.

62. Ibid., pp. 303–4.

63. Sylvia Payne to Anna Freud, May 26, 1966, reflecting back on these events: "When Jones resigned the committee formed to consider the future consisted of men returned from war work—Adrian Stephen, Rickman, Gillespie, Bowlby—Glover and I. It was voted that the President should serve for three years instead of forever, like Jones. Glover could not deal with this, and it precipitated his resignation."

64. See Grosskurth, pp. 355–56.

65. Quotations below from Kris's memorandum, which is with the Anna Freud estate in the Sigmund Freud Archives.

66. This and succeeding quotations from Anna Freud to Ernst Kris, December 12, 1945.

7: On Losing and Being Lost

1. August Aichhorn to Anna Freud, November 16, 1945.
2. Anna Freud to August Aichhorn, May 3, 1946.
3. Anna Freud to August Aichhorn, February 21, 1946.
4. Anna Freud to Richard Sterba, March 9, 1946.
5. Anna Freud to Max Schiller, February 18, 1946. Anna Freud to Ralph Greenson, January 31, 1977: "But I had my own experience with a double pneumonia 30 years ago. . . . I was told then that one really should convalesce for 6 months, which I didn't do at the time, owing to difficult circumstances. But I often wished afterward that I had followed that advice."
6. Anna Freud to Max Schur, February 24, 1946.
7. Anna Freud to Kurt Eissler, March 2, 1946.
8. Ernst Kris to Anna Freud, January 25, 1946. Roazen, *Freud and His Followers*, p. 435. Roazen also distorted many features of Ruth Brunswick's relationships with Sigmund and Anna Freud.
9. Anna Freud to A. A. Brill, February 28, 1934.
10. Anna Freud sent to Max Eitingon a copy of Ernest Jones to Ruth Brunswick, November 7, 1928, which is a letter of remarkable arrogance and condescension.
11. Anna Freud to Katá Levy, March 8, 1946; Anna Freud possessed a copy of a letter to Dr. Robert Pfeiffer of Vienna dated December 10, 1953, from the Israel Kultursgemeinde Wien about the fates of the Freud sisters.
12. Interview with David Astor.
13. Anna Freud to Hans Lampl, December 19, 1946: "Aber es hat nicht viel Sinn, von Menschen zu verlangen dass sie Helden sein sollen, besonders da sie ja alle tot weren, wenn sie es gewesen weren. Wie Du selbst auch, sagst, hat die Politik in der Analyse nich viel Sinn, sie haben jedenfalls an der Analyse festgehatten so wie sie konnten."
14. Ernst Kris to Anna Freud, January 25, 1946.
15. Anna Freud to Kurt Eissler, March 2, 1946.
16. Ernest Jones to Anna Freud, July 22, 1949.
17. Anna Freud to Eva Landauer, February 26, 1946.
18. Hanns Sachs to Anna Freud, January 21, 1946.
19. Hanns Sachs to Anna Freud, September 25, 1946.
20. Anna Freud to Hermann Nunberg, March 7, 1946.
21. Anna Freud to Robert Waelder, September 2, 1946.
22. Anna Freud to Ernst Kris, May 10, 1946; in this letter Anna Freud also suggests to Kris that he contact Robert Fliess, Fliess's son, in order to get his collaboration in the publication.
23. August Aichhorn to Anna Freud, December 24/25, 1946.
24. Anna Freud to August Aichhorn, January 6, 1947.
25. Anna Freud to Arnold Zweig, July 3, 1946. She included Zweig's current illness in her discussion of her own, and of her father's: "I have witnessed a long battle for good health and productivity and each partial victory meant incredibly much, even if, as my father liked to say, at the end the adversary will come out on top."

26. Anna Freud to Harry Freud, May 24, 1956.
27. All quotations from Anna Freud's dream material are from documents gathered in her "On Losing and Being Lost" folder, which included a long letter from Marie Bonaparte (June 18, 1948) in which the Princess copied out from Anna Freud's letters to her (1946–48) all the dreams. Interpolations in brackets are mine.
28. Kagran was a Viennese friend of Freud's, cf. Jones, III, 171.
29. Freud, *Letters*, p. 440; January 17, 1938.
30. *Writings*, IV, 302–16 (all quotations from the essay below are from this text).
31. Anna Freud found "projective identification" a useful concept—but not for infants of less than a year, i.e., before ego structuration, as Melanie Klein used it.
32. *SE*, XIV, 255 (and see also XVIII, 130–33, for Freud's own later view of mourning).
33. It is interesting to note that Anna Freud here forgot that she and Dorothy had left Freud in Cottage Sanatorium for two weeks during their first vacation together in 1927.
34. Marie Bonaparte to Anna Freud, July 1, 1961. In her 1961 letters, Marie Bonaparte frankly discussed her "penis-envy" and her fantasy that her head was a kind of phallus. (Only letters between 1959 and 1961 from Marie Bonaparte were in the Anna Freud estate.)
35. Anna Freud to Heinz Hartmann, March 27, 1947.
36. Heinz Hartmann to Anna Freud, March 17, 1947.
37. Anna Freud to Ernest Jones, June 2, 1954.
38. Anna Freud to Ernst Kris, December 16, 1946.
39. Anna Freud to Ernst Kris, February 11, 1947.
40. Anna Freud to August Aichhorn, April 3, 1948.
41. August Aichhorn to Anna Freud, April 10, 1948.
42. Anna Freud to August Aichhorn, April 23, 1948.
43. Anna Freud to August Aichhorn, December 28, 1947.
44. Anna Freud to August Aichhorn, September 21, 1948.
45. Anna Freud to August Aichhorn, July 19, 1948.
46. Anna Freud to August Aichhorn, June 8, 1949.
47. Anna Freud to August Aichhorn, September 19, 1949.
48. Anna Freud to Franz Alexander, March 26, 1947.
49. Anna Freud to August Aichhorn, July 19, 1948.
50. Anna Freud to Richard Sterba, October 26, 1949.
51. *Writings*, IV, 636.
52. August Aichhorn to Anna Freud, May 5, 1948.
53. *Writings*, IV, 637–38 (citing a letter from Aichhorn).
54. Anna Freud to Margaret Mahler, March 9, 1951.
55. Anna Freud to Ernst Kris, November 12, 1947. Deutsch was Freud's physician in 1923, when his cancer was diagnosed (see Chapter 3).
56. Ibid.
57. Anna Freud to Ernst Kris, June 4, 1947.
58. Ernst Kris to Anna Freud, December 7, 1947.
59. Anna Freud to Siegfried Bernfeld, February 28, 1950.
60. Anna Freud to Leon Shimkin, June 23, 1947.

61. Anna Freud to Ernst Kris, March 13, 1947.
62. Anna Freud to Siegfried Bernfeld, March 26, 1947. Jones's eulogy had prompted Anna Freud to a reflection on his character (to Eitingon, April 14, 1940): "It is strange how Jones could create something so beautiful and how little one notes these good feelings in him as a person."
63. Anna Freud to Ernst Jones, May 19, 1947.
64. Anna Freud to Ernst Kris, May 16, 1947 (and following quote).
65. Nancy Procter-Gregg to Anna Freud, May 12, 1947.
66. See Sachs (d. 1947), *Freud: Master and Friend*. Zweig's manuscript, discussed often in his correspondence with Anna Freud, was apparently never published, though Anna Freud gave Zweig some names of English publishers (January 27, 1951) while noting that she had read only the first half of the manuscript. When she read that first half, she wrote of it (June 28, 1948): "Ich finde das Ganze ganz besonders schön, eigentlich aufregend schön. Die Art wie Sie das Bild langsam entwickeln, durch Ihre eigene Person hindurch gesehen, verbunden mit dem Bild der ganzen Zeit, ist so wie es eben kein Biograph kann, nur ein Dichter und Schriftsteller." Zweig did publish a small article, "Die Natur des Menschen und Sigmund Freud," in *Neue deutsche Literatur* (May 1956): 89–95.
67. Anna Freud to Ernst Kris, December 10, 1951.
68. *Writings*, VIII, 352.
69. Martha Freud to August Aichhorn, July 27, 1948 (included in the Anna Freud/August Aichhorn letters).
70. Erik Erikson in *Hampstead Bulletin* 6/1 (1983), p. 53.
71. Helen Ross to Anna Freud, December 29, 1951.
72. Anna Freud to Ernest Jones, April 8, 1952.
73. Anna Freud to Ernest Jones, September 18, 1953.
74. Mabbie Schmiderer to Anna Freud, February 20, 1958.
75. Anna Freud to Ernest Jones, February 14, 1954.
76. Anna Freud to Ernest Jones, January 9, 1954. This praise may have reflected a feeling Anna Freud expressed to Jones on December 12, 1953: "by now I have acquired a guilt complex about not knowing all the details concerning the past which I am expected to know."
77. Anna Freud to Ernest Jones, November 27, 1955.
78. Ernst Kris to Anna Freud, September 6, 1955.
79. Ernest Jones to Anna Freud, February 21, 1956. In general, Jones showed Anna Freud very little of volume III, as she noted in a letter to Max Schur (May 13, 1957) that concerns Schur's prepublication reading of the volume.
80. Anna Freud to Ralph Greenson, November 16, 1969.

8: CREATIVITY AND SCIENCE

1. Anna Freud to Ernst Kris, December 8, 1947; to Heinz Kohut, December 10, 1967.
2. Anna Freud to August Aichhorn, May 30, 1948.
3. Anna Freud to Dr. M. L. Rosenheim, October 9, 1949.

4. Anna Freud to August Aichhorn, May 30, 1948.
5. Anna Freud to Martin Freud, May 28, 1947.
6. Anna Freud to Hans Lampl, November 26, 1946.
7. "Sublimation as a Factor in Upbringing," *Health Education Journal*, 6: 25–29.
8. Anna Freud to Dr. Robert Sutherland [summer 1947].
9. Anna Freud to Martin James, July 2, 1962.
10. Anna Freud to Max Schiller, February 18, 1946.
11. Dorothy Burlingham, "Twins—A Gang in Miniature," in Eissler et al., *Searchlights on Delinquency*, pp. 284–87.
12. *Writings*, IV, 163–229 (cited further below).
13. *Writings*, IV, 154.
14. *Writings*, IV, 60–74 and 489–97.
15. Anna Freud and John Bowlby set out the principles of their disagreements with each other in *PSC* 15 (1960). Anna Freud urged the journal's editors to let Bowlby reply to his critics in the next issue (Anna Freud to Ruth Eissler, May 29, 1961); she also invited James Robertson, who worked with Bowlby at the Tavistock Institute, to her Clinic for discussions (Anna Freud to James Robertson, November 4, 1959). Later, Robertson's films went a long way toward disproving Bowlby's conclusions about "separation anxiety," and Anna Freud urged that Robertson's revisionist work be published (Anna Freud to Ruth Eissler, February 28, 1971) in *PSC*.
16. *Writings*, IV, 69–72.
17. *Writings*, IV, 496–97.
18. René Spitz to Anna Freud, March 2, 1948.
19. Anna Freud to Max Schur, April 30, 1948.
20. Anna Freud to Heinz Hartmann, June 26, 1948.
21. *Writings*, IV, 245–59, cited further below. The lectures were never written out or published because Anna Freud felt that the confidentiality of her patients, who were prominent men, could not be adequately protected. She does not seem to have made use of Hermann Nunberg's "Homosexuality, Magic and Aggression," *IJP* (1930), which presents a patient like hers.
22. Jones, III, 195.
23. Anna Freud to Nancy Procter-Gregg, February 27, 1956.
24. Anna Freud to Ralph Greenson, June 16, 1963.
25. Anna Freud's position on training for homosexuals noted by Leo Rangell, 1983 San Diego Psychoanalytic Society memorial meeting (mimeo). In an October 28, 1948 letter to Dr. Gomperts she wrote about a homosexual applicant to her child study course: "I know from past experience that it is no good for any kind of course, or any kind of institution, to permit people with sexual abnormalities."
26. See Richard Isay, "On the Analytic Therapy of Homosexual Men," *PSC* 40 (1985): 235–54.
27. Robert Waelder to Anna Freud, April 22, 1950.
28. Anna Freud's preface: *Writings*, V, 488–92.
29. Milner, p. 150.

30. *Writings*, II, 125. In a letter to Heinz Kohut, December 10, 1967, Anna Freud described two or her patients in a way that indicates she had a sibling configuration in common with them as well: "I am thinking here of two of my own patients, both homosexual before their analysis, both narcissistic personalities, one of them besides an addict and the other an obsessional neurosis. Both of them had devoted mothers who never wavered in their attention to them. Both had siblings and were themselves the youngest, which means that the presence of the siblings was a given, immutable fact from the beginning, not a traumatic event. In spite of this, they acted like they had been deserted at some time by the mother, and the addiction quite obviously had to make up for this. What analysis showed was an inordinate jealousy of the siblings which turned every attention paid them by the mother into a traumatic experience."

31. Anna Freud to Kate Friedlander, September 18, 1947.

32. Anna Freud to Kate Friedlander, September 29, 1947.

33. Anna Freud to August Aichhorn, February 2, 1949.

34. Anna Freud to August Aichhorn, February 27, 1949.

35. Anna Freud to Edward Bibring, December 22, 1948.

36. Anna Freud to Grete Bibring, July 16, 1953.

37. Anna Freud to Helen Ross, September 29, 1950.

38. Anna Freud to Grete Bibring, July 16, 1953.

39. Anna Freud to Anna Maenchen, December 7, 1951.

40. "Memorandum on the Work of the Hampstead Child Therapy Course and Clinic," 1955.

41. Anna Freud to Anny Hermann, November 19, 1956. (Anny Hermann returned to London in 1958 to help organize the blind children's nursery.)

42. Anna Freud to Kurt Eissler, March 19, 1958.

43. Anna Freud to Helen Ross, January 26, 1959.

44. Anna Freud to Milton Senn, February 16, 1952.

45. Anna Freud to John E. Bell, February 23, 1950.

46. Anna Freud to Grete Bibring, February 9, 1950.

47. Anna Freud to Grete Bibring, March 14, 1950.

48. Ibid.

49. *Writings*, IV, 107–42 (cited further below).

50. Dream dated February 8, 1948 (cited in the letter from Marie Bonaparte to Anna Freud, June 18, 1948).

51. Anna Freud to Kurt Eissler, February 22, 1950.

52. Anna Freud to Clinton McCord, April 1, 1950.

53. Anna Freud to Ernst Kris, March 7, 1950.

54. Ernst Kris to Anna Freud, March 13, 1950.

55. Jean Tucker in *Worcester Daily Telegram*, April 21, 1950.

56. Dorothy Barclay in *New York Times*, April 20, 1950.

57. Anonymous, attached to a letter from Richard Sterba to Anna Freud, May 31, 1950.

58. *Writings*, IV, 143–62.

59. Clinton McCord to Anna Freud, June 21, 1950.

60. Dr. Ruth Loveland to Anna Freud, March 3, 1953; Anna Freud's reply, March 27, 1953.

9: The Director

1. Anna Freud to Berta Halberstadt, February 6, 1956.
2. Anna Freud to T. R. Fryvol (BBC), April 24, 1956.
3. Anna Freud to Margarethe Freud Magnus, October 16, 1958.
4. Ernst Freud to Mr. Rosenthal, draft, dated January 26, 1960.
5. Anna Freud to Masud Khan, July 12, 1970.
6. Maxwell Gitelson to Anna Freud, January 4, 1956.
7. Gitelson, p. 474.
8. Anna Freud to Ives Hendrick, January 17, 1955.
9. Max Schur to Anna Freud, September 7, 1956. When Jones died in 1958, Anna Freud and Willi Hoffer labored together over his obituary for *IJP* to be sure that the biography got its full due.
10. Anna Freud's remarks prepared for the Chicago Psychoanalytic Institute, read there by Charles Brenner, May 6, 1956.
11. Anna Freud to Heinz Hartmann, June 29, 1953.
12. An account (favoring Lacan) in English of these events can be found in Turkle, Chapter 4. In French: see Smirnoff, "De Vienne à Paris." Anna Freud's dislike of Jacques Lacan dated from 1936, when she heard him at the International Congress in Marienbad.
13. Anna Freud to F. J. Hacker, January 10, 1977.
14. Anna Freud to Ralph Greenson, June 12, 1956.
15. Anna Freud to Kurt Eissler, November 25 and December 16, 1957.
16. Anna Freud to R. Ralph Greenson, May 6, 1958.
17. Anna Freud to Kurt Eissler, November 25, 1957. Anna Freud refused a suggestion conveyed to her from Jean-Paul Sartre that she review a script he had written.
18. Anna Freud to Masud Khan, December 7, 1961.
19. Anna Freud to Arthur Gavshon (Associated Press), December 5, 1962.
20. Anna Freud to Robert Dorn, September 10, 1956.
21. Ruth Thomas to Anna Freud, May 15, 1956; Heinz Hartmann to Anna Freud, May 17, 1956.
22. *Writings*, V, 360.
23. The four volumes were recently reprinted: Humberto Nagera, ed., *The Hampstead Clinic Psychoanalytic Library*, 4 vols. (London: Maresfield, Reprints, 1981).
24. *Writings*, VIII, 60. On July 24, 1951, Anna Freud had written to Heinz Hartmann: "In the Kleinian psychology and others as well, perceptual processes, coordination for movement, and memory appear to be completely dependent on instinctual drives and object relations. This leads to the diagnosis, which we are fighting against today, that every disturbance of intelligence is looked at as an instinctual disruption (*Triebstörung*), and every mental deficiency as schizophrenia."
25. These two papers are in *Writings*, V, 301–14, and VIII, 34–56.
26. *Writings*, V, 41.
27. *Writings*, V, 307.
28. The Developmental Profile is presented in *Normality and Pathology*

in Childhood, Writings, VI. The phrase "line of development" seems to have come from Freud's *Inhibitions, Symptoms and Anxiety* (SE, XX, especially 107, 151).

29. This is, of course, exactly what Anna Freud did in *The Ego and the Mechanisms of Defense*—presented a *summa* and then introduced her innovations.

30. *Writings,* VI, 83.

31. For an anthology of reports on the Profile as extended and applied in different ways, see *Psychoanalytic Assessment.*

32. *Writings,* VIII, 70.

33. Anna Freud to Kurt Eissler, December 7, 1969.

34. On Margaret Mahler's work, see *Writings,* VIII, 50, 120, 287; Mahler, *On Human Symbiosis.*

35. On Spitz, see *Writings,* VII, 23; Spitz, *The First Year of Life;* Hoffer, Chapters 1–7.

36. *Writings,* VIII, 98–99.

37. *Writings,* V, 102–35.

38. Marianne Kris to Anna Freud, March 15, 1957.

39. Anna Freud to Anna Kris Wolff, March 21, 1957.

40. Grete Bibring to Anna Freud, May 31, 1961.

41. English draft of Anna Freud's memorial address, published only in French translation: *Revue Française de Psychanalyse* 29 (1965): 1–2.

42. Grete Bibring to Anna Freud, January 20, 1959.

43. Anna Freud to Ralph Greenson, September 30, 1953.

44. Anna Freud to Ralph Greenson, November 16, 1969.

45. Anna Freud to Lydia Dawes, January 17, 1972.

46. Anna Freud to Ralph Greenson, April 26, 1959.

47. Anna Freud to Helen Ross, January 26, 1959.

48. Anna Freud to Ralph Greenson, December 13, 1959.

49. Anna Freud to Ralph Greenson, June 12, 1960.

50. See Bolland et al., eds., *The Hampstead Psychoanalytic Index.*

51. Anna Freud to Ralph Greenson, December 27, 1965.

52. Seymour Lustman to Anna Freud, July 28, 1966, and see Lustman, "The Scientific Leadership of Anna Freud." Lustman wanted to use this article to promote Anna Freud for a Nobel Prize; nothing came of his effort.

53. Seymour Lustman to Anna Freud, February 1, 1968.

54. Marianne Kris to Anna Freud, January 24, 1968.

55. Heinz Hartmann to Anna Freud, January 31, 1968.

56. Anna Freud to Kurt Eissler, April 24, 1960.

57. Liselotte Frankl to Anna Freud, October 2, 1960.

58. Anna Freud to Helen Ross, December 19, 1961.

59. See the anthology cited in note 31, above, for reports on the borderline and adolescents' projects; on the nursery: Anna Freud, "The Nursery School of the Hampstead Therapy Clinic," in *Studies in Child Psychoanalysis: Pure and Applied* (PSC Monograph, 5).

60. John Bolland to Anna Freud, September 28, 1966.

61. Anna Freud to Ralph Greenson, December 29, 1960.

62. Anna Freud to Augusta Bonnard, December 4, 1956.

63. Anna Freud to Kitty Jones, December 7, 1961.
64. Nadia Ramzy to Anna Freud, September 12, 1953.
65. Anna Freud to Lynn Stein, May 6, 1958 (i.e., Freud's 102nd birthday).
66. Dorothy Burlingham to the Geensons, July 18 and September 9, 1960.
67. *Writings*, VII, 82.
68. This and quotations below from Lewin and Ross, Chapter 24.
69. Helen Ross to Anna Freud, May 3, 1962.
70. Anna Freud to Helen Ross, May 19, 1962.
71. This work was a precursor to Sandler et al., *The Technique of Child Psychoanalysis*.
72. Marianne Kris to Anna Freud, December 12, 1962.
73. Grete Bibring to Anna Freud, August 27, 1959.
74. Marianne Kris to Anna Freud, May 26, 1965.
75. This and following citations from Report of the 26th International Psychoanalytic Congress, 133rd Bulletin of the International Psychoanalytic Association, *IJP* 51 (1970): 95.

10: IN THE FACE OF ENEMY FORCES

1. *Writings*, VII, 212.
2. Anna Freud to Leo Rangell, June 9, 1971.
3. *Writings*, VII, 211–12.
4. *Writings*, VIII, 157–75.
5. Arnold A. Rostow, *The Psychiatrists*. New York: G. P. Putnam's Sons, 1970, p. 109 ("Most Outstanding Living Psychiatrists and Psychoanalysts").
6. Anna Freud to Albert Solnit, January 15, 1967. Rather less ornately but just as highly publicized was Anna Freud's receipt of the first Dolly Madison Award from the Hillcrest Children's Center in Washington, D.C., which came at a White House ceremony hosted by Muriel Humphrey, wife of the Vice President of the United States. Anna Freud's other honorifics included three doctorates in law, the one from Clark University (1950), another from the University of Sheffield (1966), her only English degree, arranged by Erwin Stengel, and Yale (1968). Honorary doctorates of science were awarded by Jefferson Medical College in Philadelphia (1964), and the University of Chicago (1966). See Chapter 11 for the continuation of the list.
7. Edwin Z. Levy to Anna Freud, June 17, 1966.
8. Anna Maenchen to Anna Freud, October 2, 1965.
9. Cited in Judith Kestenberg to Anna Freud, September 21, 1965.
10. Bornstein's paper was "The Analysis of a Phobic Child," *PSC* 3/4 (1949); 181–226; Anna Freud to Bornstein, February 4, 1949, about this paper: "without a doubt the best [case study] that has ever been written in the field of child analysis." For reasons of confidentiality, the 1965 Ritvo and Bornstein papers were not published.
11. *Writings*, VII, 204–19, cited further below.
12. Anna Freud to Evelyn Kestemberg, May 20, 1971.

13. Michael Balint to Anna Freud, December 16, 1969 (alluding to an earlier letter).

14. Clinic Administration memorandum to Council of British Society, May 21, 1970.

15. Memorandum signed by S. Leigh, Business Secretary, prepared for President's News Bulletin (no date).

16. Michael Balint to Anna Freud, October 30, 1970; Anna Freud to Michael Balint, November 12, 1970.

17. Anna Freud to Frances Gitelson, June 30, 1971.

18. Anna Freud to Leo Rangell, July 11, 1971.

19. Jeanne Lampl-de Groot to W. Gillespie, June 21, 1971; to "Friends and Colleagues," June 22, 1971; and S. Lebovici to Lampl-de Groot, July 12, 1971, copy to Anna Freud, outlines the controversy.

20. Anna Freud to Leo Rangell, July 11, 1971.

21. Anna Freud to Samuel Ritvo, June 9, 1971.

22. Anna Freud to Max Gitelson, June 19, 1964.

23. Anna Freud to Bruno Marek, March 24, 1967.

24. Mathilde Hollitscher to Anna Freud, September 20, 1968.

25. Anna Freud to Ralph Greenson, April 10, 1970. She misdated another letter to Greenson about Ernst's death "5.2.69"–the date of Oliver's funeral.

26. Ernst Freud, Lucie Freud, Ilse Grubrich-Simitis, eds., *Sigmund Freud: His Life in Pictures and Words* (New York: Harcourt, 1978).

27. Letter for Max Schur, September 23, 1967.

28. Max Schur died before he could complete *Freud: Living and Dying*. As noted in Chapter 7, Anna Freud told Schur frankly that she felt that he should not, as Freud's physician, write about Freud's illness and death; but she did not try to stand in the way of his work.

29. Letter for Helen Ross, March 16, 1970.

30. Handwritten text of April 17, 1971, speech.

31. G. G. Bunzl to Anna Freud, September 13, 1971.

32. Anna Maenchen to Anna Freud, December 30, 1970.

33. Edith Kurzweil, "The (Freudian) Congress in Vienna," *Commentary*, November 1971, p. 81.

34. Anna Freud to Grete Bibring, October 4, 1971.

35. Anna Freud to Heinz Kohut, March 16, 1971.

36. *IJP*, 137th Bulletin, p. 87.

37. Anna Freud to Ralph Greenson, May 20, 1972.

38. Anna Freud to Kurt Eissler, December 17, 1971.

39. Anna Freud to Ralph Greenson, April 2, 1973.

40. Leo Rangell in San Diego Psychoanalytic Society memorial meeting, 1983 (mimeo).

41. Anna Freud to W. Boas, January 21, 1980.

42. Sandler et al., *Analysis of Defense*, p. 343.

43. Anna Freud's preface and conclusion to Thesi Bergmann's *Children in the Hospital* are in *Writings*, V, 419–35.

44. Dr. Christine Cooper, *Bulletin of the Hampstead Clinic* 6/1 (1983): 22–25.

45. Martin Stein in San Diego Psychoanalytic Society memorial, 1983 (mimeo).

46. Anna Freud to Kurt Eissler, January 30, 1973; similarly to Helen Ross, December 10, 1974: "But after all, we have been through two world wars and one or two revolutions, so we are trained." Helen Ross praised her for voting consistently for the Liberal Party, which was the party of Anna Freud's nephew Clement Freud, MP.

47. Anna Freud to Ishak Ramzy, December 20, 1973.

48. Anna Freud to Kurt Eissler, November 24, 1974.

49. Anna Freud to G. G. Bunzl, December 11, 1973.

50. Anna Freud to Ralph Greenson, January 20, 1963.

51. Memorandum to Goldstein and Katz, kindly lent to me by Joseph Goldstein.

52. Anna Freud to Albert Solnit, April 10, 1973.

53. Dorothy Burlingham to Albert Solnit, March 22, 1973.

54. Anna Freud to Albert Solnit, January 30, 1978.

55. Anna Freud to Joseph Goldstein, October 2, 1978.

56. David Chambers, *Washington Post Book World*, March 9, 1979, p. 4. See also Rita Kramer, "The 'Psychological Parent' Is the Real Parent," *New York Times Magazine*, October 7, 1973. In legal circles, the stage had been set for the appearance of *Beyond the Best Interests of the Child* by a *Yale Law Journal* 151 (1963) Note by Goldstein's Yale group entitled "Alternatives to 'Parental Right' in Child Custody Disputes Involving Third Parties."

57. Of the many reviews of the legal impact of *Beyond the Best Interests of the Child* in America, two are of particular interest: Peggy C. Davis, "There Is a Book Out . . . ," *Harvard Law Review*, 100:1539 (1987), 1539–1603, and earlier, Richard Edelin Crouch, "An Essay on the Critical and Judicial Reception of Beyond . . . ," *Family Law Quarterly*, XIII/1 (1979): 49–70.

58. Anna Freud to Kurt Eissler, March 3, 1975.

59. Anna Freud to Judge D. H. Jacobs, November 5, 1973.

60. Anna Freud to J. C. Hill, December 20, 1973.

61. Dorothy Burlingham to Alice Colonna, July 29, 1974 (Colonna's files).

62. Anna Freud to Albert Solnit, August 16, 1974. Marianne Kris wrote a letter of retrospection, July 26, 1974: "I think about should I have tried hospitalization . . ." But she did not feel that she herself or Anna Freud had mishandled the case, as some people around the family felt, particularly those who thought that drug treatment was indicated.

63. Antony Toszeghi to Josefine Stross, copy to Anna Freud, July 21, 1976.

64. Anna Freud to Anny Katan, October 18, 1978.

65. Anna Freud to Dr. J. Groen-Prakken, July 5, 1979.

66. Anna Freud to Stephen Spender, March 26, 1979.

67. Anna Freud to F. Redlich, May 21, 1979.

68. Anna Freud to Judge D. H. Jacobs, October 24, 1979.

69. Anna Freud to Anna Maenchen, November 20, 1972.

11: FUTURE AND PAST

1. Anna Freud to William McGuire, March 6, 1973.
2. Anna Freud to William McGuire, February 27, 1973.
3. Anna Freud to Emanuel Berman, July 9, 1979.
4. Anna Freud to Harold Blum, July 29, 1976.
5. Anna Freud to Leo Rangell, February 10, 1976.
6. Writings, VIII, 184.
7. Anna Freud to Rafael Moses, July 13, 1977.
8. J. C. Hill to Anna Freud, June 6, 1977.
9. Writings, VIII, 235–37 (cited further below).
10. R. Edgcumbe and M. Burgner, "Some Problems in the Conceptualization of Early Object Relationships," Parts I and II, in PSC 27: 283–314 and 315–33; "The Phallic-Narcissistic Phase," PSC 30: 161–80; and R. Edgcumbe et al., "Some Comments on the Concept of the Negative Oedipal Phase in Girls," PSC 31: 35–61.
11. Anna Freud to Muriel Gardiner, April 24, 1980.
12. Anna Freud to Muriel Gardiner, May 29, 1980.
13. Anna Freud to Masud Khan, June 23, 1975.
14. Anna Freud supplied Eissler with her criticisms of Brother Animal, and these were incorporated into Eissler's books. Eissler always refused to reprimand Helene Deutsch for her poor judgment in sponsoring Roazen, but Marianne Kris did approach Helene Deutsch, who said that she would try to restrain Roazen—something that she either did not do or did not succeed in doing.
15. Anna Freud to Kurt Eissler, July 9, 1979.
16. Eissler, Victor Tausk's Suicide, p. 251.
17. Anna Freud to Judge D. H. Jacobs, June 27, 1975. Anny Katan to Anna Freud, April 20, 1970: "[Roazen] writes that with many others, whom he names, I told him that you were analyzed by your father. The truth is that he told me that he knew from others that this was the case and I was silent. . . . I hate these writers of books!"
18. Anna Freud to Eva Rosenfeld, February 19, 1974.
19. Roazen made this claim in a review of Reich Speaks on Freud in The Nation 206 (April 16, 1968): 510.
20. Anna Freud to Masud Khan, July 12, 1970.
21. Anna Freud to Lottie Newman, February 6, 1980, re: Uwe Peters, Ein Leben für das Kind (Munich: Kindler Verlag, 1979).
22. Muriel Gardiner in Bulletin of the Hampstead Clinic 6/1 (1983): 65; Anna Freud to Clifford Yorke, March 12, 1980.
23. Anna Freud granted the permission in a letter to Masson, November 13, 1978. Eissler (January 18, 1977) had warned her that Masson was "by temperament a Sturm und Drang type, but through and through an idealist."
24. Anna Freud to Lottie Newman, February 6, 1980. The story of Jeffrey Masson's quick rise and equally quick fall has been told by Janet Malcolm, In the Freud Archives.
25. Anna Freud to Kurt Eissler, October 14, 1978; and to Lottie Newman, January 16, 1980.

26. Anna Freud to Kurt Eissler, June 1, 1981.
27. In an August 14, 1977, letter to Anna Freud, Masson suggested that a book by Robert Fliess (Wilhelm's son) called *Symbol, Dream and Psychosis* contained an important clue: the Fliess son implied that he had been seduced, and this, Masson said, might mean that Freud had backed away from the seduction hypothesis to protect his friendship with Fliess. Robert Fliess's widow later (January 17, 1982) wrote Anna Freud a lengthy letter supporting Masson's work and elaborating on her late husband's insights.
28. See Malcolm, pp. 111–12.
29. Anna Freud to Kurt Eissler, September 10, 1981.
30. Anna Freud to Kurt Eissler, November 23, 1981.
31. Anna Freud to Kurt Eissler, November 23, 1981. Anna Freud had first heard from Swales in December 1978 when he wrote under the name Joffre de Galles; by 1979 he was Peter Joffre Swales and full of information about Freud's youth, which interested Anna Freud.
32. Muriel Gardiner to Anna Freud, August 16, 1982.
33. Anna Freud to Muriel Gardiner, August 25, 1982.
34. Anna Freud to Dr. Christine Cooper, November 5, 1981.
35. Anna Freud to Ralph Greenson, November 2, 1978.
36. Typescript of speech sent for Greenson's memorial, January 1980.
37. Anna Freud to Ruth Thomas, December 1, 1978. The staff also needed encouragement because the Clinic was then involved in an "unfair dismissal" suit by a former staff member, Bianca Gordon. The case came to trial the week after Dorothy Burlingham's death (see below) and caused Anna Freud great aggravation before it was settled.
38. *Writings*, VIII, 176–85.
39. *Bulletin of the Hampstead Clinic* 3/3 (1980): 139.
40. Ibid., p. 181. Anna Freud's opinion on emphasizing transference to the neglect of insight (letter to Arthur Valenstein, March 7, 1979): "What I hate to see or hear about is the forcing of transference onto the patient by dragging every item of material into the transference instead of waiting until the patient himself feels it and can use it as confirmation of what has happened in the past. Whereas we use the transference to elucidate the past, these others use it as something in itself, as a therapeutic agent. I think this is one of the more successful attempts to destroy psychoanalysis."
41. Muriel Gardiner to Anna Freud, November 25, 1979.
42. Anna Freud to Albert Solnit, December 17, 1979.
43. Michael Burlingham to Anna Freud, November 23, 1979.
44. Anna Freud to Hildi Greenson, February 20, 1980.
45. Hildi Greenson to Anna Freud, December 3, 1979.
46. Anna Freud to Familie Fadenberger, September 8, 1980.
47. Michael John Burlingham to Anna Freud, April 14, 1981.
48. Edmond Rostand, *Cyrano de Bergerac*, trans. Bissell and Van Wyck (Los Angeles: Ward Ritchie Press, 1947), p. 238.
49. Anna Freud to Hildi Greenson, December 16, 1980.
50. Anna Freud to Miriam Beer-Hofmann-Lens, February 9, 1981 (cited further below).

51. Anna Freud to Edna Mingo, January 6, 1982.

52. This and all quotations below of Anna Freud's direct speech are taken from Manna Friedmann's journal.

53. Anna Freud to Anna Kris Wolff, November 6, 1981.

54. Anna Freud to Anny Katan, February 15, 1982.

55. Dr. Robert Byck to K. Eissler, January 28, 1982. The publisher was Jeffrey Steinberg of Stonehill Publishing; see Malcolm, p. 94.

56. Anna Freud to Kurt Eissler, February 22, 1982. The five brief notes supposedly by Anna Freud were quoted in Sigmund Freud, *Cocaine Papers*, edited and with an introduction by Robert Byck, M.D. (New York: Stonehill Publishing Co., 1975)—based on "The Dunguin Press Edition" no date given.

57. Kurt Eissler to P. Swales March 16, 1982; Anna Freud to Kurt Eissler, March 19, 1982.

58. Anna Freud to Kurt Eissler, March 19, 1982.

POSTSCRIPT

1. Anna Freud to J. C. Hill, October 21, 1974.

2. Anna Freud to Paul Gray, October 9, 1979.

3. Greenacre, Vol. 2, pp. 488, 529 (and see Chapter 28, "Woman as Artist").

4. Anna Freud to Nancy Friday Manville, November 10, 1975.

5. Jones, II, 183 (citing a 1915 letter to Ferenczi in which Freud also says, more concretely, "My productivity probably has to do with the enormous improvement in the activity of my bowels").

6. Greenacre, p. 539, notes how common anthropomorphic thinking is among great scientists (e.g., William Harvey) as well as among visual artists.

7. Sandler et al., *Analysis of Defense*, p. 33.

8. Malcolm, p. 76.

9. Anna Freud to Lawrence Friedman, May 2, 1979.

BIBLIOGRAPHY

With the exceptions of the volumes Anna Freud coauthored with Joseph Goldstein and Albert Solnit (all available in paperback from Free Press), her major writings can be found in *The Writings of Anna Freud*, 8 vols. (New York: IUP, 1966–80). Papers from the Hampstead Clinic appear each year after 1945 in *The Psychoanalytic Study of the Child* and, after 1978, in the *Bulletin of the Hampstead Clinic*. Two important anthologies of *PSC* papers have appeared from Yale University Press: *Studies in Child Psychoanalysis: Pure and Applied* (1975) and *Psychoanalytic Assessment: The Diagnostic Profile* (1977). A bibliography of Anna Freud's works (including short pieces not collected in her *Writings*) is available in Raymond Dyer, *Her Father's Daughter: The Work of Anna Freud* (New York: Aronson, 1983) and another, updated, is being prepared for publication by Barbara R. Peltzman. In addition to Dyer's biography, there are three others, all written without access to Anna Freud's literary estate: Uwe Peters, *Anna Freud: A Life Dedicated to Children* (New York: Schocken Books, 1985; German original: 1979), Gay Coleman Collins, *Anna Freud: An Educational Biography with Implications for Teaching* (Claremont Graduate School Ph.D., 1980), and (in German) Wilhelm Salber. *Anna Freud* (Rowolt, 1986). In the *Bulletin of the Hampstead Clinic*, 6/1 (1983), there are obituaries and memorial statements about Anna Freud; the same journal, 3/2 (1980), contains memorial statements about Dorothy Burlingham and a bibliography of her writings, 1932–79. There are also collections of memorial papers in *IJP* 64 (1983) and *PSC* 39 (1984). Two volumes contain edited transcripts, and these are probably the best volumes for making an initial acquaintance with her thought: J. Sandler et al., *The Technique of Child Psycho-*

analysis: Discussions with Anna Freud (Cambridge: Harvard University Press, 1980) and J. Sandler et al., *The Analysis of Defense: The Ego and the Mechanisms of Defense Revisited* (New York: IUP, 1985). The vast literature on Sigmund Freud is well compassed in the bibliography of Peter Gay's *Freud: A Life for our Time* (New York: Norton, 1988).

Other works I have cited and a selection of those I have consulted (not including the collections of letters listed with the Notes above) are indicated below with the following abbreviations in use:

IJP = *International Journal of Psychoanalysis*
IUP = International Universities Press (New York)
JAPA = *Journal of the American Psychoanalytic Association*
PQ = *Psychoanalytic Quarterly*
PSC = *Psychoanalytic Study of the Child*

Abraham, K. "Little Hilda: Daydreams and a Symptom in a Seven-Year-Old Child." *IJP* 1 (1914): 5–14.
———. *Selected Papers*, 2 vols. New York: Basic Books, 1955.
Aichhorn, August. *Wayward Youth*. New York: Viking, 1935.
Andreas-Salomé, L. The Freud Journal of Lou Andreas-Salomé, trans. by S. Leavy. New York: Basic Books, 1964.
Arieti, S. *Creativity: The Magic Synthesis*. New York: Basic Books, 1976.
Balint, M. "On the Psychoanalytic Training System." *IJP* 29 (1948): 163–73.
Bergmann, M. S., and F. Hartman, eds. *The Evolution of Psychoanalytic Technique*. New York: Basic Books, 1976.
Bernfeld, S. *Kinderheim Baumgarten: Bericht über einen ernsthaften Versuch mit neuer Erziehung*. Berlin: Jüdischer Verlag, 1921.
———. "Some Remarks on Sublimation," *IJP* 3 (1922): 134–35 (German: *Imago* 17: 399–403).
Bertin, C. *Marie Bonaparte: A Life*. New Haven: Yale University Press, 1987.
Bibring, E. "The So-Called English School of Psychoanalysis." *PQ* 16 (1947): 69–93.
Binswanger, L. *Sigmund Freud: Reminiscences of a Friendship*. New York: Grune & Stratton, 1957.
Blos, P. *On Adolescence*. New York: Free Press, 1969.
Blum, H. P., ed. *Female Psychology*. New York: IUP, 1977.
Bolland, J., et al., eds. *The Hampstead Psychoanalytic Index*. New York: IUP, 1965.
Bornstein, B. "Masturbation in the Latency Period." *PSC* 8 (1953): 65–78.
———. "On Latency." *PSC* 6 (1951): 279–85.
Bowlby, J. "Grief and Mourning in Early Childhood." *PSC* 15 (1960): 9–52 (with replies from critics, including Anna Freud).
Brierley, M. *Trends in Psychoanalysis*. London: Hogarth, 1951.
Brome, V. *Ernest Jones: Freud's Alter Ego*. New York: Norton, 1983.
Burlingham, D. *Psychoanalytic Studies of the Sighted and the Blind*. New York: IUP, 1972.

———. *Twins: A Study of Three Pairs of Identical Twins.* London: Imago Publishing Co., 1952.

Burnham, J. C. *Jelliffe: American Psychoanalyst and Physician.* Chicago: University of Chicago Press, 1983.

Butler, R. "The Destiny of Creativity in Later Life." in *Psychodynamic Studies of Aging,* in R. J. Khana and S. Levin, eds. New York: IUP, 1967.

Cath, S., et al. *Father and Child.* Boston: Little Brown, 1982.

Chasseguet-Smirgel, J., *et al, Female Sexuality.* Ann Arbor: University of Michigan Press, 1970.

Clower, V. "Theoretical Implications in Current Views of Masturbation in Latency Girls." *JAPA* 24 and in *Female Psychology,* H. P. Blum, ed. (see above).

Coles, R. "The Achievement of Anna Freud." In *The Mind's Fate.* Boston: Little Brown: 1975.

———. *Erik Erikson.* Boston: Little Brown, 1970.

D'Amore, A. *Historical Reflections on Psychoanalysis: 1920–1970.* New York: Brunner/Mazel, 1978.

Deutsch, H. *Confrontations with Myself.* New York: Norton, 1973.

———. "Melancholic and Depressive States." In *Neuroses and Character Types.* New York: IUP, 1965.

Drucker, P. *Adventures of a Bystander.* New York: Harper & Row, 1979.

Eissler, K. R. *Talent and Genius.* New York: Grove, 1971.

———. *Victor Tausk's Suicide.* New York: IUP, 1983.

Ekstein, R., and R. Motto, eds. *From Learning for Love to Love of Learning.* New York: Brunner/Mazel, 1969.

——— et al., eds. *Searchlights on Delinquency.* New York: IUP, 1949.

Erikson, E. *Identity and the Life Cycle.* New York: IUP, 1959.

Fenichel, O. *Collected Papers,* 2 vols. New York: Norton, 1954.

———. *The Psychoanalytic Theory of Neurosis.* New York: Norton, 1945.

———. "Referate." (on the IJP 8 (1927) symposium on child analysis). *Internationale Zeitschrift fur Psychoanalyse* 14 (1928): 546–61.

Ferenczi, S. *Collected Papers,* 2 vols. New York: Basic Books, 1955.

——— and O. Rank. *The Development of Psychoanalysis.* New York: Dover, 1956 (original: 1923).

Fine, R. *A History of Psychoanalysis.* New York: Columbia University Press, 1979.

Freeman, L., and H. S. Strean. *Freud and Women.* New York: Ungar, 1981.

Freud, M. "Who Was Freud?" in *The Jews of Austria,* ed. Josef Fraenkel. London: Vallentine-Mitchell, 1967.

Friedlander, K. "Children's Books and Their Function in Latency and Prepuberty." *The American Imago,* 3/3 (1942): 129–50.

———. "Psychoanalytic Orientation in Child Guidance Work in Great Britain." *PSC* 2 (1947): 343–57.

Friedman, L. "Beating Fantasies in a Latency Girl." *PQ* 54 (1985): 569–95.

Gardiner, M. *Code Name "Mary."* New Haven: Yale University Press, 1983.

Gedo, J. "The Methodology of Psychoanalytic Biography." *JAPA* 20 (1972), 638–49.

Geleerd, E. R. "Child Analysis: Research, Treatment and Prophylaxsis." *JAPA* 12 (1964): 242–58.

———. "Evaluation of Melanie Klein's 'Narrative of a Child Analysis.'" *IJP* 44 (1963): 493–506.

Gitelson, M. "On the Identity Crisis in American Psychoanalysis." *JAPA* 12 (1964): 451–76.

Glover, E., "Examination of the Klein System of Psychology." *PSC* 1 (1945): 75–118.

———. *The Technique of Psychoanalysis.* New York: IUP, 1955.

Goodman, S., ed. *Psychoanalytic Education and Research.* New York: IUP, 1977.

Greenacre, P., ed., *Affective Disorders.* New York: IUP, 1953.

———. *Emotional Growth,* 2 vols. New York: IUP, 1971.

Greenson, R. R. "On Enthusiasm." *JAPA* 10 (1962): 3–21.

———. *The Technique and Practice of Psychoanalysis.* New York: IUP, 1967.

———. "Transference: Freud or Klein." *IJP* 55 (1974): 37–48.

Grosskurth, P. *Melanie Klein: Her World and Her Work.* New York: Knopf, 1986.

Hammerman, S. "Masturbation and Character." *JAPA* 9 (1961), 287–311.

Harley, M. "Child Analysis, 1947–1984." *PSC* 41 (1986): 129–53.

Hartmann, H. *Essays on Ego Psychology.* New York: IUP, 1964.

———. "Presidential Address." *IJP* 37 (1956): 118–20.

Hendrick, I. "The Ego and the Mechanisms of Defense." *Psychoanalytic Review* 25 (1938): 476–97.

Hill, J. C. *The Teacher in Training.* London: Allen and Unwin, 1935.

Hitschmann, E. "A Ten-Year Report on the Vienna Psychoanalytic Clinic." *IJP* 13 (1932): 245–55.

Hoffer, W. *Early Development and Education of the Child.* London: International Psychoanalytic Library and Hogarth, 1981.

Horney, K. *New Ways in Psychoanalysis.* New York: Norton, 1939.

Hug-Hellmuth, H. "On the Technique of Child Analysis." *IJP* 2 (1921), 287–305.

Jacobson, E. *The Self and the Object World.* New York: IUP, 1964.

Joffe, W. G. "A Critical Review of the Status of the Envy Concept." *IJP* 50 (1969): 533–545.

Joint Commission on the Mental Health of Children. *Crisis in Child Mental Health.* New York: Harper, 1969.

Jones, E. *Collected Papers on Psychoanalysis.* London: Baillère, Tindall & Cox, 1948.

———. *Essays in Applied Psychoanalysis,* 2 vols. London: Hogarth, 1951.

———. *Free Associations: Memories of a Psychoanalyst.* London: Hogarth, 1959.

Jung, C. G. *Collected Works of C. G. Jung*. New York and Princeton: Bollingen Series 20, 1953–79.

Kardiner, A. *My Analysis with Freud*. New York: Norton, 1977.

Kendrick, W., and P. Meisel, eds. *Bloomsbury/Freud: The Letters of James and Alix Strachey*. New York: Basic Books, 1985.

Kernberg, O. "A Contribution to the Ego Psychological Critique of the Kleinian School." *IJP* 50 (1969): 317–33.

Khan, M. M. R. *The Privacy of the Self*. London: Hogarth, 1974.

King, P. H. M. "The Life and Work of Melanie Klein in the British Psychoanalytic Society." *IJP* 64 (1983): 251–60.

Klein, M. *Contributions to Psychoanalysis: 1921–1945*. New York: McGraw-Hill, 1964 (original: 1948).

———. *Envy and Gratitude*. New York: Basic Books, 1957.

———. *The Psychoanalysis of Children*. New York: Dell, 1975 (original German 1932).

——— et al. *New Directions in Psychoanalysis*. New York: Basic Books, 1953.

Knight, R. P. "The Present State of Organized Psychoanalysis in the U.S." *JAPA* 1 (1953): 197–221.

Kohon, G., ed. *The British School of Psychoanalysis: The Independent Tradition*. New Haven: Yale University Press, 1986.

Kramer, R. *Maria Montessori*. New York: Putnam, 1976.

Kris, E. *Psychoanalytic Explorations in Art*. New York: IUP, 1952.

———. *Selected Papers*. New Haven: Yale University Press, 1975.

Krüll, M. *Freud and His Father*. New York: Norton, 1986.

Kubie, L. "The Fallacious Misuse of the Concept of Sublimation." *PQ* 31 (1962): 73–79.

———. *Neurotic Distortion of the Creative Process*. New York: Noonday, 1961.

Laufer, M. "Female Masturbation in Adolescence and the Development of Relationship to the Body." *IJP* 63 (1982): 295–302.

Leonard, L. S. *The Wounded Woman: Healing the Father-Daughter Relationship*. Boston: Shambhala, 1985.

Leonard, M. "Fathers and Daughters." *IJP* 47 (1966): 325–34.

Lester, M. "The Analysis of an Unconscious Beating Fantasy in a Woman." *IJP* 38 (1957): 22–31.

Lewin, B., and H. Ross. *Psychoanalytic Education in the United States*. New York: Norton, 1960.

Limentani, A. "Tra Melanie Klein e Anna Freud." *Rivisita Psychoanalytica* 4 (1983): 435–37.

Livingstone, A. *Lou Andreas-Salomé*. London: Gordon Fraser, 1984.

Loewald, H. *Papers on Psychoanalysis*. New Haven: Yale University Press, 1980.

Loewenstein, R. M., ed. *Drives, Affects, Behavior*, 2 vols. New York: IUP, 1953, 1965 (ed. by M. Schur).

——— et al., eds. *Psychoanalysis—A General Psychology: Essays in Honor of Heinz Hartmann*. New York: IUP, 1966.

Lorand, S., ed. *Psychoanalysis Today*. New York: IUP, 1944.

Lustman, S. "The Scientific Leadership of Anna Freud." *JAPA* 15 (1967): 810–27.

Mahler, M. *On Human Symbiosis and the Vicissitudes of Individuation.* New York: IUP, 1968.

────── et al. *The Psychological Birth of the Human Infant.* New York: Basic Books, 1975.

Malcolm, J. *In the Freud Archives.* New York: Vintage, 1985.

Marcus, I. M., and J. J. Francis, eds. *Masturbation: From Infancy to Senescence.* New York: IUP, 1975.

Milner, M. *On Not Being Able to Paint.* London: Heinemann, 1971 (original 1950).

Nagera, H. *Early Childhood Disturbances, the Infantile Neurosis, and the Adulthood Disturbances.* New York: IUP, 1966.

────── . *The Obsessional Neurosis.* New York: Aronson, 1976.

Neubauer, P., and D. Flapan. *Assessment of Early Childhood Development.* New York: Aronson, 1975.

Niederland, W. "Psychoanalytic Approaches to Creativity." *PQ* 45 (1976): 185–212.

Novick, K. K. and J. "The Essence of Masochism." PSC 42 (1987): 353–84.

Nunberg, H., and E. Federn. *Minutes of the Vienna Psychoanalytic Society,* 4 vols. New York: IUP, 1962–75.

Pollock, G. H. "The Mourning Process and Creative Organizational Change." *JAPA* 25 (1977): 3–34.

Provence, S., and R. Lipton. *Infants in Institutions.* New York: IUP, 1962.

Reich, A. "The Discussion of 1912 on Masturbation and Our Present-Day Views." In *Psychoanalytic Contributions.* New York: IUP, 1973.

Reich, W. *Character Analysis.* New York: Noonday, 1969 (first English edition, 1949).

Reik, T. *Fragment of a Great Confession.* New York: Citadel, 1965.

Reisenberg-Malcolm, R. "Melanie Klein: Achievements and Problems . . ." *Bulletin of the British Psychoanalytic Society,* 8 (1980): 15–26.

Ribble, M. *The Rights of Infants.* New York: Columbia University Press, 1943.

Roazen, P. *Brother Animal: The Story of Freud and Tausk.* New York: Knopf, 1969.

────── . *Freud and His Followers.* New York: Knopf, 1975.

────── . *Helene Deutsch.* New York: Doubleday, 1985.

Ruitenbeek, H. M., ed. *Freud As We Knew Him.* Detroit: Wayne State University Press, 1973.

Sachs, H. *The Creative Unconscious.* Cambridge: Sci-Art Publishing, 1942.

────── . *Freud: Master and Friend.* Cambridge: Harvard University Press, 1944.

Sandler, J. *From Safety to Superego.* New York: Guilford Press, 1987.

————. "The Hampstead Index as an Instrument of Psychoanalytic Research." *IJP* 43 (1962): 287–91.

Schmideberg, M. "A Contribution to the History of the Psychoanalytic Movement in Britain." *British Journal of Psychiatry* 12 (1971): 331–67.

Schur, M. *Freud: Living and Dying.* New York: IUP, 1972.

Segal, H. *Melanie Klein.* New York: Viking, 1979.

Senn, M. J. E. *Insights on the Child Development Movement in the U.S.* Chicago: Monographs of the Society for Research in Child Development, #161, 1975.

Shapiro, T. "Childhood Neurosis: The Past 75 Years." *Psychoanalysis and Contemporary Science* 4 (1975): 453–77.

Sharaf, M. *Fury on Earth: A Biography of Wilhelm Reich.* New York: St. Martin's, 1983.

Smirnoff, V. "De Vienne à Paris." *Nouvelle Revue de Psychoanalyse,* 20 (Fall 1979).

————. *The Scope of Child Analysis.* London: Routledge & Kegan Paul, 1971.

————. *The Genetic Field Theory of Ego Formation.* New York: IUP, 1959.

Spitz, R. *The First Year of Life.* New York: IUP, 1965.

Steiner, R. ". . . An Examination of the British Psychoanalytical Society's Controversial Discussions (1943–44)." *International Review of Psychoanalysis* 12 (1985): 27–71.

Sterba, R. "Clinical and Therapeutics Aspects of Character Resistance." *PQ* 22 (1953): 1–20.

————. *Reminiscences of a Viennese Psychoanalyst.* Detroit: Wayne State, 1982.

Stone, L. "The Widening Scope of Indications for Psychoanalysis." *JAPA* 2 (1954): 569–94.

"Symposium on Child Analysis." *IJP* VIII (1927).

"Symposium on Child Analysis." *IJP* 43 (1962).

Taft, J. *Otto Rank.* New York: Julian Press, 1958.

Turkle, S. *Psychoanalytic Politics: Freud's French Revolution.* New York: Basic Books, 1978.

Tyson, P. "Female Psychological Development." *Annual of Psychoanalysis* 14 (1987): 357–73.

Van der Leeuw, P. J. "On the Development of the Concept of Defense." *IJP* 52 (1971): 51–58.

Varendonck, J. *The Psychology of Daydreams.* London: Allen & Unwin, 1921.

Waelder, R. *The Basic Theory of Psychoanalysis.* New York: IUP, 1960.

————. *Psychoanalysis: Observation, Theory, Application.* New York: IUP, 1976.

Weiss, E. *Sigmund Freud as a Consultant: Recollections of a Pioneer in Psychoanalysis.* New York: Intercontinental Medical Book Corp., 1970.

Weiss, J. "Continuing Research Toward a Psychoanalytical Developmental Psychology" (panel). *JAPA* 20 (1972): 177–98.

Winnicott, D. *The Maturational Processes and the Facilitating Environment*. London: Hogarth, 1965.

―――. *Through Pediatrics to Psychoanalysis*. New York: Basic Books, 1975.

Yorke, C. "The Contribution of the Diagnostic Profile . . . To Child Psychiatry." *Psychiatry Clinics of North America* 3/3 (1980): 593–603.

―――. "Some Suggestions for a Critique of Kleinian Psychology." *PSC* 26 (1971): 129–55.

Zehn Jahre Berliner Psychoanalytisches Institut. Berlin: Berliner Psychoanalytisches Institut, 1970 (reprint of 1930).

Zetzel, E. "An Approach to the Relation Between Concept and Content in Psychoanalytic Theory, with special reference to the work of Melanie Klein." *PSC* 11 (1956): 99–121.

―――. "Defense Mechanisms and Psychoanalytic Technique" (panel). *JAPA* 2 (1954): 318–26.

―――. "The 'Depressive Position.'" In *Affective Disorders*, P. Greenacre, ed. New York: IUP, 1953.

BIBLIOGRAPHY TO
THE SECOND EDITION

Listed below are materials that have appeared since the first edition of this book. The list is mostly in English and meant to be suggestive rather than complete.

Anna Freud: Correspondences, Biographies, Studies, Anna Freud Centre Research

Anna Freud Anniversary Issue. *The Psychoanalytic Study of the Child.* New Haven: Yale University Press, 1996.

Appignanesi, Lisa, and John Forrester. *Freud's Women.* London: George Weidenfeld and Nicolson, 1992.

Bonaminio, Vincenzo. "The Virtues of Anna Freud." In *Winnicott and the Psychoanalytic Tradition,* L. Caldwell, ed. London: Karnac, 2007.

Burlingham, Michael John. *The Last Tiffany: A Biography of Dorothy Tiffany Burlingham.* New York: Atheneum, 1989.

Coles, Robert. *Anna Freud: The Dream of Psychoanalysis.* New York: Addison-Wesley, 1992.

Donaldson, G. "Between Practice and Theory: Melanie Klein, Anna Freud, and the Development of Child Analysis." *Journal of the History of Behavioral Sciences* 32 (1996): 160–76.

Edgcumbe, Rose. *Anna Freud: A View of Development, Disturbance and Therapeutic Techniques.* London: Routledge, 2000.

Etkins, Richard, and Ruth Freeman, eds. *Selected Writings of Anna Freud.* New York: Penguin, 1998.

Fonagy, Peter. *Affect Regulation, Mentalization and the Development of the Self.* New York: Other Press, 2002.

———. *Attachment Theory and Psychoanalysis.* New York: Other Press, 2001.

———. *Psychoanalytic Theory: Perspectives from Developmental Psychotherapy.* London: Whurr, 2003.

Fonagy, Peter, and Mary Target. "Mentalisation and the Changing Aims of Child Psychoanalysis." In *Psychoanalysis in Childhood and Adolescence*, K. von Klitzing, et al, eds., 129–39. Basel: Karger, 2000.

Freud, Anna. *The Harvard Lectures*. London: Karnac, 1992.

———. *Anna Freud's Letters to Eva Rosenfeld*, ed. Peter Heller, trans. Mary Weigand. Madison, CT: International Universities Press.

Freud, Sigmund, and Anna Freud. *Briefwechsel, 1904–1938*, ed. I. Meyer-Palmede. Frankfurt: S. Fischer, 2006.

Freud, Sophie. *The Legacy of Anna Freud*. Lafayette, LA: University of Southwestern Louisiana Press, 1987.

———. *My Three Mothers and Other Passions*. New York: New York University Press, 1988.

Geissman, Claudine, and Pierre Geissman. *A History of Child Analysis*. London: Routledge, 1998.

Graf-Nolde, A. *Der Fall Hermine Hug-Hellmuth. Eine Geschichte der fruhen Kinder-Psychoanalyse*. Munich: Verlag Internationale Psycoanalyse, 1988.

Heller, Peter, et al. *A Child Analysis with Anna Freud*. Madison, CT: International Universities Press, 1990.

Holder, Alex. *Anna Freud, Melanie Klein, and the Psychoanalysis of Children and Adolescents*, trans. P. Slotkin. London: Karnac, 2005.

Hurry, Anne, ed. *Psychoanalysis and Developmental Therapy*. London: Karnac, 1998.

King, Pearle, and Rudolf Steiner, eds. *The Freud/Klein Controversies, 1941–1945*. London: Routledge, 1991 (reprinted 2001).

Likierman, M. "The Debate between Anna Freud and Melanie Klein." *Journal of Child Psychotherapy* 21 (1995): 313–25.

Maclean, G., and U. Rappen. *Hermine Hug-Helmuth: Her Life and Work*. New York: Routledge, 1991.

Masson, Jeffrey M. *Final Analysis: The Making and Unmaking of a Psychoanalyst*. Reading, MA: Addison-Wesley, 1990.

Mayes, Linda. *Developmental Psychoanalysis: Integration and Innovation*. London: Karnac, 2007.

Menaker, Esther. "Anna Freud's Analysis by Her Father." *Journal of Religion and Health* 40/1 (2001): 89–96.

Peltzman, Barbara. *Anna Freud: A Guide to Research*. New York: Garland, 1990.

Rolf, Denker. *Anna Freud zur Einfuhrung*. Hamburg: Junius, 1995.

Rothe, Daria, ed. *Als kam ich heim zu Vater und Schwester: Lou Andreas Salome — Anna Freud Briefwechsel, 1919–1937*. Munich: Wallstein Verlag, 2004.

Salber, Wilhelm. *Anna Freud*. Reinbeck bei Hamburg: Rowohlt, 1997.

———. *Sigmund und Anna Freud*. Hamburg: Europa Verlag, 1999.

Sandler, Joseph, and Peter Fonagy. *Recovered Memories of Abuse: True or False*. London: Karnac, 1997.

Sayers, Janet. *Mothering Psychoanalysis: Helene Deutsch, Karen Horney, Anna Freud, and Melanie Klein*. New York: W. W. Norton, 1993.

Viner, R. "Melanie Klein and Anna Freud: The Discourse and the Early Dispute." *Journal of the History of Behavioral Sciences* 32 (1996): 4–15.

Weissensteiner, Freidrich. *Kinder der Genies*. Munich: Piper, 2007.

Yorke, Clifford. *Anna Freud*. Paris: Presses Universitaires de France, 1997.

Some Relevant Sigmund Freud Materials (since 1988)

Decker, Hannah S. *Freud, Dora, and Vienna, 1900.* New York: Free Press, 1991.

Freud, Sigmund. *The Diary of Sigmund Freud, 1929–1939: A Record of the Final Decade,* ed. and trans. Michael Molnar. London: Hogarth, 1992.

Freud, Sigmund, and Sandor Ferenczi. *The Correspondence of Sigmund Freud and Sándor Ferenczi.* Vol.1, 1908–1914, ed. Eva Brabant et al, trans. Peter T. Hoffer. Cambridge: Belknap Press of Harvard University Press, 1993.

——. *The Correspondence of Sigmund Freud and Sandor Ferenczi.* Vol. 2, 1914–1919, ed. Ernst Falzeder et al, trans. Peter T. Hoffer. Cambridge: Belknap Press of Harvard University Press, 1996.

Freud, Sigmund, and Ernest Jones. *The Complete Correspondence of Sigmund Freud and Ernest Jones, 1908–1939,* ed. R. Andrew Paskauskas, trans. Frauke Voss et al. Cambridge: Belknap Press of Harvard University Press, 1993.

Freud, Sigmund, and Eduard Silberstein. *The Letters of Sigmund Freud and Eduard Silberstein, 1871–1881,* ed. Walter Boehlich, trans. Arnold J. Pomerans. Cambridge: Belknap Press of Harvard University Press, 1990.

Gay, Peter. *Freud: A Life for Our Time.* New York: W. W. Norton, 1988.

——. *Reading Freud: Explorations and Entertainments.* New Haven: Yale University Press, 1990.

Grubrich-Simitis. *Back to Freud's Texts.* New Haven: Yale University Press, 1996.

Roazen, Paul. *Meeting Freud's Family.* Amherst: University of Massachusetts Press, 1993.

——. *How Freud Worked: First-Hand Accounts of Patients.* Northvale, NJ: Aronson, 1995.

Timms, Edward, and Naomi Segal, eds. *Freud in Exile: Psychoanalysis and Its Vicissitudes.* New Haven: Yale University Press, 1988.

Wittels, Fritz. *Freud and the Child Woman: The Memoirs of Fritz Wittels,* ed. Edward Timms. New Haven: Yale University Press, 1995.

British and American Psychoanalysts of Anna Freud's Generation: Some Biographies

Bion, Wilfred R. *The Long Week-End, 1897–1919: Part of a Life,* ed. Francesca Bion. Strath Tay, Perthshire: Clunie, 1982.

——. *All My Sins Remembered: Another Part of a Life; and The Other Side of Genius: Family Letters,* ed. Francesca Bion. Abingdon, Oxfordshire: Fleetwood, 1985.

Burston, Daniel. *Erik Erikson and the American Psyche.* New York: Aronson, 2007.

——. *The Wing of Madness: The Life and Work of R. D. Laing.* Cambridge: Harvard University Press, 1996.

Clay, John. *R. D. Laing: A Divided Self.* London: Hodder and Stoughton, 1996.

Cooper, Judy. *Speak of Me as I Am: The Life and Work of Masud Khan.* London: Karnac, 1993.

Dragstedt, Naome Rader. "Creative Illusions: The Theoretical and Clinical Work of Marion Milner." *Journal of Melanie Klein and Object Relations* 16 (1998): 425–536.

Eissler, Kurt R. *Three Instances of Injustice*. Madison, CT: International Universities Press, 1993.

Evans, F. Barton, III. *Harry Stack Sullivan: Interpersonal Theory and Psychotherapy*. London: Routledge, 1996.

Friedman, Lawrence J. *Menninger: The Family and the Clinic*. New York: Alfred A. Knopf, 1990.

———. *Identity's Architect: A Biography of Erik Erikson*. New York: Scribner, 1999.

Hazell, Jeremy. *H. J. S. Guntrip: A Psychoanalytical Biography*. London: Free Association Books, 1996.

Hoffman, Edward. *The Drive for Self: Alfred Adler and the Founding of Individual Psychology*. Reading, MA: Addison-Wesley, 1994.

Holmes, Jeremy. *John Bowlby and Attachment Theory*. London: Routledge, 1993.

Hopkins, Linda. *False Self: The Life of Masud Khan*. New York: Other Press, 2007.

Hornstein, Gail. *To Redeem One Person Is to Redeem the World: The Life of Frieda Fromm-Reichmann*. New York: Free Press, 2000.

Hughes, Athol, ed. *The Inner World and Joan Riviere: Collected Papers, 1920–1958*. London: Karnac, 1991.

Kahr, Brett. *D. W. Winnicott: A Biographical Portrait*. London: Karnac, 1996.

Kohut, Heinz. *The Curve of Life: Correspondence of Heinz Kohut, 1923–1981*, ed. Geoffrey Cocks. Chicago: University of Chicago Press, 1994.

Kotowicz, Zbigniew. *R. D. Laing and the Paths of Anti-Psychiatry*. London: Routledge, 1997.

Laing, Adrian Charles. *R. D. Laing: A Biography*. London: Peter Owen, 1994.

Little, Margaret I. *Psychotic Anxieties and Containment: A Personal Record of an Analysis with Winnicott*. Northvale, NJ: Aronson, 1990.

MacLean, George, and Ulrich Rappen. *Hermine Hug-Hellmuth: Her Life and Work*. New York: Routledge, 1991.

Mahler, Margaret S. *The Memoirs of Margaret S. Mahler*, ed. Paul E. Stepansky. New York: Free Press, 1988.

Menaker, Esther. *Appointment in Vienna: An American Psychoanalyst Recalls Her Student Days in Pre-War Austria*. New York: St. Martin's, 1989.

Mullan, Bob. *Mad to Be Normal: Conversations with R. D. Laing*. London: Free Association Books, 1995.

Paris, Bernard J. *Karen Horney: A Psychoanalyst's Search for Self-Understanding*. New Haven: Yale University Press, 1994.

Pollak, Richard. *The Creation of Dr. B: A Biography of Bruno Bettelheim*. New York: Simon and Schuster, 1997.

Quinn, Susan. *A Mind of Her Own: The Life of Karen Horney*. New York: Summit Books, 1987.

Rado, Sandor. *Heresy: Sandor Rado and the Psychoanalytic Movement*, ed. Paul Roazen and Bluma Swerdloff. Northvale, NJ: Aronson, 1995.

Reich, Wilhelm. *Passion of Youth: An Autobiography, 1897–1922*, ed. Mary Boyd

Higgins and Chester M. Raphael. New York: Farrar, Straus and Giroux, 1988.

Rodman, Robert. *Winnicott: Life and Work*. New York: Perseus, 2003.

Roudinesco, Élisabeth. *Jacques Lacan*. New York: Columbia University Press, 1997.

Scott, W. Clifford M. *Becoming a Psychoanalyst*. Binghamton, NY: esf, 1998.

Siegel, Allen M. *Heinz Kohut and the Psychology of the Self*. London: Routledge, 1996.

Sinason, Michael D. A. "Biographical Introduction." In *Life, Sex and Death: Selected Writings of William H. Gillespie*, by William H. Gillespie, ed. Michael D. A. Sinason, 3–34. London: Routledge, 1995.

Spensley, Sheila. *Frances Tustin*. London: Routledge, 1995.

Strozier, Charles. *Heinz Kohut: The Making of a Psychoanalyst*. New York: Farrar, Straus and Giroux, 2001.

Sutherland, John D. *Fairbairn's Journey into the Interior*. London: Free Association Books, 1989.

Sutton, Nina. *Bruno Bettelheim: The Other Side of Madness*. London: Gerald Duckworth, 1995.

Symington, Joan, and Neville Symington. *The Clinical Thinking of Wilfred Bion*. London: Routledge, 1996.

Van Dijken, Suzan. *John Bowlby: His Early Life; A Biographical Journey into the Roots of Attachment Theory*. London: Free Association Books, 1998.

Winnicott, Donald W. *The Spontaneous Gesture: Selected Letters of D. W. Winnicott*, ed. Robert Rodman. Cambridge: Harvard University Press, 1987.

INDEX

"Anal and Sexual" (Andreas-
    Salomé), 112
anal erotic character, 83, 112
anal-sadistic phase, 38, 104
anal stage, 329, 363, 429
"Analysis Terminable and Inter-
    minable" (S. Freud), 213
Andreas-Salomé, Lou, 64, 110–14,
    116–23, 125, 129, 133, 145, 156,
    454, 461
    A. Freud's correspondence with,
    112, 118, 119, 121, 122, 127, 133–
    34, 163–64, 186, 192, 196, 203–
    4, 207–8, 222–23
    Bonaparte compared with, 229–30
    on Burlingham, 190
    death of, 222–23
    S. Freud's correspondence with,
    63, 110, 112–14, 116, 120, 137, 161,
    217, 234, 352, 422
animals, 34, 99
Anschluss, 198, 199, 279
anti-Semitism, 69, 142, 198, 219
    Moses and Monotheism and, 205–6
    Nazism and, 195, 279–80
anxiety, 177, 184, 234
    of A. Freud, 63, 83, 94, 245, 344–
    45, 418–19
    castration, 187, 429
    defense mechanisms and, 209
    of infants, 264
    instinctual, 209, 213
    Klein's views on, 166–67
    objective, 209, 213
    Oedipal relations and, 165
    prevention of, 53
    Rank's views on, 165, 166
    separation, 321
    of S. Freud, 25, 53, 61–63, 80, 108,
    115, 173
    sources of, 209
    superego, 209, 213
APA, see American Psychoanalytic
    Association
Arden House, 349
Arendt, Hannah, 280
Arnim-Eperjesy, Hertha von, 47
asceticism, 108–9, 111, 113–14, 137, 458
Association for Child Psychoanaly-
    sis, 394

Association Psychanalytique de
    France, 355
Astor, Lord David, 357, 428
Austria:
    founding of republic of, 197
    German occupation of, 224–27
    politics in, 197–203, 224–27
Austria-Hungary, 65, 69
    breakup of, 142

Baderle, Gertrud (Trude), 50–51, 58
Balint, Michael, 366, 387, 395
Bartemeier, Leo, 282
"basic faults," notion of, 366
Bauer, Otto, 201
Baumgarten Children's Home, 99–
    100, 177
beating fantasies, 59–60, 103–9, 111,
    182, 329
    incest and, 75, 104, 107, 328
    penis-envy and, 125
"Beating Fantasies and Daydreams"
    (A. Freud), 59–60, 103–9, 111,
    126, 295, 305, 328
Beer-Hofmann-Lens, Miriam, 446
Before the Best Interests of the Child
    (A. Freud, Goldstein and Sol-
    nit), 415–18
Bell, John E., 341
Benekendorf, Joanna Kohler, 249
Bergmann, Thesi, 410
Berlin:
    child analysis in, 160
    migration of analysts to, 157–58, 160
Berlin Congress (1922), 103, 147
Berlin Policlinic, 92, 98, 142, 195,
    254, 255
Berlin Psychoanalytic Society, 103–
    4, 117
Berlin Training Institute, 142, 154
Bernays, Anna Freud, 31
Bernays, Edward, 95, 341, 348, 439
Bernays, Eli, 31, 32, 43
Bernays, Frau Emmeline (grand-
    mother), 29–32
Bernays, Judith, 348
Bernays, Martha, see Freud, Martha
    Bernays
Bernays, Minna (aunt), 29–32, 36,
    45, 55, 56, 61, 63, 77–78, 91, 119

ABOUT THE AUTHOR

ELISABETH YOUNG-BRUEHL, Ph.D., who is on the faculty of the Columbia Center for Psychoanalytic Training and Research, has a private practice in Manhattan. In addition to this biography, she is the author of many books, including *Hannah Arendt: For Love of the World* (from Yale University Press), *Creative Characters*, *The Anatomy of Prejudices*, *Subject to Biography*, *Cherishment*, *Where Do We Fall When We Fall In Love?* and *Why Arendt Matters* (also from Yale University Press).